The Sassoons

The Sassoons

Esther da Costa Meyer and Claudia J. Nahson

Jewish Museum, New York
Under the auspices of the Jewish Theological Seminary of America

Yale University Press
New Haven and London

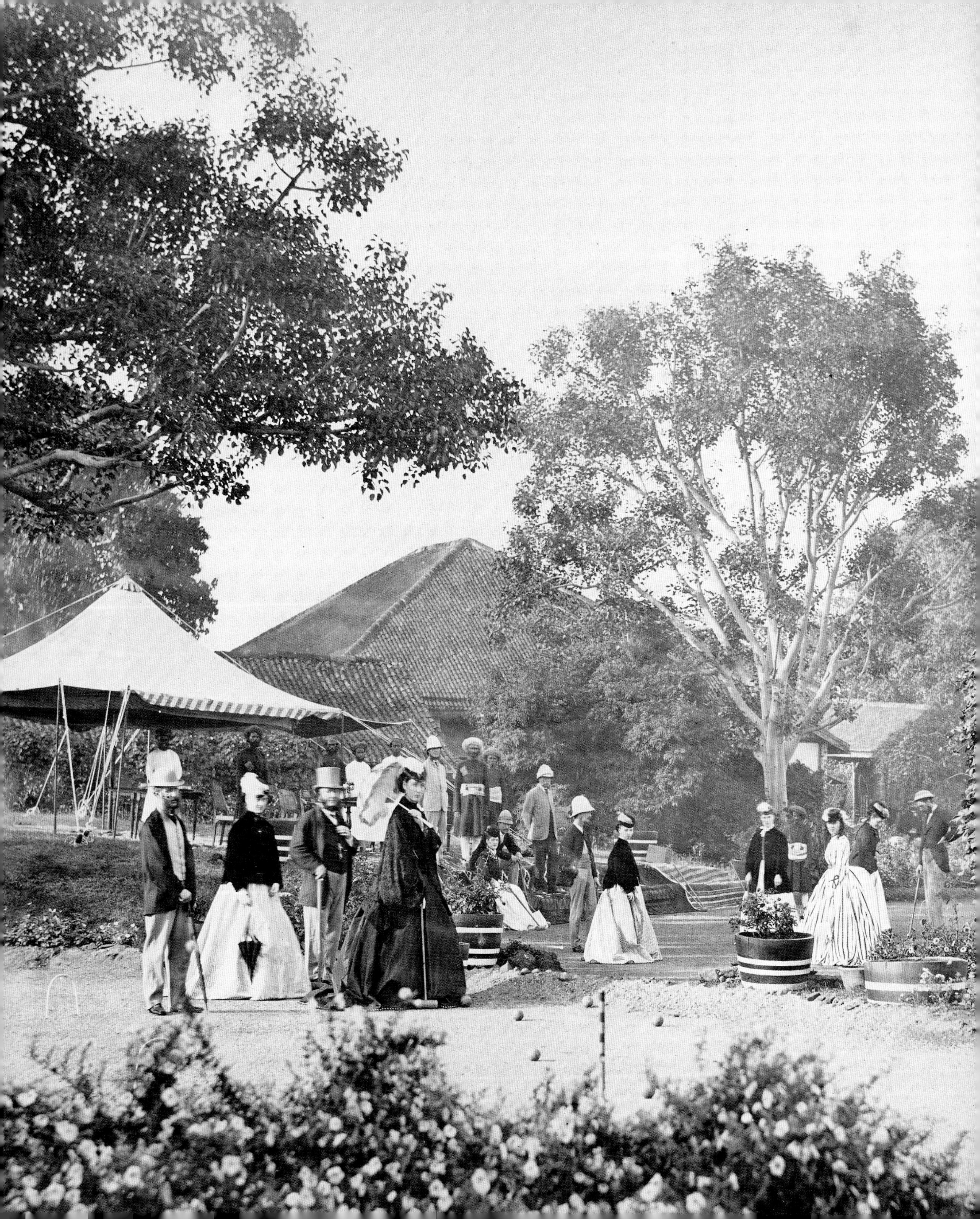

Contents

The Sassoons: An Abridged Family Tree 6

Foreword 9
Claudia Gould, Helen Goldsmith Menschel Director, Jewish Museum

Acknowledgments 11

Donors and Lenders to the Exhibition 14

Introduction 16
Esther da Costa Meyer and Claudia J. Nahson

From Commissioners to Collectors 24
Claudia J. Nahson

Art 62
Esther da Costa Meyer, with contributions by Claudia J. Nahson

Architecture: A Scattered Legacy 136
Esther da Costa Meyer

Epilogue 226
Esther da Costa Meyer and Claudia J. Nahson

Notes 242
Index 250
Jewish Museum Board of Trustees, 2023 254
Credits and Copyrights 255

The Sassoons

An Abridged Family Tree

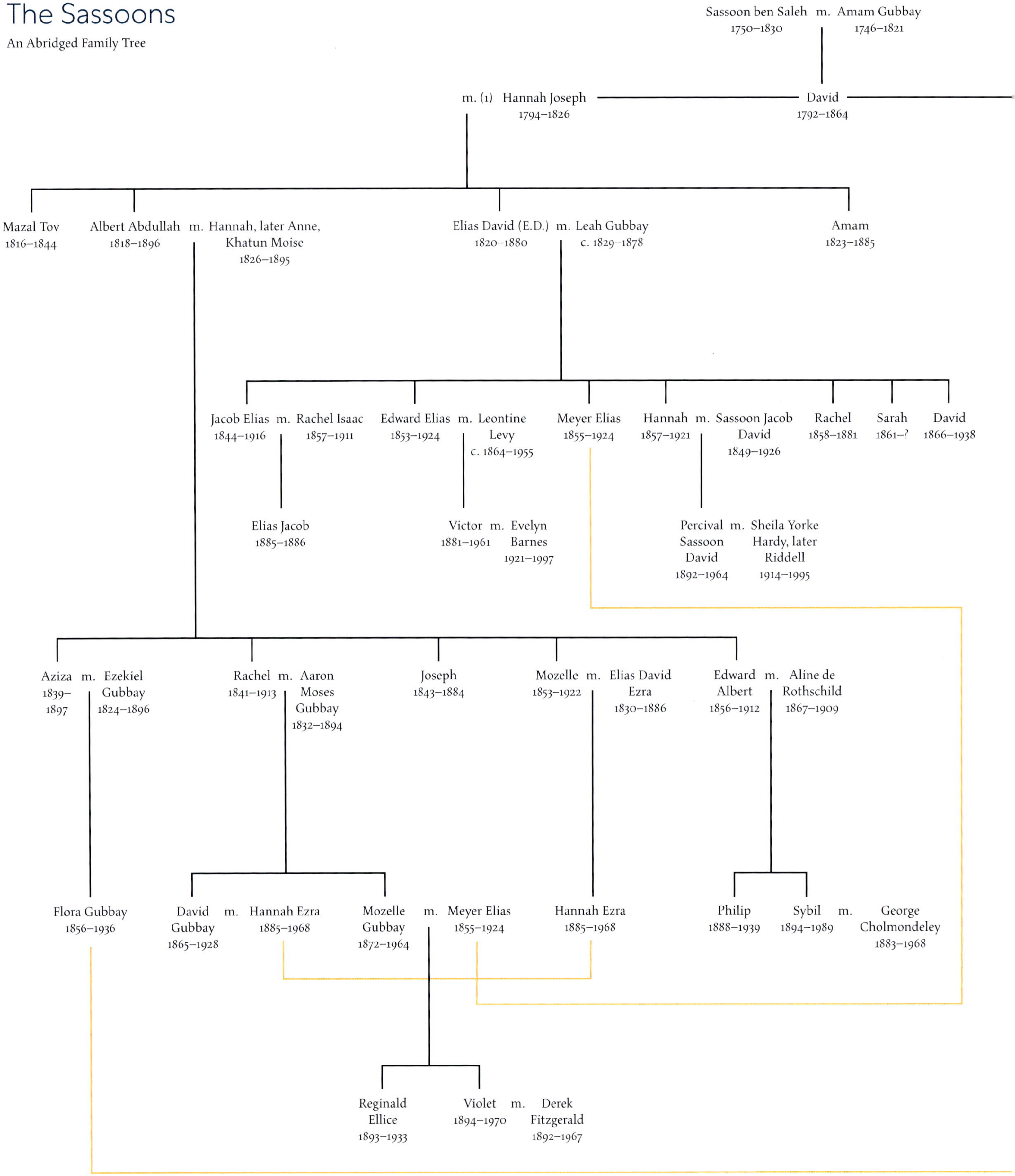

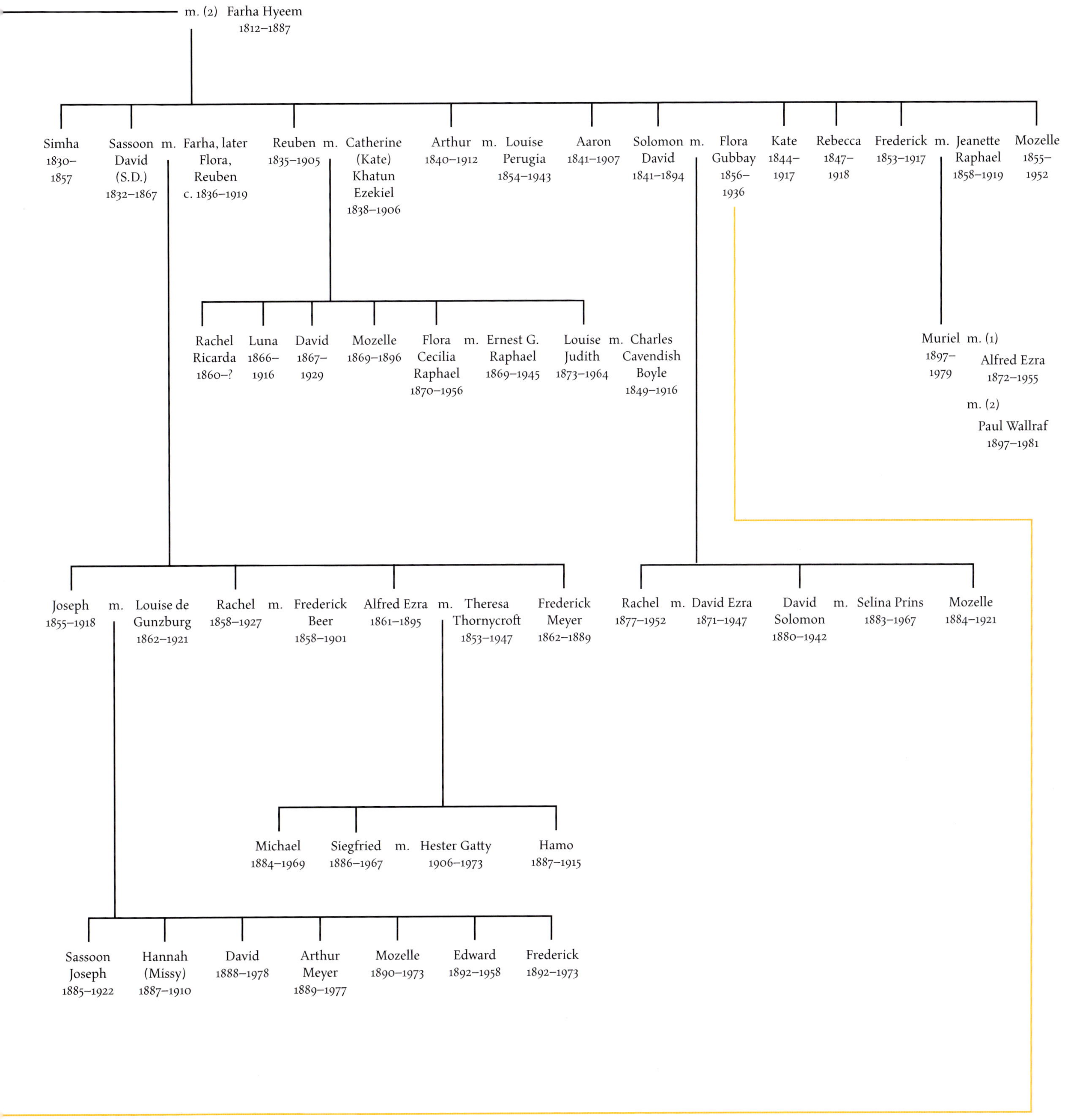
m. (2) Farha Hyeem
1812–1887
Simha
1830–
1857
Sassoon
David
(S.D.)
1832–1867
m.
Farha, later
Flora,
Reuben
c. 1836–1919
Reuben
1835–1905
m.
Catherine
(Kate)
Khatun
Ezekiel
1838–1906
Arthur
1840–1912
m.
Louise
Perugia
1854–1943
Aaron
1841–1907
Solomon
David
1841–1894
m.
Flora
Gubbay
1856–
1936
Kate
1844–
1917
Rebecca
1847–
1918
Frederick
1853–1917
m.
Jeanette
Raphael
1858–1919
Mozelle
1855–
1952
Rachel
Ricarda
1860–?
Luna
1866–
1916
David
1867–
1929
Mozelle
1869–1896
Flora
Cecilia
Raphael
1870–1956
m.
Ernest G.
Raphael
1869–1945
Louise
Judith
1873–1964
m.
Charles
Cavendish
Boyle
1849–1916
Muriel
1897–
1979
m. (1)
Alfred Ezra
1872–1955
m. (2)
Paul Wallraf
1897–1981
Joseph
1855–1918
m.
Louise de
Gunzburg
1862–1921
Rachel
1858–1927
m.
Frederick
Beer
1858–1901
Alfred Ezra
1861–1895
m.
Theresa
Thornycroft
1853–1947
Frederick
Meyer
1862–1889
Rachel
1877–1952
m.
David Ezra
1871–1947
David
Solomon
1880–1942
m.
Selina Prins
1883–1967
Mozelle
1884–1921
Michael
1884–1969
Siegfried
1886–1967
m.
Hester Gatty
1906–1973
Hamo
1887–1915
Sassoon
Joseph
1885–1922
Hannah
(Missy)
1887–1910
David
1888–1978
Arthur
Meyer
1889–1977
Mozelle
1890–1973
Edward
1892–1958
Frederick
1892–1973

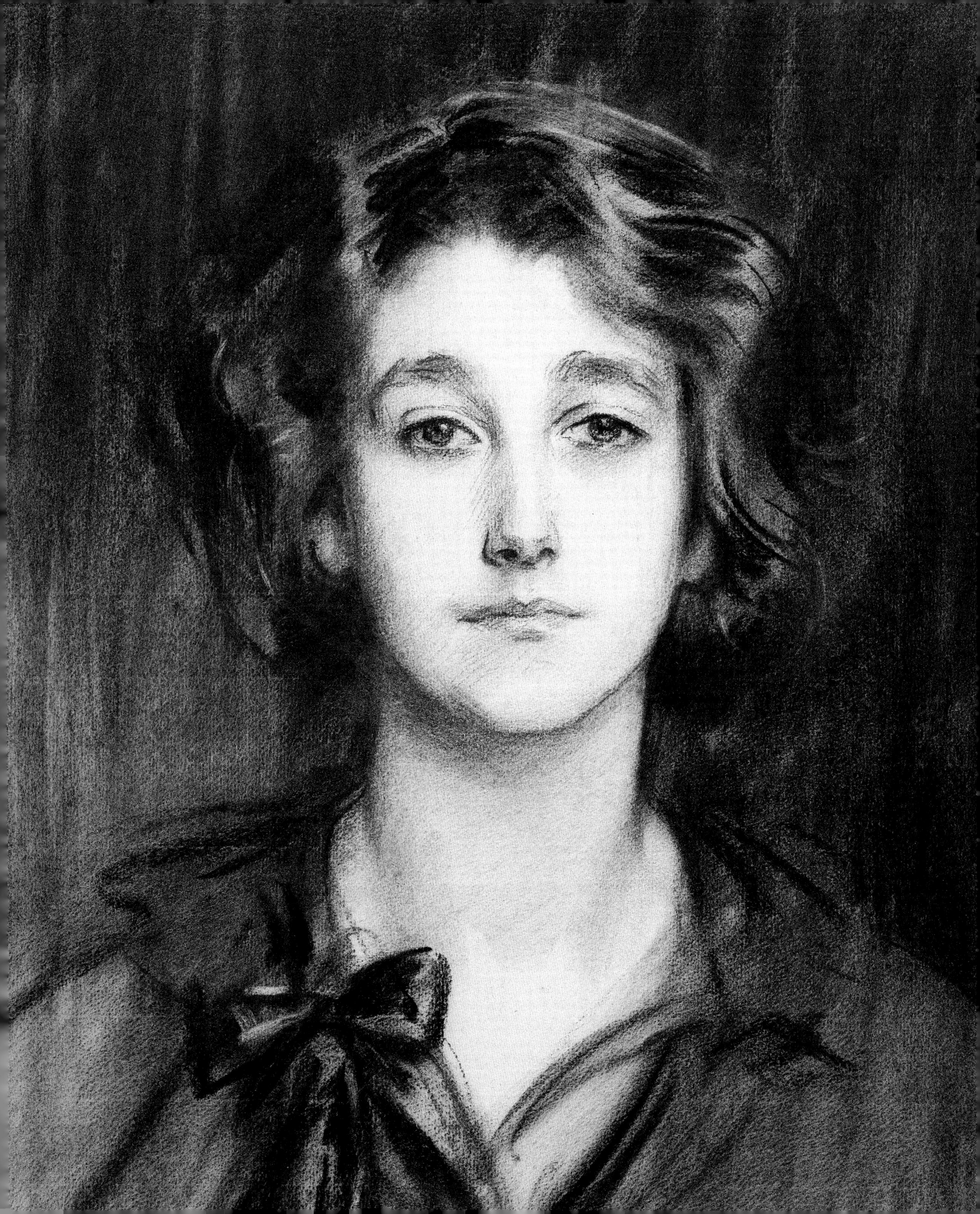

Foreword

So often the stories of Jewish culture and history are family stories. The Jewish Museum's collections include many objects and works of art that came to us as the treasures of a family, infused with memories and personal meanings. Our exhibitions frequently build upon the theme of family—family connections, family histories, family achievements, and, above all, the art and objects that family members collected, used, and loved.

We have told the stories of the Rothschilds, illustrious court financiers, and the Ephrussis, who changed the Paris art world by championing the Impressionists. We have traced the family stories of Jewish women who held literary and artistic salons, and of Jews whose art survived Nazi confiscation. We have presented exhibitions about art patrons and dealers such as Jos and Lucie Hessel, who sustained Édouard Vuillard, and Edith Halpert, the impresario of twentieth-century American art.

Often, these family stories also follow a geographic path that begins in the Ottoman Empire and may run from there to Europe, Asia, or the United States. These sagas tell a larger tale of Jewish migration, ambition, enterprise, and contributions to global culture. The Sassoons are such a family—one whose history reflects remarkable financial and intellectual achievement, connoisseurship, and cultural breadth.

Prominent for generations in Ottoman Baghdad, they were expelled from the city in 1830 and moved to India in 1832. There they became successful merchants, first in textiles and spices, and later in dyes, pearls, and—we must not equivocate—the lucrative opium trade. Over the course of the nineteenth century they founded businesses throughout Asia, including shipping, manufacturing, and other mercantile concerns, and expanded to London. In England they entered the highest echelons of society, building grand homes, filling them with art, and engaging in large works of philanthropy. By the nineteenth century, the family included many forward-thinking, highly educated women, who were themselves influential in all these areas.

In the succeeding decades the Sassoons collected precious antique Hebrew manuscripts and religious objects; became patrons of John Singer Sargent; produced one of the great modern poets, Siegfried Sassoon; published two of London's most influential newspapers; and commissioned architectural gems in the cities where they lived.

As is often the case, their story of ambition, influence, and achievement ended abruptly with the advent of World War II. Although the Sassoons largely escaped the Holocaust, their presence on the world stage faded, leaving synagogues, hospitals, and schools, poems and art collections that bear their name.

For their work in reviving this remarkable family story, I am deeply grateful to the curators, Claudia J. Nahson, the Morris and Eva Feld Senior Curator at the Jewish Museum, and Esther da Costa Meyer, professor emerita at Princeton University. They jointly conceived and executed this breathtaking publication and exhibition. I extend my warm thanks to the accomplished staff of the Jewish Museum, who helped them bring the project to fruition. Miko McGinty, who designed the book, and Leslie Gill, who designed the exhibition, met the challenge of the Sassoons' own splendor with exceptional flair and style.

Numerous private and institutional collectors graciously lent works to the exhibition and gave unstintingly of their knowledge and time in the research for it. I especially thank the members of the Sassoon family who so generously opened their doors and archives to us. I offer my warm appreciation in particular to Lord Sassoon, Lord Cholmondeley, Charles Cholmondeley, Edwina Sassoon, and Adrian Sassoon.

Our donors continue to sustain our work with munificence, and I am profoundly grateful to them and to our Board of Trustees, our most steadfast supporters, under the leadership of Chairman Robert A. Pruzan.

Claudia Gould
Helen Goldsmith Menschel Director
Jewish Museum, New York

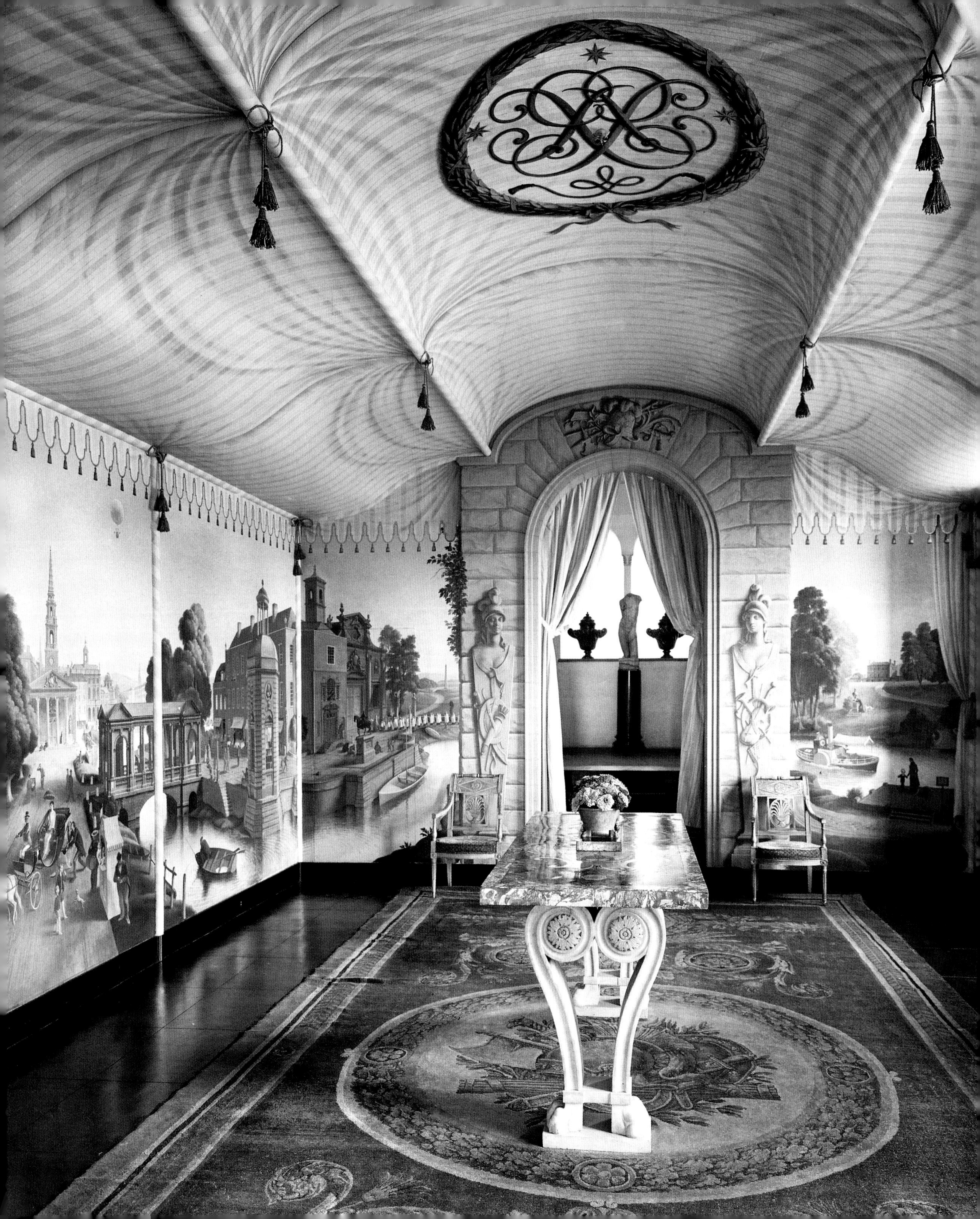

Acknowledgments

Over the course of a century, the Sassoons created a commercial empire that stretched across different continents, leaving behind magnificent collections of manuscripts, fine and applied arts, and imposing public and private buildings. This volume and the accompanying exhibition explore these legacies through a range of artworks, artifacts, photographs, and documents that tell the story of this remarkable family and highlight the contributions of several of its members, the women and men who created a world of elegance and played a central role in the social, political, and cultural life of Britain, where they finally settled.

During our research we were able to locate many of the family's treasures scattered in public and private hands in Europe and the United States, and we are both honored and excited to bring them together for the first time. Organizing a large-scale exhibition with international loans and a publication is always a challenge, but doing so during a global pandemic raised the bar considerably. Over a year into developing the exhibition we went into lockdown, and our research plans were severely curtailed: travel, libraries, archives suddenly became insurmountable obstacles. That we were able to bring the project to fruition at all is thanks to the help of many curators, scholars, private collectors, friends, and colleagues who went out of their way to help us obtain the necessary loans, documentation, photographs, and permissions.

We are deeply indebted to the Sassoon family members who endorsed our project wholeheartedly from its inception. Our heartfelt thanks to Lord Sassoon for embracing our exhibition idea in its nascent stages and facilitating introductions to other family members. His wife, Lady Sassoon, received us warmly at their home and contributed to our research. The exhibition is greatly enriched by important loans from the Houghton Hall Collection. Lord Cholmondeley graciously hosted us at his magnificent family home and shared stories about his grandmother, the Marchioness of Cholmondeley, née Sybil Sassoon; his great-uncle Sir Philip Sassoon; and his great-grandmother Lady Sassoon, née Aline de Rothschild. Edwina Sassoon was an avid champion and ambassador of our exhibition. Her warmth and generosity of spirit kept us going during the worst of the pandemic, as she indefatigably shared newly discovered connections of interest for our research. Charles Cholmondeley was extremely supportive throughout the various stages of the project, graciously elucidating several issues related to the Sassoons' works of art. We are also very grateful to Adrian Sassoon for sharing his connoisseurship.

Several colleagues lent advice and expertise over the course of the project. Special thanks to Caroline Corbeau-Parsons, former curator of British art 1850–1915 at the Tate, who provided valuable input, and to Mallica Kumbera Landrus, keeper of the Eastern Art Department at the Ashmolean Museum, who devoted much time offering critical advice as we conceptualized the exhibition. We also extend our gratitude to Cary Liu, Nancy and Peter Lee Curator of Asian Art at the Princeton University Art Museum, for his careful reading and many suggestions concerning Percival David's collections.

In Britain, many colleagues generously shared their collections and knowledge. At the British Museum we are grateful to Jessica Harrison-Hall, head of the China Section and curator of the Sir Percival David Collections. Ilana Tahan, lead curator of Hebrew and Christian Orient Studies at the British Library, and her colleague Malini Roy, head of Visual Arts at the Asia and Africa Collections, welcomed us and facilitated our viewing of their important holdings, while Jayesh Tailor deftly processed our loan request. Thanks are also due to Susan Foister, deputy director and curator of early Netherlandish and German painting at the National Gallery; the staff of the National Gallery Archive; and Clare Freestone, curator of photographs at the National Portrait Gallery. At the National Trust, we are indebted to Katherine Carter, project curator at Chartwell, for her warm welcome during our visit, and Sophie Chessum, senior curator at Clandon Park, for providing valuable information on the Hannah Gubbay Collection. James Dobson, photographer at the National Trust, gave us crucial and timely assistance. At the Royal Collection Trust, thanks go to Sally Goodsir, curator of decorative arts. Melanie Aspey, director of the Rothschild Archive, and Justin Cavernelis-Frost, archivist, generously shared their holdings and expertise. At the Victoria and Albert Museum,

Kirstin Kennedy, curator, and Alice Minter, curator of the Rosalinde and Arthur Gilbert Collection, were enthusiastic supporters. Silvia Davoli and Thomas Stammers, of the Jewish Country Houses core research team, greatly added to our visit with their knowledge. Elizabeth Loughran, assistant registrar, and Daryl Tappin, former assistant registrar, also lent their help. Thanks also to Alan Wakefield, head of First World War and Early 20th-century Conflict at the Imperial War Museums, and Kathrin Pieren, former collections manager and curator of social and military history at the Jewish Museum in London.

Jessica Gardner, university librarian and director of library services, and her wonderful staff at Cambridge University Library were extremely supportive. We are deeply grateful to John Wells, senior archivist, for facilitating our research during our visit to Cambridge, and to Jill Whitelock, head of special collections; Benjamin Outhwaite, head of the Genizah Research Unit; and the conservator Shaun Thompson for their valuable assistance. At the Fitzwilliam Museum we are thankful to Elena Saggers, acting registrar, and David Packer, former registrar. Thanks are also due to Adrian Green, director of the Salisbury Museum, and to Fiona Campbell, collections assistant at the National Museums Liverpool.

Madeleine and Freddie Mossanen hosted us warmly and lavishly at their London home, and our dear friends Maria Kell and Tabitha (Tabsy) Pring were the perfect partners during a splendid research day in Kent. Tabsy was tireless and full of good cheer as she drove us to Chartwell and Port Lympne. Gordon Franks and the late Godfrey Gould, our wonderful cicerones in Brighton, shared their deep knowledge of the Sassoons' past in Brighton-Hove, their former homes, and their many contributions to the magnificent Middle Street Synagogue. Thanks also to Marina Brounger for her timely help.

At the Louvre, we would like to thank Sébastien Allard, head of the paintings department. Guillaume Faroult, chief curator in the paintings department, graciously led us through the museum's beautiful new installation of British paintings. We are also much obliged to Janet McLean, curator of European art, 1850–1950 at the National Gallery of Ireland. Cristina Portell, Eduard Valles, and Mariàngels Fondevila at the Museu Nacional d'Art de Catalunya in Barcelona kindly facilitated our viewing of the panels by Josep Maria Sert once owned by Philip Sassoon and shared research. Thanks also to our dear friends in the Wing for Jewish Art and Life at the Israel Museum, Jerusalem: Daisy Raccah-Djivre, long-serving chief curator, and her successor Rachel Sarfati; Sharon Weiser-Ferguson, curator; Anna Nizza, assistant curator; Gioia Perugia, storage and collection manager; and Shani Zahavi, loans and shipping coordinator. We also extend our warm thanks to Professor Yaron Ben-Naeh at the Hebrew University of Jerusalem. Philip Goldberg deserves our deep gratitude for generously allowing us to use his wonderful photos.

In India, many people welcomed us and shared their knowledge about the Sassoons' legacy in Mumbai and Pune. We would like to thank Mr. Solomon Sopher, chairman and managing trustee of Sir Jacob Sassoon Charity and Allied Trusts, as well as E.E.E. Sassoon High School, and a leader of the Baghdadi Jewish community, who greeted us at the Magen David Synagogue in Byculla, and Lalita Sharma, who guided us through the adjacent buildings. We are much indebted to the kind reception of Hemant Bhalekar, president of the David Sassoon Library, and trustees Shruti and Kunal Ved during our visit. Shekhar Krishnan spent hours leading us through the Sassoon Textile Mills, and Vikas Dilawari, conservation architect, who completed a remarkable restoration study on David Sassoon's home Sans Souci, now the Masina Hospital, visited the building with us. At the Dr. Bhau Daji Lad Museum, the curator Ruta Waghmare-Baptista showed us around the facilities. The architect Abha Narain Lambah kindly allowed us to publish images of her studio's magnificent restoration of Keneseth Eliyahoo Synagogue. In Pune, Eliyahoo Penkar, caretaker of Ohel David, opened the synagogue and the adjacent mausoleum of David Sassoon and guided us through the Jewish cemetery, while the staff at the Niwara David Sassoon Old Age Home made every effort to show us the premises and answer our questions. We were also graciously hosted by Mr. and Mrs. J. Jehangir and Dr. and Mrs. Farrokh Wadia, who kindly shared their knowledge of the Sassoons' history in Pune.

Closer to home, staff at several institutions contributed generously to our project. At the Metropolitan Museum of Art, in the Department of European Sculpture and Decorative Arts, we wish to thank Sarah E. Lawrence, Iris and B. Gerald Cantor Curator in Charge, and Denny Stone, general manager for collections. Thanks also to Joseph Scheier-Dolberg, Oscar Tang and Agnes Hsu-Tang Associate Curator of Chinese Paintings. We wish to express our gratitude to Martina Droth, deputy director and chief curator at the Yale Center for British Art. At the Museum of Fine Arts, Boston, thanks go to Art of Europe Department Chair Frederick Ilchman; Marietta Cambareri, senior curator of European sculpture and Jetskalina H. Phillips Curator of Judaica; and Simona Di Nepi, Charles and Lynn Schusterman Curator of Judaica. Erica Hirshler, Croll Senior Curator of American Paintings, was equally supportive. At the Cleveland Museum of Art we are grateful to Clarissa von Spee, chair of Asian art and James and Donna Reid Curator of Chinese Art.

At the New York Public Library we thank Lyudmila Sholokhova, curator of the Dorot Jewish Collection, and Deborah Straussman, head registrar. Naomi Steinberger, director of library services at the Library of the Jewish Theological Seminary, was also supportive. At Princeton University, Sharon Brown, special collections assistant at the library, lent continued help, and in the Department of Art and Archaeology, Maureen Killeen, manager of finance and administration, offered indispensable assistance; Stacey Bonette helped secure images; and the photographer John Blazejewski kindly accommodated last-minute image requests. Arthur Kiron, Schottenstein-Jesselson Curator of Judaica Collections, and Abby Lang, registrar and collections and metadata management coordinator, at Penn Libraries; Nadav Sharon, Judaica librarian at the Thomas Fisher Rare Book Library at the University of Toronto; Abra Cohen, archivist at the American Jewish Joint Distribution Committee; our dear friend Diane Saltzman, director, Office of Constituency Engagement, and Suzy Snyder, curator, at the United States Holocaust Memorial Museum, all lent their support. Thanks also to Anne E. Peterson, curator of photographs, and Cindy Boeke, digital collections librarian in the DeGolyer Library, at Southern Methodist University.

We would also like to acknowledge the help and support of private collectors, art galleries, and auction houses: Toby Campbell of Rafael Valls Ltd.; Sandra Hindman of Les Enluminures Ltd.; Katherine Drake of Museum Services at Christie's New York; Nicholas White, formerly at Christie's London; Julian Gascoigne at Sotheby's London; and the staff at Kedem auction house in Jerusalem. Sharon Liberman Mintz, senior consultant of Judaica at Sotheby's New York, was particularly helpful in fielding many queries. Special thanks to Joyce and Kenneth X. Robbins for their warm hospitality and for enriching the exhibition with an important loan from their wonderful collection.

At the Jewish Museum, many staff members made the exhibition and this catalogue possible. We are deeply indebted to Claudia Gould, Helen Goldsmith Menschel Director, for her leadership and support; Ruth K. Beesch, former senior deputy director, programs and strategic initiatives, for her guidance in the early stages of this project; Darsie Alexander, senior deputy director and Susan and Elihu Rose Chief Curator, for her constant support; Jody Heher, director of program administration, for shepherding the exhibition schedule and budget; and to Elizabeth Abbarno, former assistant director, exhibitions, and Maureen Merrigan, exhibitions manager. Nelly Silagy Benedek, deputy director, education and programs; Jenna Weiss, assistant director of public programs; and Holly Harmon, manager of interpretive media, devised insightful programming. Warmest thanks also to Katie Hollander, chief development officer, Allison Curran, former director of institutional and major gifts, and Genesis Mullis, senior development officer, exhibitions, for their continued fundraising efforts, and to Sarah Supcoff, deputy director, audience development, and her team for diligently promoting the exhibition. Intern Emily Cao deftly researched the Sassoons' presence in her native China in the local press. Susan L. Braunstein, Senior Curator Emerita, and Sharon Wolfe, former assistant curator, were particularly supportive. Susan Higman Larsen was a patient and generous editor and Rebecca Merriman, rights and reproductions coordinator, nimbly procured the images that illustrate this catalogue. We are also extremely thankful to the staff at Yale University Press.

Julie Maguire, head registrar, is to be particularly commended for overseeing the complex arrangements of international loans during a global pandemic and for coordinating the exhibition installation. Thanks also to Derya Kovey, interim associate registrar. Michael Stafford, director of facilities, security and engineering; Val Ognev, associate director, operations; and their staffs did everything possible to prepare the galleries for installation and tended to many details. Exhibition designer Leslie Gill turned our curatorial vision into a splendid reality, together with Adam Johnston and Ines Yupanqui, an early contributor, while Miko McGinty was responsible for the beautiful exhibition graphics and book design.

On a personal note, we would like to thank our long-suffering husbands, who were enlisted many a time to edit, counsel, and safely deliver two nondriving curators to research appointments, with equanimity and good humor.

Claudia J. Nahson
Morris and Eva Feld Senior Curator

Esther da Costa Meyer, Professor Emerita
Guest Co-curator

Donors to the Exhibition

The Sassoons is made possible by The Achelis and Bodman Foundation; The American Friends of the Shanghai Museum; The David Berg Foundation; The Starr Foundation; E. Rhodes and Leona B. Carpenter Foundation; Barbara Tober, The Acronym Fund; The Gladys Krieble Delmas Foundation; David Keidan; the Oded Halahmy Foundation for the Arts; and The Nancy Sidewater Foundation.

Additional support is provided by the Horace W. Goldsmith Exhibitions Endowment Fund; The Joan Rosenbaum Exhibitions Endowment; The Centennial Fund; and the Dorot Foundation.

The publication is made possible, in part, by Denise Littlefield Sobel, the Arthur F. and Alice E. Adams Charitable Foundation, and the Barr Ferree Publication Fund at Princeton University.

Lenders to the Exhibition

British Library, London
British Museum, London
Cleveland Museum of Art
Emeric Hahn Gallery, Paris
Les Enluminures Ltd.
Fitzwilliam Museum, Cambridge, UK
Houghton Hall Collection, Norfolk, UK
Imperial War Museums, London
Israel Museum, Jerusalem
The Library of the Jewish Theological Seminary, New York
Metropolitan Museum of Art, New York
Musée du Louvre, Paris
Museum of Fine Arts, Boston
National Gallery, London
National Gallery of Ireland, Dublin
National Trust, UK
New York Public Library
Private collection, London
Private collections
Rafael Valls Ltd., London
Rare Book and Manuscript Library, University of Pennsylvania, Philadelphia
Kenneth X. and Joyce Robbins Collection
Royal Collection Trust, London
Collection of Adrian Sassoon
Syndics of Cambridge University Library, UK
Tate, London
Victoria and Albert Museum, London
Walker Art Gallery, National Museums, Liverpool
Yale Center for British Art, New Haven
Collection of Jane and Stuart Weitzman
Benjamin Zucker Family Collection

Introduction

There are multiple challenges to telling the story of the Sassoons, a transnational, multigenerational dynasty. It is a story of rupture and continuity, of exile and assimilation, which proceeded unevenly as the family grew and its paths diverged. It is a story of both globalization and of diaspora, and as the anthropologist James Clifford notes, diasporas "connect and disconnect, forget and remember, in complex, strategic ways." Covering a period of more than one hundred years, the Sassoons' sweeping narrative led them from Baghdad to Mumbai (formerly Bombay), Hong Kong, Shanghai, and London, with several way stations in between, linking East and West through trade, art collecting, architectural patronage, philanthropy, and communal and civic engagement.[1]

Although there have been attempts to connect the Sassoons to Sephardic roots, the family is of Mizrahi (Eastern) origin. Their status was legendary: they came to be linked to the Princes of Captivity, or *Roshei Galuta*, who ruled over Mesopotamian Jewry after the Exile to Babylon in the early sixth century BCE, and, by extension, to King David himself. The family's modern history begins in Ottoman Iraq in the early 1830s, with the patriarch David Sassoon (1792–1864), scion of a family that for generations had served as treasurers to the pashas and leaders of the Jewish community in Baghdad. Situated on the Tigris River, the city was home to a diverse population. Jews, Christians, and some Muslims dwelled on the river's east bank, with the Jewish quarter occupying the northeastern area. The west bank was inhabited solely by Muslims. Wealthy Jews lived along the river, in houses built on brick walls rising directly from the water. The homes had latticed windows, which allowed for natural ventilation, and flat roofs, where the inhabitants slept when it was hot. Beit "Abu-Reuben," the Sassoons' ancestral home, was one of the largest and finest houses in Baghdad. It had a huge courtyard planted with orange trees and was surrounded by a covered balcony (*shanasheel*), supported by slender wooden columns and elaborate muqarnas capitals. It was still occupied by the family in 1910, when David Sassoon's grandson David Solomon visited the city with his mother and sisters, though it had deteriorated. A few objects linked to the family's past in Iraq are known, including a magnificent ketubbah, or wedding contract, from Baghdad, witnessed by their ancestor Saleh ben David ben Jacob. Documenting a marriage in 1764, it is the oldest known ketubbah from that city.[2]

When the Mamluk ruler Dawud Pasha (c. 1767–1851) took control of the area roughly comparable to modern-day Iraq, he began a ruthless persecution against the Jews of Baghdad. David Sassoon, one of his targets, was forced to leave the

Attributed to William Melville, *Portrait of David Sassoon* (b. Baghdad 1792–d. Pune, India, 1864), mid-nineteenth century, oil on canvas, 41½ × 33 in. (105.4 × 83.8 cm), private collection. In the background are the hill of Malabar and Back Bay in Mumbai.

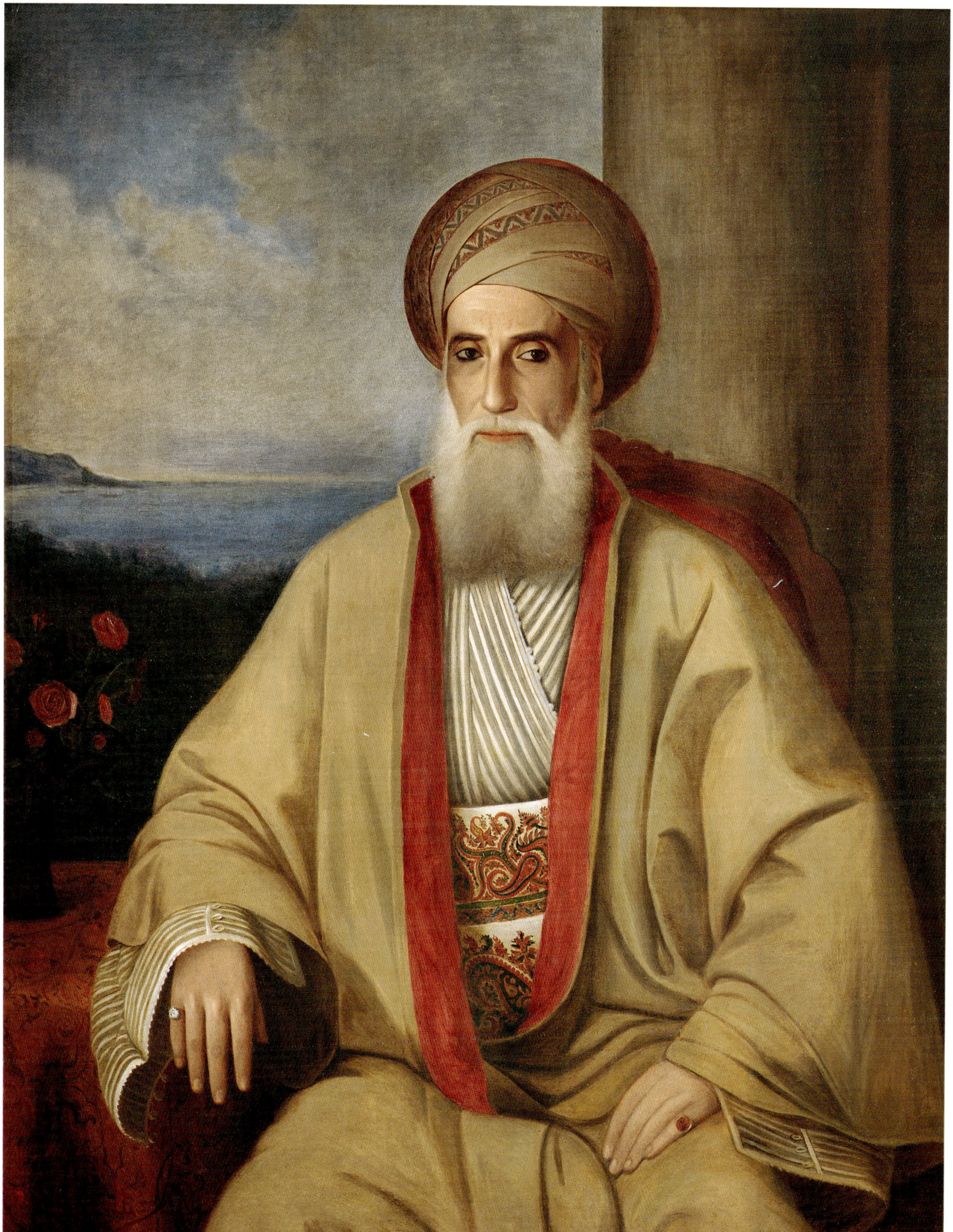

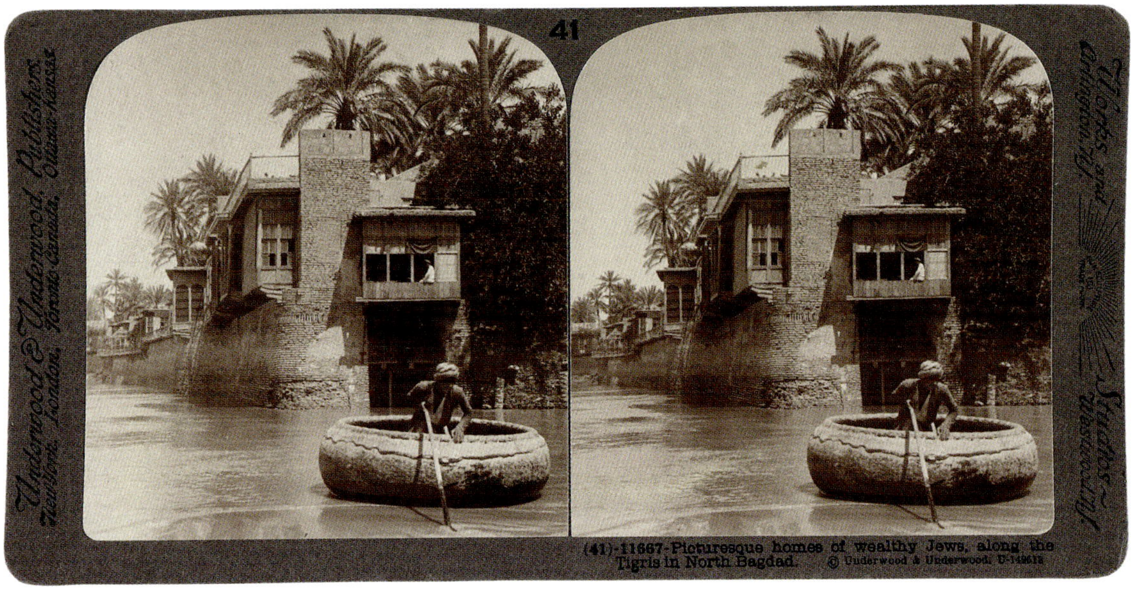

Keystone View Company, New York, Chicago, and London, England, "Picturesque Homes of Wealthy Jews along the Tigris in North Baghdad," Iraq, c. 1914, Jewish Museum exhibition purchase. Such stereograms exoticized Baghdadi Jews and their lifestyle.

city in 1830. Two years later, after a brief stint in Bushehr, he settled in Mumbai, where he joined a small community of Baghdadi Jews. Although he began modestly, trading in spices, cotton, wool, wheat, and pearls, he soon built up an increasingly successful business with a tight-knit organization, heavily reliant on family members. To ensure loyalty and confidentiality among his employees, he would hire young Jewish men from Baghdad, providing for their basic and religious needs, as well as the education of their children.

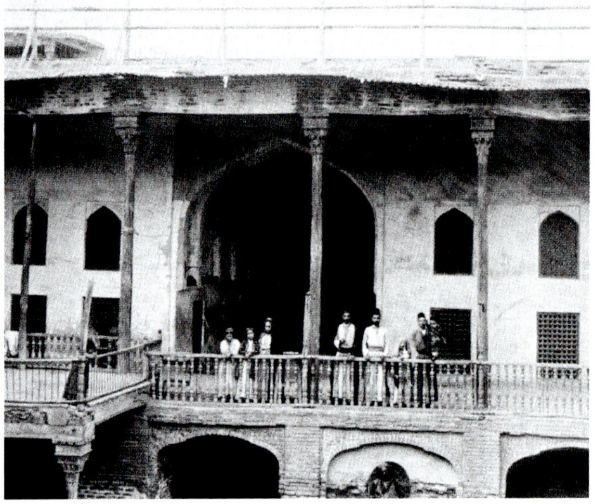

Beit "Abu-Reuben," ancestral home of the Sassoon family, Baghdad, late nineteenth–early twentieth century.

The Sassoons have repeatedly been called the "Rothschilds of the East." Yet as the historian Yaron Ben-Naeh points out, Jewish families from Islamic lands should not be seen through the lens of European Jewish history. Placing them within the context of other affluent merchant Jewish families in the Ottoman Empire, such as the Camondos of Istanbul and the Farhis of Damascus, he views the Sassoons as nineteenth-century Jewish *tujjars*, or merchants, operating between East and West in a manner akin to that of the medieval *tujjars* who traded across borders between the Islamic and Christian worlds.[3]

Following the First Opium War of 1839–42, waged by the British Empire against China, which opposed the harmful trade, the Chinese were forced to cede Hong Kong to Britain and open five of their ports, including Guangzhou (formerly Canton) and Shanghai. These treaty ports, as they came to be known, were granted extraterritorial status, meaning they were subject only to British law, which considered opium a legal commodity. These ports thus became gateways for the distribution of the drug in exchange for Chinese goods, primarily tea and silk.

Embracing the booming opium market, David Sassoon expanded his activities from his branches in Mumbai, Kolkata (formerly Calcutta), and Karachi to China (Hong Kong and later Shanghai), Japan (Kobe), Myanmar (formerly Burma), and Malaysia. The Sassoons also traded in other products, such as indigo and alum. His eight sons were soon deployed in various countries to oversee the family's burgeoning commercial empire, which had become deeply entwined with British colonial interests. In the early 1840s, David Sassoon's son Elias David (1820–1880) had been the first member of the family to set foot in China, where he had gone to explore business prospects. The Hong Kong–based Jardine, Matheson & Co., named after its Scottish proprietors, dominated the opium traffic from 1842 until the early 1870s, when David Sassoon & Co. took the lead,

OPPOSITE
Marriage contract signed by David Sassoon's grandfather, Saleh ben David ben Jacob, one of the witnesses, Baghdad, Iraq, 1764; groom: Mikhael, son of David Yeshu'ah Gubbay; bride: Sarah, daughter of Saleh Aaron Gubbay, ink on German appliqué decorative paper, 25⅜ × 18⅞ in. (65.5 × 48 cm), Benjamin Zucker Family Collection (Z241), formerly in the David Solomon Sassoon Collection (no. 204).

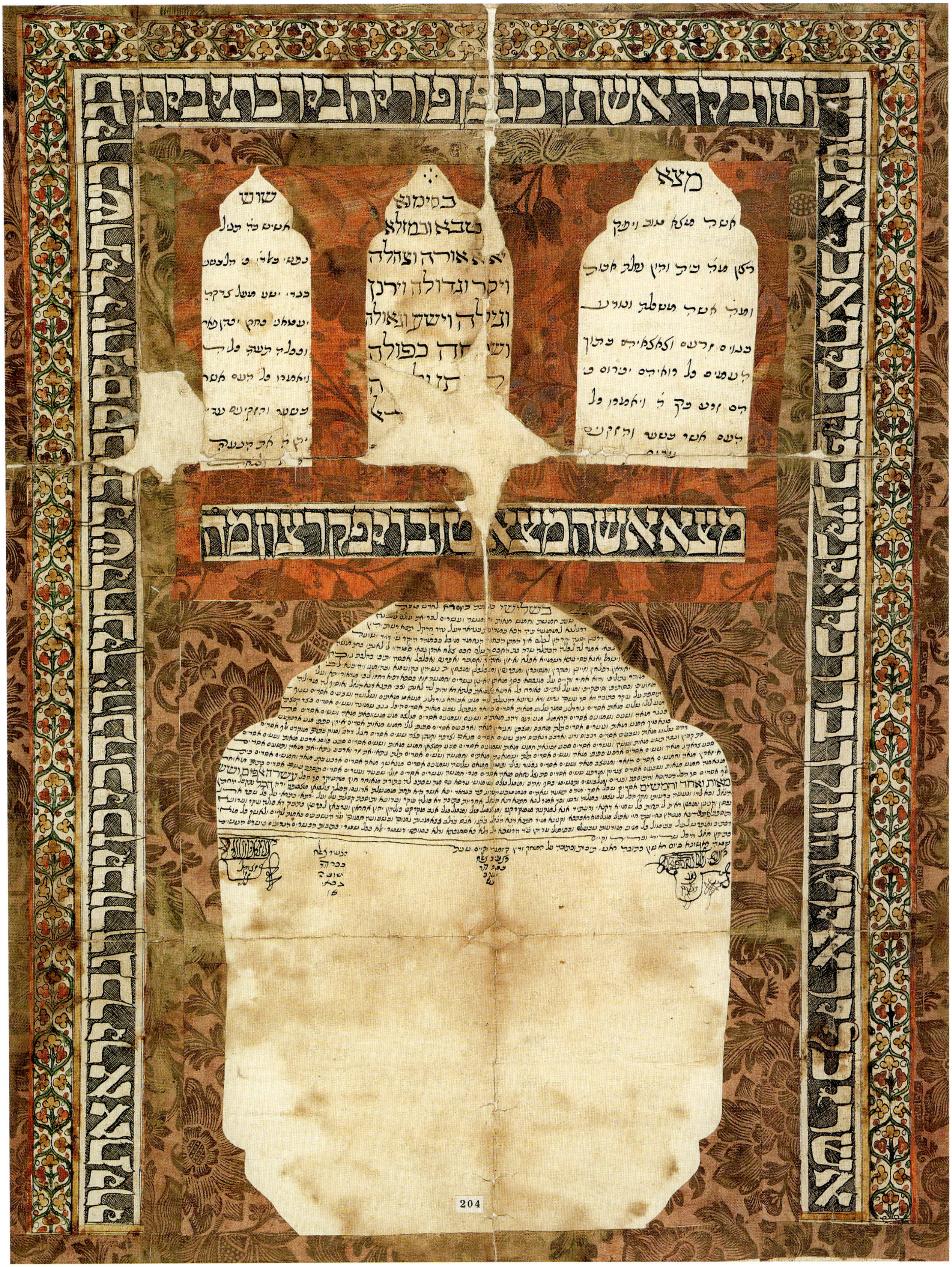
מצא אשה מצא טוב ויפק רצון מה
מצא
שוש

becoming the main traders of opium. To distribute Indian opium in China, the Sassoons relied on swift-sailing clippers. By 1854, "the *Henry Ellis*, owned by Messrs David Sassoon and Sons, was the only Jewish-owned opium ship among the six well-manned and armed opium ships . . . moored at Saddle Island, at the mouth of the Pearl River in the vicinity of Guangzhou."[4] The sons were later involved in several banks in different countries.

David would officially cement his relationship with the Crown in 1853, when he became a citizen, and he would later be granted a coat of arms. He signed an oath of allegiance in Hebrew, as, despite being multilingual, he never mastered English.[5] In 1858, Sassoon David Sassoon (1832–1867) left for London to open an office of David Sassoon & Co. A photograph shows the patriarch with his three eldest sons, including Sassoon David Sassoon, shortly before his departure from Mumbai to England, the first member of the family to settle there.

Looking back at this history from the perspective of the present day, we cannot help but wonder how David Sassoon and his sons were able to reconcile deep Jewish religious observance with their participation in a pernicious trade. The principle of *pikuach nefesh* in Jewish law (based on Lev. 18:5) places the preservation of human life above most religious duties. A rare item in the collection of Hebrew manuscripts amassed by David Sassoon's grandson, David Solomon Sassoon, is a Hebrew Prayer for Dreams that would reveal figures to secure success at an opium auction. A bizarre intersection of religion and commerce, it combines biblical passages on divine revelation, including excerpts from the story of Jacob's dream and the book of Ezekiel, with incantations that imbue the text with an amuletic quality.[6] The fact that the scribe, Joseph Rahamim, copied it in Kolkata in 1917, at a time when opium trade was being eradicated, attests to the drug's endurance despite its harmful effects.

David Sassoon may not have been fully aware of or concerned about the detrimental effects of the opium trade on the population of China, a distant place he never visited and knew only vicariously through his sons who were posted there. He did use part of his immense wealth to build important charitable institutions in the land that had welcomed him and to benefit the Jewish community of Iraq, the ancestral homeland he had been forced to leave behind. In fact, the opium trade and philanthropy were directly intertwined in the family's dealings, as attested in the Sassoons' business ledgers, in

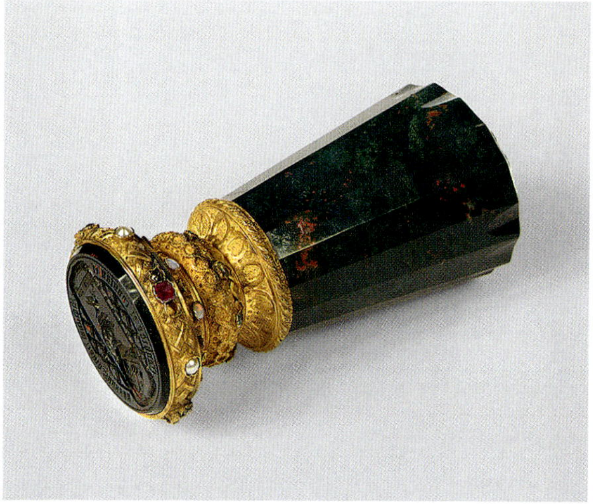

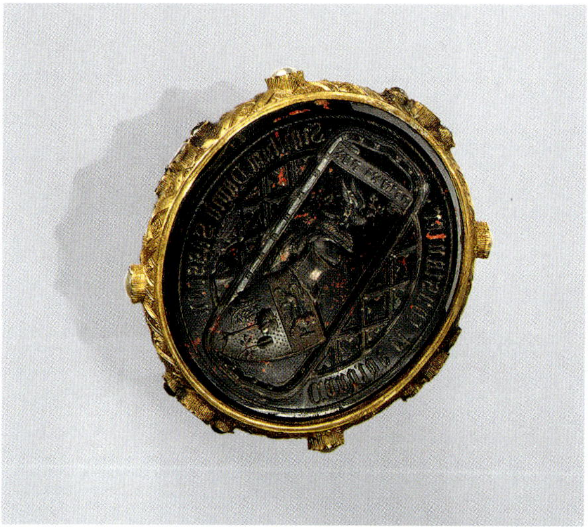

TOP AND CENTER
David Sassoon's desk seal, probably 1863 or 1864, bloodstone, seal set with gold, precious stones, and pearls, Norfolk, UK, Houghton Hall Collection. David Sassoon was granted arms on December 20, 1862. The seal bears the Sassoons' motto, "Truth and Faith," in both Latin, *Candide et Constanter*, and Hebrew, *Emet ve-emunah*. The phrase is recited after the *shema*, a central Jewish prayer. The lion passant holding a rod refers to the verse "The scepter shall not depart from Judah" (Gen. 49:10), asserting the Sassoon family's legendary Davidic ancestry. The palm tree is an allusion to Psalms 92:13: "The righteous bloom like a date-palm." To the right of the tree is a pomegranate, recalling the saying in the Babylonian Talmud "as full of good deeds as the pomegranate is full of seeds" (Sanhedrin 37a), stressing the central role of philanthropy in the family. At left of the tree is a branch of laurel, traditionally signifying harmony, and a dove with an olive branch in its beak is over the helmet surmounting the shield.

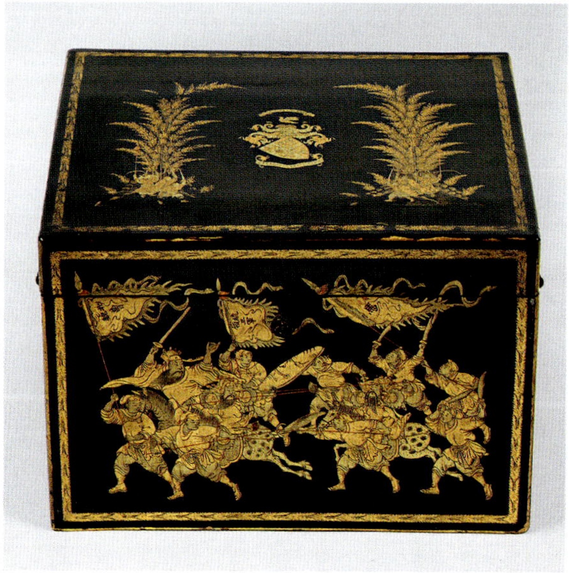

BOTTOM
Box with the Sassoon family coat of arms on the cover, probably China, nineteenth century, lacquered wood, Norfolk, UK, Houghton Hall Collection.

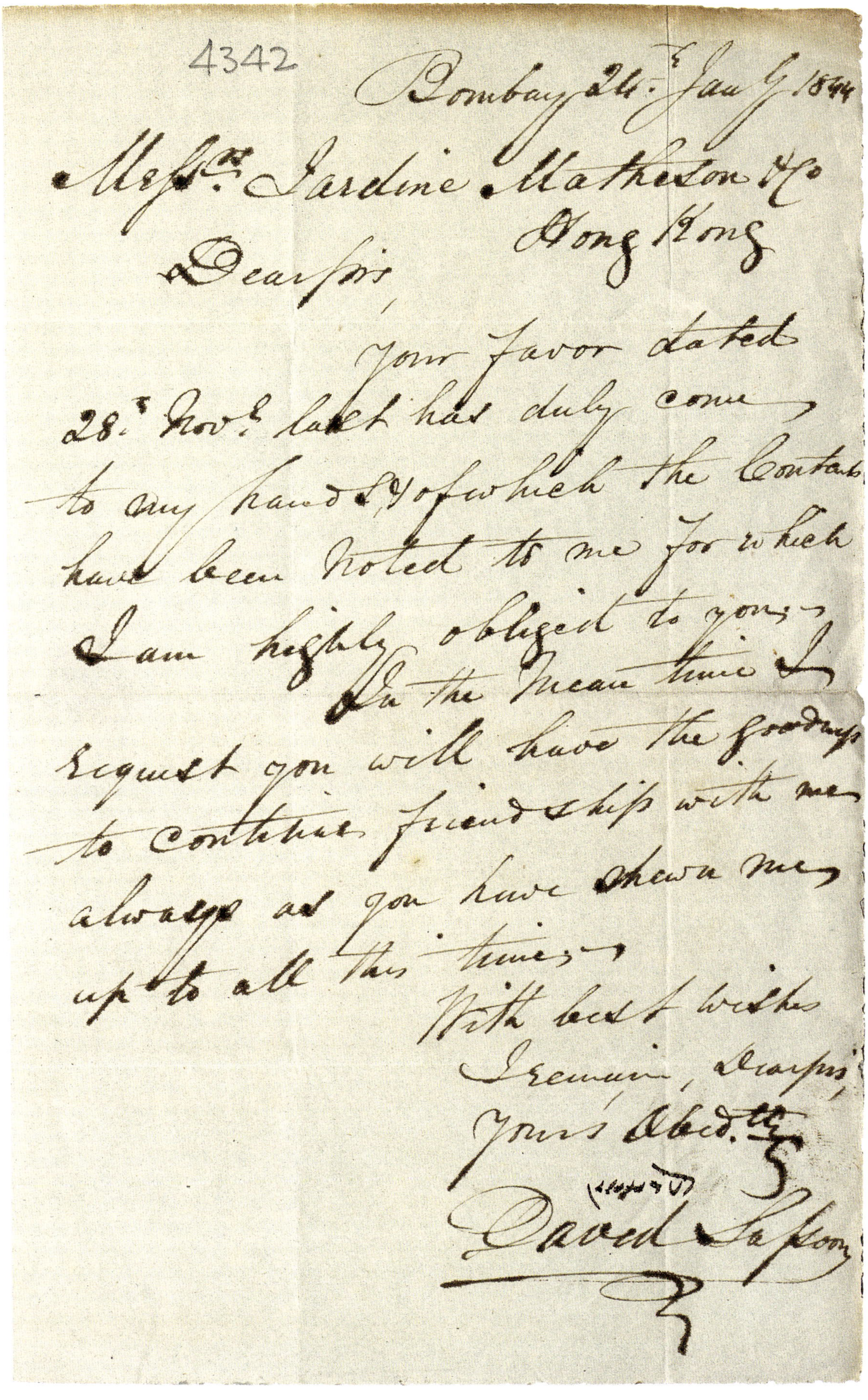
4342

Bombay 24th Jany 1844

Messrs. Jardine Matheson & Co
Hong Kong

Dear Sir,

Your favor dated 28th Novr. last has duly come to my hand & of which the Contents have been Noted to me for which I am highly obliged to you. In the mean time I request you will have the goodness to continue friendship with me always as you have shewn me up to all this time.

With best wishes
I remain, Dear Sir,
Yours Obedt. Servt.

David Sassoon

Business letter from David Sassoon to Jardine, Matheson & Co., future rivals in the opium trade, Mumbai, January 24, 1844, Cambridge University Library, UK, ms. JM B6/4/4342. Sassoon's signature is in Hebrew, as he never mastered English.

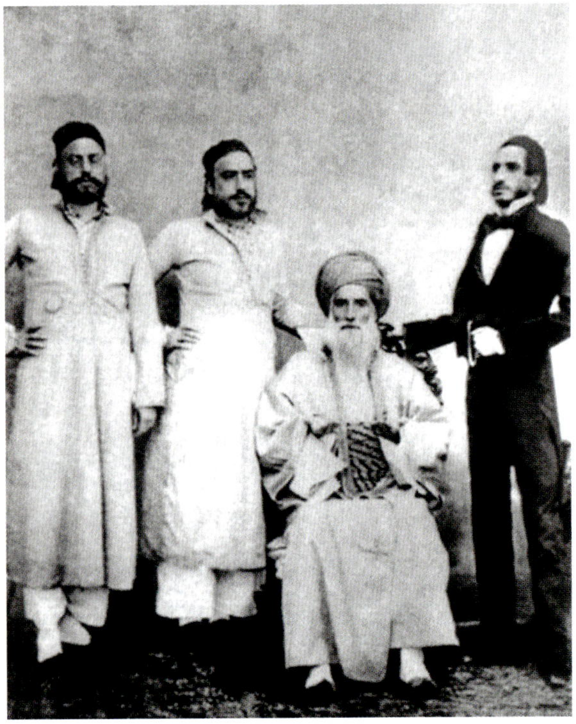

David Sassoon (seated) with his three eldest sons, Elias David, Albert Abdullah, and Sassoon David Sassoon. Sassoon David is shown in Western attire before his departure for England in 1858.

which a set percentage earmarked for charity was charged as cost on each transaction.[7] What David Sassoon accomplished in the last few years of his life would lay the foundation for the family's extraordinary religious and cultural legacy. In India, and later China, the family left an indelible architectural footprint. In Iraq, he and his family would enable the restoration and upkeep of Jewish holy sites, and would continue to play a leading role in the community despite no longer residing there. But it was Britain that would be the ultimate home for most of his descendants.

By the late nineteenth century, the Sassoons who had settled in England were approaching the pinnacle of their social, cultural, and political aspirations. They had strengthened their ties to the Continent through intermarriage with distinguished Ashkenazi dynasties, including the Rothschild and de Gunzburg families, and in Britain, their friends and intimates included politicians at the highest levels of government, as well as members of the aristocracy and the royal family. The economic and social forces that increased the Sassoons' affluence and influence also enabled them to collect art of exceptional quality. Several Sassoons were renowned and influential hosts; distinguished collectors of Asian, European, and British fine and applied arts; and major benefactors of both cultural and social institutions. What had begun as a pragmatic alliance with British imperialism had developed into a deeply felt identification and patriotic loyalty to British culture.

In the present exhibition and the accompanying catalogue, we seek more inclusive ways of telling the story of this patrician and patriarchal family. To this end, we underscore the role of the women, who have traditionally been excluded from the narrative. A long Hebrew poem in the Magen David Synagogue in Mumbai extols the founding patriarch and his male offspring as "King David Sassoon and the sons of David, priests, ministers, and deputies," but it is silent about the mothers who birthed and raised them, and their sisters, wives, and daughters.[8] Many of their names and contributions have been left out of publications on the Sassoons, although they played a major role in the family's philanthropy, business, and cultural endeavors. The Sassoons' close collaboration with other social, political, and religious groups, without which their achievements would not have been possible, has also received little attention.[9] The buildings they erected, the homes in which they lived, and the objects they collected and cherished all contribute to this narrative. Each has its own story, but here, together, they evoke both an era and a family at the convergence of politics and religion, commerce and culture, social aspiration, and public service.

From our present perspective, this is also a modern story of exile and immigration, of belonging and exclusion, though we must resist facile comparisons to the refugees of today. The chronicle of the affluent Sassoon family cannot serve as an allegory of the modern condition. Nevertheless, we cannot ignore the forms of dispossession that all refugees have in common, regardless of their position in life: the loss of the grounding safety of the originary home, the mother tongue, and everyday habits of cherished routine. Driven from Baghdad by persecution, the first generation of Sassoons assumed the precarious status of stateless Jews. Memories of their Iraqi homeland provided a measure of cultural stability, but it was the Torah that anchored their identity. In time, as their physical and spiritual homeland grew more distant, new homes brought new loyalties and new identities.

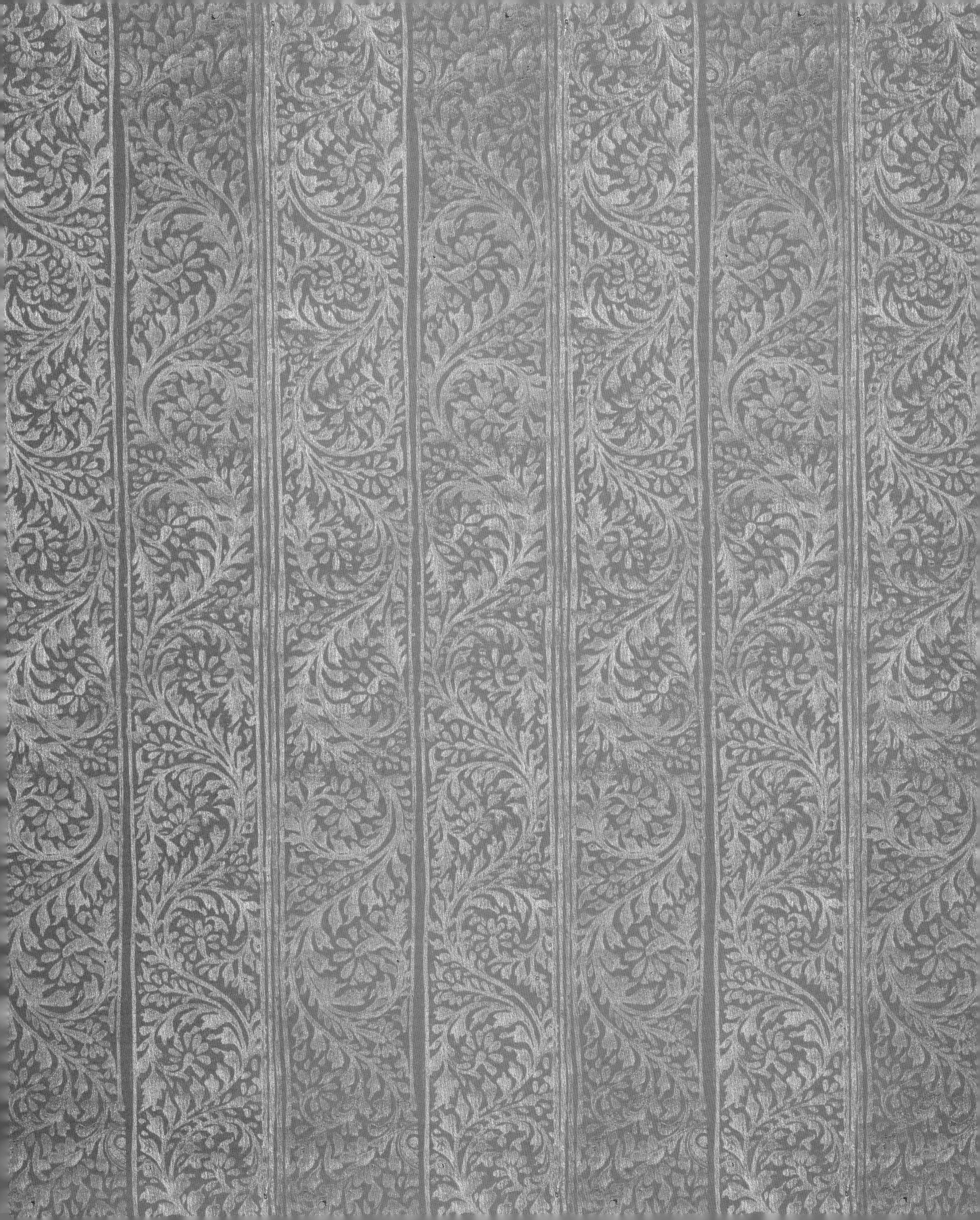

From Commissioners to Collectors

The immense wealth of the Sassoons enabled them to collect splendid works of art, which represent the various cultures that welcomed them: Jewish ceremonial art from Iraq; Indian marriage contracts; ceramics and ivories crafted in China; European decorative arts; and Western paintings from the eighteenth to the early twentieth century. The Sassoons' first interest was in Jewish ceremonial art. Gradually, they turned from commissioning such objects for communal or private use to collecting superbly crafted Judaica. The early commissions aimed to express the family's Jewish identity through beautiful objects while allowing future generations to develop a deep appreciation for their spiritual and aesthetic value.

The earliest known Jewish ritual objects commissioned by a Sassoon are three Torah scrolls in decorated silver cases dedicated by Sason ben Saleh ben David (David Sassoon's father, known as Sheikh Sassoon), to the Great Synagogue of Baghdad. He presented the first, dated 1790/91, in honor of Ezra the Scribe. Baghdadi Jews would dedicate Torah scrolls in memory of deceased relatives, but if they commissioned one for themselves it had to be devoted to Ezekiel the Prophet, Ezra the Scribe, or Joshua the High Priest, whose tombs were traditionally believed to be in Iraq. The Sassoons would be involved in the upkeep of these holy sites. In 1809/10, Sheikh Sassoon dedicated a second Torah scroll in memory of his eldest son, Reuben, who had died in the plague of 1802. A third scroll, which Sheikh Sassoon presented in 1821, honored Amam (née Gubbay), his deceased wife. In 1910 his great-grandson, David Solomon Sassoon (1880–1942), visited the synagogues of Baghdad. He found the Torah scrolls to be the oldest and largest ones in cases and recorded their inscriptions. In doing so, he was both preserving the memory of the heirlooms for his descendants and following his bibliophile's impulse to catalogue and document, occupying a key role among the family collectors.[1]

David Solomon related that while in Baghdad he "tried to find old ritual objects made of silver that were used in the synagogue, but I only succeeded in purchasing a pair of finials and a singleton. The ones used today are new and the rest were sold from time to time for the sake of paying the government tax on behalf of the poor."[2] This charitable purpose may have trumped the injunction against sale or pawning stated in the Hebrew inscriptions on a pair of silver-gilt Torah finials from Iraq once in the Sassoon family. (A similar warning appears on two of the Torah scrolls in cases dedicated by Sheikh Sassoon.) The beautifully decorated pair may well be the one he acquired. Each finial is crowned by a small *hamsah*, the hand-shaped symbol, bearing on one side the

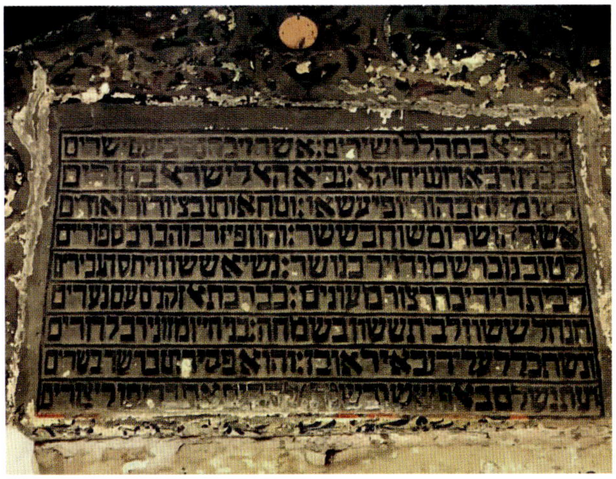

Hebrew inscription at the Tomb of the Prophet Ezekiel in Al-Kifl, Iraq, with poem by Hakham Abdallah el-Khdeir commemorating the restoration of the shrine by David Sassoon in 1858/59.

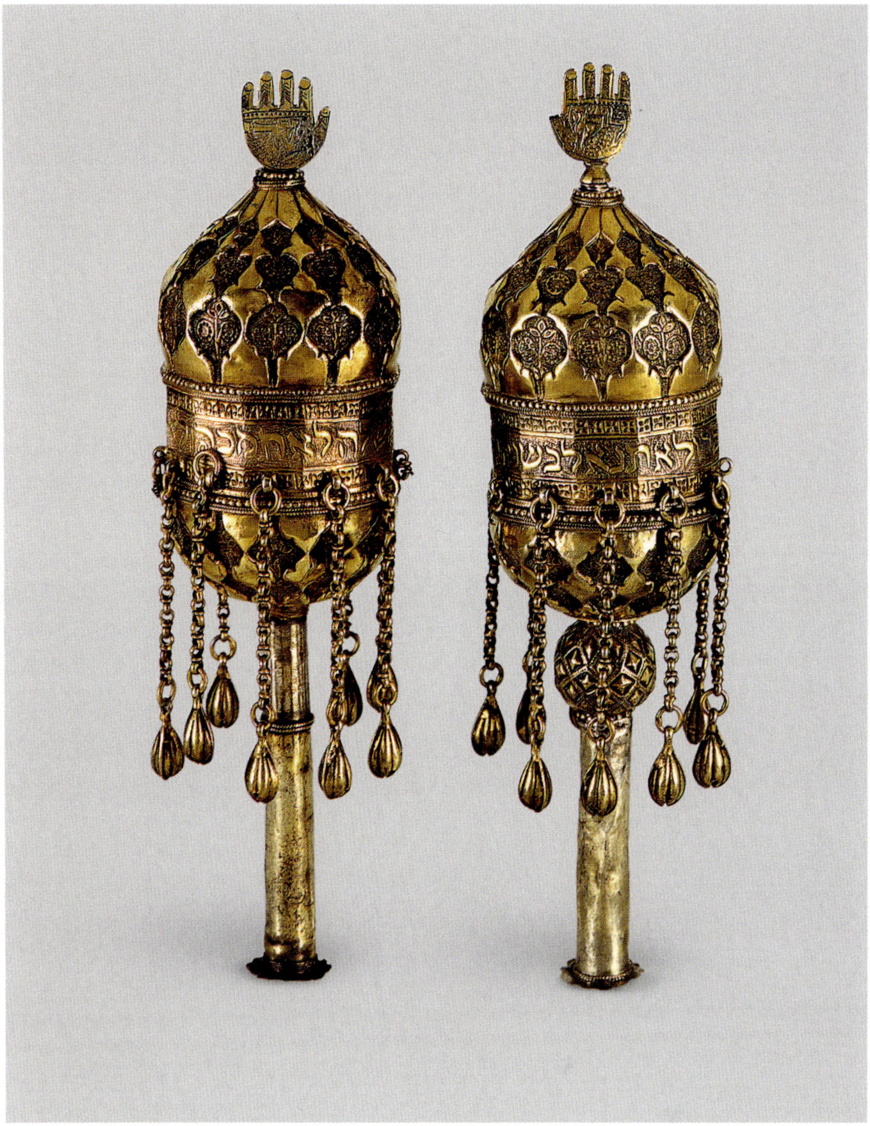

Torah finials, Iraq, 1741/42, silver gilt, each 10¼ in. (26 cm), Jerusalem, Israel Museum, extended loan from the collection of René and Susanne Braginsky, Zurich, 147/412, formerly in the Sassoon Family Collection.

acronym for "I wait for your deliverance, O Lord" (Gen. 49:18), and on the reverse, "Shaddai," one of the divine names. These inscriptions, often found on Jewish amulets, imbue the finials with an apotropaic quality. Dedicated in 1741/42, the pair is probably the earliest dated one that survives from Iraq. As for the singleton, one such finial, bearing an inscription in memory of Ma'atuka, daughter of Sheikh Sassoon, was also once owned by the Sassoon family. In the Great Synagogue of Baghdad, David Solomon also saw a white calico Torah curtain, c. 1800, used on Simhat Torah, the holiday of the Rejoicing of the Law. On the curtain, Rabbi Sason ben Mordecai Shindookh (1747–1830), a kabbalist and author, had drawn the plans of the division of Israel and of the Temple according to Prophet Ezekiel. The collector would purchase it ten years later.[3]

A *hamsah*-shaped pilgrimage standard, formerly in David Solomon's collection, is a rare remnant of a distinctive Iraqi Jewish practice—the pilgrimage to the sacred tombs. The silver banner, which would have been carried on a pole, bears the Hebrew inscription "Presented by . . . Joseph Abdullah Elyahu in honor of our master the Prophet Ezekiel . . . in the year 5587 [=1826/27]." When a child or a woman became ill, it was customary for relatives to visit the tombs of Ezra the Scribe or Ezekiel the Prophet bearing banners. In

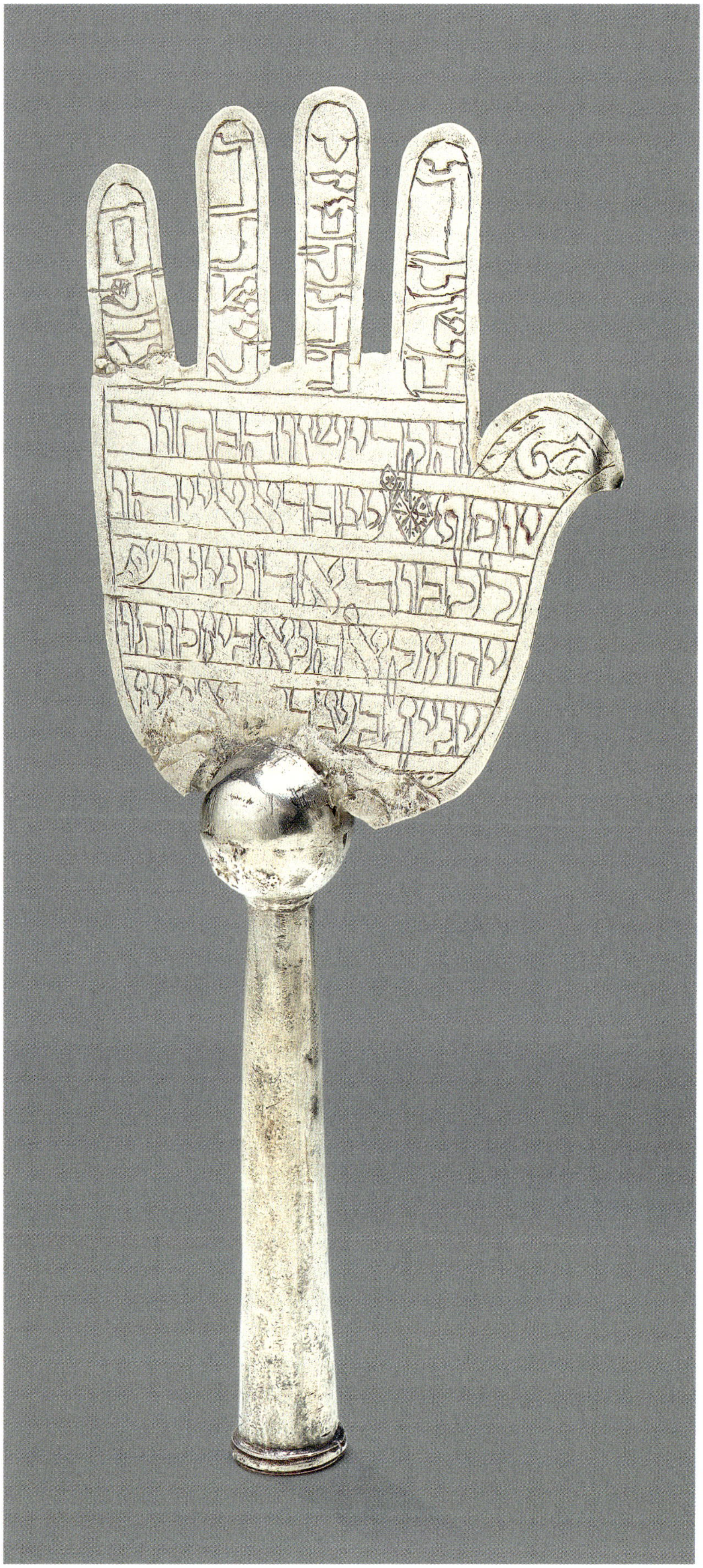

LEFT
Standard carried during pilgrimage to the shrine of the Prophet Ezekiel in Al-Kifl, Iraq, 1826/27, silver, 9⅞ × 4½ in. (25.1 × 11.4 cm), New York, Jewish Museum, purchase: Judaica Acquisition Fund, 2000-49, formerly in the David Solomon Sassoon Collection.

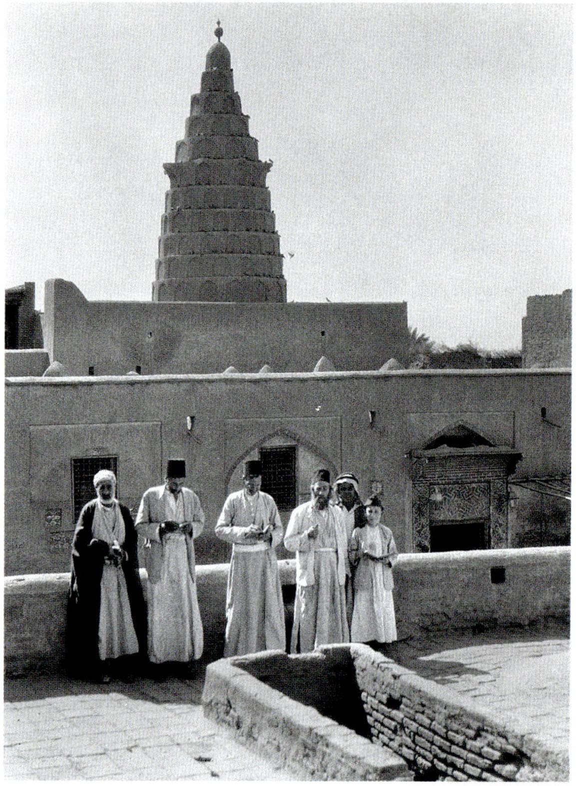

Jews at the Tomb of the Prophet Ezekiel in Al-Kifl, Iraq, 1932. Jews customarily visited the site, sacred also to Muslims, during the holiday of Shavuot.

preparation, a ceremony would be held involving a bowl in which several items would be placed, including silk threads, a long silk cloth, a piece of wood covered with silver foil, and a silver hand-shaped banner inscribed with the name of the sick person. The "Miracle of the Silver Hand" is said to have occurred on Shavuot, "when a pilgrim came from afar bringing with him such a silver hand as a gift to Ezra, and before landing, it fell into the river, yet by miracle the hand was found floating in the river, and was laid by him on the catafalque." In 1853, David Sassoon gifted a beautifully embroidered cover for the bier of Prophet Ezekiel. The textile was inscribed with a poem by the Baghdadi Hakham Abdallah el-Khdeir, which honored the prophet and extolled the donor of the precious cloth. An additional Hebrew dedication mentioned that the textile, no longer extant, was sent by David Sassoon "from the city of Bombay to the city of his birth Baghdad," the two main centers of his life.[4]

By 1862/63 David Sassoon had also erected an eponymous synagogue in Hillah, the town near Al-Kifl where the Shrine of Ezekiel is located. According to his grandson's description: "The size of the *tevah* (pulpit) is as large as the synagogue which is itself quite small. In a corner inside the synagogue is a big tree said to be over one hundred years old." David and his son Albert Abdullah were also important donors to the Alliance Israélite of Baghdad established in 1864. The Collège A. D. Sassoon for boys, named after its benefactor Albert Abdullah, featured a synagogue. Ties with Ottoman Palestine were also maintained by the first generations of Sassoons, who contributed to causes there through emissaries, including Shneur Zalman of Hebron, whom they hosted in Mumbai in the 1850s. He obtained from them a donation for the erection of the Tzemach-Tzedek Habad Synagogue in Jerusalem. The 1888 edition of *Sefer Zikhron Yerushalayim*, Shneur Zalman's account of his fundraising travels, features an illustration of the synagogue with the English inscription: "This synagogue was built by Messrs Dawid Sassoon & Sons in Jerusalem the Holy Land."[5]

The Sassoons also dedicated ritual objects to synagogues in Ottoman Palestine. A silver plaque inscribed in memory of Hannah Khatun Sassoon (Lady Anne, née Moise) (1826–1895), and once affixed to a Torah curtain, bears the Hebrew inscription: "This Torah ark curtain is consecrated upon the passing of the noble, modest, elder Lady Hannah Khatun daughter of Noam, may she abide in Eden, wife of Sir Abdallah David Sassoon . . . to the Yagel Yaakov Synagogue in the Holy City of Jerusalem. . . . She passed away in Bombay on Wednesday 13 Tevet 5655 [January 9, 1895]. May her soul be bound up in the bond of life." A second inscription embroidered on velvet, also once part of a Torah curtain, was dedicated to Shalom Shabazi Synagogue in Jerusalem by Hannah Khatun's niece Rachel Sassoon (née Isaac) (1857–1911), wife of Jacob Elias (1844–1916). Women hoping for children would visit the tomb of Rabbi Shabazi in Yemen and synagogues dedicated to him outside Yemen. Having lost her only child in infancy, Rachel must have dedicated the Torah curtain for that reason.[6]

In Jewish communities, it was not uncommon for members who donated ritual objects for synagogue use to maintain ownership and use them on special occasions. Nevertheless, Sheikh Sassoon set stringent conditions for the use of the Torah scroll he presented in 1790/91. His great-granddaughter Mozelle (1884–1921) writes in her diary about attending Rosh Hashanah services at the Great Synagogue of Baghdad together with her family in 1910:

> Grandpapa, Sheikh Sassoon's *Sefer* [Torah scroll] was brought out as *Sefer Rishon* [the first Torah scroll]. It is contained in a beautiful, chased silver case (*tik*) much tarnished with age. He . . . made a condition that it should be brought out first for *Kol Nidre* [the prayer that ushers in Yom Kippur] and every holiday including the Festivals and *Hol Hamoed* [the working days within the weeks of Passover and Sukkot] and [on three] Sabbaths . . . and one of the direct descendants from the paternal side is to be called up to the *Sefer*. . . . Our family here have the original document . . . and it is signed by the Rabbis of those days. A few years ago, others . . . wanted to do away with this time-honored right. . . . The descendants . . . also have a right to sit in the middle *Hekhal* which is the principal one and where our ancestor Sheikh Sassoon sat.

The number of privileges described by Mozelle is a remarkable testament to the Sassoons' continued status as leaders of the Jewish community of Baghdad.[7]

Her ancestor's "beautiful, chased silver case (*tik*) much tarnished with age" may have particularly resonated with Mozelle. Years earlier, her mother, the devoted Flora (1856–1936), had

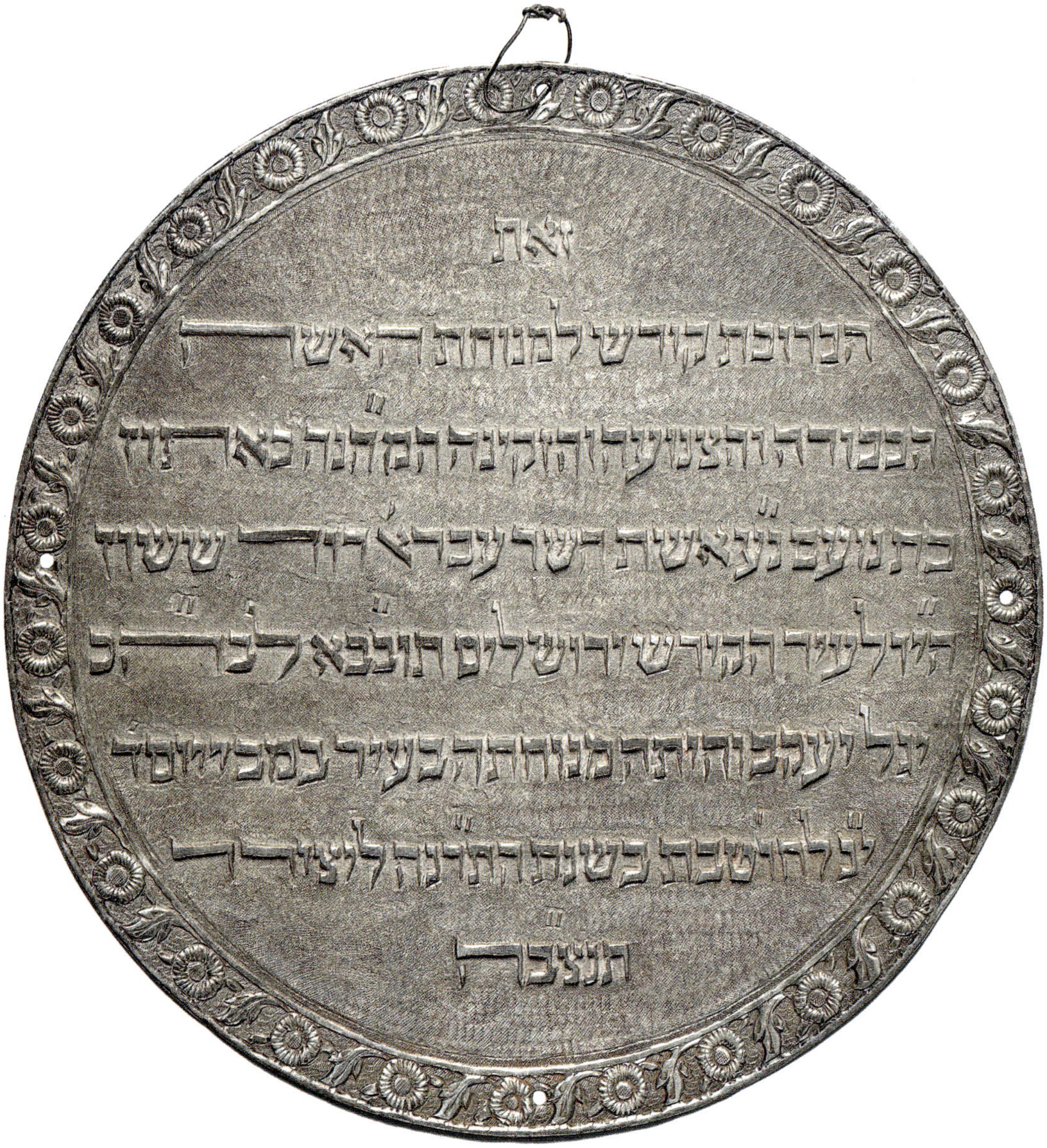

Plaque from a Torah ark curtain in memory of Hannah Khatun Sassoon, probably Mumbai, 1895, silver, 6½ in. (16.5 cm) in diameter, New York, Jewish Museum, purchase: Judaica Acquisitions Committee Fund, 2021-1.

OPPOSITE
Inscription from a Torah ark curtain dedicated by Rachel Sassoon, probably Mumbai, c. 1886–90, velvet and metallic thread, 10¼ × 9¾ in. (26 × 24.8 cm), New York, Jewish Museum, purchase: gift of Dr. Harry G. Friedman, by exchange, 1993-211. The Hebrew inscription reads: "Holy to the Lord/ heartfelt gift of . . . Mrs. Rachel wife of the notable honored Yaakov Elihau David Sassoon . . . from the city of Bombay may they perform good deeds and have long life . . . in the name of the Godly kabbalist/ Rabbi Shalom Shabazi. . . . In his synagogue in the Holy City of Jerusalem, may it be built and inaugurated soon in our time." Heart-shaped dedicatory inscriptions are often found on Torah ark curtains dedicated to Baghdadi Jewish synagogues in India.

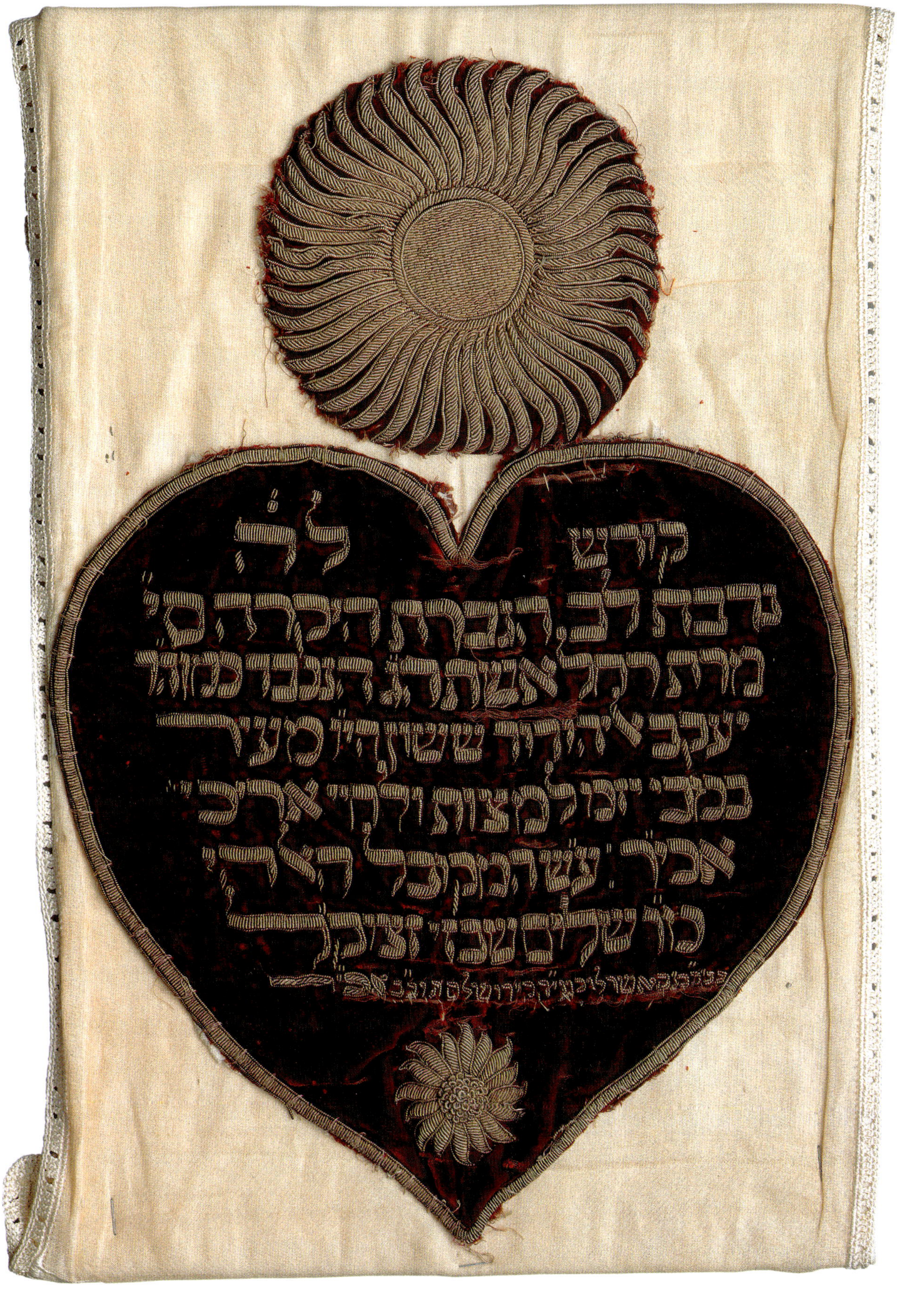
קודש לה'
ידבה לבה הגברת היקרה ס'
מרת רחל אשת הר"ג הנכבד כמוה"ר
יעקב יהודה ששון הי"ו

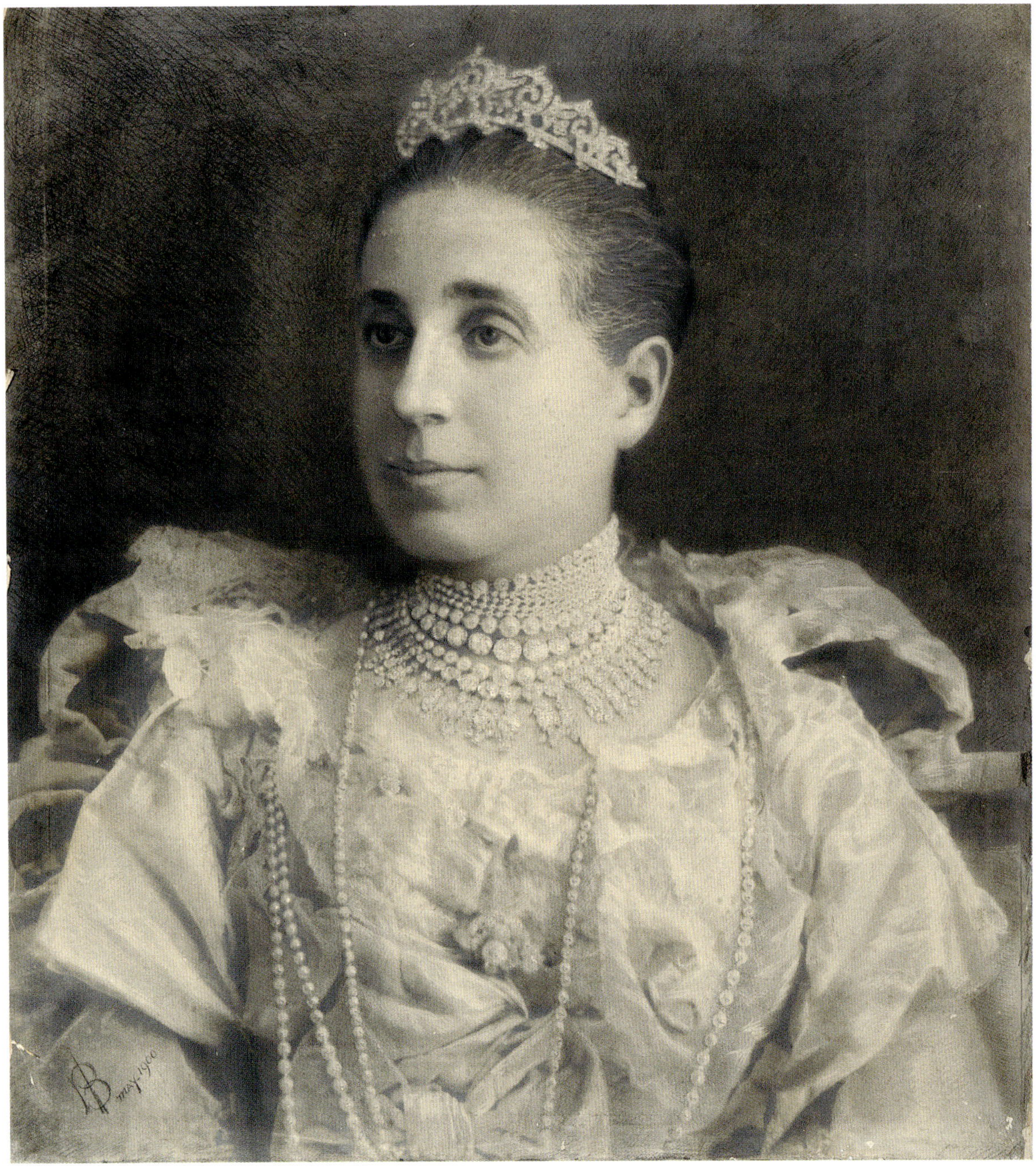

Flora Sassoon, photographed in 1900. Following the death of her husband, Solomon, in 1894, Flora, known for her scholarship, managed the Mumbai (Bombay) office of David Sassoon & Co. until 1901—the only woman in the family to oversee a branch of the firm.

commissioned a set of Torah and haftarah scrolls in superb cases bearing Hebrew inscriptions in her honor. With its scrolls produced in Iraq, kept within silver-gilt cases crafted in China, commissioned for use in Mumbai, and later taken to England, this exceptional set encompasses the breadth of the Sassoons' journey from East to West, while continuing the family's tradition of honoring the Torah through its beautification. Rabbi Joseph Hayyim (the Ben Ish Hai) (1832–1909), the spiritual leader of Iraqi Jews, had sent Flora the Torah scroll from Baghdad, and possibly also the haftarah scroll, containing the corresponding readings from the Prophets that follow the weekly Torah portions. In his letter of March 8, 1888, the rabbi notes that he had been pleased to hear that Flora had received a scroll he had sent (possibly the haftarah scroll) and reports that the copying of the Torah scroll is almost complete and will probably reach her by Shavuot of that year. He also mentions a second Torah scroll being prepared for Mozelle (Sassoon) Ezra, the daughter of Albert Abdullah, another woman in the family who actively commissioned ritual objects and contributed to the preservation of the Shrine of Ezra the Scribe in Iraq.[8]

The matching cases, made of wood, are sheathed with silver panels embellished with

OPPOSITE
Torah and haftarah scrolls in cases commissioned by Flora Sassoon, Iraq and China, c. 1888–93, cases: silver gilt and enamel, 37⅜ in. (95 cm) and 30 in. (76.2 cm), scrolls: ink on parchment, private collection.

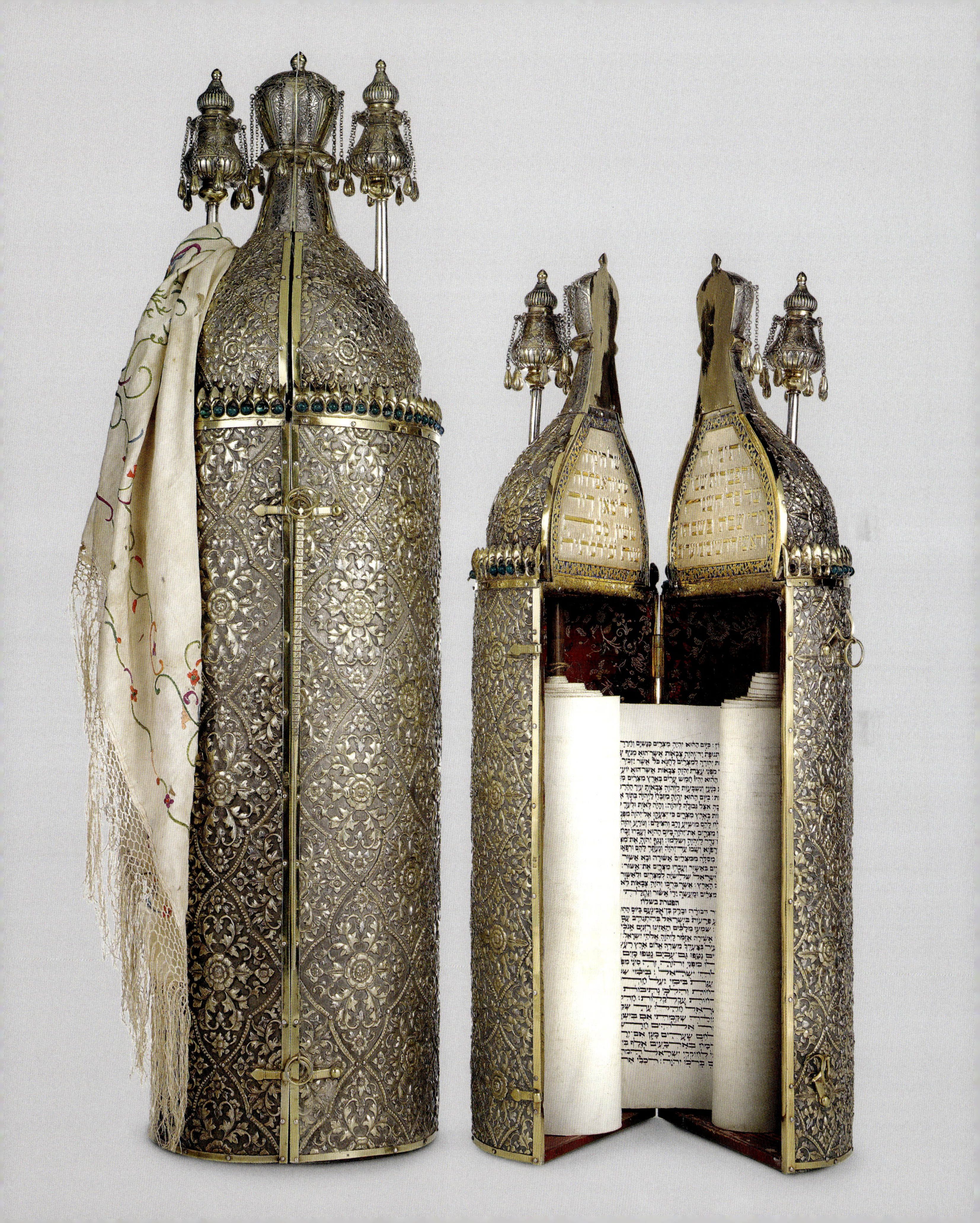

foliage motifs in a trellis pattern. Inside they bear Hebrew inscriptions rendered in relief and framed by decorative bands in blue and green enamel, not drawn behind glass as had been customary in Iraq—a change effected by Chinese silversmiths who created these elaborate cases for Baghdadi Jews in India. The inscription on the Torah case reads: "This is the Torah that Moses set before the Israelites [Deut. 4:44]. These are the laws, rules, and instructions that the Lord established, through Moses on Mount Sinai, between Himself and the Israelite people [Lev. 26:46]. This *tik* [case] and the Torah scroll within it belong to the precious Señora Farha [wife of] Sliman David Sassoon, more blessed than the women of the tent, in the year 'and I shall bless her' [Gen. 17:16] [chronogram for the year [5]643=1882/83]." The inscription on the second case reads: "This *tik* and the *haftarot* for the entire year—each Sabbath, New Moon, and festival—within it belong to the precious Señora Farha [wife of] Sliman David Sassoon, more blessed than the women of the tent, in the year 'and I shall bless her.'" According to Avraham Ben-Ya'akov, the case for the Torah had been ordered from China and arrived in Mumbai, where the scroll had been placed in it in 1893. As suggested by Sharon Liberman Mintz, the ten-year disparity between the date on the inscription and the date reported by Ben-Ya'akov may be attributed to a mistake by the Chinese silversmith, who left the letter *yod*, whose numerical value is ten, unmarked in the chronogram. Another Torah scroll in a similar case would be dedicated more than a decade later to the Keneseth Eliyahoo Synagogue in Mumbai by Flora's niece Rachel, the wife of Jacob Sassoon.[9]

Flora's devotion and deep ties to Baghdad had been instilled in her by her parents, Aziza (1839–1897; Anne and Albert Abdullah's daughter) and Ezekiel Gubbay (1824–1896). Ezekiel had immigrated to Mumbai in 1842 and traveled to China the following year, one of the first Baghdadi Jewish traders to do so. Three miniature manuscripts, including one containing "Afternoon and Evening Prayers for Weekdays and Sabbaths according to the Rite of Baghdad" and a Passover Haggadah, were penned by Ezekiel in 1840–42, serving as a portable library to aid him in the observance of Judaism during his transient life as a trader.[10] His magnificent bridegroom robe, made of sumptuous Indian silk, is fashioned in the Baghdadi style. The simple yet elegant cut of the robe follows Baghdadi Jewish tradition for men's wear, while its luxurious red fabric embroidered with gold thread renders it magnificent wedding attire. This adherence to the dress practices and other traditions of the Jewish community in Iraq was typical of the early generations of Baghdadi Jews in India.

Another Torah and case commissioned by a Sassoon, also dedicated in memory of a family member, is listed among the possessions of the Bevis Marks Synagogue in London, where several Sassoons served as officers. Described as "Baghdadi hand. The wooden case bears an inscription recording a gift of David Sassoon 1868," the Torah in case was eventually transferred to the Lauderdale Road Synagogue, opened in 1896 to accommodate the flow of Bevis Marks's congregants to West London. The Torah in case is likely the one lent by Reuben Sassoon (1835–1905) to the *Anglo-Jewish Historical Exhibition* in 1887, held in London at the Royal Albert Hall. In the catalogue, the description reads: "Scroll of the Law. In red plush case. Writing of great beauty. Fitted with curious silver bells [Torah finials] and pointer (Indian workmanship). Hebrew inscription: 'Presented by David Sassoon in memory of his brother, Sassoon David Sassoon, 5628 [=1868].'" The translation of the inscription seems incomplete. All sons of Sassoon bore his first name as their middle name, so if the presenter was a brother of Sassoon David Sassoon, then his first name (probably Reuben) is missing. Sassoon David had died in 1867, and the Torah in case was likely offered on the first anniversary of his death. Whether it was kept by Reuben after its presentation and used for private worship or remained at Bevis Marks and was later lent by him to the *Anglo-Jewish Historical Exhibition* is not known.[11]

The display of the Torah scroll in case within an exhibition context signals the family's appreciation of ritual objects as art to be admired and collected. As we have seen, commissioning and dedicating ritual objects was not uncommon in Jewish communities, but the interest shown by descendants of David Sassoon in collecting Judaica was unusually strong, especially in the late nineteenth and early twentieth centuries, when the practice was not widespread.[12] The *Anglo-Jewish Historical Exhibition* provided the first public stage for the display of Sassoon family collections. Held in the year of Queen Victoria's Golden Jubilee, the exhibition was mounted "to promote a knowledge of Anglo-Jewish history" and "to create a deeper interest in its records and relics, and to aid in their preservation as well as to determine the extent of the materials which exist for the compilation of a History of the Jews in England." These goals, however, should be considered against the background of Eastern

Wedding robe in which Ezekiel Gubbay married Aziza Sassoon on January 17, 1853, India, c. 1852, silk, gold metallic thread, and cotton, 54 in. long (137.2 cm), private collection.

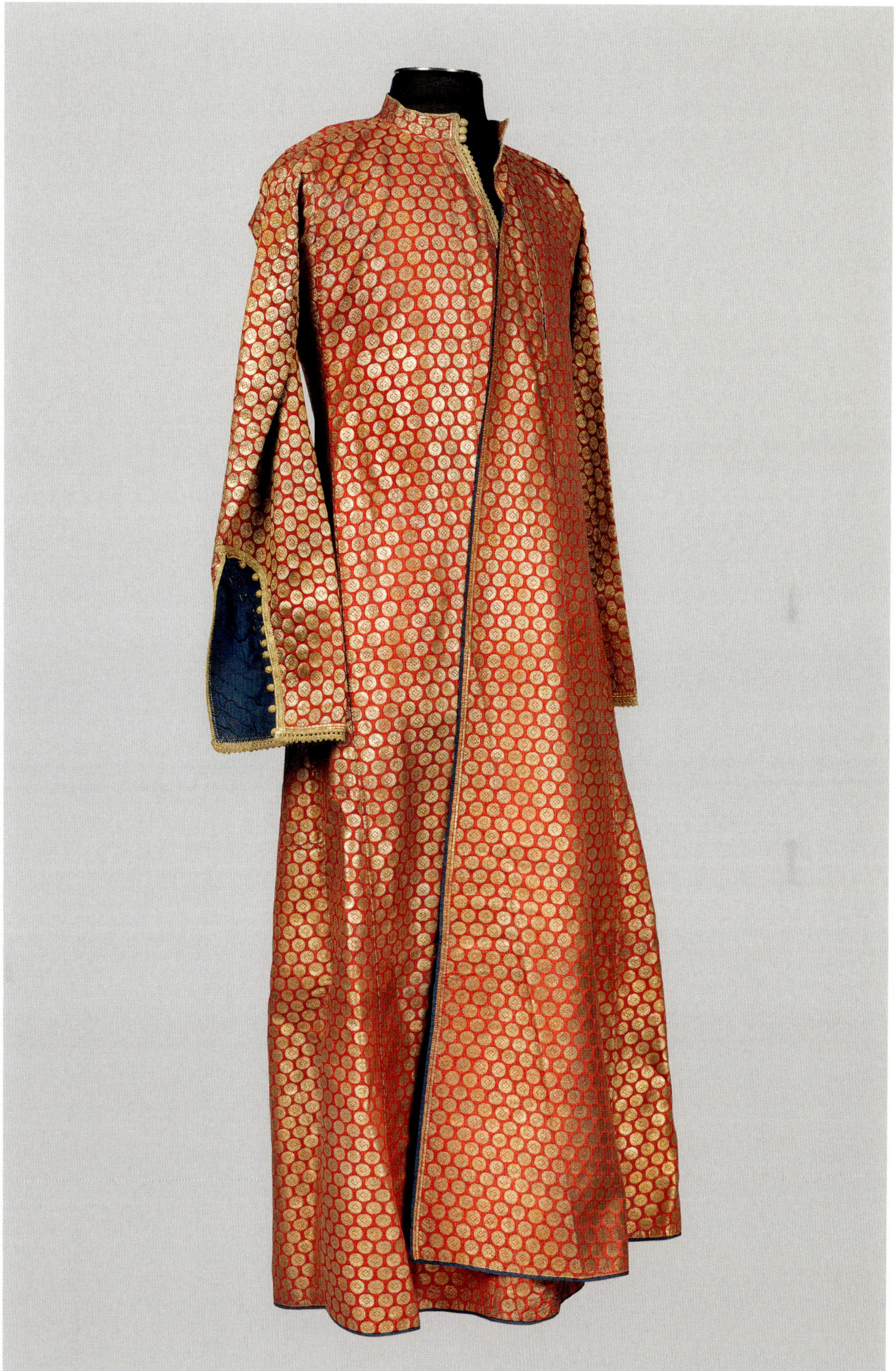

European Jewish immigration to Britain, which had begun to surge in the early 1880s, causing disparate reactions within the established Anglo-Jewish community. That the first Select Committee on Immigration and Emigration was formed in 1888, a year after the *Anglo-Jewish Historical Exhibition*, indicates that the issue of Jewish immigration was becoming more and more critical, and that the exhibition may have had the further yet unstated purpose of diverting attention from the debate.[13]

Some 12,000 people saw the groundbreaking exhibition during a twelve-week period, and its display of ceremonial art would serve as a prototype for Jewish museums that would soon begin to emerge in Europe and the United States. The contribution of Sassoon family members to this unprecedented endeavor cannot be overestimated. Albert Abdullah (1818–1896), David Sassoon's eldest son, was one of the guarantors, and he and his brother Arthur (1840–1912) were part of the exhibition's General Committee. Among the lenders was Joseph Sassoon (1855–1918). His father, Sassoon David, had been born in Mumbai, educated in Baghdad, sent to Shanghai to expand the family business, and finally settled in England. At Ashley Park, his magnificent Tudor residence near London, Sassoon David was able to withdraw from business to devote himself to the study of rare Hebrew books; his interest in collecting manuscripts has been little mentioned in the literature.[14]

Joseph, the eldest son, followed in his footsteps, likely inheriting his father's considerable holdings along with his passion for collecting Hebrew books. His marriage in 1884 to Louise (1862–1921), the eldest daughter of Baron Horace de Gunzburg, head of the prominent Russian Jewish family, may have also expanded Joseph's collecting horizons and sources for acquisitions. The significant group of Jewish ceremonial works he lent to the *Anglo-Jewish Historical Exhibition*, which was described in nineteen entries in the catalogue, some comprising multiple objects, included works of Baghdadi and Indian as well as Ashkenazi origin. Among them were a Torah scroll in silver case, probably from India; a fifteenth-century Sephardic mahzor; and a pair of silver candlesticks from Germany decorated with rampant lions and biblical scenes. One of the three Esther scrolls he lent to the exhibition was kept in a beautifully crafted silver-gilt case. Created in Baghdad for use in India, and later taken to Britain, "living objects" such as this straddle the line between precious ritual artifacts and collectors' items, exemplifying the Sassoons' rich journey across geographic regions and cultures. Also included were two wedding rings, one dated to the sixteenth century. These objects had become ubiquitous in the nineteenth century, as forged examples imitating medieval rings were circulated by dealers among European collectors. At the *Anglo-Jewish Historical Exhibition*, twenty-five examples were on view, including fifteen belonging to Isaac Strauss, the pioneering collector of Judaica who had lent 130 works. Beyond the scope of the *Anglo-Jewish Historical Exhibition*, Joseph Sassoon's collecting activities seem to have extended to fine arts, as attested by a group of ten paintings auctioned in 1918, shortly after his death, which included a *Portrait of Cosimo I, Duc de Medici*, said to be by the sixteenth-century painter Bronzino, and four works by Godfrey Kneller, a court painter and leading portraitist in England during the late seventeenth and early eighteenth centuries.[15]

The collection of Joseph's uncle Reuben, however, was the one singled out in the catalogue, under the heading "The Sassoon Collection of Hebrew Ecclesiastical Art." The Report to the Members of the General Committee read: "In the region of Ecclesiastical Art, we were fortunate enough to obtain the collections of M. Strauss, of Paris, and of Mr. R. D. Sassoon, of London, the most important of their kind in existence, and these were supplemented by the more modern examples lent by the Chief Synagogues and many private individuals." Reuben seems to have been the one who inspired further Judaica collecting within the family. Whether he had any say in its commission or not, the ketubbah celebrating his marriage to Catherine (Kate) Ezekiel is magnificent. Illuminated with shell gold and profusely decorated with floral designs, tigers, and peacocks, the ketubbah is a superb example of a type that was adopted by Baghdadi Jews in India, featuring the actual text of the contract at the bottom of the page written in semicursive rabbinic script, and surmounted by two panels bearing blessings and salutations. Floral and animal motifs, as well as the eschewing of human figuration, were also common in ketubbot created for the Bene Israel and for the Jews of Kochi (formerly Cochin), who excelled in this art form. The type differs greatly from decorated ketubbot extant from Iraq (see page 19), and, according to Shalom Sabar, "seems to have taken shape with the start of Baghdadi settlement in India and . . . had definite influence on the Bene Israel."[16] A Mumbai ketubbah from 1859

Sassoon David Sassoon, with Persian inscriptions inspired by Sufi poetry, Baghdad, January 18, 1850, gouache (?) on paper, 9 × 7 in. (22.9 × 17.8 cm), private collection, London. This delicate portrait was created shortly before the wedding of Sassoon David Sassoon to Flora (Farha) Reuben on February 17, 1850. The portrait bears both the Gregorian calendar date and the month and year in the Islamic calendar "Rabi' ul-awwal [the third month], 1266," corresponding to January 14 through February 13, 1850. It was probably offered as a wedding gift by a commissioner whose name is only partially decipherable. The poem is by Hazīn Lāhījī (1692–1766) after Sa'adi Shirazi (d. 1292). The honorific *Khwāja* is used for spiritual mentors. The term *bigāna*, a mystical Sufi concept, can also signify a denier, rejector, refuser, or atheist. The indigent refers to the religious mendicant or dervishes.

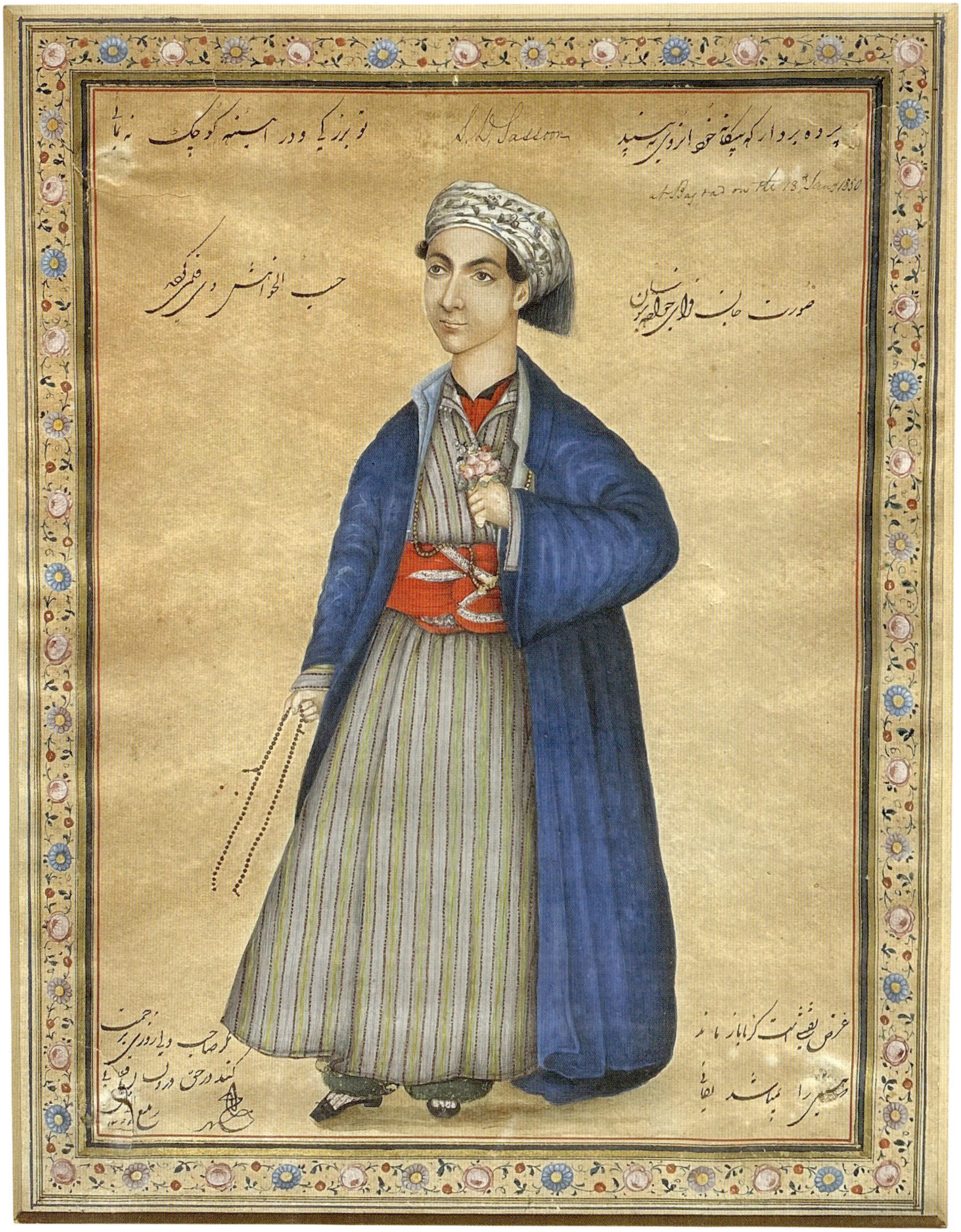

The inscriptions read: "At the behest of Di Filmar K . . .
The soul-nourishing image of Khwāja Sassoon
Unveil so the stranger [*bigāna*] may see your face for himself
You are big and appear small in the mirror.
Thus, this image has been made as it may become our memorial
As the body shall not live forever
A kindhearted person one day, out of mercy may offer a prayer for the indigent."

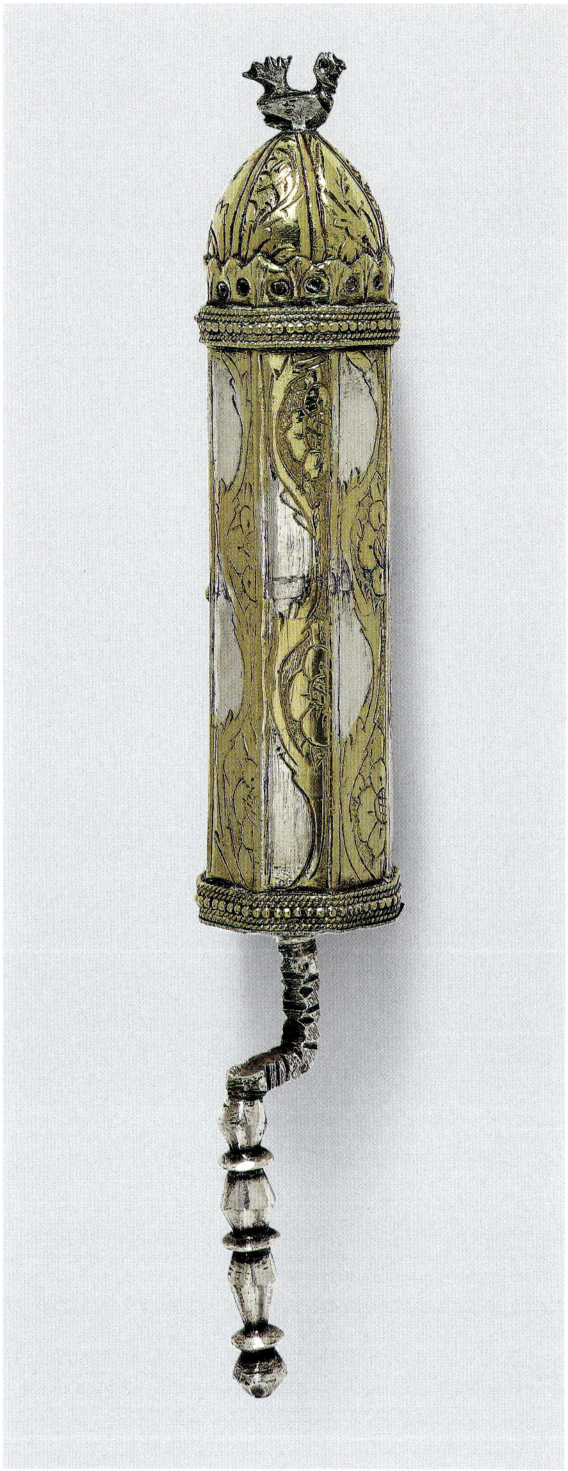

Esther scroll in case, probably Baghdad, mid-nineteenth century, case: silver gilt, 7 × 2⅝ in. (17.8 × 6.7 cm), scroll: ink on parchment, formerly in the Joseph S. Sassoon Collection.

probably documenting a Bene Israel wedding, formerly in the collection of David Solomon Sassoon, presents a very similar design to the one for his uncle Reuben's wedding.

Besides the Torah scroll in case in memory of his brother Sassoon David, Reuben lent many objects to the *Anglo-Jewish Historical Exhibition*, the bulk of which he had acquired from the collection of his neighbor Philip Salomons, a financier, sheriff of Sussex, and warden of the New Synagogue in London who eventually settled in the seaside town of Hove. His home at 26 Brunswick Terrace had a private rooftop synagogue; its domed outline is visible to this day. After Salomons's death in 1867, Reuben purchased most of his Judaica holdings, reflecting a collector's impulse and an appreciation for ritual objects as art.[17] The works he acquired were primarily of Ashkenazi origin with some artifacts from Italy, representing different traditions from that of his own Baghdadi Jewish upbringing in India, thus broadening his knowledge of different styles and forms in Jewish ceremonial art. Among these works is a pair of silver-gilt Dutch Torah finials, finely worked in filigree, dating to the eighteenth century. As with other Judaica pieces from the Salomons collection, they bear the engraved inscription "P. Salomons, Esq" on their shafts within a thin band, surrounded by delicate floral and scroll decoration.

Exceptional among Reuben's loans to the exhibition was a large group of dressed Torah scrolls, nine of which are listed as fully fitted with rich mantles and lavish Torah ornaments, including three Torah shields dating to the late eighteenth or early nineteenth century, likely made in Lviv (Lemberg). All three are relatively small and feature decoration on both sides. The Decalogue is at center, surmounted by a crown and flanked by a pair of columns topped by baskets overflowing with fruits and flowers. Facing crouching lions are at the bases, and a pair of flanking birds seemingly bears the weight of these architectural elements. On one of the shields, Moses and Aaron appear abutted to the columns. The columns and the crown are rendered sculpturally, adding three-dimensionality to these remarkably intricate pieces. The contrast of the gilt openwork against a plain silver background adds depth to the composition, which is quasi-symmetric, as the animals within cartouches along the sides all face the same direction. The creatures that appear within lobed plaquettes and intertwined within foliage, and the horror vacui of the compositions, are typical of Eastern European Jewish papercut art and no longer extant carved wooden Torah arks. Similar animal menageries

OPPOSITE
Marriage contract of Reuben and Kate Ezekiel, Mumbai, 6 Adar I, 5613 (February 14, 1853), ink and shell gold on paper, 19½ × 15¼ in. (50 × 39 cm), Kenneth X. and Joyce Robbins Collection, formerly in the Sassoon Family Collection.

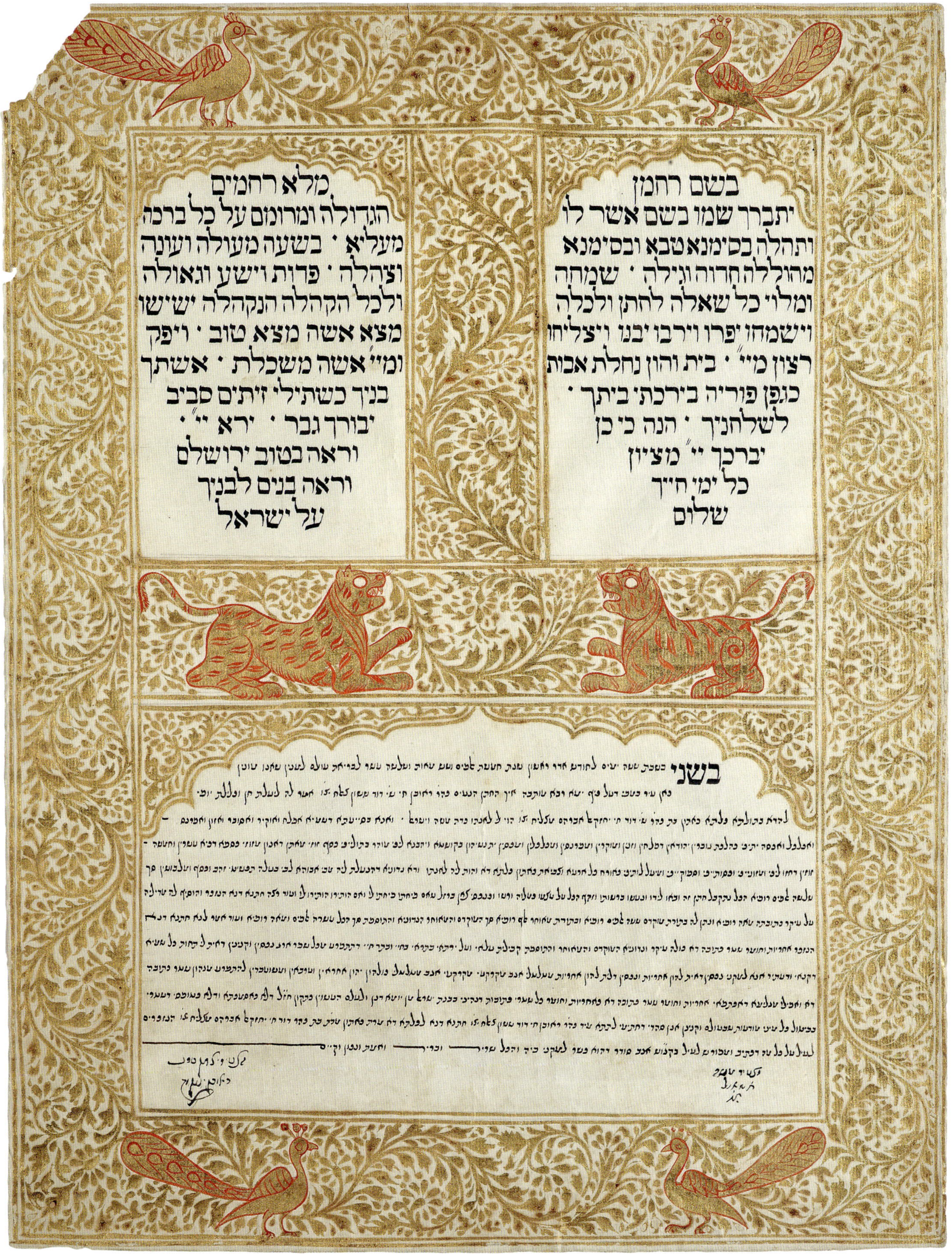
בשם רחמן
יתברך שמו בשם אשר לו
ותהלה בסימנא טבא ובסימנא
מהוללה חדוה וגילה · שמחה
ומלוי כל שאלה לחתן ולכלה
וישמחו יפרו וירבו יבנו ויצליחו
רצון מיי״ · בית והון נחלת אבות
כגפן פוריה בירכתי ביתך ·
לשלחניך · הנה כי כן
יברכך יי״ מציון
כל ימי חייך
שלום
מלא רחמים
הגדולה ומרומם על כל ברכה
מעלי״א · בשעה מעולה ועונה
וצהלה · פדות וישע וגאולה
ולכל הקהלה הנקהלה ישישו
מצא אשה מצא טוב · ויפק
ומיי״ אשה משכלת · אשתך
בניך כשתילי זיתים סביב
יבורך גבר · ירא יי״ ·
וראה בטוב ירושלם
וראה בנים לבניך
על ישראל
בשני

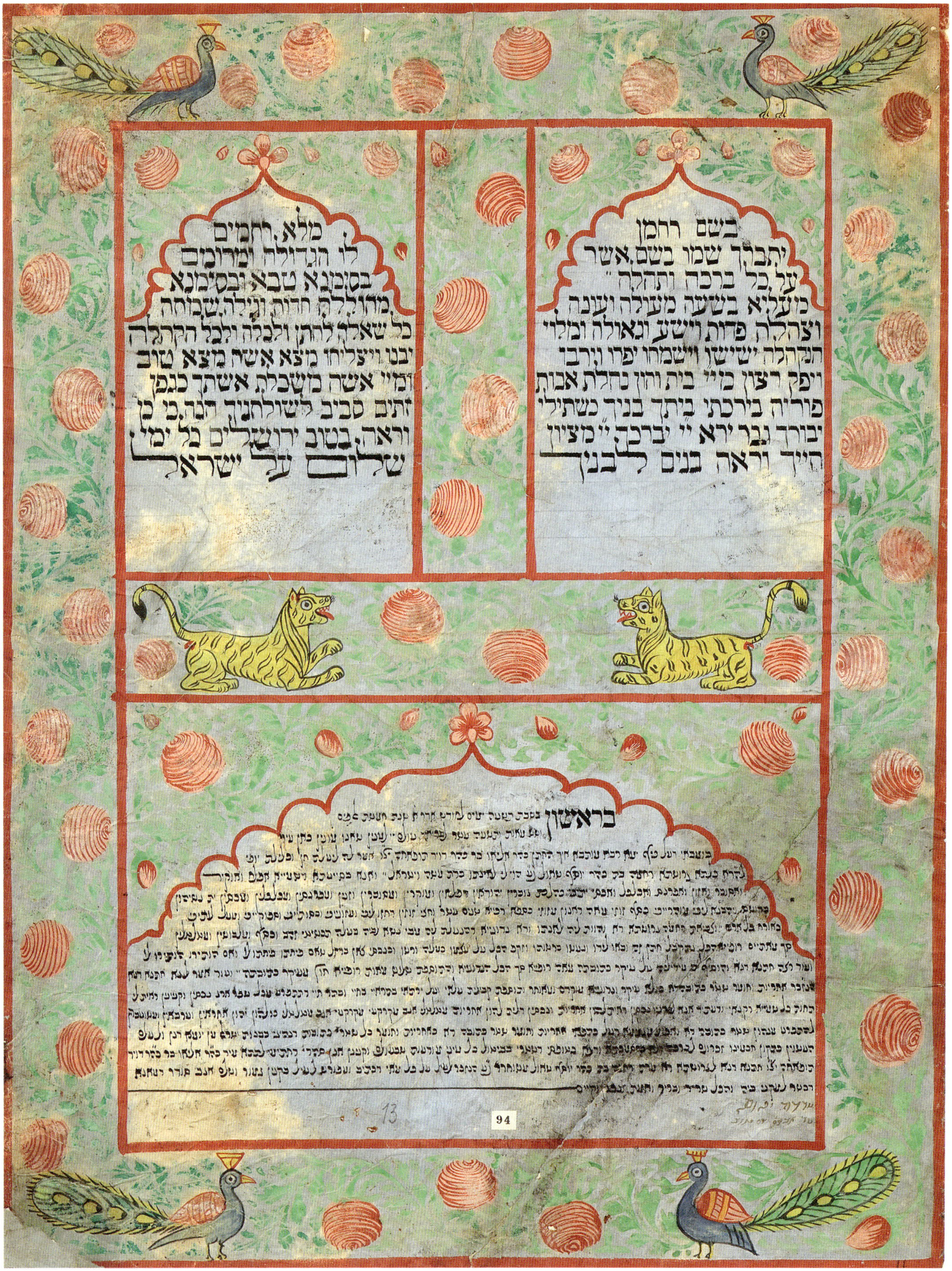
בשם רחמן
יתברך שמו בשם אשר
על כל ברכה ותהלה
כעליא בשעה מעלה ועונה
וצהלה פדות וישע וגאולה ומלוי
התהלה ישישון וישמחו יפרו וירבו
ויפק רצון מיי בית והון נחלת אבות
פוריה בירכתי ביתך בניך כשתילי
יבורך גבר ירא יי יברכך יי מציון
הייך וראה בנים לבניך
מלא רחמים
לו הגדולה ומרוממים
בסימנא טבא ובסימנא
מהוללה חדוה וגילה שמחה
כל שאלה לחתן ולכלה ולכל הקהלה
יבנו ויצליחו מצא אשה מצא טוב
ומיי אשה משכלת אשתך כגפן
זתים סביב לשולחניך הנה כי כן
וראה בטוב ירושלים כל ימי
שלום על ישראל
בראשון
94

OPPOSITE
Marriage contract, Mumbai, 1859, ink and gouache on paper, 19½ × 15 in. (49.7 × 38.3 cm), New York, Jewish Museum, gift of Barbara and Benjamin Zucker Family in honor of Daniel M. Friedenberg, 2009-26, formerly in the David Solomon Sassoon Collection (no. 94).

RIGHT
Torah finials, Netherlands, c. 1780, silver gilt, each 15⅜ × 3⅞ in. (39 × 10 cm), London, Victoria and Albert Museum, presented by Lady Marjorie Gilbert through the American Friends of The Art Fund (M.27-2009 and M.28-2009), formerly in the Reuben Sassoon Collection.

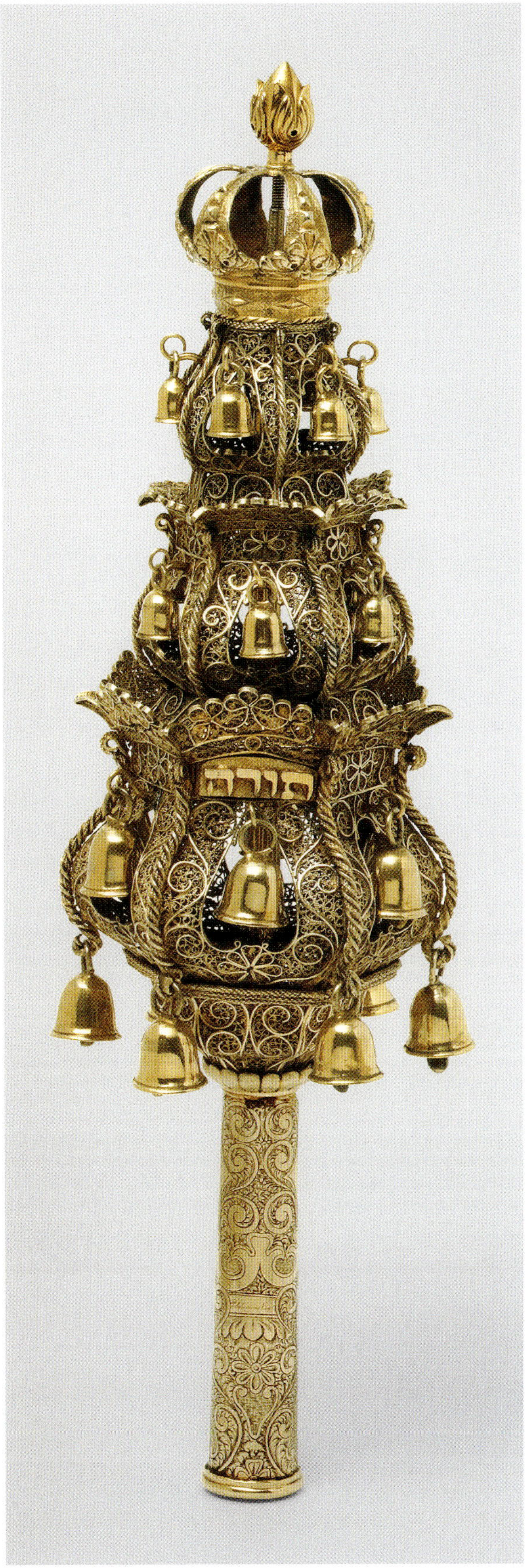

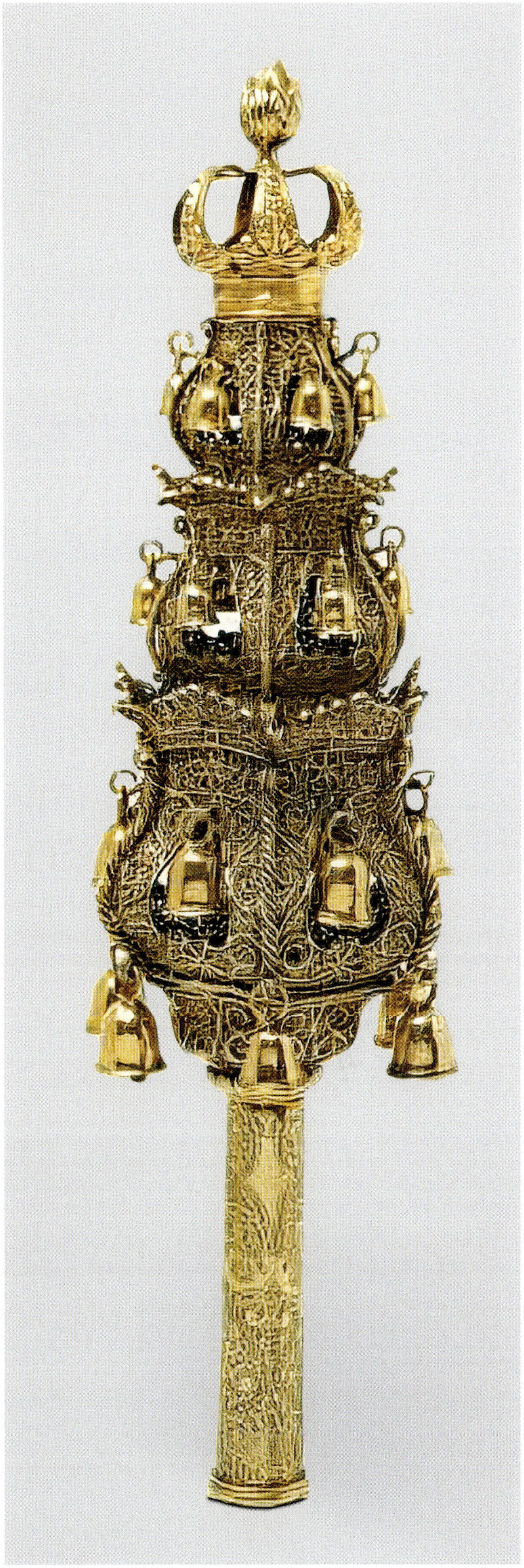

Elimelekh Tzoref, Torah shield (front and back), 1782, silver, parcel gilt, with enamel, niello, and stones, 8 × 6⅛ in. (20.4 × 15.5 cm), Boston, Museum of Fine Arts, museum purchase with funds donated by the Phillip Leonian and Edith Rosenbaum Leonian Charitable Trust, Jacques Aaron Preis, Trustee (2021.58), formerly in the Reuben and Flora Sassoon Collections.

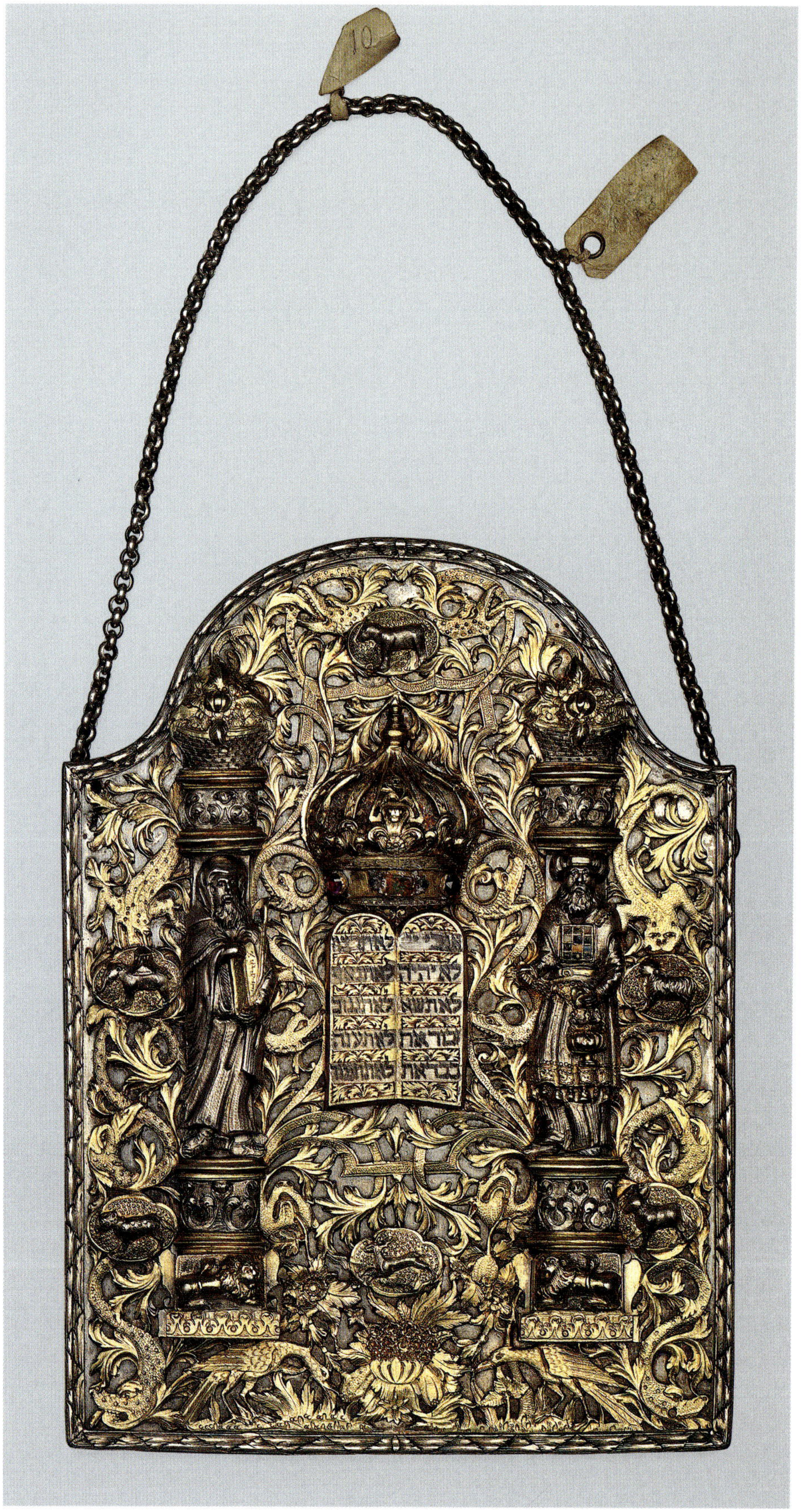

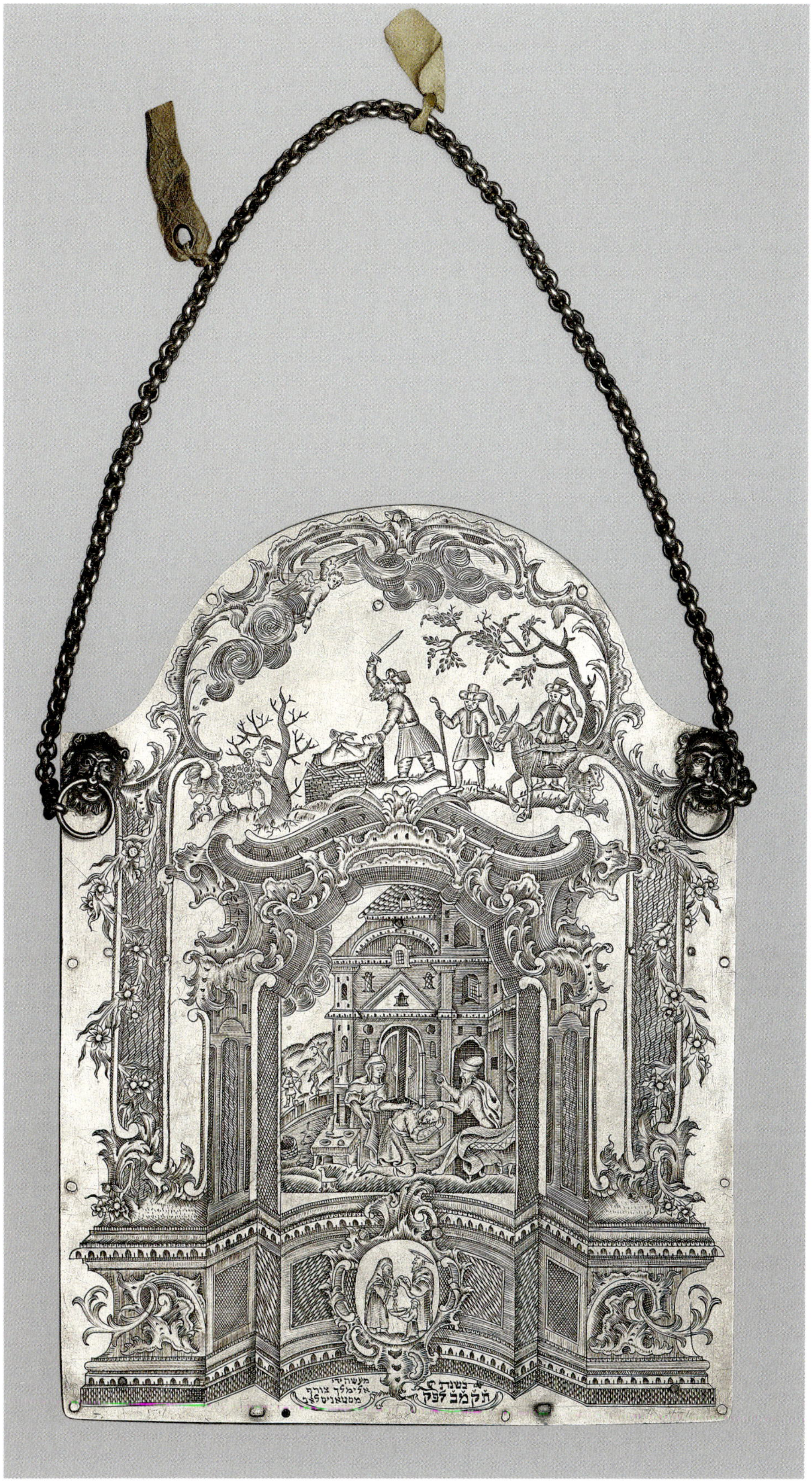

also populated the painted ceilings of Eastern European synagogues destroyed during the Holocaust. As Liberman Mintz suggests, an illustrated version of *Perek Shira* (Chapter of Song) may have also been a source for these creatures.[18] An ancient Hebrew text in which various creations, including animals, praise God, *Perek Shira* offered wonderful possibilities for scribes who were also illustrators. The *Meshal ha-kadmoni*, a collection of animal fables, was also popular, and illustrated copies showing pairs of animals "discussing" the Talmud and "conversing" in biblical Hebrew circulated widely.

The three Torah shields are also fully decorated on the back, which is rare, finely engraved in a style akin to that of manuscript illuminations. Two feature a plan of the Jerusalem Temple and the third, a depiction of the Blessing of Isaac—all three are topped by a representation of the Binding of Isaac. The shield now in the Museum of Fine Arts, Boston, stands apart from the other two. Featuring Moses and Aaron on its front and the Blessing of Isaac on the reverse, the piece is signed and dated. A Hebrew inscription on its back reads: "In the year [5]542 (=1781/82)/The work of my hands Elimelekh Tzoref of Stanislav." In Hebrew, "tzoref" means both goldsmith and silversmith, and is also used as a last name. Given their stylistic similarities, the three shields have been attributed to the artist. Two of the shields bear early nineteenth-century control marks for Lviv (Lemberg), leading to the suggestion that he may have been active in that city, an important center of Jewish life. Although Torah shields originating from Galicia at the time were usually modest in size and scope, fine Torah ornaments created in the region in the late eighteenth and early nineteenth centuries are known, including a shield and a pair of finials, and a superb crown, in the collection of the Jewish Museum, New York.[19]

The three Torah shields entered Reuben's collection sometime before the *Anglo-Jewish Historical Exhibition*. Whether they were part of the Judaica holdings from the late Philip Salomons is difficult to ascertain, as their decoration would not have allowed room for his inscription of ownership. We do not know who commissioned the three Torah shields, but the depiction of a Levite washing the hands of a Cohen within a medallion on the reverse of the one at the Museum of Fine Arts, Boston, likely indicates that the owner was a Levite. Given that biblical scenes relating to Isaac appear on all three shields, the owner's name may have been Isaac. The elaborate decoration on the back of each shield raises the question as to whether those sides would have been meant for display on special occasions. The shields may have been commissioned to celebrate an important family event, such as the bar mitzvah of a boy named Isaac, a Levite, whose Torah portion reading was *Toldot* (Gen. 25:19–28:9). This parashah includes the episode in which Abraham is tricked into blessing Isaac instead of Esau, his first-born, the scene depicted on the shield in the Museum of Fine Arts, Boston. Moreover, the supplemental reading or haftarah for *Toldot*, Malachi 1:1–2:7, addresses God's dissatisfaction with the sacrifices being offered in the Temple, which may account for the detailed plan of the Jerusalem Temple depicted on the back of the two other shields, with rows of worshipers dutifully bringing in their offerings.

Reuben died in 1905, followed by his wife, Kate, in 1906. Their five surviving children—their only son David and four daughters—were adults at the time; a fifth daughter, Mozelle, had died in 1896. Their daughter Luna had married Maurice Gubbay of Kolkata, and her sister Flora Cecilia had wed Ernest Raphael, son of a prominent Sephardic banking family, in 1893. Her uncle Frederick also married a Raphael a year later. Reuben and Kate's two other surviving daughters, Rachel and Louise Judith, would later marry outside the Jewish faith.

The disposal of Reuben's assets had started some ten years before his death. Two notices in *The Statist* in 1894 announced the sale of his mansion at 1 Belgrave Square and much of its contents: furniture, Sèvres porcelain, jardinières, and cloisonné enameled vases, as well as paintings "by or attributed to" Antonio Canaletto, Claude Vernet, and Jean-Baptiste Pater, among other artists—casting a doubt on their authenticity and the auctioneers' connoisseurship. Silver plate and jewelry owned by Reuben were auctioned at Christie, Manson & Woods on June 29 and July 13, 1905; Kate's jewelry was sold in April 1906.[20]

According to Ben-Ya'akov, Reuben's Judaica holdings went directly to his nephew David Solomon. Harry M. Rabinowicz, who visited David Solomon's library at Letchworth, which was still owned by the family in the 1960s, reported that "apart from manuscripts and books, Sassoon inherited and acquired many priceless items of ecclesiastical art. Some of these were collected by Reuben D. Sassoon and exhibited in the Anglo-Jewish Historical Exhibition." But in the catalogue for the *Exhibition of Jewish Art and Antiquities* held at London's Whitechapel Art Gallery in 1906, most of the objects Reuben had lent are listed as loans from Mrs. S. D. Sassoon (i.e., Flora Sassoon, David Solomon's mother; see page 30).[21] Whether the collection passed to Flora by sale or descent cannot be ascertained.

The Sassoons not only loaned works but also contributed to the cost of the Whitechapel exhibition. Arthur, his nephew Edward (1856–1912), and sister-in-law Flora Sassoon were listed as financial supporters, and Flora's son David Solomon was a member of the organizing committee.[22] Flora's loans included the three Lviv (Lemberg) Torah shields and an exquisite pair of English Torah finials made in 1804, probably in London. Once in Salomons's collection, they had probably been lent by Reuben to the *Anglo-Jewish Historical Exhibition*, forming part of a dressed Torah. They were listed as "small silver-gilt bells with small brackets and fir cones," similarly to their description in the Whitechapel exhibition catalogue but omitting the Hebrew inscription, which is identical on both shafts: "A donation from that which God has bestowed upon me, Judah Aryeh, known as Leib, son of the departed Yitzhak Isaac, of blessed memory, in the year [5]595 [1834/35]" and "Judah is a lion's [in Hebrew, "aryeh"] whelp" [Gen. 49:9] within a band above a rampant lion.[23] Topped with silver-gilt pineapple (rather than fir cone) motifs, also nestled within leaves rendered in green enamel, and with acanthus chasing on the shafts, the finials are visually arresting. The pineapple was a symbol of luxury and viewed as "exotic" since its introduction in Europe from the Caribbean in the seventeenth century. The fascination with the fruit may account for the existence of several versions of the painting *Charles II Presented with a Pineapple*, said to depict John Rose, the royal gardener, presenting the monarch with the first one grown in England, though the fruit may still have been imported during his reign. One of the copies, by the seventeenth-century Dutch artist Hendrick Danckerts, who was active in England and Italy, would later be owned by Philip Sassoon (1888–1939).[24] Philip's mother, Lady Sassoon, was also represented in the Whitechapel exhibition with two of her own studies, listed among the watercolors and pastels, and a depiction of David Sassoon, possibly the same engraving that had been shown at the *Anglo-Jewish Historical Exhibition*, was also included.[25]

Held at the Whitechapel Art Gallery in London's East End, an area teeming with Eastern European Jewish immigrants, the *Exhibition of Jewish Art and Antiquities* was meant to open in 1905 but was delayed until late 1906. By then, the Aliens Act had passed in August 1905, curtailing Jewish immigration into Britain and signaling the

Torah finials, England, probably London, 1804, dedicated in 1834/35 (Hebrew inscription date), silver parcel gilt and enamel, 6 in. (15.2 cm), Collection of Jane and Stuart Weitzman, formerly in the Reuben and Flora Sassoon Collections.

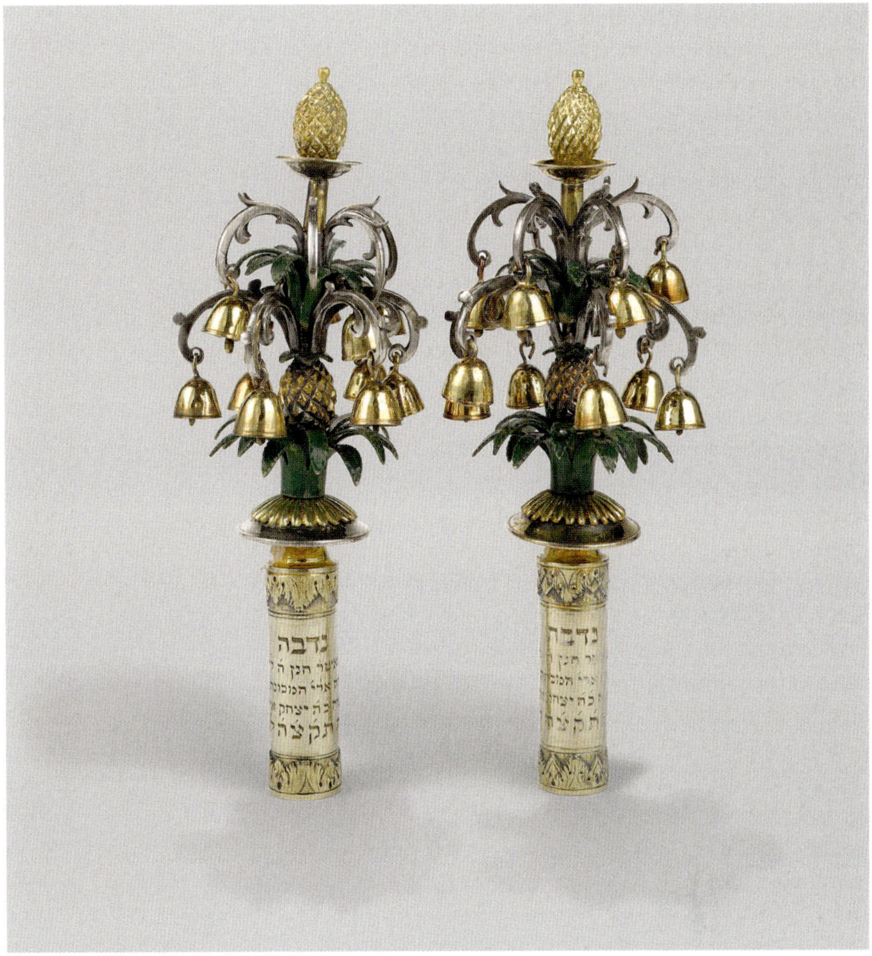

continued rise of antisemitism. As was the case with the *Anglo-Jewish Historical Exhibition* of 1887, the Whitechapel exhibition was probably intended to influence the immigration debate and prevent the enactment of anti-Jewish immigration policy. Thus, as stated by Juliet Steyn, "the proximity of these two exhibitions to political processes and legislation which could directly affect the Jews cannot be mere coincidence and must be seen as part of the sub-text of the shows."[26] As stated in its catalogue, the goal of the Whitechapel exhibition was to highlight the contributions of Anglo-Jewry while aiding in the assimilation of recent arrivals by exposing them to works by English Jewish artists, as well as "many pictures by foreign painters," such as "the illustrious Jozef Israels." Also included was the work of Alfred Wolmark, who had been endeavoring to call attention to the plight of his Jewish brethren in Eastern Europe. Having emigrated from Poland as a child, he exemplified the very integration into British society the exhibition sought to advance. On view for six weeks, and offering free admission and late opening hours to accommodate low-income and working-class visitors, the exhibition was viewed by some 151,000 people—an unprecedented number for exhibitions of similar duration at the Whitechapel Gallery since its establishment in 1901 and a staggering number when compared with the 12,000 visitors to the *Anglo-Jewish Historical Exhibition* during its twelve-week run. In addition, some 20,000 catalogues were sold at the affordable price of one penny.[27]

By 1906, David Solomon had been collecting rare books for some time, and he lent several manuscripts and two ancient Jewish tombstones from Iraq to the Whitechapel exhibition. As he states in the preface of *Ohel Dawid*, his comprehensive two-volume catalogue of his collection published in 1932, he had begun collecting at a young age: "The first item of my collection was not a [manuscript], but a rare printed booklet, namely the Scroll of Ruth in Arabic, as printed for the use of the Baghdad Jews in India, dated Bombay 1859. I was eight years old when I got it by exchanging a kite with a boy." The first manuscript to enter his collection was "an illuminated Scroll of Esther . . . which originally belonged to one of my uncles." The initials "A.S.D.," for his uncle Arthur's Hebrew name, Abraham Shalom David, were engraved on the silver handle of the scroll. His uncle Reuben owned a similar Esther scroll, inscribed "R. D. Sassoon," which he had lent to the *Anglo-Jewish Historical Exhibition,* but it is not listed among the loans to the Whitechapel exhibition or in *Ohel Dawid*. It appears to have found its way to his nephew after 1932. David Solomon would come to own Arthur's ketubbah documenting his marriage to Louise Perugia (1854–1943) in Trieste on January 19, 1873; Arthur was the first son to wed in Europe. The text is set within an arched frame inscribed with biblical verses and surmounted by a decorative flower rendered with verses from Psalm 45 in micrography. The simplicity of the design belies the couple's prominent social standing. According to Shalom Sabar, the waning of ketubbah decoration came about in Trieste with Jewish emancipation in 1782. David Solomon's uncle Frederick's and cousin Mozelle's marriage contracts would also become part of his collection. By 1893, the budding collector had received his second manuscript, also an Esther scroll, from the great Baghdad Rabbi Joseph Hayyim as a gift for his bar mitzvah, celebrated in Pune (formerly Poona) on December 15 of that year. The scroll's text columns end with letters that make up the recipient's name in Hebrew: David ben Sliman David Sassoon.[28]

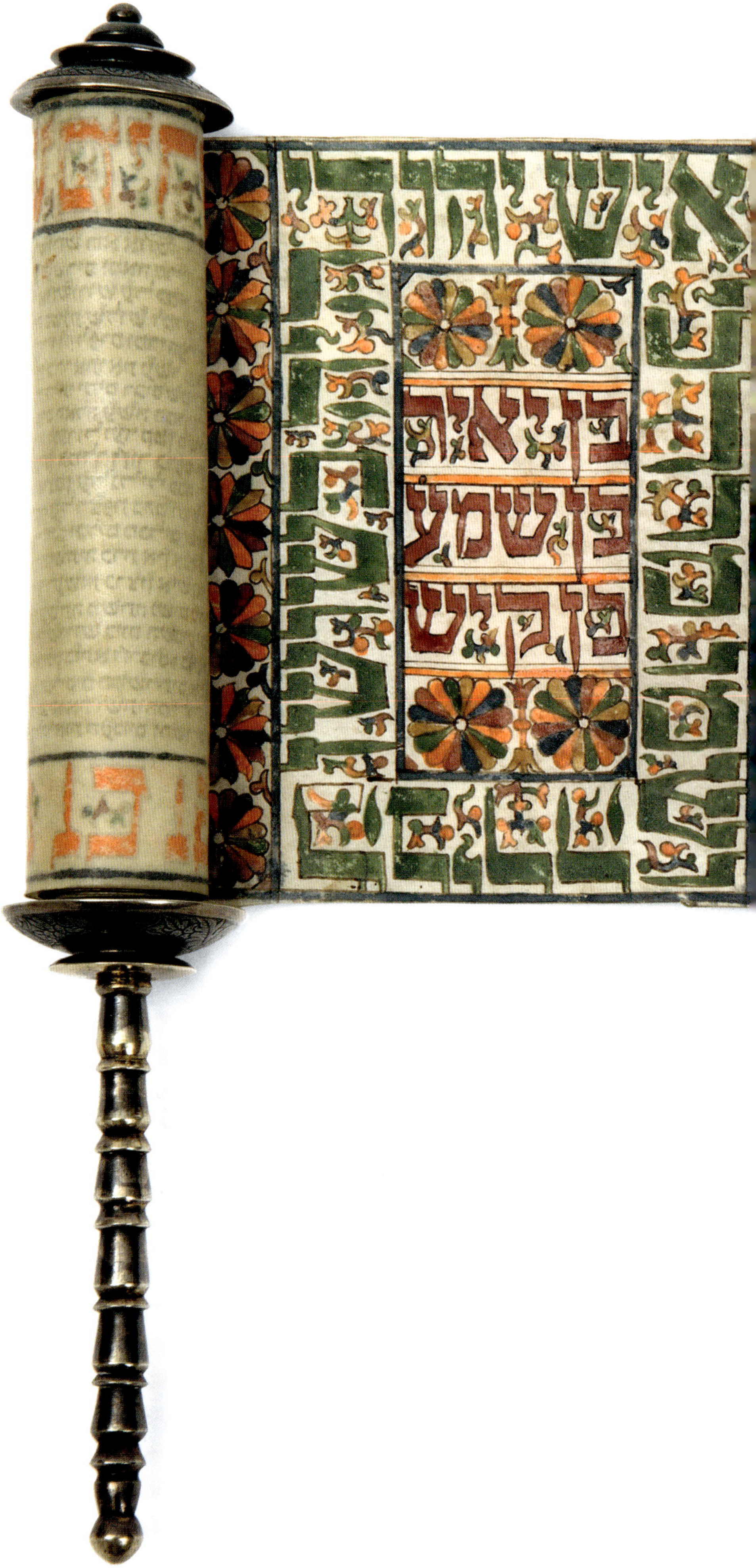

Esther scroll of Reuben Sassoon, Baghdad, mid-nineteenth century, paint on parchment, scroll: 4⅛ in. (10.5 cm), with handle 7⅞ in. (20 cm), Collection of Jane and Stuart Weitzman.

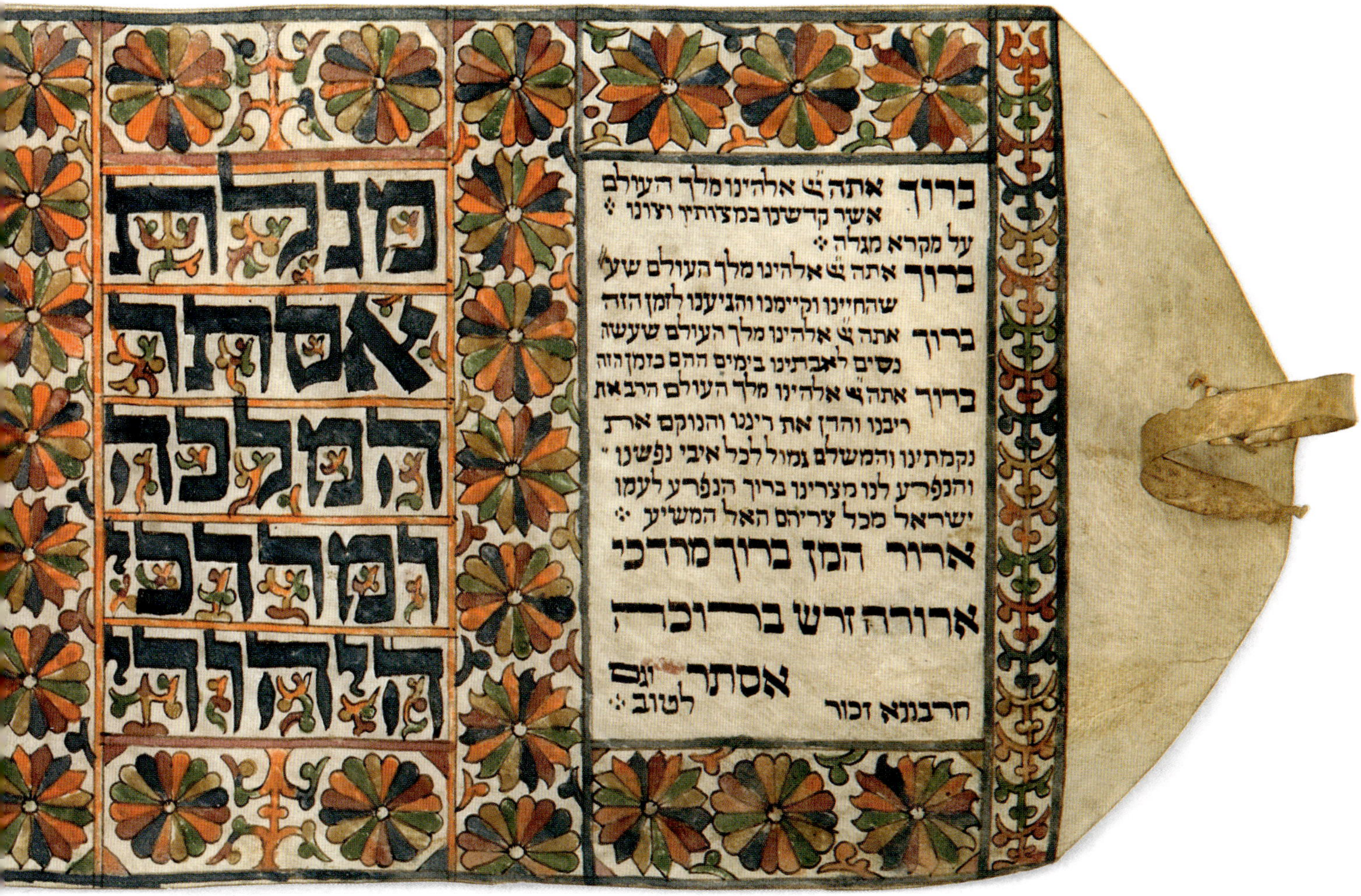

מגלת אסתר המלכה והמהדר
ברוך אתה ײַ אלהינו מלך העולם
אשר קדשנו במצותיו וצונו
על מקרא מגלה
ברוך אתה ײַ אלהינו מלך העולם שע״
שהחיינו וקיימנו והגיענו לזמן הזה
ברוך אתה ײַ אלהינו מלך העולם שעשה
נסים לאבתינו בימים ההם בזמן הזה
ברוך אתה ײַ אלהינו מלך העולם הרב את
ריבנו והדן את דיננו והנוקם את
נקמתינו והמשלם גמול לכל איבי נפשנו
והנפרע לנו מצרינו ברוך הנפרע לעמו
ישראל מכל צריהם האל המשיע
ארור המן ברוך מרדכי
ארורה זרש ברוכה
אסתר וגם
חרבונא זכור לטוב

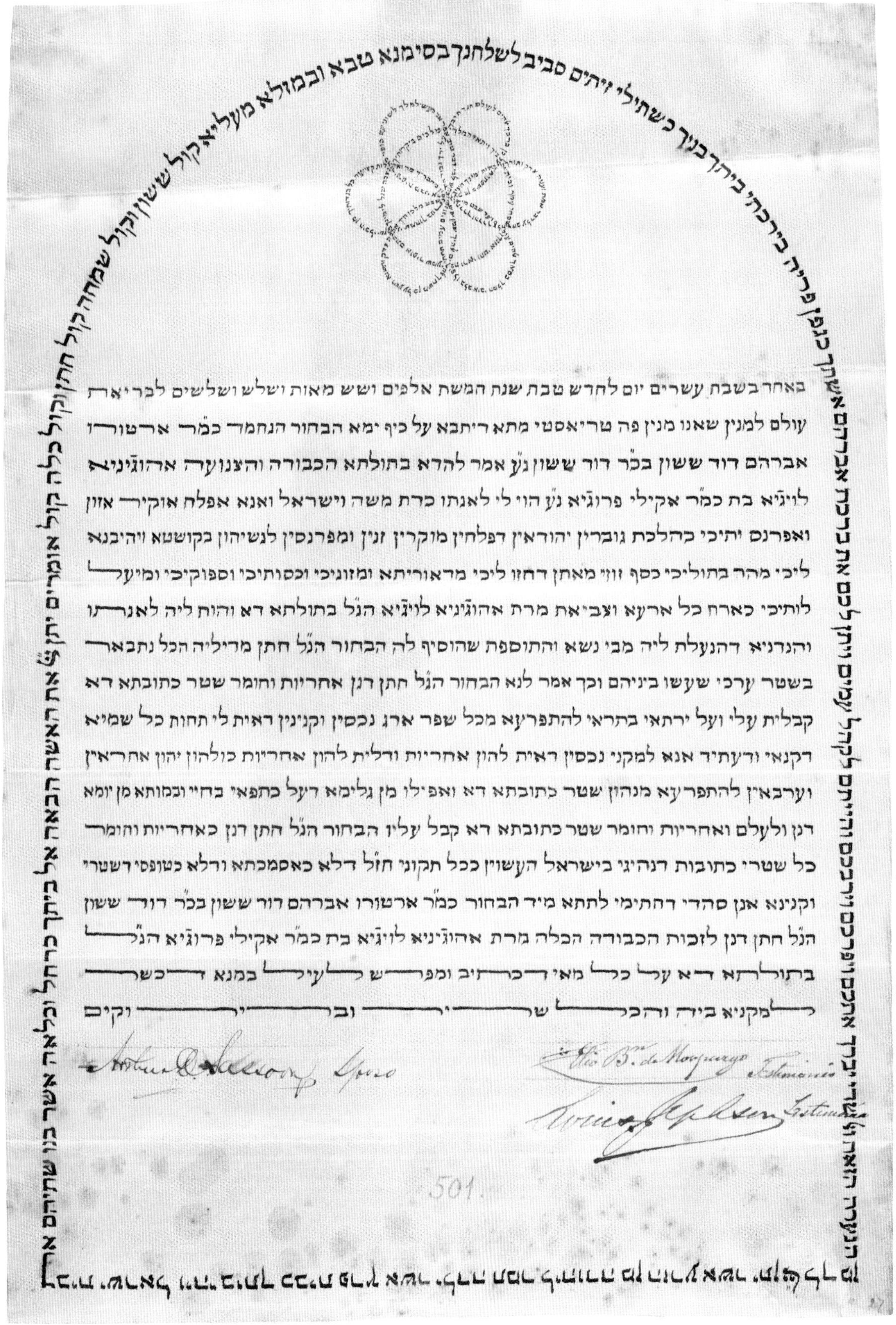
באחד בשבת עשרים יום לחדש טבת שנת חמשת אלפים ושש מאות ושלש ושלשים לבריאת
עולם למנין שאנו מנין פה טריאסטי מתא דיתבא על כיף ימא הבחור הנחמד כמ"ר ארטורו
אברהם דוד ששון בכ"ר דוד ששון נ"ע אמר להדא בתולתא הכבודה והצנועה אהוגיניא
לויג'א בת כמ"ר אקילי פרוג'א נ"ע הוי לי לאנתו כדת משה וישראל ואנא אפלח אוקיר ואזון
ואפרנס יתיכי כהלכת גוברין יהודאין דפלחין מוקרין זנין ומפרנסין לנשיהון בקושטא ויהיבנא
ליכי מהר בתוליכי כסף זוזי מאתן דחזו ליכי מדאוריתא ומזוניכי וכסותיכי וספוקיכי ומיעל
לותיכי כאורח כל ארעא וצביאת מרת אהוגיניא לויג'א הנ"ל בתולתא דא והות ליה לאנתו
והנדוניא דהנעלת ליה מבי נשא והתוספת שהוסיף לה הבחור הנ"ל חתן מדיליה הכל נתבאר
בשטר ערכי שעשו ביניהם וכך אמר לנא הבחור הנ"ל חתן דנן אחריות וחומר שטר כתובתא דא
קבלית עלי ועל ירתאי בתראי להתפרעא מכל שפר ארג נכסין וקנינין דאית לי תחות כל שמיא
דקנאי ודעתיד אנא למקני נכסין דאית להון אחריות ודלית להון אחריות כולהון יהון אחראין
וערבאין להתפרעא מנהון שטר כתובתא דא ואפילו מן גלימא דעל כתפאי בחיי ובמותא מן יומא
דנן ולעלם ואחריות וחומר שטר כתובתא דא קבל עליו הבחור הנ"ל חתן דנן כאחריות וחומר
כל שטרי כתובות דנהיגי בישראל העשוין ככל תקוני חז"ל דלא כאסמכתא ודלא כטופסי דשטרי
וקנינא אנן סהדי דחתימי לתתא מיד הבחור כמ"ר ארטורו אברהם דוד ששון בכ"ר דוד ששון
הנ"ל חתן דנן לזכות הכבודה הכלה מרת אהוגיניא לויג'א בת כמ"ר אקילי פרוג'א הנ"ל
בתולתא דא על כל מאי דכתוב ומפורש לעיל במנא דכשר
למקניא ביה והכל שריר וברור וקים

LEFT

Marriage contract of Arthur Sassoon and Louise Perugia, Trieste, 20 Tevet 1873 (January 19, 1873), ink on parchment, 16⅜ × 11⅜ in. (41.5 × 29 cm), Benjamin Zucker Family Collection (Z72), formerly in the David Solomon Sassoon Collection (no. 501). Arthur's bride, Louise Perugia, belonged to an affluent Italian Jewish family. Arthur and Louise were frequent hosts of King Edward VII at both their Brighton home and their hunting lodge in Tulchan, Scotland.

OPPOSITE

Marriage contract of Frederick Sassoon and Jeanette Raphael, London, 4 Tishrei 5655 (October 4, 1894), ink on paper, 16½ × 12⅞ in. (42 × 33 cm), Benjamin Zucker Family Collection (Z40), formerly in the David Solomon Sassoon Collection (no. 502). Frederick Sassoon married Jeanette Raphael, of Dutch Portuguese Jewish descent, who belonged to a prominent banking family. Their wedding was held at the Spanish and Portuguese Holy Congregation Gate of Heaven, known as Bevis Marks, the oldest synagogue in London.

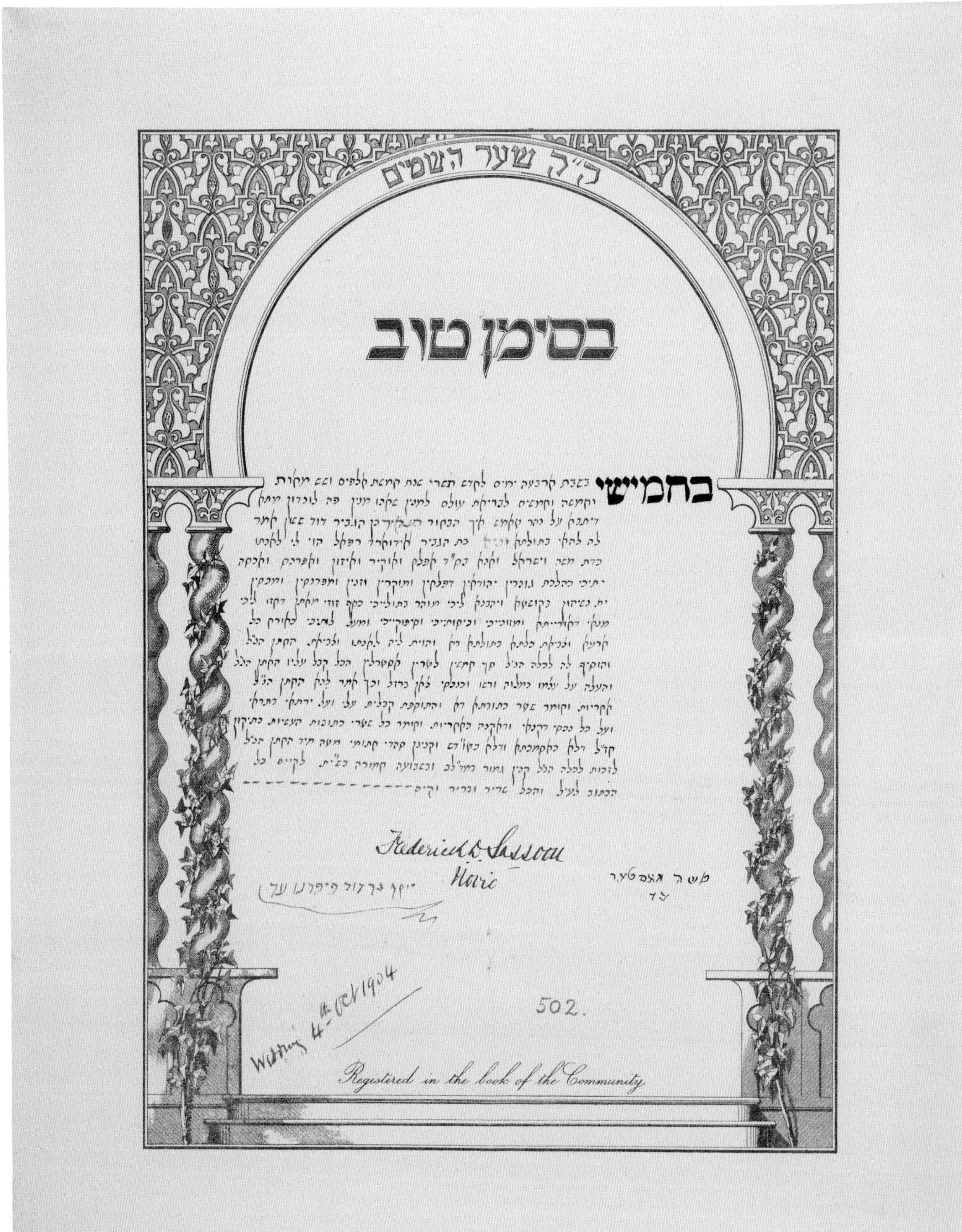
ק״ק שער השמים

בסימן טוב

בחמישי

Frederick D. Sassoon

502.

Wedding 4th Oct 1904

Registered in the book of the Community

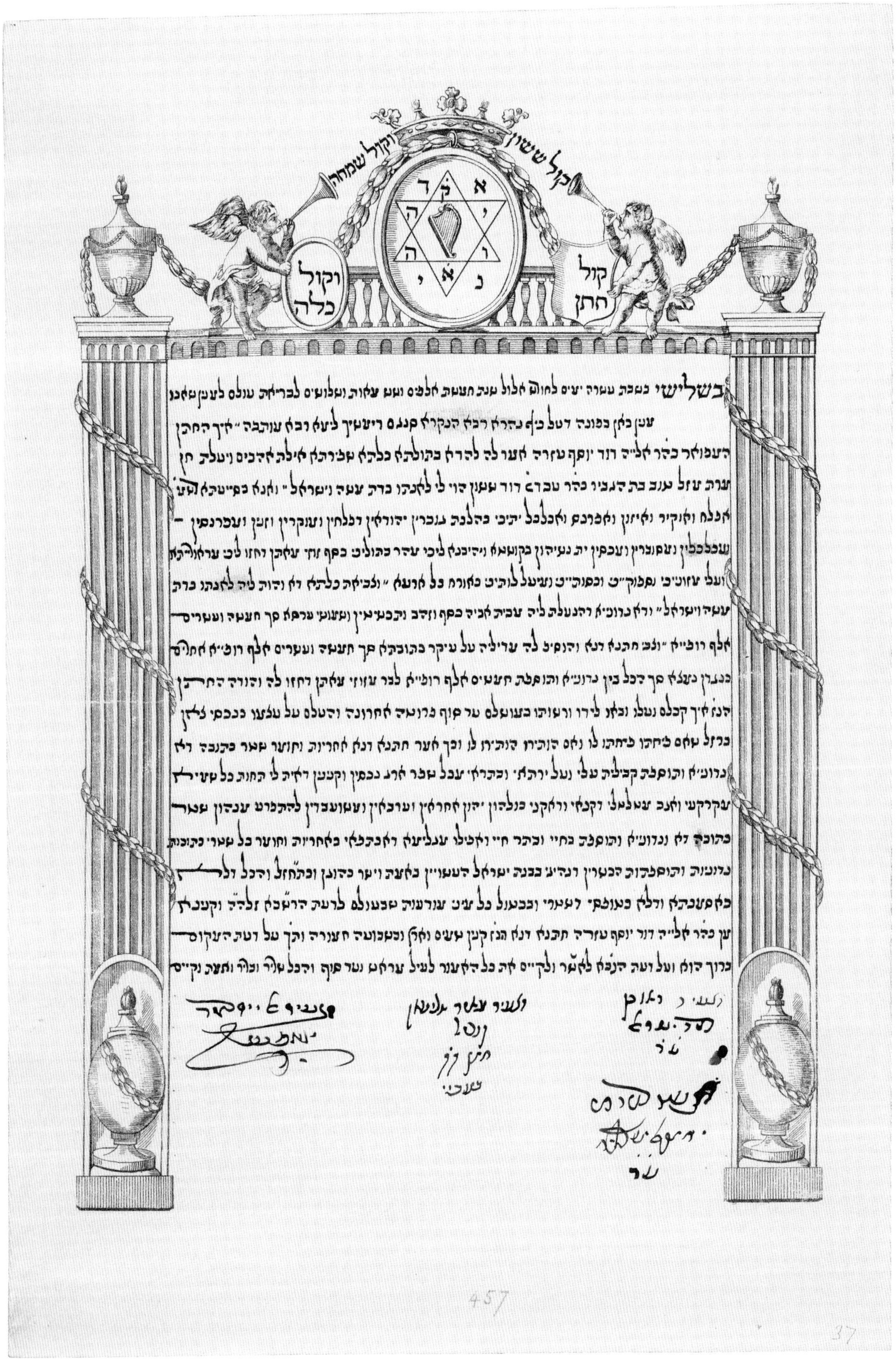

Marriage contract of Mazal Tov (Mozelle) Sassoon and Elias Ezra, Pune, India, Elul 10, 5630 (September 6, 1870), print and ink on parchment, 13¾ × 9¼ in. (35 × 23.5 cm), Benjamin Zucker Family Collection (Z56), formerly in the David Solomon Sassoon Collection (no. 457). Mozelle was the daughter of Hannah Khatun and Albert Abdullah Sassoon, David Sassoon's oldest son. Her bridegroom, Elias, belonged to another prominent Baghdadi Jewish family, the Ezras, who were based in Kolkata. The wedding took place in the Ohel David Synagogue in Pune, founded by the bride's grandfather. The decorative program of the marriage contract follows a Dutch model, a short-lived trend among Baghdadi Jews.

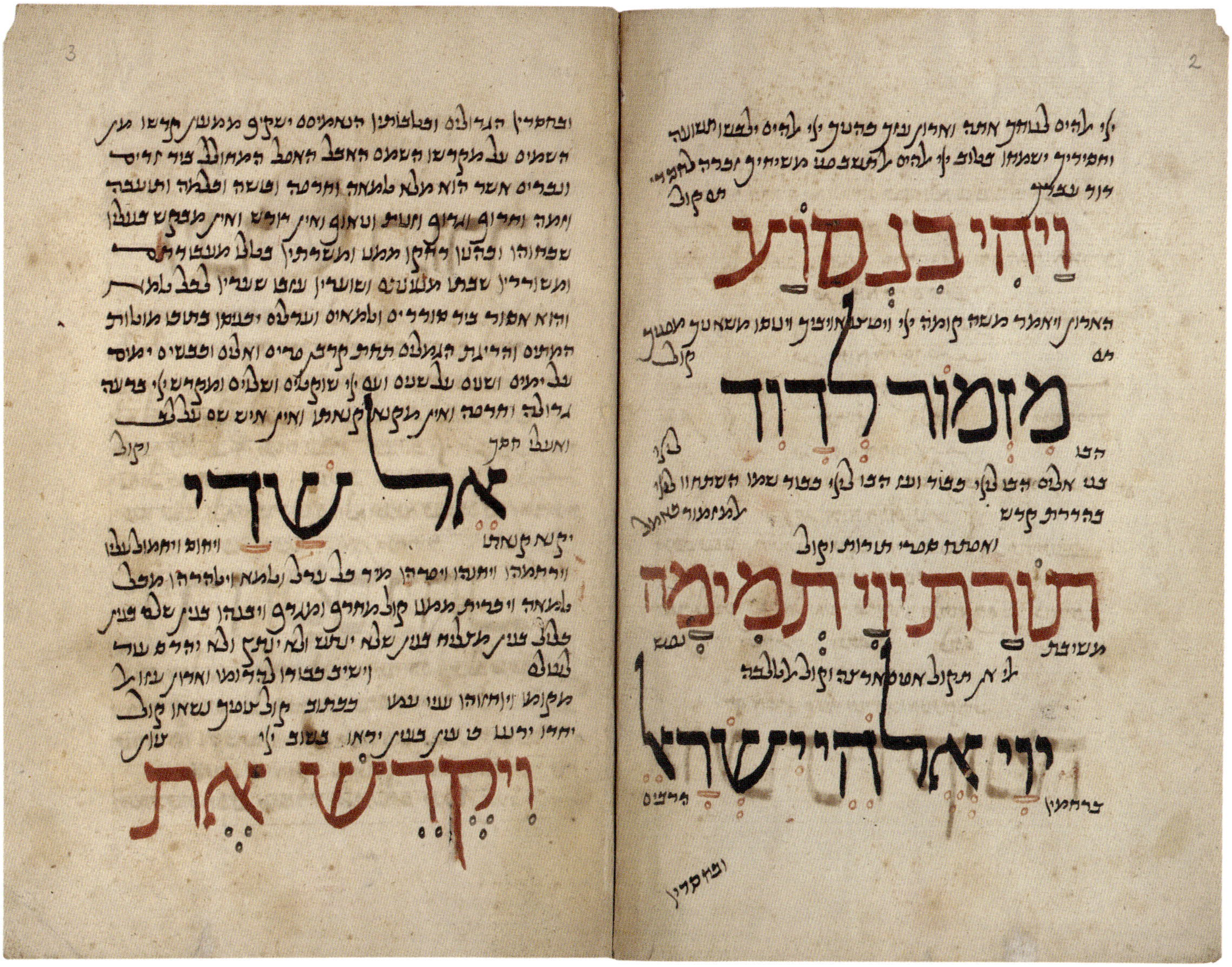

Liturgical fragment according to the Rite of the Karaites, from the Cairo Genizah, cursive Karaite hand, sixteenth century, ink on paper, 10 × 6¼ in. (25.2 × 16 cm), Cambridge University Library, UK, ms. Or. 2243, formerly in the David Solomon Sassoon Collection (no. 227).

The manuscripts collected by David Solomon include some of the oldest extant Hebrew Bibles and superbly illuminated Hebrew manuscripts ever assembled.[29] His first significant acquisition was the Rashba Bible, so called after Rabbi Solomon ben Abraham Adret (known as Rashba), the grandfather of its first owner, Astruc ben Isaac. Copied in Cervera, Catalonia, in 1383, and filled with illuminations incorporating birds, animals, and fish, the Bible reached Damascus, probably following the late fifteenth-century expulsions from the Iberian Peninsula, where the collector purchased it in 1902. He would later write about the trials he endured to secure it: "I was subjected to an examination, testing my ability in reading a portion from the Law before the congregation. This was done to guard against a repetition of earlier attempts made by missionaries to obtain the [manuscript]."[30] According to Katrin Kogman-Appel, the work belongs to a group of Hebrew Bibles from Barcelona and its environs that share common features: Temple implements depictions (beautifully illuminated in the Rashba Bible), Gothic elements, and lack of carpet pages. This acquisition was so meaningful to the collector that he would recall its date for years to come. On November 4, 1937, he would write in his journal that the first of the Jewish month of Kislev was a special day for him: thirty-five years earlier he had bought the Rashba Bible, and ten years later he had become engaged to Selina Prins.[31] On his return journey from Damascus to India via Egypt, in December 1902, he would make yet another important purchase: fragments from the Cairo Genizah—the Ben Ezra Synagogue storeroom where thousands of ancient, worn-out texts were

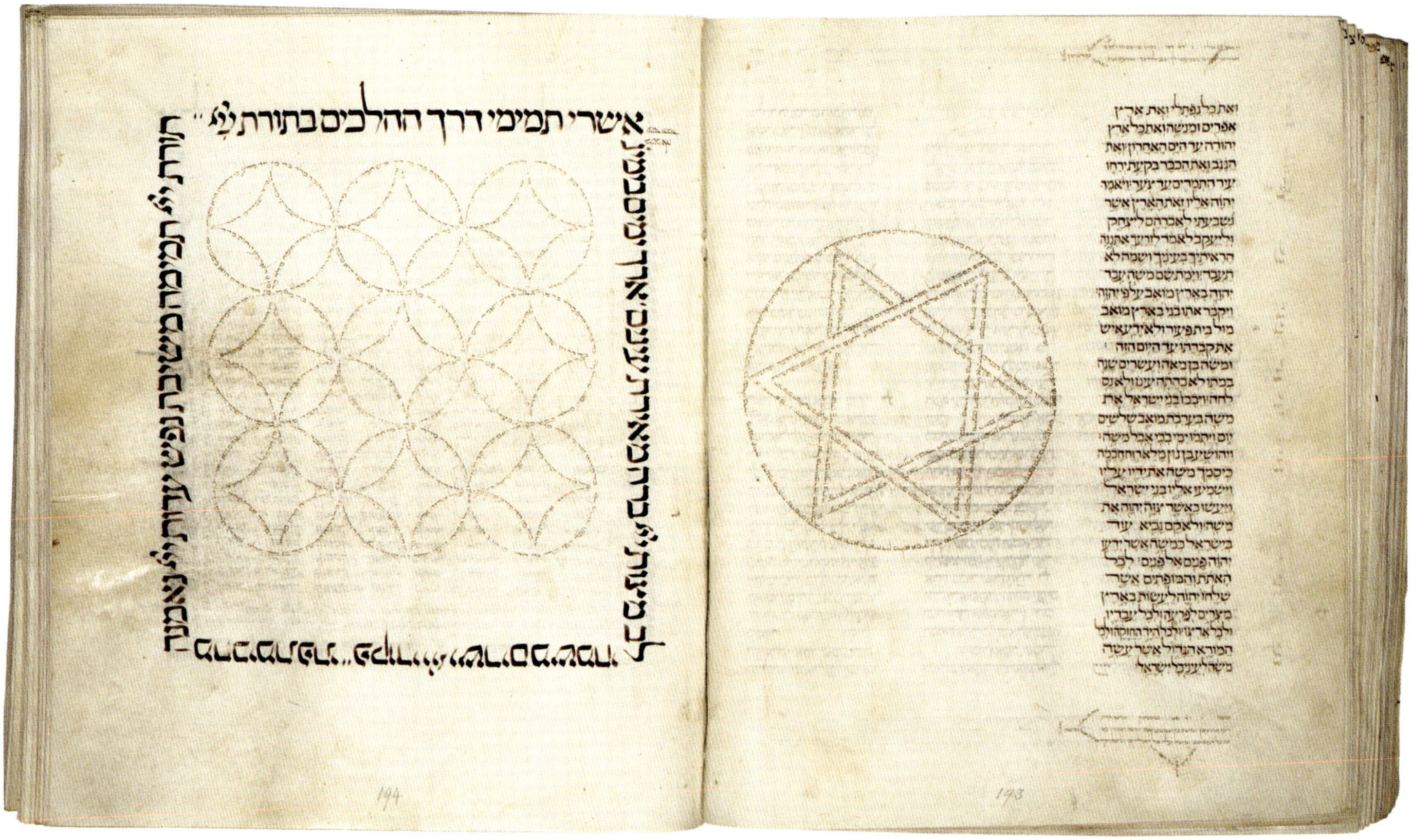

deposited. Among his acquisitions were liturgical texts used by Karaites, followers of a movement within Judaism that emerged in the eighth to ninth century and adhered to the Hebrew Bible as the only source of Jewish law, eschewing rabbinic interpretations set forth in the Talmud.[32]

A Hebrew Bible completed in Toledo in 1307 by Joseph ben Judah ibn Merwas shows the strong influence of Islamic art. Its bold calligraphy framing the Masoretic lists at the beginning of the book and micrographic carpet pages characterize the work of the scribe, who also copied two other Bibles.[33] During his sojourn in Baghdad in 1910, David Solomon purchased a fifteenth-century Sephardic Hebrew Pentateuch with haftarot and Five Scrolls at the Great Synagogue. A dedication in the manuscript records that "the owner, a Baghdadian, Yahya b. Mordecai by name, in memory of his father, Mordecai b. Abraham b. Sason, in the year 1676, handed over this [manuscript] for the use of the Great Synagogue in Baghdad, where it was held in great reverence."[34] It contains illuminated comparison tables, listing the differences between the Masoretic Bible versions of Ben Naphtali and Ben Asher, and illuminated initial letters and words. The manuscript had been used during circumcisions in a traditional Baghdadi ceremony—the "Bond of the Myrtle" (Áqd-el-yas). On the eighth night after the boy's birth, the synagogue's Elijah chair—reserved for the prophet, who is believed to be present at every circumcision—would be taken to the house of the newborn. The Pentateuch would be placed on the chair decorated with Torah finials and covered with rich textiles, flowers, myrtle leaves, and rue. Myrtle was used due to the similarity between the Arabic name for the plant el-yas, believed to ward off evil forces, and the name of the prophet Khidr Elyas.[35]

David Solomon would follow this tradition on the circumcision of his son Solomon in 1915, held at his private prayer room in the library of his London home. He would place one of his most prized possessions on the Elijah chair—the Farhi Codex—which he had recently acquired. One of the most magnificent Hebrew illuminated manuscripts ever produced, the codex combines lavish miniatures featuring the implements of the Temple set against diapered backgrounds in Gothic style with thirty carpet pages influenced by Islamic art. It also contains "quite a small library . . . which embodies over fifty smaller and larger treatises of different branches of Biblical literature, like

OPPOSITE
Carpet page and geometric motifs influenced by Islamic book art, Hebrew Bible, Toledo, Spain, 1307, scribe: Joseph ben Judah ibn Merwas, ink on parchment, 10⅛ × 8½ in. (25.7 × 21.6 cm), University of Toronto, Thomas Fisher Rare Book Library, Friedberg mss. 5-001, pp. 193–94, formerly in the David Solomon Sassoon Collection (no. 508).

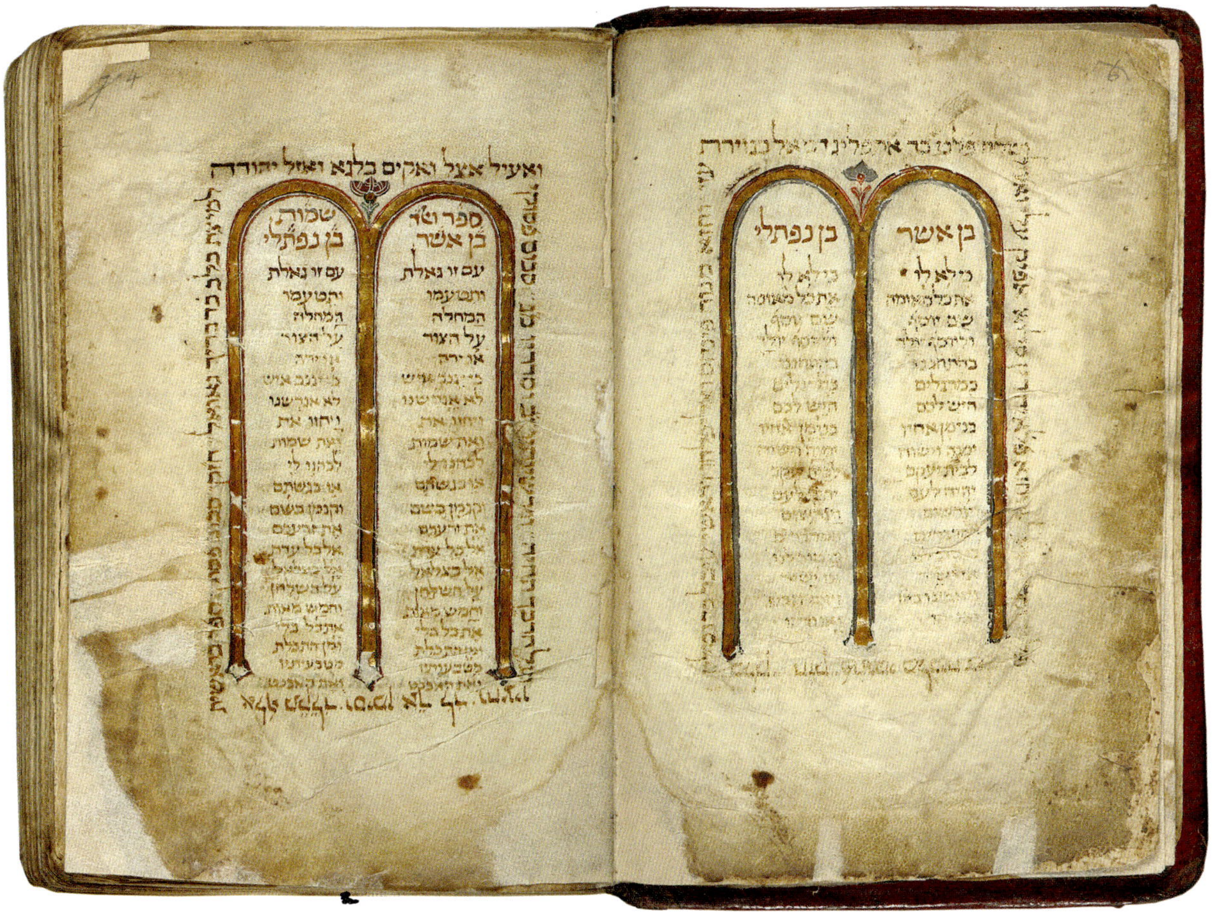

Tables listing the differences between the Masoretic Bible versions copied by Ben Naphtali and Ben Asher in the tenth century, Hebrew Bible (Pentateuch with haftarot and Five Scrolls), Spain, fifteenth century, ink and paint on parchment, 6⅞ × 4¹¹⁄₁₆ in. (17.4 × 11.9 cm), London, British Library, ms. Or. 14054, fols. 3v–4r, formerly in the David Solomon Sassoon Collection (no. 199).

Midrashim, works of chronology, and a Biblical introduction."[36] The scribe and illuminator, Elisha ben Abraham Bevenisti Cresques of Majorca (1325–1387), was also a cartographer in the service of King Peter IV of Aragon (r. 1336–87). He worked on the *mikdashyah*, or "sanctuary of the Lord," as he refers to his masterwork in the colophon and as these illuminated Sephardic Hebrew Bibles are termed, for seventeen years (1366–83). It is not surprising, therefore, that it would take David Solomon almost as much time to secure this treasure. He purchased the Bible in 1913 during his first visit to Aleppo, but the painstaking process of its acquisition had begun more than a decade earlier when he overheard, from fellow travelers on a boat, that the manuscript was still available. The Bible belonged to the prominent Farhi family of Syria and it was held in Aleppo by the British Consul. After years of trying to obtain it through correspondence to no avail, he traveled there to plead his case and was successful.[37]

David Solomon's collection contained significant Yemenite holdings, which he acquired beginning in 1911, when, as he put it, "a new source of [manuscripts] was opened to me by a Jew in Yemen."[38] Among these are important Pentateuch books known as *tijan* (singular, *taj*), or crowns, in Arabic. A superb two-volume *taj* manuscript exemplifies the Yemenite tradition of producing fine biblical codices, featuring the Masorah text in micrography forming geometric patterns, a delicate decorative program, and full pages with mnemonic text for the weekly Torah portions within Exodus, Leviticus, and Numbers.[39] The manuscript is further enhanced by a double colophon. On the first page of the first volume, the scribe states: "This was my portion from all of my labors: I, the humble Salim ibn Joseph al-Aziri, may his soul be bound up in the Bond of Life. I have donated this object; he who reads it shall rejoice, while he who steals it shall be obliterated—and the nation of God shall dwell in peace." On the second colophon at the beginning of the second volume, the scribe refers to his manuscript as *taj*:

> This was my portion from all of my labors: I, the humble Salim, son of my master, my father Joseph ben Salim al-Aziri, may his soul be bound up in the Bond of Life. I have donated this object, known as the holy *taj* [. . .] to my synagogue, which God gave me the opportunity to build in the

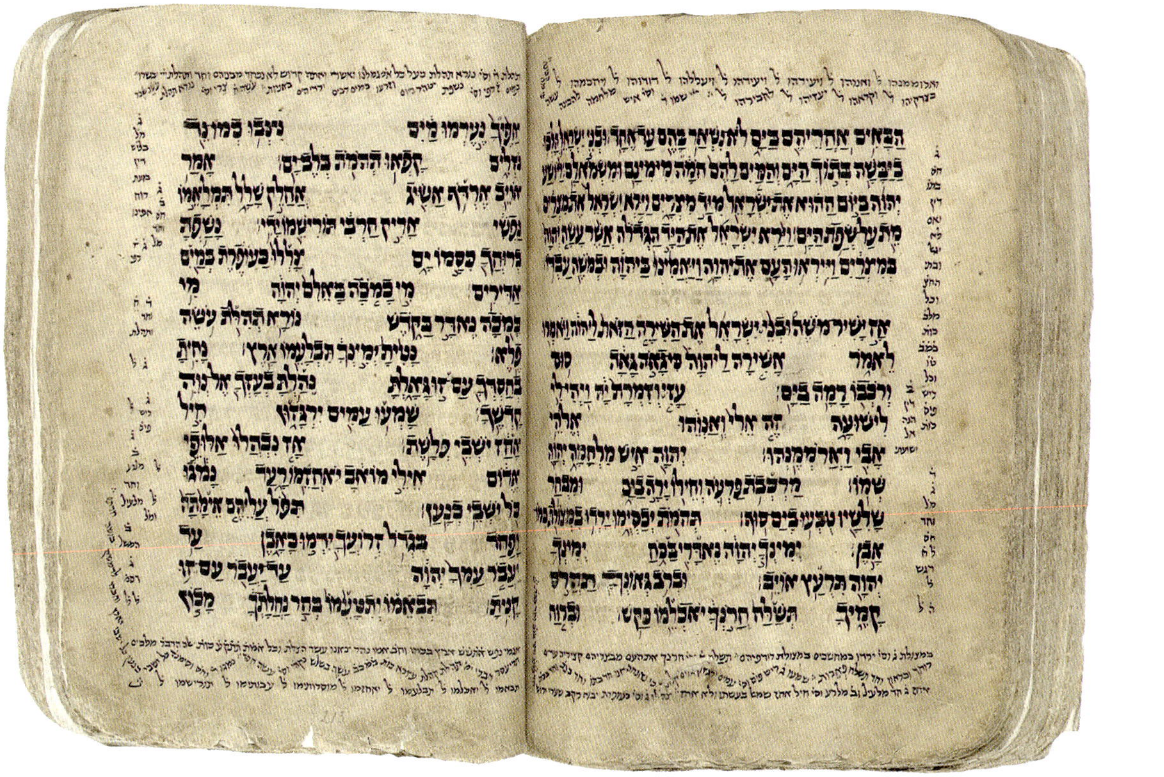

Exodus 14:28–31 and the Song of the Sea (Exod. 15:1–17), *Taj* (Yemenite Hebrew Pentateuch), vol. 1: Genesis and Exodus, Yemen, sixteenth century, ink on paper, 10⅜ × 7½ in. (26.5 × 19 cm), Les Enluminures Ltd., formerly in the David Solomon Sassoon Collection (no. 330).

city Asade [?], may the Uppermost prosper it. It shall be called by my name as a source of merit and as a remembrance. He who reads it shall rejoice, while he who steals it shall be obliterated—and the nation of God shall dwell in peace.

Among the Ashkenazi manuscripts in the Sassoon collection, the De Castro Pentateuch, so called after David Henriques de Castro, the Dutch Jewish collector who owned it in the late nineteenth century, stands out.[40] Completed in 1344, it is beautifully penned in square and semicursive Ashkenazi script, comprising also the haftarot and Five Scrolls. The Pentateuch text is surrounded by the Aramaic translation Targum Onkelos and by a rare version of the commentary by Rashi (Rabbi Solomon ben Isaac, 1040–1105). Each of the five books of the Pentateuch and the Five Scrolls open with decorated initial words colored with tempera and embellished with silver leaf, some illustrated, as in the book of Genesis featuring Adam and Eve in the Garden of Eden. The book of Esther concludes with a full-page illustration of the hanging of Haman and his ten sons, its vibrant colors belying the gruesome scene. Given the manuscript's monumental size and rich decorative program, it is likely that Joseph ben Ephraim, who commissioned it, intended it both for private use as well as for synagogue reading of the haftarot. As was often the case in a production of this scope, work would be divided between two scribes: one copied the main text, and a second, the masorator, added the vocalization and was responsible for the Masorah, or notes that ensure the accurate transmission of the biblical text, with each scribe adding his own colophon. In the De Castro Pentateuch, Levi ben David Ha-Levi proudly signed the Bible, detailing in his colophon that he masoreted and vocalized it, and wrote the text of the Pentateuch in small script in the lower margins. But the colophon of the scribe who penned the main text is missing, and it is left to the reader to guess his name, possibly a Netanel [ben] Daniel, hinted with markings over these names when they appear in the main text. David Solomon noted that the main text, the Targum Onkelos, and the Rashi commentary were done by an older hand, which may explain the absence of a colophon by the main scribe. It is possible that he was no longer alive or unable to sign his work by the time the manuscript was completed.[41]

Similar in scope and also produced in Ashkenaz at about the same time is a copy of the *Mishneh Torah*, Maimonides's masterwork of rabbinic law. The manuscript's fascinating journey is

OPPOSITE
Initial word panel for the Song of Songs, De Castro Pentateuch, Germany, 1344, scribe: Netanel [ben] Daniel (?), masorator: Levi ben David Ha-Levi, ink, tempera, and silver leaf on parchment, 18⅛ × 12¼ in. (46 × 31 cm), Jerusalem, Israel Museum, acquired on the advice of Joseph and Caroline Gruss and with the assistance of Friends of the Israel Museum, 180/094, fol. 333r, formerly in the David Solomon Sassoon Collection (no. 506).

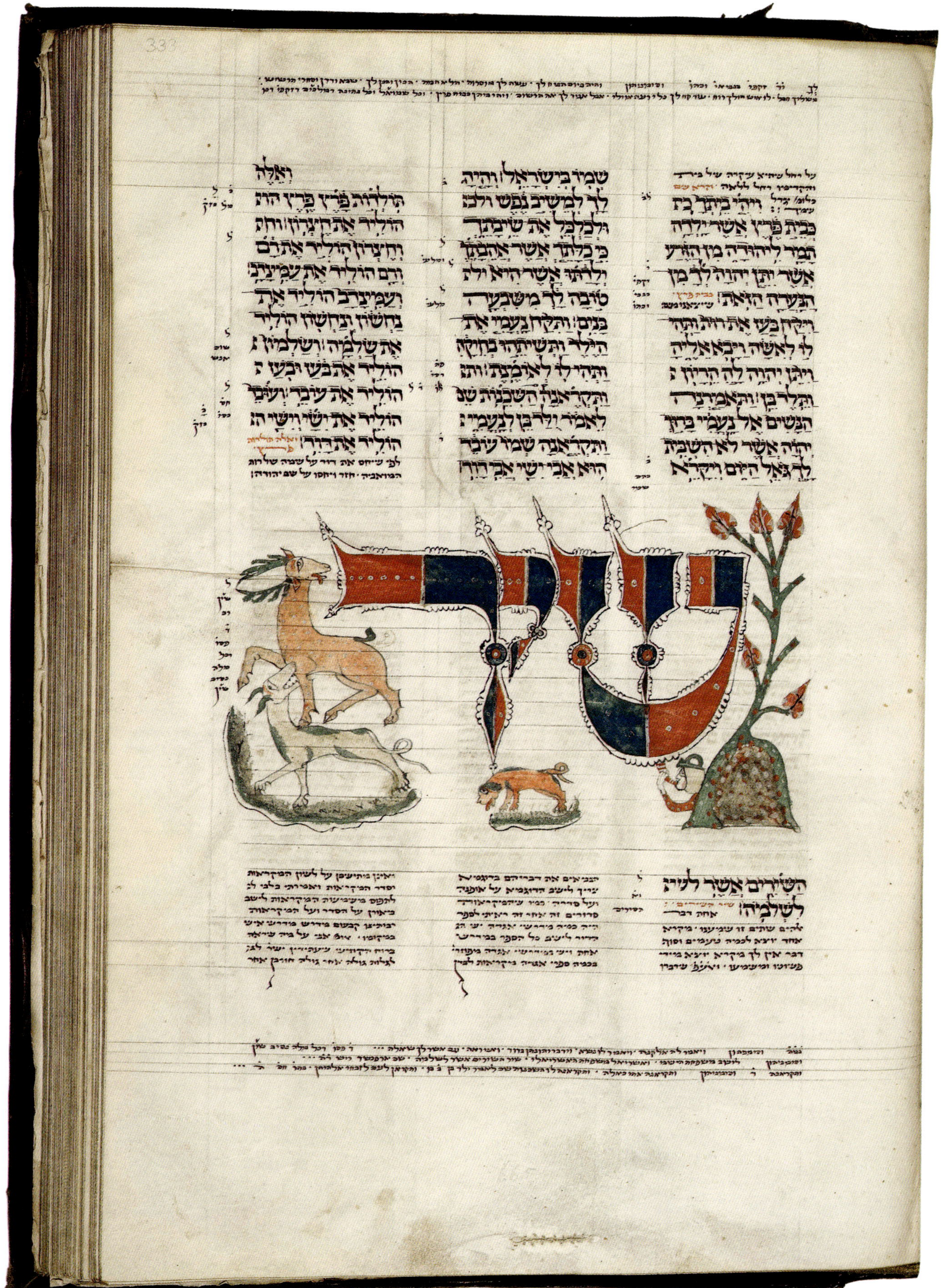

ויהי ביתך כבית
בית פרץ אשר ילדה
תמר ליהודה מן הזרע
אשר יתן יהוה לך מן
הנערה הזאת׃
ויקח בעז את רות ותהי
לו לאשה ויבא אליה
ויתן יהוה לה הריון
ותלד בן׃ ותאמרנה
הנשים אל נעמי ברוך
יהוה אשר לא השבית
לך גאל היום ויקרא
שמו בישראל׃ והיה
לך למשיב נפש ולכל
כל את שיבתך
כי כלתך אשר אהבתך
ילדתו אשר היא טו
בה לך משבעה
בנים׃ ותקח נעמי את
הילד ותשתהו בחיקה
ותהי לו לאמנת׃ ות
קראנה לו השכנות שם
לאמר ילד בן לנעמי
ותקראנה שמו עובד
הוא אבי ישי אבי דוד׃
ואלה
תולדות פרץ פרץ הו
ליד את חצרון׃ וחצ
רון הוליד את רם
ורם הוליד את עמינדב׃
ועמינדב הוליד את
נחשון ונחשון הוליד
את שלמה׃ ושלמון
הוליד את בעז ובעז
הוליד את עובד׃ ועבד
הוליד את ישי וישי
הוליד את דוד׃

שיר השירים אשר
לשלמה׃

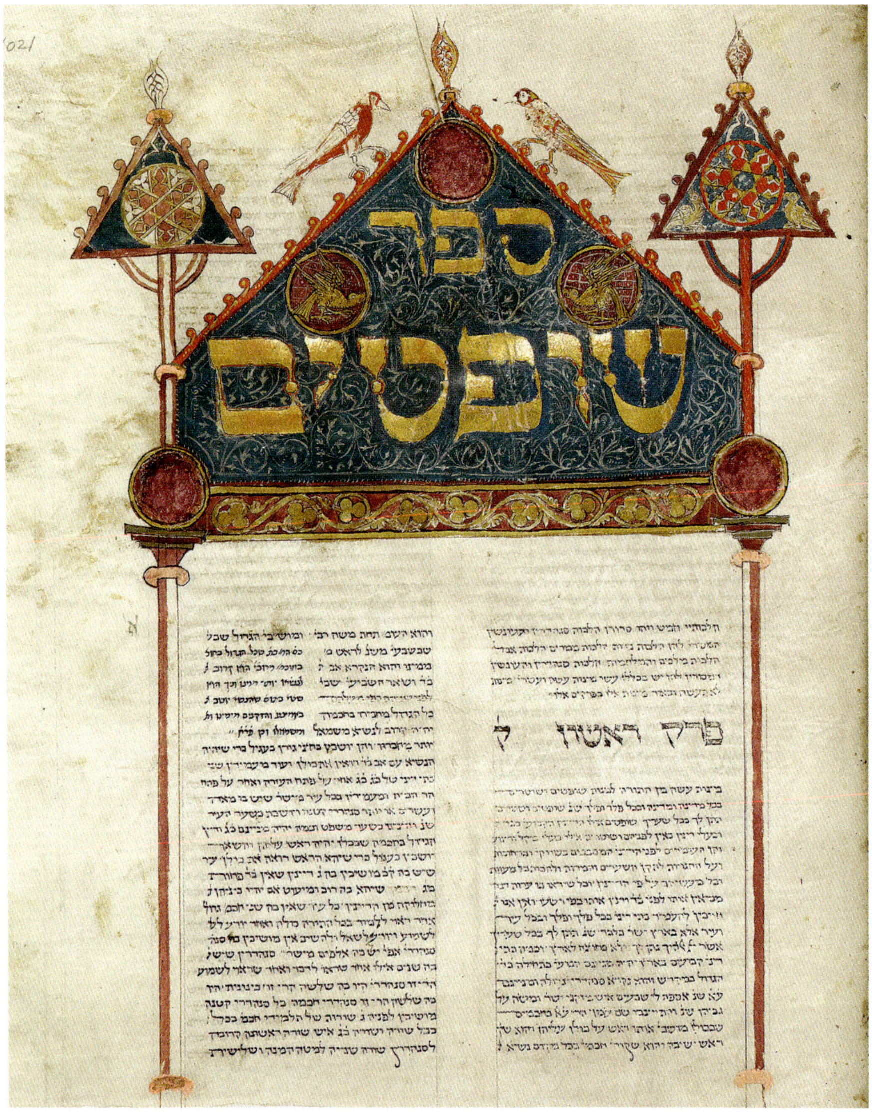

Initial decorated page for the Book of Judges, Maimonides, *Mishneh Torah* with *Haggahot Maimunyyot* (Maimonidian Comments) and *Teshuvot Maimunyyot* (Maimonidian Responsa) by Meir ben Yekutiel ha-Kohen of Rothenburg, Germany, 1355–56, scribe: Jacob, son of Joseph Halevy, ink, tempera, and gold leaf on parchment, 19½ × 13¾ in. (49.3 × 35 cm), Zurich, Braginsky Collection, BC 345, formerly in the David Solomon Sassoon Collection (no. 1043).

described by the collector: "written in Germany by Jacob b. Joseph Hallevy for Mordecai b. Moses in the year 1355–6, found its way to Mardin, Turkey, in Asia Minor, where it remained from the second half of the sixteenth century—first in private, afterwards in communal possession—till it reached me."[42]

Probably the most revered manuscripts formerly in the Sassoon collection are the two volumes of Maimonides's autograph *Commentary on the Mishnah*.[43] Divided into six orders or *sedarim* (singular, *seder*), the Mishnah is the oldest collection of Jewish law, and the two Sassoon volumes of Maimonides's commentary on it were part of the author's own working copy. Written by Maimonides (1138–1204) in Judeo-Arabic (Arabic in Hebrew script), it also includes diagrams that he drew to explicate his text. It is possible that the main text was copied by a scribe rather than the author himself, with emendations and deletions in Maimonides's own hand. The rabbinic authority, philosopher, and royal physician, who lived a transient life due to persecutions of Jews in his native Spain, completed the *Commentary* in Egypt after he settled there in 1168 but continued to revise his text as he created other works. Notes were also added by Maimonides's son, Rabbi Avraham Maimuni (1186–1237), and a later descendant who took the book to Aleppo in 1375. There the manuscript was divided and sold in parts, with commentary on five of the six *sedarim* of the Mishnah extant. The two volumes once in the Sassoon collection comprise Seder Moed (from the middle of tractate *Eruvin*), pertaining to the laws of the Sabbath and festivals, and Seder Nashim, concerning laws of marriage and divorce. Three more *sedarim* survive in two tomes, both in the collection of the Bodleian Libraries, acquired from two Christian Hebraists in the 1600s.[44] David Solomon was able to secure his two volumes more than two centuries later. The collector often

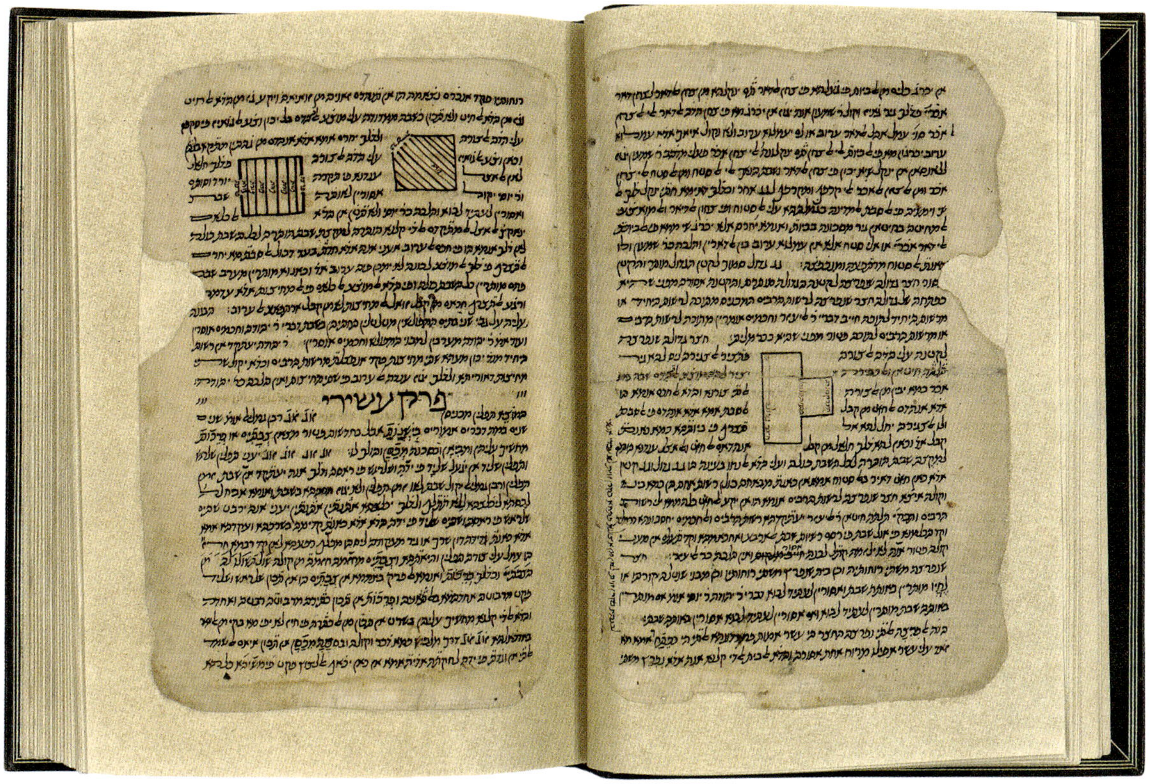

Seder Moed, tractate *Eruvin*, end of chapter 9 and beginning of chapter 10, Maimonides, ***Commentary on the Mishnah***, in Judeo-Arabic with corrections and emendations in Maimonides's hand and notes by his son Avraham Maimuni and others, completed in Egypt after 1168, ink on paper, 10⅞ × 7¾ in. (27.6 × 19.8 cm), National Library of Israel, Heb. 4°5703, formerly in the David Solomon Sassoon Collection (no. 72).

spoke publicly about his holdings and hosted visitors to his library. According to his journal entry for May 10, 1925, he had lectured that day at his home for more than one hundred members of the Sephardic Literary Society. When he showed them some of his treasures, they were awed by Maimonides's *Commentary*: "Many of the viewers touched the manuscripts with their fingertips and kissed them in an admiring way."[45]

A copy of Maimonides's *Guide of the Perplexed*, his major philosophical work, was also once in the Sassoon collection. In that treatise, the author addresses students well-versed in the Torah and observant of its precepts who are confounded by the seeming contradictions between philosophical teachings and religious tradition. Written by the Rambam in Arabic, the work was translated into Hebrew during his lifetime by Samuel ben Judah ibn Tibbon. The manuscript (British Library, ms. Or. 14061) was richly illuminated in Catalonia in the fourteenth century and bears similarities to a signed copy of the *Guide* in the Royal Library of Copenhagen (cod. Heb. 37) penned by the scribe Levi ben Isaac ben Caro of Salamanca and illuminated in the Barcelona workshop of the fourteenth-century Christian painter Ferrer Bassa, court artist to King Peter IV of Aragon. His atelier was responsible for the creation of altarpieces as well the decoration of manuscripts. Rich in illuminated initial-word panels, the manuscript once in the Sassoon collection has two full illuminated pages, including a miniature featuring a rampant crowned golden lion, a heraldic motif, in a panel with a diapered blue background surrounded by scrollwork.[46] Also produced in the fourteenth century in the same geographic milieu is a Passover Haggadah that has come to be known as the Sassoon Haggadah, following its acquisition by the State of Israel in 1975 at one of several auctions of David Solomon's former holdings. The manuscript dates to about 1320 and was probably copied in Spain or southern France. It is filled with colorful illustrations of the text, at times quite literal, often rendered within word panels illuminated with gold and silver leaf and decorated with grotesques and animals. Gothic-style arcades incorporate the text on some pages. Poems were later added, including Had Gadya, the ten-verse Aramaic song chanted at the conclusion of the Passover ceremonial meal or seder. As is the case with many medieval Jewish manuscripts, the Haggadah's journey is only partly known. Its passage through Italy is documented by the signature, dated 1687, of censor Antonio Francisco Enriquez, active in Urbino in 1683–88, as expurgation of Hebrew books in Italy was relaxing. A letter sent to David Solomon in 1919 by Librairie M. Lipschutz in Paris, in answer to a query from the collector as to

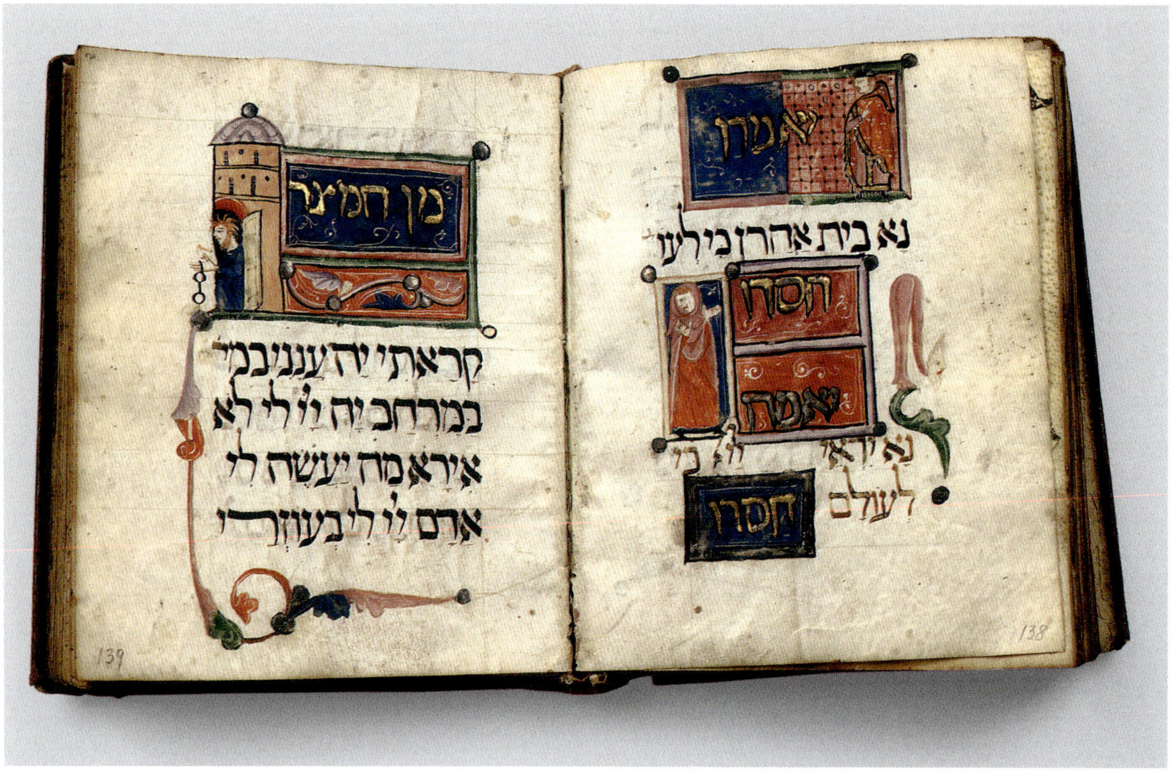

Illustrations to "Let the house of Aaron declare . . . In distress I called on the Lord; the Lord answered me and brought me relief" (Pss. 118:3–7). Sassoon Haggadah, Spain or southern France, c. 1320, ink, tempera, and gold and silver leaf on parchment, 8¼ × 6½ in. (21 × 16.5 cm), purchased by the State of Israel through an anonymous donor, London, formerly in the David Solomon Sassoon Collection (no. 514).

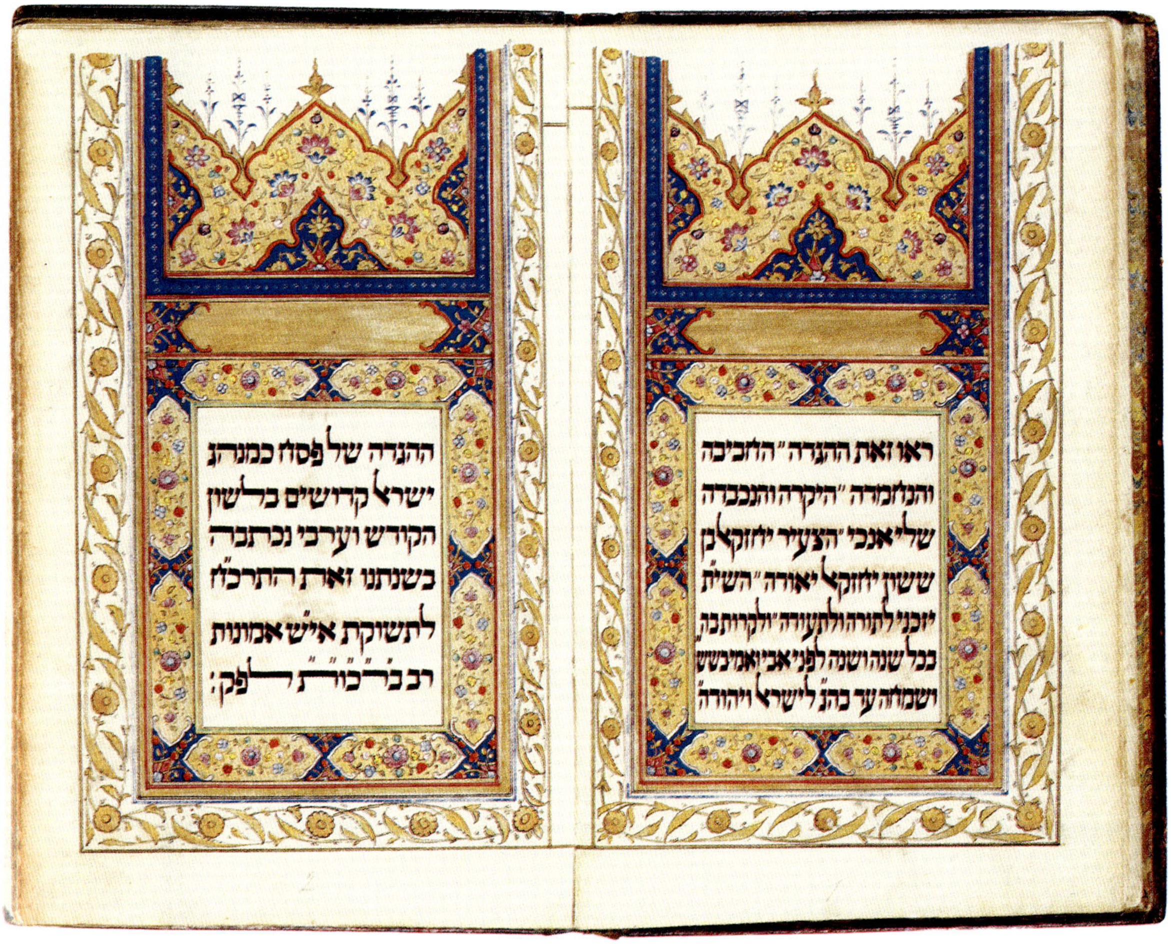

Passover Haggadah, Kolkata, 1868, ink, gouache, and shell gold on paper, 7⅝ × 5 in. (19.4 × 12.7 cm), Collection of Jane and Stuart Weitzman, formerly in the David Solomon Sassoon Collection (no. 363).

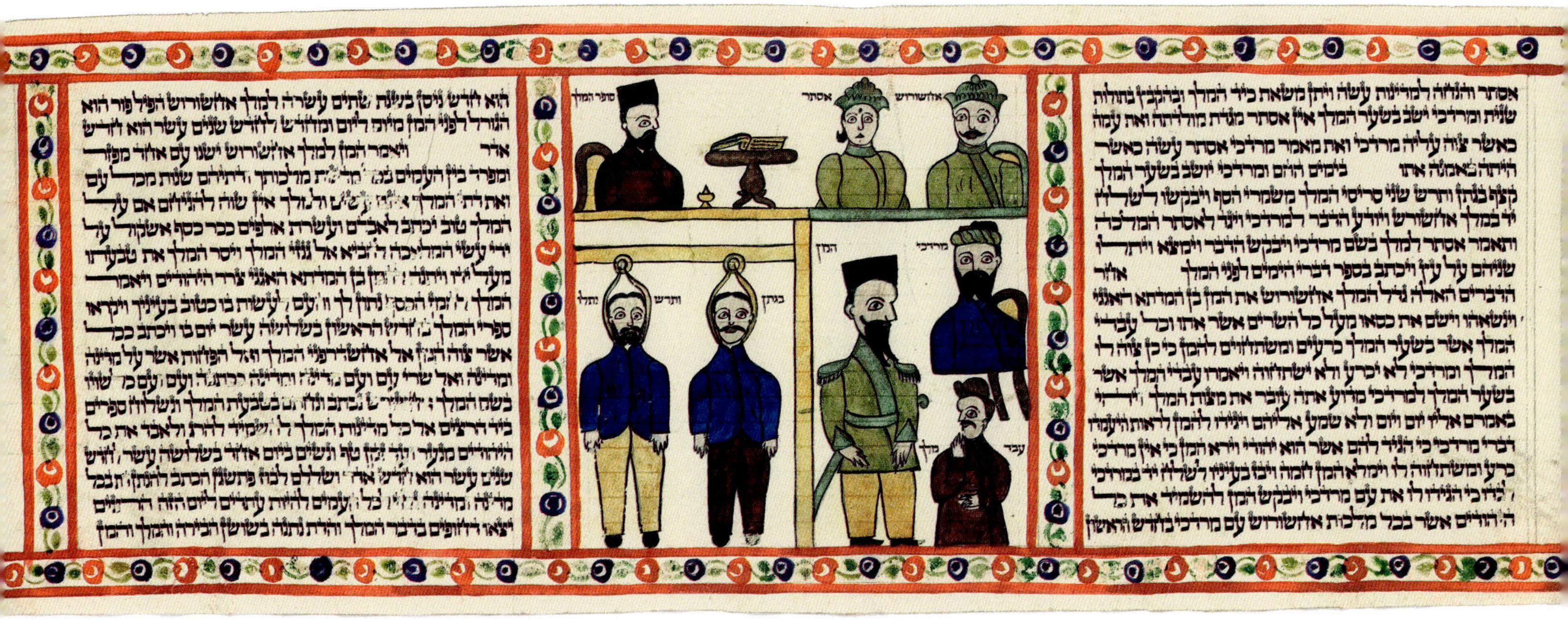

Esther scroll, India, c. 1900, ink and gouache on parchment, 8 × 23 ft. ⅜ in. (20.2 × 702 cm), Zurich, Braginsky Collection, Megillah BCS 58, formerly in the Sassoon Family Collection.

the origins of the Haggadah "in his possession," indicates that he owned it by that time.[47]

Another Passover Haggadah formerly in the Sassoon collection is an exquisite and rare example of Hebrew illumination from India, replete with vibrant illustrations embellished with shell gold depicting the elements of the seder and the various related rituals. Commissioned in 1868 for the youth Ezekiel by his father Sassoon Ezekiel Judah of Kolkata, the Haggadah follows the Baghdadi Rite, with Judeo-Arabic translation to facilitate the boy's understanding of the ceremonial meal. Like the Sassoons, the Judahs were a Baghdadi family that rose to prominence in India through prosperous trade.[48] While the decorative program of the Haggadah eschews human representation, another manuscript from India—an Esther scroll—celebrates it.[49] An unusual departure from the classic aniconic Baghdadi examples with floral decoration (see pages 44–45), this *megillah* is richly illustrated and vibrantly colored, with depictions of the characters of the Purim story in both Western and Eastern dress, with some women wearing the Hindu bindi on their foreheads. This melding of traditions in a single manuscript speaks to the various cultures the Sassoons inhabited.

A lavish Judeo-Persian manuscript is also richly figurative. Created in Iran between 1675 and 1724, it is an incomplete copy of the epic *Fath-Nāma* (Book of Conquest), the poetical paraphrase of biblical stories from the books of Joshua, Ruth, and Samuel, composed by the Isfahani Jewish poet 'Imrani (1454–1536).[50] The manuscript is decorated with small panels containing animals and birds or delicate flowers, and features seven miniatures depicting episodes from the book of Joshua, including the carrying of the Ark of the Covenant across the Jordan River with a haloed Joshua looking from above (Josh. 4:18), and the priests sounding *shofarot* (horns) at the walls of Jericho (Josh. 6:20). Vera Moreen, the preeminent scholar of Judeo-Persian manuscripts, has described the *Fath-Nāma* as "one of the most beautiful illuminated Judeo-Persian manuscripts known," attesting to David Solomon Sassoon's highly discerning eye as a collector.

Kabbalistic literature was well represented in the Sassoon collection. An early acquisition is a collection of philosophical and kabbalistic treatises in a Byzantine hand.[51] The scribe, Moses ben Jacob ben Mordecai ben Jacob ben Moses, signed his work not once but three times, dating the first two colophons to 1465 and 1468. The text contains a copy of *Sefer ha-razim* (The Book of Secrets), one of the earliest treatises of Jewish magic, with a full page of symbols for magical writing. The treatise deals with incantations, supernatural remedies, and witchcraft—a rare occurrence in Hebrew literature. Believed to date to the late third or early fourth century, the *Sefer ha-razim* was only reconstructed in its complete form in the 1960s by Mordecai Margalioth, underscoring the importance of the Sassoon manuscript.

The Sassoon collection also included important works on astronomy, astrology, and the calendar. An astronomical anthology produced in

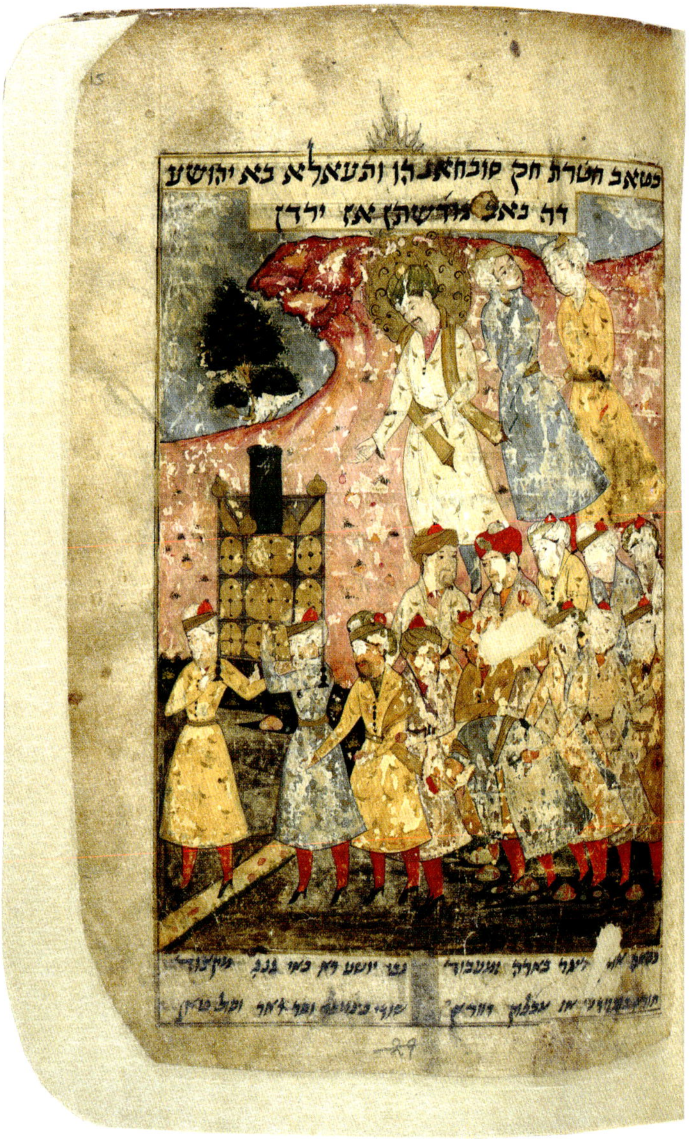

Joshua and the Israelites crossing the Jordan River, carrying the Ark of the Covenant, ʿImrani (1454–1536), *Fath-Nāma* (Book of Conquest): A paraphrase of biblical stories from the books of Joshua, Ruth, and Samuel, in Judeo-Persian, Iran, 1675–1724, ink and gouache on paper, 11¼ × 7⅞ in. (28.5 × 20 cm), London, British Library, ms. Or. 13704, fol. 15r, formerly in the David Solomon Sassoon Collection (no. 614).

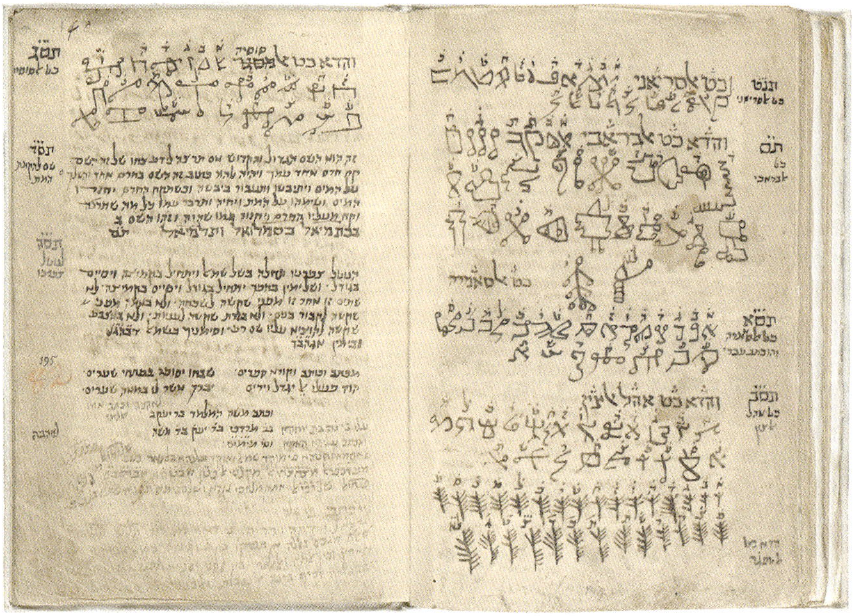

End of *Sefer ha-razim*, a book on magic, with scribe's colophon, Collection of philosophical and kabbalistic treatises, Greece, 1465–68, scribe: Moses ben Jacob ben Mordecai ben Jacob ben Moses, ink on paper, 10 × 6⅝ in. (25.4 × 16.8 cm), New York Public Library, ms. Heb. 190, formerly in the David Solomon Sassoon Collection (no. 56).

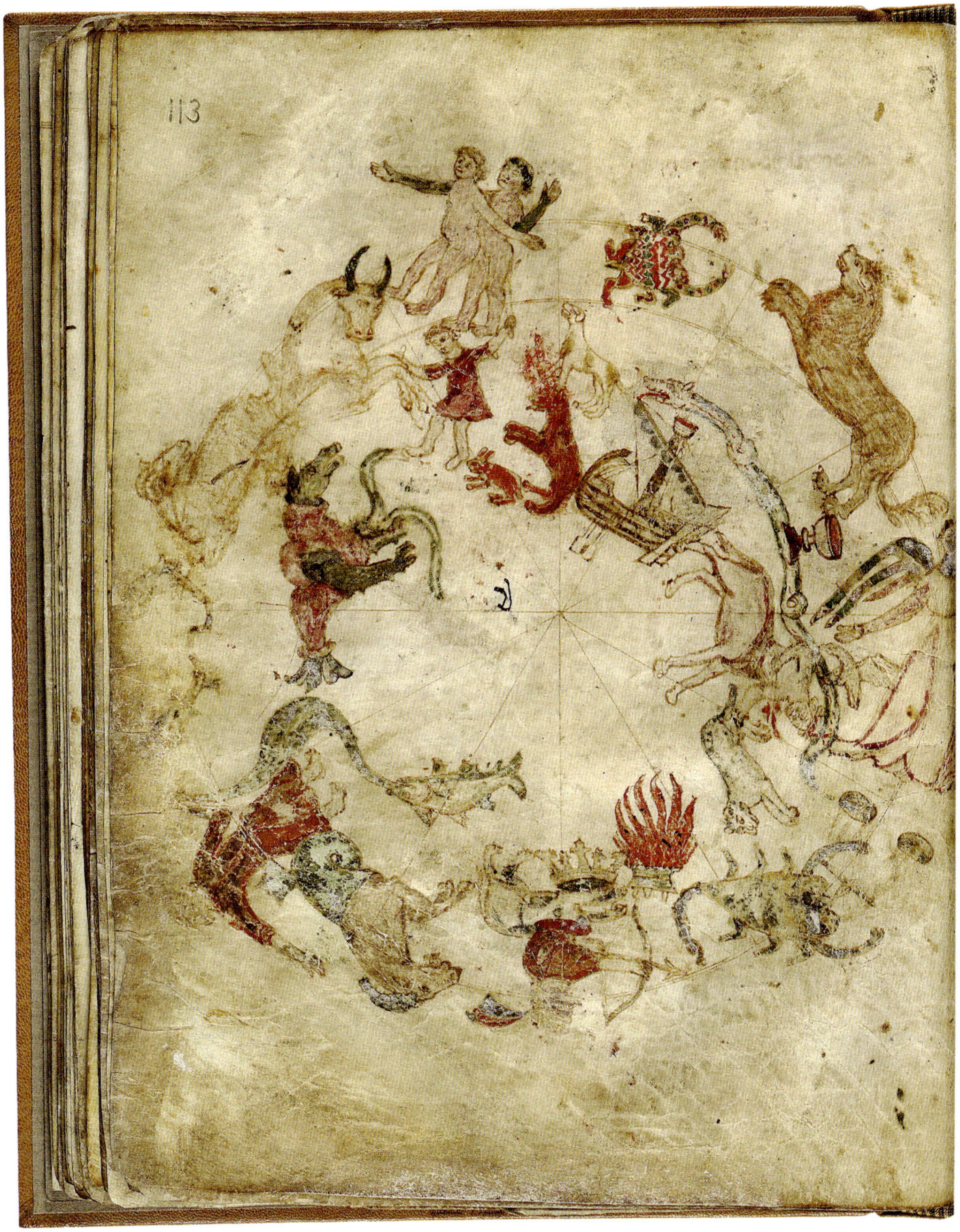

Constellation map, Astronomical anthology, Catalonia, c. 1361, ink and paint on parchment, 11⅜ × 8¾ in. (28.8 × 22.4 cm), Philadelphia, Rare Book and Manuscript Library, University of Pennsylvania, LJS 57, formerly in the David Solomon Sassoon Collection (no. 823).

Catalonia in about 1361 comprises astronomical tables originally compiled for King Peter IV of Aragon by Jacob ben David ben Yomtob (Bonjorn, in Catalan); a Hebrew translation of Ptolemy's *Almagest*; and brief astrological works by the renowned Jewish scholar Abraham Ibn Ezra (1089–1164), who was also a poet, a scientist, and a Hebrew grammarian.[52] The manuscript is a product of the fertile exchange among Muslims, Christians, and Jews in medieval Iberia. Ancient Greek science and philosophy reached Christian Europe through the Islamic world, and Spanish Jews translated works from the Arabic and contributed scientific writings of their own. The manuscript is richly illustrated with two full pages featuring maps of the constellations, and depictions of the constellations are rendered throughout in gouache and accented in gold. Particularly rare are the Samaritan calendrical treatises. The collector owned significant Samaritan holdings, including biblical and liturgical manuscripts, as well as halakhic compendia and community annals.

Following the 1932 publication of *Ohel Dawid*, his extensive catalogue of the 1,153 manuscripts then in his possession, David Solomon would continue to add to his collection. Indeed, as

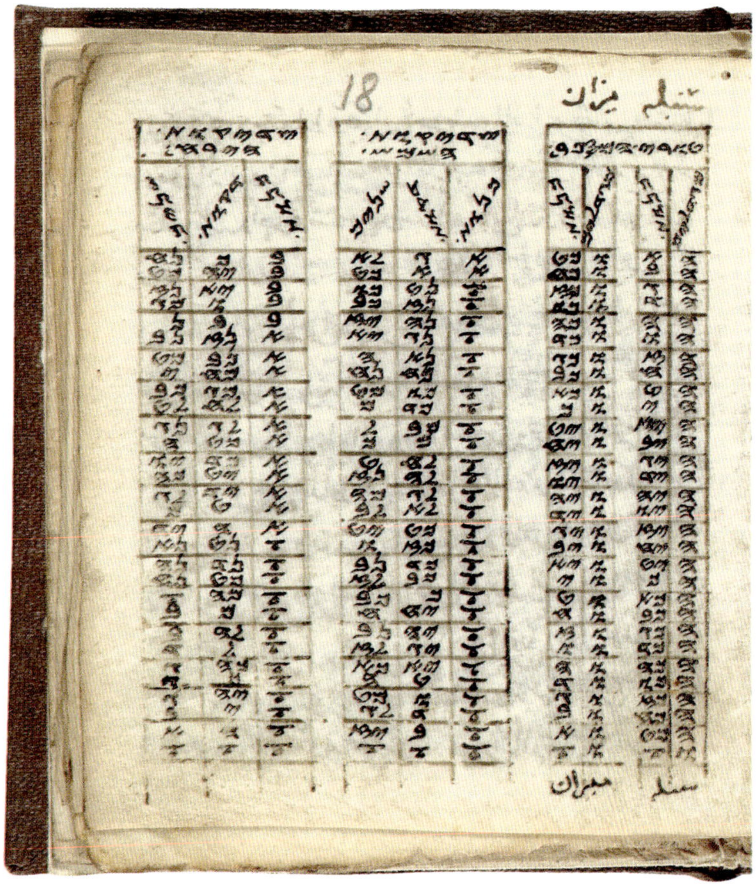

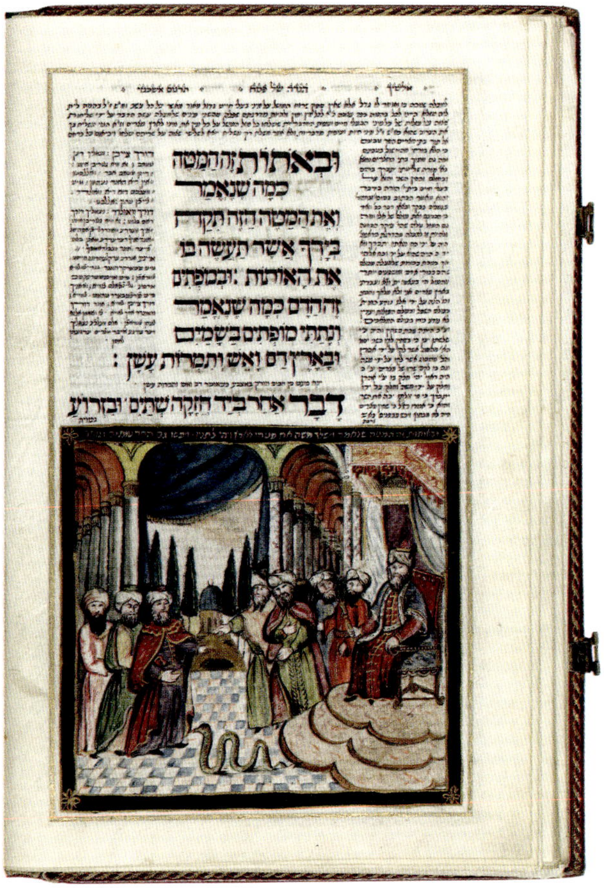

he was writing the preface, it already totaled 1,220 volumes.[53] But his unparalleled career as a bibliophile would soon come to a close as Europe entered World War II. Following the Anschluss in 1938, he began to fear for the safety of his precious collection. "I was afraid lest the Nazis bombard London," he wrote presciently in his diary on April 11, 1938. "I felt it my duty to preserve my manuscripts." Some books were sent to the National Library of Wales at Aberystwyth for safekeeping. Others he took to Winchester Safe Deposit in London: "I placed them in the strong box. I embraced and kissed them, and I reflected whether I should set my eyes on them again."[54] This emotional parting speaks to the relationship David Solomon had with his priceless possessions—his was a living collection that had been cherished, used in daily rituals and on important events in his life, studied, and shared with a wide community of scholars. As his London house was bombed during the Blitz, he was forced to move in the fall of 1940 to Letchworth, not far from the city, where he spent the last two years of his life. It was during these tumultuous times that he made his last acquisition, a Passover Haggadah penned and illustrated by Hijman (Hayyim ben Mordecai) Binger in 1796, and an important example of the manuscript production of the eighteenth and early nineteenth centuries in the Germanic lands as this extraordinary renaissance was ending.[55] His son Rabbi Solomon David Sassoon would inherit the collection, which, beginning in the early 1970s, would be sold in great part in successive auctions, dispersing its contents widely among public and private collections to this day.

ABOVE LEFT
Ishban Kashtah, Samaritan calendrical treatise, Samaritan square and Arabic scripts, Mamluk Palestine, early fourteenth century, ink on parchment, 3⅞ × 3½ in. (9.8 × 8.8 cm), Les Enluminures Ltd., formerly in the David Solomon Sassoon Collection (no. 772).

ABOVE RIGHT
Moses conjuring a snake before Pharaoh, Passover Haggadah, 1796, scribe and illustrator: Hijman (Hayyim ben Mordecai) Binger, ink and gouache on parchment, 12 × 7¾ in. (30.4 × 19.7 cm), Zurich, Braginsky Collection, BC 285, formerly in the David Solomon Sassoon Collection (no. 1274).

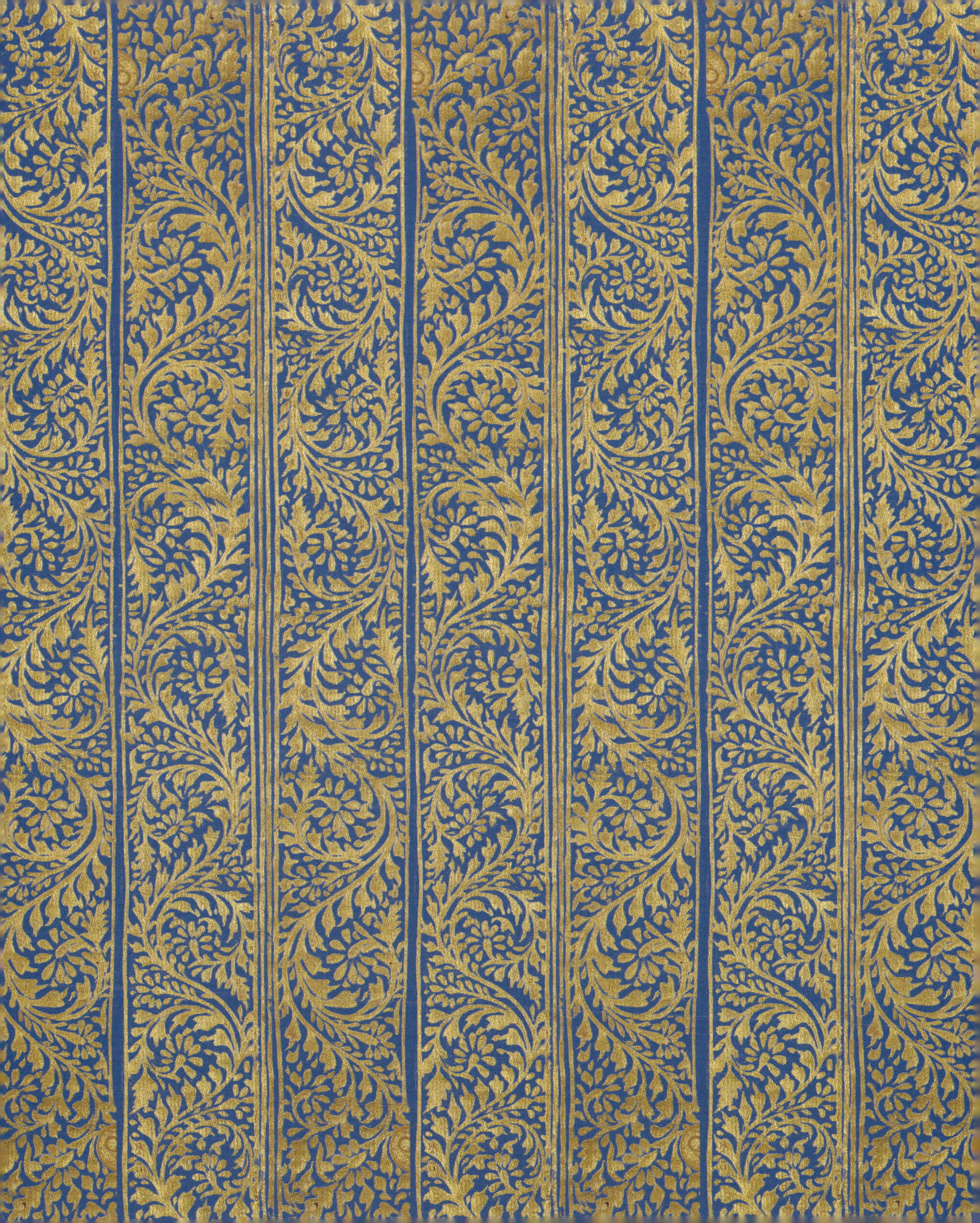

Art

Diaspora made collectors of the Sassoons: the objects they sought bore the traces of homelands both lost and acquired. The first generations of the family cast their gaze toward the past and their roots in Baghdad, the great center of Jewish learning, and their collections reflected a yearning for enduring identities. But collecting also reflects the mutations of identity, another kind of yearning that seeks to belong, to slough off the past and fill the voids of forgetting with discovery and acquired affinities.

The affinities of the children and grandchildren of David Sassoon were shaped by the world of colonial consolidation, in which cultural acquisition was the perquisite of power. Yet, as they moved through different countries, their tastes were also shaped by a genuine engagement with the cultures at each station of their expanding mercantile empire. Later generations, the family members born or educated in London, strove to establish impeccably English and European credentials. For these connoisseurs, collecting was also the means of establishing a legacy, either through service or bequests to British museums. Although their cultural philanthropy was largely secular at this point, it also reflected the rise of what the British historian Abigail Green describes as "emancipated and self-consciously patriotic 'national' Jewries within the emerging European framework of nation-states."[1]

Rachel

The Sassoon women, although less known than their male relatives, were also discerning collectors. Rachel Sassoon Beer (1858–1927) was probably the earliest and one of the most important collectors of paintings in the family. Born in Mumbai, she grew up in England. Her father, Sassoon David Sassoon, had been the first of the patriarch's sons to settle in Britain. Rachel was well educated and musical, and showed early interest in art. Her friend Mary Gladstone, daughter of British Prime Minister William Ewart Gladstone, wrote an entry in her diary in April 1883 about their visit to the studios of the artists Frederic Leighton, Edward Burne-Jones, and George Frederic Watts. Rachel would come to own drawings by Burne-Jones and Watts's sensual painting *Orpheus and Eurydice*, one of two versions now in the Watts Gallery. The two also viewed the plaster model for the marble statuette *A Sonata of Beethoven*, showing Rachel seated gracefully on a piano stool holding a sheet of music, by Hamo Thornycroft. Displayed at the Royal Academy of Arts that year, the plaster model drew praise from *The Observer*.[2]

Four years later, Rachel would marry the owner of that newspaper, Frederick Beer (1858–1901), a descendant of Frankfurt Court Jews who had attained prominence in the eighteenth century. As a child, Frederick had been baptized in the

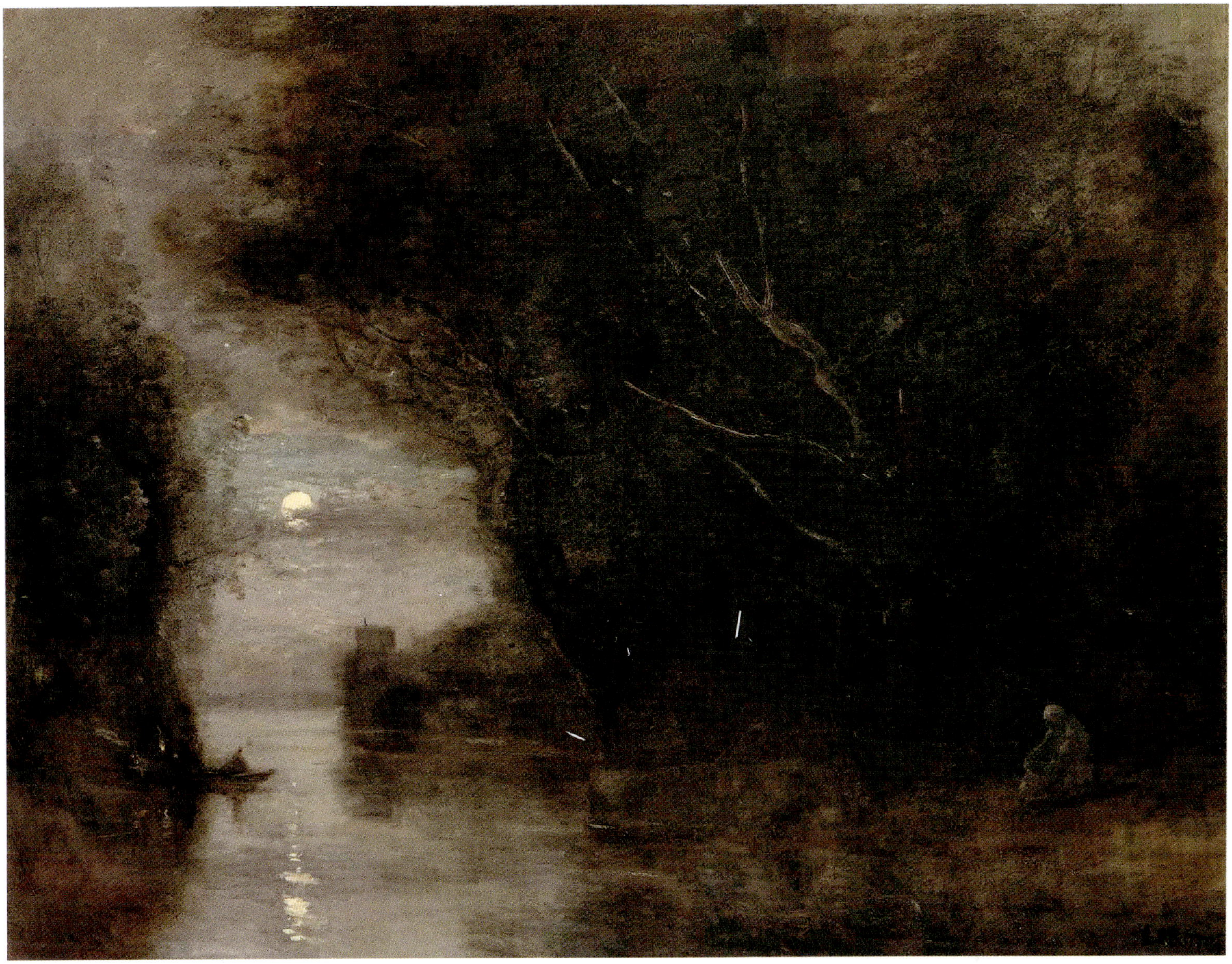

Jean-Baptiste-Camille Corot, *Moonlit Landscape,* 1874, oil on canvas, 35½ × 45½ in. (90.2 × 115.6 cm), formerly in the Rachel Sassoon Beer Collection.

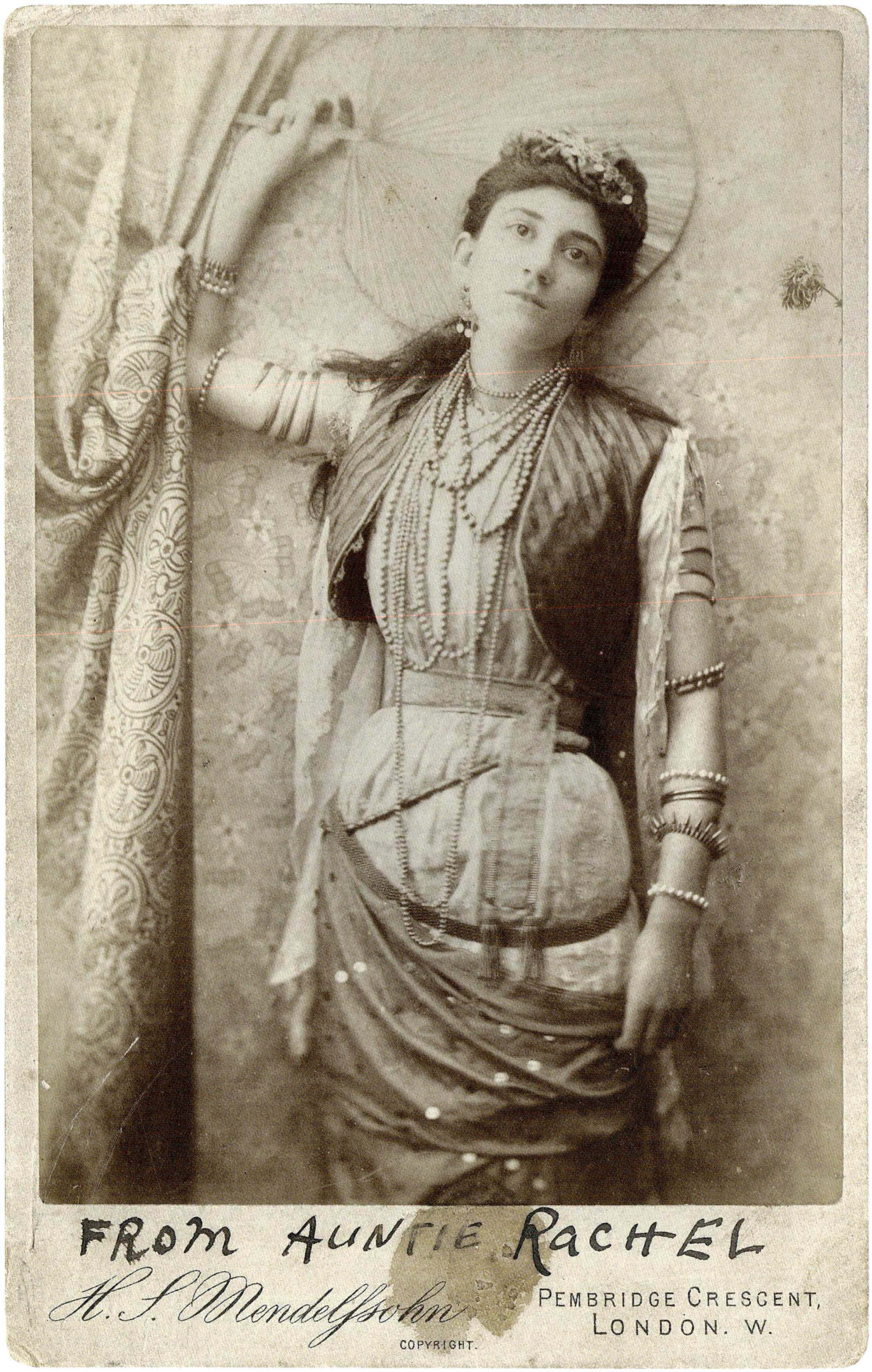

Hayman Selig Mendelssohn, Rachel Sassoon Beer, New Haven, Beinecke Rare Book and Manuscript Library, Gen. mss. 523. This *carte de visite* was inscribed "From Auntie Rachel" by Rachel's young nephew Siegfried Sassoon.

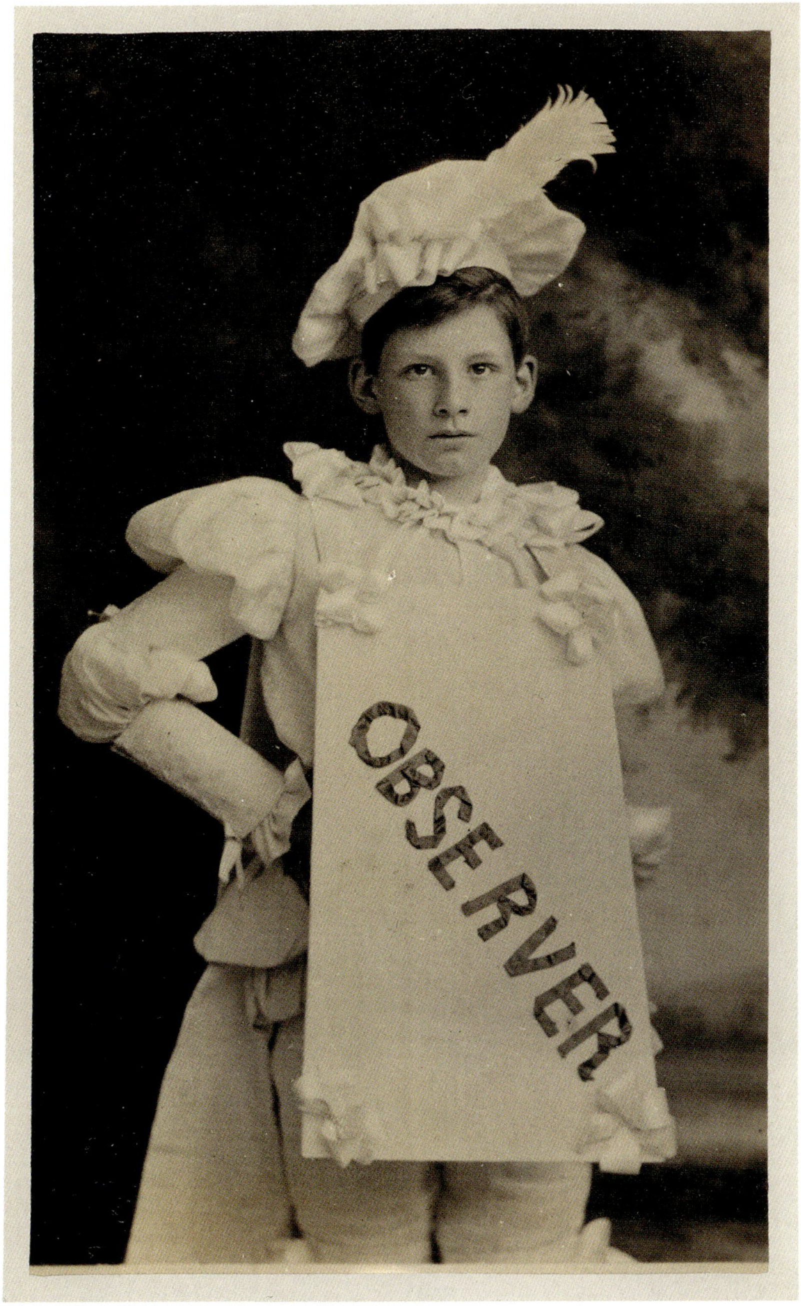

Thomas Ashby Flemons, Young Siegfried Sassoon dressed as a page for *The Observer*, 1896, Cambridge University Library, UK, ms. Add.9454/163/1.

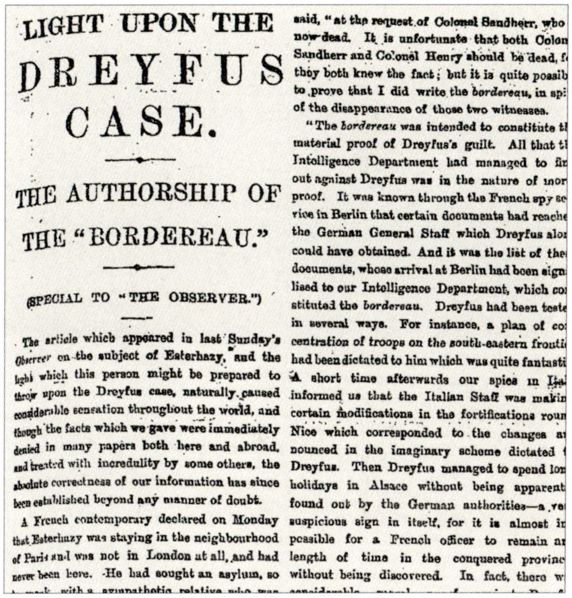

LIGHT UPON THE DREYFUS CASE.

THE AUTHORSHIP OF THE "BORDEREAU."

(SPECIAL TO "THE OBSERVER.")

The article which appeared in last Sunday's *Observer* on the subject of Esterhazy, and the light which this person might be prepared to throw upon the Dreyfus case, naturally caused considerable sensation throughout the world, and though the facts which we gave were immediately denied in many papers both here and abroad, and treated with incredulity by some others, the absolute correctness of our information has since been established beyond any manner of doubt.

A French contemporary declared on Monday that Esterhazy was staying in the neighbourhood of Paris and was not in London at all, and had never been here. He had sought an asylum, so

said, "at the request of Colonel Sandherr, who now dead. It is unfortunate that both Colon Sandherr and Colonel Henry should be dead, f they both knew the fact; but it is quite possib to prove that I did write the *bordereau*, in sp of the disappearance of those two witnesses.

"The *bordereau* was intended to constitute t material proof of Dreyfus's guilt. All that t Intelligence Department had managed to fi out against Dreyfus was in the nature of mor proof. It was known through the French spy se vice in Berlin that certain documents had reach the German General Staff which Dreyfus alo could have obtained. And it was the list of the documents, whose arrival at Berlin had been sign lised to our Intelligence Department, which co stituted the *bordereau*. Dreyfus had been test in several ways. For instance, a plan of co centration of troops on the south-eastern fronti had been dictated to him which was quite fantasti A short time afterwards our spies in Ita informed us that the Italian Staff was makin certain modifications in the fortifications roun Nice which corresponded to the changes a nounced in the imaginary scheme dictated Dreyfus. Then Dreyfus managed to spend lo holidays in Alsace without being apparent found out by the German authorities—a ve suspicious sign in itself, for it is almost i possible for a French officer to remain a length of time in the conquered provinc without being discovered. In fact, there w

"Light upon the Dreyfus Case: The Authorship of the 'Bordereau,'" *The Observer*, September 25, 1898. One of two newspaper articles published in *The Observer* featuring Rachel Sassoon Beer's breakthrough reporting on the French military officer Ferdinand Esterhazy, the real culprit in the Dreyfus affair, who had fled to England.

Anglican church, and so the marriage caused a rift with Rachel's family. The couple came to view journalism as an agent for social change. By 1893, Rachel was working full-time at *The Observer*. A photograph shows her beloved nephew, a young Siegfried Sassoon (the future war poet), as a page advertising the newspaper. With the Beers' purchase of the *Sunday Times*, Rachel became the first woman in Britain to edit two newspapers. She would play a crucial role reporting on the Dreyfus affair in Britain.[3] In 1898, four years after Captain Alfred Dreyfus, a Jewish officer in the French army, had been falsely accused of treason, court-martialed, and incarcerated, the discovery of new evidence led to the real culprit, French officer Ferdinand Esterhazy. He fled to London, where he tried to rally support while profiting from the sale of his story to newspapers. Rachel interviewed Esterhazy and obtained incriminating information, which, in a journalistic breakthrough, she published in *The Observer*. A new trial would still find Dreyfus guilty, however, and he would not be exonerated until 1906.

Frederick, like Rachel, had been exposed to art early in life. His father, Julius Beer, was a collector and owned John Everett Millais's

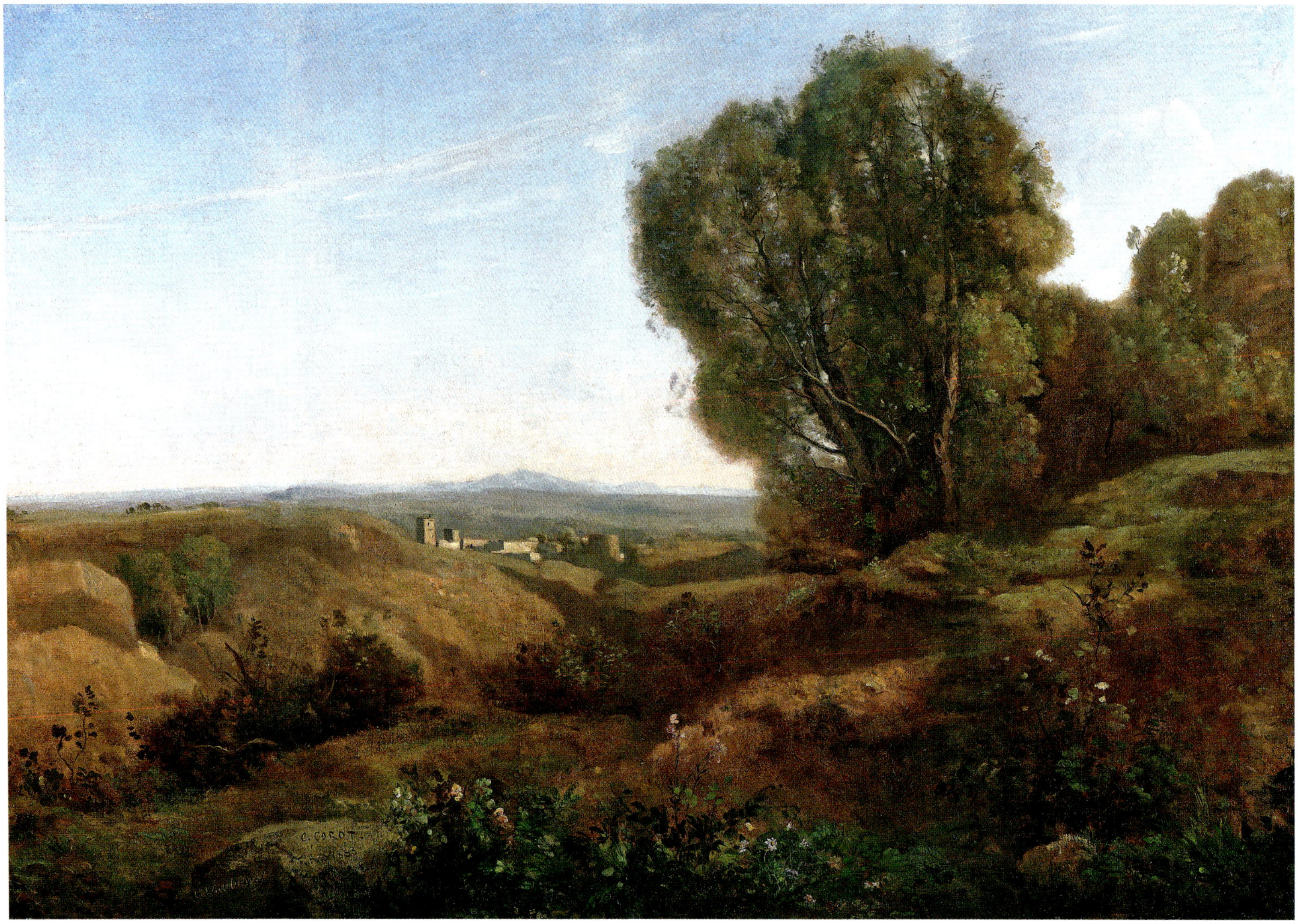

Jean-Baptiste-Camille Corot and Charles-François Daubigny, *Souvenir of Roquemaure in the Gard*, 1853, oil on canvas, 55⅞ × 81½ in. (142 × 207 cm), Dublin, National Gallery of Ireland, purchased, 1931, formerly in the Rachel Sassoon Beer Collection.

controversial *Christ in the House of His Parents (The Carpenter's Shop)*, now at the Tate. Soon after their marriage, the couple commissioned Henry Jones Thaddeus to paint pendant portraits. Rachel's is as monumental as it is romanticized, showing her in ethereal silk holding an ostrich feather. The French painter Jean-Baptiste-Camille Corot became a favorite artist, and his bewitching *Moonlit Landscape* occupied pride of place at their home. Frederick died in 1901. For solace during his illness, Rachel wrote poetry inspired by their art, which she would then publish in her editorials. Her remarkable collection, primarily of nineteenth-century landscapes and genre scenes, sold at auction in 1927, shortly after her death. Among the 160 paintings, 27 drawings, and one engraving were three paintings by Peter Paul Rubens, two by Gustave Courbet, and one by John Constable; one drawing and fifteen paintings by Corot; and works by such women artists as Laura Alma-Tadema and Rosa Bonheur. The collection was widely dispersed, and only a few notable works can be traced today, including *Souvenir of Roquemaure in the Gard*, a fireplace screen from 1853 that was a collaboration between Corot and Charles-François Daubigny, and Constable's *Salisbury from the Fields* of about 1820. The Beers' matching portraits were also sold in the auction. The one of Rachel was acquired by her nurse, Ethel Ross, who later sold it to Siegfried Sassoon.[4]

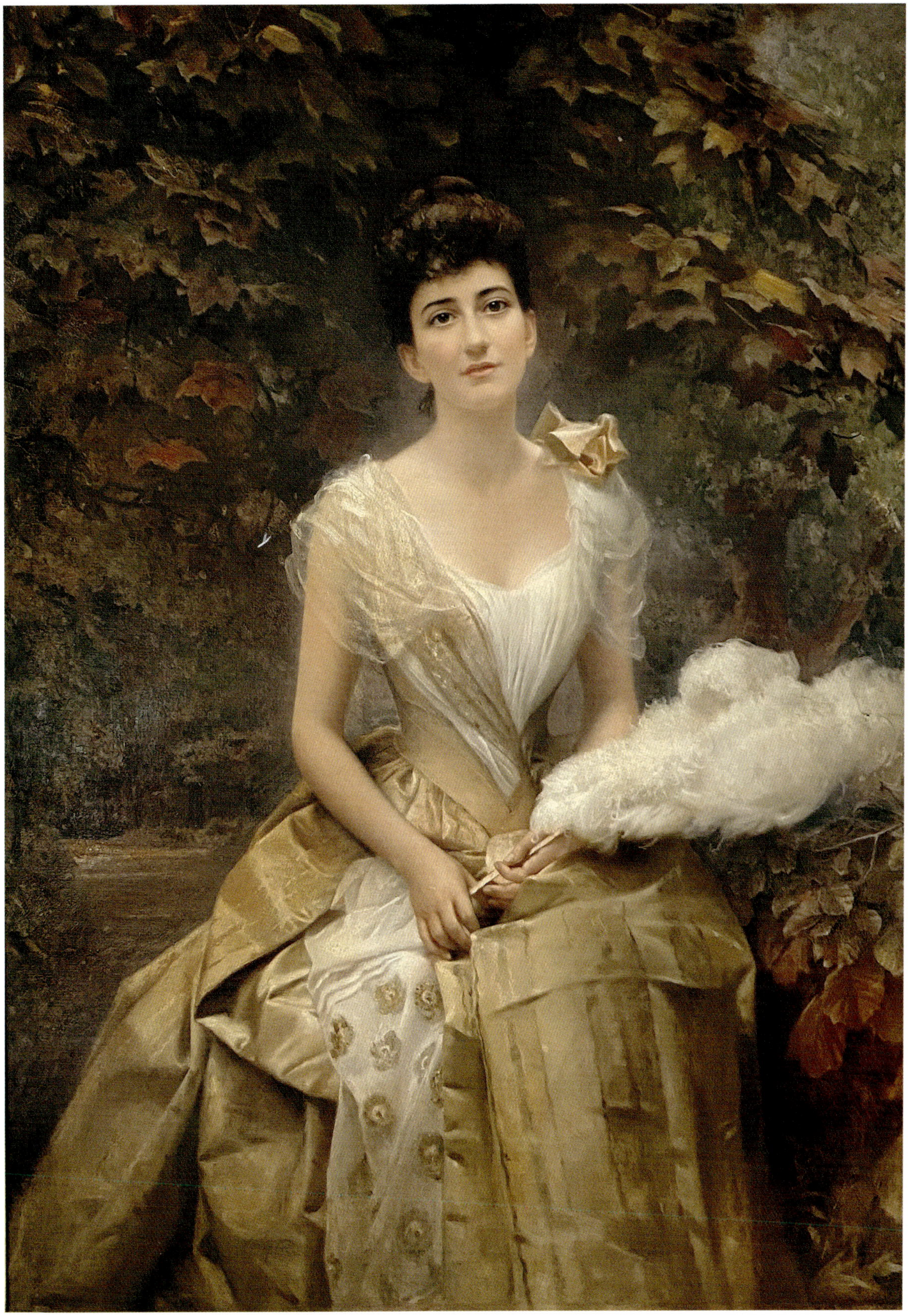

Henry Jones Thaddeus, *Rachel Sassoon Beer,* 1887, oil on canvas, 52 × 37 in. (132.1 × 94 cm), private collection, London.

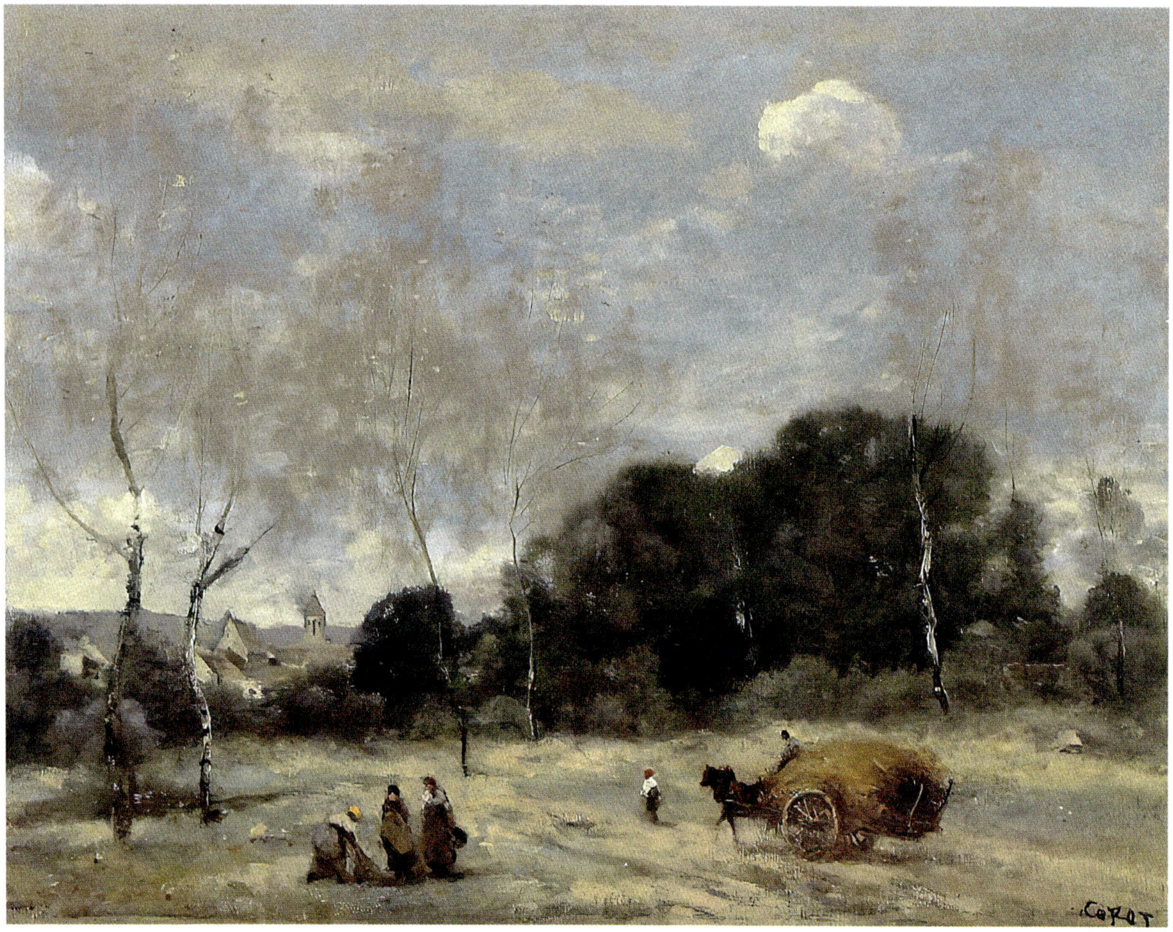

Jean-Baptiste-Camille Corot, *Return of the Hayers to Marcoussis,* 1870–74, oil on canvas, 17 × 21⅞ in. (43.2 × 55.6 cm), formerly in the Rachel Sassoon Beer Collection.

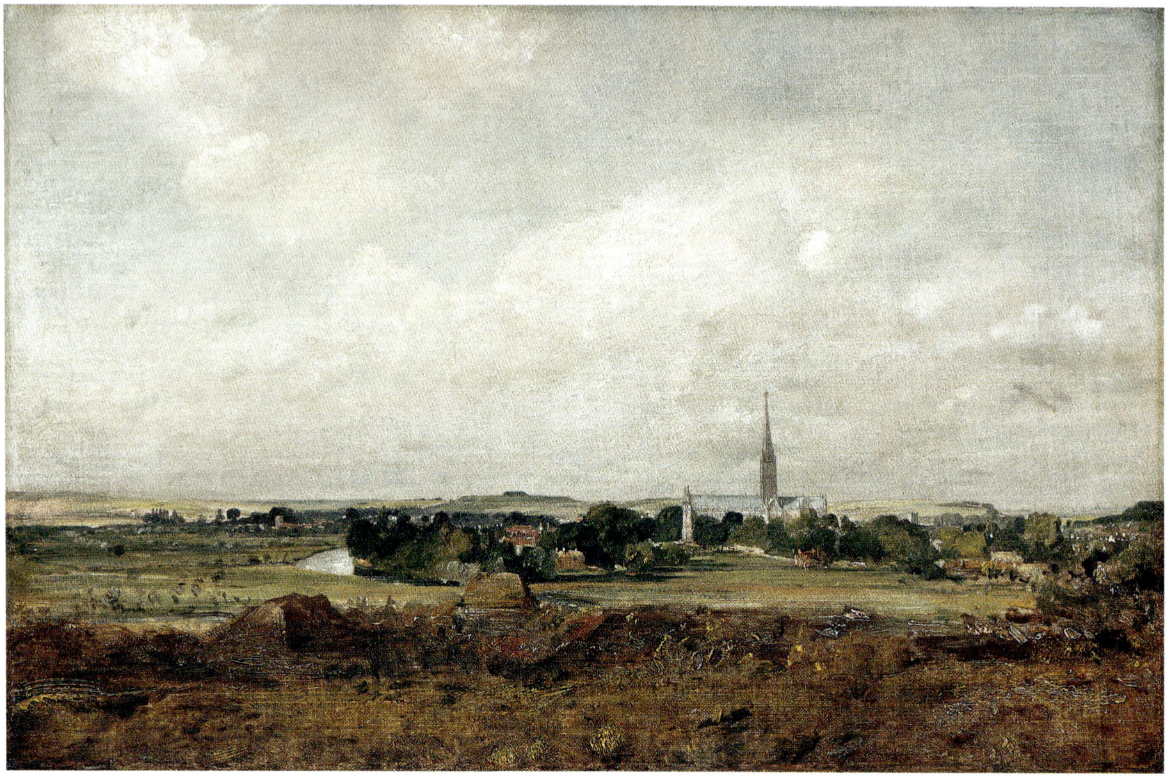

John Constable, *Salisbury from the Fields,* c. 1820, oil on canvas, 13¾ × 20 in. (35 × 51 cm), Paris, Musée du Louvre, formerly in the Rachel Sassoon Beer Collection.

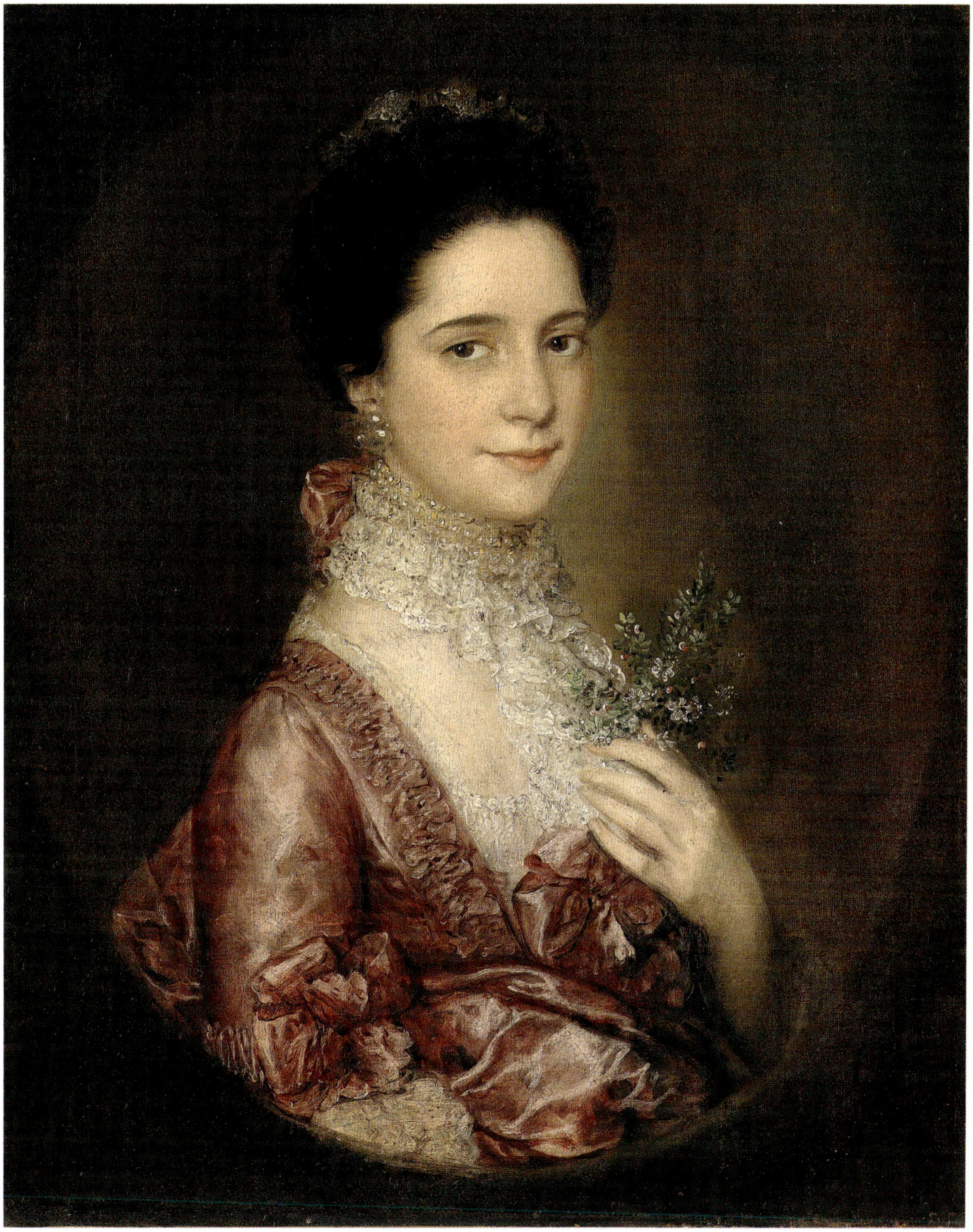

Thomas Gainsborough, *Mrs. David Richards,* c. 1764, oil on canvas, 30 × 25 in. (76.2 × 63.5 cm), private collection, England, formerly in the Frederick Sassoon Collection.

Frederick

Frederick Sassoon (1853–1917), David's youngest son and the only one to marry in England, was closer to the third generation in age and interests. He seems to have pioneered a new collecting trend in the family: eighteenth-century art. In 1905 he acquired Thomas Gainsborough's *Portrait of Mrs. David Richards*, thought to depict the wife of a violinist who played for theaters in London and Bristol. The work represents the height of the painter's career. The exquisite treatment of the diaphanous chemise with ruffled collar is reminiscent of the work of the seventeenth-century Flemish painter Anthony van Dyck, who worked in the British court. The sitter holds a sprig of myrtle, symbol of love and virginity, probably indicating that it was commissioned to celebrate her

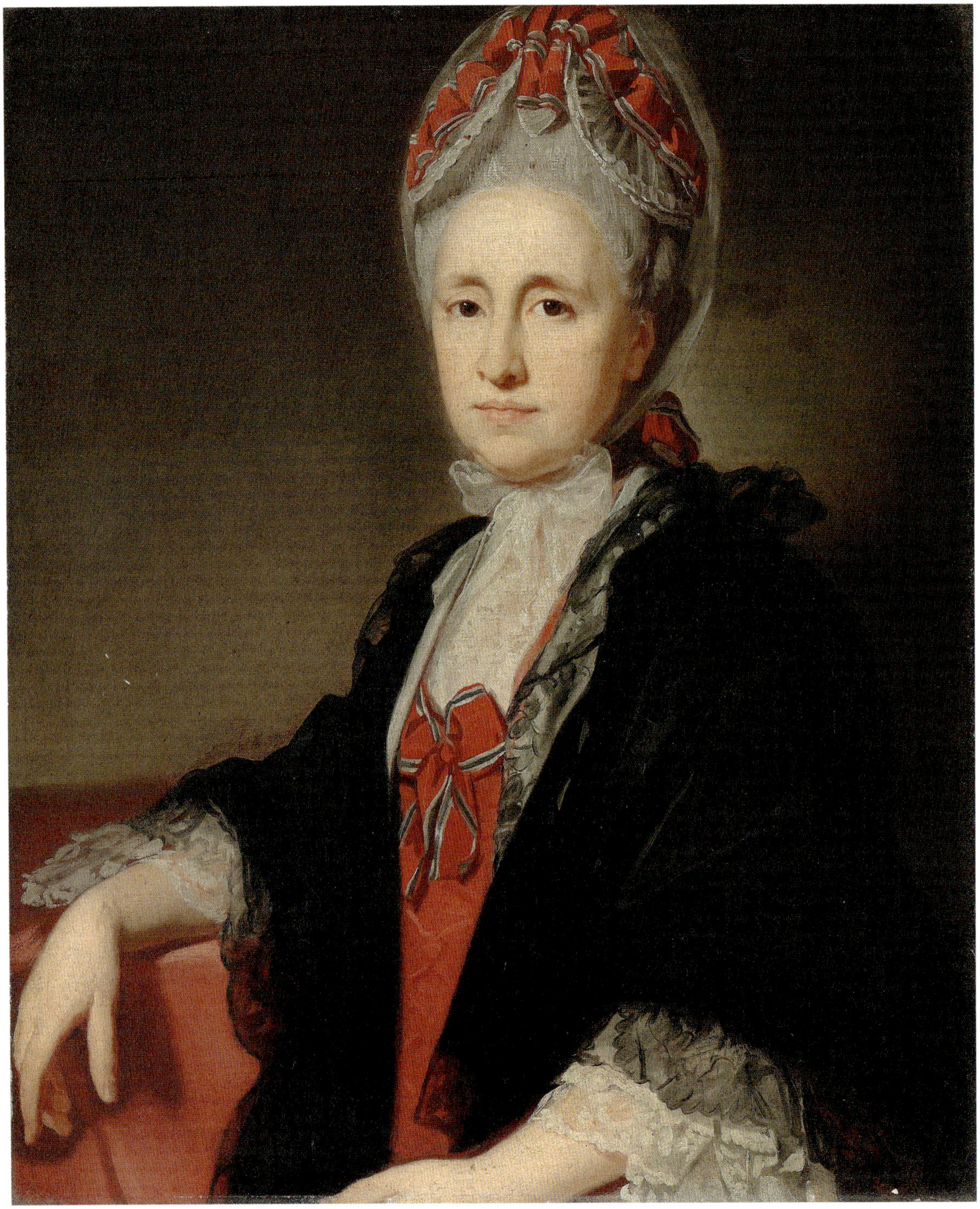

George Romney, *Hester, Countess of Clanricarde,* c. 1772, oil on canvas, 30 × 25 in. (76.3 × 63.5 cm), private collection, formerly in the Frederick Sassoon Collection.

wedding. That same year, Frederick purchased a George Romney portrait, said to be of Mrs. Trevean but later identified as Hester, Countess of Clanricarde. More neoclassical in style is the *Portrait of Mrs. Harriet Ker-Seymour* by Thomas Lawrence. Other paintings in Frederick's collection included *Portrait of Miss Bullock*, attributed to Joshua Reynolds; *Portrait of Nelly O'Brien* by Reynolds's studio, after the eponymous work by Reynolds in the Hunterian Art Gallery; and the charming *A Marmoset Taking Sweets on a Painted Commode*, also referred to as *The Thieving Marmoset*, attributed to Louis Tessier or Jean-Jacques Bachelier. The paintings were inherited by Frederick's daughter Muriel (1897–1979), who first married Alfred Ezra (1872–1955), a member of another prominent Baghdadi Jewish family. Muriel's second husband, Paul Wallraf (1897–1981), was a collector of Old Master drawings and a member of the German family that founded the Wallraf-Richartz Museum in Cologne.[5]

Thomas Lawrence, *Mrs. Harriet Ker-Seymour,* c. 1806, oil on canvas, 30 × 25 in. (76.2 × 63.5 cm), London, Rafael Valls Ltd., formerly in the Frederick Sassoon Collection.

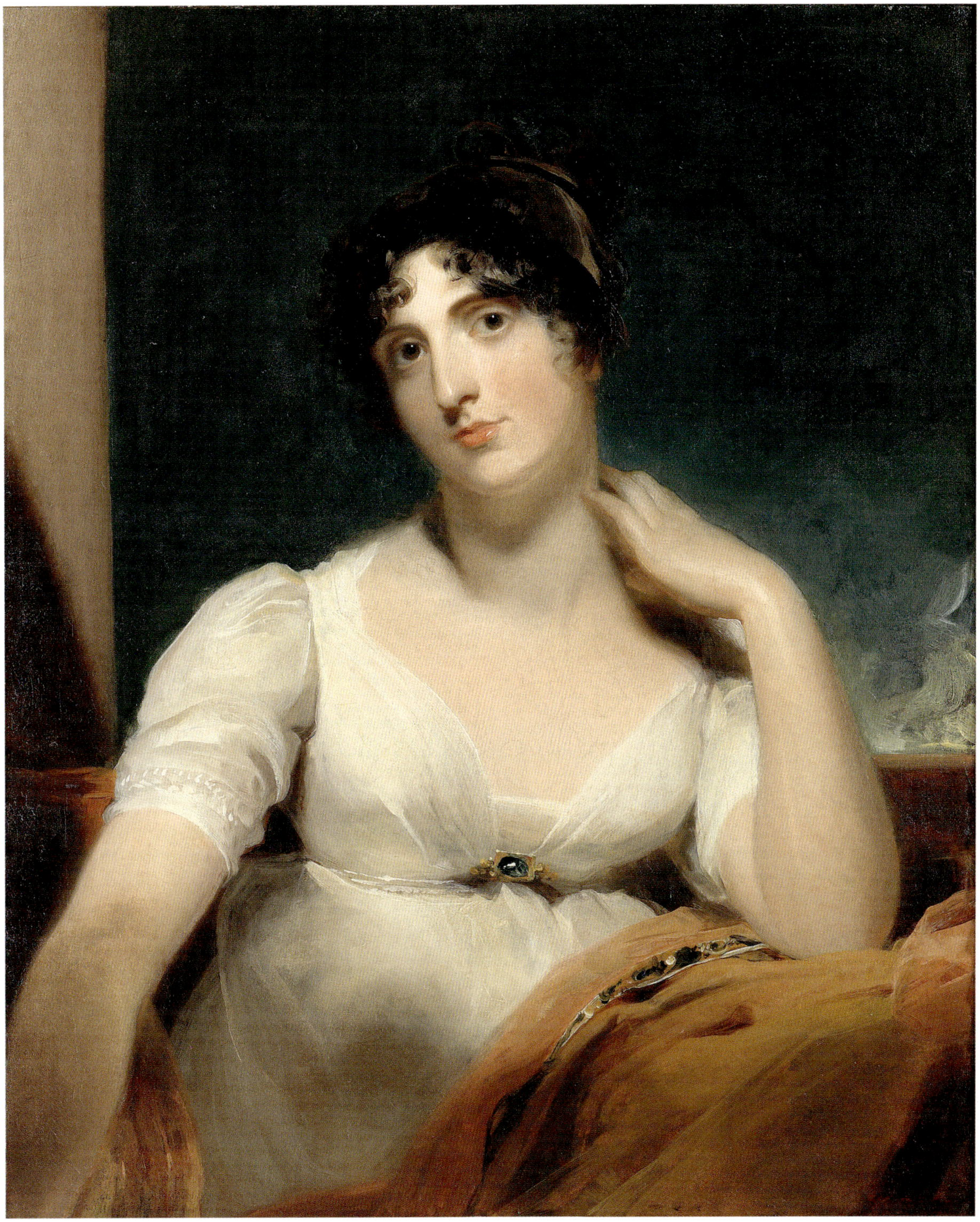

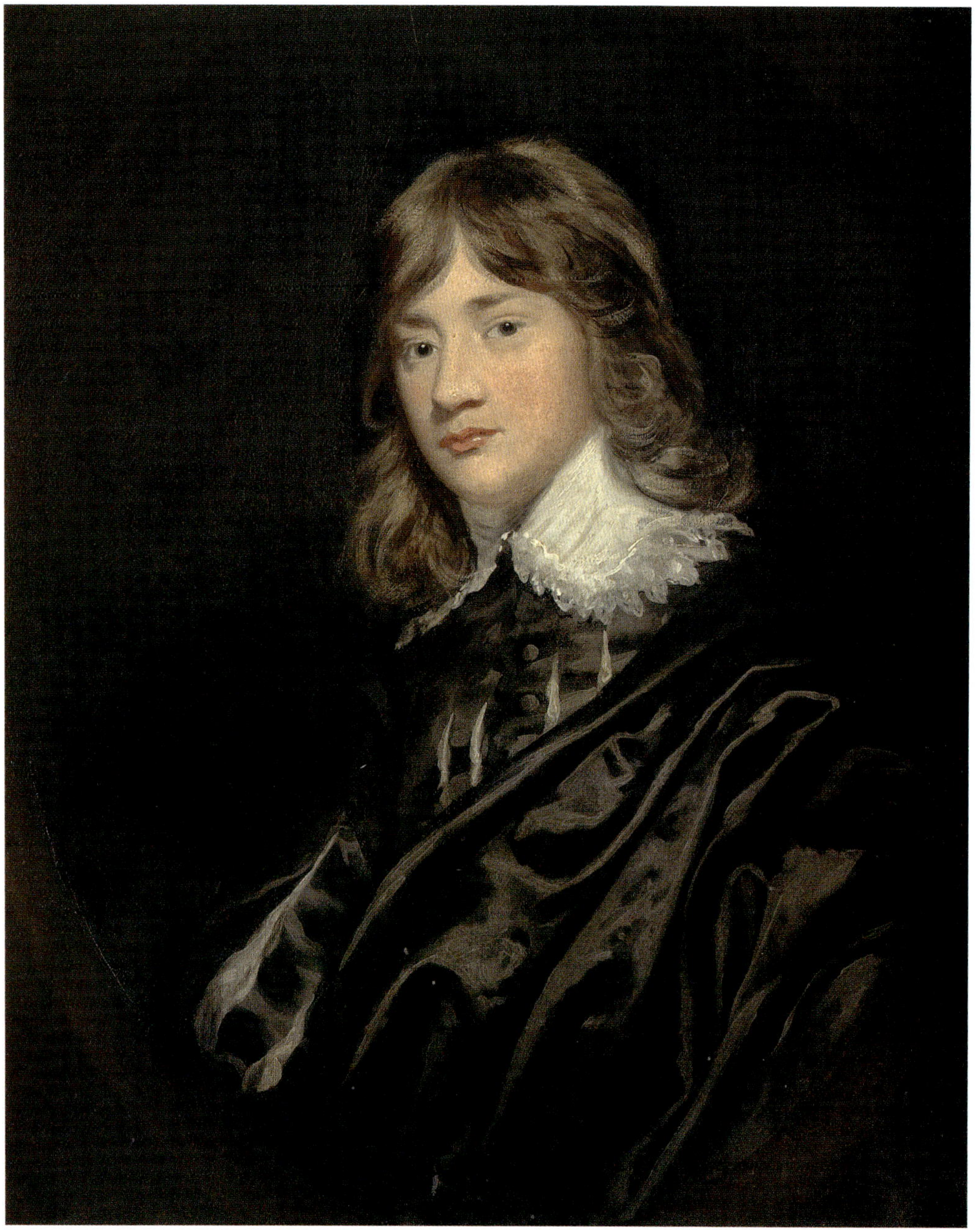

Attributed to Joshua Reynolds, *Andrew Drummond of Ridgeway*, possibly 1766, oil on canvas, 30 × 24⅞ in. (76.3 × 63 cm), private collection, formerly in the Leontine, Lady Sassoon Collection.

OPPOSITE
Leontine (née Levy), Lady Sassoon, photographed by Bassano, 1922, London, National Portrait Gallery, given by Bassano and Vandyk Studios, 1974.

Leontine

Frederick's niece Leontine (née Levy), Lady Sassoon (c. 1864–1955), was also drawn to eighteenth-century paintings and decorative arts. Born in Egypt to an affluent Jewish family, she married Sir Edward Elias Sassoon (1853–1924), a grandson of the patriarch, in 1880. An avid collector, she owned at least two works by Gainsborough: an undated grand pastoral landscape and the portrait of Robert Hamby (c. 1752), listed as "Hornby" based on a late inscription.[6] *Lake, Ruin, and Pine Trees* (c. 1765–70), attributed to Richard Wilson, a Welsh landscape painter who worked in Britain and Italy, was bequeathed by Leontine to the Tate. She also owned eight paintings by the Flemish master Pieter Casteels III (1684–1749), active in England and known for flower and bird compositions. In 1923 she acquired the portrait of Andrew Drummond of Ridgeway, attributed to Reynolds, featuring its subject clad in a Van Dyck costume.[7]

Equally passionate about furniture, Leontine owned several eighteenth-century pieces, including a Louis XVI commode by the French *ébéniste* Pierre Roussel, a Queen Anne card table, and a George II mirror with a giltwood frame in fantastic "Chinese Chippendale" style.[8]

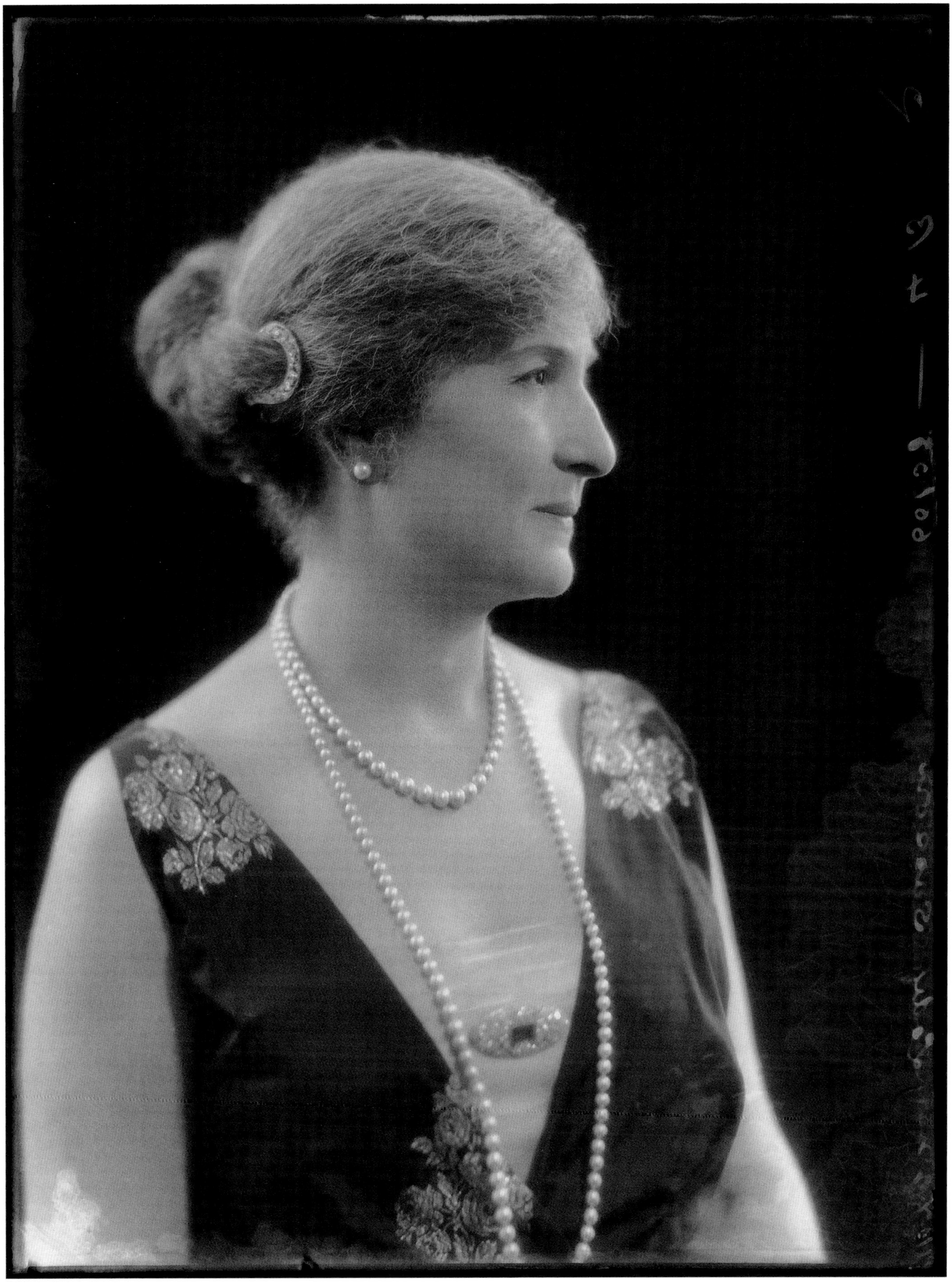

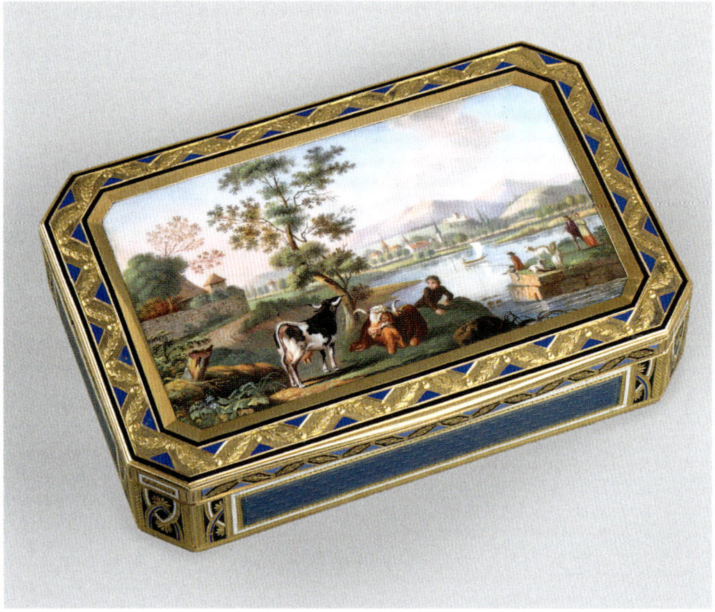

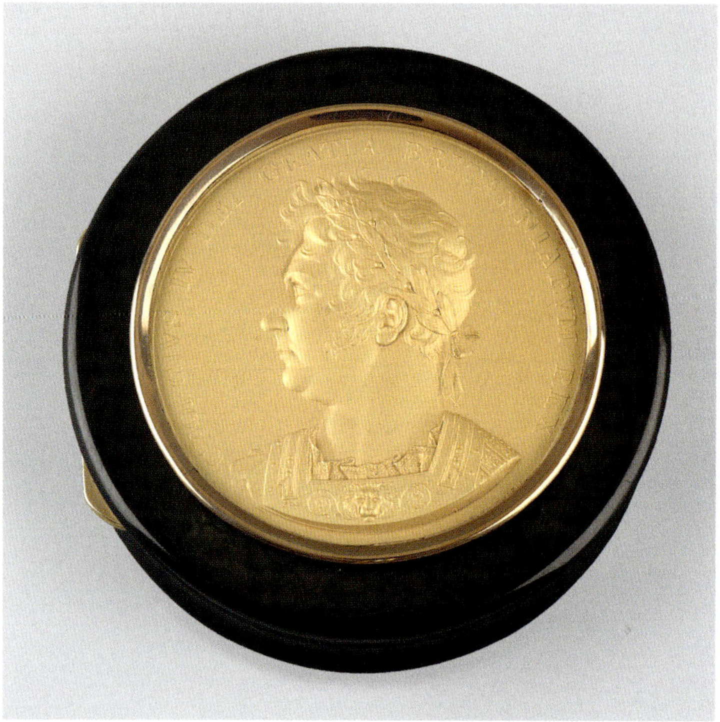

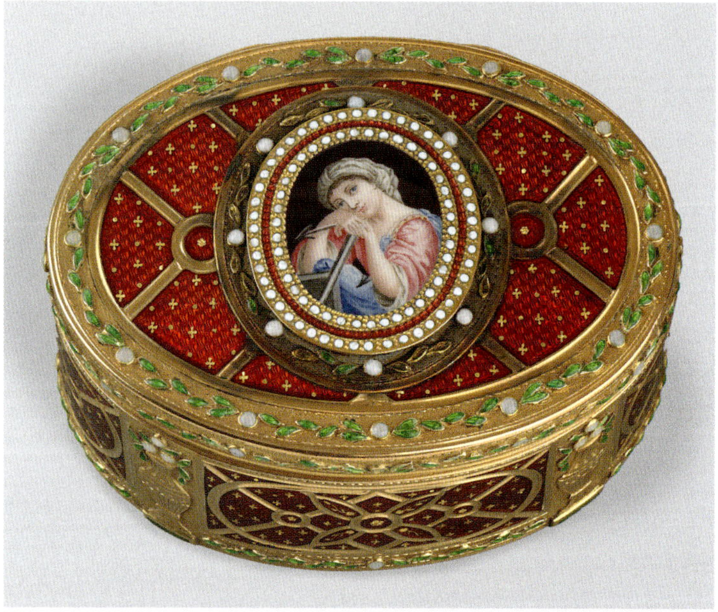

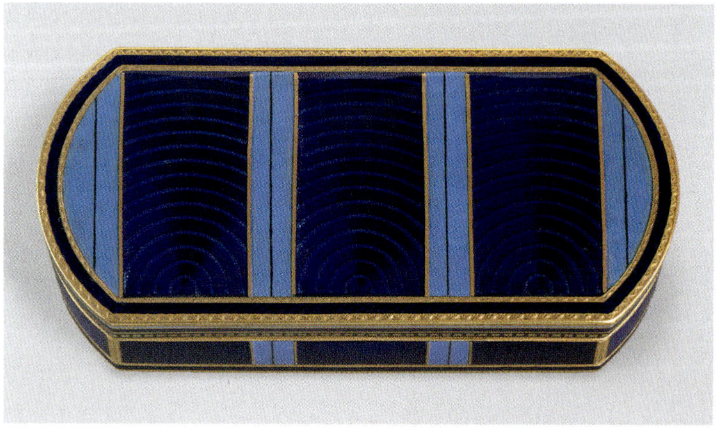

ABOVE
Guidon, Gide and Blondet, snuffbox, Geneva, Switzerland, 1801–4, gold, enamel, and paint, ¾ × 3½ × 2¼ in. (1.9 × 8.9 × 6 cm), presented to the Prince of Wales, later King Edward VII, by Arthur Sassoon in 1891, London, Royal Collection Trust.

ABOVE RIGHT
Rundell Bridge and Rundell, box with George IV accession medal, 1820–30, tortoiseshell, gold, and glass, 1¼ × 3¾ in. in diameter (3.2 × 9.4 cm), presented to King Edward VII by Reuben Sassoon, London, Royal Collection Trust.

Jean-Jacques Prévost, snuffbox, Paris, gold, pearl, sablé, opal, and enamel, ¼ × 2½ × 1¾ in. (3.1 × 6.2 × 4.5 cm), presented to Queen Mary by Mozelle Sassoon, Christmas 1934, London, Royal Collection Trust.

Boeck (Carl Albrecht Boeck), snuffbox, probably Vienna, 1799, gold, enamel, and paint, ⅞ × 3¾ × 1⅝ in. (2.1 × 9.4 × 4.3 cm), presented to Queen Mary by Hannah Gubbay, Christmas 1941, London, Royal Collection Trust.

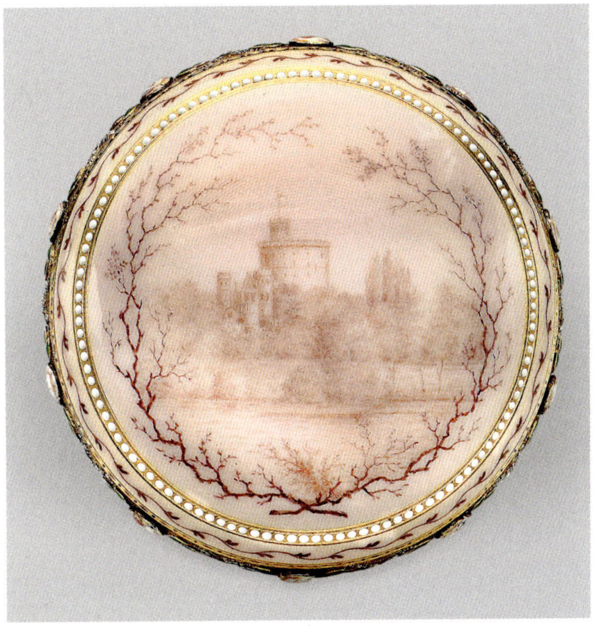

Henrik Immanuel Wigström, Fabergé bonbonnière with a view of Balmoral Castle, St. Petersburg, Russia, 1907, gold, enamel, and rose diamonds, 1 × 2¼ in. in diameter (2.5 × 5.7 cm), presented to Queen Mary by Sir Philip Sassoon for her birthday in 1934, London, Royal Collection Trust.

Cousins, Collectors, and Curators

Younger generations also collected judiciously and at a very high level. Philip Sassoon, a member of Parliament, was a visible public figure, twice appointed Undersecretary of State for Air, a position that united his love of flying with his resolve to strengthen air defense and civil aviation.[9] But his abiding passions were art and architecture. He was born in the Paris home of his maternal grandparents, Baron Gustave de Rothschild and Cécile Anspach, whose salon was frequented by major figures of the art world, such as Marcel Proust and the composer Reynaldo Hahn. Philip's studies at Oxford University laid the foundation for his deep knowledge of the eighteenth century.

Two of Philip's cousins, Hannah Gubbay (1885–1968) and Mozelle Sassoon (1872–1964), shared his love of the eighteenth century. Hannah, whose mother was a Sassoon, was born in Mumbai and partly educated in London; her husband, David Gubbay, became chairman of David Sassoon & Co. on the death of his cousin Frederick, the youngest son of David Sassoon. Hannah's focus on English decorative art reflected her enthusiastic embrace of her adopted country. Mozelle, another granddaughter of Albert Abdullah Sassoon, was one of the family's most cosmopolitan members. Born in Malabar Castle, Mumbai, she moved in her early years to Paris, where her parents had a townhouse on the fashionable Boulevard Malesherbes. The recipient of a superb French education, Mozelle remained a lifelong Francophile and a discriminating collector. Philip, Hannah, and Mozelle traveled in the same circles and had close ties to the British royal family. Together with Reuben and Arthur Sassoon, all sent annual birthday greetings to King Edward VII and Queen Mary in the form of precious *objets de vertu*. Philip's younger sister Sybil (1894–1989), later Marchioness of Cholmondeley, was exposed to great art from birth. She would play an important role as muse to notable artists, and as a connoisseur whose talent and knowledge enabled her to restore a major architectural landmark, Houghton Hall.

Percival David (1892–1964) and Victor Sassoon (1881–1961), nephews of Mozelle, amassed collections focused on China. Percival had been born and educated in Mumbai. His mother, Hannah, was the sister of Mozelle's husband Meyer Sassoon (1855–1924); his father, Sassoon David, was chairman of the Bank of India. After completing his studies, Percival moved to London in 1913 and embarked on a career in banking. A year later he purchased the first piece of what would become one of the finest collections of Chinese ceramics.

Victor was the son of Edward Elias and Leontine Sassoon. When his father died in 1924, he inherited the baronetcy and assumed the reins of E. D. Sassoon & Co. After establishing himself in India, he bought more textile mills for the family firm and invested the profits in Shanghai real estate. Increasingly interested in Shanghai, he moved there in 1931. While expanding and diversifying the family firm, he also acquired an impressive collection of Chinese ivories. Although he spent most of his life abroad, he was well acquainted with his aunt Mozelle and his cousins in Britain.

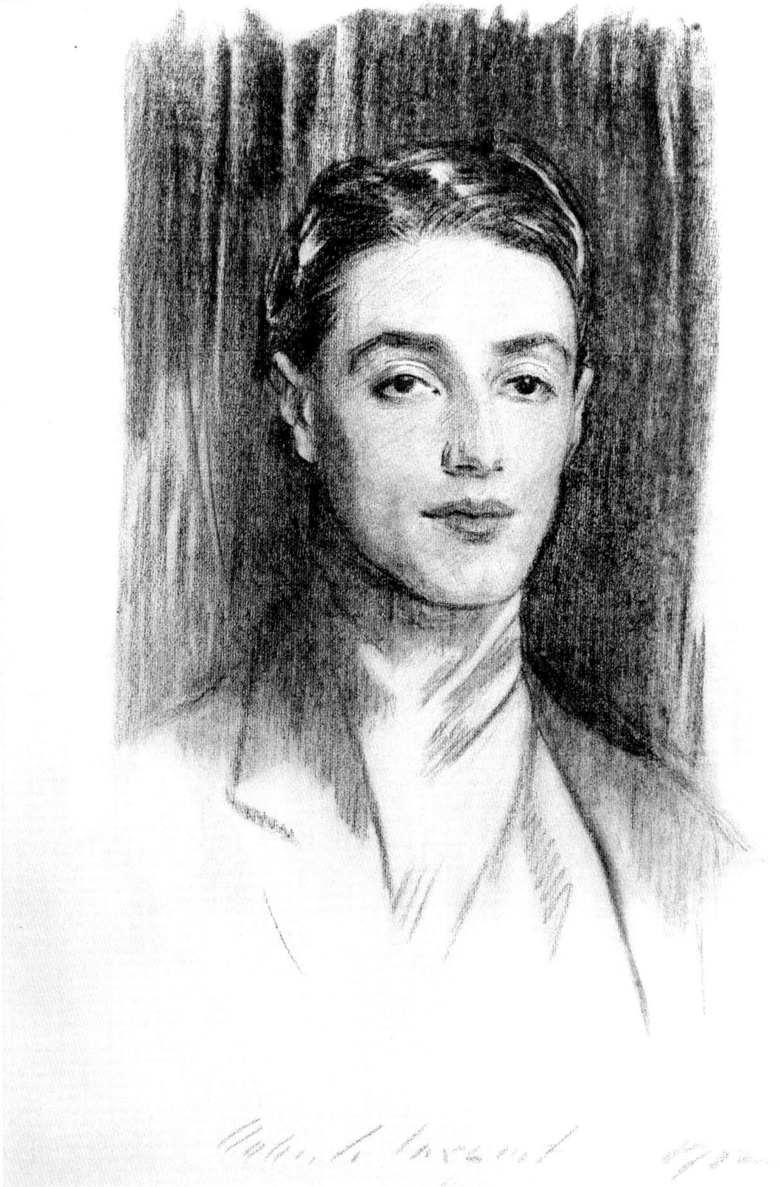

John Singer Sargent, *Philip Sassoon*, 1912, charcoal on paper, 25⅛ × 20⅛ in. (63.8 × 51.1 cm), Norkfolk, UK, Houghton Hall Collection.

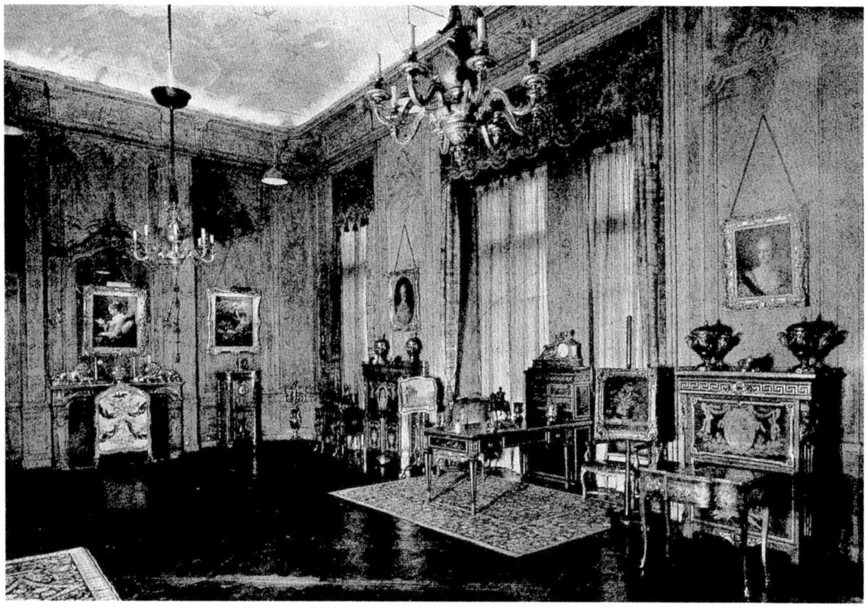

BELOW LEFT
Installation view of the 1933 *Three French Reigns* exhibition at Philip Sassoon's residence at 25 Park Lane, London. Fragonard's *A Young Girl Reading*, c. 1769, can be seen in the background.

Philip

Philip's collection, dominated by eighteenth-century art, was divided among his three homes: Park Lane, in central London; Trent Park, in north London; and Port Lympne, in Kent. Park Lane housed most of his collection, including works by Gainsborough, Reynolds, Johan Zoffany, William Hogarth, Jean-Baptiste Perronneau, Jean-François de Troy, and Jean-Baptiste Oudry, as well as a portrait of Philip IV by Diego Velázquez, and several oils and charcoal drawings by John Singer Sargent. From his parents, Edward and Aline (née de Rothschild, 1867–1909), and grandparents he had inherited hundreds of pieces of furniture, tapestries, and porcelain, but he sold them, perhaps because their styles did not fit with his carefully curated interiors. Surprisingly, these included Jean-Auguste-Dominique Ingres's *Odalisque with Slave* (1842, Walters Art Museum, Baltimore) and Giovanni Antonio Boltraffio's beautiful *Portrait of a Youth* (c. 1495/98, National Gallery of Art, Washington, DC). While Philip's collections have received serious attention, his curatorial work has not.

A self-taught art historian, Philip made significant contributions to British cultural policy. Emulating his great-uncle Reuben, Philip opened his house for concerts and exhibitions. With the help of his cousin Hannah, Philip curated ten superb exhibitions in his elegant Park Lane home to benefit the Royal Northern Hospital. These ranged from thematic shows on different reigns in England and France, to monographic exhibitions on Gainsborough and Reynolds. All were immensely successful and attended by members of the royal family, celebrities, and the general public, drawn by the opportunity to see rarely displayed pieces from storied properties. The sheer number and quality of artworks he exhibited

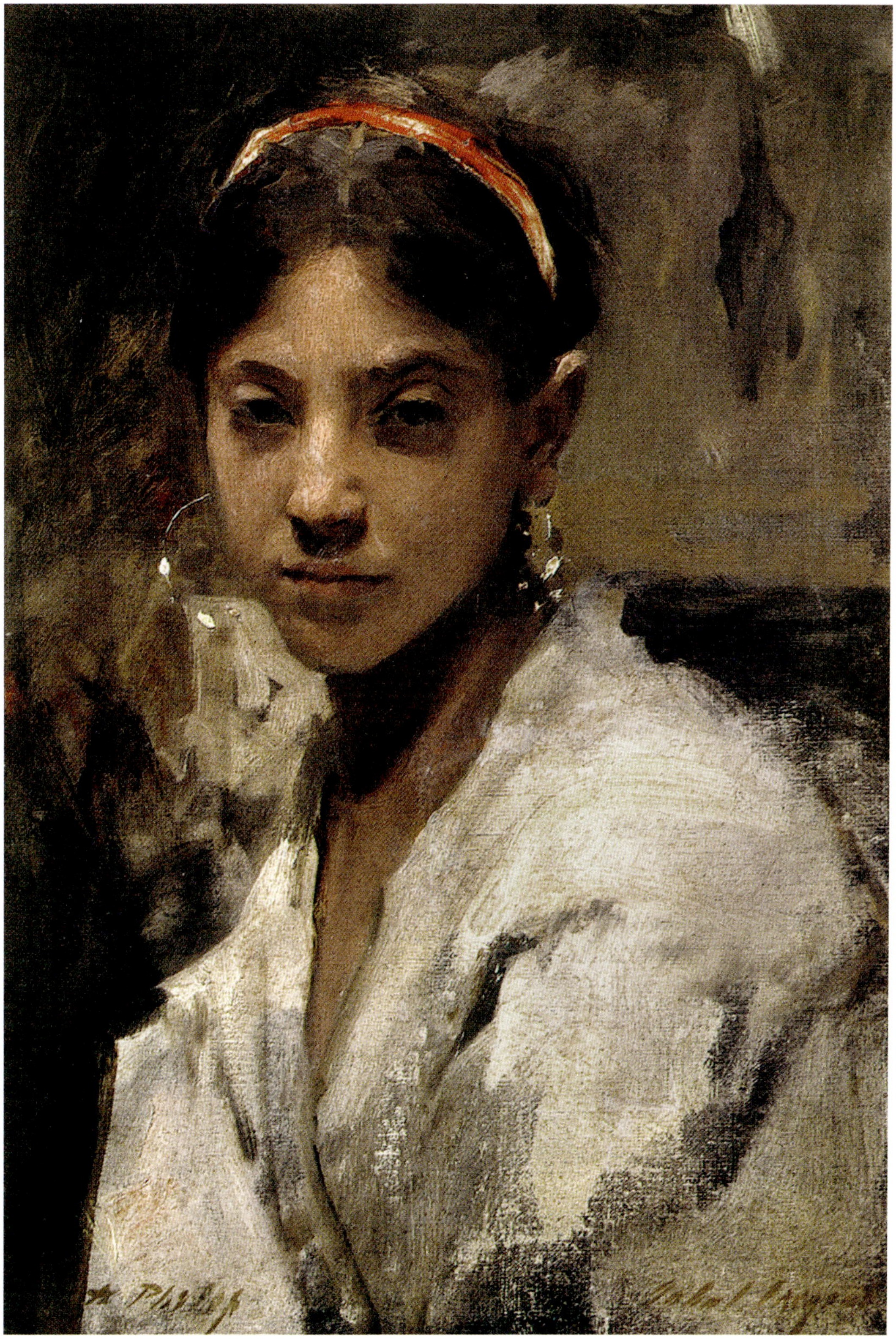

John Singer Sargent, *Head of a Capri Girl*, 1878, inscribed "To Philip," oil on canvas, 17 × 12 in. (43.2 × 30.5 cm), private collection, formerly in the Philip Sassoon Collection.

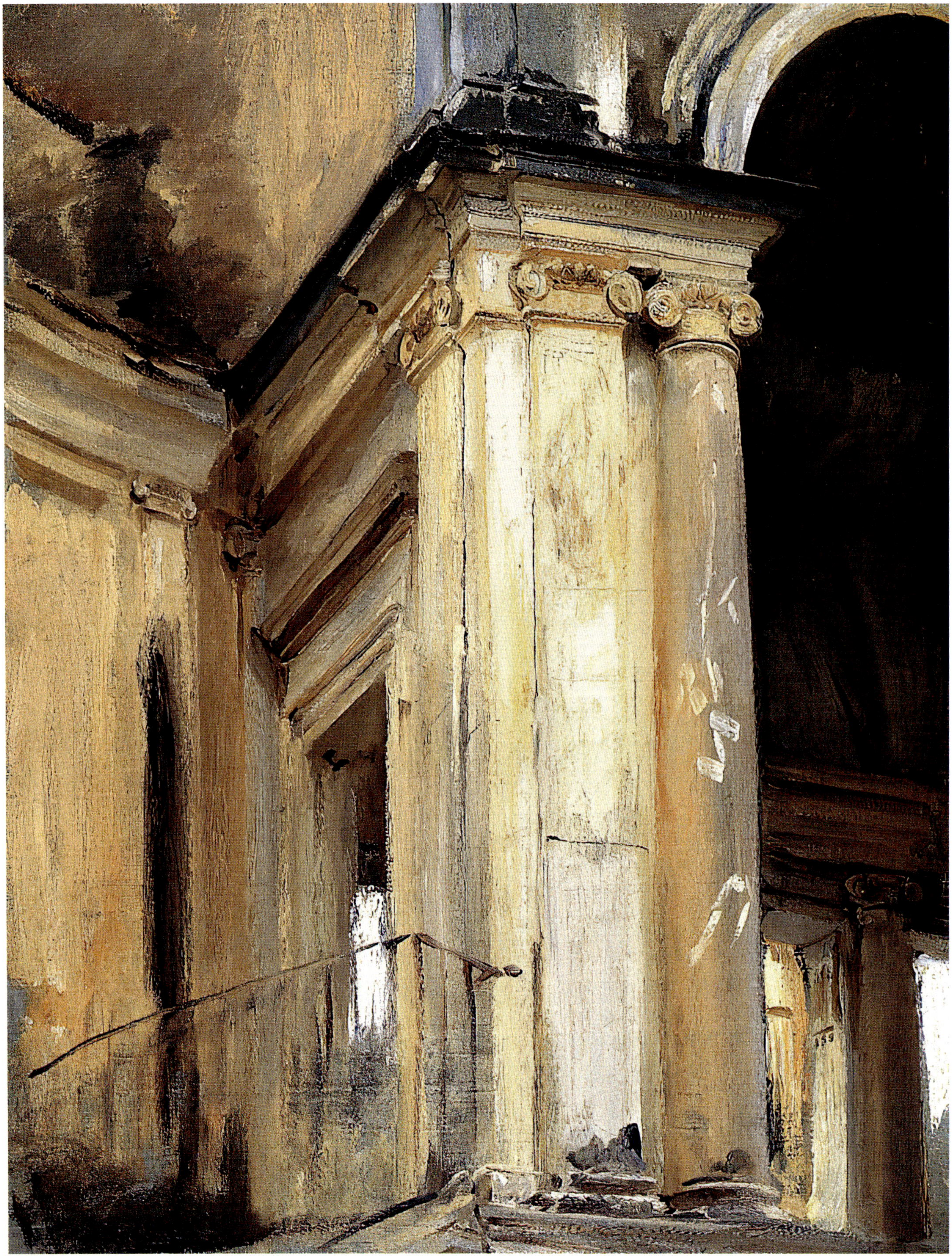

John Singer Sargent, *Roman Architecture*, 1907, oil on canvas, 27½ × 22 in. (69.8 × 55.9 cm), private collection, formerly in the Philip Sassoon Collection.

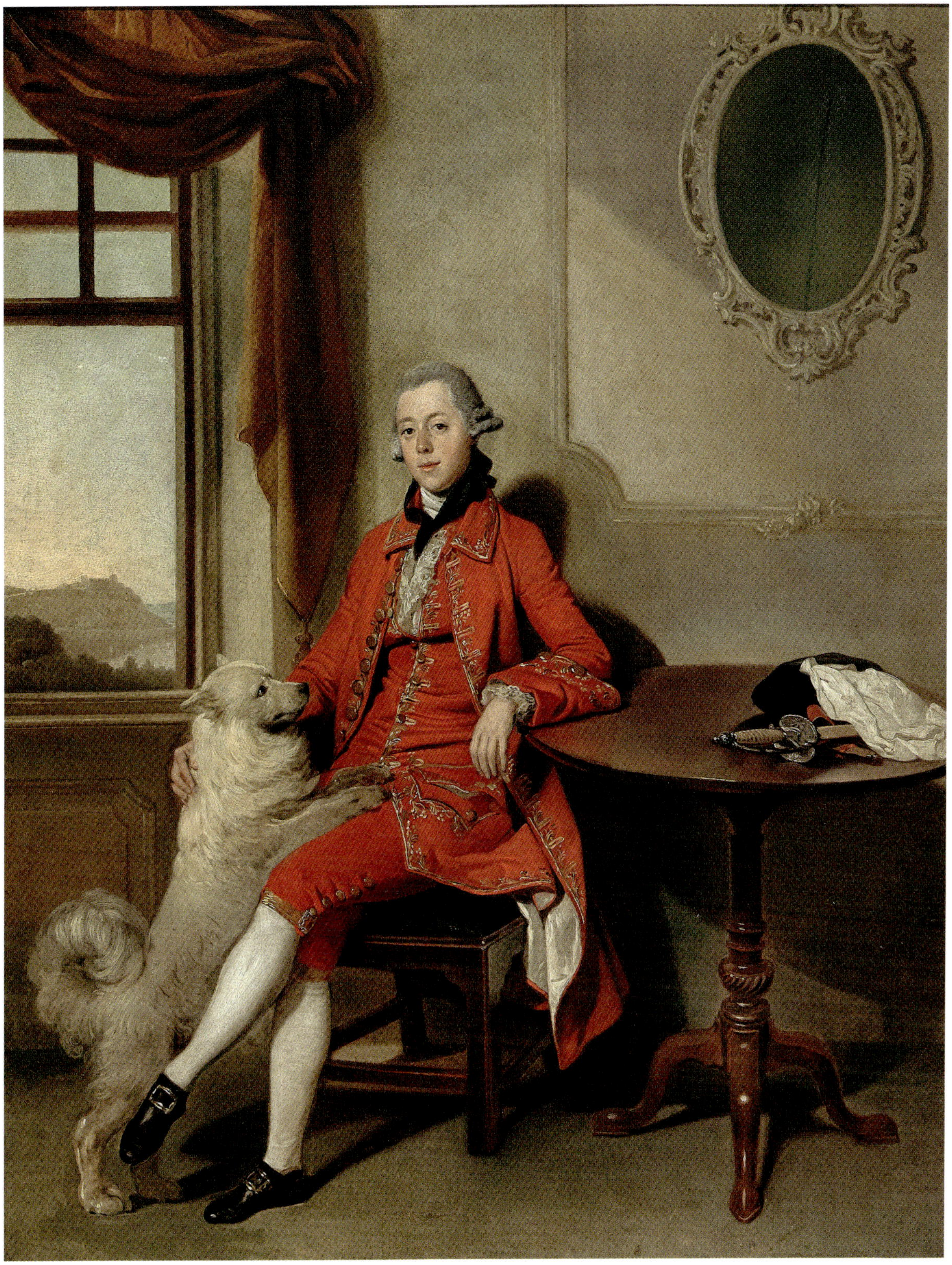

Johan Zoffany, *Richard Henry Alexander Bennett*, c. 1770, oil on canvas, 36 × 27 15/16 in. (91.5 × 71 cm), Norfolk, UK, Houghton Hall Collection, formerly in the Philip Sassoon Collection.

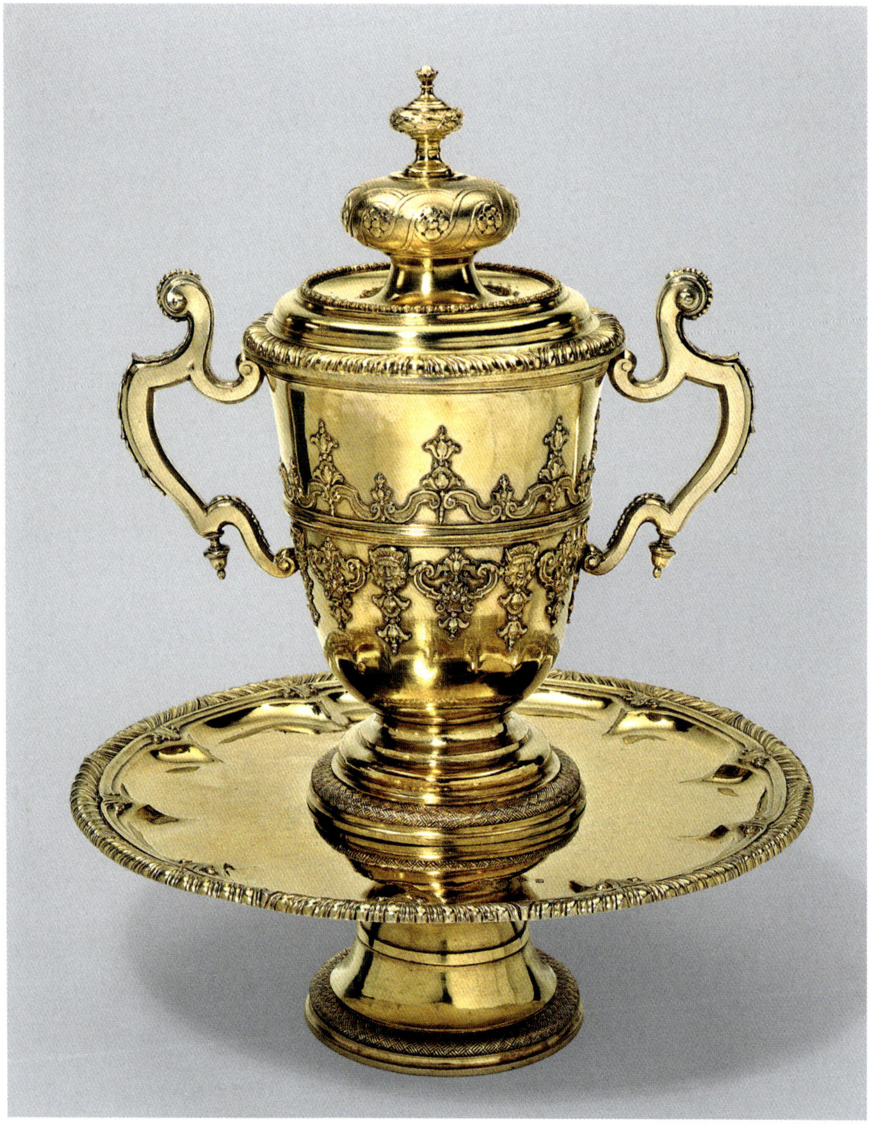

Philip Rollos the Elder, Bingley Cup, London, c. 1713 (one of a pair), silver gilt, cup and cover: 15 × 14 × 8⅛ in. (38 × 35.5 × 20.5 cm), salver: 15⅞ × 5¼ in. (40.4 × 13.5 cm), London, Victoria and Albert Museum, accepted by HM Government in lieu of Inheritance Tax and allocated to the Victoria and Albert Museum, 2008, formerly in the Philip Sassoon Collection. Made for official use by the 1st Baron Bingley (Robert Benson) when he was appointed ambassador to Spain in 1713, the cup and salver are engraved with the royal emblem and the cover bears the monogram of Queen Anne (r. 1702–14). The set was later acquired by Philip Sassoon, who included it in the exhibition *Old English Plate*, held at his London residence at 25 Park Lane, in 1929.

OPPOSITE
Johan Zoffany, *The Family of Sir William Young*, 1767–69, oil on canvas, 45 × 66 in. (114.5 × 167.5 cm), Liverpool, National Museums, Walker Art Gallery, formerly in the Philip Sassoon Collection.

were staggering. The catalogue to *Early English Needlework and Furniture* lists 574 objects, and the one to *Old English Plate* numbers 873 pieces.[10] Philip convinced friends (the king and the queen among them) to lend prized possessions, and he was advised by noted art historians such as Kenneth Clark, William George Constable, and Ellis Waterhouse. He also sought loans from the best dealers in Europe: Duveen Brothers, Seligmann of Paris, Frank Partridge, and Harris & Sons.[11] Philip's secretary Grace Boyce worked indefatigably to make the exhibitions a success. Additional priceless pieces were lent by the Sassoon cousins.

As a politician whose "Oriental" roots were brandished repeatedly by friends and foes, Philip was keen to assert himself as a connoisseur and major collector of English art, the subject of seven of the ten exhibitions. These displays of rare treasures, many on loan from great ancestral homes, drew such large crowds that the shows often had to be extended for a few days. *Conversation Pieces*, mounted in 1930, was the most famous and influential of the exhibitions, and presented a rediscovery of both the genre and one of its important practitioners—Zoffany. In his brief but masterful introduction to the catalogue, Philip captured the genre's main traits and defined the term, popularized by Hogarth, as "a representation of two or more persons in a state of dramatic or psychological relation to each other." Noting that "the figures are considerably smaller than life-size and more intimate and personal than in a portrait group," Philip wrote that "the Conversation Piece stands half-way between the portrait group and the genre picture."[12]

Philip lent two of his paintings by Gainsborough and four by Zoffany. The latter's *Family of Sir William Young* (1767–69) exemplifies

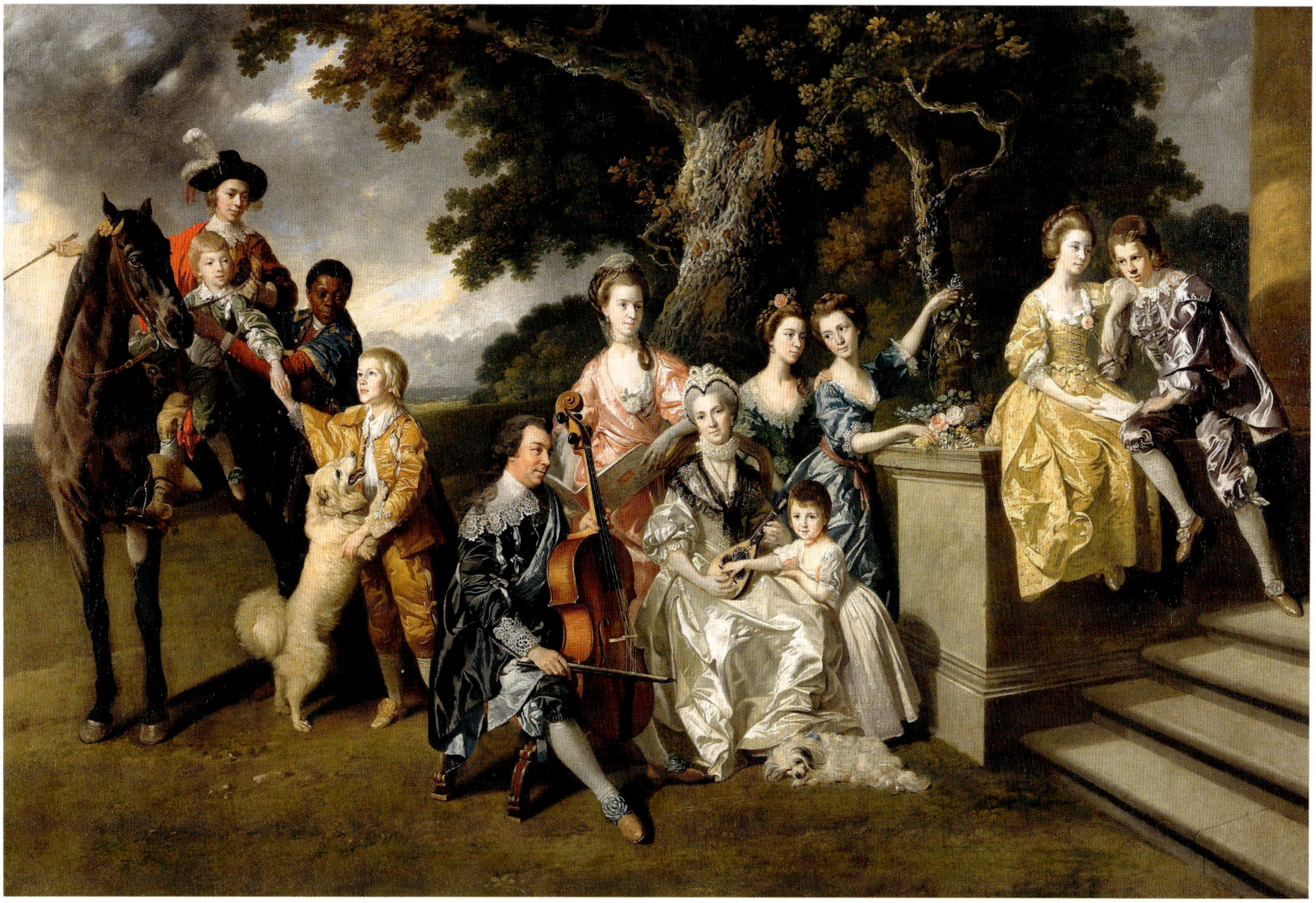

the intimacy, polite sociability, and material possessions critics have admired in the genre. Family members are shown in elegant Van Dyck costume, their musical instruments a sign of their pretensions to culture. The well-dressed Black groom belies this pastoral quietude. Shown in an ancillary position, serving the family, he is a reminder of the role played by Young in the First Carib War (1769–73), when the British sought to usurp land from the Indigenous peoples of St. Vincent. Young, owner of sugar plantations in the Caribbean, and once a governor of Dominica, inherited almost 900 enslaved workers from his father.[13]

Philip's other exhibitions, *The Four Georges*, *Three French Reigns*, *Gainsborough*, and *Reynolds*, were equally successful. Philip enticed American collectors to lend great works that had not been seen in London for years. *The Four Georges* charted the rise of a new class of wealthy landowners, enriched by their plantations in the West Indies or businesses in India. *Three French Reigns* featured superb works from the Paris collections of the Louvre, the French Rothschilds, the Comte de Camondo, the banker David David-Weill, and the designer Jean Puiforcat, as well as fourteen works from U.S. lenders and a few from the British elite. The catalogue had a preface by the French writer André Maurois (Émile Salomon Wilhelm Herzog). Philip's interiors at Park Lane, with their own exquisite French furnishings, enhanced the magnificent works on display.[14]

The Gainsborough exhibition received accolades from the critics, not least because after the opening, the king lent eight portraits never shown in public. Philip included Gainsborough's *Portrait of the Artist with His Wife and Daughter* and a striking self-portrait in a tricorne, dashed off with verve and brilliance. Gainsborough's beloved landscapes were singled out for praise, as were their preparatory sketches with loose, impressionistic brushwork.[15] Waterhouse and Martin Davies of the National Gallery in London assisted in the overall conception and the catalogue entries. An exhibition on Reynolds followed, with 101 works from distinguished U.S. and British collections.

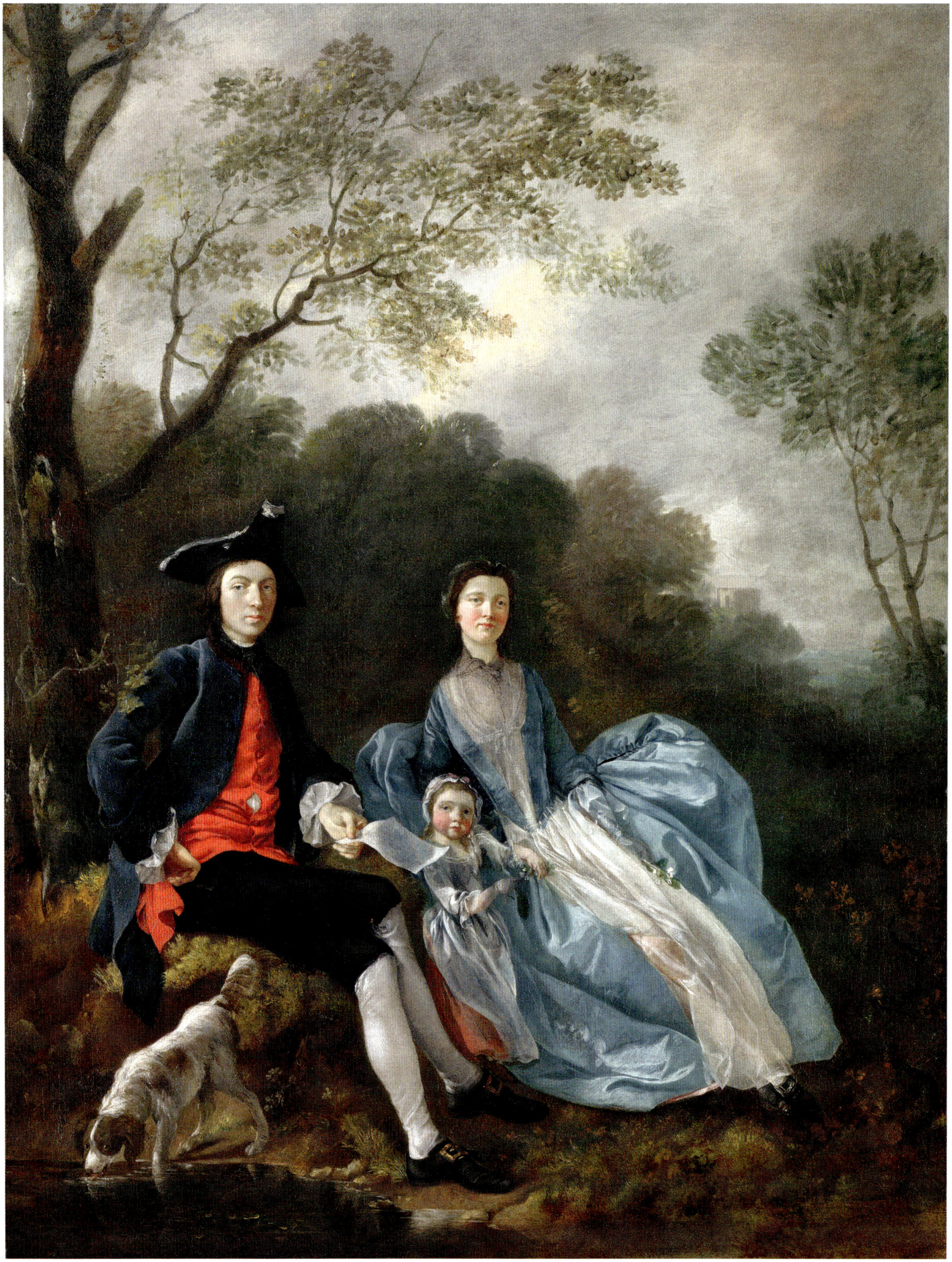

Thomas Gainsborough, *The Artist with His Wife and Daughter*, c. 1748, oil on canvas, 36¼ × 27¾ in. (92.1 × 70.5 cm), London, National Gallery, acquired under the acceptance-in-lieu scheme at the wish of Sybil, Marchioness of Cholmondeley, in memory of her brother, Sir Philip Sassoon, 1994, formerly in the Philip Sassoon Collection.

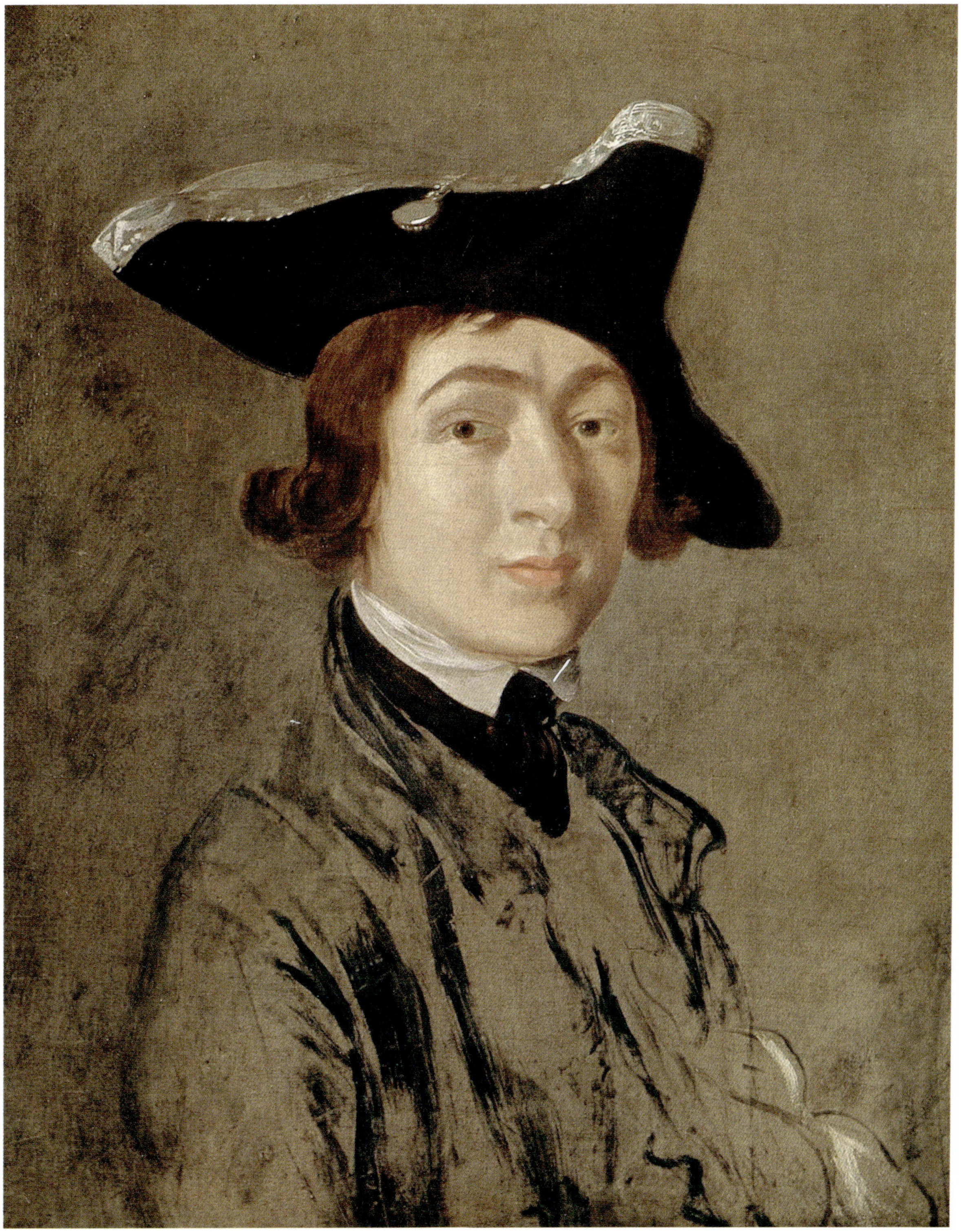

Thomas Gainsborough, *Self-Portrait*, 1754, oil on canvas, 21¼ × 18⅞ in. (54 × 48 cm), Norfolk, UK, Houghton Hall Collection, formerly in the Philip Sassoon Collection.

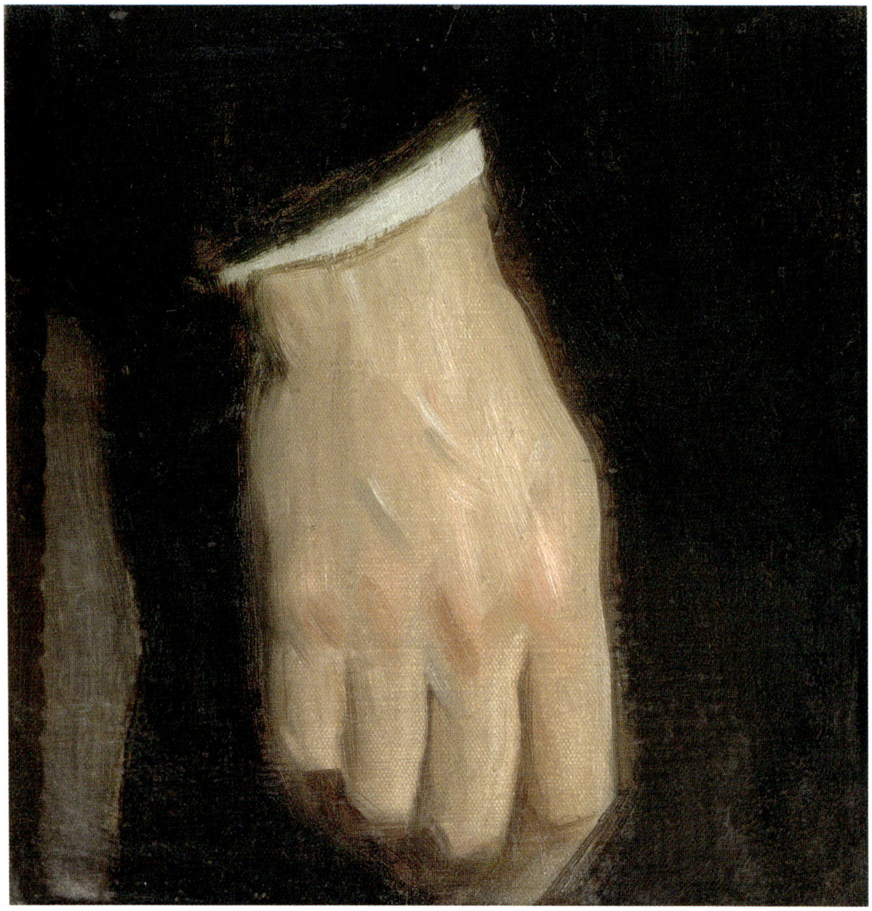

John Singer Sargent, *Hand of Philip Sassoon*, 1923, oil on canvas, 8¼ × 8¼ in. (21 × 21 cm), private collection. An inscription by Philip Sassoon on the back of the frame indicates that the hand was cut from his 1923 portrait.

Philip eschewed the avant-garde for figurative artists of high quality. He owned an extensive collection of works by John Singer Sargent, who captured Philip's elegance and fastidious taste in a remarkable portrait. Josep Maria Sert, Rex Whistler, and Glyn Philpot produced murals for Philip's houses, which were portrayed by Whistler, William Orpen, John Lavery, and E. H. Shepard. Philpot and Philip de László both painted Philip. A great admirer of the Ballets Russes, Philip owned several drawings by the Russian Jewish artist Léon Bakst, who designed scenery and costumes. Philip also bought Philpot's striking *Nijinsky before the Curtain*, a symphony of reds, as well as a charcoal drawing and bust-length oil of a Black model known as "Billy."[16] Philip was a patron of David Bomberg, and also had works by Augustus John and Philip Wilson Steer.

As a trustee of the National Gallery, the Wallace Collection, the Tate, and the British School in Rome, and as a member of the Royal Commission on National Museums and Galleries, Philip rendered valuable services to the arts through his social and political connections.[17] In 1922 he convinced the House of Commons to assist museums and galleries in protecting works of national importance from sale abroad. Philip also believed strongly in broadening access to the arts. "I do not think it is sufficiently realized," he argued in Parliament, "how largely our national galleries and museums in London and in the provinces that are now open to the public exist for the benefit of the poorer sections of the population, or how largely they are frequented by people who have no other means of gratifying their love for rare and beautiful things."[18] To this end, he offered students and workers discounted tickets to his exhibitions, and in 1934 he urged Kenneth Clark, then director of the National Gallery, to extend opening hours on selected days to enable workers to visit the museum before closing time.[19]

John Singer Sargent, *Sir Philip Sassoon*, 1923, oil on canvas, 37½ × 22¾ in. (95.2 × 57.8 cm), London, Tate, bequeathed by Sir Philip Sassoon Bt, 1939.

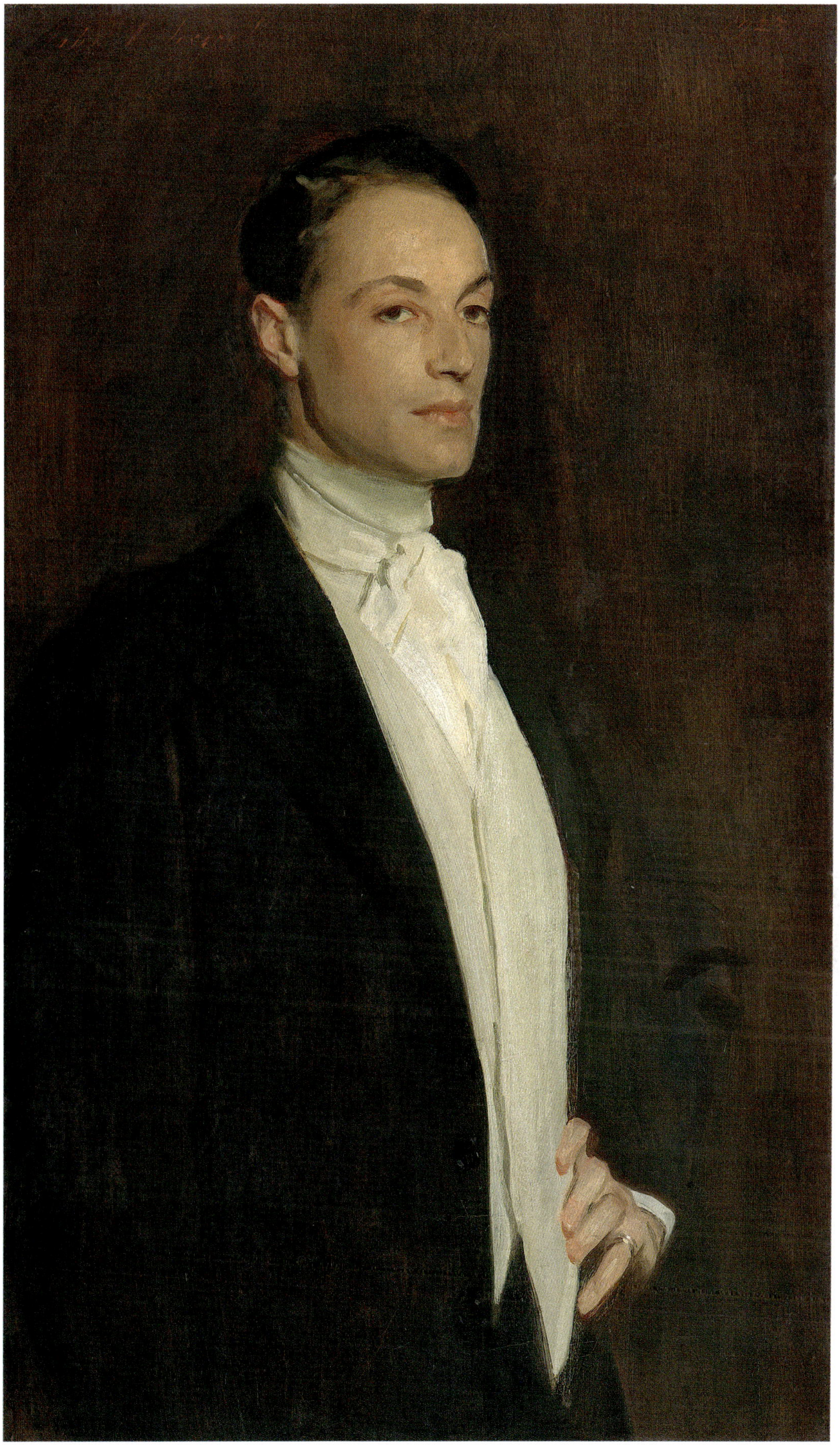

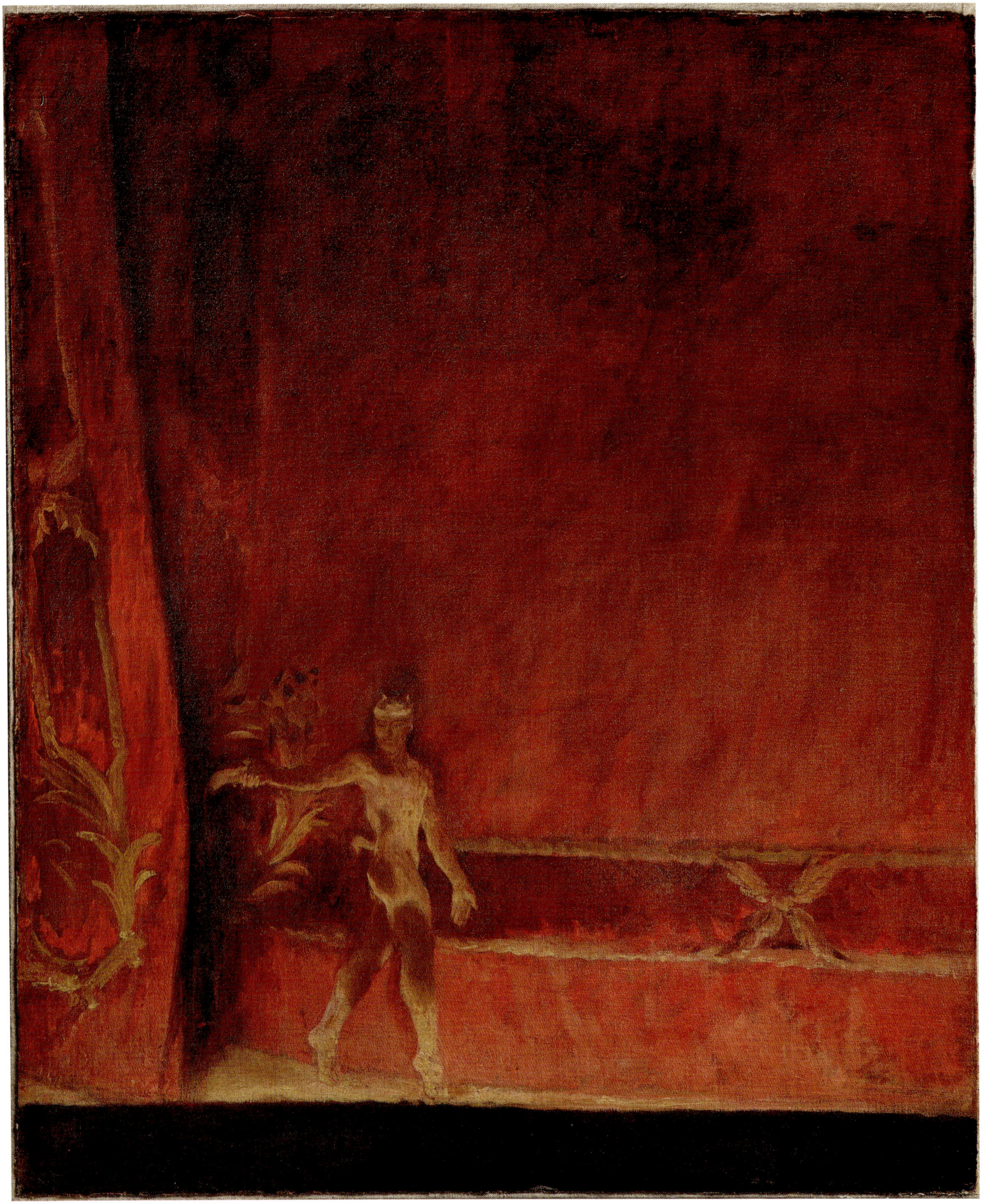

Glyn Warren Philpot, *Nijinsky before the Curtain*, 1913, oil on canvas, 29 × 24 in. (75.5. × 62.5 cm), formerly in the Philip Sassoon Collection. This painting depicts the Russian dancer Vaslav Nijinsky in costume as the Faun, taking a curtain call after a performance of *Afternoon of a Faun* at the Royal Opera House in Covent Garden, London. Based on the eponymous poem by Stéphane Mallarmé, the ballet featured music by Claude Debussy, choreography by Nijinsky, and costumes and sets by Léon Bakst.

Glyn Warren Philpot, *Head of Billy*, 1912–13, oil on canvas, 20 × 16 in. (50.8 × 40.6 cm), private collection, formerly in the Philip Sassoon Collection.

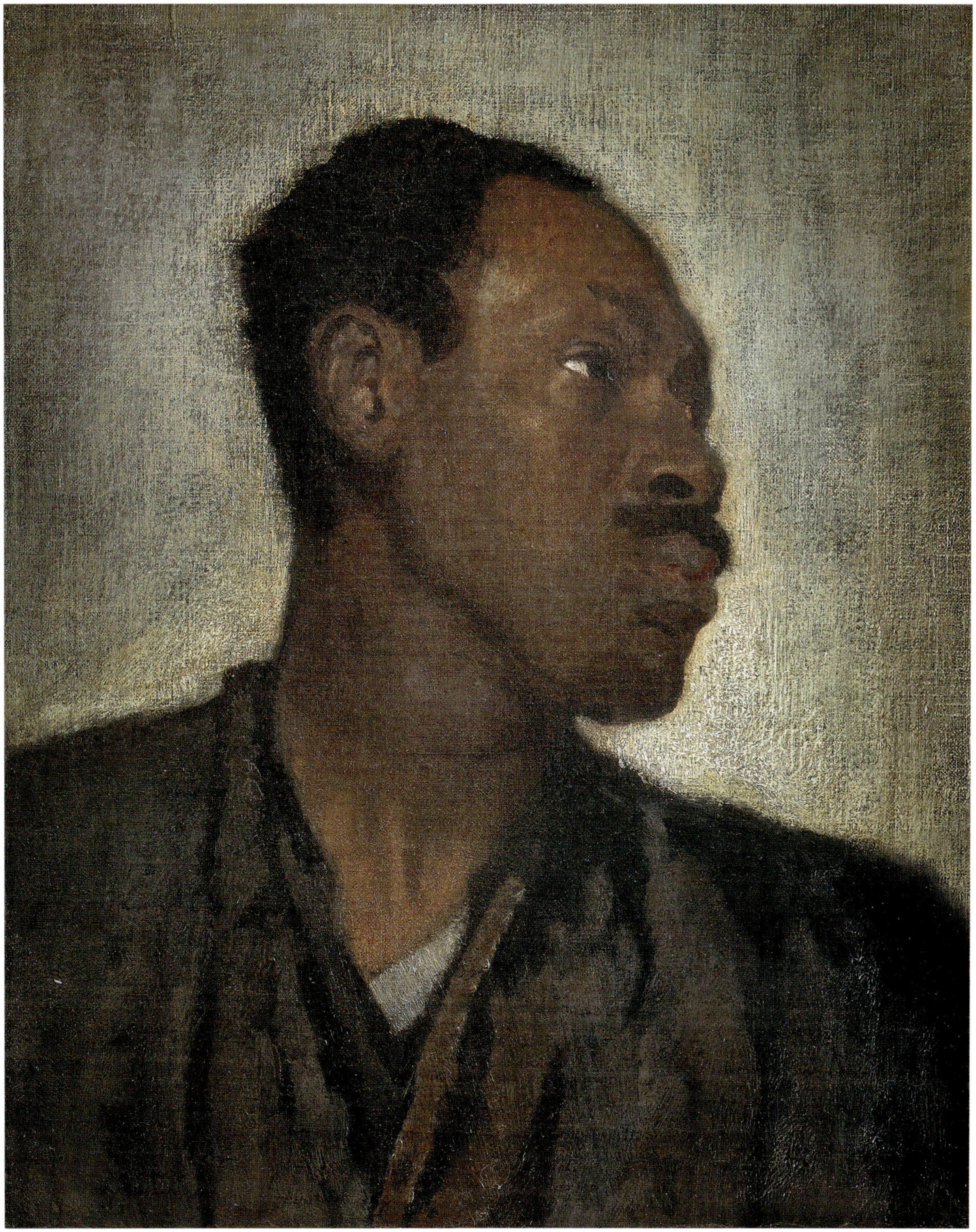

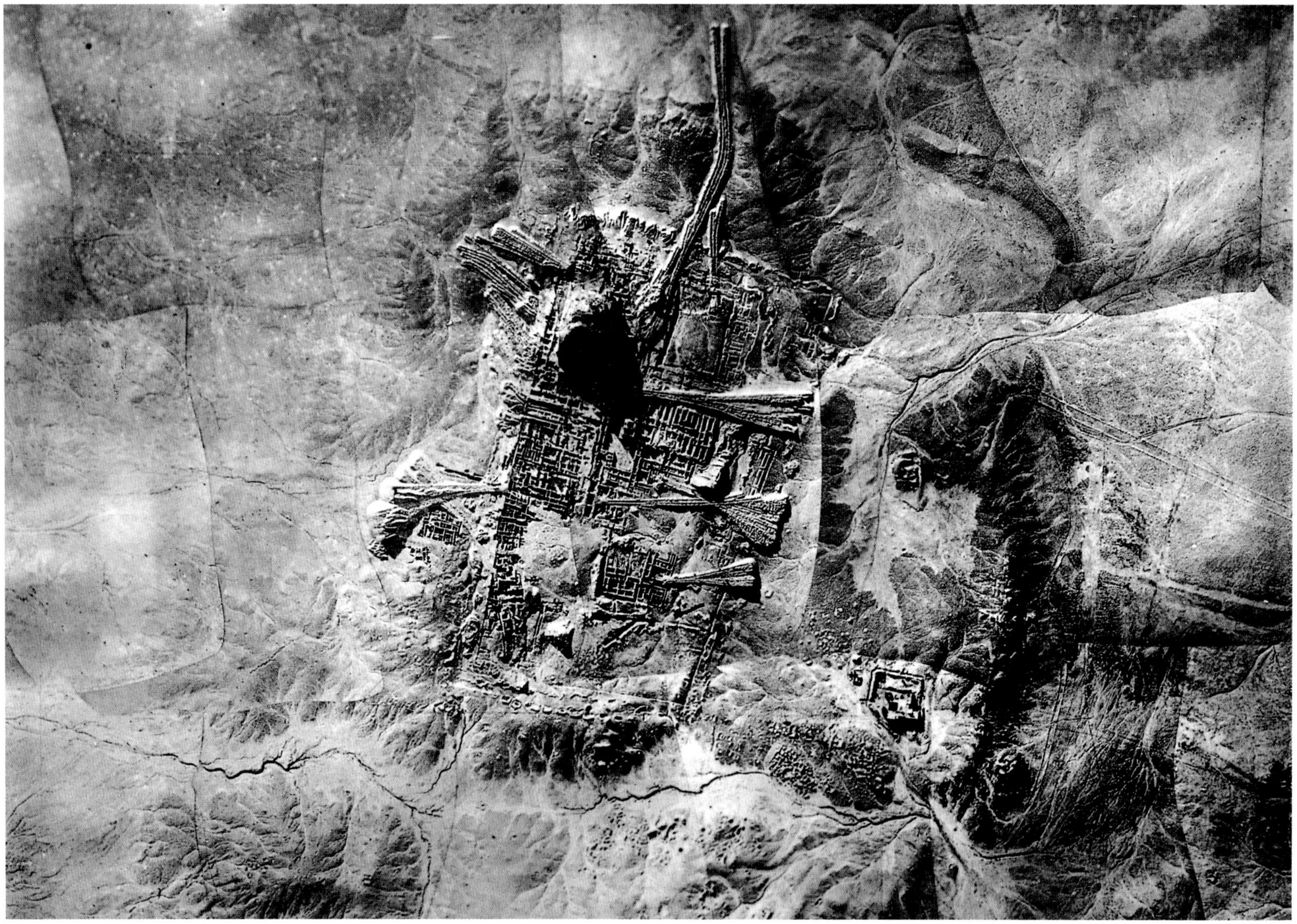

Aerial view of the ruins of the ancient Sumerian city of Ur (today, Tell el-Muqayyar, Iraq), photographed by Philip Sassoon, December 7, 1928.

As Undersecretary of State for Air, Philip wanted to build up the air force. Encouraging air travel was another way of achieving that aim. In 1928, he embarked on a long journey by plane and flying boat from London to Mumbai, stopping in several cities, including Baghdad and Bushehr, cities associated with his great-grandfather. Philip's text makes no reference to the Sassoons' past in Baghdad, nor did he try to visit Beit "Abu-Reuben," the family home. During his flights, he took remarkable aerial photographs of Jerusalem and ancient sites such as Philae, Erbil, Ur, and Ctesiphon, as well as New Delhi, where the architect Edwin Lutyens was designing the capital with the help of Herbert Baker, the architect of Philip's country house at Port Lympne. The photographs were later published in his account of the journey, *The Third Route*, in 1929.

Appointed First Commissioner of Works in 1937, a position he had long coveted, Philip put his impressive knowledge to work for his country. No one was better suited for the job: his "exceptional artistic taste," wrote the historian Cecil Roth, "was a national asset."[20] Responsible for the upkeep of all property, parks, and gardens owned by the government, he devoted his considerable energies to the restoration of landmarks, such as Inigo Jones's Marlborough House Chapel; the excavation of Whitehall Palace; and the painting, upholstering, and refurnishing of ministerial offices according to his own exacting standards.

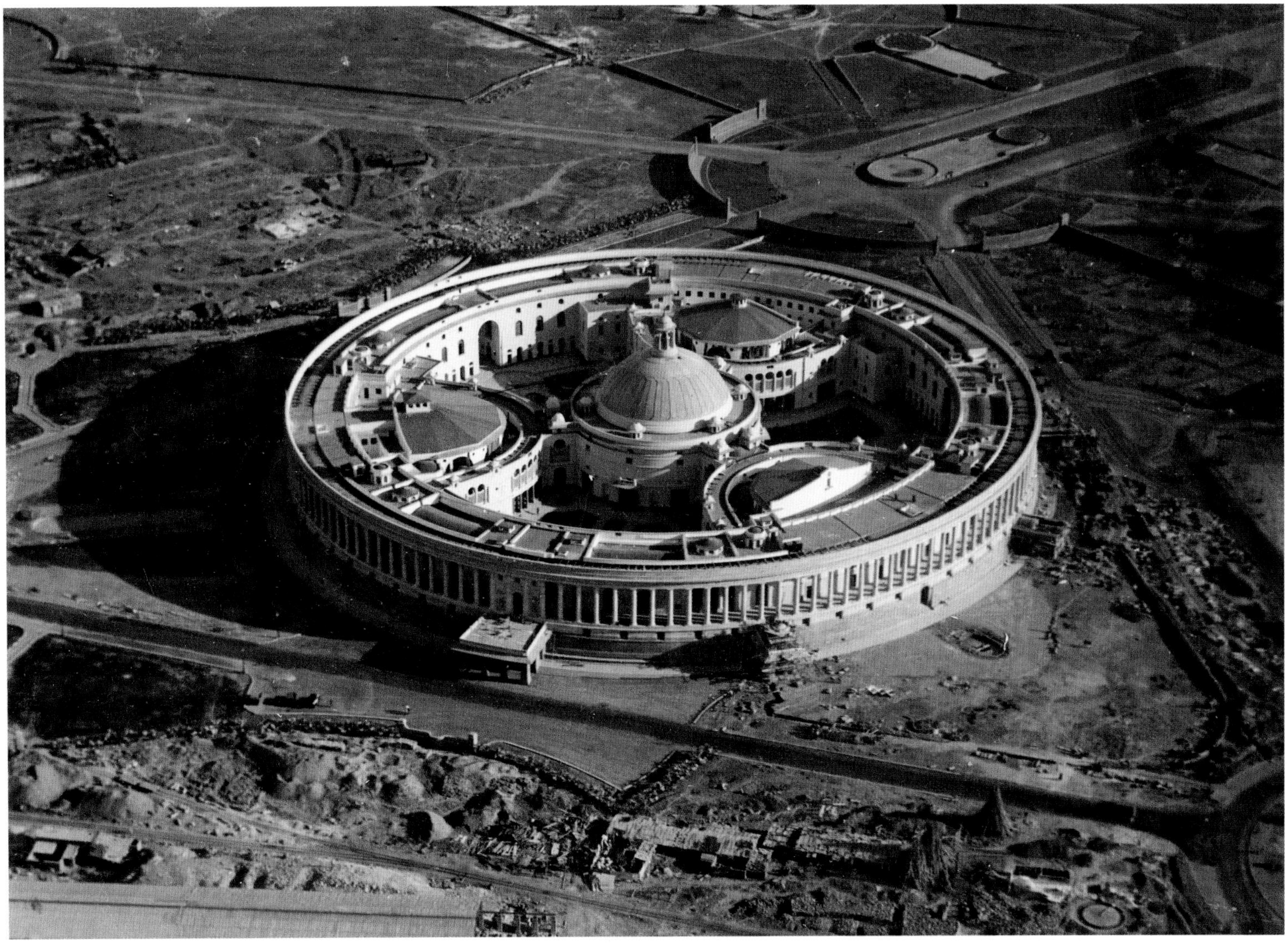

Aerial view of the Legislative Assembly, New Delhi, photographed by Philip Sassoon and published in *The Third Route,* 1929, Norfolk, UK, Houghton Hall Collection. Philip documented his journey by air from London to Mumbai, which began September 29, 1928.

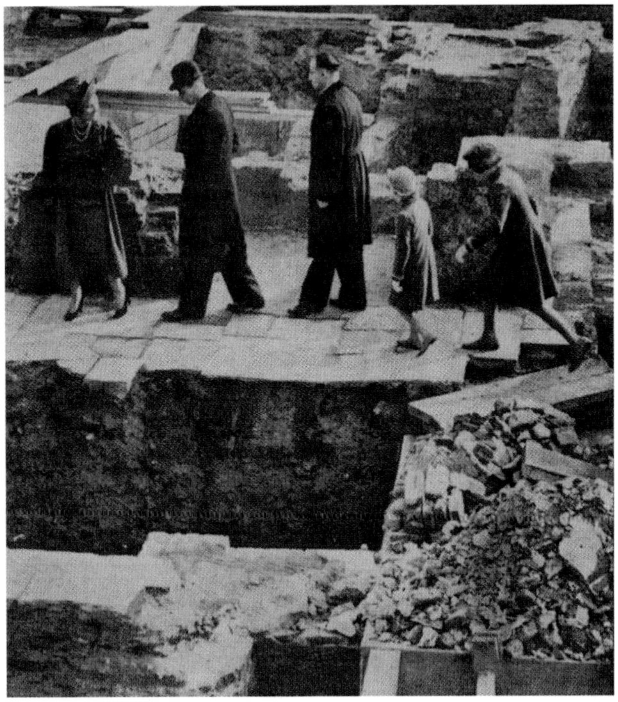

LEFT
In his capacity as First Commissioner of Works, Philip Sassoon tours the excavations of old Whitehall Palace in Westminster, London, with King George VI, the Queen, and Princesses Elizabeth and Margaret, March 11, 1939.

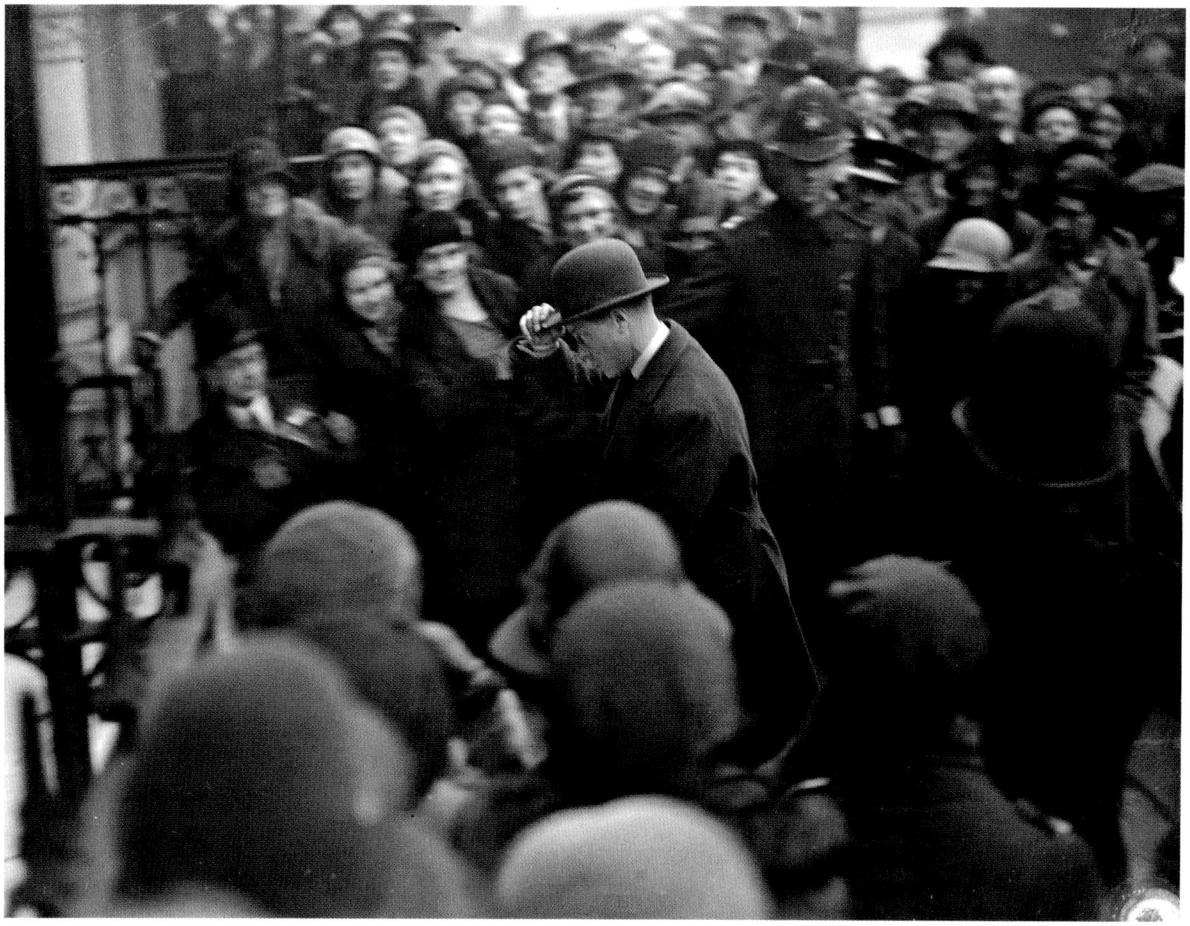

The Prince of Wales arriving at Philip Sassoon's London residence at 25 Park Lane to inaugurate the exhibition *The Age of Walnut*, organized by Philip and his cousin Hannah Gubbay, February 23, 1932.

Hannah

Whereas Philip acquired paintings and decorative arts to furnish his beautiful homes, Hannah had the single-minded determination that distinguishes dedicated collectors, tracking down her treasures in country-house sales or antique dealers in Bond Street, often accompanied by Queen Mary.[21] With its aristocratic allure, Georgian art exercised particular fascination on foreign-born collectors, and on those viewed as "outsiders." Masterworks from Hannah's extraordinary collection of decorative arts, on loan to several important exhibitions, received considerable attention in the press. Philip respected her expertise, and she was acknowledged as the actual organizer of some of his exhibitions, although her name does not always appear in the catalogues.[22] *The Age of Walnut*, mounted in 1932, was inaugurated by the Prince of Wales (later King Edward VIII), a close friend of both Hannah's and Philip's. Covering the years from the Restoration (1660) to the end of Queen Anne's reign (1714), the exhibition featured fifty-one of Hannah's matchless pieces, making her the biggest lender.

As Philip was unmarried, Hannah and his sister Sybil often helped host his receptions. When Sybil's children and responsibilities came to demand more of her attention, Hannah took over, particularly after the death of her husband in 1928. In recognition of her support, Philip bequeathed Port Lympne and Trent Park to Hannah. With her husband and cousin gone, Hannah gave up her home in Hertford Street, Mayfair, but never got a chance to live in Trent Park: during World War II, the house and its surroundings were requisitioned by the government to house German officers held for questioning. When the conflict ended, Trent Park was placed under a compulsory order that forced Hannah to sell. She was given Dower House, an eighteenth-century cottage on the estate. Known as Little Trent Park, it was filled with her museum-quality collection of decorative arts.

Hannah focused on furniture, old textiles and needlework, carpets, porcelain, and metalwork. Seeking out rare pieces judiciously and competitively, she amassed a selection of unequaled quality in several fields. Her eighteenth-century porcelain included Meissen, Vincennes, Sèvres, Tournai, Chelsea, and Wedgwood. A pair of

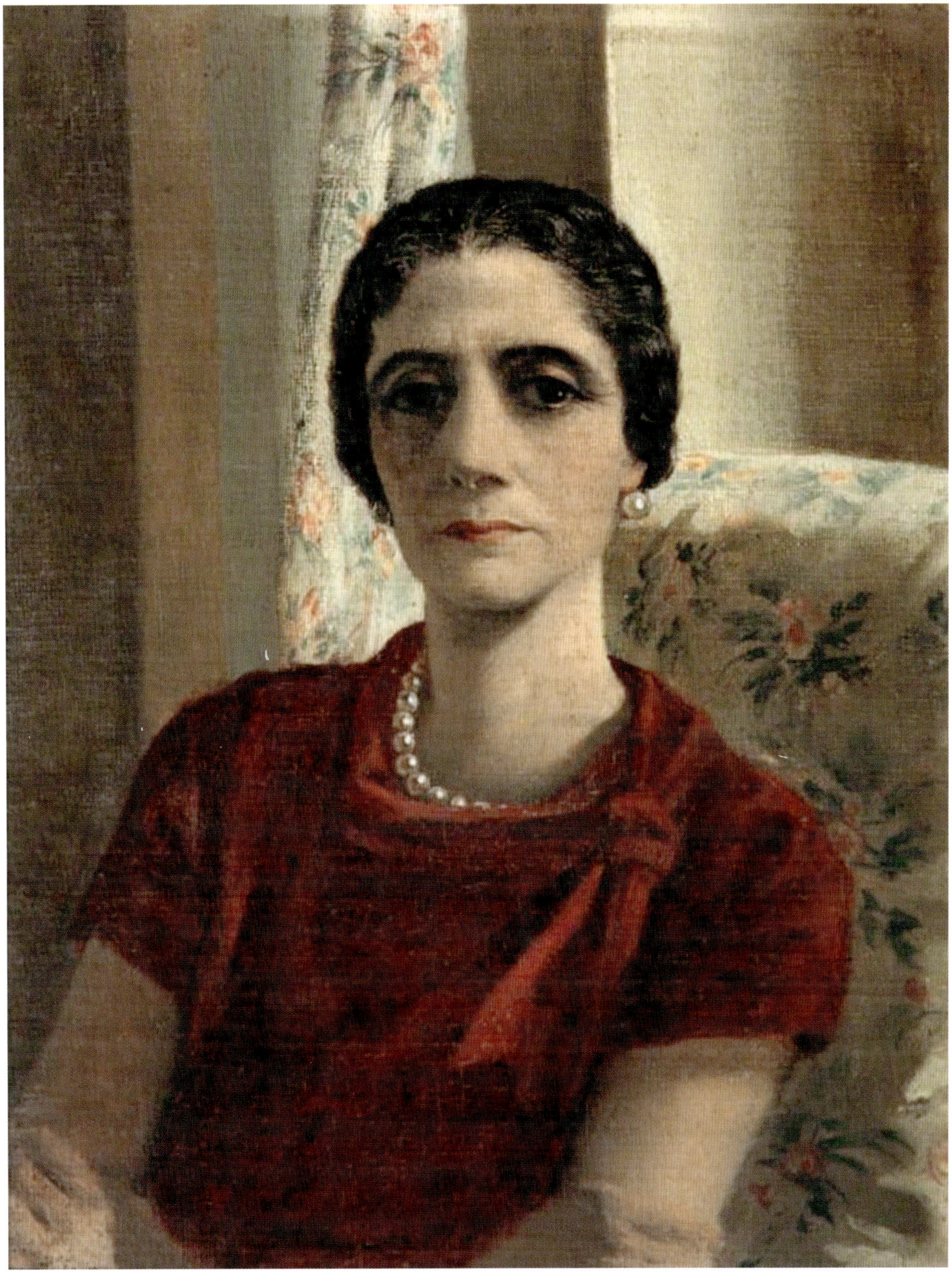

Rex Whistler, *Hannah Gubbay,* 1933–34, oil on canvas, 17½ × 14½ in (44.5 × 36.8 cm), Hannah Gubbay Collection, Clandon Park, Surrey, UK, National Trust. This portrait was destroyed on April 29, 2015, in a fire.

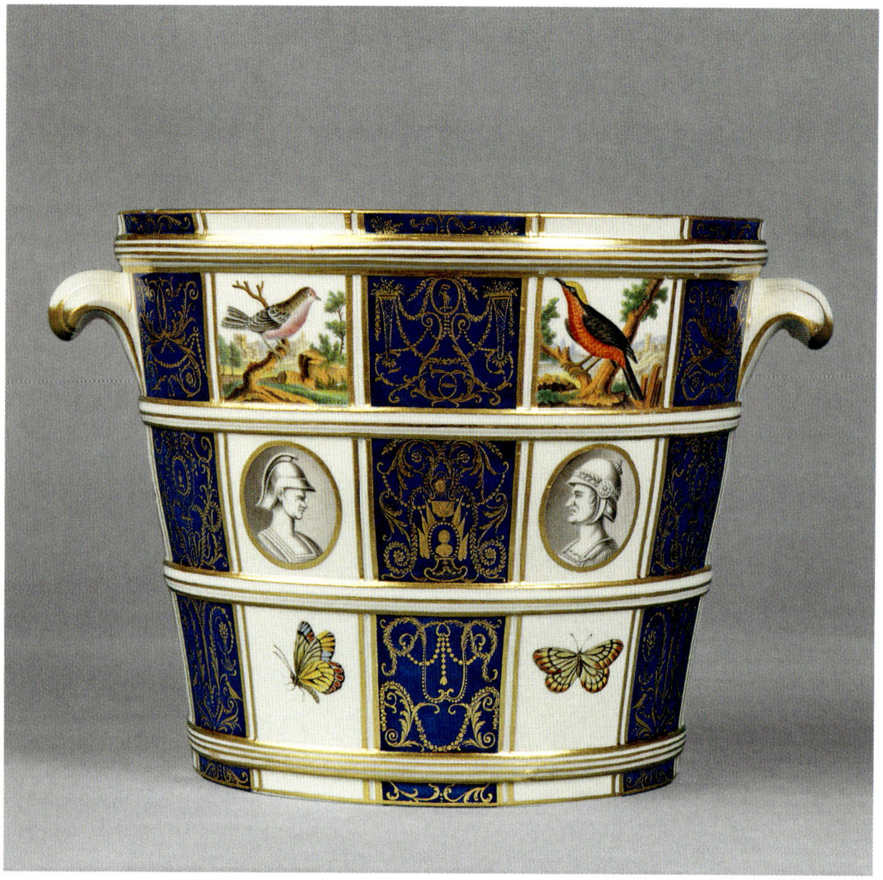

Jean-Ghislain-Joseph Mayer, pail commissioned by the Duc d'Orléans (later Philippe Égalité), with birds based on Buffon's *Natural History* (one of a pair), Tournai, France, 1787, ceramic, 7½ in. high (19 cm), Hannah Gubbay Collection, Clandon Park, Surrey, UK, National Trust.

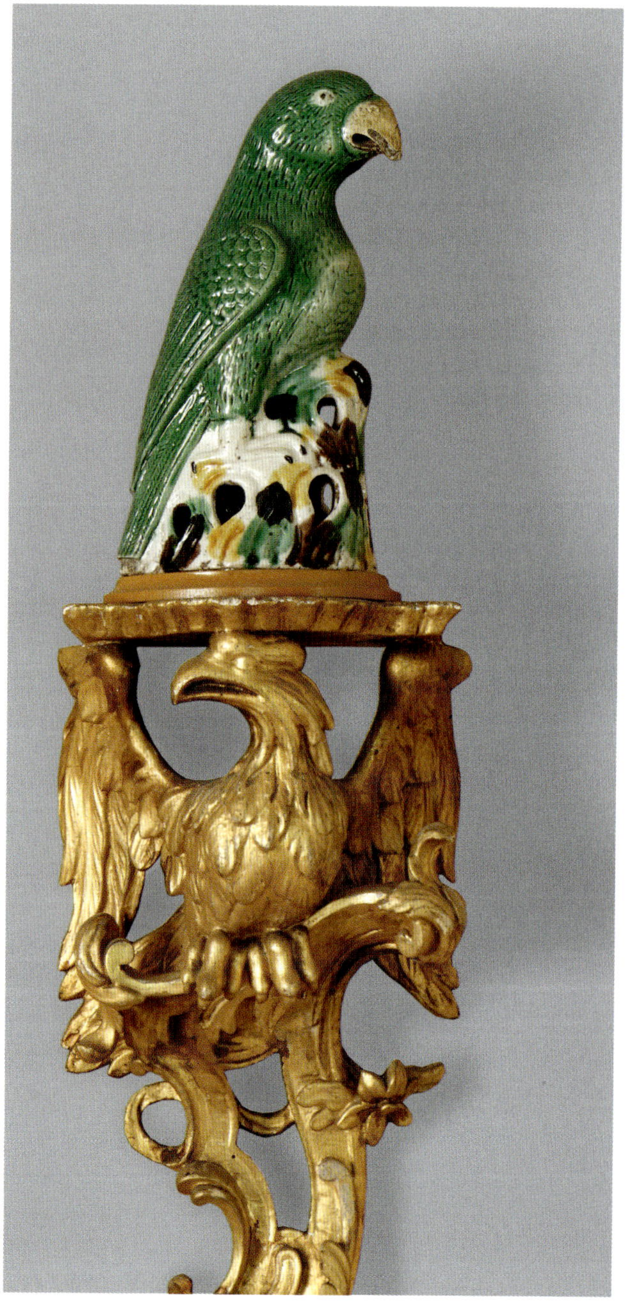

Biscuit green parrot on domed rockwork base on a Rococo bracket, China, Kangxi period, 1662–1722, parrot: ceramic, 9 in. high (23 cm), bracket: gilt wood and gesso, 16⅛ × 7⅞ in. (41 × 20 cm), Hannah Gubbay Collection, Clandon Park, Surrey, UK, National Trust.

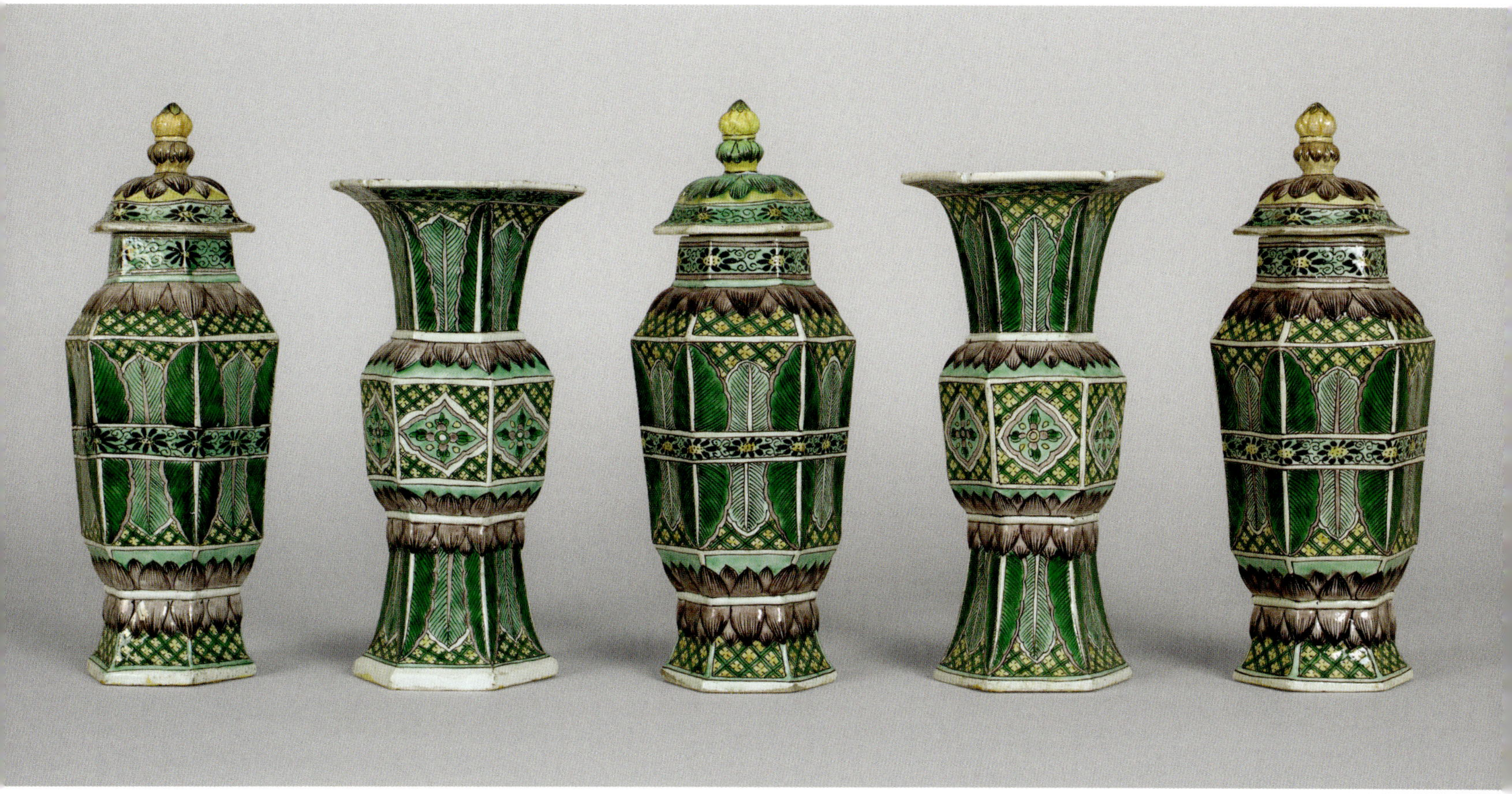

Famille verte garniture de cheminée (mantelpiece ornaments), China, Kangxi period, 1662–1722, ceramic and hard-paste porcelain, each approx. 10⅝ × 4¼ in. (26.9 × 10.9 cm), Hannah Gubbay Collection, Clandon Park, Surrey, UK, National Trust.

porcelain pails from a table service commissioned in 1787 by the Duc d'Orléans (later Philippe Égalité) had birds taken from Buffon's *Natural History*, revealing the influence of the Enlightenment. Executed by the manufactory of Tournai, the pails had centurion heads in grisaille and butterflies on a sumptuous lapis blue background with stylized, golden foliage. With their gilt accents, such pieces were deliberately designed to reflect the radiance of the flickering candelabra on the table, creating a play of golden light dancing across the room.[23]

Birds played a prominent role in Hannah's porcelain, furniture, and textile collections. From Asia there were Chinese, Japanese, and Korean porcelain birds, elegantly displayed on gilt Rococo brackets that were also rare. Most of the Chinese birds dated from the reigns of the first Qing emperors, but a Korean celadon duck could be traced to the Koryŏ dynasty (935–1392). Among her many treasures from China is a gorgeous *famille verte* mantelpiece garniture in hard-paste porcelain from the reign of Kangxi (1662–1722). "No comparable collection of these valuable objects has been, or is ever again likely to be, amassed in this country," wrote the architectural historian Gervase Jackson-Stops, "and its particular value is that a study of the techniques, the colours and glazes of each one in relation to its neighbours helps to date more precisely these early results of the Chinese export trade to Europe."[24]

Hannah's tall mirrors from the late seventeenth to the early eighteenth century were also unique. Encased in carved wooden frames, gilt, silvered, or in *verre églomisé*, they had historical and art-historical significance as an index of the growth of the English manufacture of mirror plates that slowly eclipsed that of Venice, formerly the great center of the trade.[25] In their day, the complexity of the available technology made mirrors expensive items of exclusivity.

In furniture, Hannah preferred satinwood and walnut, inlaid with precious woods and lacquered. The vogue for Asian lacquer dates back to the years of King Charles II (r. 1660–85). While he was in exile in the Netherlands, his court was exposed to luxurious examples of Japanese and, later, Chinese lacquer introduced by the Dutch East India Company. Successful attempts to apply lacquer to wood in the Netherlands were eagerly followed in England, where how-to books flourished, beginning with the influential *A Treatise of Japaning and Varnishing* by John Stalker and

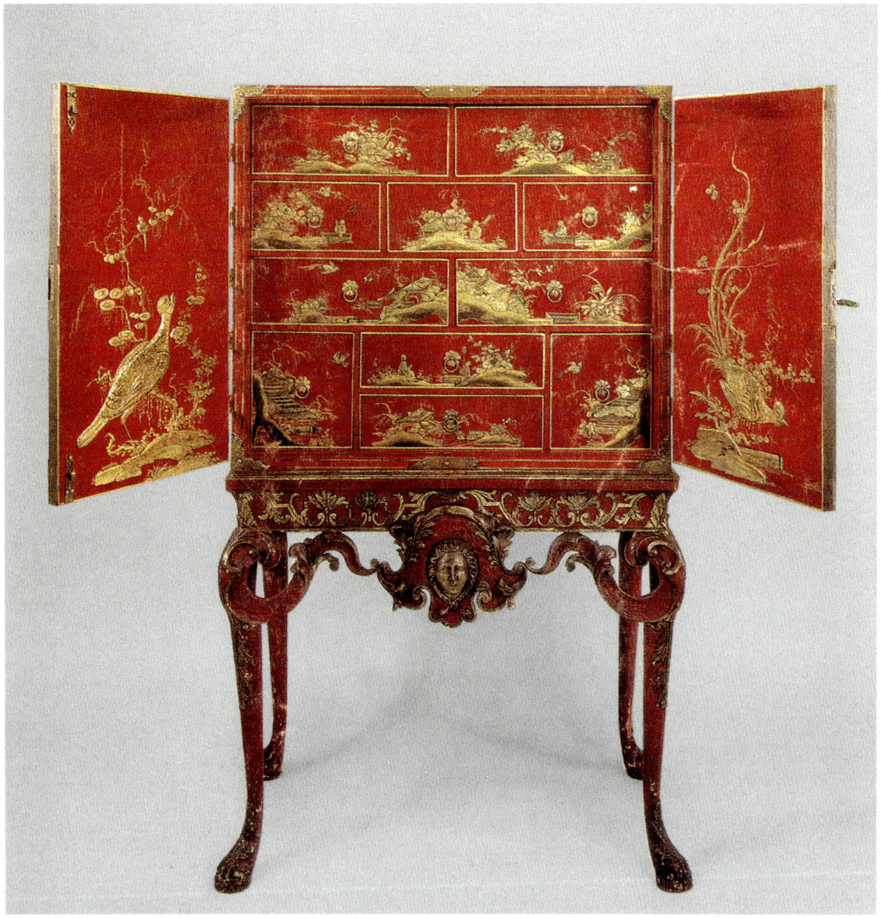

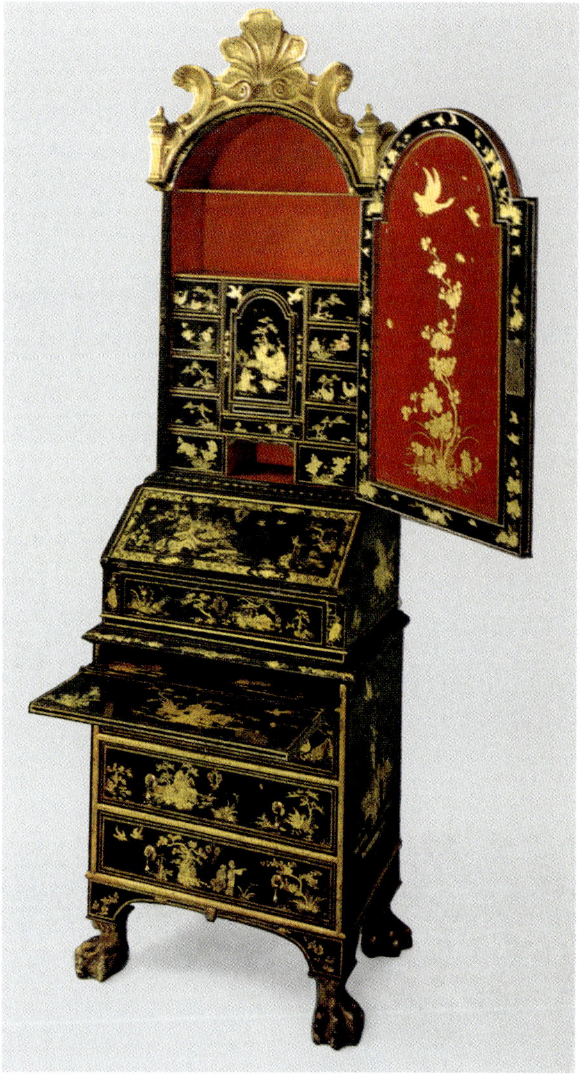

Cabinet, japanned in silver on scarlet ground, c. 1710, 58 × 35⅜ × 19¾ in. (147.3 × 90 × 50.2 cm), London, Victoria and Albert Museum, bequest of Mrs. Hannah Gubbay of Trent Park. Of a later date, the stand on which the cabinet sits, originally gilt, was considerably altered to match it.

George Parker (1688). Though not of the same quality as the delicate pieces from the East, European imitations, known as Japan work, rose sharply, partly due to the exorbitant price of the imports, although English examples were also labor intensive. Hannah's William and Mary lacquered bureau is a lovely example of European chinoiserie. A drawer for ladies' toiletries still shows the original vivid green and scarlet hues. Another superb piece is a Queen Anne cabinet in vermilion lacquer, dating to about 1710, with low relief in gesso and silver mounts chased with flowers and foliage.[26]

Needlework, an old aristocratic genre, was a particular passion for Hannah. *Early English Needlework and Furniture* included specimens by Mary, Queen of Scots, and Queen Caroline, wife of George II. Hannah's friend Edward, Prince of Wales, learned needlepoint from his mother, Queen Mary. A superb needlewoman herself, Hannah gave examples of her work to members of the royal family.[27] One of her outstanding possessions was a rare, luxurious Louis XIV Savonnerie fire screen in glorious color, boldly signed by Pierre Parisot. A defrocked Capuchin, Parisot recruited weavers who fled the royal manufactory of Savonnerie and introduced the knotted-pile technique to England, where he founded a short-lived workshop at Fulham. Hannah's beloved birds dominate: a brilliant red pheasant from China looks to the sky, with a wood duck from North America at his feet, while a kingfisher flies overhead. The iconography is unique. In the background is a well-known property: Claremont (Surrey), built for the Whig politician Thomas Pelham-Holles (later bought by Robert Clive—"Clive of India") and landscaped by William Kent, who designed the *tempietto* in the background.[28]

Although paintings were not the main focus of her collecting, Hannah owned Zoffany's *Samuel Foote as Major Sturgeon and Robert Baddeley as Sir Jacob Jollop in "The Mayor of*

OPPOSITE
Green japanned cabinet, c. 1688–1702, wood, 74 × 22 × 15 in. (188 × 56 cm × 38 cm), Hannah Gubbay Collection, Clandon Park, Surrey, UK, National Trust. The drawers of this William and Mary bureau are covered with the original brocaded silk.

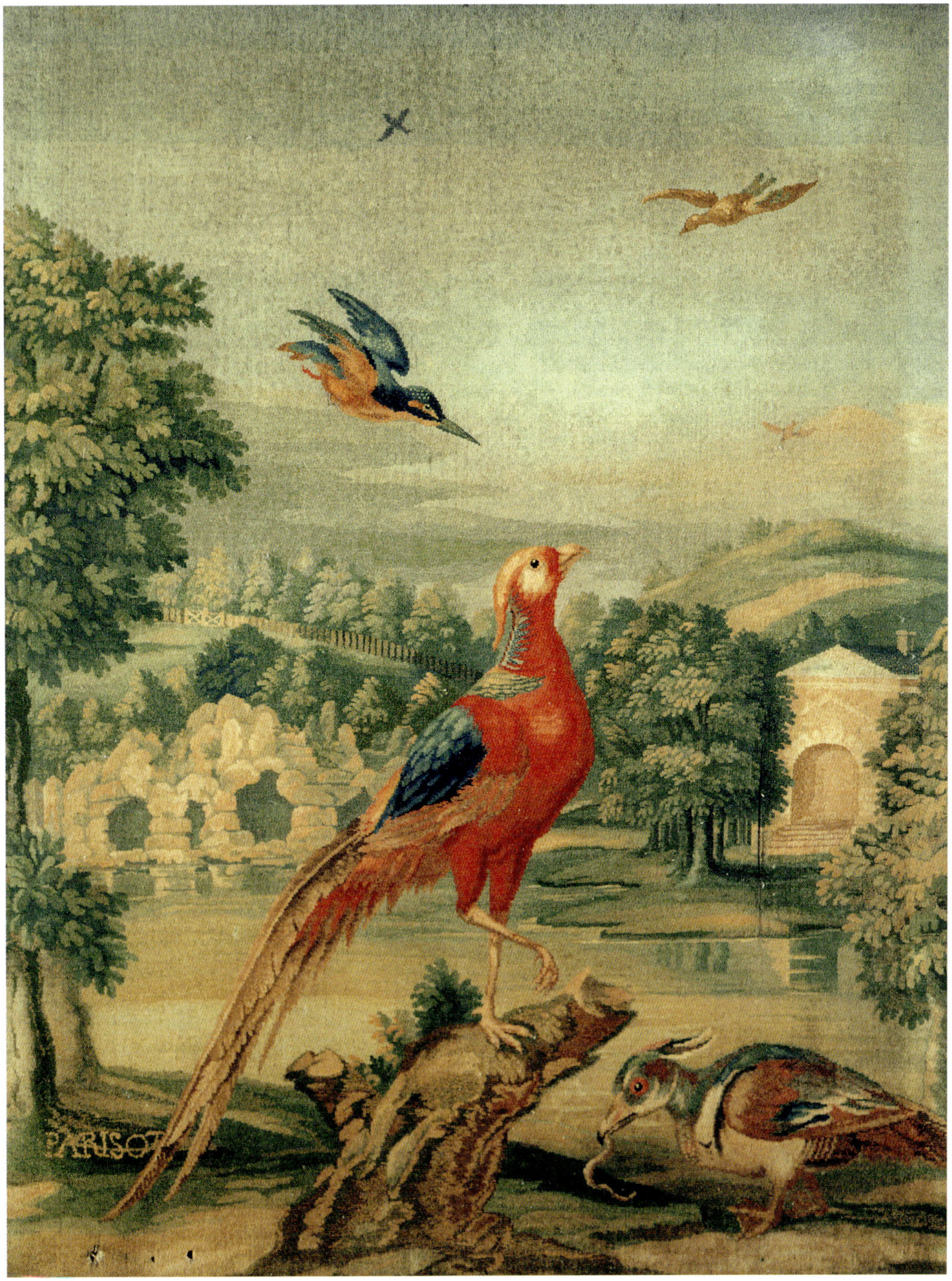

Pierre Parisot, fire screen, Fulham, London, c. 1750–55, textile and wood, 43¾ × 31⅛ in. (111 × 79 cm), Hannah Gubbay Collection, Clandon Park, Surrey, UK, National Trust.

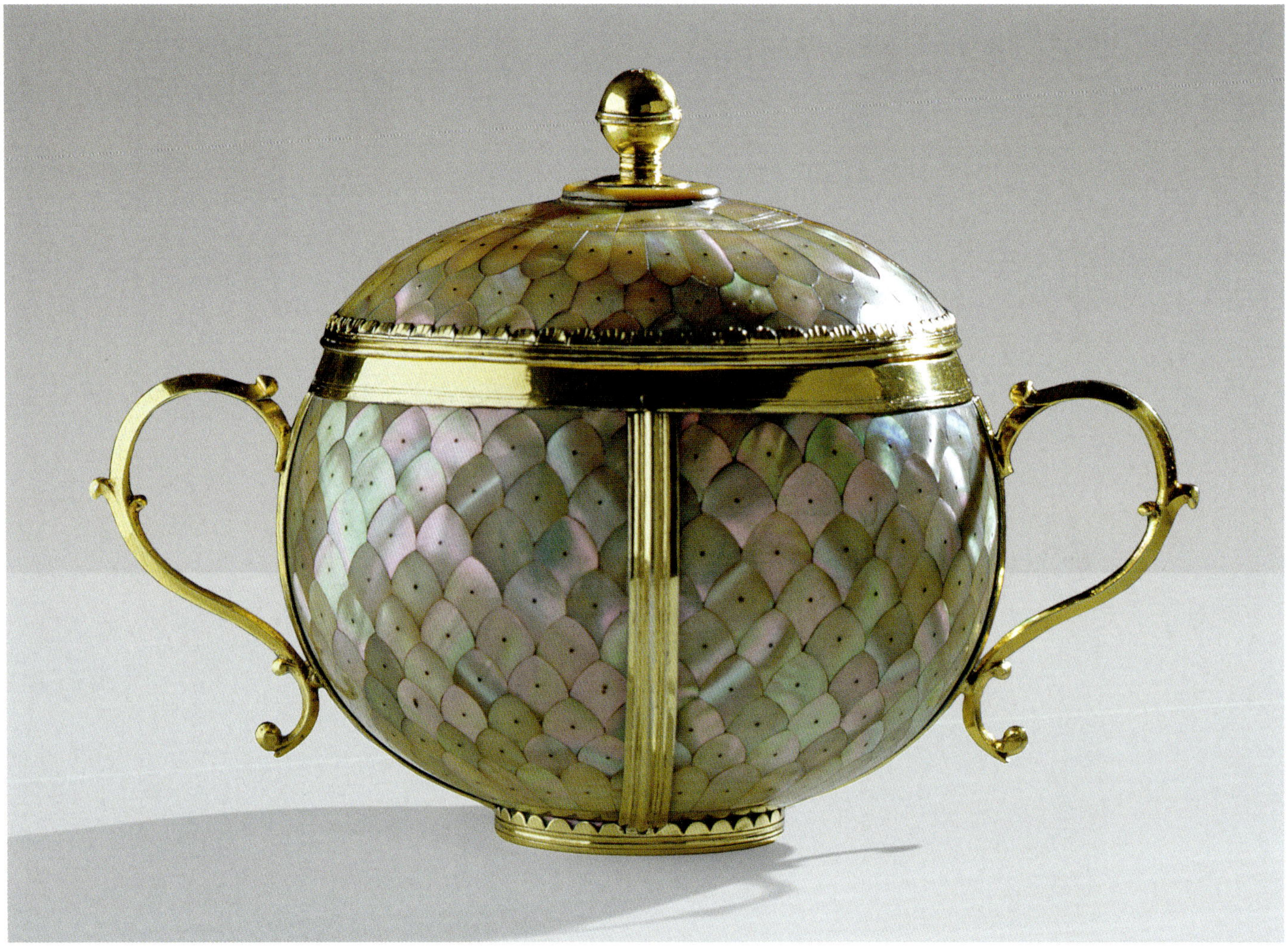

Garratt" (1764), which she lent to the exhibition *Conversation Pieces*. She had several oils by John Singer Sargent, but these may have been inherited from Philip. Sargent had executed a charcoal drawing of her husband, David Gubbay, in 1925. Eugène Boudin's *The Laundresses* also hung in her home, but this too may have been one of Philip's acquisitions. Hannah also commissioned a portrait from Rex Whistler, who worked on Philip's homes at Port Lympne and Trent Park. She appears with splendid pearls around her neck, sitting on a chintz-covered armchair with matching curtains behind her.

Hannah's collection boasted two sumptuous pieces from India: an early seventeenth-century covered cup and a bowl, both made in Gujarat, a center of luxury goods in western India. Exported to England, the thin petals of mother-of-pearl were fastened with brass pins before being given silver-gilt mounts in London. Such refined objects were highly prized by the Mughals, in whose courts European traders first saw them. By the seventeenth century, these wares were aimed at foreign as well as domestic markets, and were given forms familiar to Western clients. With their shimmering, iridescent surfaces, these nonutilitarian objects served as markers of wealth and distinction.

Though well known among critics and collectors of her day, Hannah has been dismissed with the usual stereotypes reserved for women: "She did not possess Sir Philip's depth of connoisseurship and she was unlikely to have been a

OPPOSITE
Bowl and cover, Gujarat, India, mounted in London, c. 1621–22, mother-of-pearl plaques fastened with brass pins and silver-gilt mounts, 6¼ × 9⅞ in. (16 × 25 cm), London, Victoria and Albert Museum, bequeathed by Mrs. Hannah Gubbay.

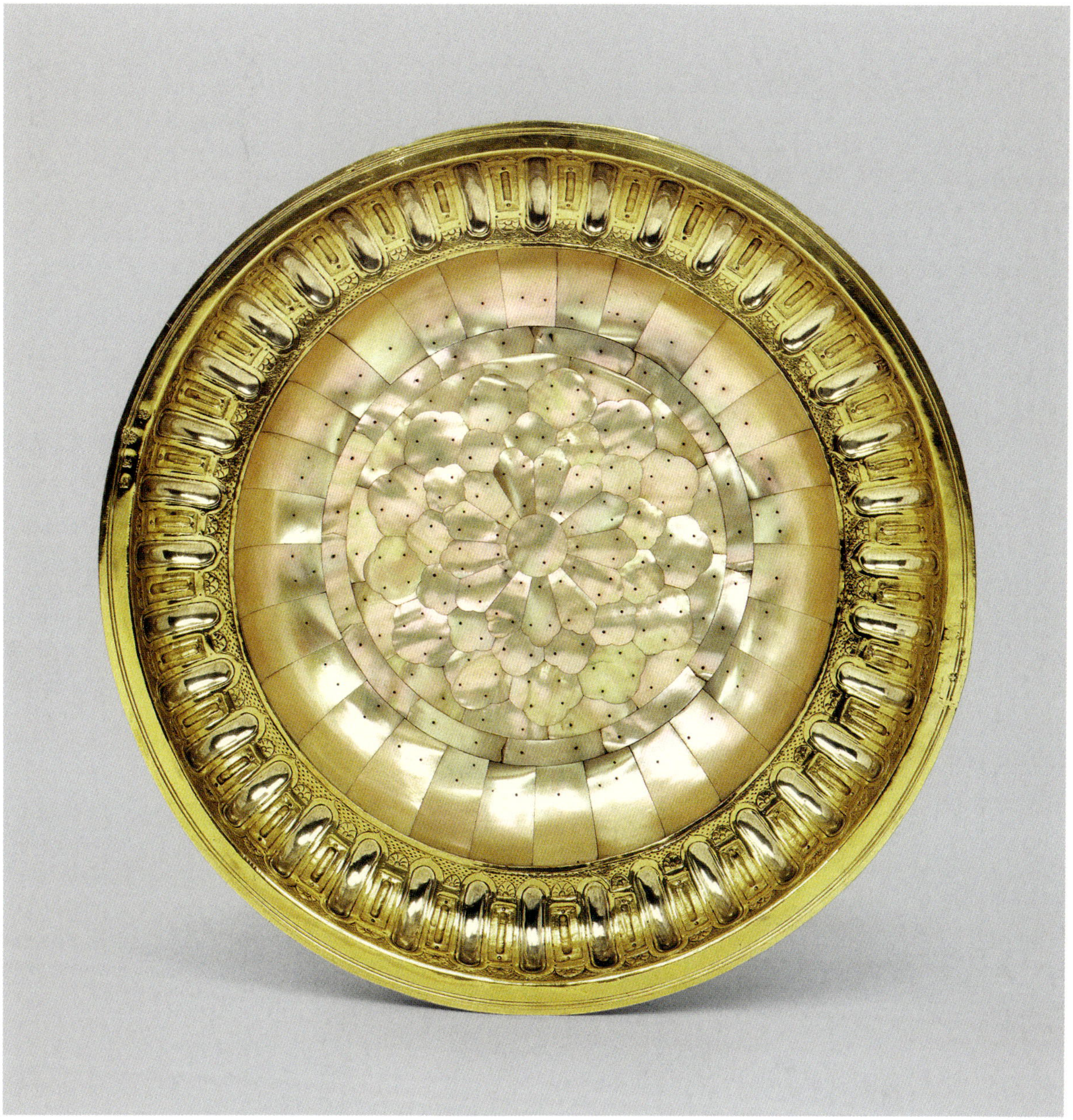

Bowl, Gujarat, India, mounted in London, early seventeenth century, mother-of-pearl with silver-gilt mounts, 3⅜ × 9½ in. in diameter (8.5 × 24 cm), London, Victoria and Albert Museum, bequeathed by Mrs. Hannah Gubbay. This bowl was displayed in the exhibition *Old English Plate*, organized by Philip Sassoon and Hannah Gubbay.

close reader of the latest publications," wrote John Cornforth and Jackson-Stops, who claimed instead that "she had a *natural* eye for objects." That many of Hannah's porcelain pieces were made up of figures or animals was due, they concluded, to "a strong down-to-earth streak in Mrs. Gubbay. High art and book learning were not for her." This is the same woman the art historian John Pope-Hennessy described as "a collector of genius" in his obituary of her in *The Times*: "Not only was Mrs. Gubbay in a formal sense the ideator of these exhibitions," he wrote, "but their opulence and the selectiveness and taste by which they were informed, stemmed directly from her personality."[29]

After a lifetime of collecting, Hannah gave several pieces to the Victoria and Albert Museum but gifted about 450 items to the National Trust in 1968, along with one million pounds and the stipulation that the collection be kept together. The Trust placed the bequest in Clandon Park, a grand eighteenth-century Palladian mansion designed by Giacomo Leoni and landscaped by Capability Brown. With this munificent gift, Clandon Park became one of the most important repositories of decorative arts in Britain, a great boon to specialists who now had a range of related pieces at their disposal.[30]

On April 29, 2015, Clandon Park burned down, along with "one of the greatest art collections ever to come into national ownership."[31]

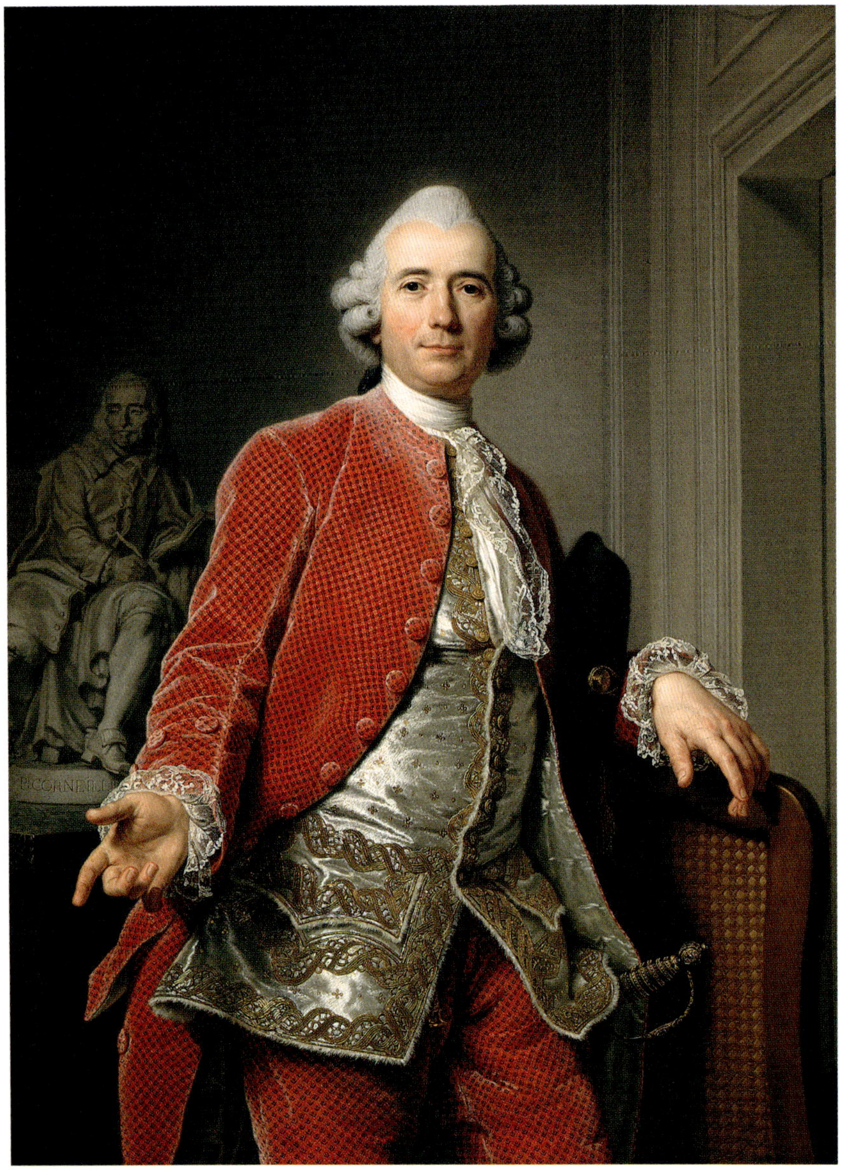

Adolf Ulric Wertmüller, *Jean-Jacques Caffieri*, 1784, oil on canvas, 50¾ × 37¾ in. (128.9 × 95.9 cm), Boston, Museum of Fine Arts, Ernest Wadsworth Longfellow Fund, formerly in the Mozelle Sassoon Collection.

Mozelle

At the age of twenty, Mozelle married her cousin Meyer Elias Sassoon. The couple moved to London and then Shanghai. On their return to London, they purchased an elegant home in Hamilton Place, near Rothschild Row and around the corner from her cousin Philip. Like Philip, Meyer and Mozelle were part of the glittering high society and entertained on a grand scale. "There is no sign in this house of the departure of Israel's glory," wrote the Clerk of the Council after attending a grand ball in 1904, reporting that "everything shines with the greatest lustre."[32]

A distinguished *dix-huitièmiste*, Mozelle amassed an extraordinary collection of paintings, furniture, and the decorative arts. Even her country house, Pope's Manor, in Berkshire, had an unimpeachable eighteenth-century pedigree as the former home of the poet Alexander Pope (1688–1744). Her taste enriched by travels and residence in different continents, Mozelle had a fine eye for art and did not hesitate to return a painting when it did not meet her expectations.[33] At Philip's exhibition *Three French Reigns*, she first saw two masterpieces she would later acquire. The first was the splendid portrait of French sculptor Jean-Jacques Caffieri by the Swedish artist Adolf Ulric Wertmüller, formerly attributed to Jacques-Louis David. Wertmüller depicts Caffieri in court dress, the velvet, silk, and lace vividly rendered, with his statue of the seventeenth-century dramatist Pierre Corneille in the background. The second was Nicolas de Largillière's most famous painting, *La Belle Strasbourgeoise*.[34] The artist clearly relished demonstrating his prowess in rendering

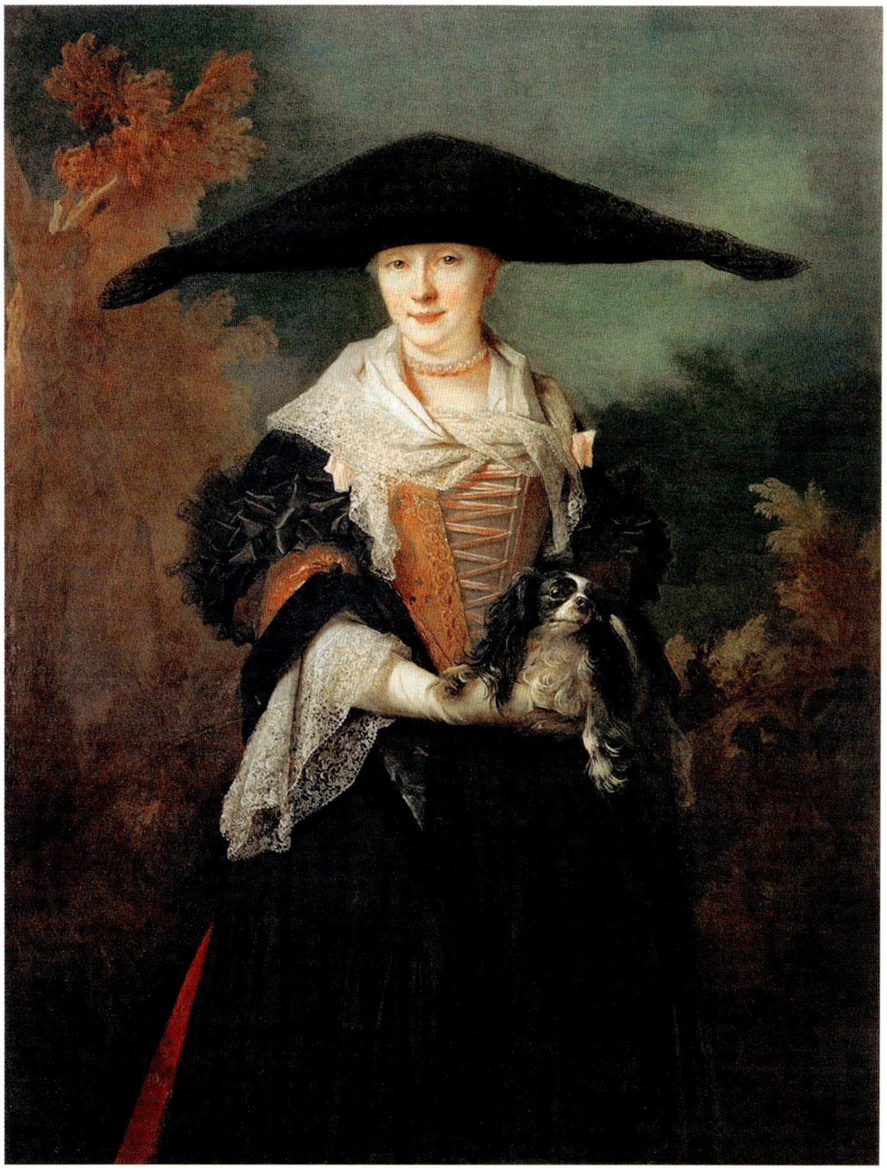

Nicolas de Largillière, *La Belle Strasbourgeoise,* 1703, oil on canvas, 54⅜ × 41¾ in. (138 × 106 cm), Strasbourg, Musée des Beaux-Arts, formerly in the Mozelle Sassoon Collection.

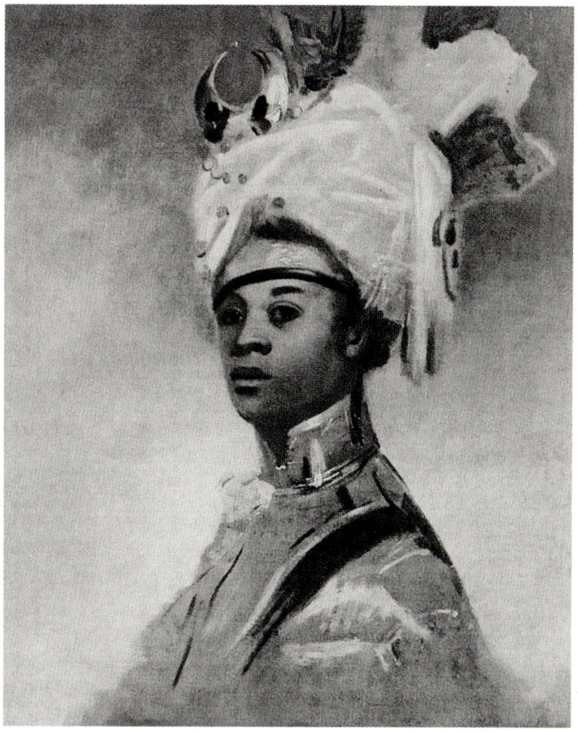

Joshua Reynolds, *Young Man in a Turban* (previously called *Omai*), c. 1776, oil on canvas, 29¼ × 24⅛ in. (74.3 × 61.3 cm), private collection, formerly in the Mozelle Sassoon Collection, seen here in a monochrome reproduction.

textures—lace, silk, fur—but wisely confined that approach to the sitter, a patrician lady wearing the stylish attire of her class and her city, sporting a ravishing outsize hat. In contrast to the sharp clarity and detail of the costume, sky and foliage dissolve into a hazy sfumato that throws the figure into relief.

Mozelle also owned a superb oil sketch by Reynolds, then thought to be a portrait of "Omai," a young man from Raiatea brought to England from the Pacific Islands in 1774. Scholars now question this identification: Ma'i (his true name) caused such a stir in London society when he arrived that several portraits of Black men were named after him. Mozelle's painting shows a spirited young man in an extravagant turban crowned by a crescent, an Orientalist signifier of otherness.[35] By means of quick strokes fading in a *non finito* effect, the headdress and armor serve as a foil to the more accomplished features of the sitter.

Like her cousins, Mozelle lent paintings and decorative arts to several exhibitions. In 1935, to help Philip, who had taken a year off from curating on behalf of the Royal Northern Hospital, Mozelle opened her house to the public. Paintings, porcelain, eighteenth-century furnishings, almost all French, blended together harmoniously, wrote the enthusiastic critics of *The Times*, who described her home "as perhaps one of the most thorough collections to be found in London, for everything is in the period."[36] Her other eighteenth-century paintings included a portrait of the Baron de Longepierre by Jean-François de Troy; two fêtes galantes by Jean-Baptiste Pater, *Fête Champêtre* and *L'Escarpolette*; *The Old Dovecote* by François

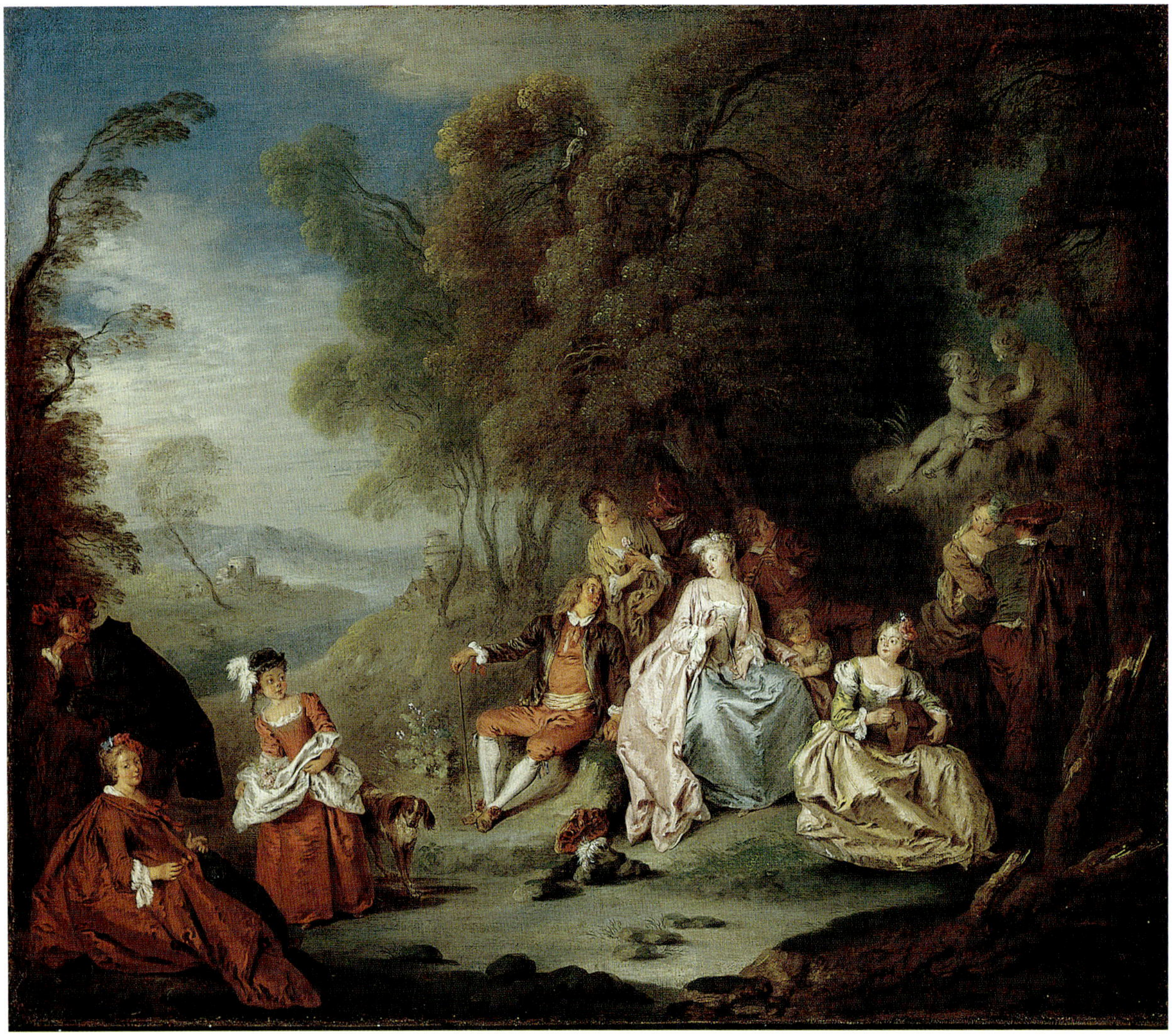

Jean-Baptiste Pater, ***Fête Champêtre***, c. 1730, oil on canvas, 22⅛ × 26 in. (57.9 × 66 cm), Pasadena, Norton Simon Museum, formerly in the Mozelle Sassoon Collection.

Boucher; and works by Jean-Marc Nattier and François-Hubert Drouias.

Luxurious French snuffboxes were another interest of Mozelle's. Made of chased gold, often set with pearls or precious stones, these tiny, jeweled treasures combined the flawless expertise of the goldsmith and the painter, reflecting "in miniature the life and customs of the fashionable world of their day."[37] Small as they were, their delicately worked surfaces often had portraits or reproductions of famous paintings. In *ancien régime* Paris, grandees of the court could have several hundred for storing different things and even for different seasons.

Mozelle's collection of Chelsea scent bottles had no equal, a profusion of figurines in hard and soft paste, often gilt-mounted. Although Mozelle's porcelain came from several manufactories, she had a predilection for Sèvres. Here she was following British precedent. Members of the royal family and the aristocracy had long been avid

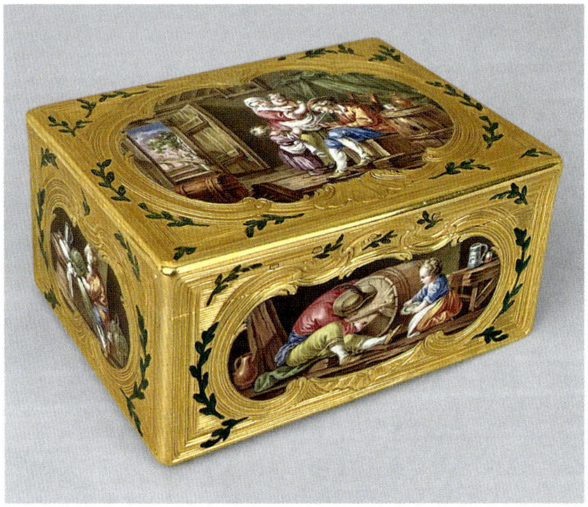

Jean Ducrollay, snuffbox, 1757–58, gold and enamel, 1⅝ × 3⅛ × 2⅜ in. (4.1 × 8.1 × 6 cm), New York, Metropolitan Museum of Art, gift of James Donahue, 1954, formerly in the Mozelle Sassoon Collection.

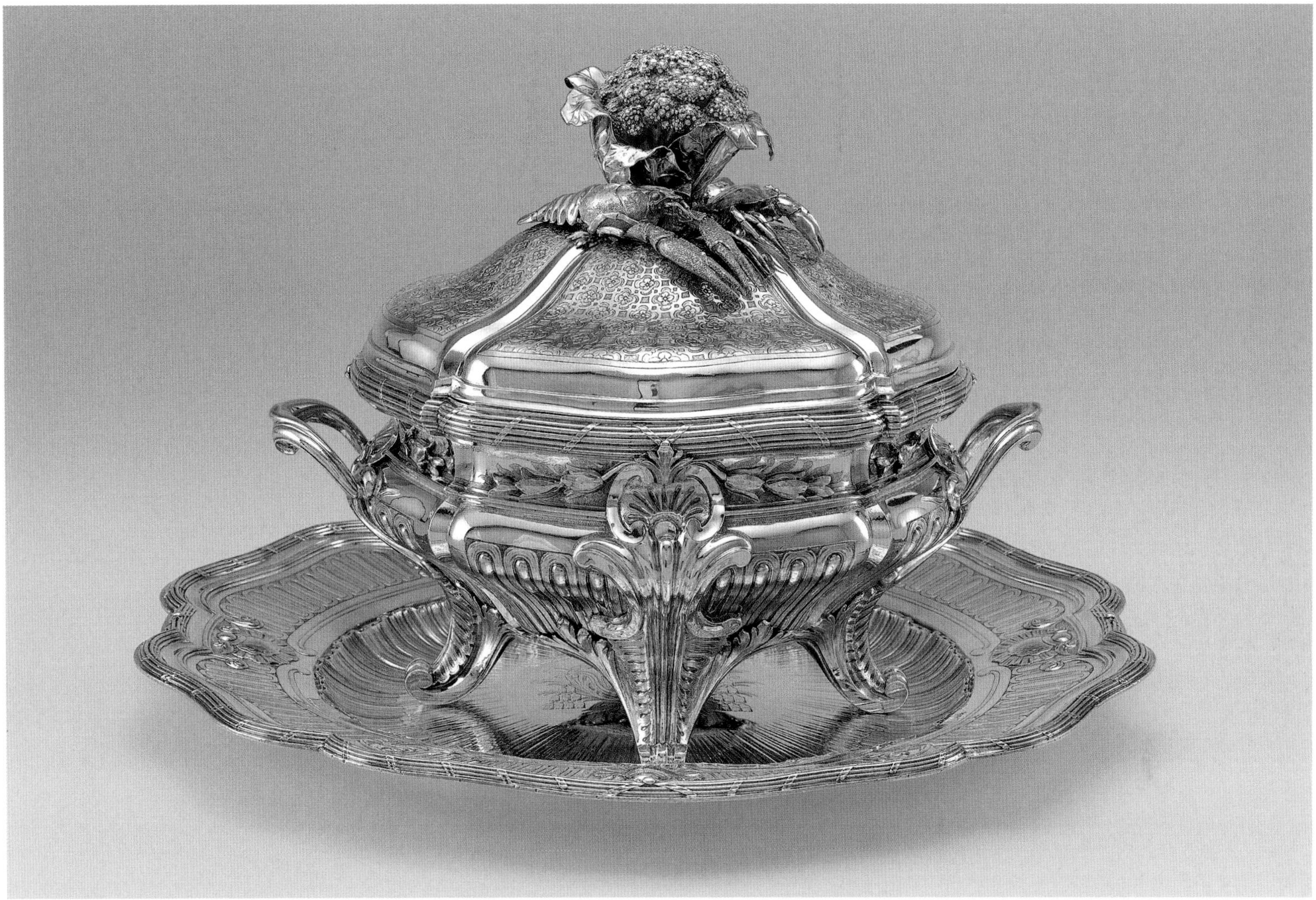

Thomas Germain, lidded tureen, liner, and stand (one of a pair), Paris, c. 1744–50, silver, 11⅛ × 13¾ × 11⅛ in. (28.4 × 34.9 × 28.3 cm), Los Angeles, J. Paul Getty Museum, formerly in the Mozelle Sassoon Collection.

collectors, and King George IV had amassed the best collection in existence. Of unsurpassed technical quality, these exquisite, labor-intensive products relied on a specialized division of labor, from the Sèvres chemists who developed vivid colors to the modelers who created molds, to the gilders and artists. A single plate could take more than a year to produce, and the services often numbered hundreds of pieces. The aesthetic side was just as compelling: each item was an opulent, brilliantly colored microcosm, freighted with references to art, literature, mythology, opera, or natural history.

Among Mozelle's prized Sèvres possessions was a pair of green-ground pot-pourri vases with foliate handles in soft paste. The cartouches show bucolic scenes after Boucher—*Ismène and Daphnis* and *The Bagpipe*—an artist much copied at Vincennes and Sèvres, sometimes with a certain amount of license. A cabaret set dated 1758 also shows scenes *dans le goût de Boucher*.[38] There is a bold contrast between the apple-green scrolls framing the cartouches and the *gros bleu* background with *oeil de perdrix* (partridge eye: the dotted circles introduced in the eighteenth century). Painted and signed by the artist André-Vincent Vieillard, the set shows children playing music or working in the garden.

In his work on the Sassoon dynasty, Cecil Roth attributes the art collecting exclusively to Mozelle's husband, Meyer. Though interested in the arts, Meyer died in 1924, and Mozelle's greatest portraits were all bought in the 1930s. After her husband's death, she gained control of her finances, which enabled her to increase the scale and quality of her acquisitions and broaden her philanthropy considerably. In 1927, she donated funds to build a library for the British Institute in Paris. In 1936, the Mozelle Sassoon High Voltage X-Ray Therapy Department opened in St. Bartholomew's Hospital for cancer research, one of many hospitals she assisted. Mozelle's cultural philanthropy was generous and open-minded. When St. Paul's

BELOW
Chelsea Porcelain Manufactory, England, scent bottle, Red Anchor period, c. 1755, soft-paste porcelain, 4⅛ in. high (10.6 cm), New York, Metropolitan Museum of Art, gift of Irwin Untermyer, 1971, formerly in the Mozelle Sassoon Collection.

BELOW RIGHT
Meissen Manufactory, Germany, theater figure, 1750–52, hard-paste porcelain, 8¼ in. high (21 cm), New York, Metropolitan Museum of Art, gift of Irwin Untermyer, 1964, formerly in the Mozelle Sassoon Collection.

RIGHT
Sèvres Manufactory, France, Sèvres dark blue and green cabaret set, 1758, painted by André Vincent Vieillard, soft-paste porcelain with enamel and gilding, teapot: 4¾ × 6⅝ × 3½ in. (12 × 17 × 9 cm), cup and saucer: 2¾ × 5½ in. in diameter (7 × 14 cm), collection of Adrian Sassoon, formerly in the Mozelle Sassoon Collection.

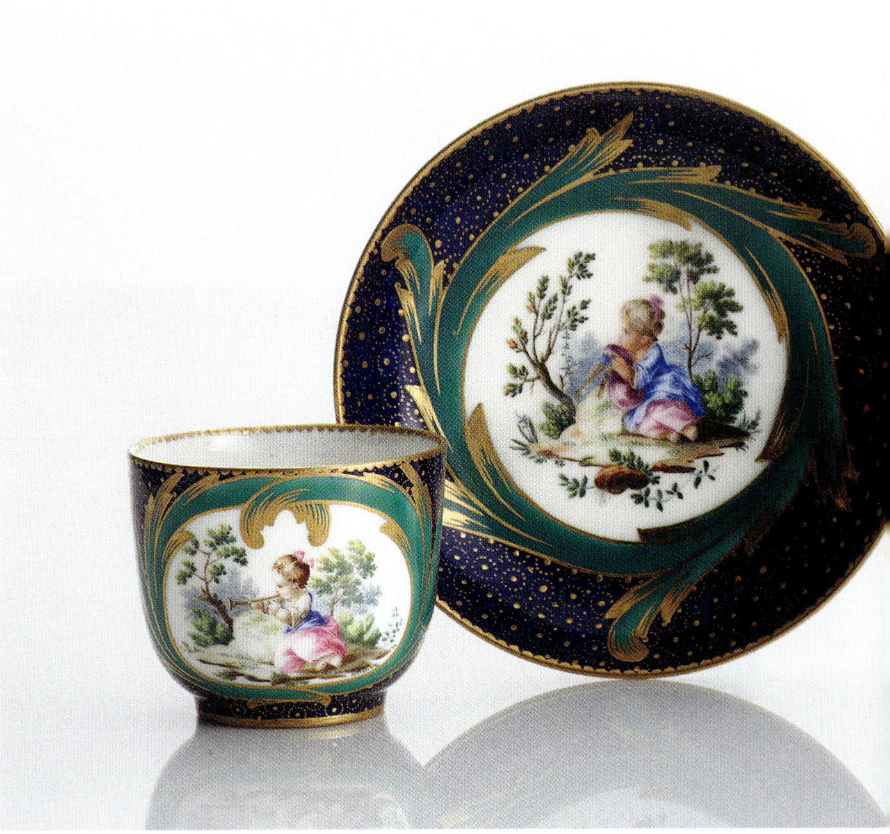

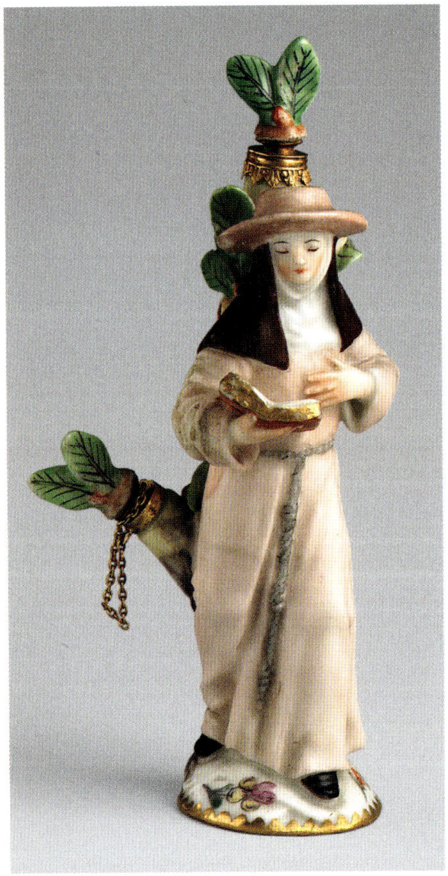

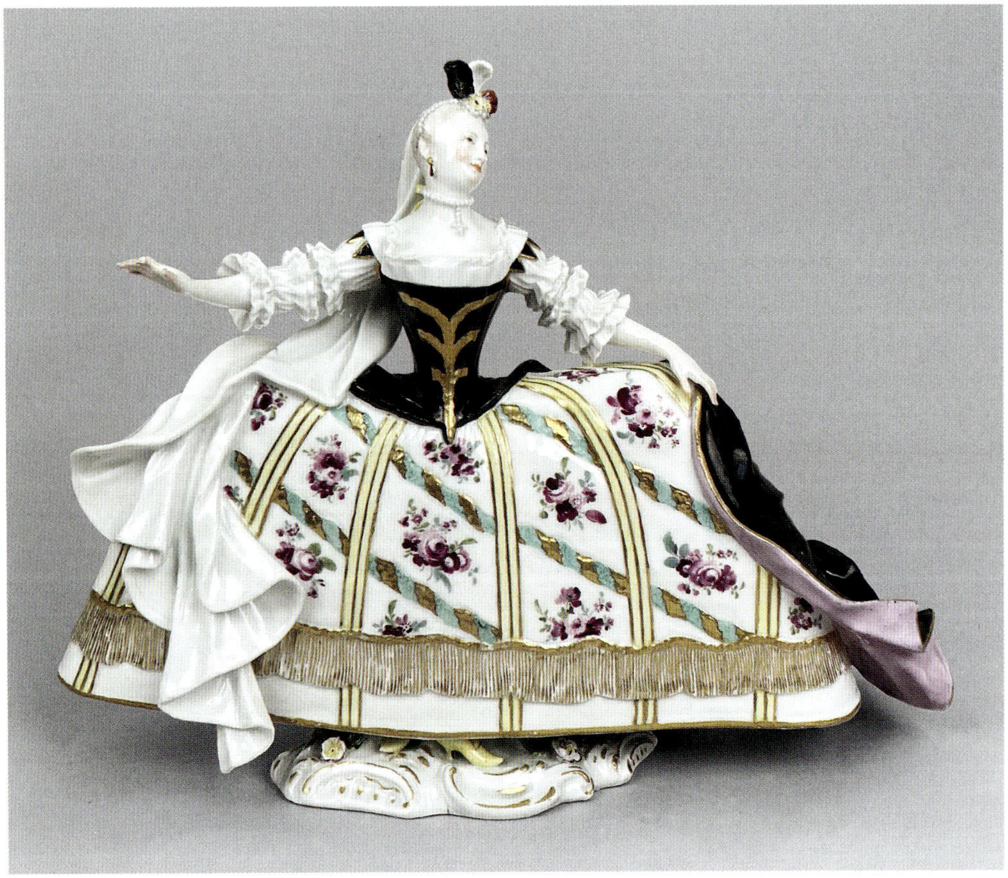

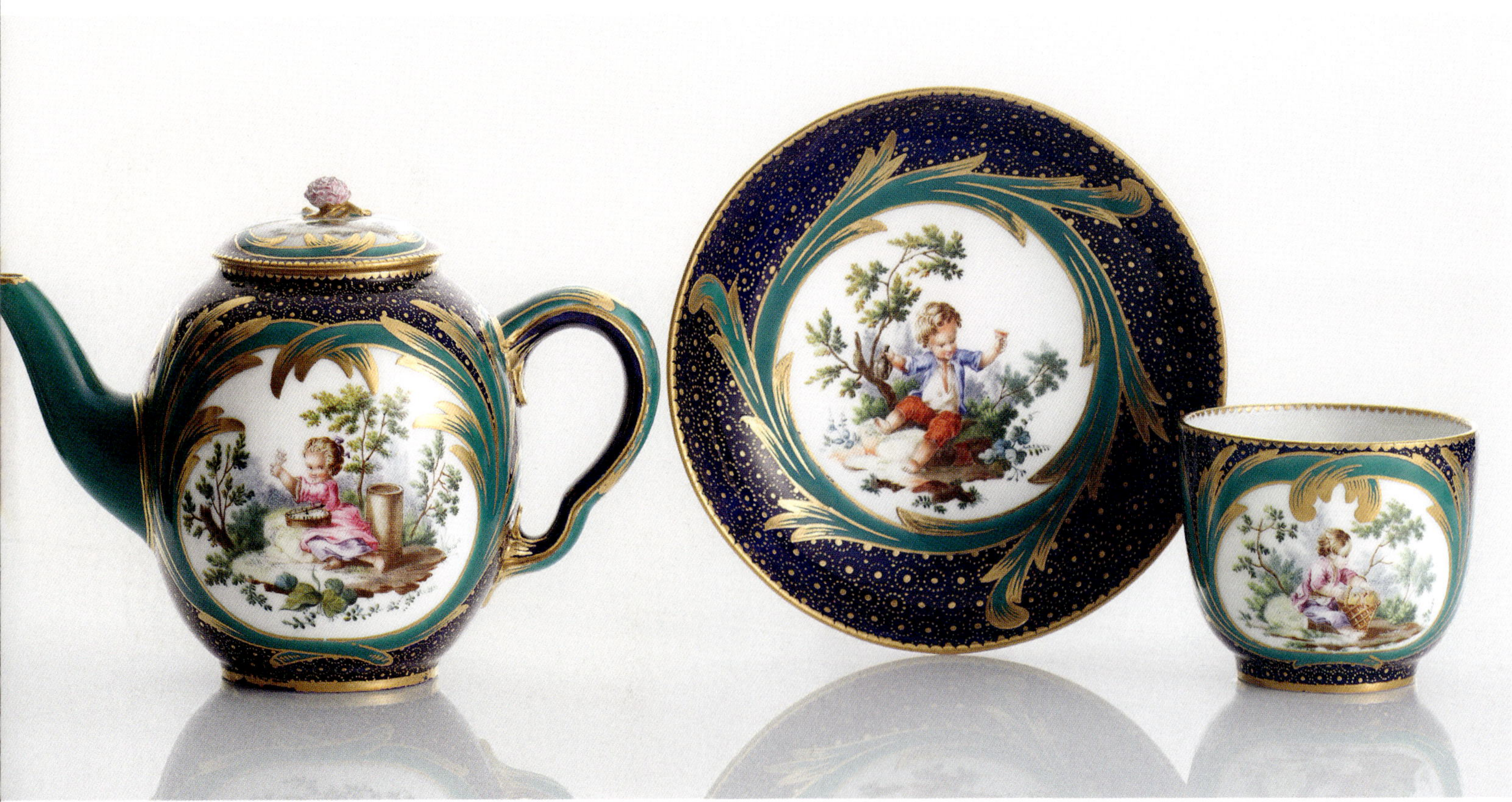

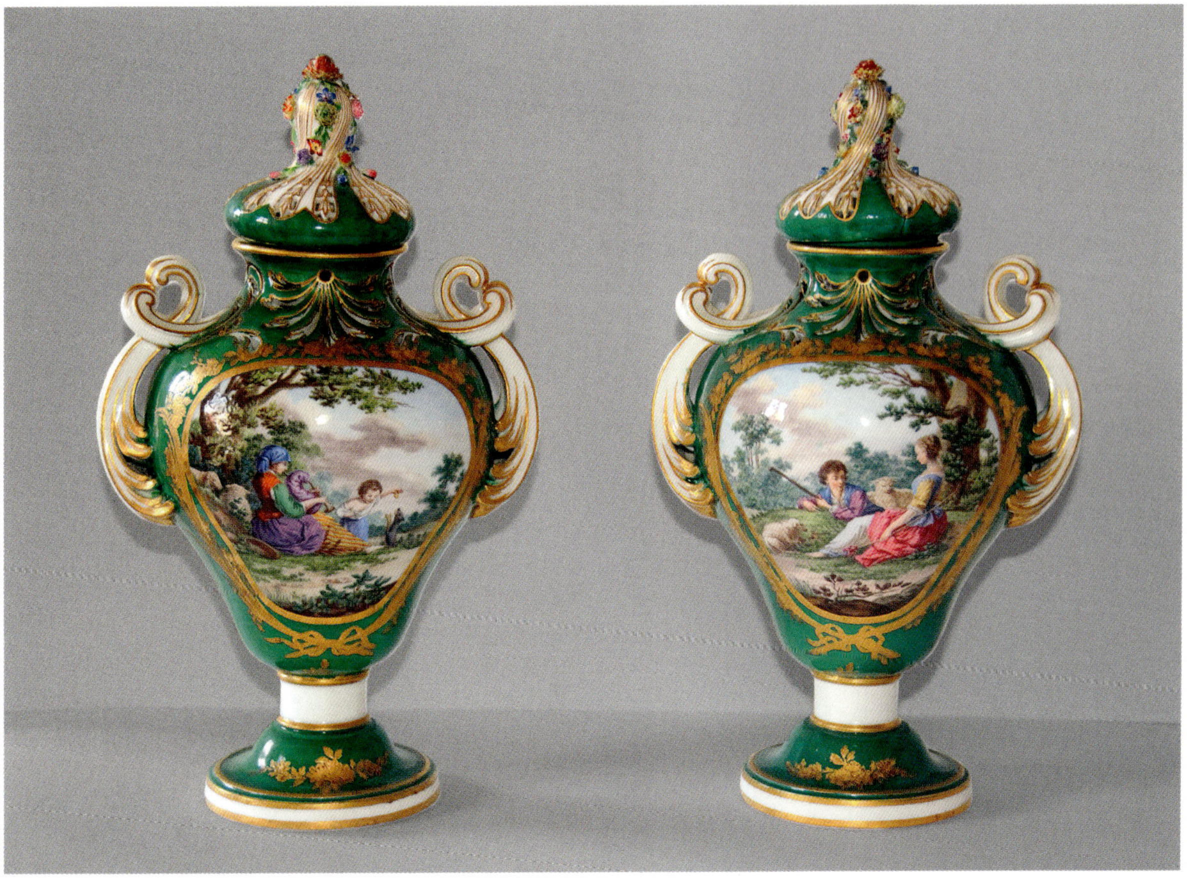

Sèvres Manufactory, France, pair of Sèvres green-ground pot-pourri *feuilles de mirte* vases and two covers, 1763, painted by Pierre-Nicolas Pithou, soft-paste porcelain with enamel and gilding, 11¼ in. high (28.5 cm), private collection, France, formerly in the Mozelle Sassoon Collection.

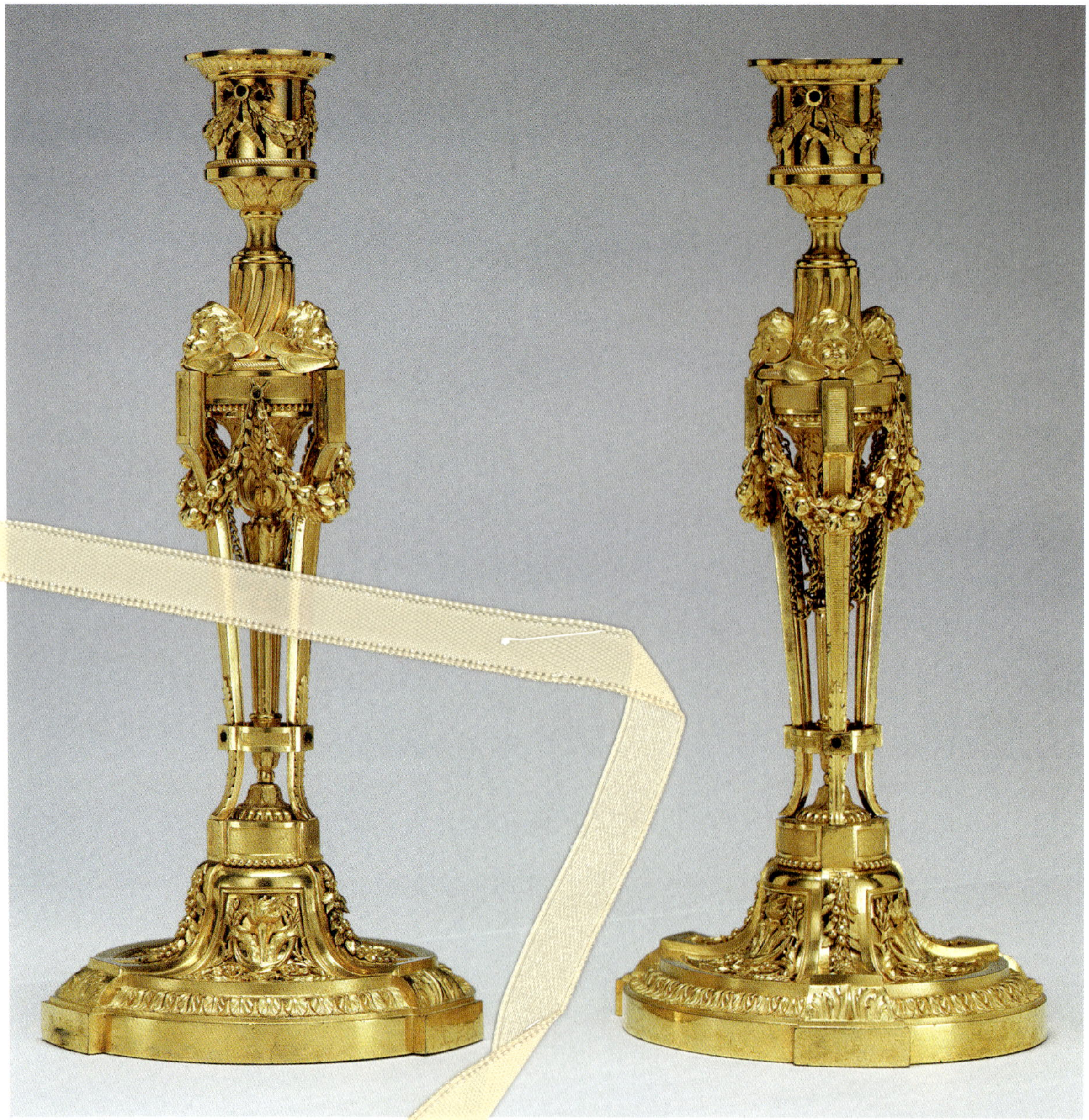

Étienne Martincourt, pair of candlesticks, Paris, c. 1780, gilt bronze, 11¾ × 5⅜ in. (29.9 × 13.7 cm), Los Angeles, J. Paul Getty Museum, formerly in the Meyer Sassoon Collection.

Cathedral was damaged during World War II, she contributed substantial amounts to its restoration. Two years before she died, Mozelle was one of the donors whose largesse allowed the National Gallery to buy Leonardo's Burlington House Cartoon showing the Virgin and Child with Saint Anne and John the Baptist. Several articles were written about Hannah's collection during her lifetime, but there is almost nothing about Mozelle's despite her connoisseurship, exhibition loans, and munificent philanthropy.[39]

Neither Mozelle nor Hannah has been accorded the place they deserve in the history of British art. Connoisseurship was long attributed almost exclusively to empirical observation rather than intellection, and denied its collaborative aspects. In recent decades, scholars have reassessed our notions of women as collectors and shed light on the specifically Jewish contribution to the field through international networks linking collectors, dealers, donors, and their cultural politics.[40] Cultivated, well-traveled, and multilingual, Hannah and Mozelle had considerable income at their disposal and ready access to notable private collections that enabled them to widen the scope of their expertise. Wealth gave them access to the finest art dealers, facilitating acquisitions. Living with art honed their taste and allowed close reading and careful analysis. Their collections, carefully assembled around pieces of similar quality, origin, and age, made significant contributions to scholarship.

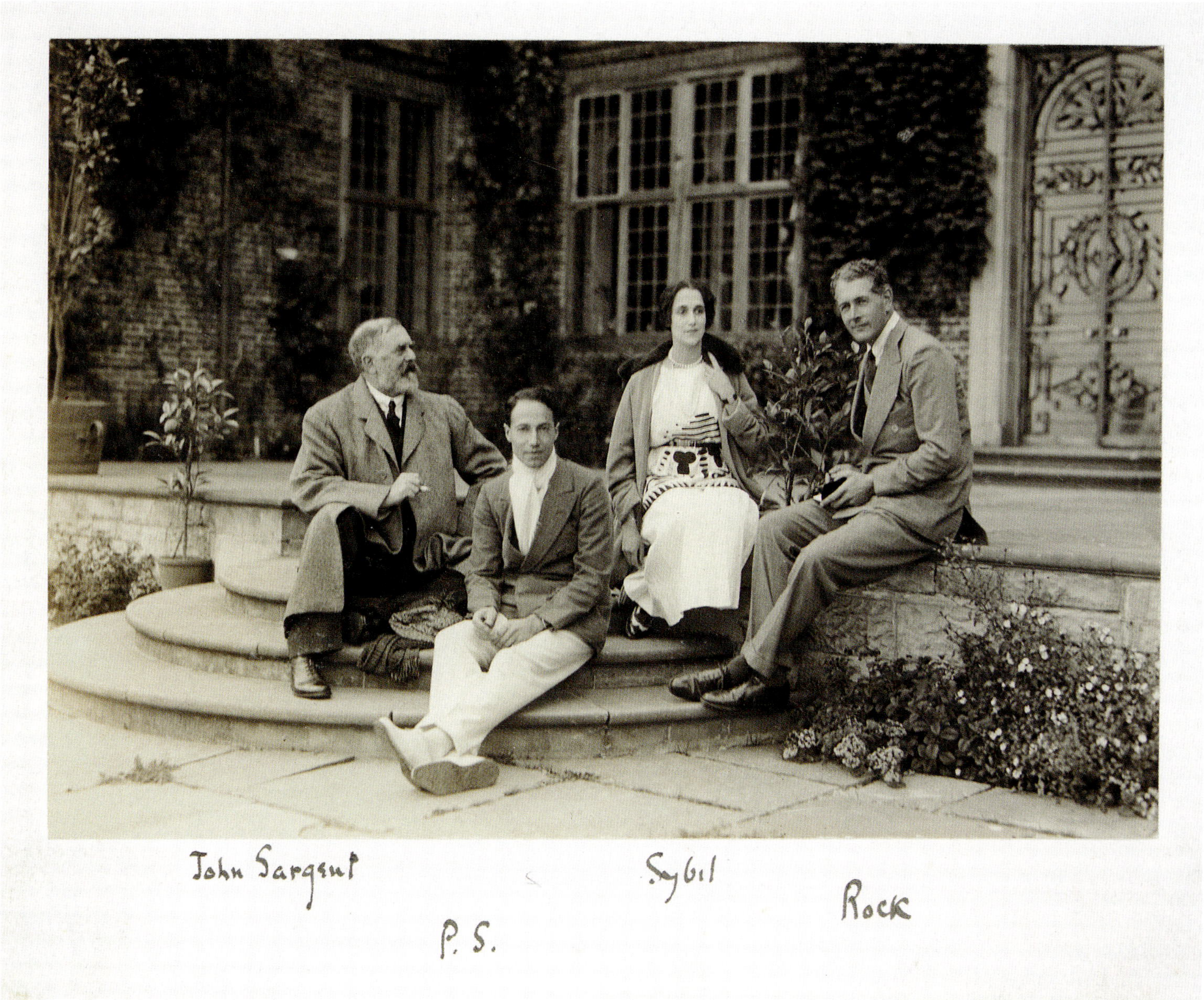

Left to right: John Singer Sargent, Philip Sassoon, Sybil Sassoon, Countess of Rocksavage, and George ("Rock"), Earl of Rocksavage, August 30, 1920, from the Port Lympne visitors' book, vol. I, 1919–28, private collection.

Sybil

Sybil Sassoon, unlike other women in her family, has received considerable attention in the literature. She and her brother, Philip, grew up surrounded by exquisite art and prominent artists. Like her mother, Lady Sassoon, young Sybil kept an autograph book, her own intimate "collection" of works by the likes of Sargent, Orpen, Philpot, and Max Beerbohm. Sargent, a close friend, rendered Lady Sassoon and her children in magnificent oil paintings and several charcoal portraits. Sybil became his favorite subject. He had first captured her in a drawing in 1910, while she was in mourning for her mother and living with her aunt Louise, who commissioned the portrait. In 1905, Sargent had depicted another member of the family in mourning, likely his first rendering of a Sassoon. His magnificent portrait of Flora (Mrs. Ernest G. Raphael) shows her in a fitted black dress, probably following the death of her father, Reuben, Sybil's great-uncle.[41] Sybil's 1913 oil portrait, a present from the artist upon her marriage to George Cholmondeley, Earl of Rocksavage (and future 5th Marquess of Cholmondeley), shows the beautiful young sitter enveloped in a woolen shawl Sargent had also gifted her. In 1922, when he had almost abandoned portraiture, he depicted her on a monumental canvas, clad in a Spanish court–style dress he had commissioned from the House of Worth. Sargent also persuaded the American sculptor Paul Manship to create a bust of Sybil and drew

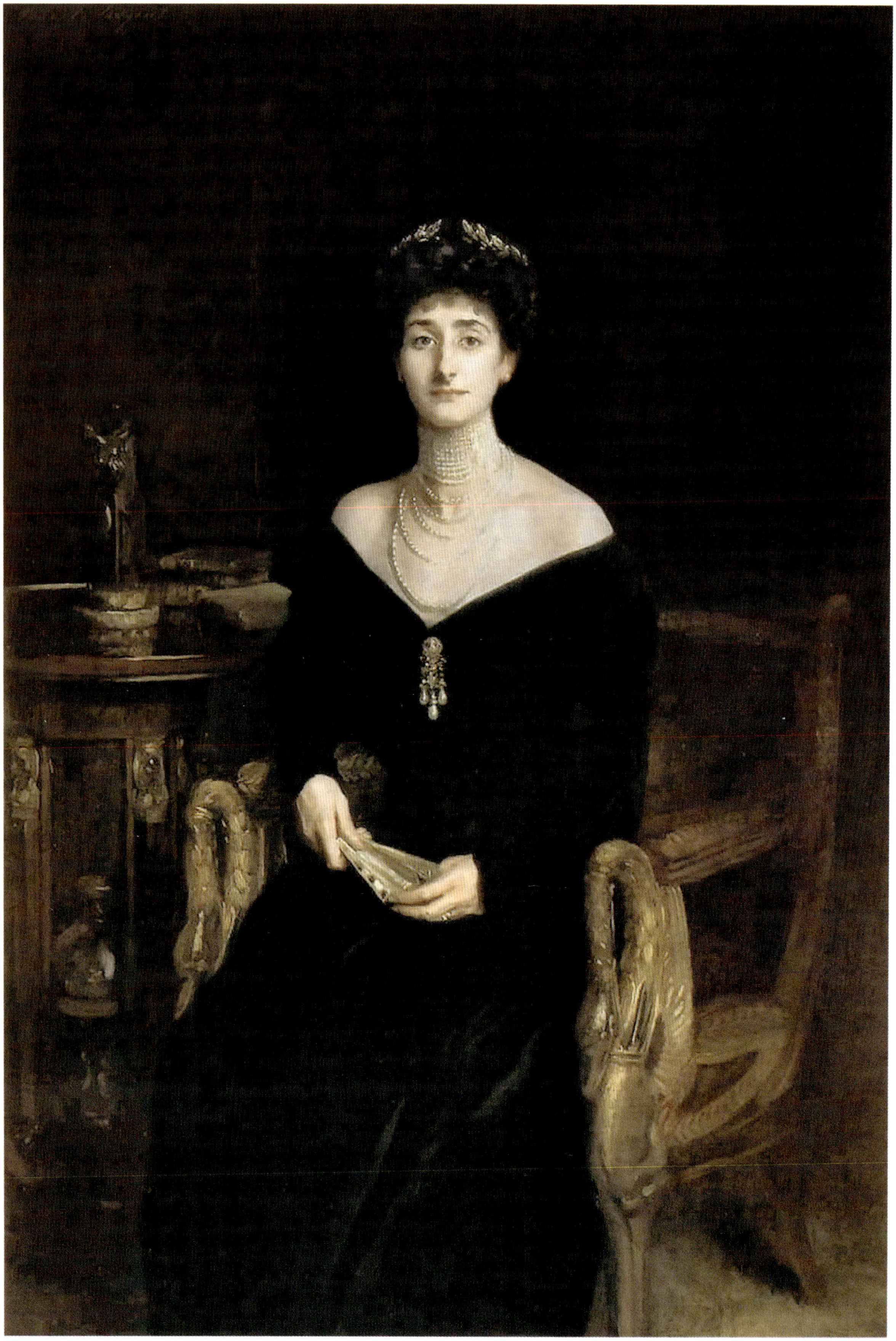

John Singer Sargent, *Mrs. Ernest G. Raphael* (Flora Cecilia Sassoon), 1905, oil on canvas, 64½ × 45 in. (163.8 × 114.3 cm), private collection.

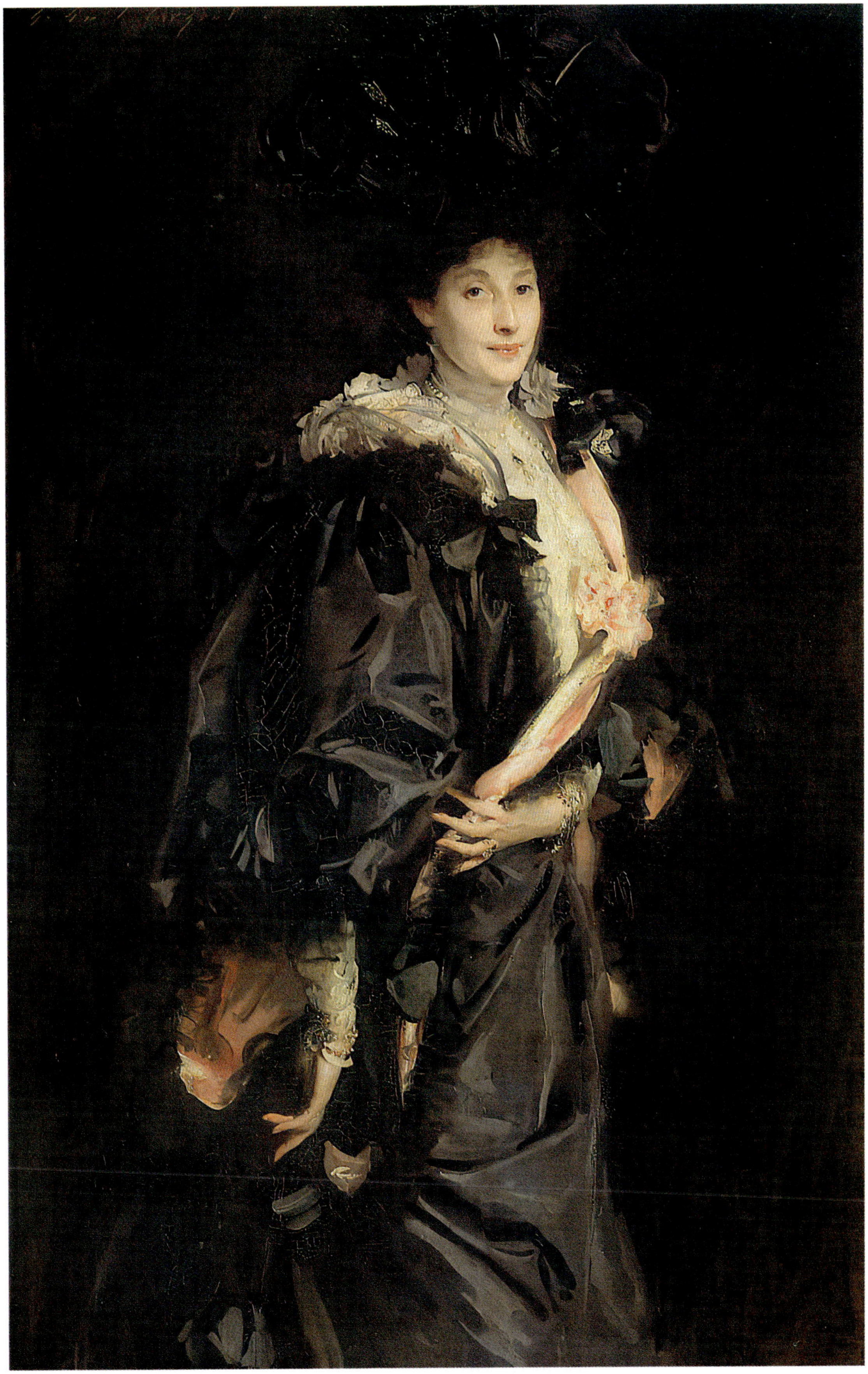

John Singer Sargent, *Aline de Rothschild, Lady Sassoon,* 1907, oil on canvas, 64¼ × 42½ in. (163 × 108 cm), Norfolk, UK, Houghton Hall Collection.

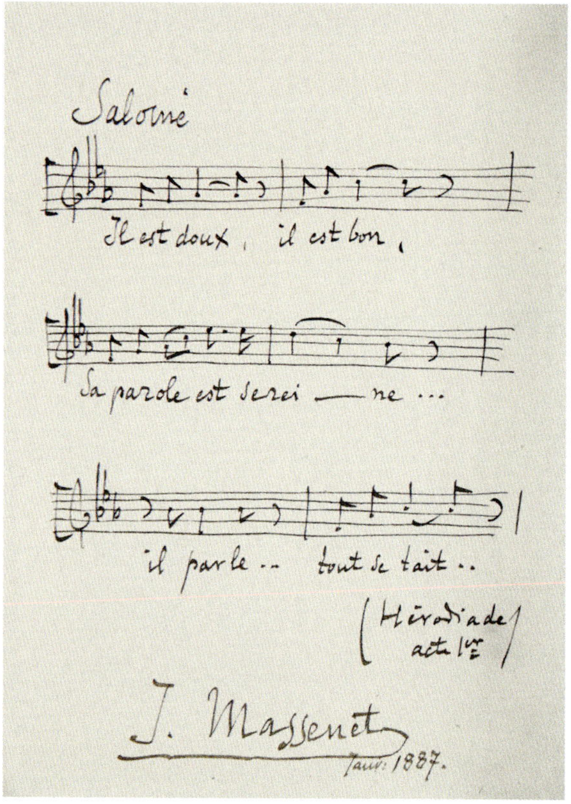

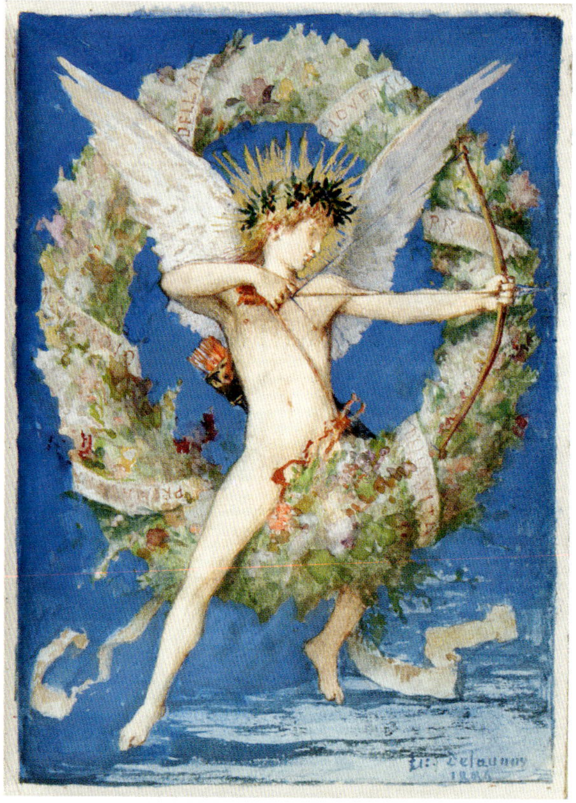

Jules Massenet, "Il est doux, il est bon," Salome's aria from his 1881 opera *Hérodiade*, 1887, ink on paper, 9½ × 6¼ in. (24.1 × 15.9 cm), from the autograph book of Aline de Rothschild, containing sketches, notes, and music scores, Norfolk, UK, Houghton Hall Collection.

Jules-Élie Delaunay, *Personification of Spring*, 1886, watercolor or tempera on paper, 9½ × 6¼ in. (24.1 × 15.9 cm), from the autograph book of Aline de Rothschild, containing sketches, notes, and music scores, Norfolk, UK, Houghton Hall Collection.

Manship in her autograph book, making a preparatory sketch.[42] Other admiring artists also created portraits of her. Orpen depicted her in 1913 in a glamorous Fortuny dress. Joseph Duveen acquired the work and presented it to Sybil. Charles Sims emphasized her stylish figure, painting her in long décolleté dresses at the ballroom of Philip's Park Lane residence and at home with her young son. An art connoisseur, Sybil was the one to discover in the Cholmondeley holdings a painting that turned out to be a masterpiece: Hans Holbein's *A Lady with a Squirrel and a Starling* (*Anne Lovell*?), c. 1526–28, now in the National Gallery, London.[43]

Sybil's major undertaking was to restore Houghton Hall, in Norfolk, to its former glory. The Cholmondeleys' grand Palladian house for generations, it had been built originally for Robert Walpole, the first British prime minister. Over the years, Sybil would acquire important works of art for the house, some connected to its history, such as a portrait of Walpole as a hunter by John Wootton and others created by artists in her circle, such as *The Play Scene from Hamlet* by Orpen.[44] After Philip's death in 1939, she inherited much of his art collection, which she incorporated into Houghton Hall.

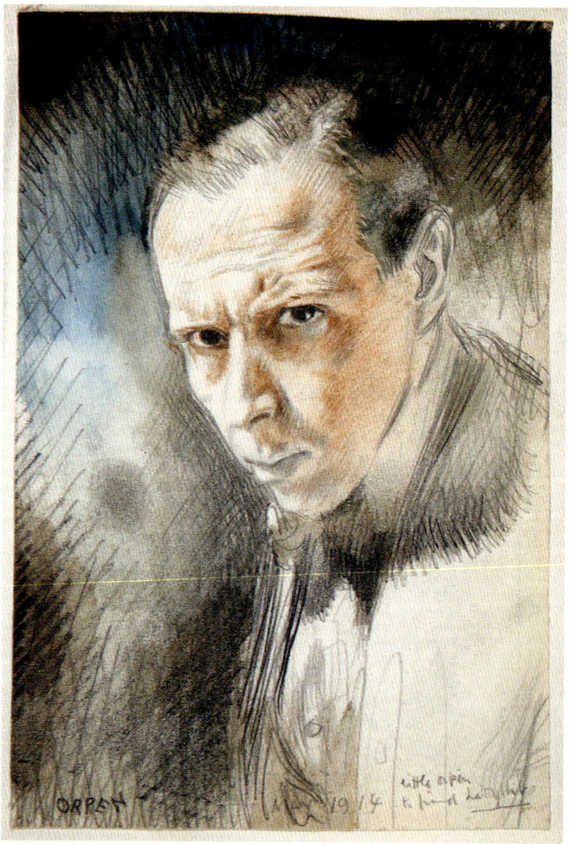

William Orpen, *Self-Portrait*, 1914, pencil and pastel (?) on paper, 9½ × 7½ in. (24.1 × 19.1 cm), from the autograph book of Sybil Sassoon, containing sketches, notes, and music scores, inscribed: "Little Orpen to friend . . . Lady Sybil," Norfolk, UK, Houghton Hall Collection.

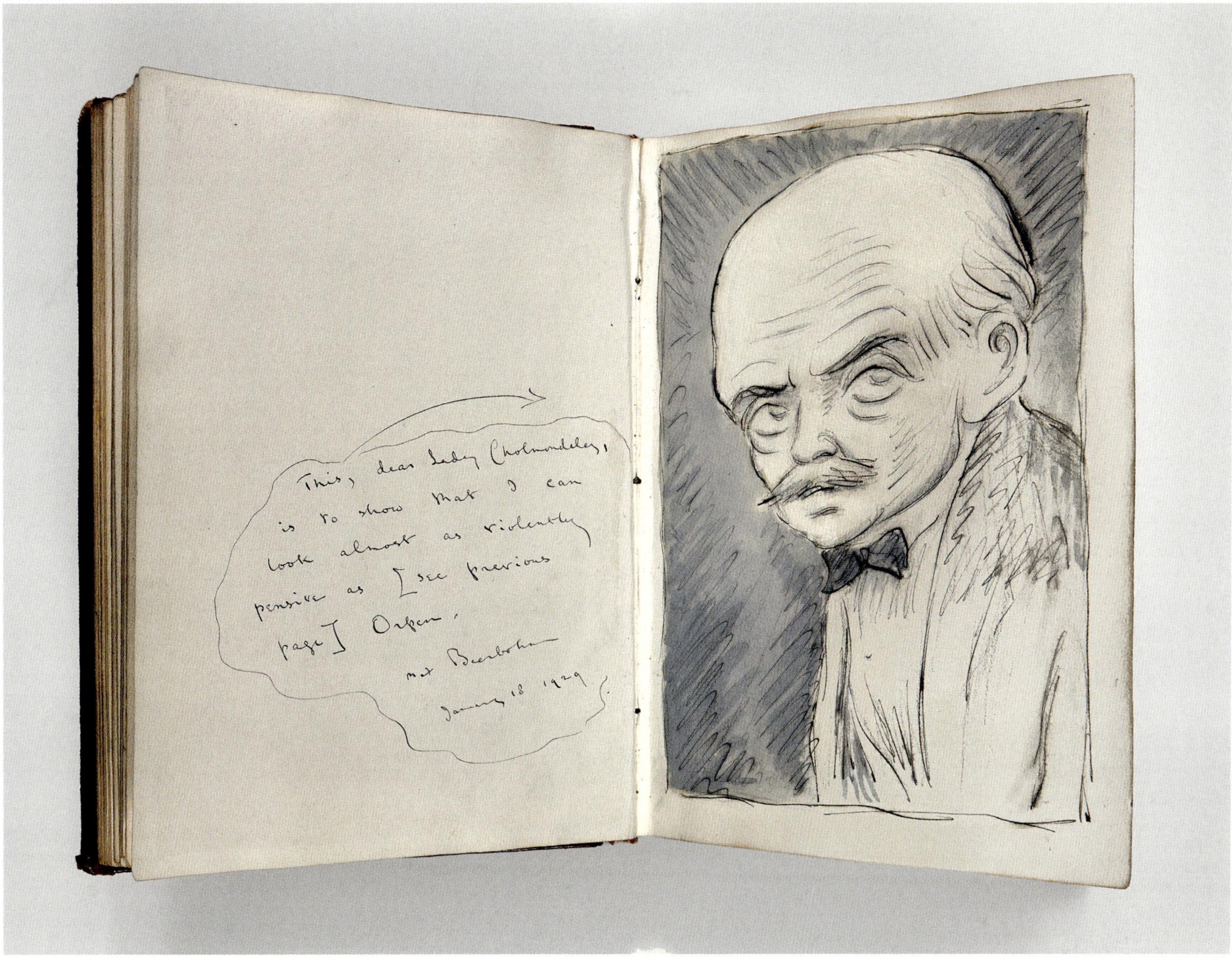

Henry Maximilian "Max" Beerbohm, *Self-Portrait*, 1929, pencil on paper, 9½ × 7½ in. (24.1 × 19.1 cm), from the autograph book of Sybil Sassoon, containing sketches, notes, and music scores, inscribed to her: "This, dear Lady Cholmondeley, is to show that I can look almost as violently pensive as (see previous page) Orpen. Max Beerbohm, January 18, 1929," Norfolk, UK, Houghton Hall Collection.

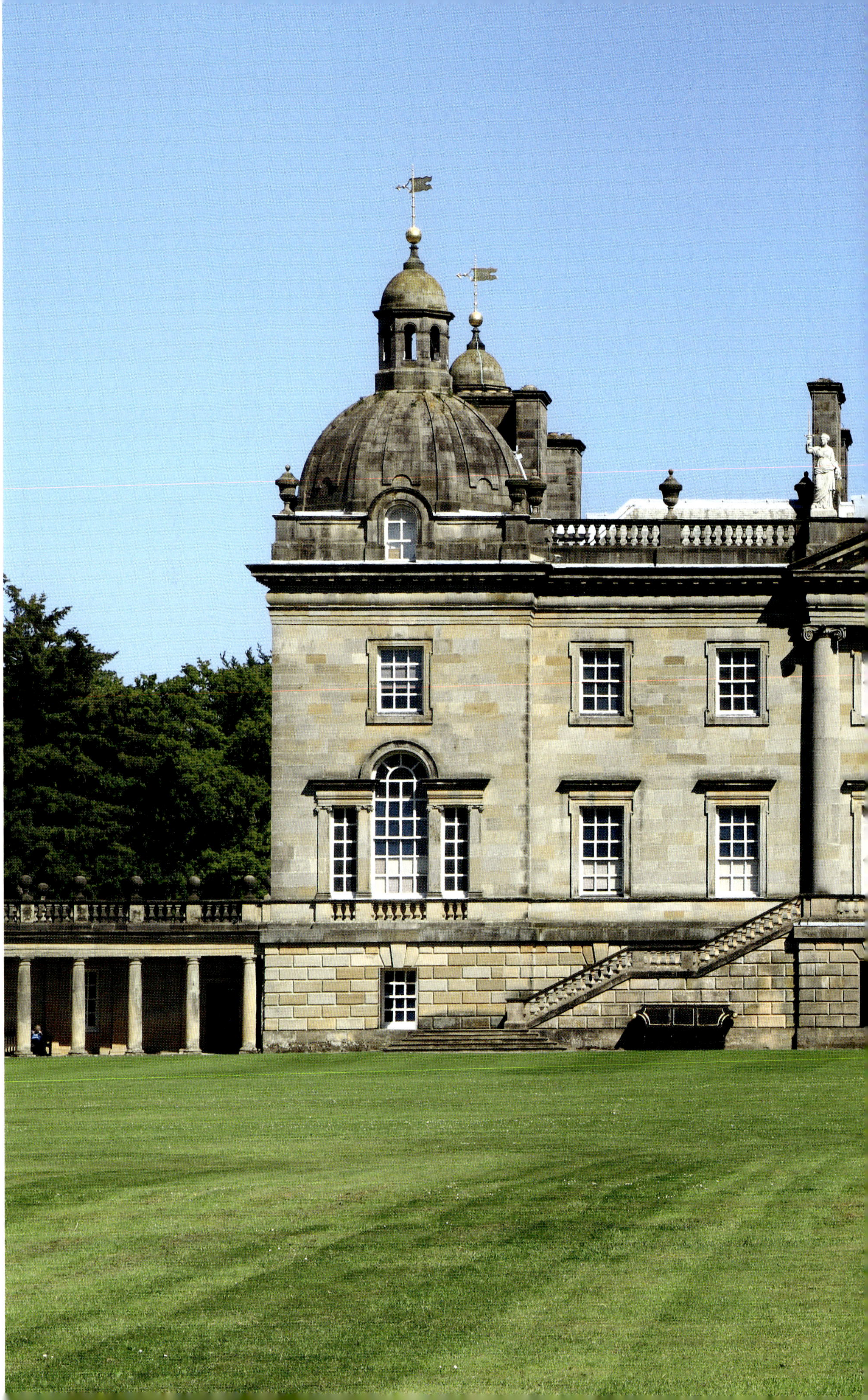

Houghton Hall, Norfolk, home of the Marquess of Cholmondeley, Colen Campbell and James Gibbs, architects, interiors by William Kent. Houghton Hall was built in the 1720s for Robert Walpole, first prime minister of England, and was inherited by the 1st Marquess of Cholmondeley in the late eighteenth century. In 1916, three years after his marriage to Sybil Sassoon, George, Earl of Rocksavage, was given the house by his father. The couple settled at Houghton Hall in 1919.

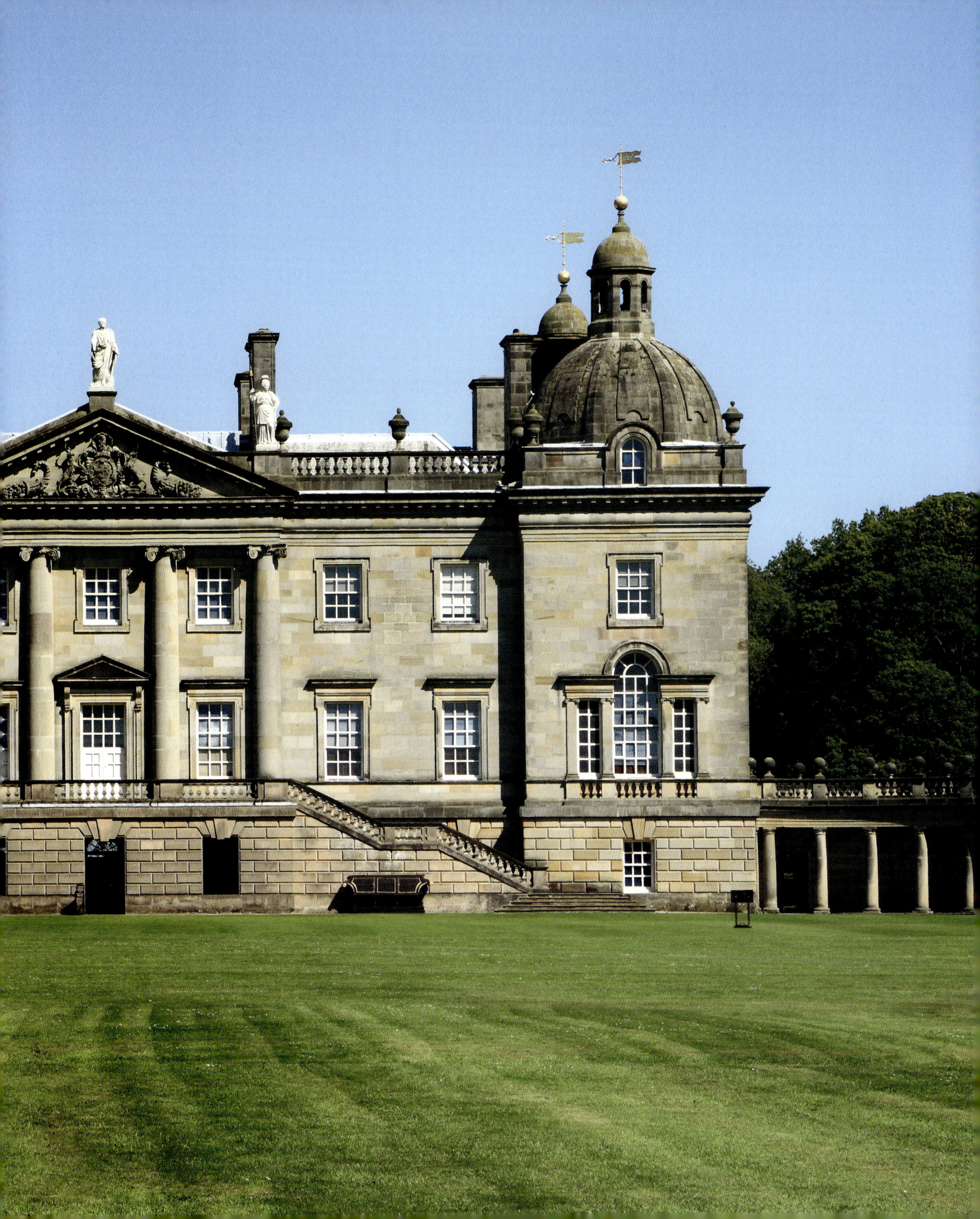

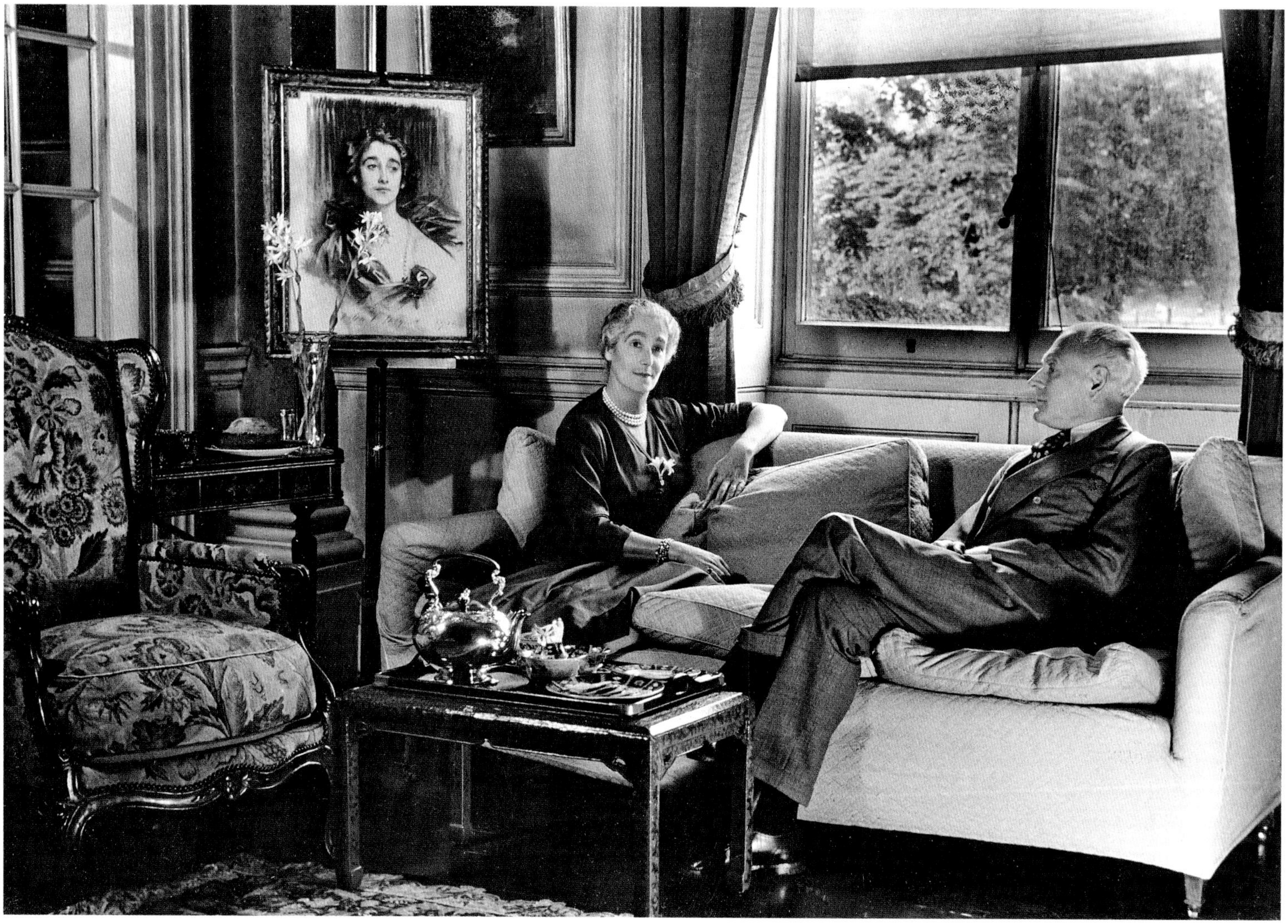

Sybil (Sassoon), Marchioness of Cholmondeley, and her husband at 12 Kensington Palace Gardens, late 1950s or early 1960s, Norfolk, UK, Houghton Hall Collection. At left is John Singer Sargent's 1912 charcoal portrait of her.

OPPOSITE
John Singer Sargent, *Sybil Sassoon*, 1910, charcoal on paper, 29¾ × 24⅛ in. (75.5 × 61.2 cm), private collection.

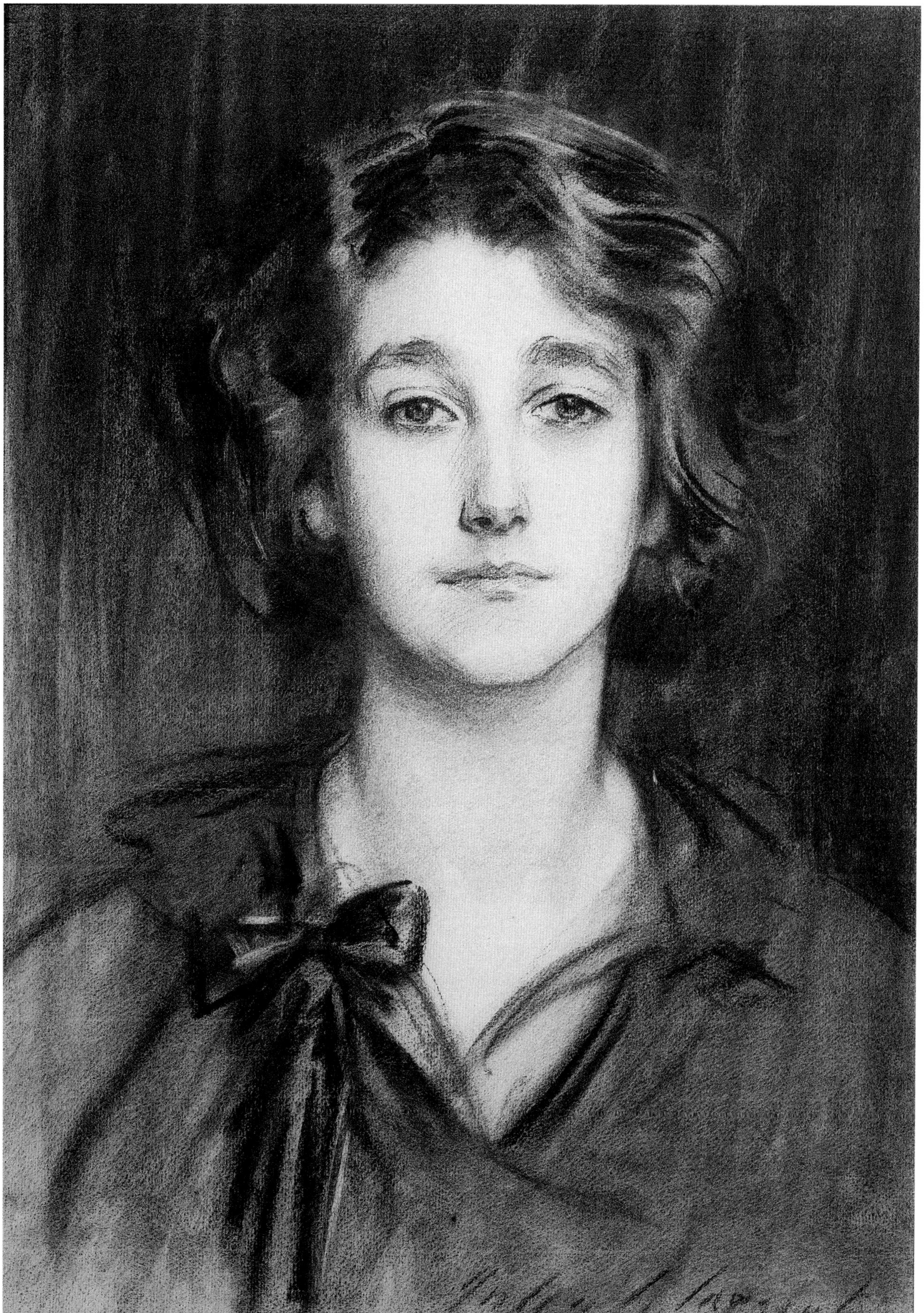

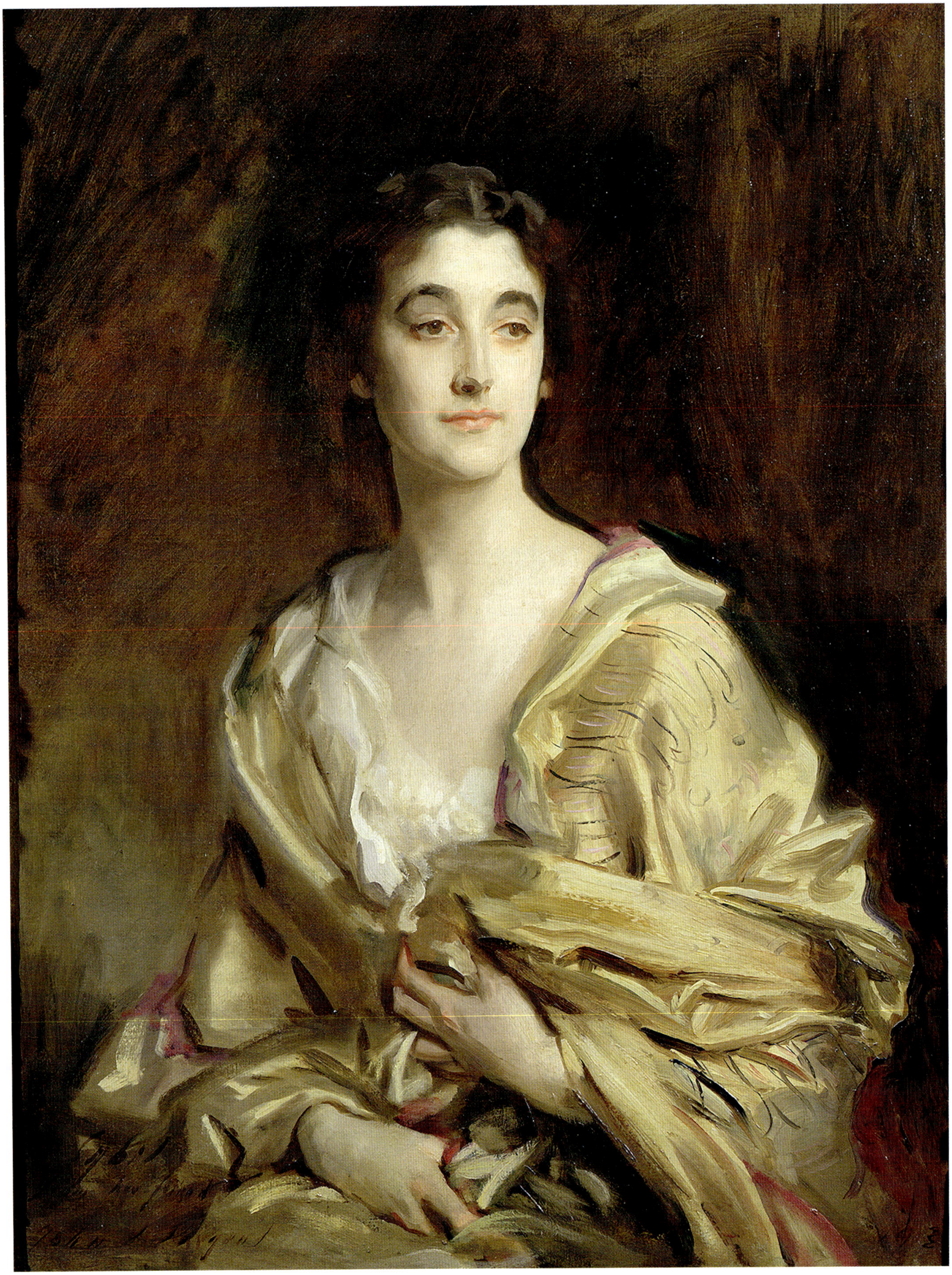

OPPOSITE
John Singer Sargent, *Sybil, Countess of Rocksavage*, 1913, oil on canvas, 33⅞ × 26 in. (86 × 66 cm), inscribed: "To Sybil from her friend John S. Sargent," Norfolk, UK, Houghton Hall Collection.

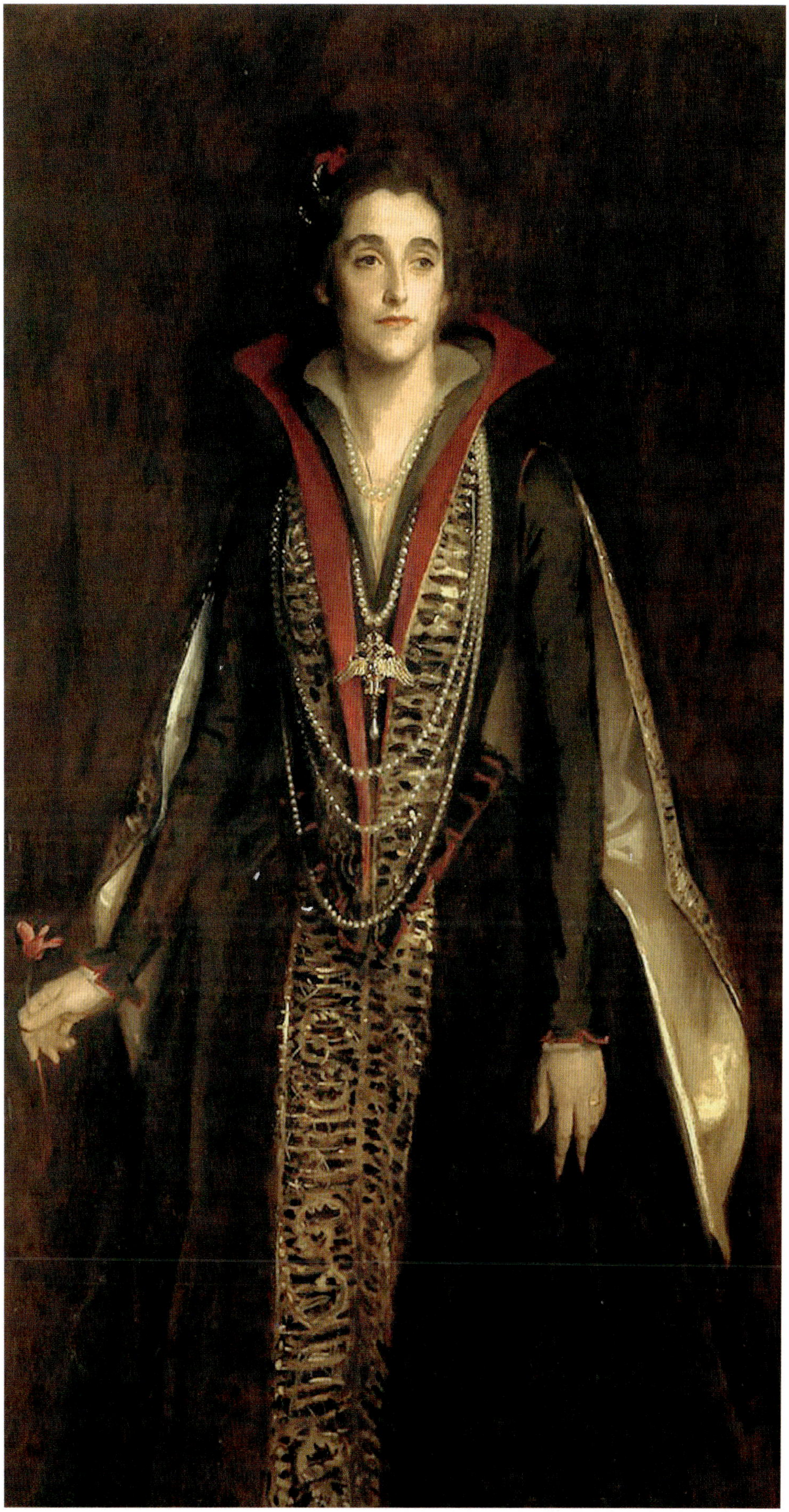

John Singer Sargent, *Sybil, Countess of Rocksavage*, 1922, oil on canvas, 63½ × 35⅝ in. (161.3 × 89.8 cm), Norfolk, UK, Houghton Hall Collection.

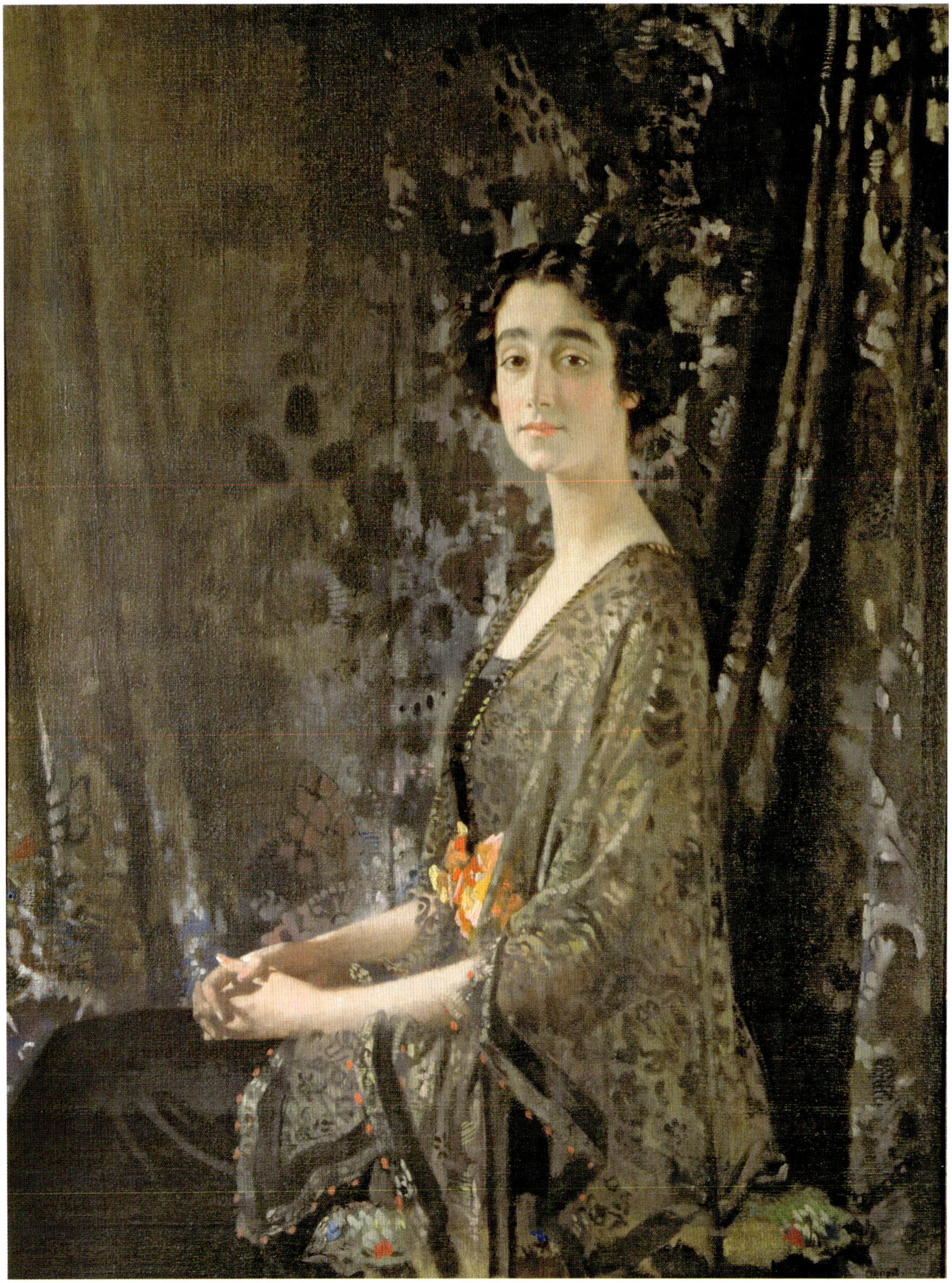

William Orpen, ***Sybil Sassoon, Countess of Rocksavage***, 1913, oil on canvas, 48 × 37¼ in. (121.9 × 94.6 cm), private collection.

OPPOSITE
Sybil at her brother Philip Sassoon's residence, 25 Park Lane, London, with Hans Holbein's *A Lady with a Squirrel and a Starling (Anne Lovell?)*, photographed by Cecil Beaton in the 1920s, London, National Portrait Gallery, accepted in lieu of tax by HM Government and allocated to the Gallery, 1991.

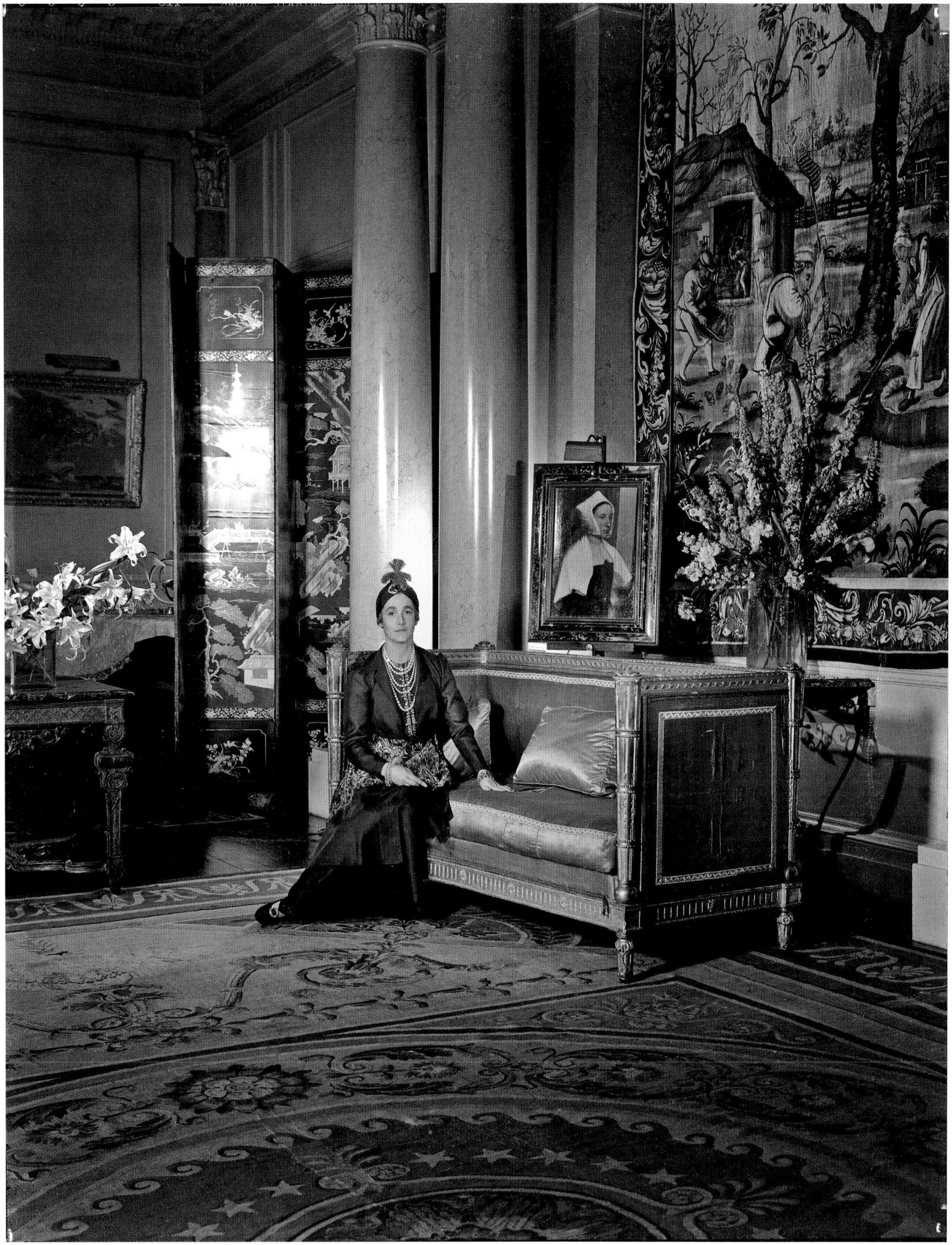

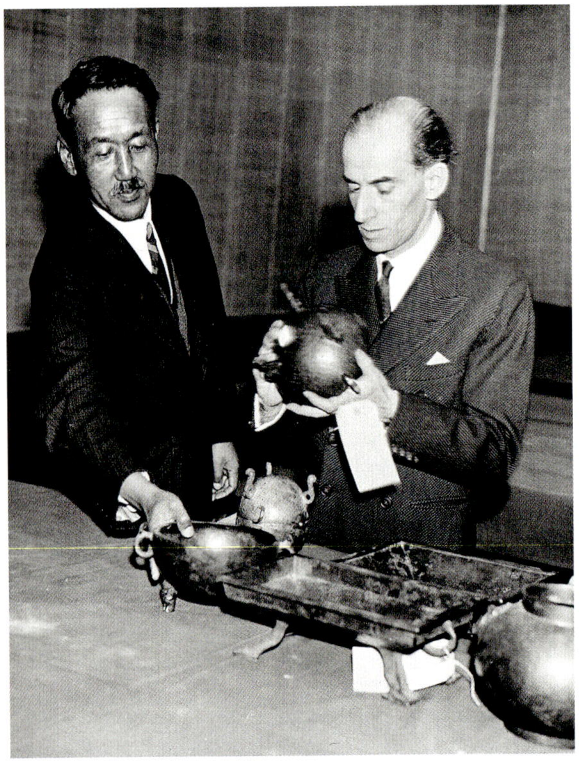

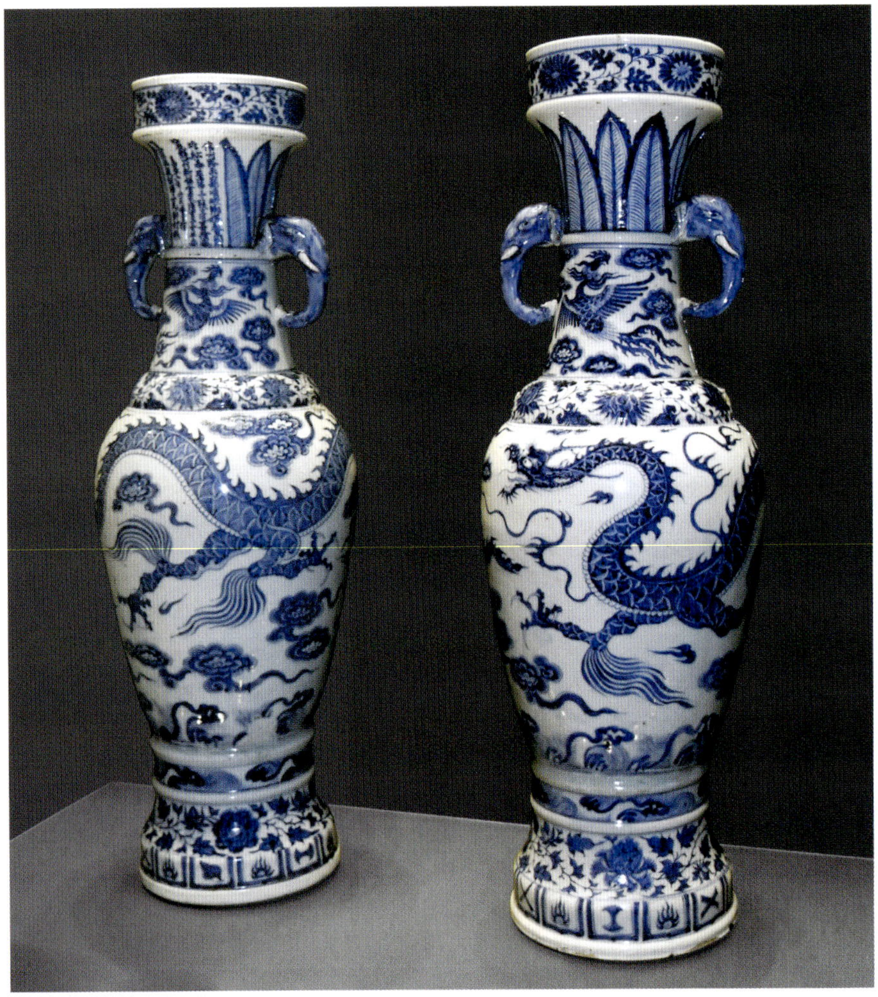

Percival David, exhibition committee director of the *International Exhibition of Chinese Art*, held at the Royal Academy of Arts in London in 1935–36, and Tang Xifen, exhibition secretary, examining exhibits in 1935.

The David vases, 1351, Jingdezhen, China, Yuan dynasty (1271–1368), porcelain, 25 × 8⅛ in. in diameter (63.6 × 20.7 cm), London, British Museum, on loan from the Sir Percival David Foundation of Chinese Art.

Percival

Chinese art was well represented in a family with so many connections to Asia. Although Percival began collecting porcelain in London, his travels in China slowly transformed his taste and whetted his appetite for older and more valuable specimens. In 1925, the Palace Museum in the Forbidden City opened its doors to the public. After the fall of the Qing dynasty, hundreds of antiquities were stolen from royal residences across China.[45] Percival became a major donor in efforts to support the Palace Museum, and his vision of Chinese art would be shaped by what he saw there. In 1927, however, he managed to acquire fifty choice pieces of porcelain from the imperial collections through complicated negotiations that would not meet today's ethical standards concerning provenance and cultural appropriation.[46]

The superlative quality of Percival's collection required more than wealth. His visual acumen and deep knowledge of Chinese art were enhanced by his love of travel and research, which enabled him to carefully study artifacts. In Japan, he spent time in Nara, examining the holdings of the imperial treasures in the Shōsō-in repository of Tōdai-ji Temple; it boasts an extraordinary collection of Japanese, Chinese, and Korean artifacts acquired over the centuries, which he later published.[47] Thanks to his funding, the excavations of the Seobongchong Tomb in South Korea yielded notable pieces of Korean pottery and porcelain. Together with Robert Lockhart Hobson, an expert on Far Eastern ceramics, he studied and published the superb collection of Chinese porcelain from the Yuan and Ming dynasties housed in Istanbul's Topkapı Palace.[48]

In 1929 Percival began to publish in academic journals, focusing mainly on ceramics, thereby strengthening his international credentials as a scholar. To work with primary sources, including his own collection of rare Chinese books, he learned both modern and, apparently, classical Chinese. This allowed him to translate a late fourteenth-century treatise on Chinese connoisseurship, the *Ko Ku Yao Lun*, which appeared in print after his death. Although the edition has been subject to critique, it nonetheless bears witness to the scope of Percival's intellectual ambitions and self-confidence.[49] In that work he was consciously emulating "traditional Chinese connoisseurs who themselves made a priority of scholarship and previous commentary in their quest for authenticity."[50]

Among other important publications, Percival sponsored an edition of Marco Polo's *Description of the World*, based on an eighteenth-century Latin manuscript Percival had found in the Cathedral Library of Toledo. The four resulting volumes went beyond translation, relying on a thorough comparison with other extant manuscripts in different parts of the world. For this project Percival enlisted Paul Pelliot, a French sinologist and orientalist, and Arthur Christopher Moule, professor of Chinese at Cambridge. He likewise financed the publication of Hobson's *A Catalogue of Chinese Pottery and Porcelain in the Collection of Sir Percival David* in 1934.

Percival was aware of the cultural importance of his cousin Philip's exhibitions, particularly *Porcelain through the Ages*, held in 1934 and to which he had lent remarkable works. But Percival had greater ambitions. That very year, he spearheaded negotiations with the Chinese government to organize a massive exhibition of Chinese art in London. The *International Exhibition of Chinese Art*, held at the Royal Academy, Burlington House, in 1935–36, was the largest exhibition of Chinese art ever mounted. It featured more than 3,000 pieces from several museums in China, Europe, and private collections, roughly ten percent of which came from his own collection.[51] Seen by more than 400,000 people, the show was a huge success and sparked a flurry of professional publications.[52]

Developing a visionary plan for the teaching and appreciation of Chinese art in Britain, Percival helped shift it from a pursuit of wealthy collectors to an academic endeavor.[53] He had initially planned to bequeath his collection to the University of London, with the stipulation that it be housed together in a separate building. After a final agreement with the university, he donated it to the School of Oriental and African Studies (SOAS) in 1950. Housed in Bloomsbury Square, it was run by the Percival David Foundation of Chinese Art. Opening to the public in 1952, the collection moved to the British Museum in 2006, though it is still administered by the foundation. Seeing teaching as a fundamental component of his gift, Percival had already financed a chair of Chinese of art and archaeology at SOAS in 1931.

Percival's princely gift encompassed roughly 1,400 items, largely from the Yuan dynasty (1271–1368) to the reign of Qianlong (1711–1799), all distinguished by imperial taste. The extraordinary David vases, originally from a Daoist temple, are famous for the important dedications inscribed on their necks. As the earliest inscriptions in blue and white Chinese porcelain then known, they were a revelation. Though their form was based on Chinese bronze altar vases, these were made under the Mongols (who sacked Baghdad, among other cities). Blue and white porcelain, synonymous with China, had Muslim origins in what is now Iran and Iraq (this last, another irony), the source of the vivid cobalt blue of the underglaze design. Slim, bearded dragons writhe around the body of the vases, trailing wisps of clouds. The bright blue zones are designed so as to create aesthetically pleasing voids, striking a perfect balance with the white areas. Handles shaped like elephant heads were further refinements. Though known as the "David vases," they had once belonged to two other collectors of Chinese ceramics, Percival's friend William Mountstuart Elphinstone and Charles Ernest Russell.[54] Percival reunited the pieces after buying the first from Elphinstone in 1927 and acquiring the second at auction in 1935. Elphinstone—great-grandson of that other Elphinstone, Governor of Bombay, whom Percival's own great-grandfather, David Sassoon, hosted in a magnificent dinner in 1859—donated his collection to the Percival David Foundation before it opened to the public in 1952.

Also in the British Museum is a beautiful *famille rose* moon flask with the rose-hued enamel introduced during the reign of Yongzheng (1723–35). It shows the superb achievements of the Qing emperors, who admired older ceramics while encouraging both stylistic and technological innovations. There is a clear separation between the dazzling white body with cloud scroll handles, and the birds and blossoms delicately rendered in color. Yongzheng and his son Qianlong were highly

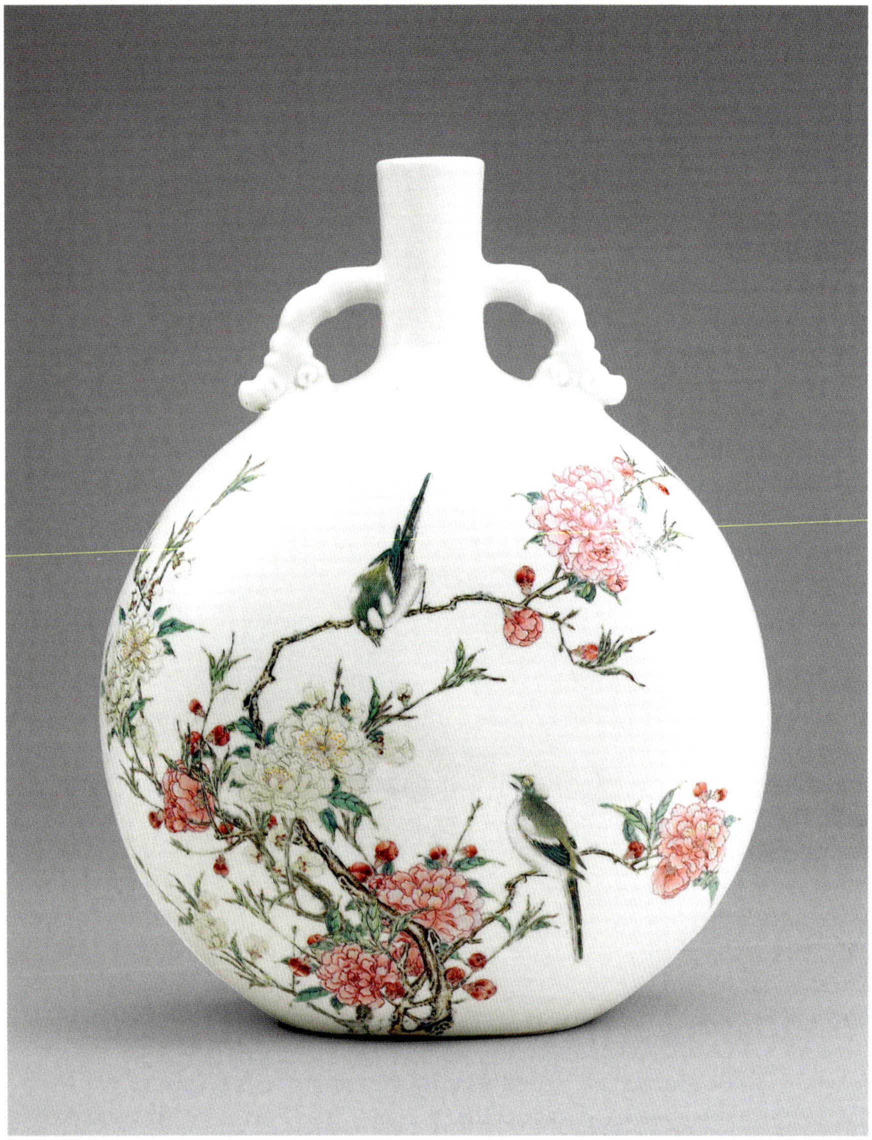

Famille rose moon flask with birds on flowering branches, Jingdezhen, China, Qing dynasty, Yongzheng mark, 1723–35, porcelain, 11½ in. high (29.3 cm), London, British Museum, on loan from the Sir Percival David Foundation of Chinese Art.

cultured scholar-emperors. Their knowledge of old ceramics encouraged the deliberate archaisms found in the rarefied imperial porcelains of their time, such as the shape of this particular flask. A porcelain bowl in the Victoria and Albert Museum, edged in copper, exemplifies the quiet sophistication of the Song dynasty, with elegantly molded lotus flowers and foliage, its creamy, off-white effect enhanced by monochrome glazes. Made for the imperial court in northern China, at one of the five classic kilns of the Song dynasty, Ding ware has an understated luxury that was greatly admired centuries later by Emperor Qianlong, who valued its beauty and antiquity.

Percival also collected artworks in different mediums. Among the imperial pieces that he bought from the Forbidden City in Beijing were superb archaizing jade cups, of the kind favored by Qianlong. Inscribed by the emperor, they were inspired by ancient bronze vessels and carved in relief. An exquisite rhyton, or wine cup, in pale green jade is decorated with a dragon that covers the body of the flaring vessel, terminating in the handle. A pair of white jade tripod cups, their legs patterned with clouds, displays friezes with dragons and phoenixes. The memorable silver raft cup, once in Qianlong's possession, evokes the story of an immortal sailing down a river only to find himself in the Milky Way, as one of its inscriptions explains. Dating from the Yuan dynasty or slightly later and attributed to the silversmith Zhu Bishan, this astonishing wine vessel was made with

Bowl, China, Song dynasty (960–1279), porcelain with decoration molded in relief, Ding ware, 1¾ × 5½ in. in diameter (4.4 × 14 cm), London, Victoria and Albert Museum, given by Sir Percival David, Bt. The bowl bears the labels of the Elphinstone and David (no. 174) Collections.

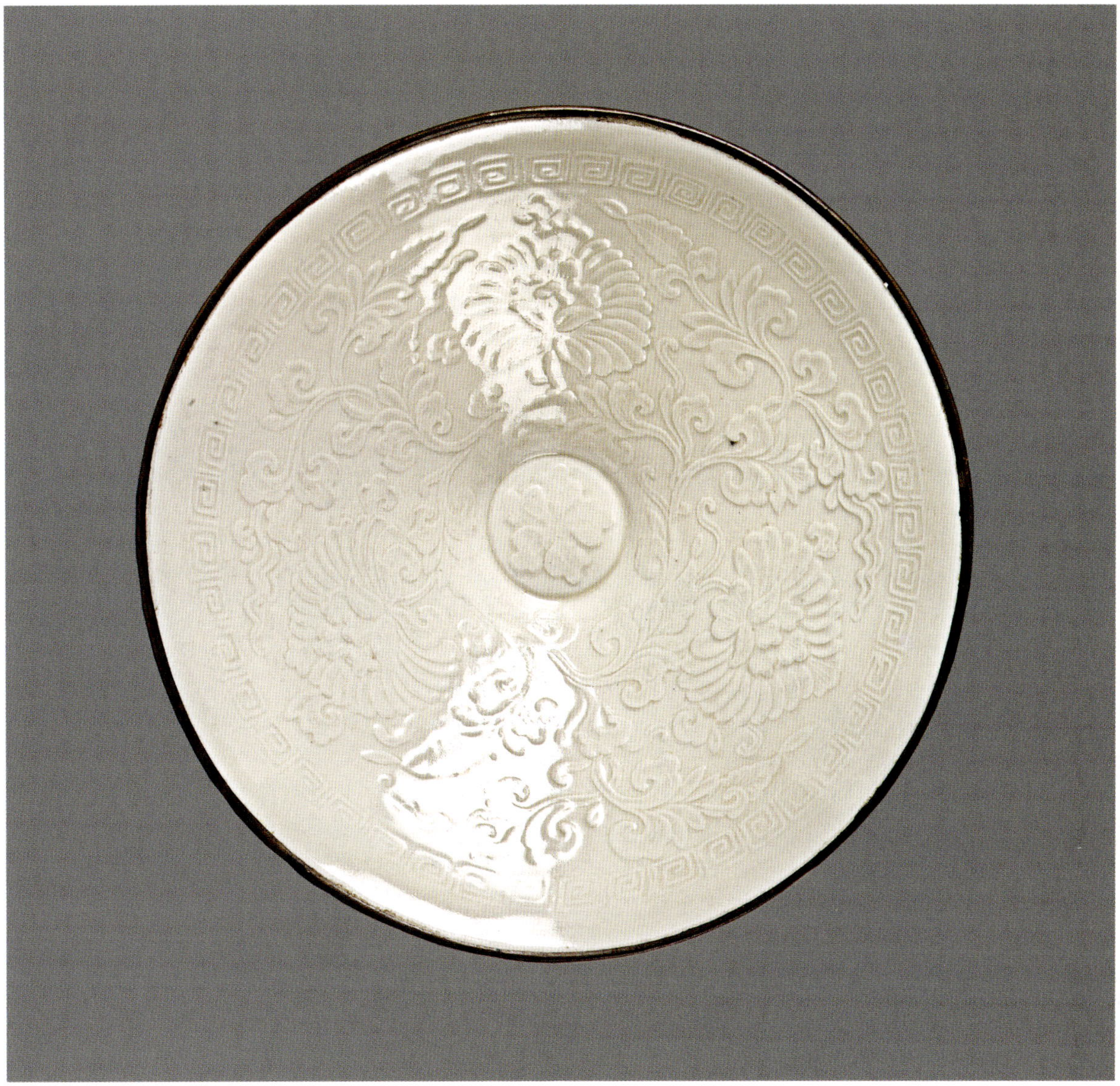

consummate skill by soldering different pieces of sheet silver together. The virtuosity of the chasing, which conceals the seams, is particularly remarkable in its treatment of bark. The traveler, his head upturned as if in ecstasy, is meant to confront the drinker who raises the cup to the lips, a brilliantly conceived piece that nevertheless exceeds and hinders functionality.[55]

Another magnificent object from the Yuan dynasty is a wooden plate with peony decorations in carved cinnabar lacquer, first exhibited in the famous exhibition of Chinese art of 1935–36. Requiring time-consuming and highly specialized labor, such luxury items were not meant for utilitarian purposes. Numerous layers of lacquer were slowly superimposed to build up a thick coating that could then be carved. The background, of darker color, acts as a foil to the peonies and leaves that stand out in relief. The lush red density of the lacquer, its cost, and superb craftsmanship give the plate a sense of opulence. Made between the late thirteenth and the early fourteenth centuries, the plate is signed by Yang Mao, a renowned master from Zhejiang province.

Percival's favorite medium in Chinese art, however, was painting. As he wrote to the art historian Fritz Saxl, then director of the Warburg Institute, Percival considered his own handscrolls as "perhaps the most valuable and significant part of my collection, an opinion with which several Chinese connoisseurs who are acquainted with them have expressed agreement."[56] Older than his porcelain and absolutely priceless, his paintings are now in the Metropolitan Museum of Art.

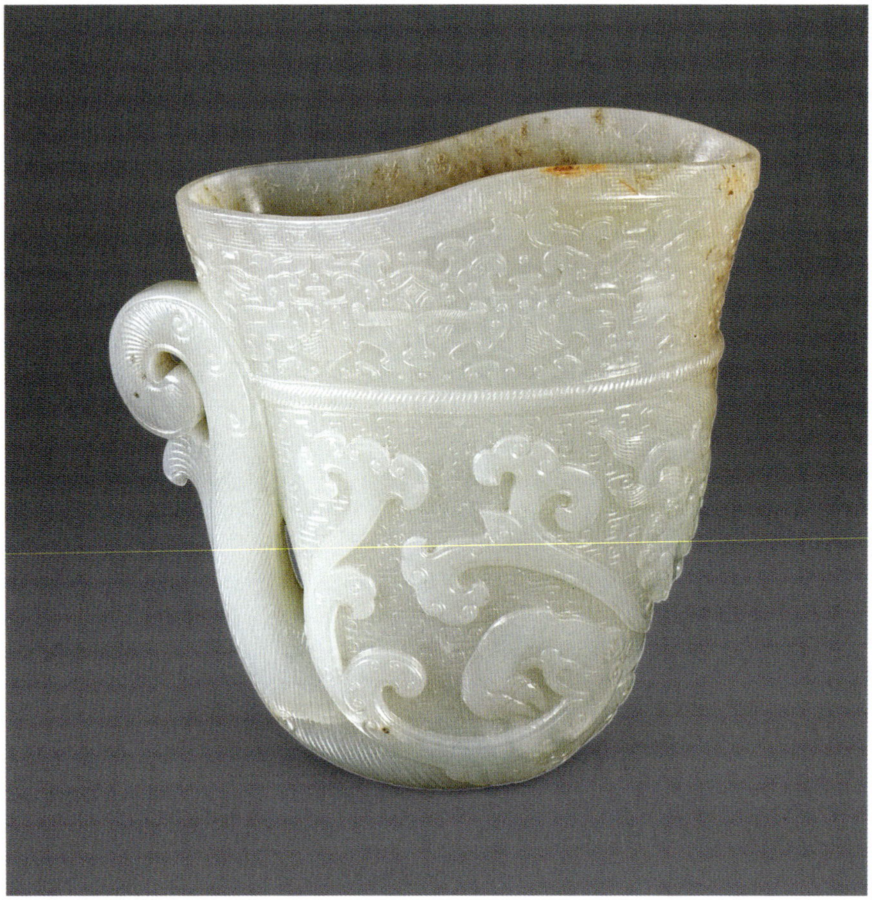

Rhyton, China, Qianlong period (1736–95), inscription dates to Emperor Qianlong in the second moon of the cyclical year Ding Wei (1787), jade, 6⅛ × 6⅛ in. (15.5 × 15.5 cm), Cambridge, UK, Fitzwilliam Museum, Oscar C. Raphael Bequest, 1941, received 1946. Sir Percival David bought this vessel from the Palace Treasure in 1929 and gave it to Raphael in 1931.

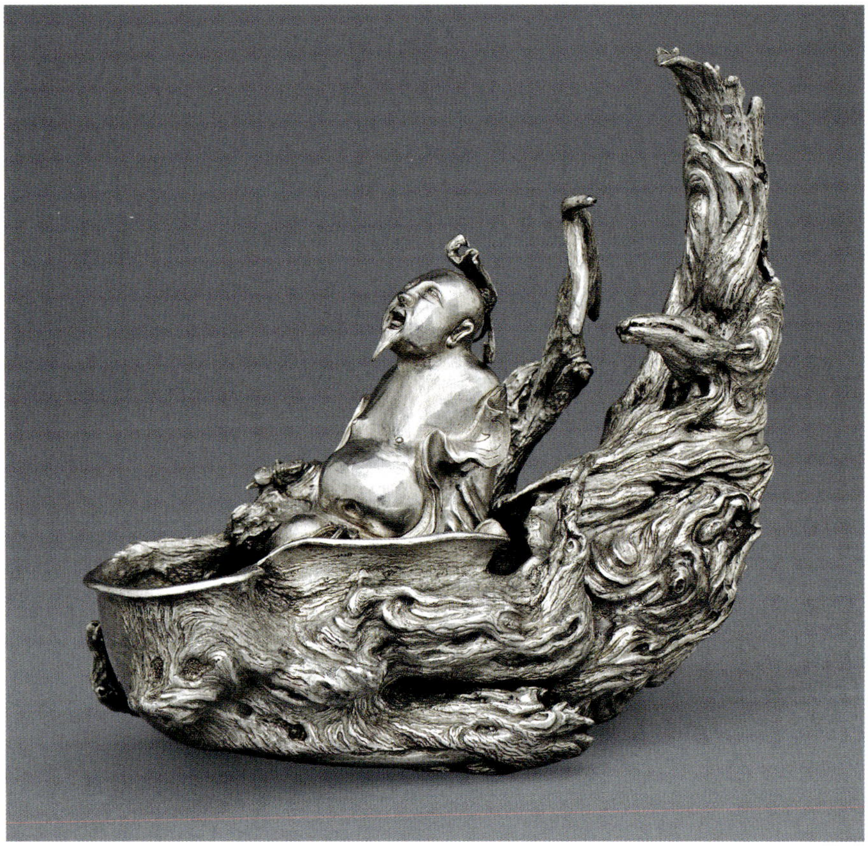

Attributed to Zhu Bishan, Raft cup, 1345, China, Yuan dynasty (1271–1368) or later, silver, 6¼ in. long (16 cm), Cleveland Museum of Art, John L. Severance Fund, formerly in the Percival David Collection.

OPPOSITE
Yang Mao, plate with peony decoration, China, Yuan dynasty (1271–1368), carved cinnabar lacquer on wood, 6½ in. in diameter (16.5 cm), Cleveland Museum of Art, John L. Severance Fund, formerly in the Percival David Collection.

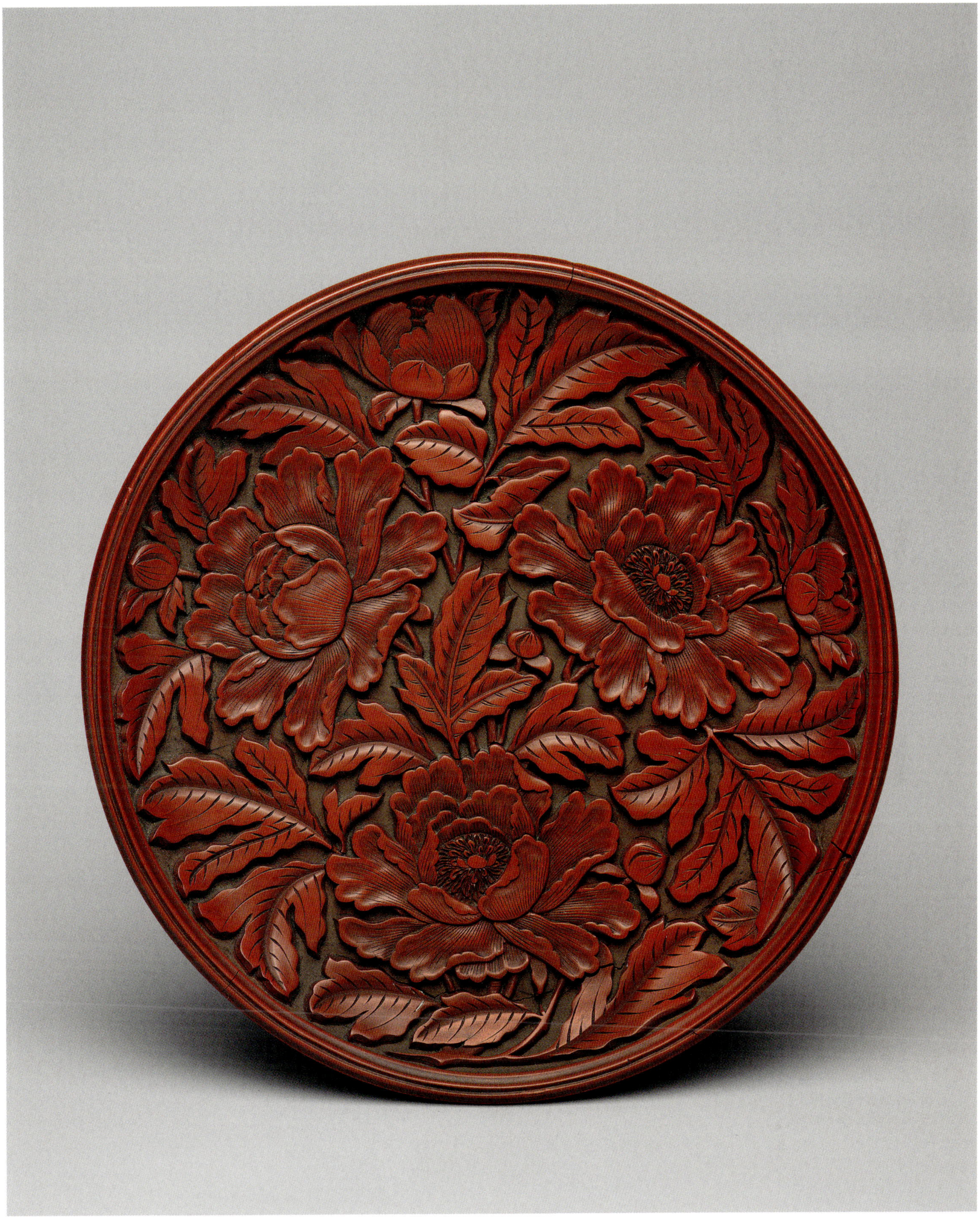

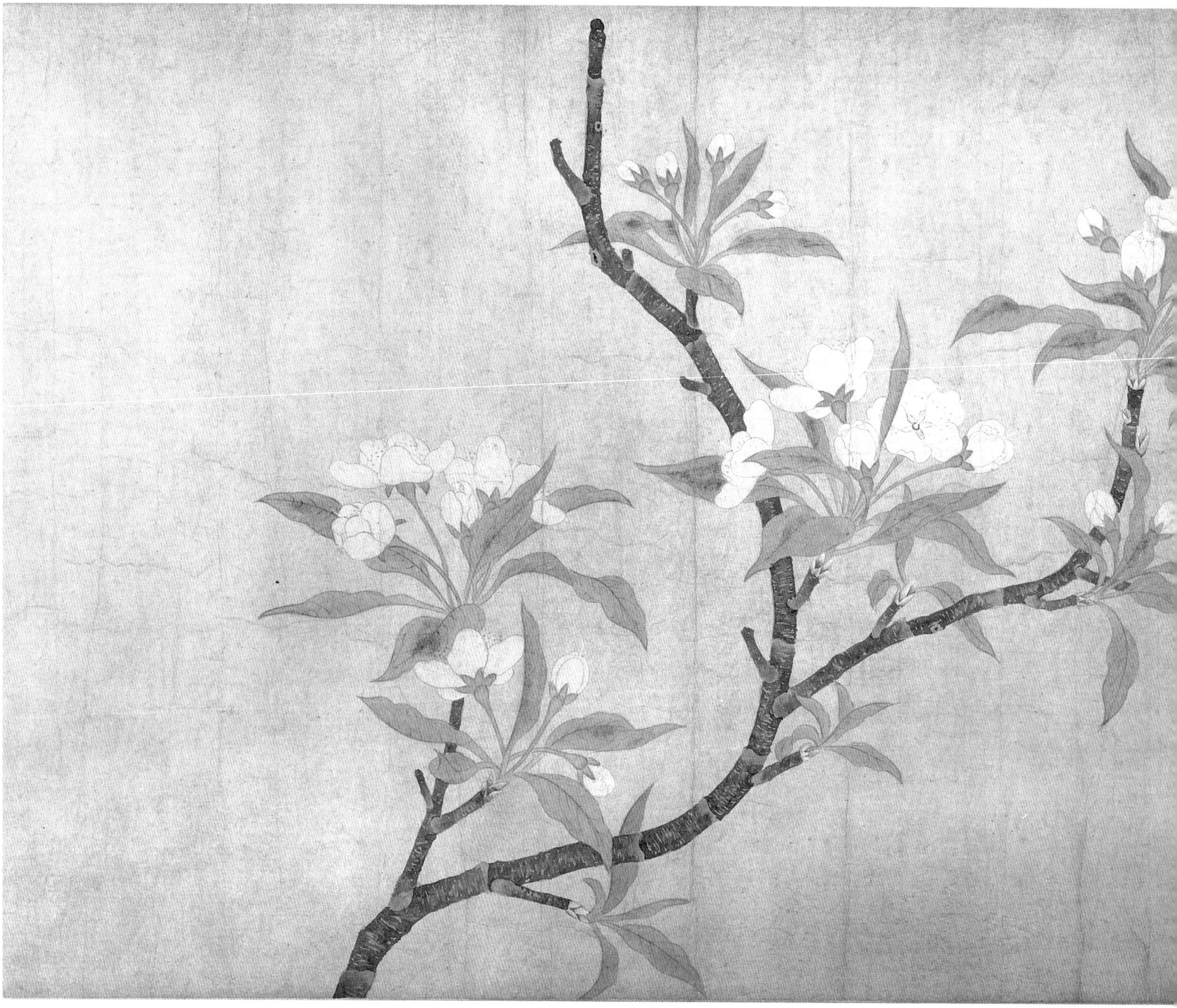

They include *In the Palace*, a twelfth-century copy of an earlier work by Zhou Wenju who portrayed ladies from the court of Li Yu, ruler of the Southern Tang; and *Scholars of the Liuli Hall*, dating from the thirteenth century, by an unknown artist. Now believed to be based on a painting by Qian Xuan (Ch'ien Hsüan, 1239–1301), *Pear Blossoms*, c. 1280, is characteristic of literati painting of the Southern Song. A fragile branch with pear blossoms is paired with a poem of such wistful melancholy that it gives added poignancy to the image of flowers on the bough:

The lonely tear-stained face, teardrops drenching the
branches,
Though washed of make-up, her old charms remain.
Behind the closed gate, on a rainy night vainly sorrowing,
How differently she looked bathed in golden waves of
moonlight before darkness fell.

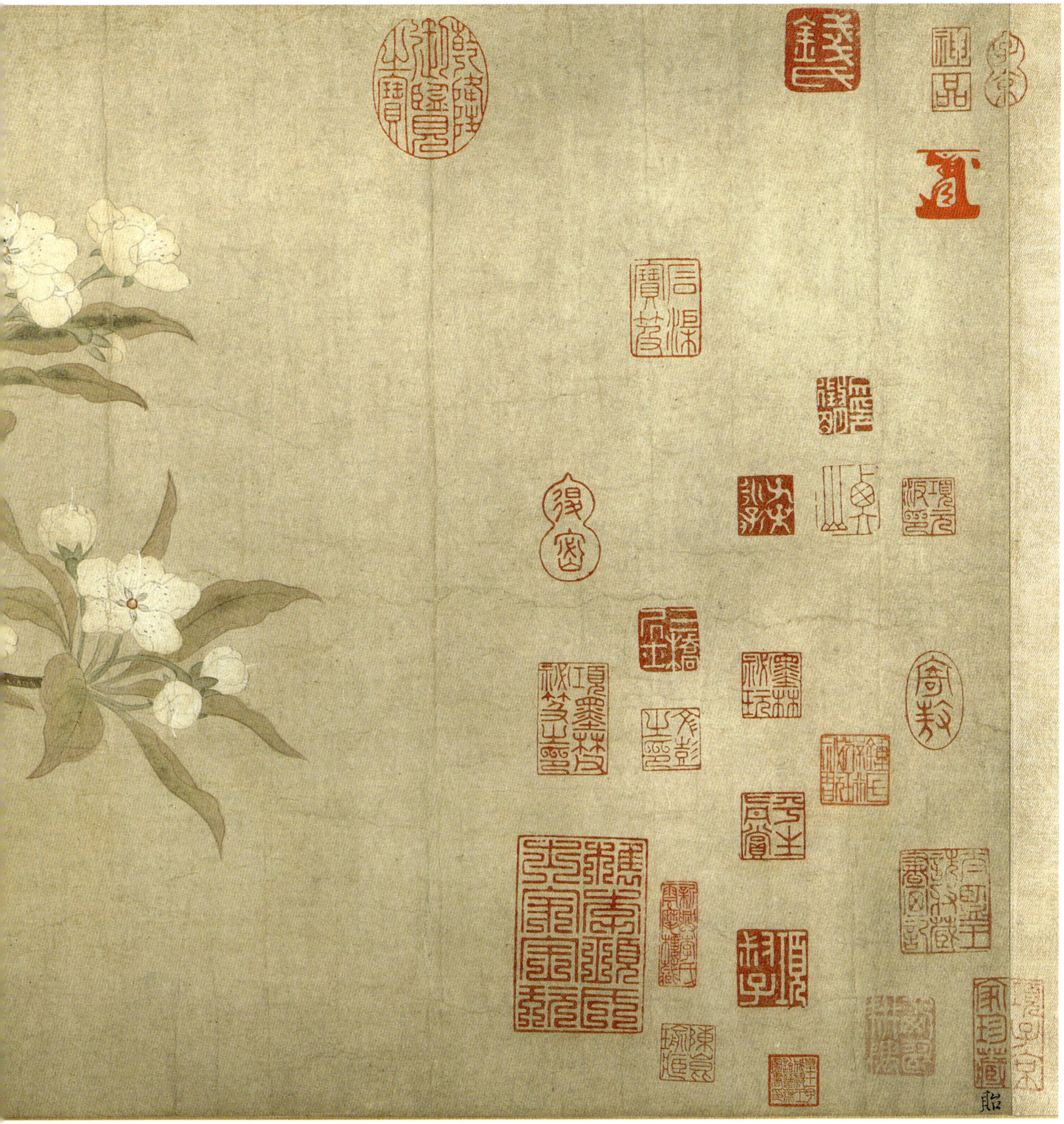

After Qian Xuan, *Pear Blossoms* (detail), c. 1280, China, Yuan dynasty (1271–1368), ink and color on paper handscroll, 12⅝ in. × 34 ft. 9⅛ in. (32.1 × 10.6 m), New York, Metropolitan Museum of Art, purchase, Dillon Fund Gift, 1977, formerly in the Percival David Collection.

Cultured members of the Song court would have no difficulty reading the poem's allusions to court poetry from the Tang dynasty.[57] But the anonymous artist went beyond erudite citation. Equally at home in poetry, art, and calligraphy, he chose his graphic means carefully, seeking a close relationship among three different mediums, rendering the blossoms in a nonnaturalist way, and lending the calligraphy some of the affect of the image. Qian Xuan, to whom the painting was once attributed, was an influential scholar-painter who epitomized what the distinguished art historian Wen Fong called "the epochal shift from pictorial representation to calligraphic self-expression [that] occurred between the Song and Yuan dynasties, at the end of the fourteenth century."[58]

The glory of Percival's original collection, however, was the great *Night-Shining White*, an eighth-century handscroll from the Tang dynasty. It is an unrivaled masterpiece by Han Gan, a legendary horse painter, tasked with portraying the charger of Emperor Xuanzong. With monochrome ink, the artist captures the emotional intensity of the stallion in an image that transcends portraiture and

Han Gan, *Night-Shining White* (detail), c. 750, China, Tang dynasty (618–907), ink on paper handscroll, 14 in. × 37 ft. 5⅛ in. (35.4 cm × 11.4 m), New York, Metropolitan Museum of Art, purchase, Dillon Fund Gift, 1977, formerly in the Percival David Collection.

evokes the celestial steeds of Chinese myths.[59] In a moving colophon, Qianlong pays tribute to its pride and impetuousness:

> *Unrolling the scroll, I see the lofty spirit of the horse*
> *By tilting its head, the horse is recalling previous battles.*
> *Though muzzled, the horse refuses to be saddled.*

Now mounted on a long handscroll, the seals and colophons record the names of several collectors, including two (perhaps three) emperors, during almost thirteen centuries—a testament to the painting's compelling power.

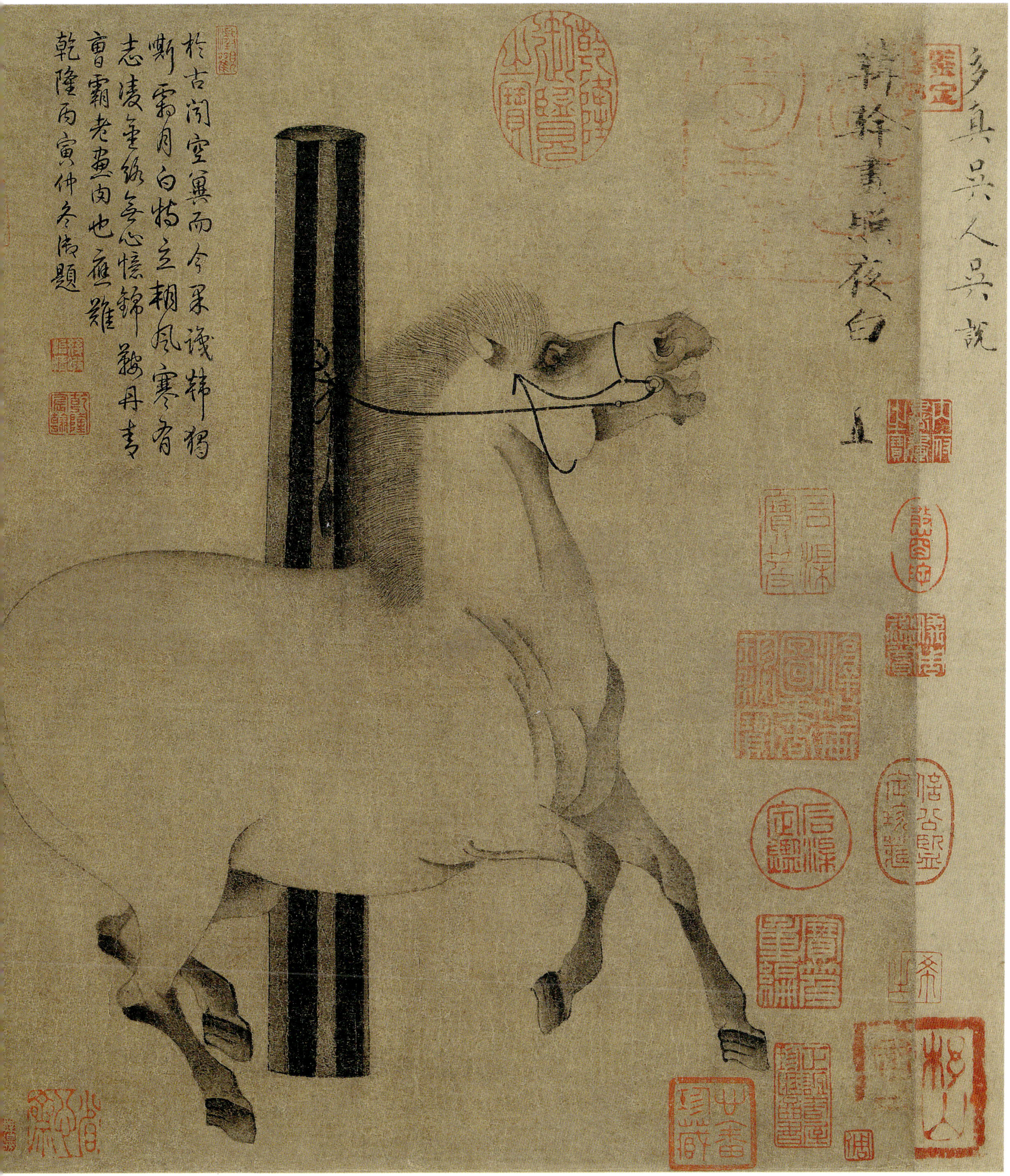
韓幹畫照夜白
乾隆丙寅仲冬御題

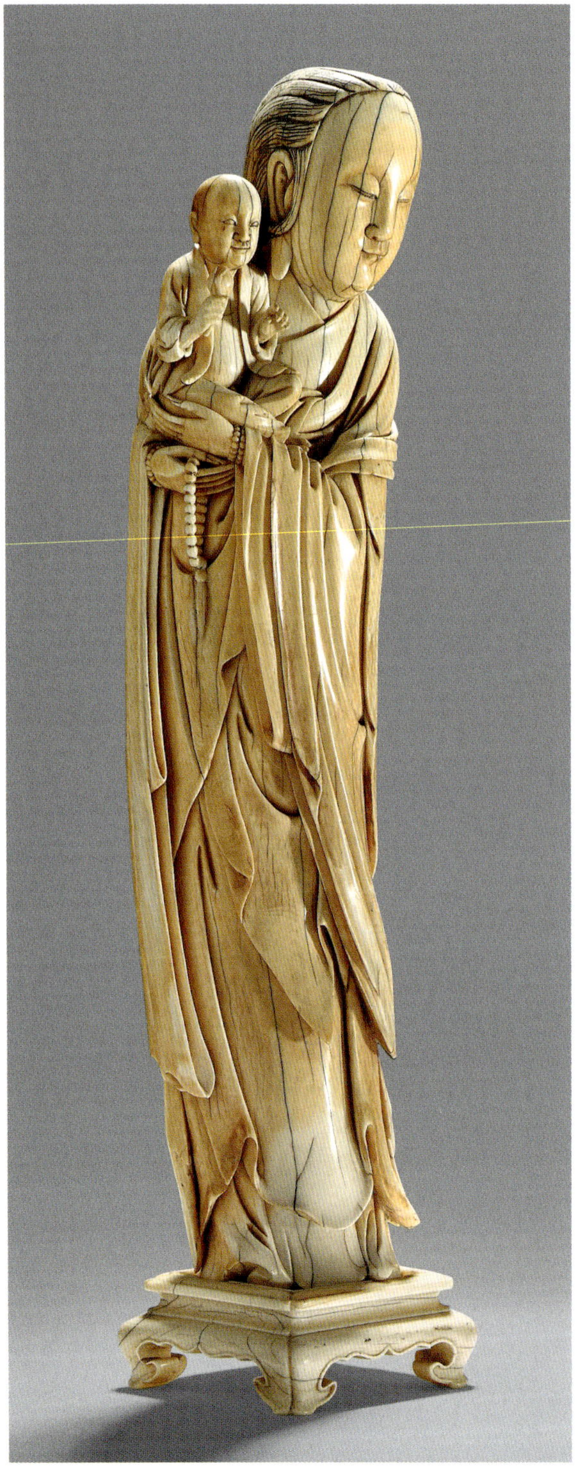

Bodhisattva Guanyin as the Sender of Sons, China, late Ming dynasty, sixteenth–seventeenth century, ivory, 13⅜ in. high (34 cm), London, British Museum, Sir Victor Sassoon Chinese Ivories Trust.

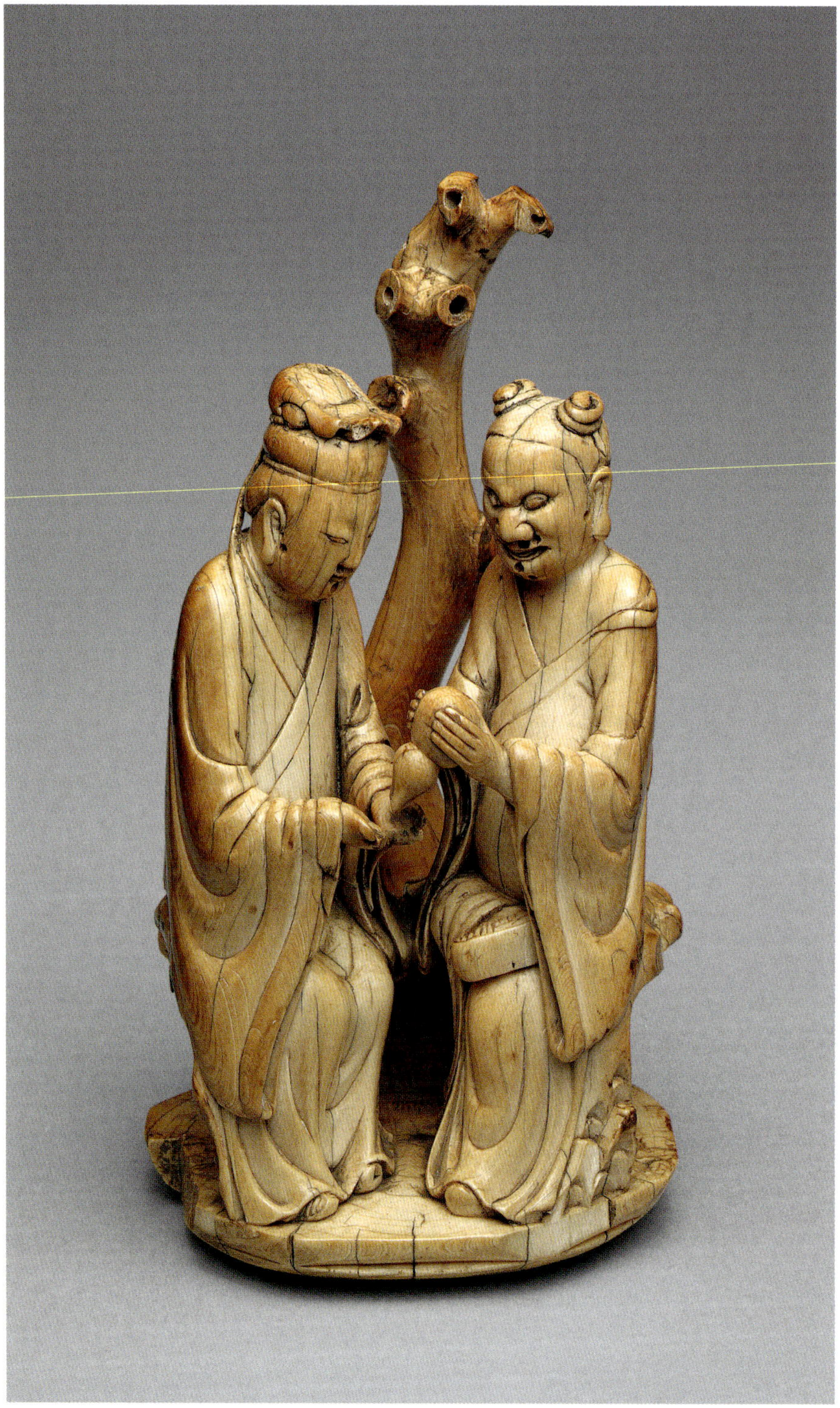

Two men, one thought to be Bian Qiao, China, seventeenth century, ivory, 5½ × 3 × 2⅜ in. (14 × 7.5 × 6 cm), London, Victoria and Albert Museum, Sir Victor Sassoon Chinese Ivories Trust.

Victor

We do not know how Percival David's cousin Victor assembled his collection of Chinese ivories. According to a luxurious three-volume catalogue, published in 1950 and compiled by his friend Sydney Edward Lucas, Lucas bought the ivories in Beijing between 1915 and 1927. Stanley Jackson, however, wrote that Victor relied on agents who scoured the country to procure ivories for him, buying from Manchu families and Buddhist and Daoist temples in need of repair. Victor had hoped the catalogue would help secure a permanent place for his collection in the British Museum. When this failed, he set up the Sir Victor Sassoon Chinese Ivories Trust in 1955. In 2016, the trustees published a handsome volume summarizing what was known about the collection. Victor's cousin Elizabeth Mary Humphrey-Owens, a trustee, knew Lucas well, and stated that Victor bought Lucas's collection in 1937 or 1938. In 2018, the trust donated 556 Chinese ivories to the British Museum.[60]

Victor and Lucas were not scholars, and their catalogue did not receive good reviews. Despite his criticism of its contents, the *Times Literary Supplement*'s anonymous reviewer, now known to be Leigh Ashton, then director of the Victoria and Albert Museum, ended by acknowledging that while the catalogue was difficult to use, "the immense amount of folk-lore that can be dug out of its pages, the identification of obscure groups and legends, which will ease the task of recognizing scenes and subjects, makes this catalogue an important repertory for all interested in Chinese tales."[61] Victor's collection, however, was much more than a compendium of historic and mythological figures. The number and diversity of the ivories provide a comparative framework enabling scholars to track stylistic traits, analyze craftsmanship and geographic particularities, and shed light on Chinese workshops and the networks that fed export to the West.

Ivory carving flourished initially in Fujian province, in southeastern China, before spreading to other cities and even Japan. By means of its port city Zhangzhou, Fujian merchants established lucrative commercial exchanges with the Spanish, who had conquered the Philippines in the sixteenth century. As Asia began to supply Spain and Mexico with religious ivories, a robust trans-Pacific commerce emerged via the Manila galleon trade.[62] An image of Guanyin from the Ming dynasty shows a mother holding her child, carved of a piece with its elegant stand. Age cracks and the warm patinated surface of the ivory enhance the quality of the work. The gentle curve of the statuette, underscored by the deep folds of the tunic, echoes the natural contour of the elephant tusk from which it came. To Westerners, such images of the bodhisattva of compassion inevitably evoked the Virgin and Child. The iconographic similarity appealed to Spanish and European audiences, partly because clients in Europe and New Spain were keen for high-quality artifacts showing superb Chinese craftsmanship and "exotic" styles. Cross-cultural influences ran both ways, however; Fujian audiences loved the foreign appeal of ivories reflecting Western models.[63] A related piece is the seventeenth-century ivory said to represent the partly mythological Bian Qiao, a fifth-century physician credited with almost supranatural powers. Beautifully burnished by time and use, the votive figures may reflect the influence that Christian images had on the production of ivories for Asian markets.

A miniature mountain from the Qing dynasty, carved in high relief out of a single piece of ivory, is probably a representation of the famous rock bridge at Mount Tiantai (T'ien-t'ai Shan), a mountain sacred to the Buddhists.[64] It contrasts the unpredictability of nature—crags, gnarled pine trees, and capricious mountain torrent—to a group of Buddhist priests who had attained Nirvana and calmly ascend the mountain, talking serenely to one another as they go. These pieces were much admired for the great skill of the carvers and the originality shown in the depiction of well-known themes. A table screen dated 1775 shows the garden of Gao Pian (821–887), a Tang writer and general. On one side, all is pastoral tranquility: two gentlemen sit under a tree, surveying scenes of rural labor. A poem by Gao Pian, inscribed on the top right, celebrates the oneness with nature shared by all, including man-made things:

> *Green trees and shade during the long*
> *summer day*
> *Pavilion and reflections from the pond.*[65]

The other side shows Daoist immortals in a paradisical setting, a subject frequently depicted on table screens. Swirling clouds part to reveal foaming water, while soaring cliffs overhang the otherwise ethereal landscape where immortals tread on insubstantial air, stand aloft on leaves or cloth, or sit astride mythological beasts.

A growing transnational market enabled workshops to reproduce successful items for export. A carved figure of the Daoist immortal

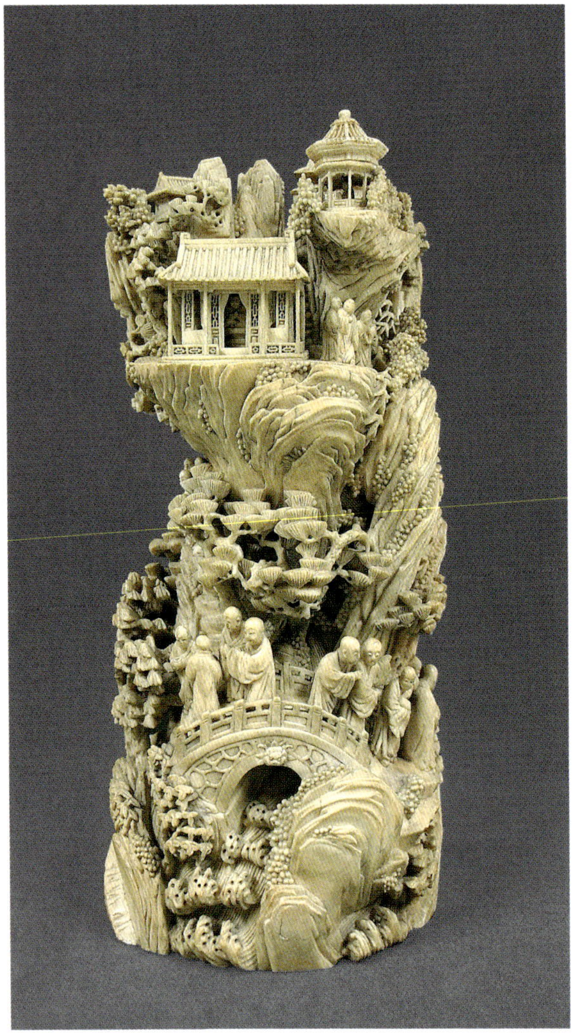

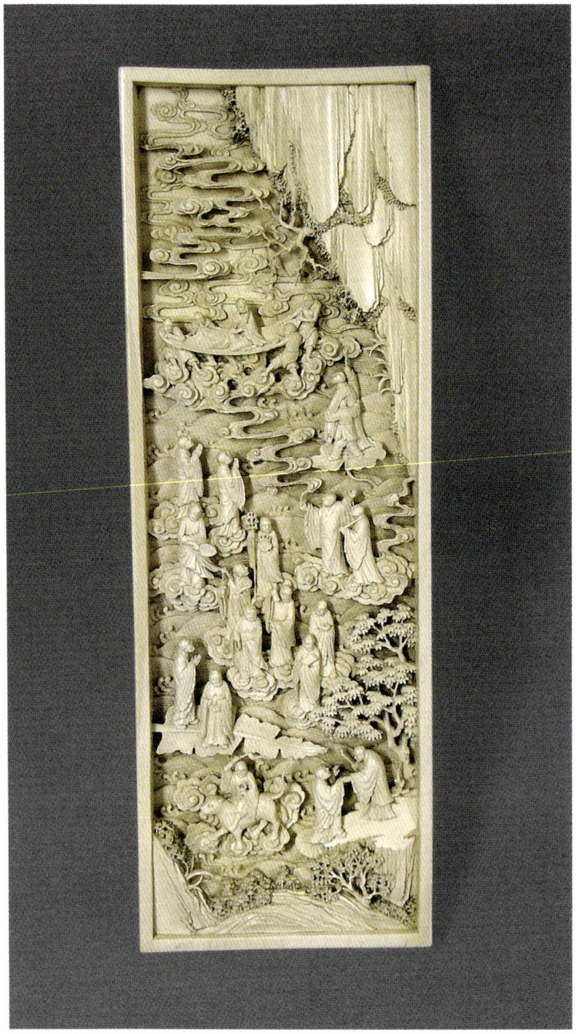

Miniature mountain, China, Qing dynasty, probably nineteenth century, ivory, 12¼ × 4½ in. (31 × 13.5 cm), London, British Museum, Sir Victor Sassoon Chinese Ivories Trust.

Table screen, China, Qing dynasty, 1775, ivory, 11⅜ × 3⅞ in. (29 × 10 cm), London, British Museum, Sir Victor Sassoon Chinese Ivories Trust.

OPPOSITE TOP LEFT
Figure of the Daoist immortal Li Tieguai, China, Republican period, twentieth century, ivory, 19⅛ in. high (48.5 cm), London, British Museum, Sir Victor Sassoon Chinese Ivories Trust.

OPPOSITE TOP RIGHT
Casket, China, Qing dynasty, early nineteenth century, ivory, 4½ × 9⅞ × 4⅝ in. (11.5 × 25 × 11.8 cm), London, British Museum, Sir Victor Sassoon Chinese Ivories Trust.

OPPOSITE BOTTOM LEFT
Box, Guangzhou, China, c. 1808, lined in Dublin, silversmith: James England, ivory and silver gilt, 3½ × 6⅛ × 4⅝ in. (9 × 15.7 × 11.9 cm), London, Victoria and Albert Museum, given by Sir Victor Sassoon Chinese Ivories Trust.

OPPOSITE BOTTOM RIGHT
Mortar, China, seventeenth century, ivory, 3⅞ × 2⅛ in. (9.8 × 5.3 cm), London, Victoria and Albert Museum, Sir Victor Sassoon Chinese Ivories Trust.

Li Tieguai made in the early twentieth century exists in several versions. The contrapposto pose makes great demands on the carver: as the top-heavy statuette is open at the bottom, the figure has to be able to stand on slender supports. A nineteenth-century casket carved on all sides was also meant for export, as the horror vacui implacably reveals. In the front, a hunt is in progress: servants carry their prey in a landscape interspersed with pavilions. The underside of the lid shows a painted view of the fortified Bocca Tigris, a strait on the Pearl River delta, which had played a seminal role during the First Opium War. A second intricately carved lid covers the interior compartments. These ivories attest to the supply and demand chains of ivory production, and the colonial networks in which they circulated.

Victor was not a connoisseur like his cousins Philip, Hannah, Mozelle, or Percival. Several of his pieces date from the early twentieth century; others, passed off to Lucas as Chinese, were possibly made in Japan.[66] In contrast to Percival, whose collection deliberately excluded Chinese export porcelain, Victor's had numerous items made for the West. Most of his pieces date from the end of the Qing dynasty, whereas Percival hewed to the prevailing views of the time that saw the Qing dynasty as decadent after the eighteenth century. Yet Victor paid close attention to Percival, like him producing a catalogue and trying to interest the British Museum in his collection just as his cousin was negotiating with the University of London over the final destination of his ceramics. Intensely patriotic, Victor wanted to place his ivories so that they could serve an educational purpose.

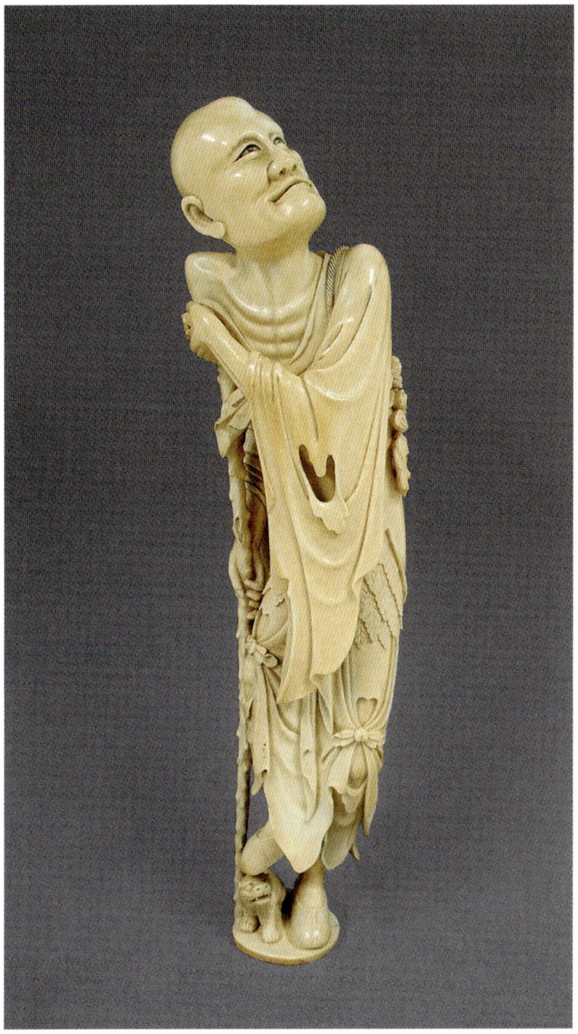
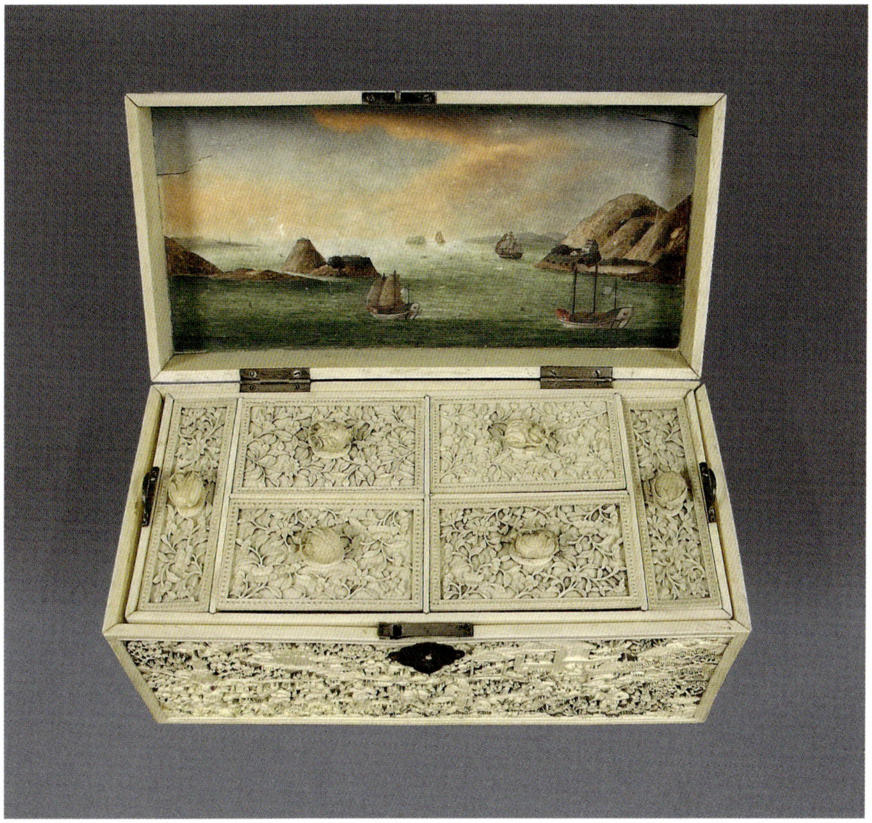
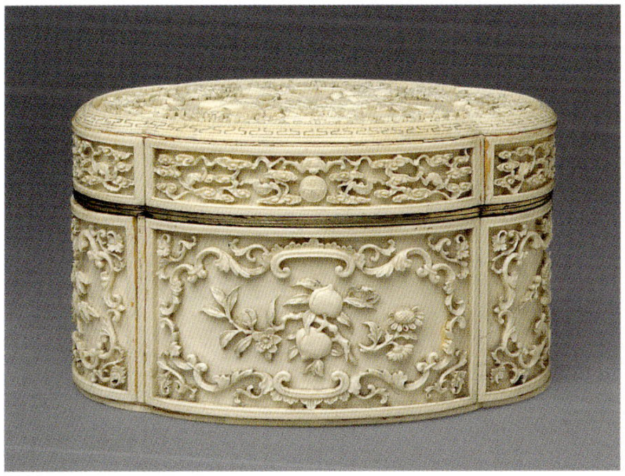
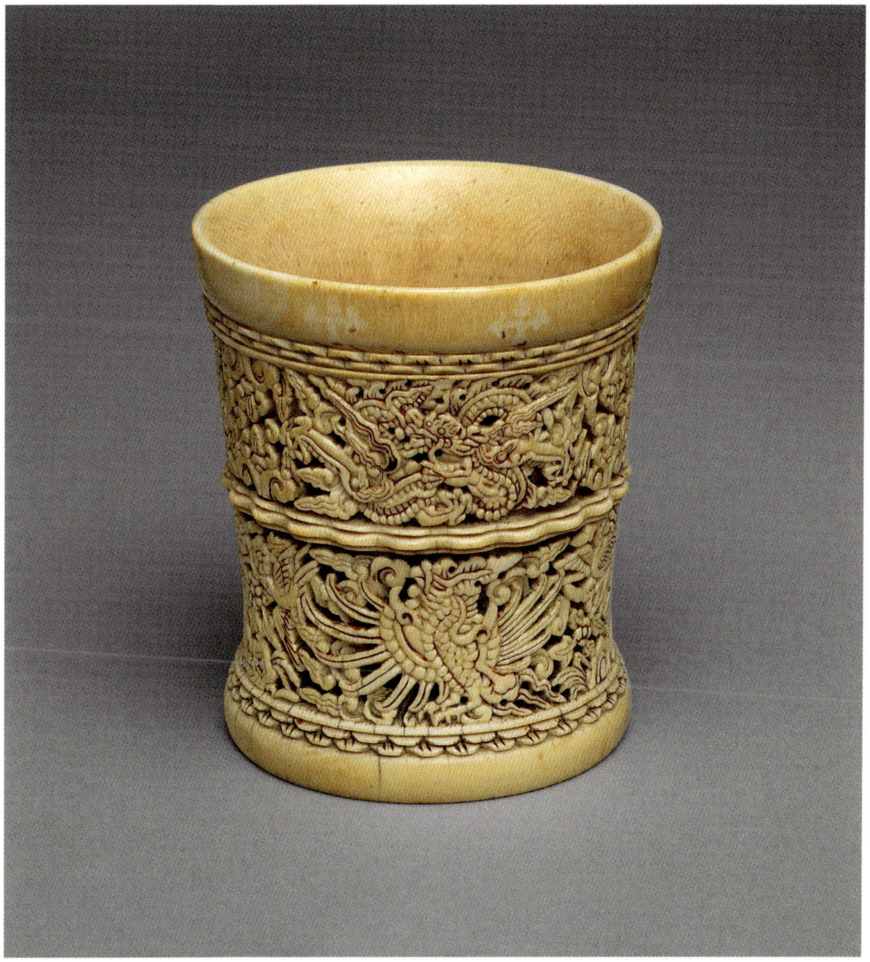

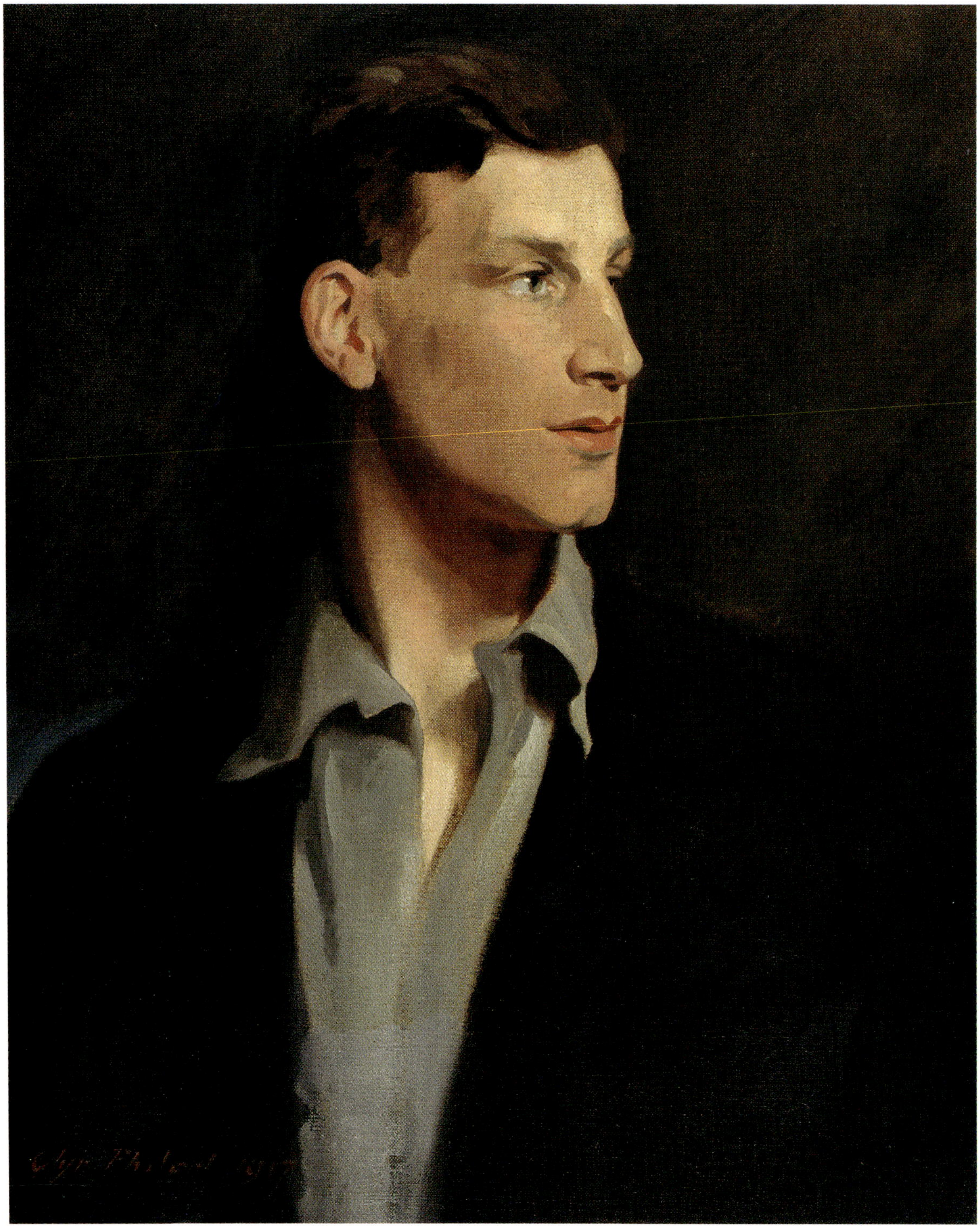

Glyn Warren Philpot, *Siegfried Sassoon*, 1917, oil on canvas, 24 × 20 in. (61 cm × 50.8 cm), Cambridge, UK, Fitzwilliam Museum, given by Siegfried Sassoon, 1924.

Siegfried

Siegfried Sassoon (1886–1967), who distinguished himself as a soldier during World War I and would become best known as a poet and writer, also developed an interest in the arts. A great-grandson of David Sassoon, he grew up estranged from his Sassoon relations. His father, Alfred, had married outside the faith and was disowned by his mother, Flora. Only Siegfried's aunt Rachel (Beer) and his great-aunt Mozelle maintained contact. After the war, he eventually met Philip and Sybil, but they were never close. Siegfried both envied and loathed everything Philip stood for: the storied country houses, the front-page fame. And yet the Tory socialite and the sometime Socialist had much in common. Both were friends of the Sitwells, T. E. Lawrence (Lawrence of Arabia), Max Beerbohm, Ottoline Morell, Lord Berners, and the artists Rex Whistler and Glyn Philpot (who painted

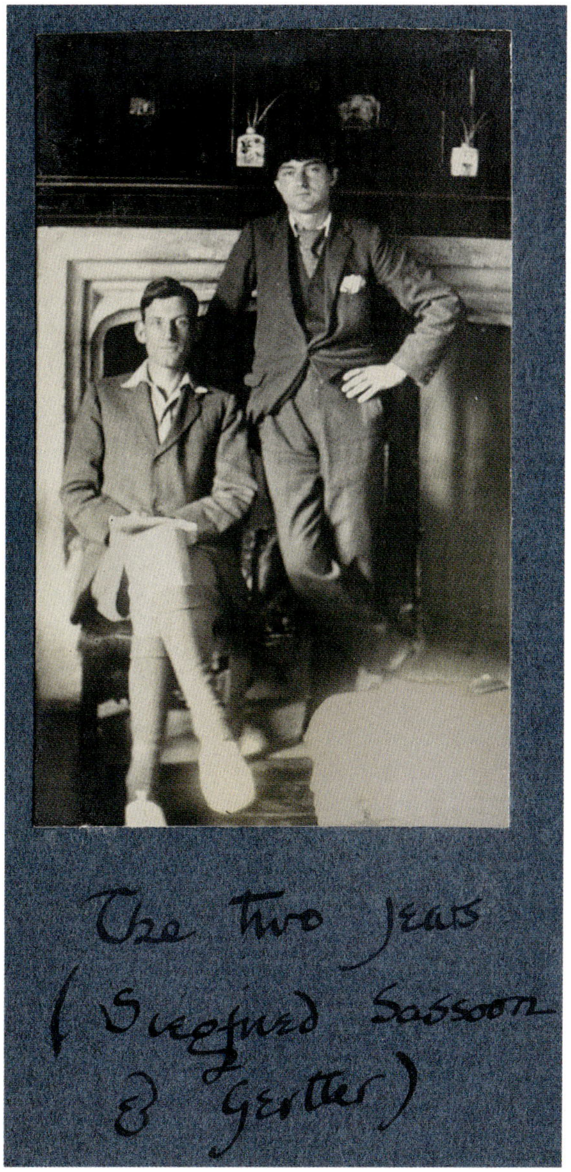

NEAR RIGHT
Siegfried Sassoon and the painter Mark Gertler photographed in 1921 by Lady Ottoline Morrell, who captioned the photograph "The Two Jews," London, National Portrait Gallery, purchased with help from the Friends of the National Libraries and the Dame Helen Gardner Bequest, 2003. While Gertler, a son of Polish Jews, had a Jewish upbringing, Siegfried Sassoon was raised by his Roman Catholic mother.

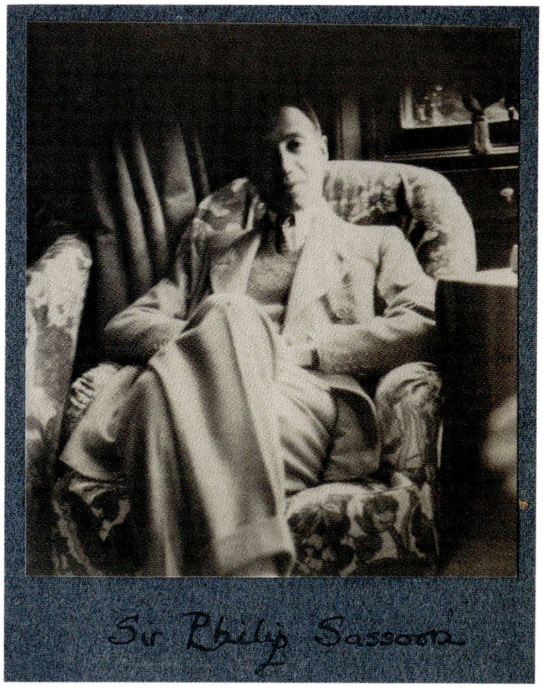

FAR RIGHT
Philip Sassoon, photographed in 1925 by Lady Ottoline Morrell, London, National Portrait Gallery, purchased with help from the Friends of the National Libraries and the Dame Helen Gardner Bequest, 2003.

both men). They shared a dislike of dissonant varieties of modernism in art, music, and literature but admired the Ballets Russes. Philip's love of Georgian art and architecture was matched by Siegfried's love of pastoral England, its countryside, and rural life.

Although he was a homosexual, Siegfried fell in love with Hester Gatty (1906–1973), whom he married in 1933. With the substantial inheritance he received from his aunt Rachel, he purchased Heytesbury House, a large Georgian mansion surrounded by parkland; her portrait hung in the library.[67] When the couple separated in 1948, Hester took her beautiful paintings and furniture, leaving Siegfried to fill the house with new acquisitions, largely from Frost and Reed, a gallery in Bristol: works by Giovanni Paolo Panini, J. M. W.

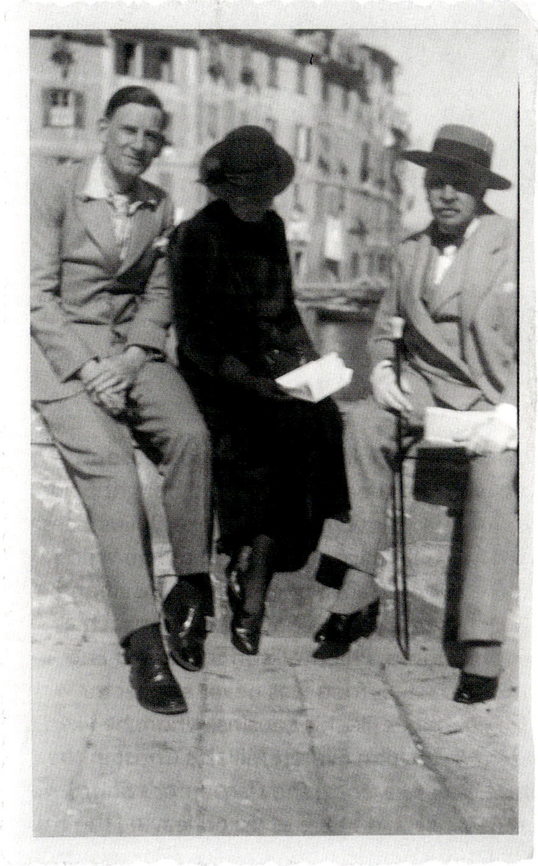

Left to right: Siegfried Sassoon, Florence (née Kahn), Lady Beerbohm, Max Beerbohm, c. 1937, London, National Portrait Gallery.

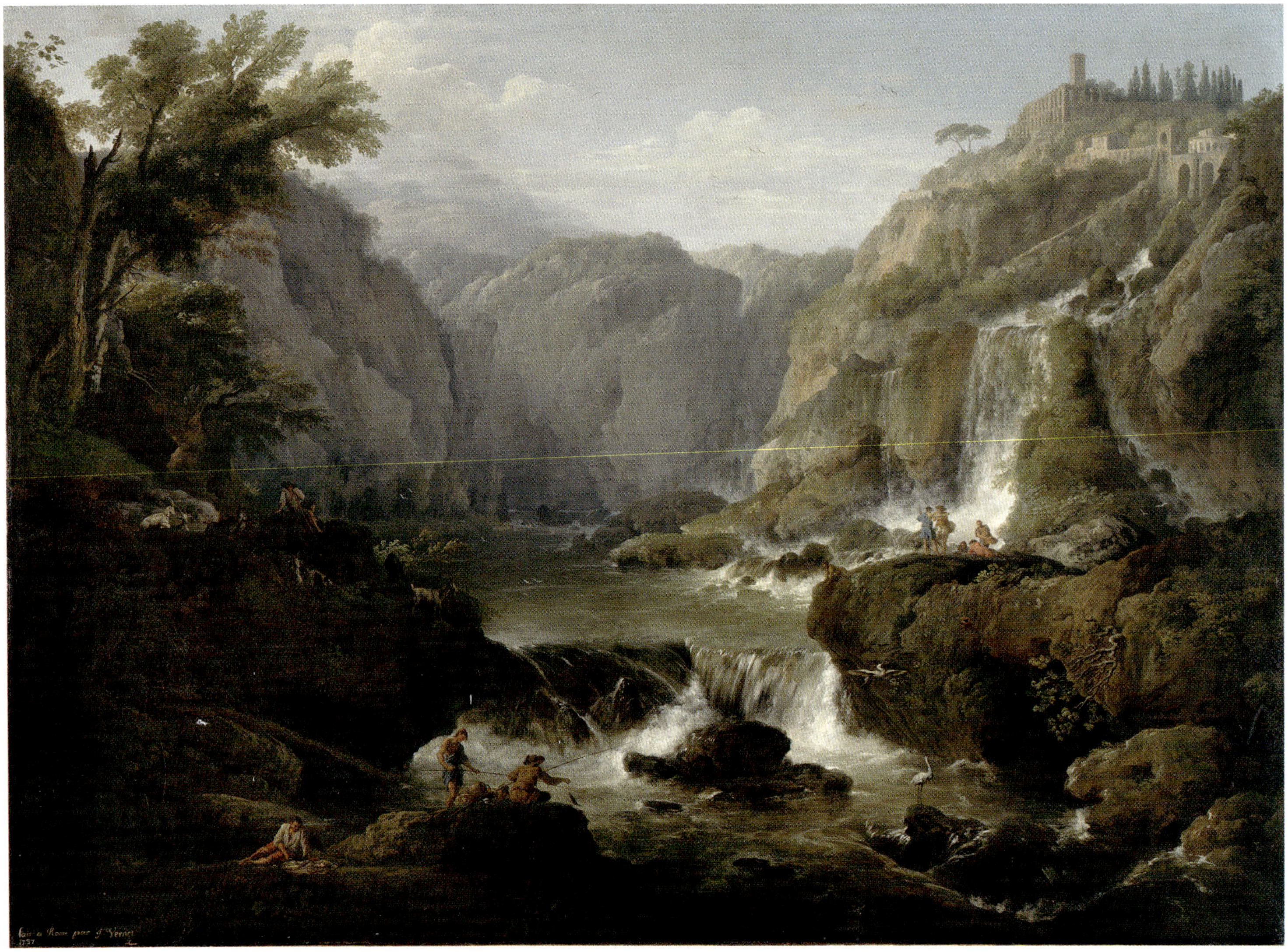

Claude-Joseph Vernet, *The Waterfalls at Tivoli*, 1737, oil on canvas, 48½ × 67⅞ in. (123.2 × 172.6 cm), Cleveland Museum of Art, Leonard C. Hanna, Jr. Fund, formerly in the Siegfried Sassoon Collection.

Turner, Copley Fielding, and Claude-Joseph Vernet.[68] Over the years Siegfried bought paintings and drawings by William Blake, Julius Caesar Ibbetson, Jules Jacquemart, Samuel de Wilde, and Edward Williams; portraits of himself and friends; and works by contemporaries such as Max Beerbohm, Philip Wilson Steer, and Eric Kennington. Siegfried was never a collector with a particular focus like his cousins, whom he liked to tease. When John Everett Millais's *Christ in the House of His Parents (The Carpenter's Shop)* was put up for sale in 1921 and risked leaving the country, Siegfried wrote a humorous open letter to *The Nation & The Atheneum*, asking "some Sassoon, more affluent than myself, to come forward with the money needed to retain a pre-Raphaelite masterpiece in one of our National Art galleries."[69] To the Tate he donated the portrait of Walter Richard Sickert by Sylvia Gosse, and Richard Dadd's *Fairy Feller's Master-Stroke*, this last in memory of Julian Dadd, the artist's grand-nephew, with whom Siegfried had served, and of Dadd's two brothers, who had all died in World War I.

The Sassoons' wealth accorded them a secure place in England's still-rigid class system along with the appurtenances of privilege reflected in their homes and collections. But these collections were far more than emblems of privilege; they spoke of a deep sense of belonging, which, noblesse oblige, the Sassoons channeled toward social institutions and cultural enlightenment, investments of public beneficence fueled by a deep sense of patriotism.

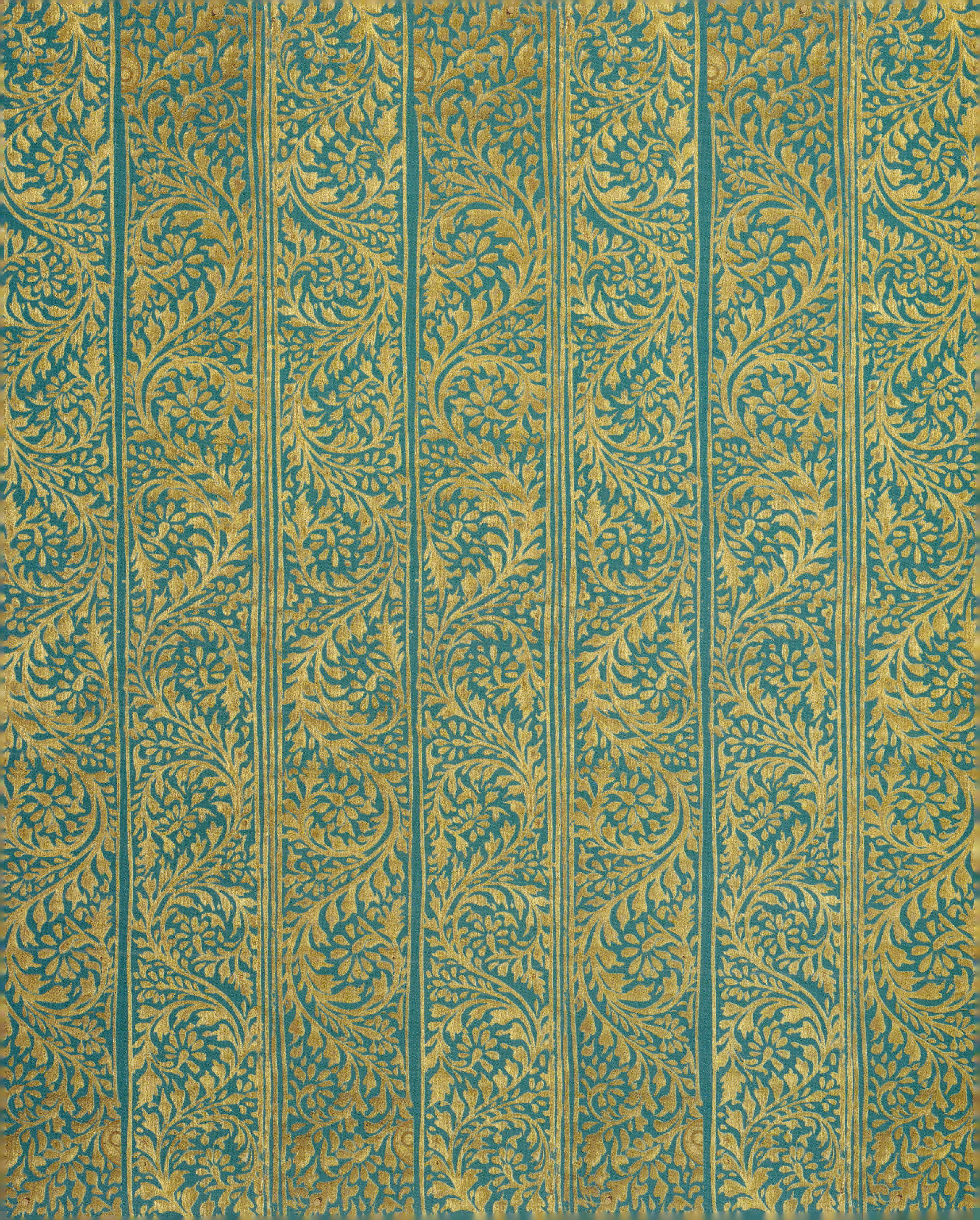

Architecture
A Scattered Legacy

It was in Asia that the interests of the Sassoons were most closely intertwined with empire, and it was through architecture that their political and commercial influence was most visible. But for stateless minorities, establishing themselves in colonized lands and cities differed radically from settling in independent nations.[1] Whether in India or China, it was not possible for the Sassoons to transplant what they had known in Baghdad; as in other Jewish communities, they "were forced to adapt to the particular challenges of being Jewish in colonial environments distant from major centers of Jewish life."[2] Architecture thus represents another aspect of the spatial and cultural dislocations of diaspora, a complex dialectic between place and identity.

Accordingly, the Sassoons paid homage to the aesthetic canons of the ruling elites: in its different modalities, European culture "gave access to power."[3] At the same time, their experience of geographic, linguistic, and cultural diversity became an empowering engine of cultural syncretism as they sought to adapt their architectural ambitions to a succession of cultural and political contexts. The resulting hybridity of their synagogues, schools, hospitals, and commercial structures served as emblems of self-representation for the Baghdadi community within the framework of local contingencies. In the long run, it was an unstable amalgam, a slippery cusp where diaspora and colonialism intersected.

Creating a meaningful architectural legacy involves more than financial patronage; it also requires the considerable affective and psychological investment of its donors. The homes and synagogues that witnessed so many rites of passage—births, bar and bat mitzvahs, marriages, funerals—had become repositories of memory. But unlike art collections, buildings are not portable, and each migration took an emotional toll on the family, as these structures had to be left behind: traces of presence that took on new meanings as they were appropriated by other groups.

The dialectic between place and identity would change one last time when England became home, and architecture, an investment in permanence.

India

When David Sassoon disembarked in Mumbai in 1832, it was a bustling, cosmopolitan, and multilingual port, a great cultural crucible inhabited by Hindus, Muslims, Parsis, Jains, Armenians, Portuguese, Baghdadis, and large numbers of Eurasians, as well as a city of caste, class, and enslaved individuals.[4] The "Baghdadis" included Jews from other cities in Iraq, Syria, Yemen, Persia, and Afghanistan. The monopoly of the East India Company had ended, but the Europeans still huddled within the walled precincts of the Fort. Water supply and proper sewerage were lacking. Public lighting, introduced in 1843, was limited to an insufficient number of oil lamps. By the time David died in 1864, Mumbai was a city transformed, not least through the profits of opium, a major source of wealth for both Indians and Europeans since the 1820s.[5] As in Mumbai, a vibrant Baghdadi community established itself in Kolkata, under the leadership of the Ezras. The Sassoons, who had offices there, were deeply engaged in all aspects of local life.

Sir Henry Bartle Frere, Governor of Bombay from 1862 to 1867, endowed the city with

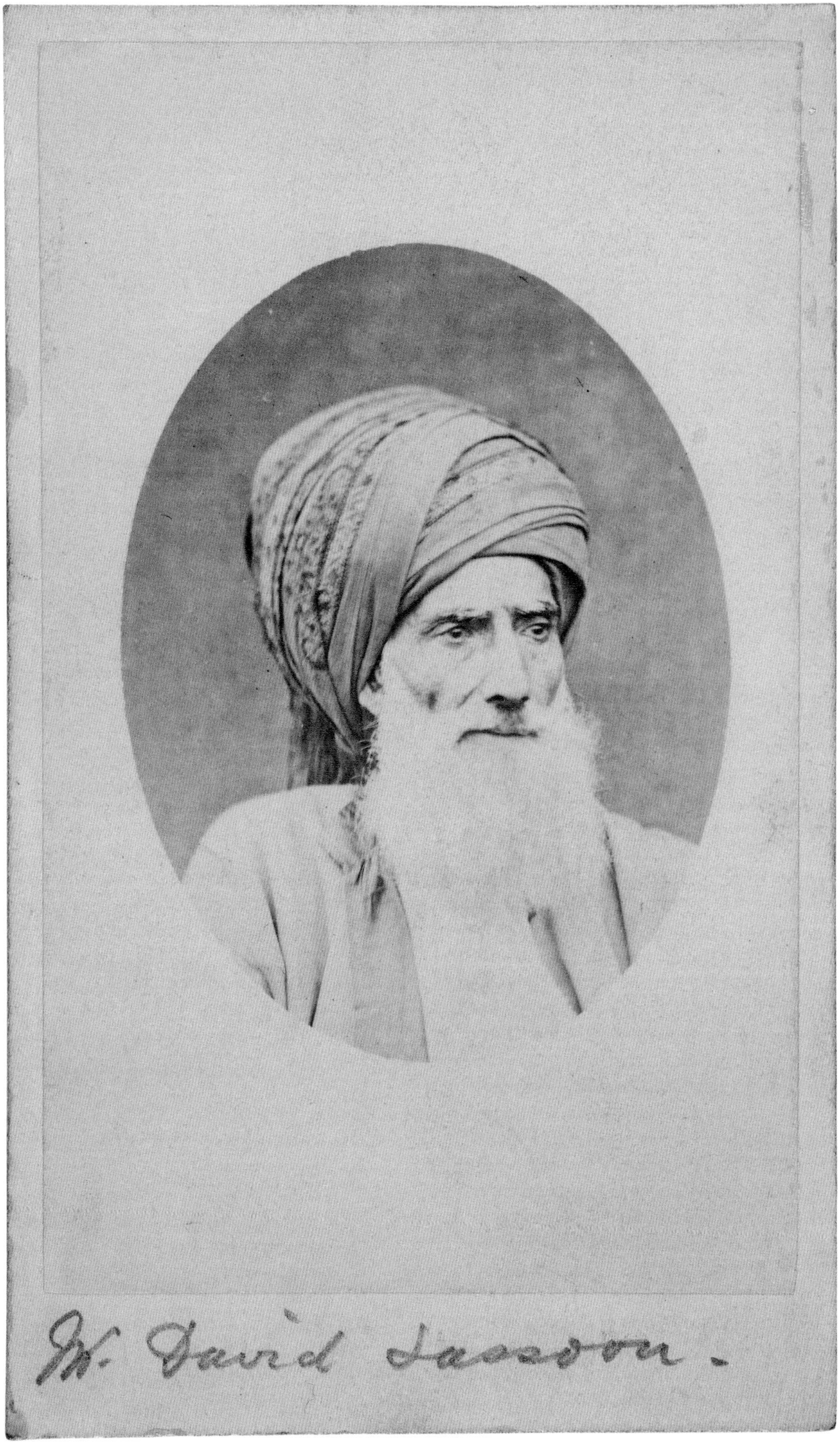

David Sassoon, c. 1858–64, from "Indian worthies non Indian," in *Archaeological Survey of India Collections: India Office Series*, vol. 44, London, British Library, Visual Arts Collection. This portrait of David Sassoon evokes a description of him by James Douglas in *Glimpses of Old Bombay and Western India with Other Papers*, 1900: "A quiet unpretending man in Eastern dress, he comes out like Isaac at eventide, making his ways by Church Gate."

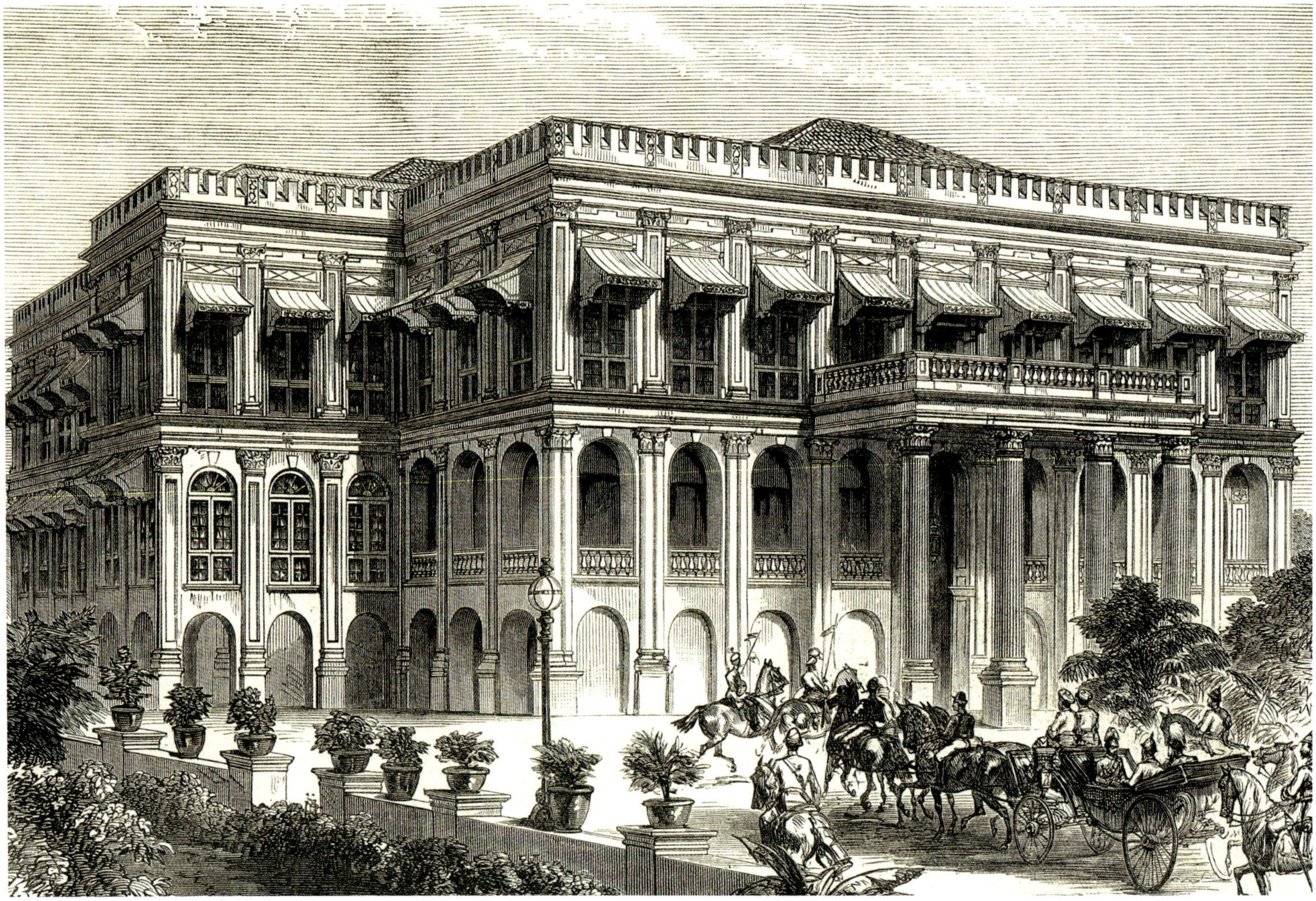

modern infrastructure, razing the walls, moat, and the glacis that surrounded the Fort to make more land available for building. These changes were only possible with the active participation and initiatives of the Indians, as well as the Parsis, Baghdadis, and other ethnic minorities. Inevitably, heritage suffered. "Almost every old landmark of the Fort of 1850 and 1855 has vanished from view," lamented the Parsi politician Dinshaw Edulji Wacha.[6]

When the Sassoons arrived, there were already between twenty and thirty "Arabian" Jewish families in Mumbai.[7] A much older Jewish community, the Bene Israel, had lived in India for centuries.[8] Indistinguishable from the Indians, they were part of the "unselfconscious cosmopolitanism" of the area, residing, as the architectural historian Smita Dalvi pointed out, "cheek by jowl with Hindus, Muslims, Christians, Parsis, and Jains, religiously distinct but socially one with the polyglot of Bombay and the Konkan."[9] The Bene Israel received the Baghdadis warmly, welcoming them to their synagogues and opening their cemetery to the newcomers. The Sassoons responded with many benefactions, but fissures soon appeared between the orthodox Baghdadis and the more self-consciously Indian Bene Israel.[10] In 1836, ten Mizrahi Jews, including David Sassoon, asked permission from the authorities to build a wall inside the Jewish cemetery to separate Baghdadis and Bene Israel (the Baghdadis would later build their own cemetery).[11] And in the following decades, the Baghdadis in Mumbai and Kolkata would petition the authorities repeatedly to have themselves classified as Europeans. In the deeply stratified social landscape of colonial Bombay, minorities who were part of the entrepreneurial elites sought to emphasize their special status, an ambition Frere was quick to exploit, writing in 1862 that the Baghdadis "are, like the Parsees, a most valuable link between us and the natives—oriental in origin and appreciation—but English in their objects and associations, and, almost of necessity, loyal."[12]

In traditional accounts, Baghdadi Jews appear as unwavering supporters of the colonial

Visit of the Prince of Wales to Sans Souci, Mumbai, David Sassoon's former home (now the Masina Hospital), November 17, 1875, published in the *Illustrated London News*, February 5, 1876.

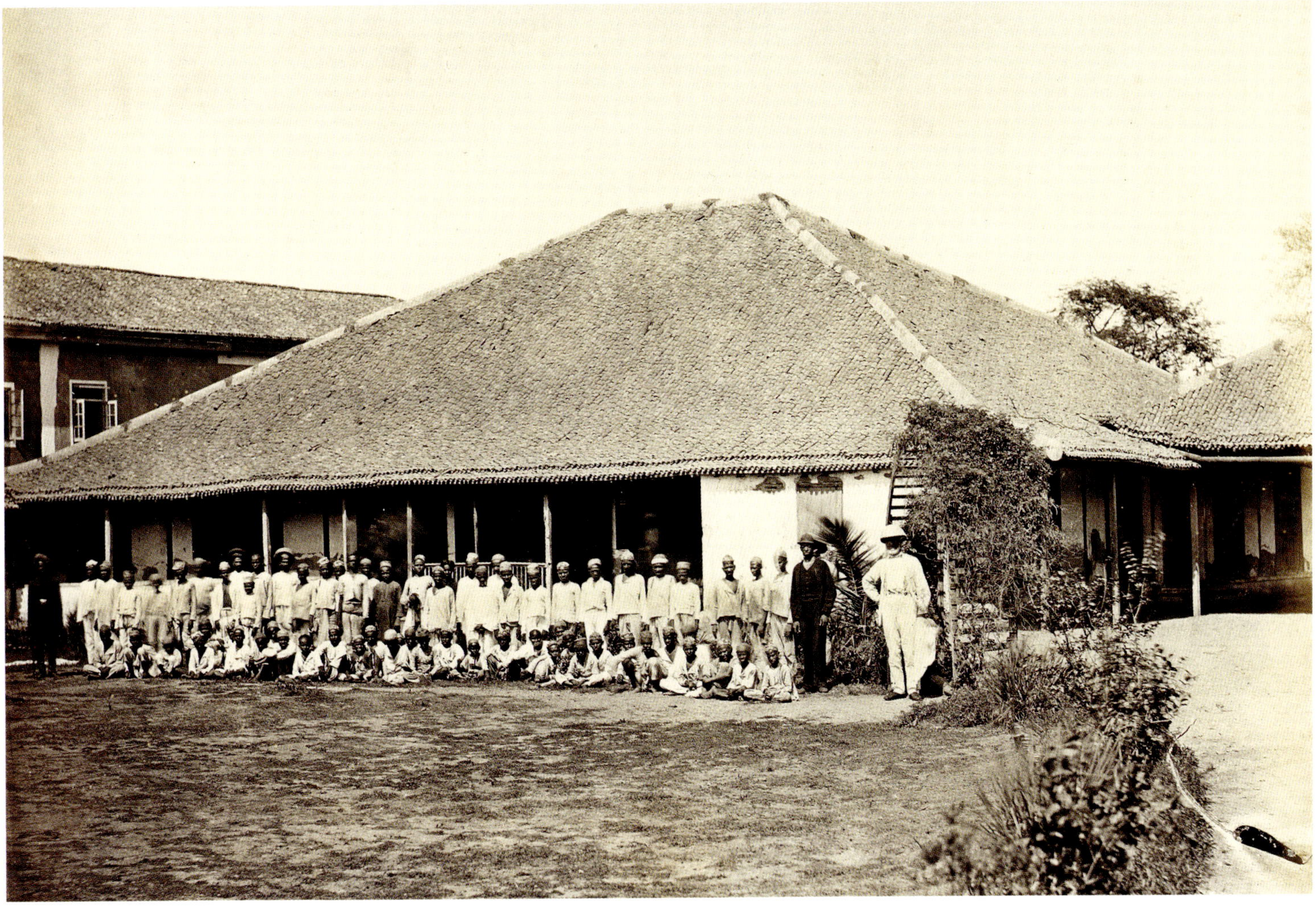

The David Sassoon Industrial and Reformatory Institution in Mumbai, c. 1869, photographed by Tandy and Co. (?), from an album of photographs of the Mumbai properties belonging to the Sassoon family, 1869, London, British Library, Visual Arts Collection, given by Edwina and Sybil Sassoon. David Sassoon donated the house and money for its upkeep in 1857.

powers, with little contact with other ethnic and religious groups. However, public and private realms were hardly watertight.[13] David was close to several Parsis, like his friend Jamsetjee Jeejeebhoy, a Parsi businessman and philanthropist. Albert Abdullah Sassoon, David's son, frequented and entertained Indian nobility. Far less is known about the role played by the Sassoon women, but they, too, forged affective ties with other groups. In 1875, when Albert Abdullah was in London, his wife, Hannah (1826–1895), received the Prince of Wales and his entourage during his visit to Mumbai, and after her husband moved permanently to England, she remained behind due to poor health, overseeing all the charities supported by David Sassoon & Co.[14] Her death was mourned even by the Bene Israel, who remembered her generosity and influence.[15]

Flora Sassoon received progressive Hindu, Parsi, Muslim, and European women in her palatial home. Together with Lady Dhunbai Cowasji Jehangir, member of a distinguished Parsi family and the head of several women's organizations, and Fanny Mackay, wife of Lord Reay, Governor of Bombay, Flora was one of the leaders of the anti-purdah movement, which opposed the practice of secluding women.[16]

On arrival, David found modest dwellings in Tamarind Lane, in the Fort. As his business grew (trade in textiles, spices, pearls), he became a highly respected member of the city and the biggest employer of the Baghdadi Jews. Eager to acquire a new home commensurate with his growing prestige, in 1851 he bought and remodeled an imposing mansion in Byculla, the new upscale residential area north of the city center. Surrounded by gardens and fountains, the three-story classical villa—now the Masina Hospital—was renamed Sans Souci, after Frederick the Great's palace at Potsdam. A long allée led from the gate to the entrance, an elegant portico framed by Corinthian columns. Inside, the coat of arms of the Sassoons was conspicuously displayed on the first landing of the impressive staircase. Two glazed courtyards,

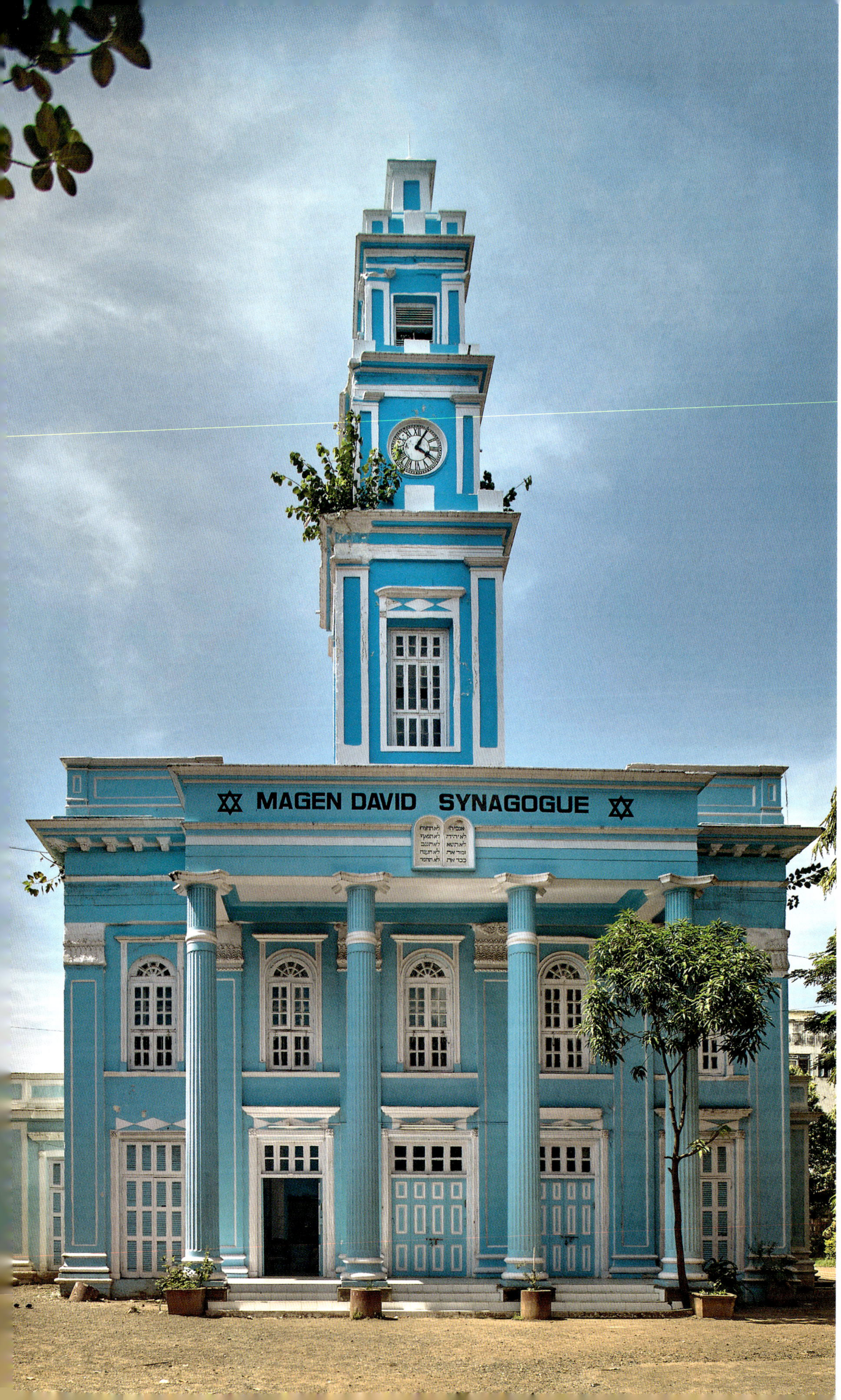

Magen David Synagogue, 1857–61, Byculla, Mumbai.

OPPOSITE
Magen David Synagogue, Byculla, Mumbai, interior.

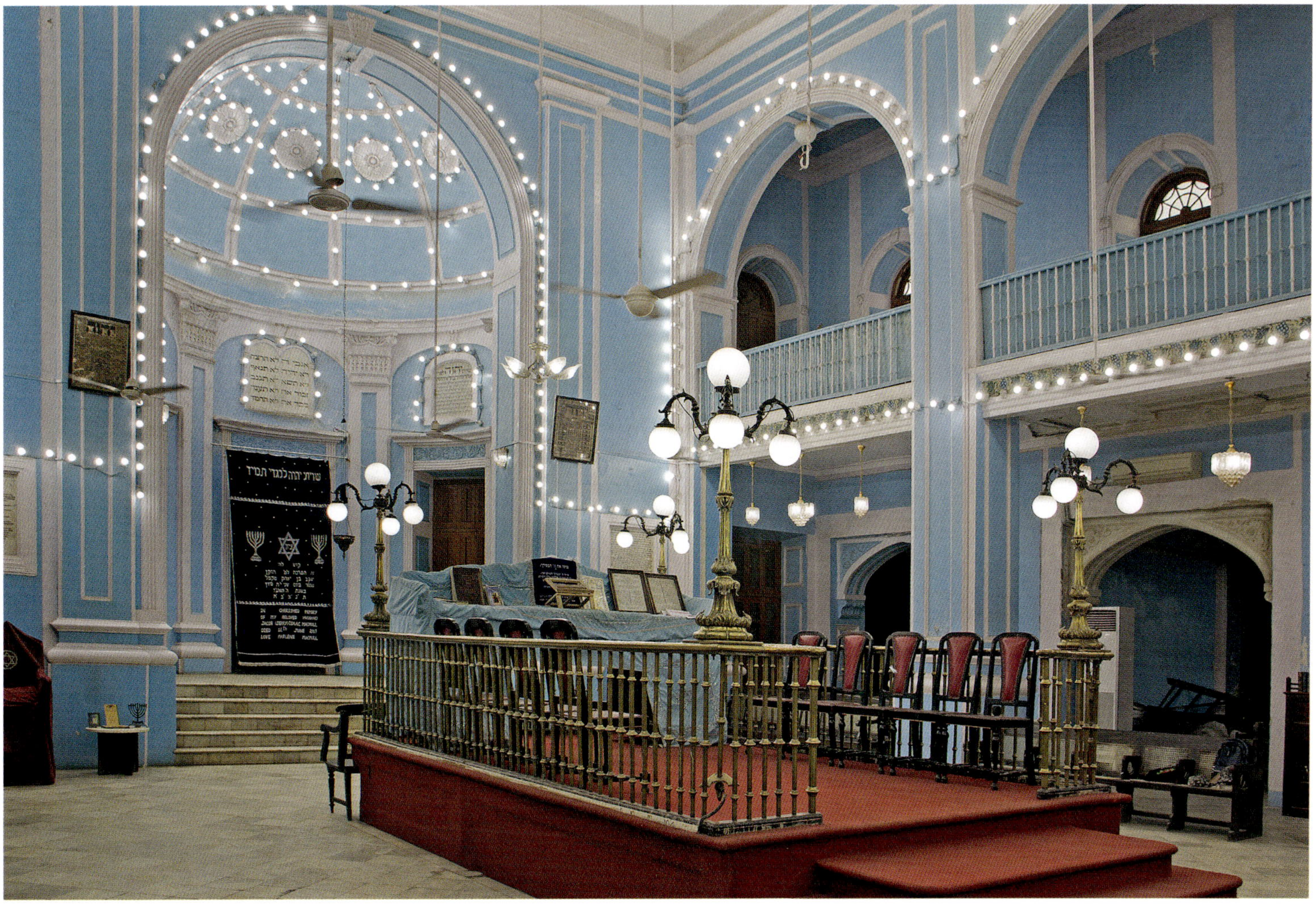

ingeniously ventilated, brought light and air into the building. Its magnificent crystal chandeliers are now in the city's Royal Opera House. One of the grandest houses in Mumbai, Sans Souci became the site of receptions for the elite. In 1859, when the government of India passed from the East India Company to Queen Victoria, David gave a ball for 500 people. After dinner, John Elphinstone, Governor of Bombay, thanked his host for his magnificent hospitality, praised him for the recently endowed Reformatory Industrial Institution, and expressed gratitude for the loyalty shown by the Jewish community during the Indian Rebellion of 1857, the first movement of independence against the British.

If David lost no opportunity to affirm his ties to Britain, he remained proudly Jewish, as shown by the beautiful synagogue he built in Mumbai. Magen David (1857–61), situated near Sans Souci, was part of a large compound that came to include schools, a dispensary, an oven for matzot, a ritual bath or mikvah, a club, and later still, a guesthouse. With its two-story portico and clock tower, the classical façade echoes that of the nearby Anglican Christ Church (1832–33). Both houses of worship were based on James Gibbs's St. Martin-in-the-Fields in London, the prototype for churches in India. But Magen David was no slavish imitation of its Christian model. Little given to impetuous gestures, David considered everything with the cautious deliberation of a chess player, pondering consequences and implications before acting. The synagogue's inspired hybridity reflects both religious devotion and political calculation. His cultural kinship to the British also served to distance the Baghdadis from the Bene Israel, whose synagogues resembled their domestic architecture and reflected their lower economic status.[17]

Despite the synagogue's monumental scale, its classical details and white trim give it a pronounced delicacy, inside and out. The exterior was clad in chunam, polished lime plaster. As the side porticoes have been enclosed, the darkened

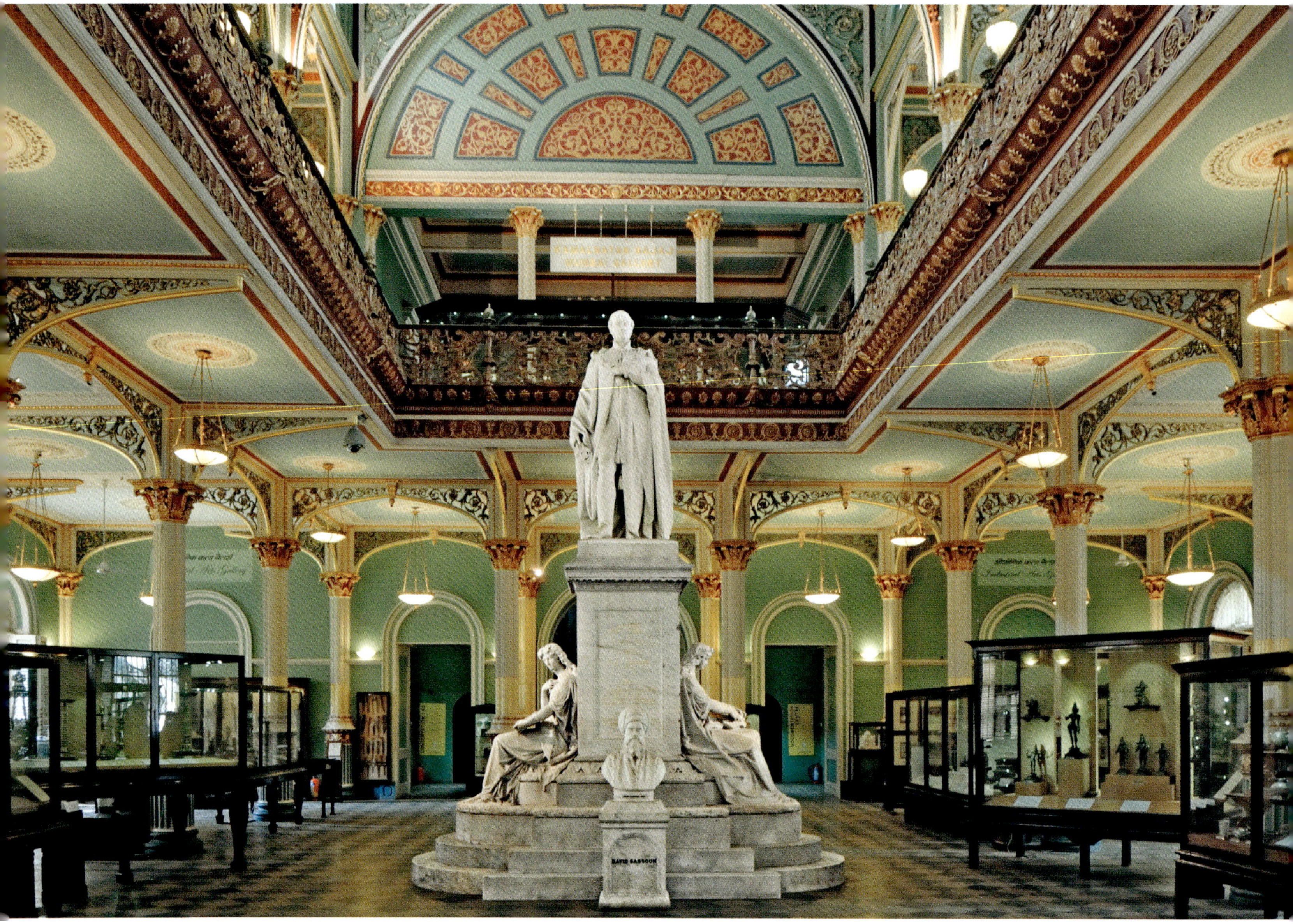

Dr. Bhau Daji Lad Museum (the former Victoria and Albert Museum), Mumbai, 1862–71, with Matthew Noble's 1864 statue of Prince Albert, donated by David Sassoon.

interior is now lit by numerous electric lights, added in the twentieth century, and carefully designed to underscore the main lines of the building. When Magen David proved too small for the growing community, it was enlarged by David's grandson Jacob Elias Sassoon in 1910. Next to it stood an equally handsome building, designed to match the synagogue: the David Sassoon Benevolent Institution, a primary school, long since demolished.

Other projects supported by David addressed both British and Indian interests. In 1862, the authorities decided to create a permanent building for Mumbai's first museum, the Victoria and Albert, renamed the Dr. Bhau Daji Lad Museum in honor of the renowned philanthropist, physician, and Sanskrit scholar. Situated in Victoria Gardens, now Jijamata Udyan, the grounds served as the botanical garden. Along with Jamsetjee Jeejeebhoy and the philanthropist and social reformer Jagannath Shanker Sheth, David contributed funds. He also gifted to the museum a marble statue of Prince Albert by Matthew Noble, with a dedicatory inscription in Marathi, Gujarati, Persian, English, and Hebrew. Sassoon did not live to see the completion of the building. In his honor, friends commissioned Thomas Woolner to make a bust of David for the museum. A clock tower donated by David was built in the gardens by Scott, McClelland and Company in 1864, an Italianate structure with a rusticated base, imported Minton tiles, and terracotta panels. There, too, a marble bust of Sassoon was installed inside after his death.

The Mechanic's Institute, now the David Sassoon Library (1867–73), is a testament to

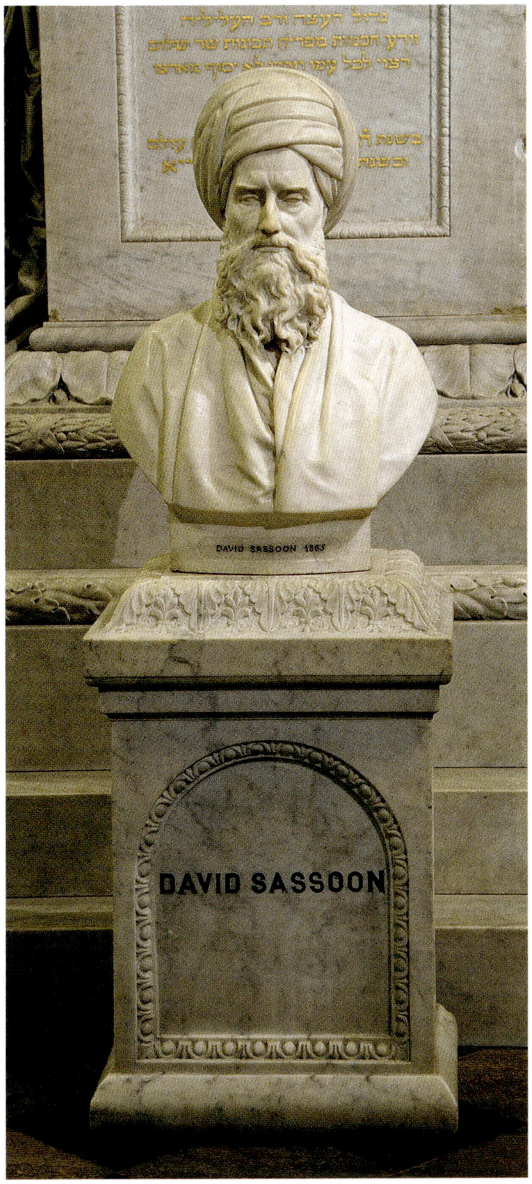

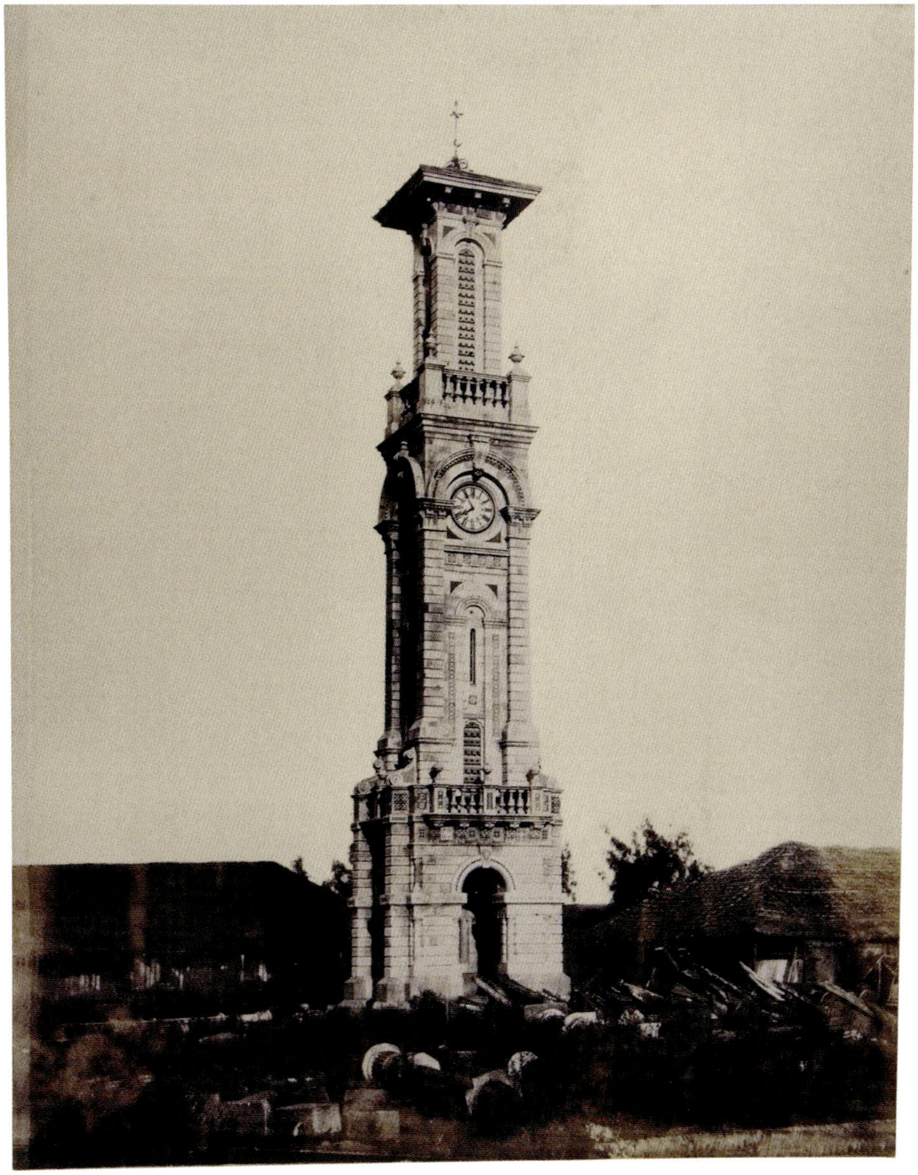

Thomas Woolner, bust of David Sassoon, 1865, in the Dr. Bhau Daji Lad Museum, Mumbai; behind him is the Hebrew dedicatory inscription for the statue of Prince Albert.

David Sassoon Clock Tower, Jijamata Udyan, Byculla, Mumbai, 1864, from an album of photographs of the Mumbai properties belonging to the Sassoon family, 1869, London, British Library, Visual Arts Collection, given by Edwina and Sybil Sassoon, 2012.

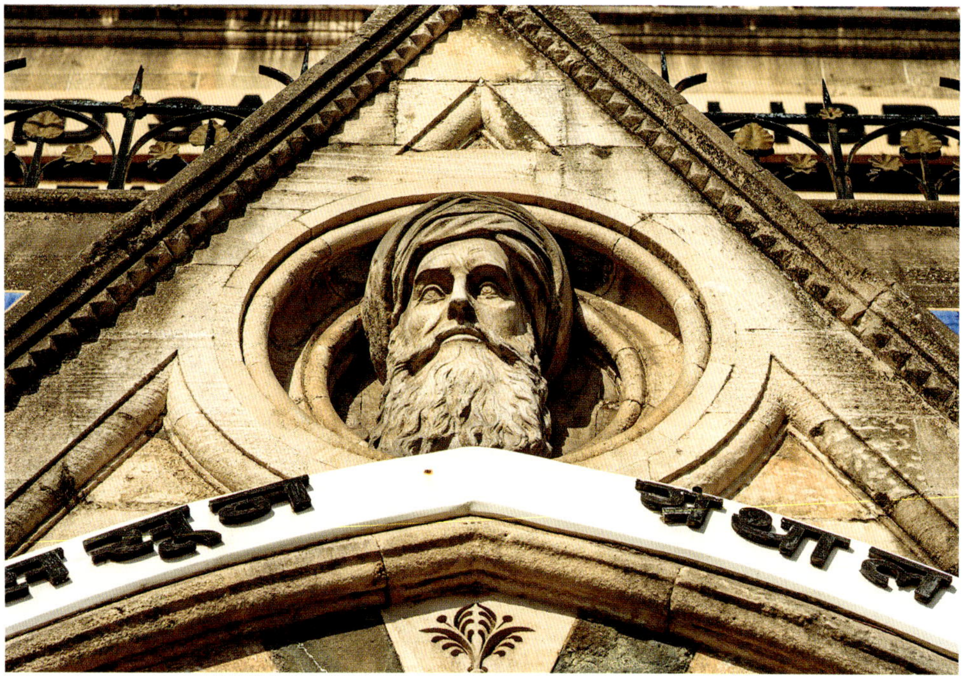

John Lockwood Kipling, portrait of David Sassoon on the façade of the David Sassoon Library, Mumbai, c. 1870–73.

David's interest in educating citizens beyond his community. It is one of the best known buildings of Victorian Mumbai, built on a prime location on the Esplanade. Founded in the 1840s to provide a forum for lectures and discussions, the organization met in rented premises until Sassoon's bequest. As the Gothic Revival was in full swing in Britain and its colonies, architects David Ebenezer Gostling and John Campbell of Scott, McClelland and Company chose the Venetian Gothic, then gaining popularity in Mumbai. The architects were aided by the engineers John Augustus Fuller and Khan Bahadur Muncherji Cowasji Murzban. The latter was responsible for much of the detailing, including the furniture and floor patterns.[18]

As it stands, this small, lovely library sparkles with creative flourishes. Whenever possible, the architects sought contrasting forms, colors, and materials (Kurla, Porbandar, and Vasai stone). To impart variety to the façade, each of the three floors is treated differently. The beauty of the wrought iron, woodwork, and delicately carved fruit and foliage of the capitals reflects the exceptional quality of local craftsmanship. Two statues of David Sassoon adorn the building: a medallion by John Lockwood Kipling (father of Rudyard Kipling) on the façade and, at the instigation of Frere, a life-size statue by Thomas Woolner in the foyer, to which the Rothschilds, the Montagus, the Mocattas, Gladstone, Parsi philanthropists, and even Lancashire mill workers (whom David had helped in the past) contributed.[19]

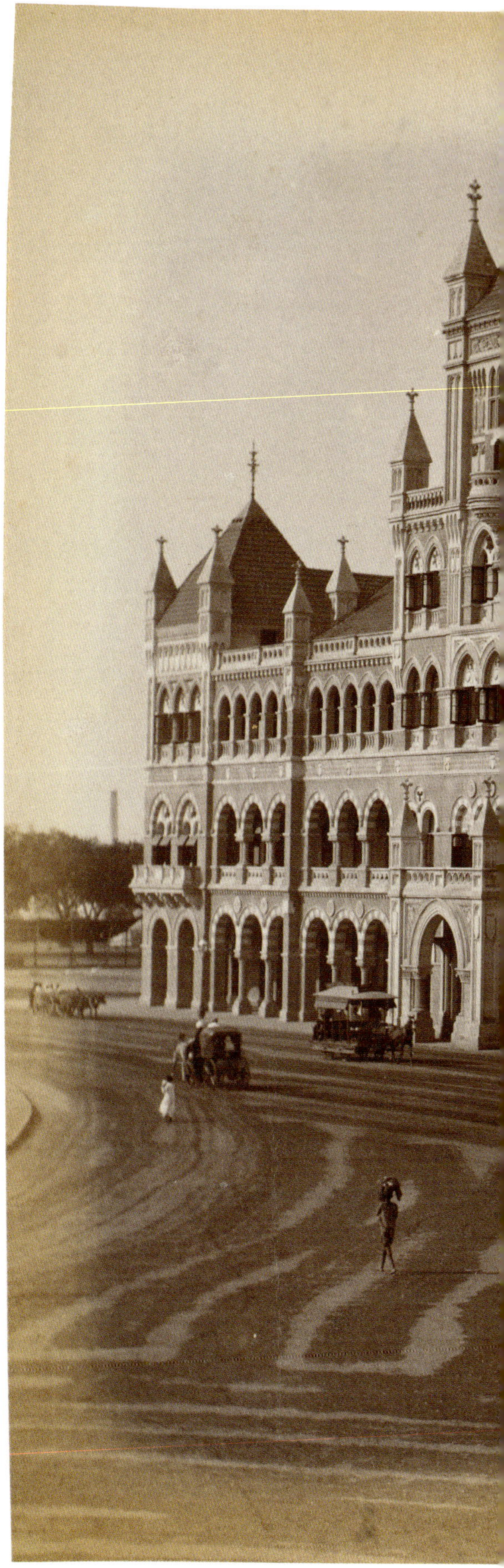

View of the Elphinstone College from the junction of Rampart Row and Esplanade Road, Mumbai—with a view of the Sassoon Library and equestrian statue of the Prince of Wales (known as Kala Ghoda), a statue commissioned by Albert Abdullah Sassoon, c. 1890, London, British Library, Visual Arts Collection.

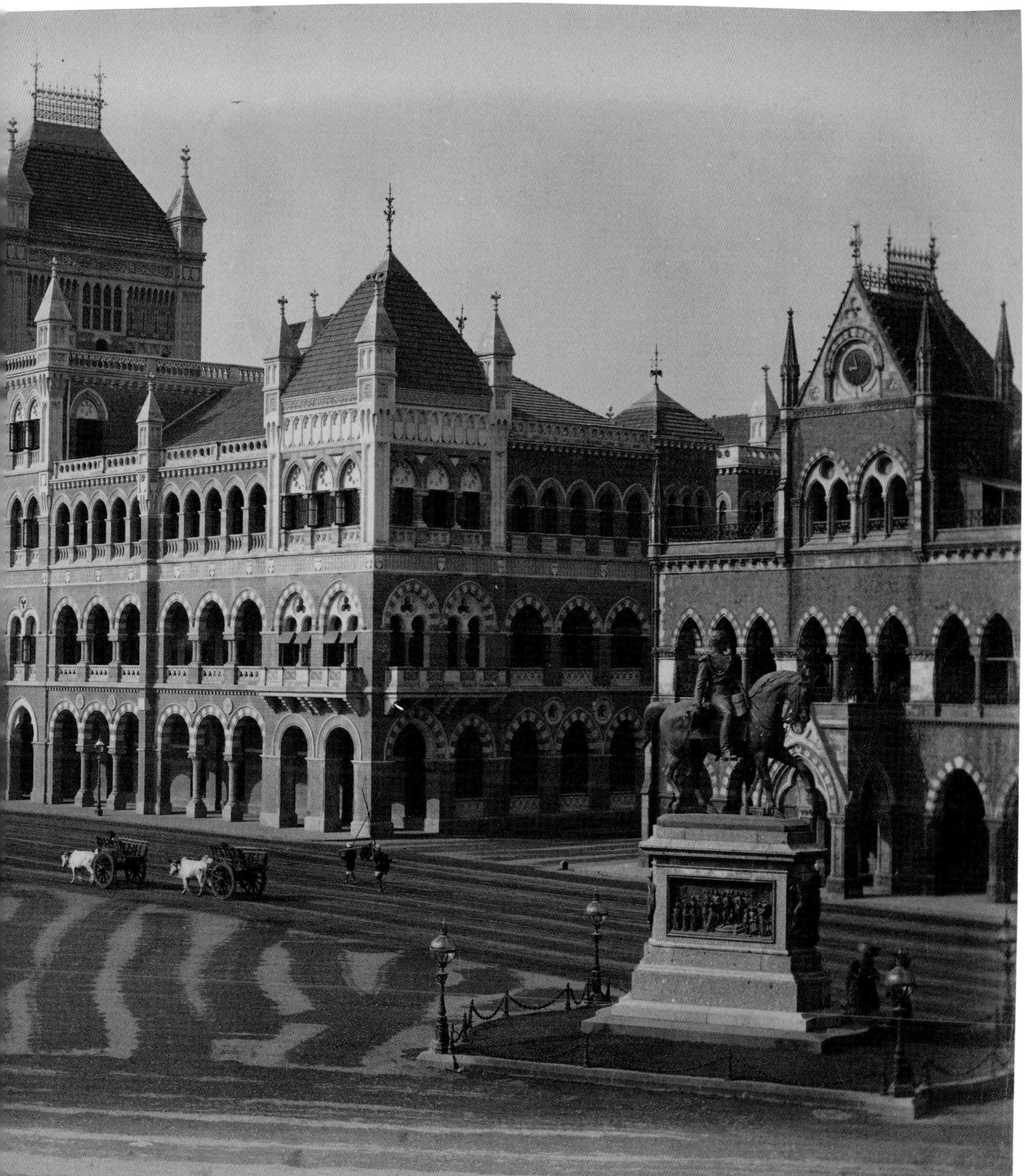

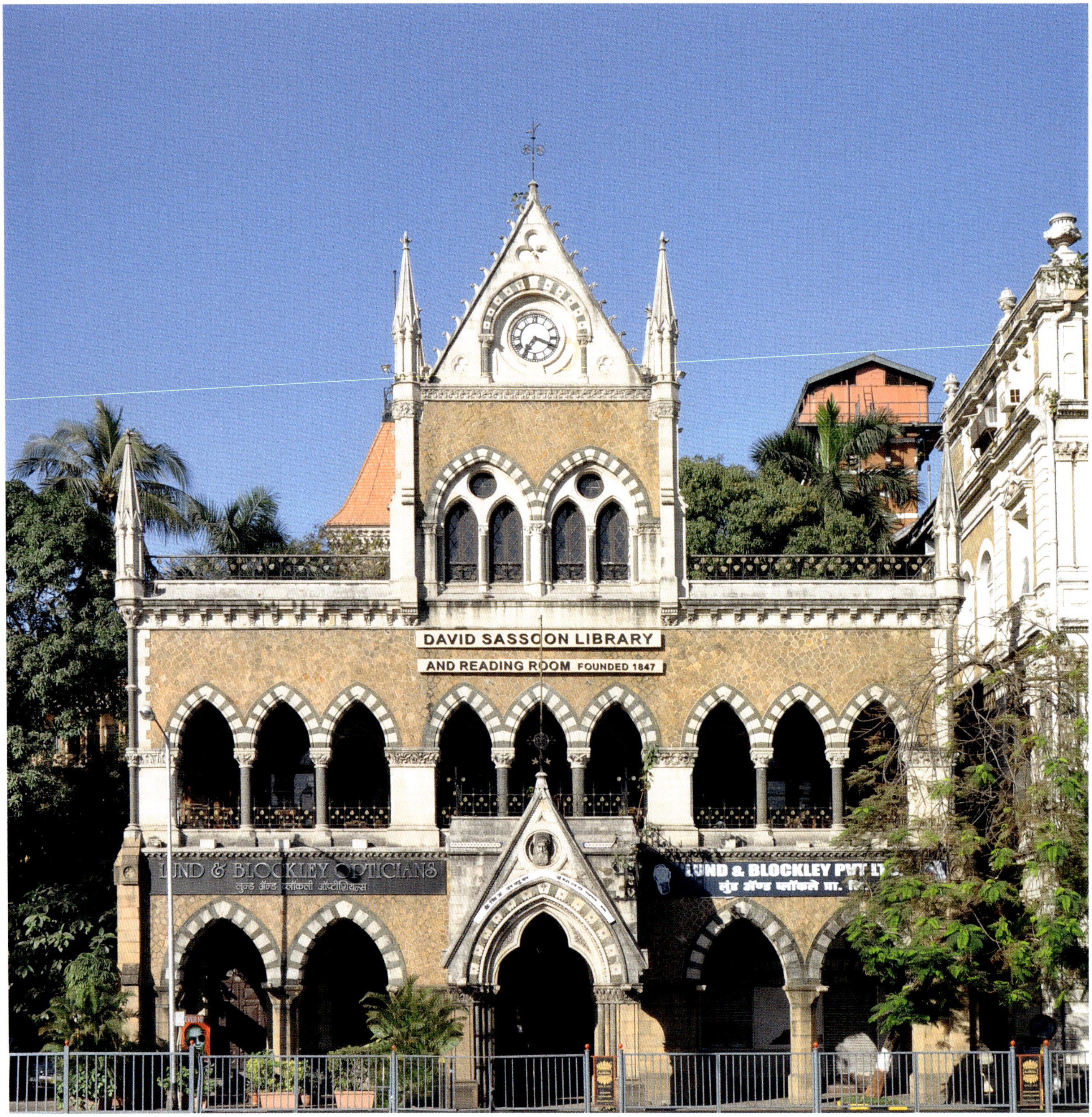

David Sassoon Library, Mumbai, 1870, David Ebenezer Gostling and John Campbell of Scott, McClelland and Company, architects, John Augustus Fuller and Khan Bahadur Muncherji Cowasji Murzban, engineers.

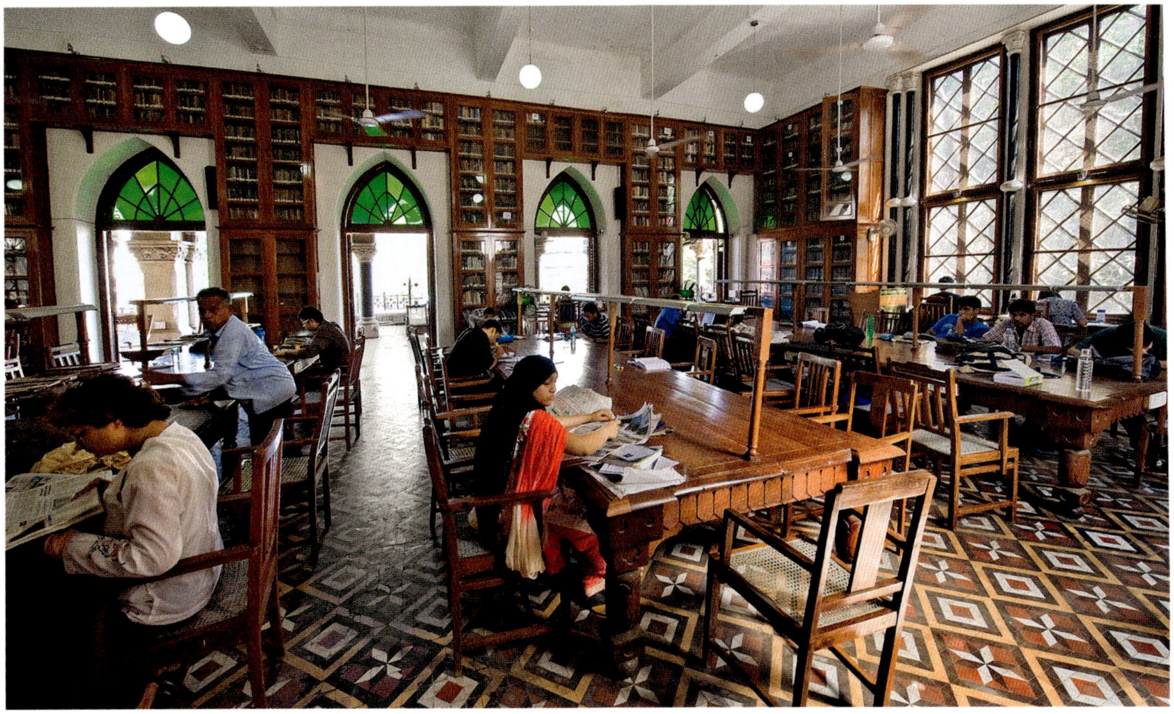

David Sassoon Library, Mumbai, interior.

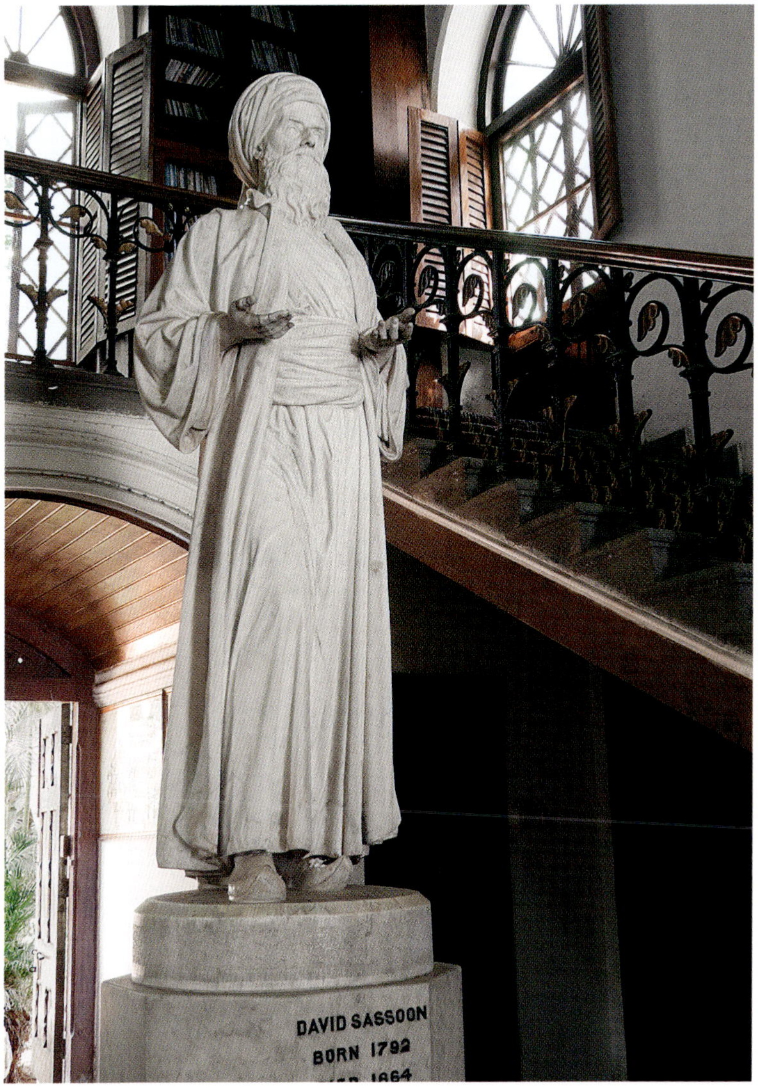

Thomas Woolner, *David Sassoon*, 1865, marble, David Sassoon Library, Mumbai.

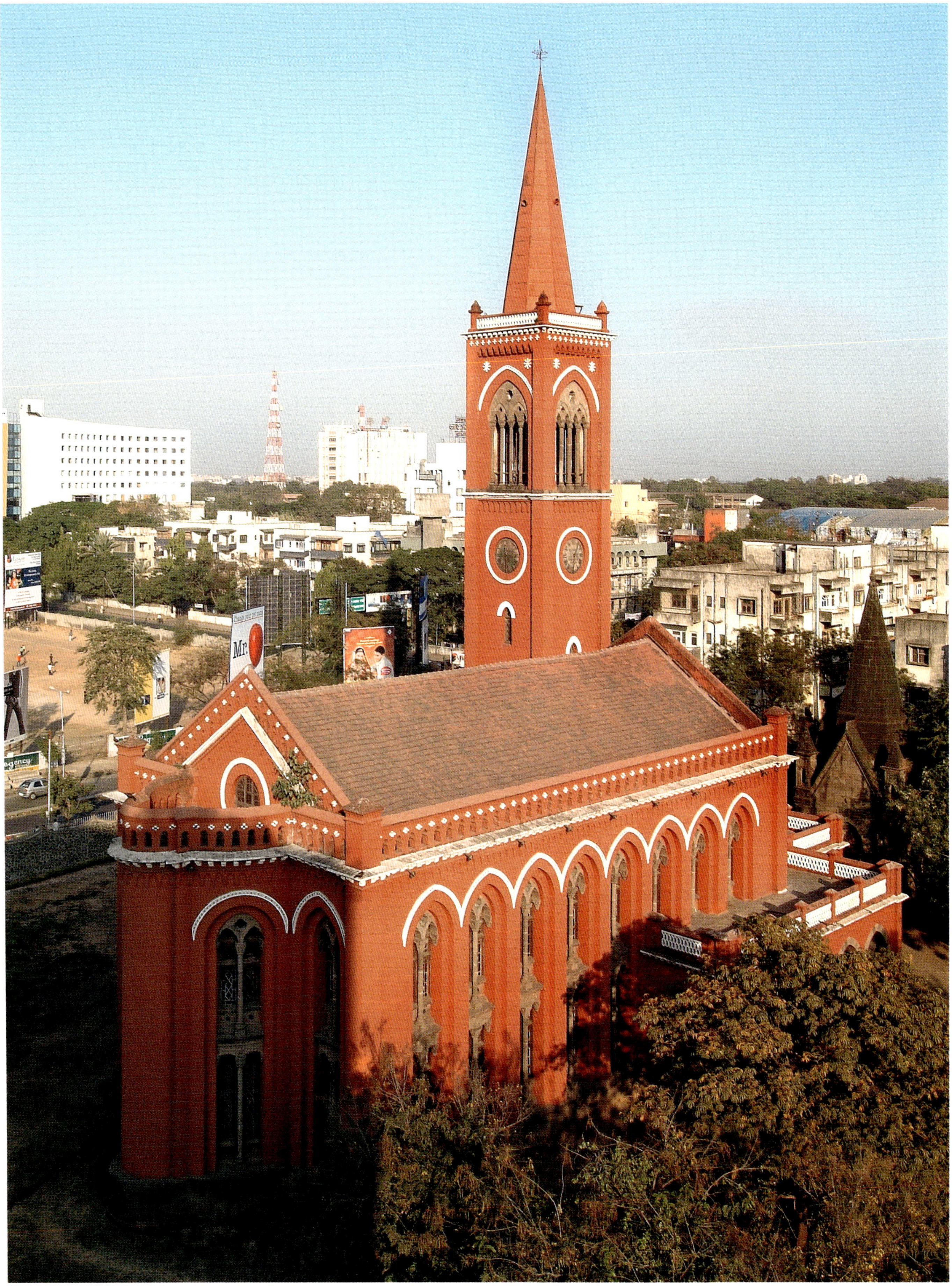

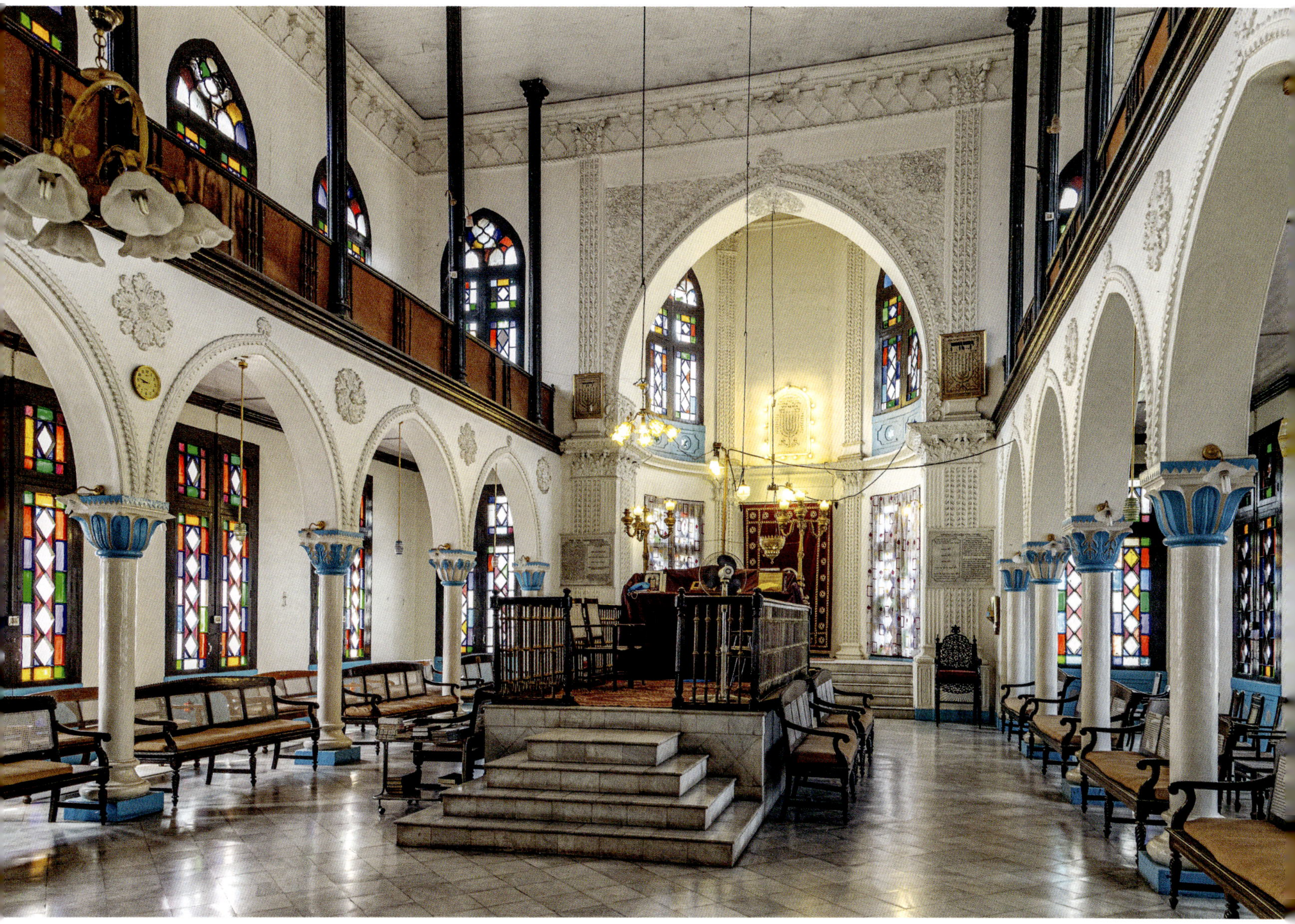

Ohel David Synagogue, Pune, 1863–67, Henry Saint Clair Wilkins, architect.

Ohel David Synagogue, Pune, 1863–67, interior.

Pune

Like other members of the elite, the Sassoons spent the monsoon season in Pune, a fashionable resort then part of the Bombay Presidency. In Pune, David sponsored a hospital, a leper asylum, the Niwara Old Age Home, and a beautiful neo-Gothic synagogue, Ohel David (1863–67), designed by Henry Saint Clair Wilkins, an officer in the East India Company. As in the case of Magen David, the synagogue resembled the nearby Anglican church of St. Paul's, which was under construction at the same time. Both have a tall steeple to the right of the nave (equipped with a clock, in the case of Ohel David), a front portico serving as entrance, and another to the side. Known as the red synagogue, Ohel David offers a striking contrast between the sleek neo-Gothic design and vivid un-Gothic color. The spacious, airy feeling of the nave, flooded with light streaming through stained-glass windows, comes from the façade's close-set, two-story ogival windows. Wilkins also designed Sassoon's tomb within the premises of the synagogue, a cube pierced by four neo-Gothic arches and gables and surmounted by a tapering spire, all in Deccan basalt. The Hebrew epitaph extols David Sassoon and his philanthropic works, as the builder of the synagogues Magen David in Mumbai and Ohel David in Pune, who also erected a hospital and a reformatory for young men, for people of all creeds, and whose generosity knew no boundaries, extending from Jerusalem to London. In Jewish tradition, mausoleums are unusual.[20] Other Sassoon family members would make use of them in Mumbai and in Brighton.

Before he died, in Pune, David donated funds for the Sassoon General Hospital (1863–67),

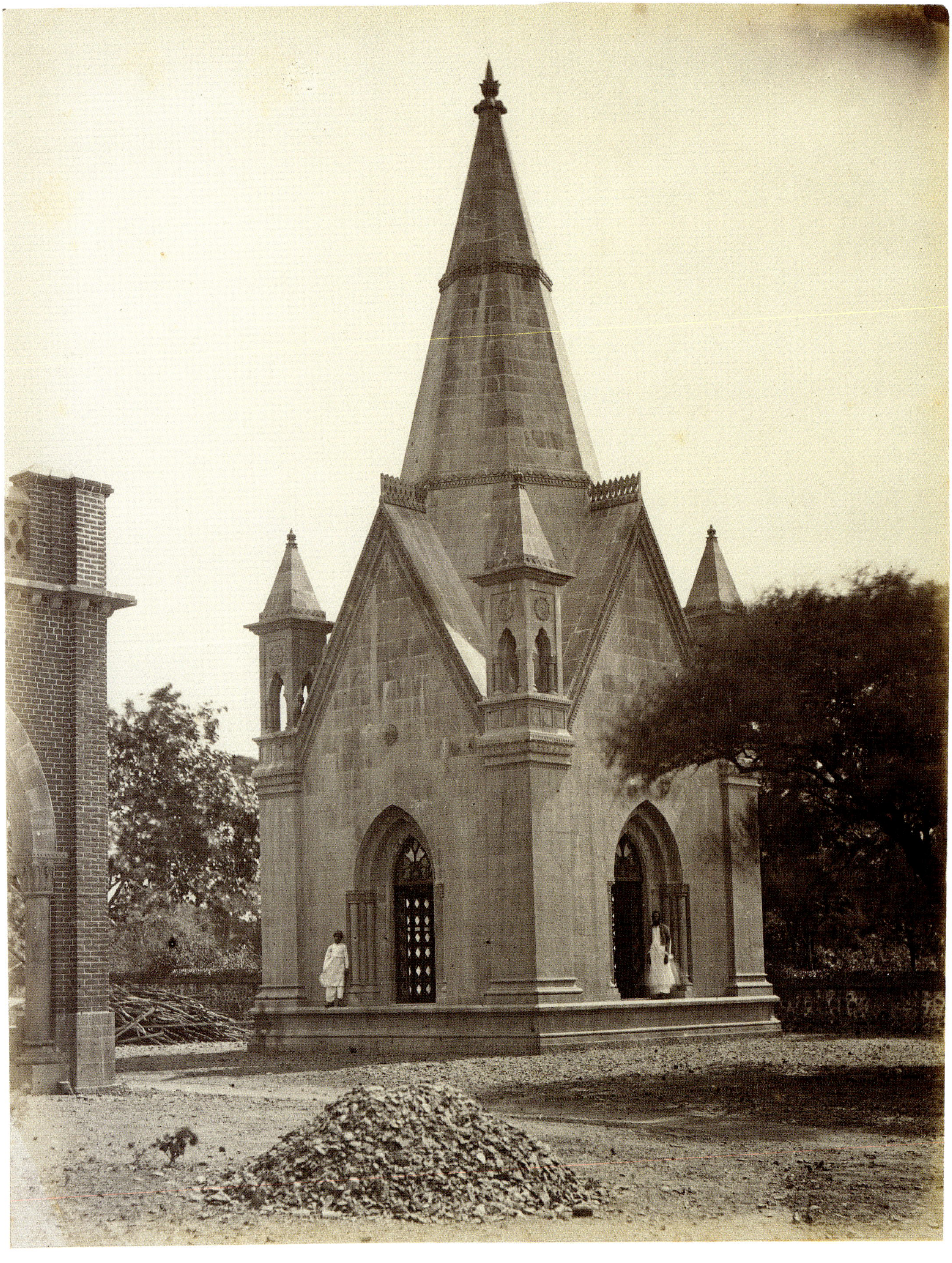

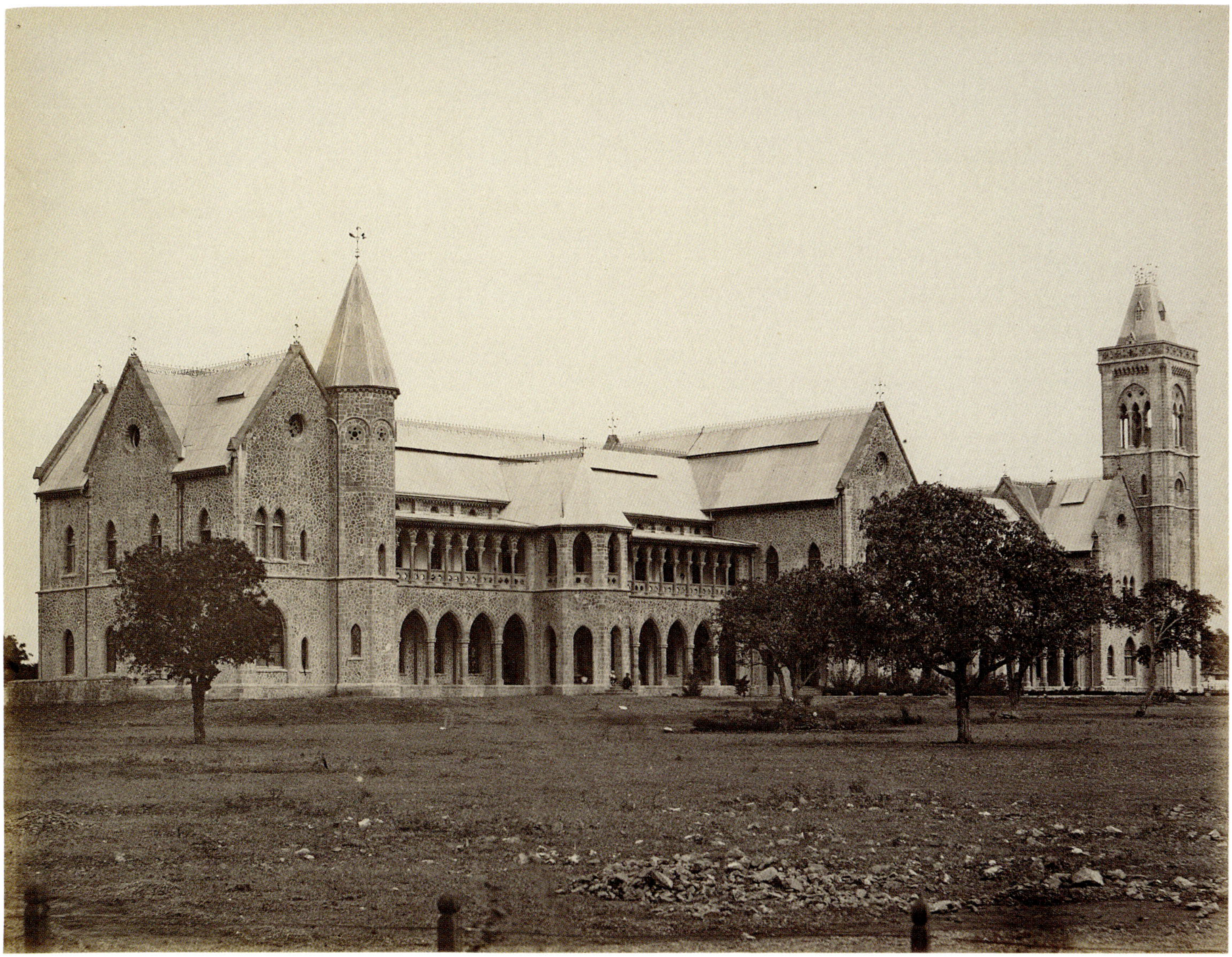

OPPOSITE
David Sassoon's mausoleum on the grounds of the Ohel David Synagogue, 1864, Henry Saint Clair Wilkins, architect, from an album of photographs of the Pune properties belonging to the Sassoon family, 1869, London, British Library, Visual Arts Collection, given by Edwina and Sybil Sassoon, 2012.

Sassoon Hospital, Pune, 1863–67, Henry Saint Clair Wilkins, architect, from an album of photographs of the Pune properties belonging to the Sassoon family, 1869, London, British Library, Visual Arts Collection, given by Edwina and Sybil Sassoon, 2012.

also designed by Wilkins. The long neo-Gothic building was broken up by several short wings, a turret, and a clock tower similar to that of Ohel David. On one side, two stories of arcades produce a welcome contrast to the walls in basalt and gray trap stone. At the time, it was rare to find hospitals that admitted all groups and castes, due to notions of ritual purity and propriety. As the *Illustrated London News* put it, with a touch of colonial superiority, the dispensary was open "to all, Hindoo or Mahommedan, or of whatever creed or nation, who come to seek the help of European science."[21]

Sons and Grandsons

Albert Abdullah, David's oldest son and heir, continued to expand the Sassoon business while working to complete his father's public projects.[22] He, too, sought to balance colonial and local interests, using Sans Souci to entertain lavishly. When Frere named him a Companion of the Order of the Star of India in 1867, Albert gave a ball for 300 people, earning praise from the *Bombay Gazette* for excluding "natives" from the guest list.[23] However, on November 25, 1872, Albert Abdullah gave a sumptuous dinner in honor of the Viceroy of India, Lord Northbrook, with more than 1,400 guests, including Indian dignitaries. According to a British eyewitness, the reception "was the most gorgeous and brilliant ever given in Bombay, and it will never be forgotten by anyone who took part in that magnificent entertainment."[24]

In Pune, where the family's legendary hospitality continued during the monsoon season, Albert Abdullah bought a magnificent neo-Gothic residence, Garden Reach, from Jamsetjee Jeejeebhoy, whose coat of arms adorned the stained-glass windows. Designed by Wilkins between 1862 and 1864, it was surrounded by gardens that sloped toward the river. The asymmetrical façade has towers, wings, and porticoes, giving a lively rhythm to the massing. The interior boasted refined detailing, metalwork, stained glass, and marble floors.[25] Along with other elite families, the Sassoons had additional summer homes in the hills at Mahabaleshwar, far above sea level, 150 miles from Mumbai.

Many of Albert Abdullah's benefactions were in the form of charitable trusts, often to support institutions founded by his father. Others involved construction. Among his most important contributions to Mumbai were the Sassoon Docks (1872–75). Realizing that the opening of the Suez Canal would significantly cut travel time with the Mediterranean and increase trade, he bought land at Colaba and built the first wet dock of the city, excavated out of solid granite. It was an ambitious project. Warehouses for cotton, the main export crop, were built along the piers, close to the railway. The large gateway marking the entrance to the docks was capped by a clock tower, a sign of Western punctuality and discipline characteristic of the British Raj, the period from 1858 until 1947 during which the Indian subcontinent was subject to direct rule by Britain.[26]

In honor of Mountstuart Elphinstone, Governor of Bombay, Albert Abdullah founded the David Sassoon Building for Elphinstone Technical

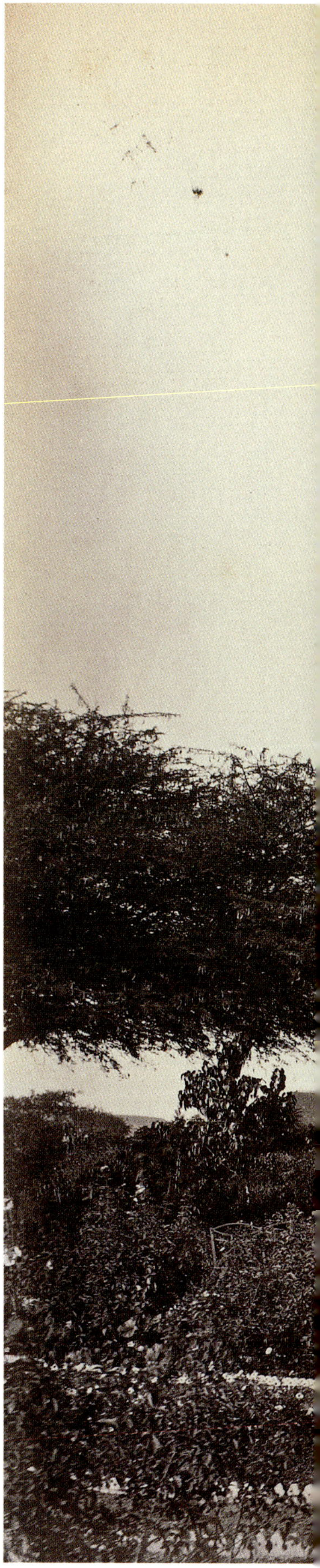

Albert Abdullah Sassoon residence, Garden Reach, Pune, 1862–64, Henry Saint Clair Wilkins, architect, photograph taken during the visit of Alfred, Duke of Edinburgh and Saxe-Coburg-Gotha, c. 1870, London, Royal Collection Trust.

OVERLEAF
Members of the Sassoon family at one of their homes in Pune, where they spent the monsoon season, from an album of photographs of the Pune properties belonging to the Sassoon family, 1869, London, British Library, Visual Arts Collection, given by Edwina and Sybil Sassoon, 2012.

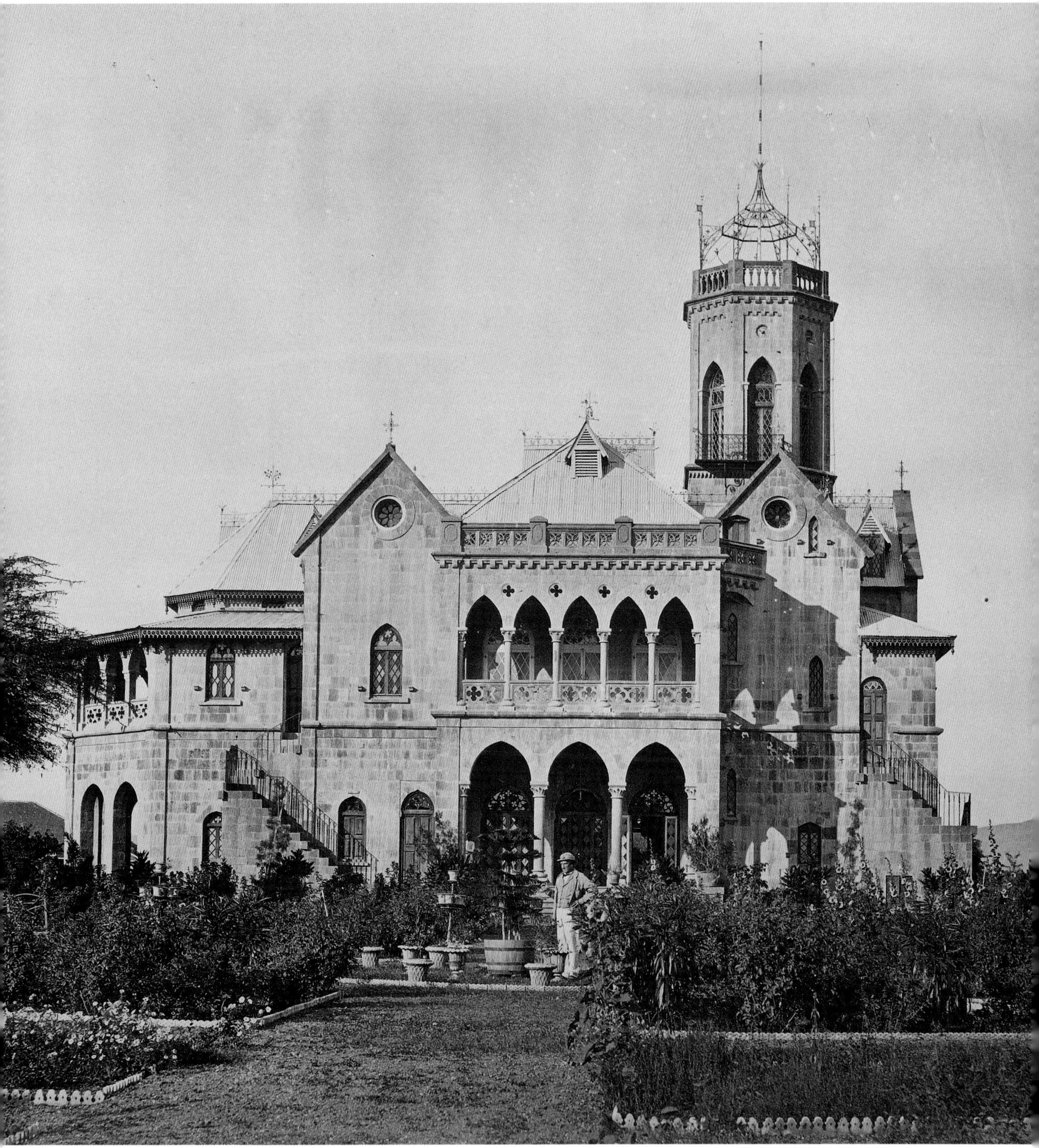

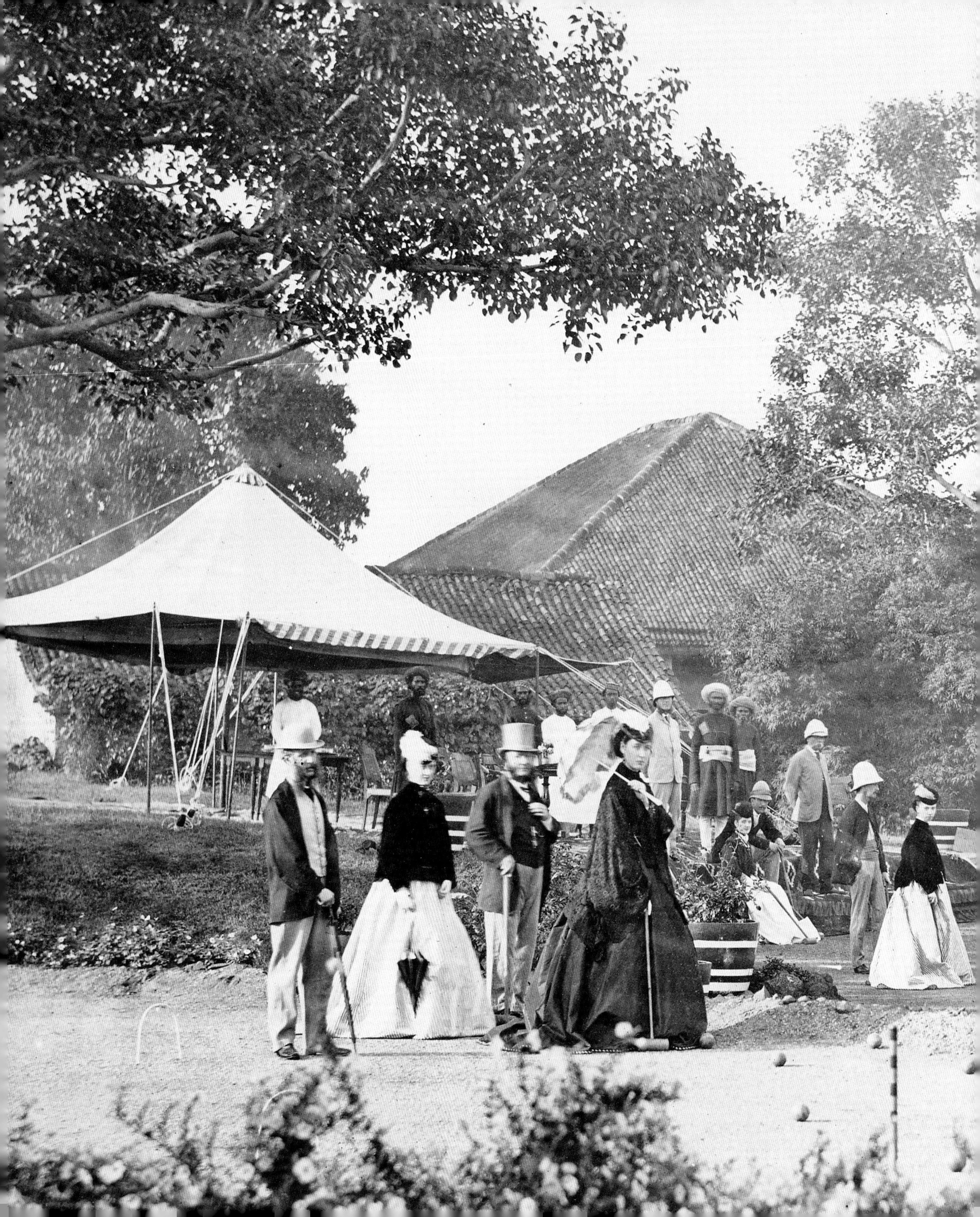

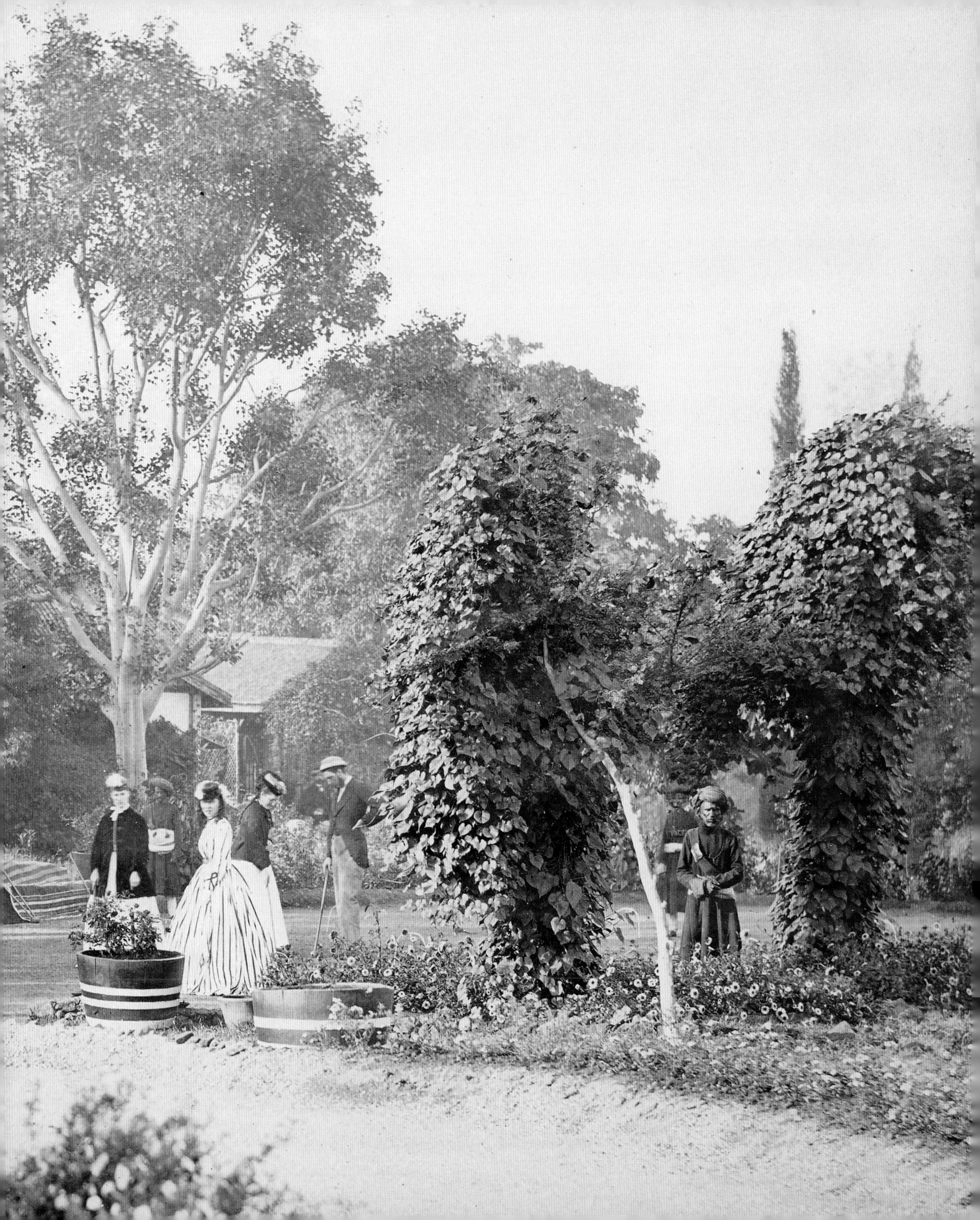

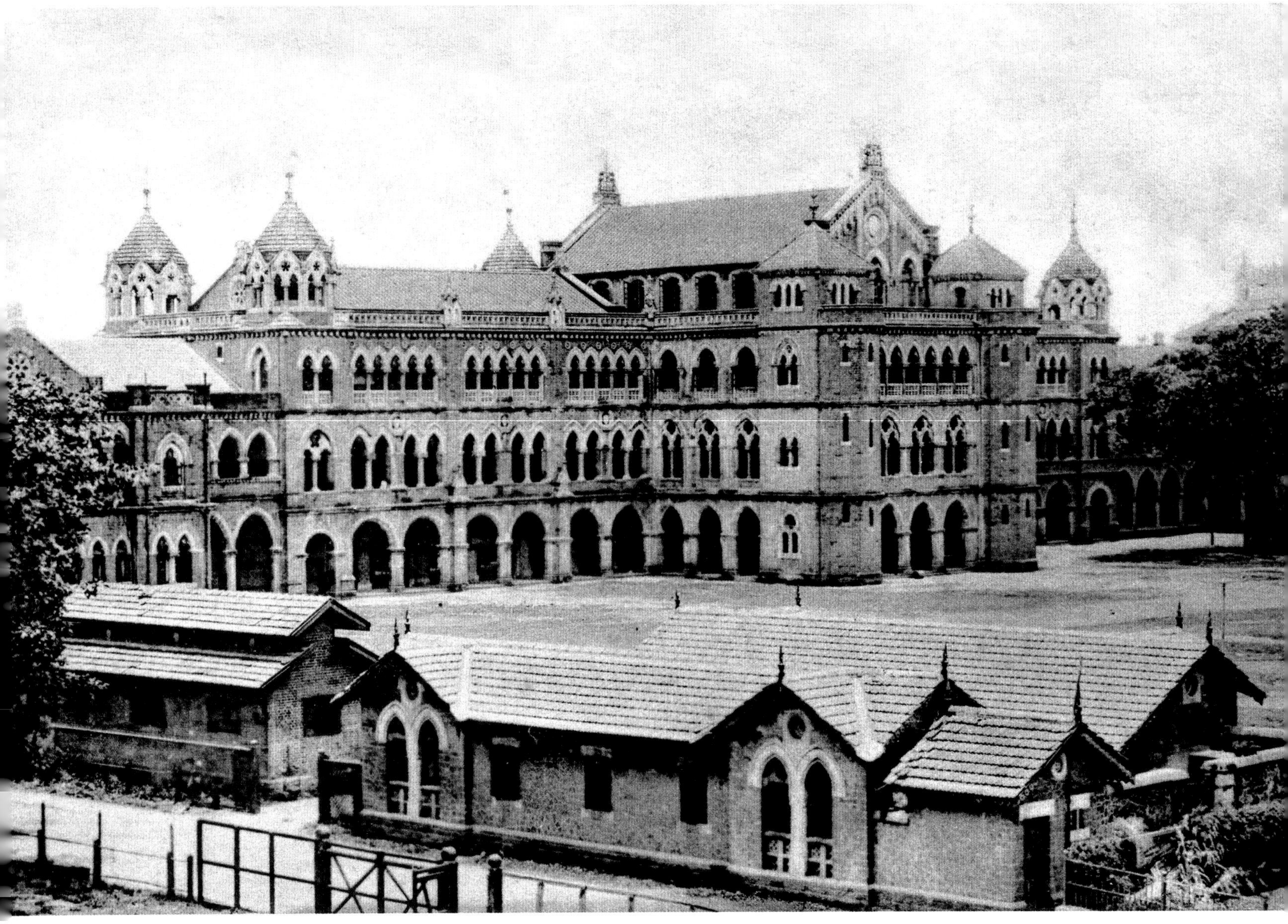

David Sassoon Building for Elphinstone Technical High School, Mumbai, built by Albert Abdullah Sassoon, 1872–79, George Twigge Molecey, architect.

Chinchpokli Jewish cemetery, Mumbai, 1878, built by Elias David Sassoon, with the twin mausoleums of Jacob and Rachel Sassoon.

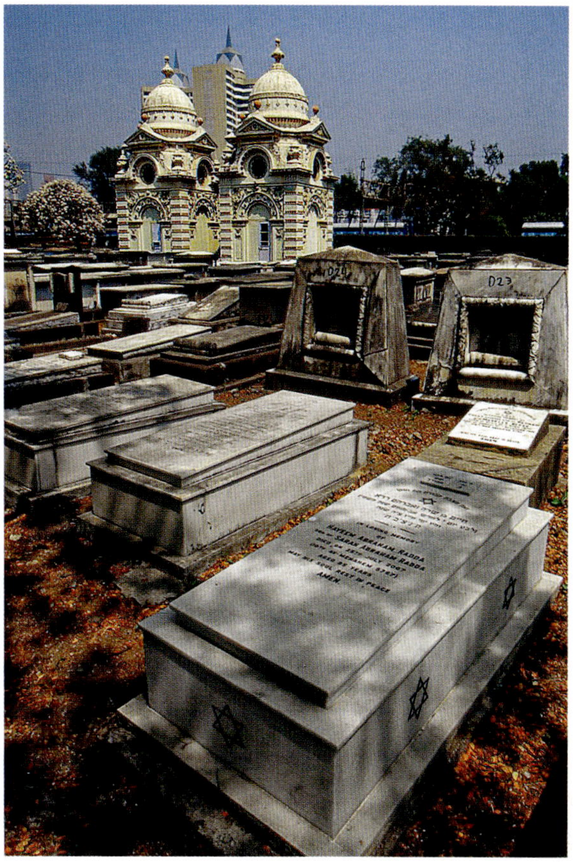

High School. Designed by George Twigge Molecey, the robust neo-Gothic structure is clad in Kurla stone, perforated by ogival porticoes and windows that provide shade and coolness to the interior classrooms, one of the strategies used by architects and engineers to adapt the Gothic to the native climate. Local craftsmen created the imaginative carved capitals and superb wrought-iron metalwork.[27]

Albert Abdullah scored a major coup by commissioning an equestrian statue to commemorate the visit of the Prince of Wales in 1875. As Matthew Noble—the sculptor originally tasked with the work—had died, the job went to Joseph Edgar Boehm. The prince was present for the casting in London. Horse and rider were placed on a tall granite pedestal; the sides were hung with panels representing different moments of the prince's arrival in Mumbai. When the statue was unveiled in 1879, Albert Abdullah was in London, but he was represented by his son, Edward, who appears in one of the panels, and by his brother Solomon David (1841–1894).[28] Called Kala Ghoda (the Black Horse), the statue eventually gave its name to the entire district. In 1965, however, it was moved to the gardens of the zoo, along with other remnants of the colonial period, and its panels were dispatched to the storeroom of the Dr. Bhau Daji Lad Museum.

David's children and grandchildren soon began building mansions in fashionable Malabar Hill, a socially segregated enclave.[29] Given the price of real estate, almost all have now given way to high-rises. The largest, aptly named Il Palazzo, was built by his pious son Solomon David and his wife, Flora. Designed by John Campbell and completed in 1901, its scale alone was staggering. The façade, overlooking Chowpatty Beach, resembled different villas attached to one another without transitions. A four-story eclectic block, loosely based on Indian models, with porticoes and shaded balconies, was interrupted by two classical pavilions with pediments and Italianate towers. A synagogue was enclosed.

Elias David Sassoon, David's second son, broke away from the family business in 1867 to found his own extremely successful firm.[30] Engaged in expanding its commercial reach, he had less time for cultural and charitable projects. But in 1878, when his son Joseph died, he built a cemetery in Chinchpokli for the Baghdadi Jews of Mumbai.

The American Civil War (1861–65) marked a turning point in the Sassoon fortunes. As the

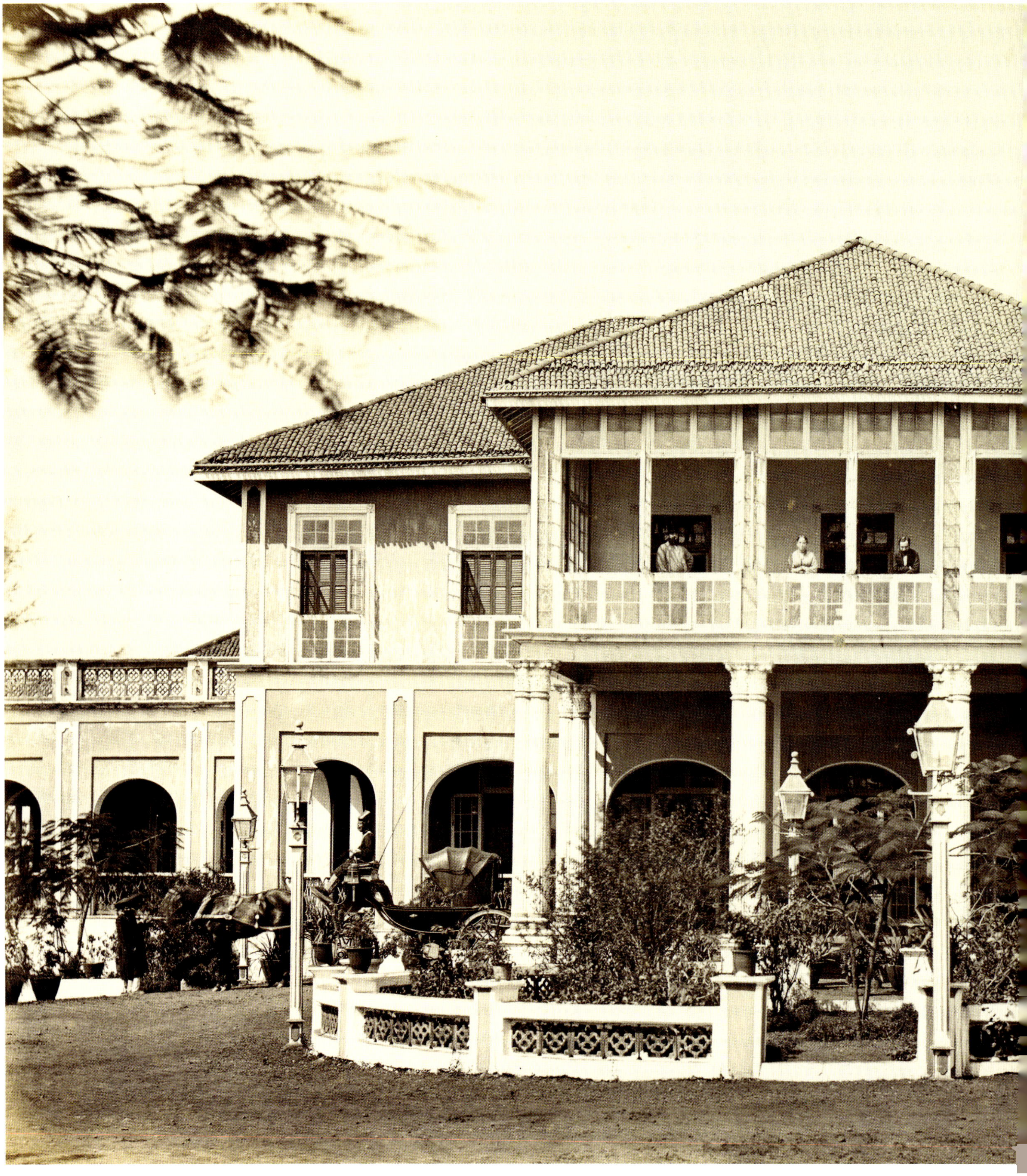

Confederate States could not export cotton, Manchester turned to India. Mumbai had a fledgling cotton industry, railroads, telegraph lines, and a major port. Elias David saw his chance. In 1880, he bought Alexandra Mill, originally an oil mill converted into a cotton one by the Parsi industrialist Jamsetji Nusserwanji Tata, and began renovations. Elias David's sons completed the monumental weaving shed, an elegant building designed according to the classical tenets of the early Renaissance. David Sassoon & Co. had already opened a mill in 1877. Jacob Elias Sassoon (1844–1916), Elias David's son, would transform his father's company into India's largest textile conglomerate, exporting cloth to Asia, the Middle East, and Britain. Employing 25,000 workers, its eleven mills were thought to have the most advanced technologies in the field. As benefits, E. D. Sassoon & Co. offered night school, reading rooms, day care for the children of women workers, and sports clubs. Since the days of David Sassoon, the family had employed almost exclusively co-religionists from Baghdad, providing schools, medical services, synagogue, and burial grounds. As the business grew, however, they took in a growing number of Bene Israel and Hindu workers. In 1886, Jacob went to England and a year later opened offices of his firm in Manchester and London.[31]

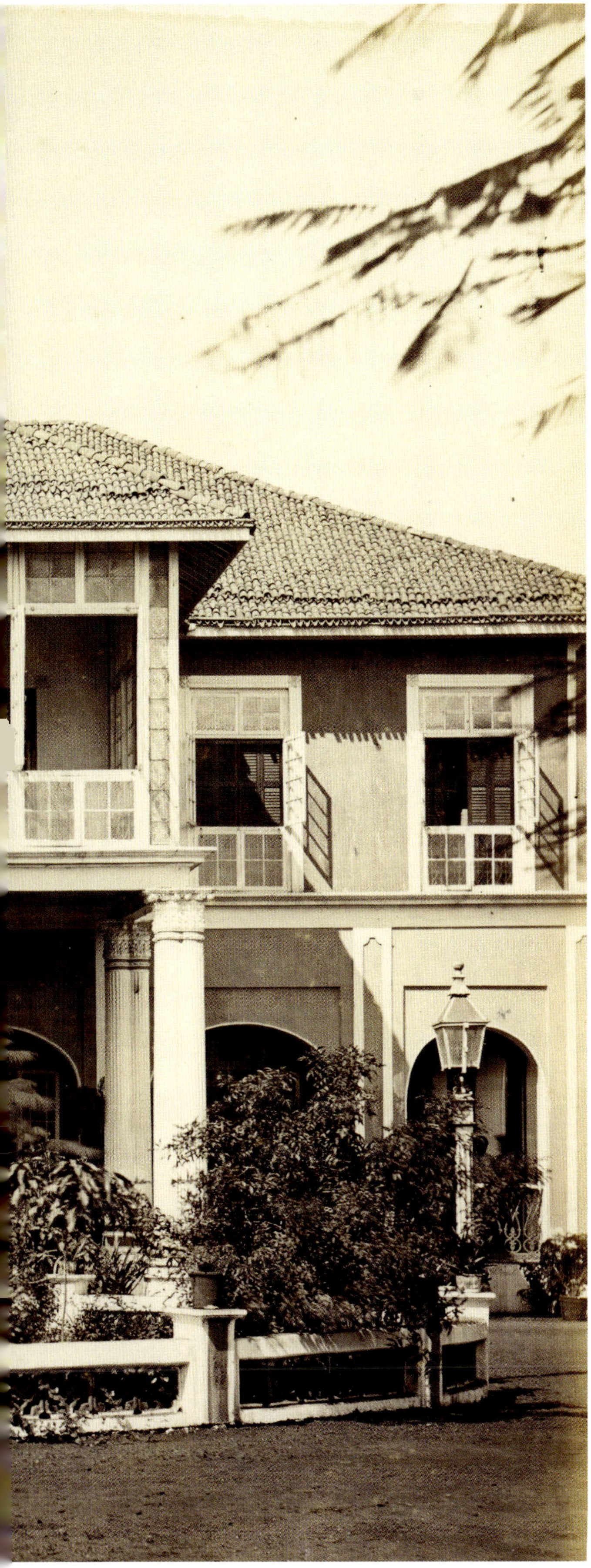

Malabar Castle, Malabar Hill, Mumbai, c. 1869, childhood home of Mozelle Sassoon, granddaughter of Albert Abdullah Sassoon, Tandy and Co. (?), from an album of photographs of the Mumbai properties belonging to the Sassoon family, 1869, London, British Library, Visual Arts Collection, given by Edwina and Sybil Sassoon, 2012.

Jacob, head of a hugely successful firm, had three princely residences: Braganza Hall in Byculla; Ashley House in Pune; and Glen Ogle in the cool hills at Mahabaleshwar. In Kala Ghoda, near the David Sassoon Library, he built the lovely Keneseth Eliyahoo Synagogue (1882–84) in honor of his father Elias (Eliyahoo). Designed by David Ebenezer Gostling and James Morris, and beautifully restored in 2019 by the architect Abha Narain Lambah, it has a compact neo-Renaissance exterior with two windowed stories resting on a rusticated base. The dark blue façade forms a striking contrast with the rich ornamentation in white stucco. The interior is breathtaking. Everything seems to be insubstantial, from the slender Gothic arches to the graceful cast-iron columns of the skeletal structure. Stained glass, gilded capitals, and light-fingered metalwork on the women's gallery bathe the space with golden light. Color contrasts, remarkable for their delicacy, have been restored to their original state.

As Jacob's surviving uncles had moved to London and no longer supported the charities founded by David Sassoon, Jacob was left to take over his grandfather's benefactions.[32] When the school next to Magen David risked closing for lack of funds, Jacob set up a charitable trust to support

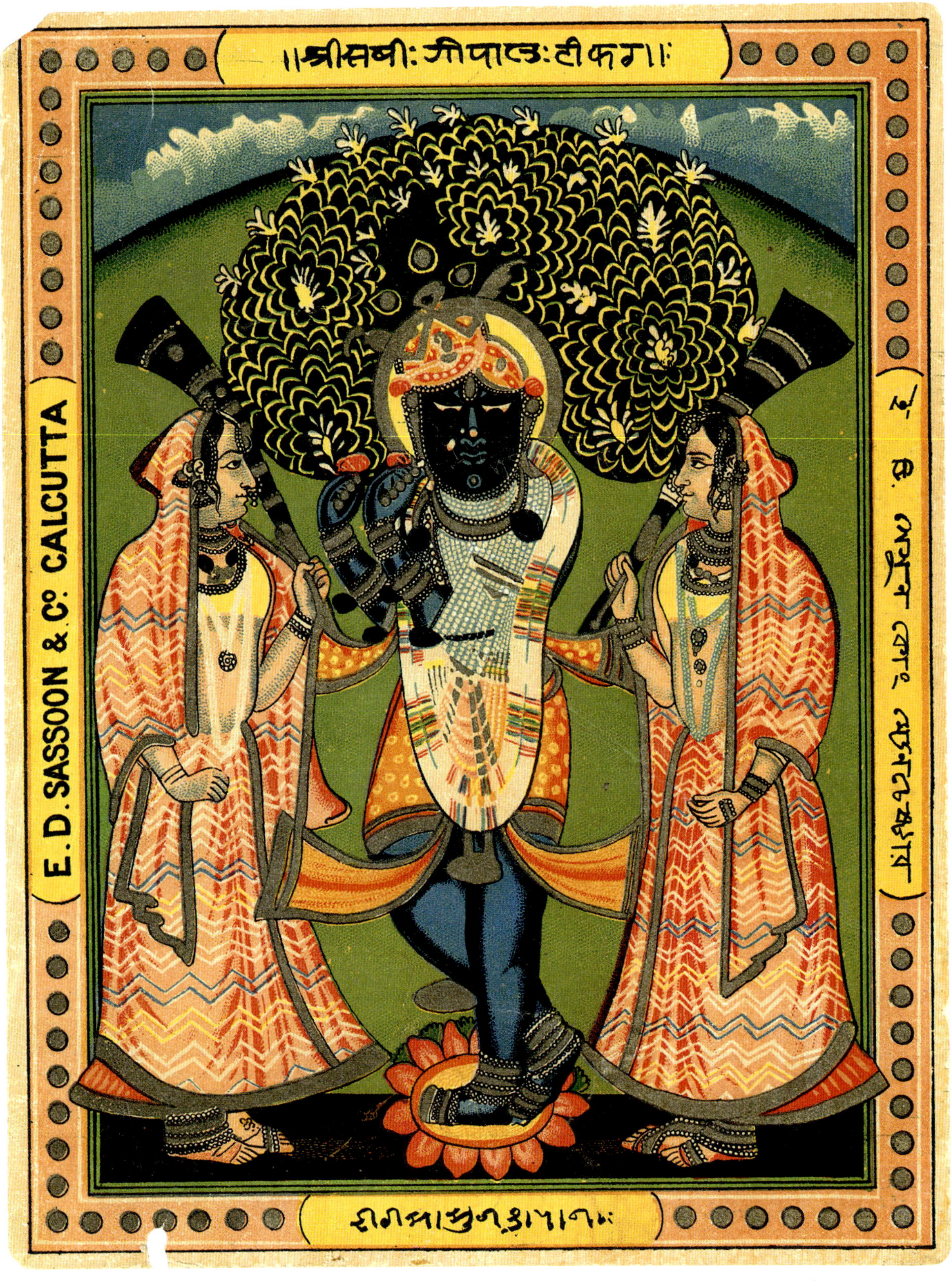

Textile trade label for E. D. Sassoon & Co. Ltd., Mumbai, early twentieth century, chromolithograph, 7½ × 5⅞ in. (19 × 14.9 cm), Jewish Museum exhibition purchase.

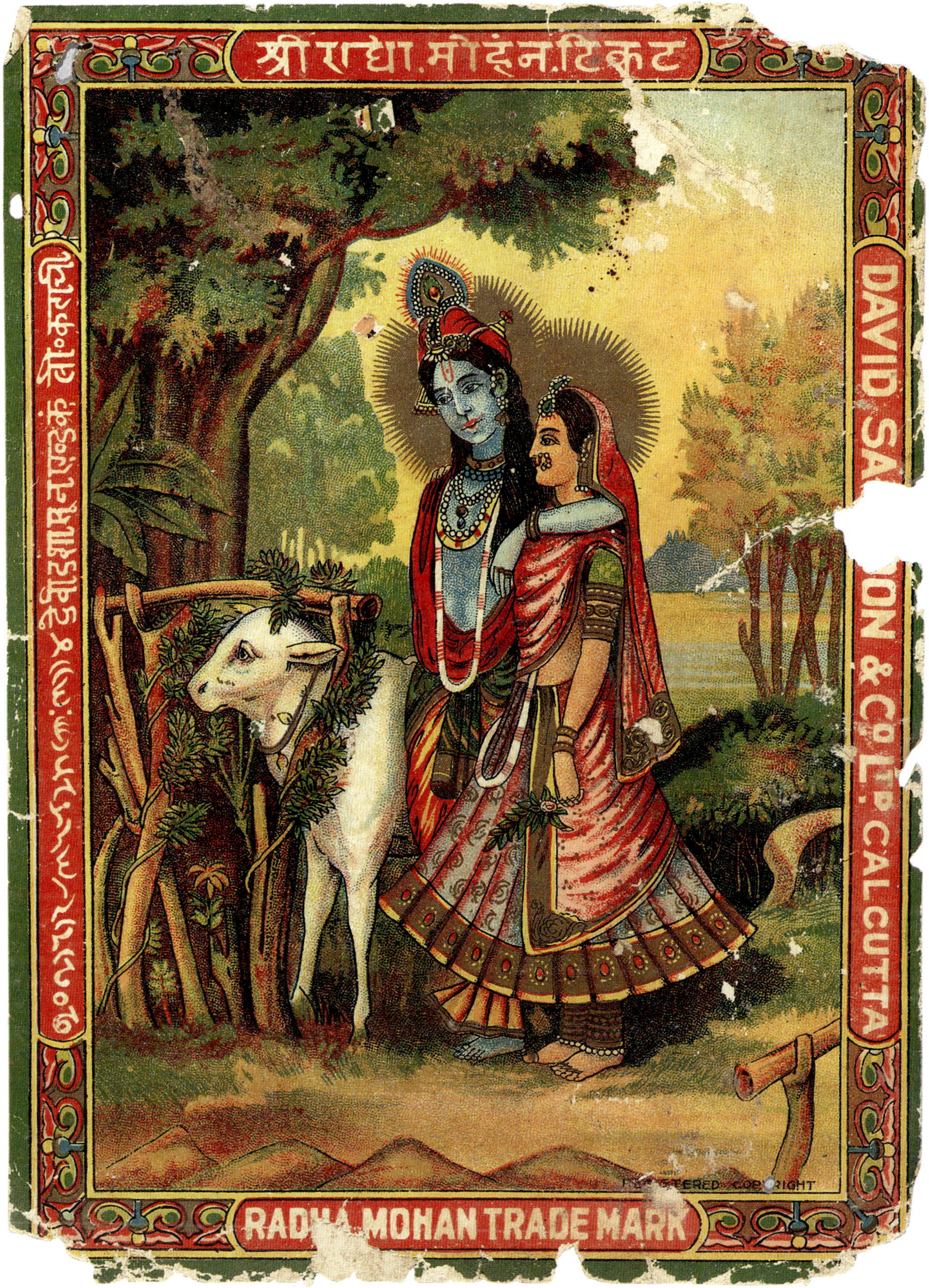

Textile trade label for David Sassoon & Co. Ltd. showing Krishna and Radha, Mumbai, 1910–30, chromolithograph, 7 × 5¼ in. (18 × 13.3 cm), Royal Ontario Museum, purchase made possible with the generous support of the South Asia Research and Acquisition Fund.

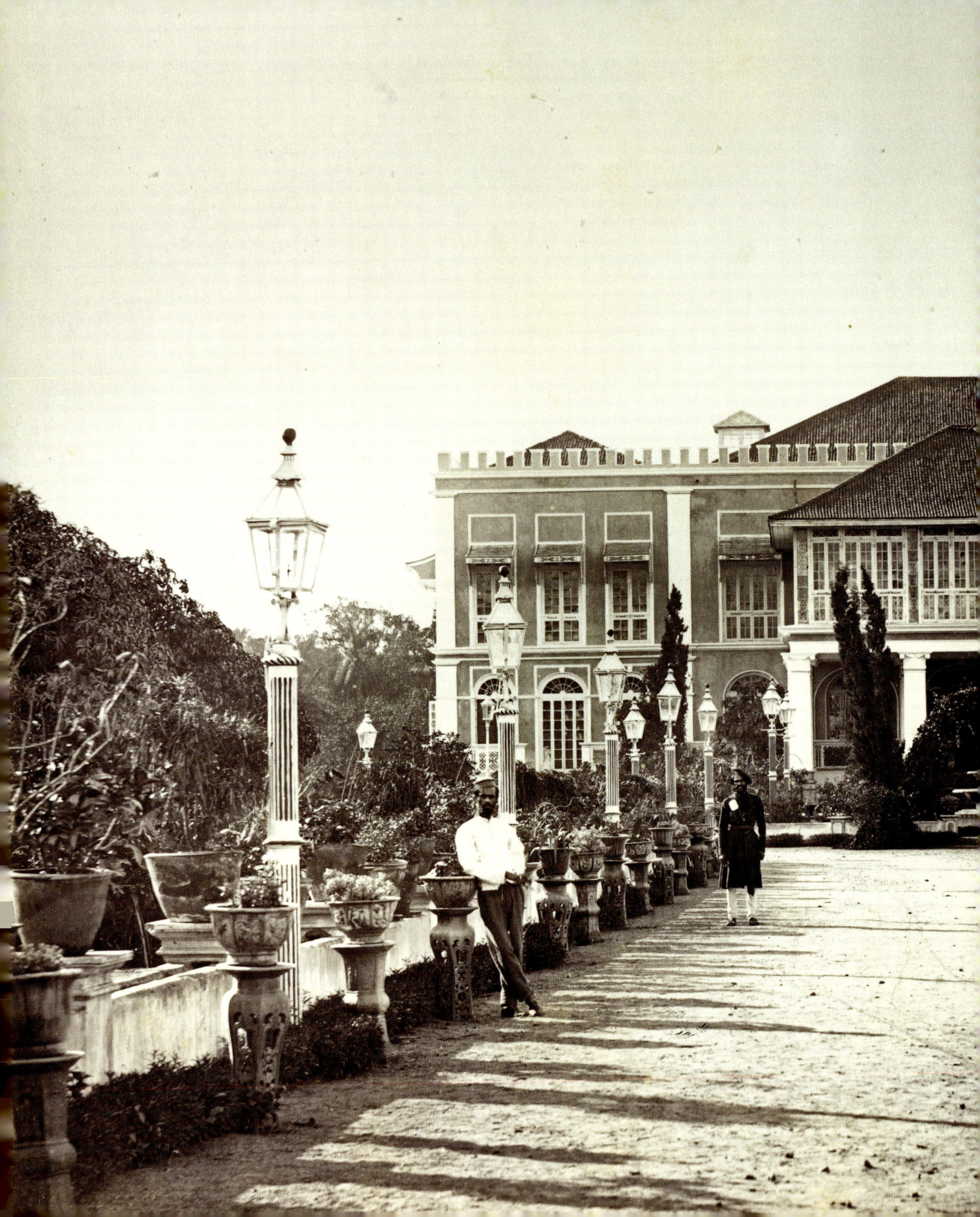

it. Tearing down the old building, he replaced it with the Sir Jacob Sassoon High School, which opened in 1903. The clauses of Jacob's charity trusts excluded the Bene Israel, who were barred from the Baghdadi burial grounds and not welcome in their synagogues.[33] Over the years, however, the Bene Israel supplied distinguished teachers and headmasters to the schools founded by the family. Today, the situation is reversed. Few Baghdadis remain in Mumbai. The Bene Israel frequent the Sassoon synagogues, while the Sir Jacob Sassoon High School now serves primarily the children of the impoverished Muslim neighborhood surrounding the compound.[34]

If the Sassoons established watertight partitions between themselves and the Bene Israel, they suffered discrimination at the hands of the British. While the British did not pass up invitations to the lavish balls held in Sans Souci, they did not admit Jews in their segregated clubs, enclaves of intra-European exclusivity. Yet the Baghdadis themselves had segregated clubs. The Sassoons' status in British India was ambiguous. Not only were they wealthier than the colonial authorities, but in England they had closer connections to the Royal House.[35]

Together with other merchant princes, Jacob helped fund the Royal Institute of Science (1924), designed by George Wittet, consulting architect to the government of Mumbai. In addition, Jacob was the major donor of the monumental Gateway of India, also by Wittet, rising dramatically on the waterfront at Apollo Bunder. Built to celebrate the visit of King George V and Queen Mary to India between 1911 and 1912, the gestation of the structure was long and complex. Stylistically, it followed what the British then called the "Indo-Saracenic," now considered a colonial artifact. It was, in fact, a classical triumphal arch given an

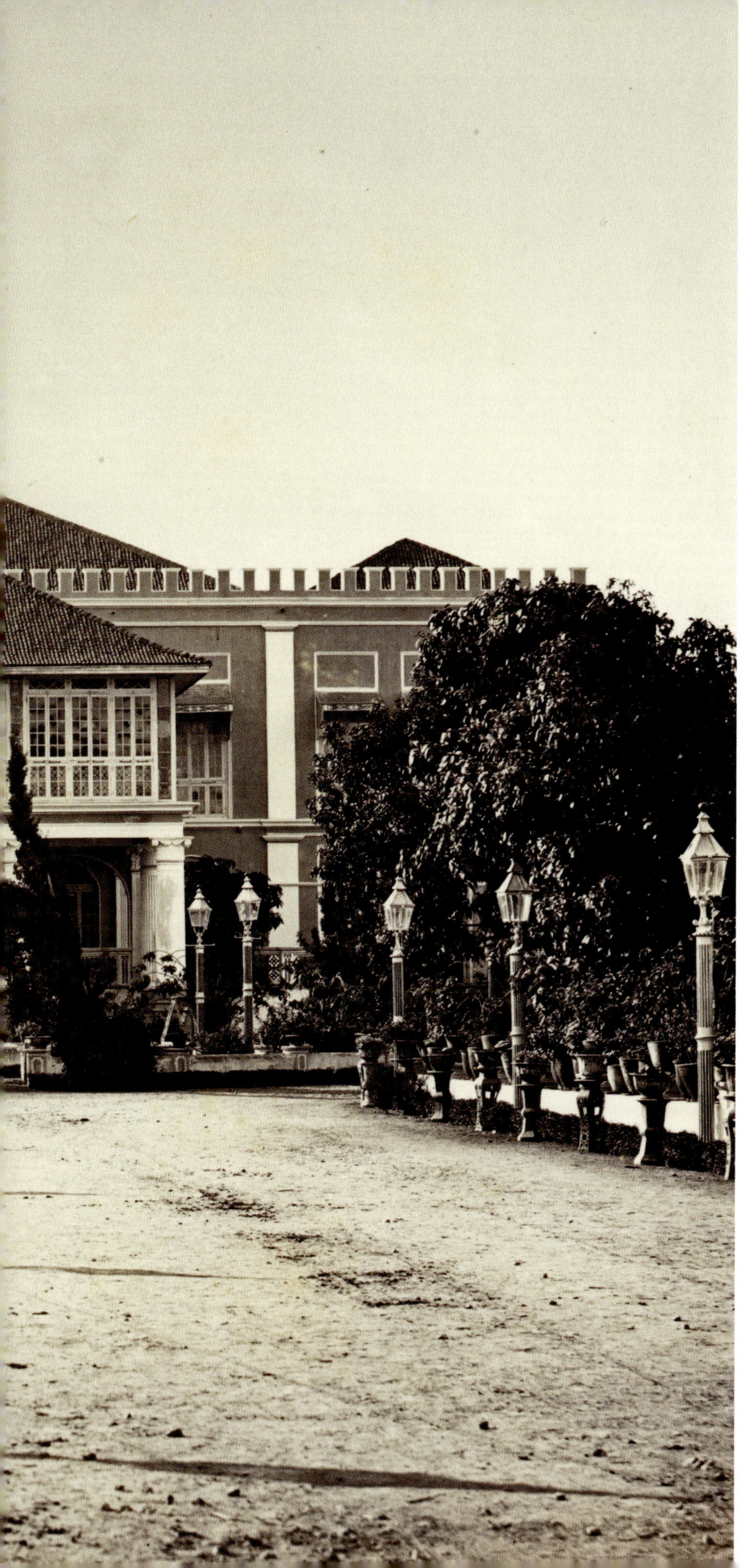

Braganza Hall, Victoria Road, Mumbai, before 1869, Tandy and Co. (?), from an album of photographs of the Mumbai properties belonging to the Sassoon family, 1869, London, British Library, Visual Arts Collection, given by Edwina and Sybil Sassoon, 2012.

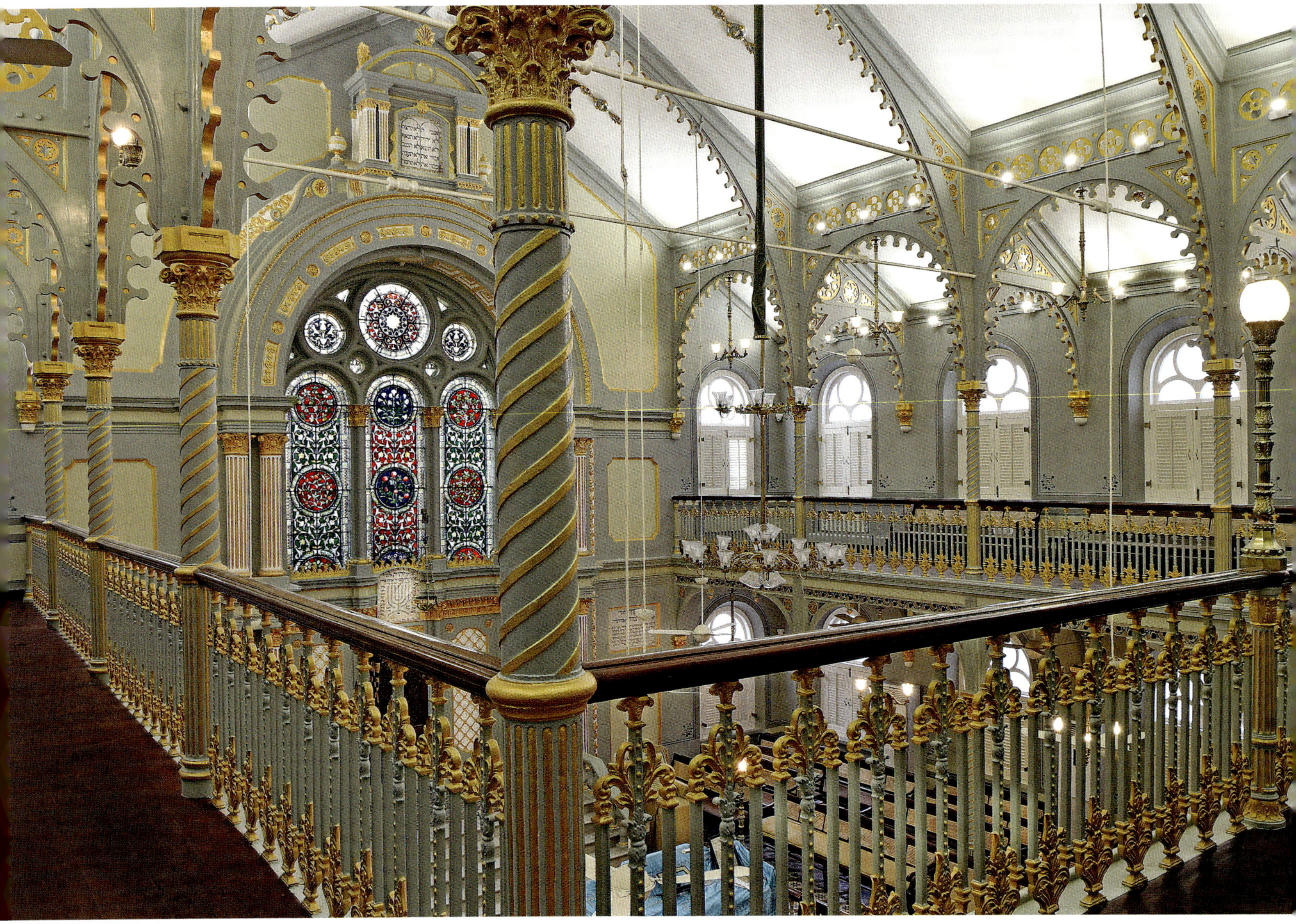

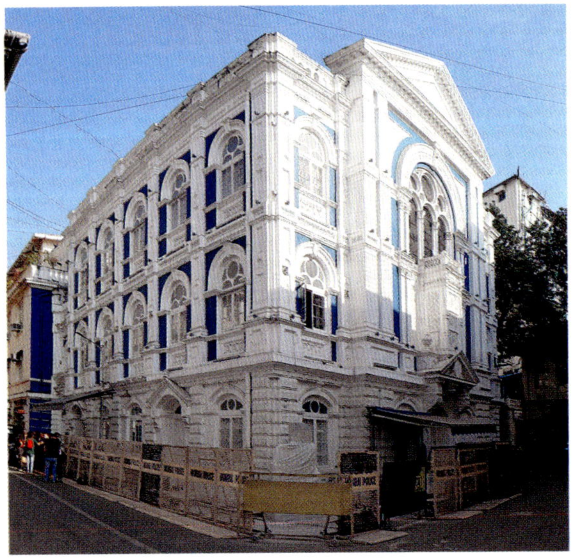

Keneseth Eliyahoo Synagogue, 1882–84, restored by architect Abha Narain Lambah in 2019, interior showing the women's gallery.

Keneseth Eliyahoo Synagogue, Mumbai, built by Jacob Sassoon in honor of his father, Elias; David Ebenezer Gostling and James Morris, architects.

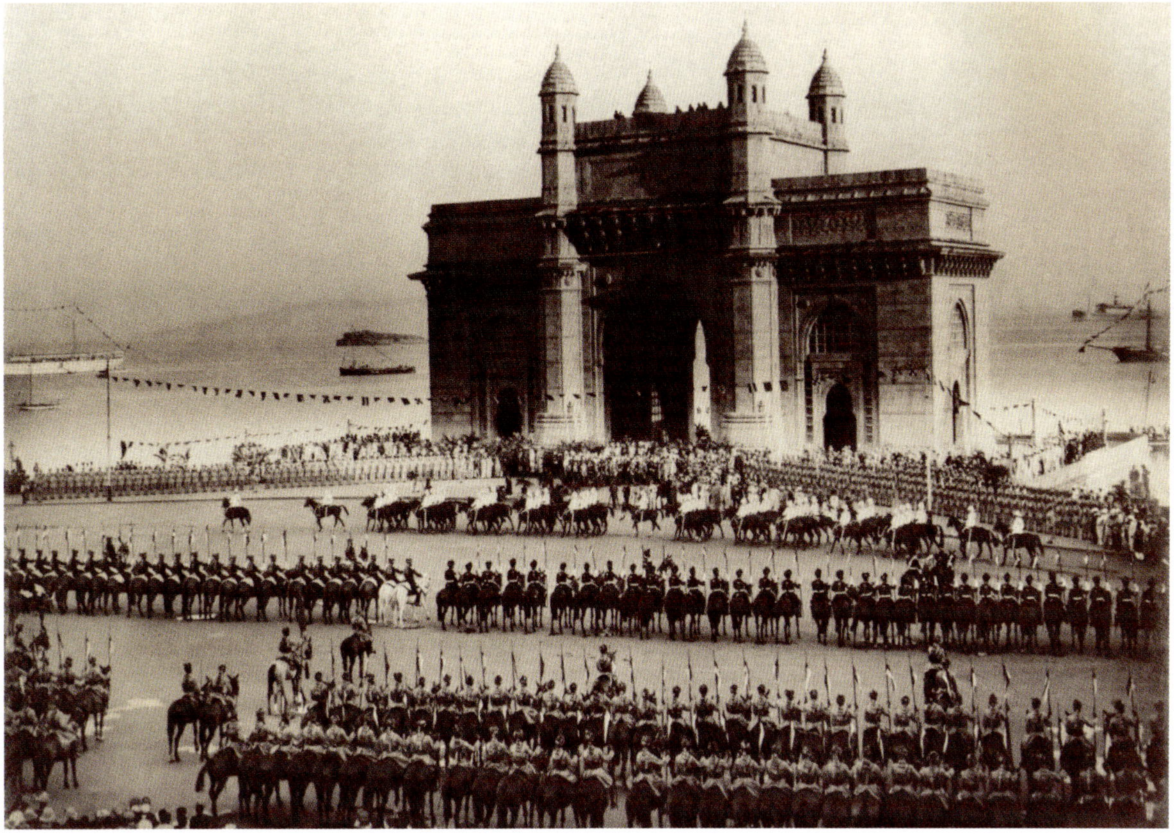

The inauguration of the Gateway of India, Mumbai, 1924, photograph attributed to the Myers Brothers. The Gateway, to which Jacob Sassoon was a major contributor, was designed by George Wittet and built to celebrate the visit of George V and Queen Mary to India.

Orientalist dressing. The architect Edwin Lutyens suggested some changes to the building, which was overseen by the engineer Rao Bahadur Yeshwantrao Harishchandra Desai.[36]

In Pune, Jacob funded the neo-Gothic Jacob Sassoon Hospital for Europeans (1905–6). Though smaller than his grandfather's hospital, it had stylistic similarities. Here, too, turrets and pavilions in basalt stone interrupt the façade, which is enlivened by porticoes on two stories. Founded to commemorate the visit of the Prince and Princess of Wales, this second hospital was timely: the bubonic plague arrived in India in 1896. Pune, a military cantonment, had an extremely high mortality rate. Given the escalating number of cases, "it would be more advisable," declared Jacob, "to retain the present Hospital for Natives, and to build an entirely new one, complete and up-to-date, for Europeans with a certain number of beds for Jews."[37] Segregated hospitals were common; they had to accommodate issues of caste and purity in the case of Hindus, and kosher dietary laws for the Baghdadis.[38] The plague only disappeared from India in the early 1920s thanks to the Ukrainian bacteriologist Waldemar Mordecai Haffkine, a protégé of Flora Sassoon's, who developed the first vaccine after testing it on himself.[39]

When Victor Sassoon took over as the head of E. D. Sassoon & Co. in 1924, he had already moved from London to Mumbai. By then the textile industry was the company's principal source of profit, as both the British government and China had agreed to bring the opium trade to an end in 1917, though it lingered for several years after that. In Mumbai, Victor built little apart from the Sir Sassoon David Hospital in 1928 and the new offices of E. D. Sassoon & Co. in the Ballard Estate.[40] Designed by architect David William Ditchburn, the large, heavy building was completed in 1926. At Pune, Victor built a large bungalow, Eves, and a horse stud. As it became clear that India would gain independence, the Baghdadis felt uneasy. They had thrown their lot in with the colonial powers, and many had begun to emigrate. Victor continued to spend part of the year in India, as required by his father's will, but with the end of the Raj now only a question of time, he began to transfer assets to Shanghai before moving there in 1931.[41]

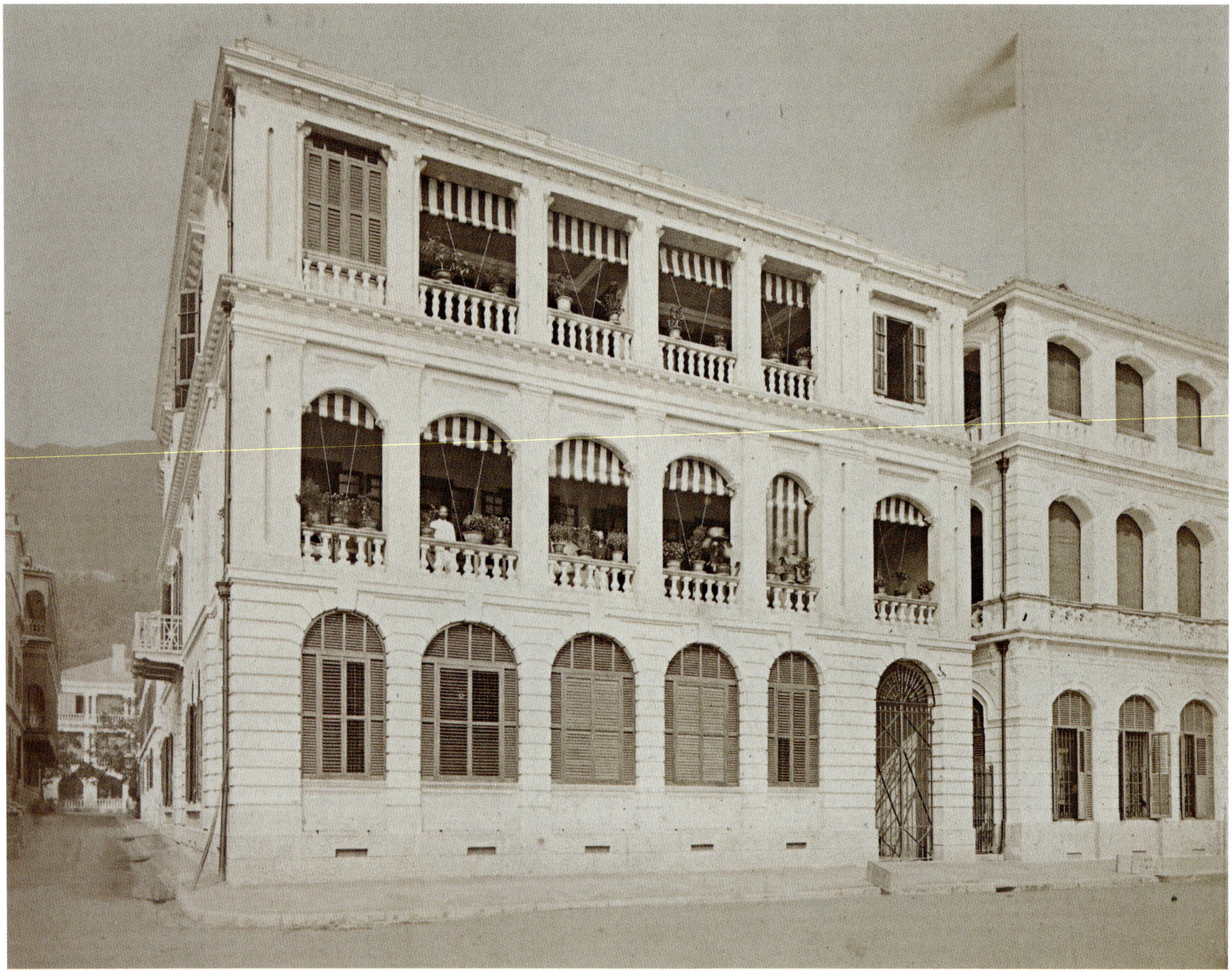

Hong Kong

Hong Kong played a key role in the trade diaspora of the Baghdadis. It was a central hub not only of their Chinese ventures but also of their operations in the Middle East, colonial India (Mumbai, Kolkata, Karachi, Chennai [formerly Madras]), Southeast Asia (Yangon [formerly Rangoon], Java, Singapore), and Japan (Yokohama, Nagasaki, Kobe). There, as elsewhere throughout their merchant empire, the Sassoon family's interests were intertwined with the political and commercial ambitions of the British, including one of their principal sources of profits: opium.

The British had long wanted a larger share of the Chinese market, but the Chinese did not care for their goods, and expected tea and silk to be paid for with silver. Opium, premised on the principle of "free" trade, became the means to reestablish the balance. The violent First Opium War ended with the Treaty of Nanjing in 1842, which forced China to open up five treaty ports to trade and ceded the coveted deep-water port of Hong Kong to the British.

Elias David Sassoon, sent to China by his father in the early 1840s, bore the brunt of the harsh pioneering work required to lay foundations for the family firm, living for months at a time in boomtowns, far from his family, often in difficult conditions. Eventually, other brothers took turns in Hong Kong managing the business. They began with office buildings and warehouses, and then rental properties and residences. All were characteristic of "compradoric" architecture, with large windows, verandas, or porticoes.[42] Almost nothing survive of the buildings erected by the Sassoons.

David Sassoon Sons & Co. office and dwelling, Praya, Hong Kong, from an album of photographs of the Hong Kong properties belonging to the Sassoon family, 1875, Norfolk, UK, Houghton Hall Collection.

OPPOSITE

Offices of E. D. Sassoon & Co., Queens Road, Hong Kong, from an album of photographs of the Hong Kong properties belonging to the Sassoon family, 1875, Norfolk, UK, Houghton Hall Collection.

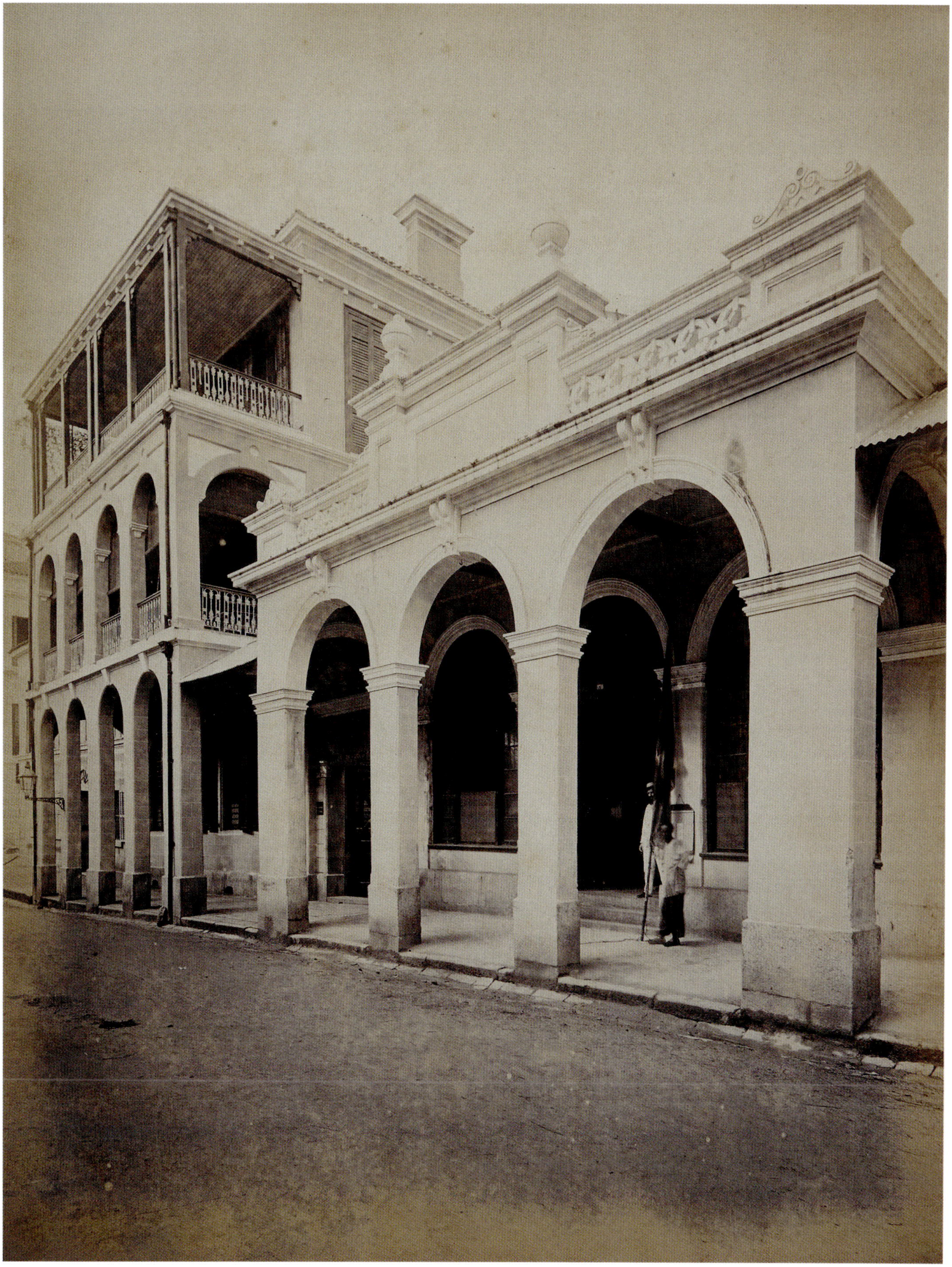

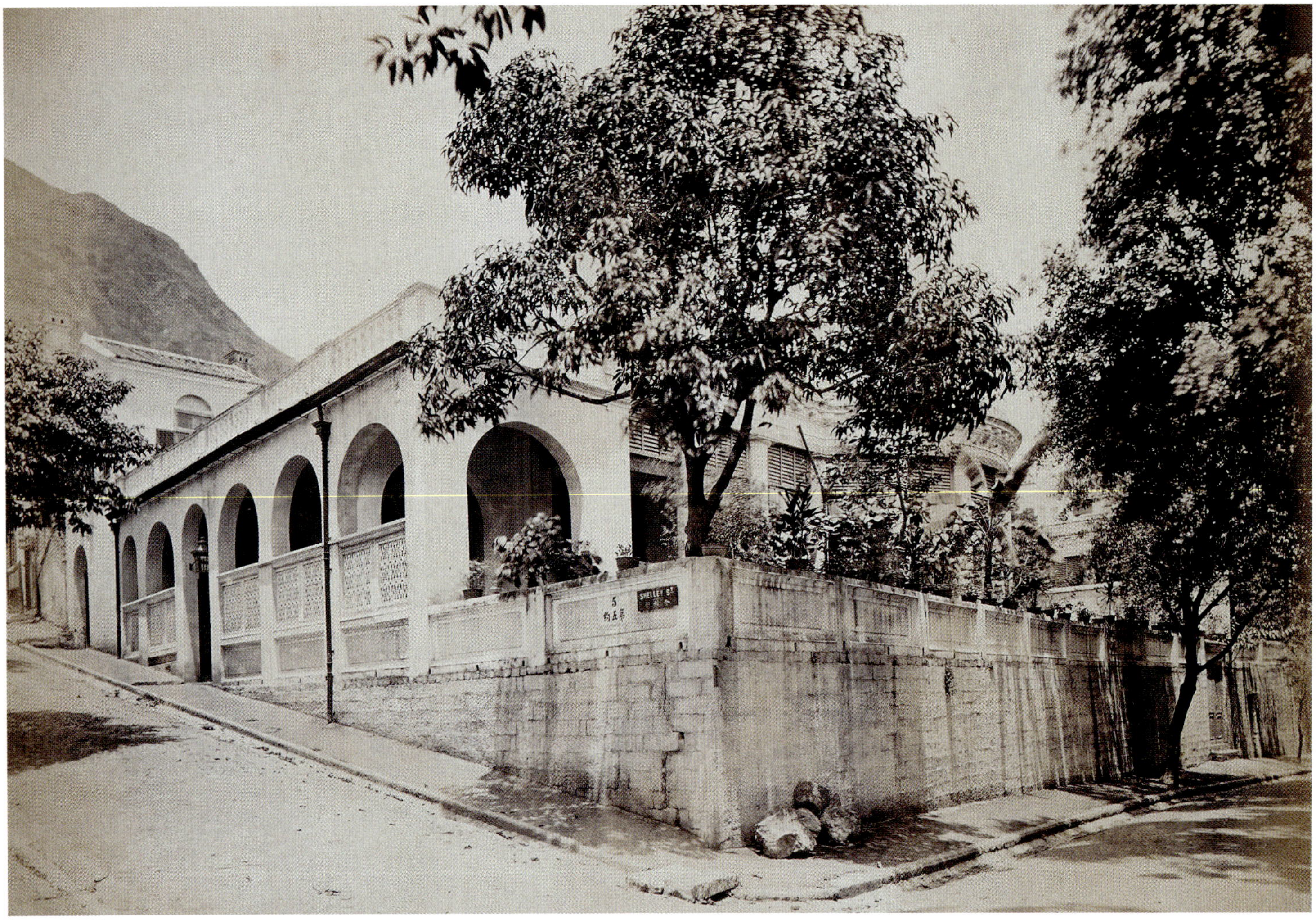

A port city rising in a hurry, Hong Kong did not have the architectural culture of Mumbai but offered greater freedom from accepted canons. As the Jewish community grew, the Sassoon brothers set aside first one, then another villa to serve as synagogues in a prosperous, leafy enclave of the city. In 1901, Jacob and his brothers Edward and Meyer Sassoon commissioned the Ohel Leah Synagogue in memory of their mother. Spectacularly sited on Victoria Peak, with views of the harbor and the islands, it is now hemmed in by tall skyscrapers. The original red brick walls with white trim have since been covered over with white stucco. In the interior, a low barrel vault reinforced by ribs spans the prayer hall. There were marble floors, wood carvings, and metalwork, as well as stained-glass windows. The actual arrangement of the furnishings was influenced by the Ashkenazi, who eventually made up the majority of the congregation. A thorough restoration (1997–98) returned part of the original beauty, which had been obscured when work was carried out to build a fire escape on the exterior, improve lighting, and install air-conditioning.[43]

In Hong Kong, with its gold-rush atmosphere, Baghdadis, Parsis, and other minorities found a more complex situation than in India. Discrimination against the Chinese was harsh and unremitting. Jews also faced strong prejudice in the colony's tight social circles. Jewish members of the Legislative Council, for instance, including Frederick Sassoon, could not join the Hong Kong Club.[44] In response, the Kadoories, major Baghdadi benefactors, built the Jewish Recreation Club on the premises of the synagogue in 1905.

Synagogue, Shelley Street, Hong Kong, from an album of photographs of the Hong Kong properties belonging to the Sassoon family, 1875, Norfolk, UK, Houghton Hall Collection.

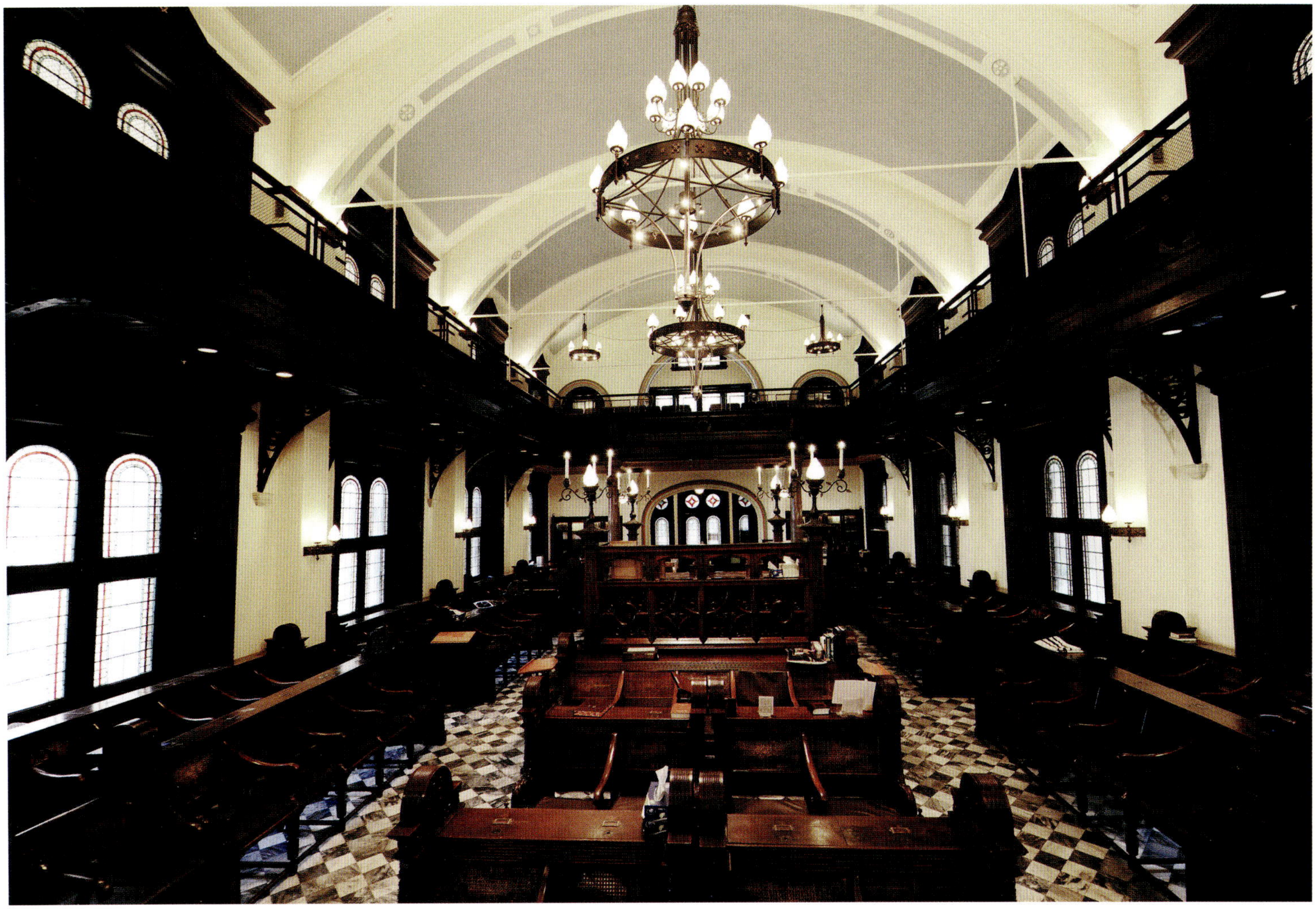

Interior view of Ohel Leah Synagogue, Hong Kong, photographed in 1996.

Ohel Leah Synagogue, Hong Kong, 1901–2, Leigh and Orange, architects, photographed in 2018.

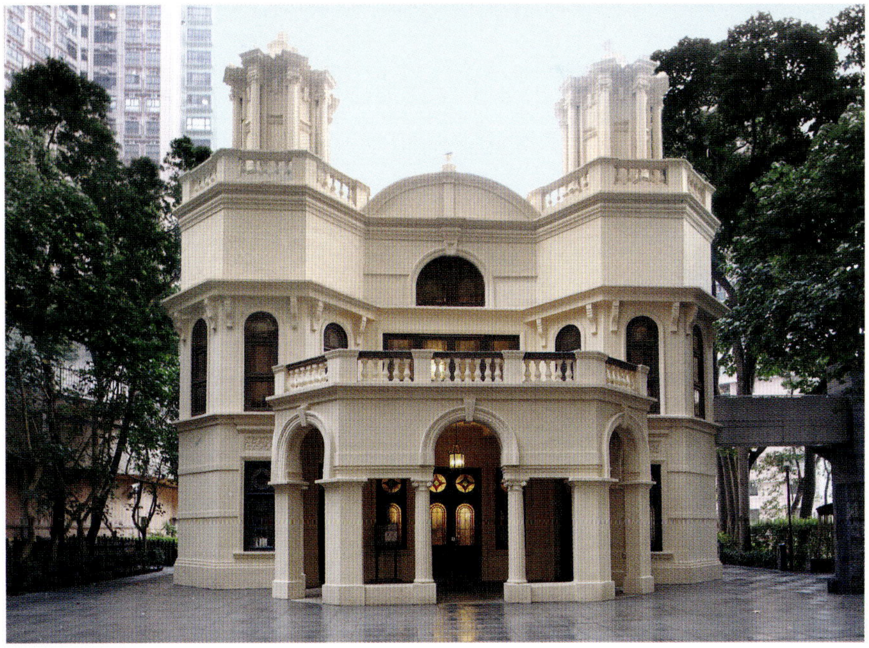

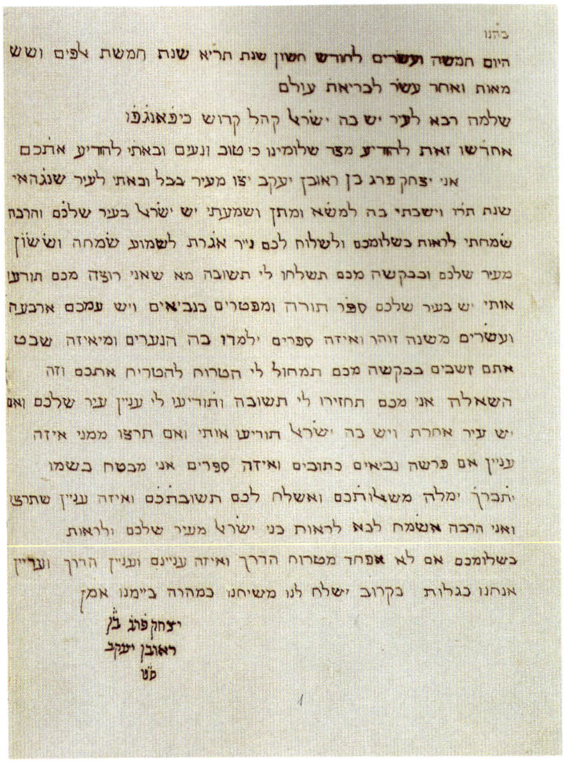

בה״ו
היום חמשה ועשרים לחודש חשון שנת תר״יא שנת חמשת אלפים ושש
מאות ואחר עשר לבריאת עולם
שלמה רבא לעיר יש בה ישרא׳ קהל קדוש כיפאנגפו
אחרשו זאת להודיע מצד שלומינו כי טוב ונעים ובאתי להודיע אתכם
אני יצחק פרג בן ראובן יעקב יצו מעיר בבל ובאתי לעיר שנגהאי
שנת ת״ח וישבתי בה למשא ומתן ושמעתי יש ישרא׳ בעיר שלכם והרבה
שמחתי לראות בשלומכם ולשלוח לכם נייר אגרת לשמוע שמחה וששון
מעיר שלכם ובבקשה מכם תשלחו לי תשובה מא שאני רוצה מכם תורעו
אותי יש בעיר שלכם ספר תורה ומפטרים בנביאים ויש עמכם ארבעה
ועשרים משנה זוהר ואיזה ספרים ילמדו בה הנערים ומיאיזה שבט
אתם יושבים בבקשה מכם תמחול לי הטרוח להטריח אתכם וזה
השאלה אני מכם תחזירו לי תשובה ותודיעו לי עניין עיר שלכם ואם
יש עיר אחרת ויש בה ישרא׳ תודיעו אותי ואם תרצו ממני איזה
עניין אם פרשה נביאים כתובים ואיזה ספרים אני מבטח בשמו
יתברך ימלה משאלותכם ואשלח לכם תשובתכם ואיזה עניין שתרצו
ואני הרבה אשמח לבא לראות בני ישרא׳ מעיר שלכם ולראות
בשלומכם אם לא אפחד מטרוח הדרך ואיזה עניינם ועניין הדרך ועדיין
אנחנו בגלות בקרוב ישלח לנו משיחנו במהרה בימנו אמן
יצחק פרג בן
ראובן יעקב
ס״ט

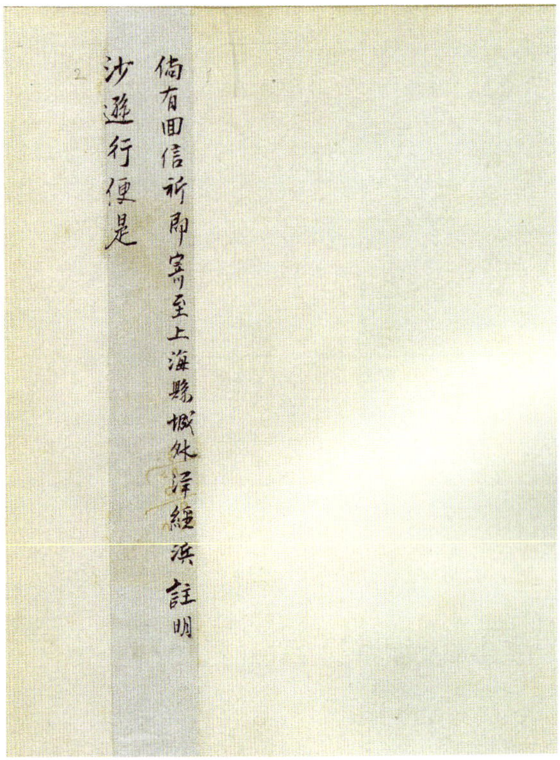

A letter in Hebrew from the Baghdadi Jewish trader Isaac Faraj ben Reuben ben Jacob to the Jewish community of Kaifeng, China, inquiring about their well-being and religious practices, October 31, 1850, formerly in the David Solomon Sassoon Collection (no. 54). An inscription in Chinese reads, "If you have a letter [in reply to this] send it to Shanghai town care of Sassoon Company."

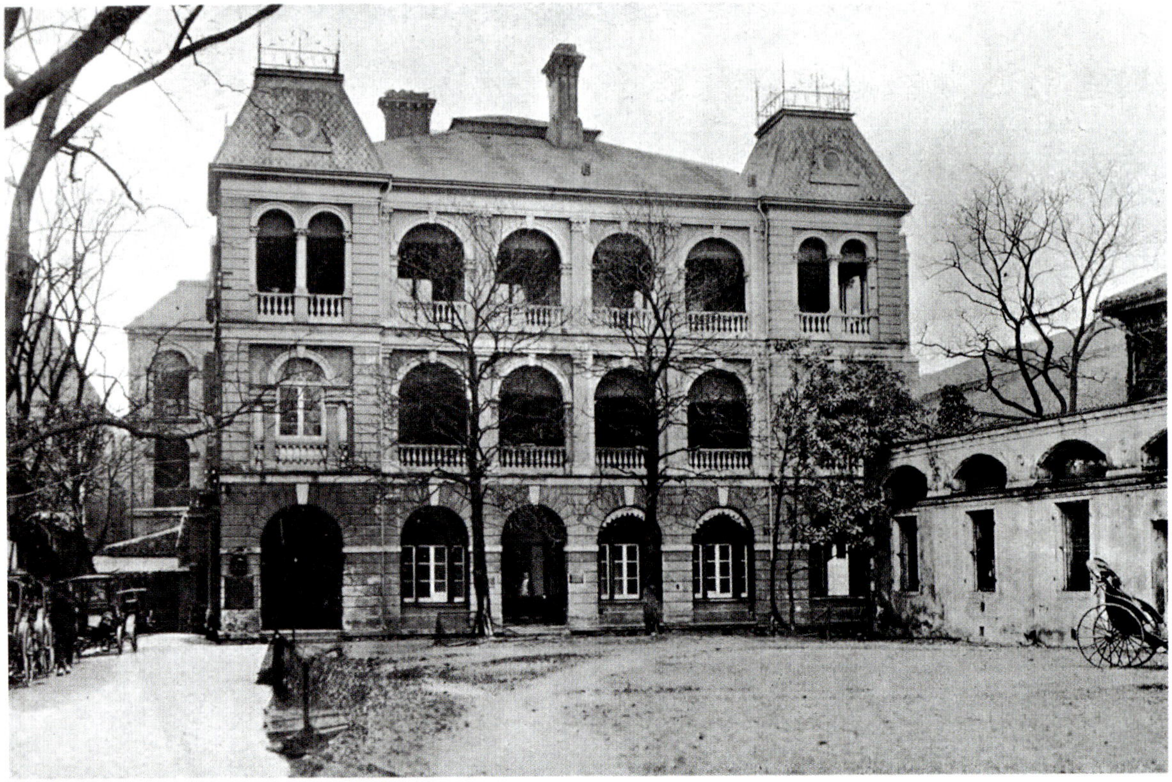

The Shanghai offices of David Sassoon & Co., c. 1907–8.

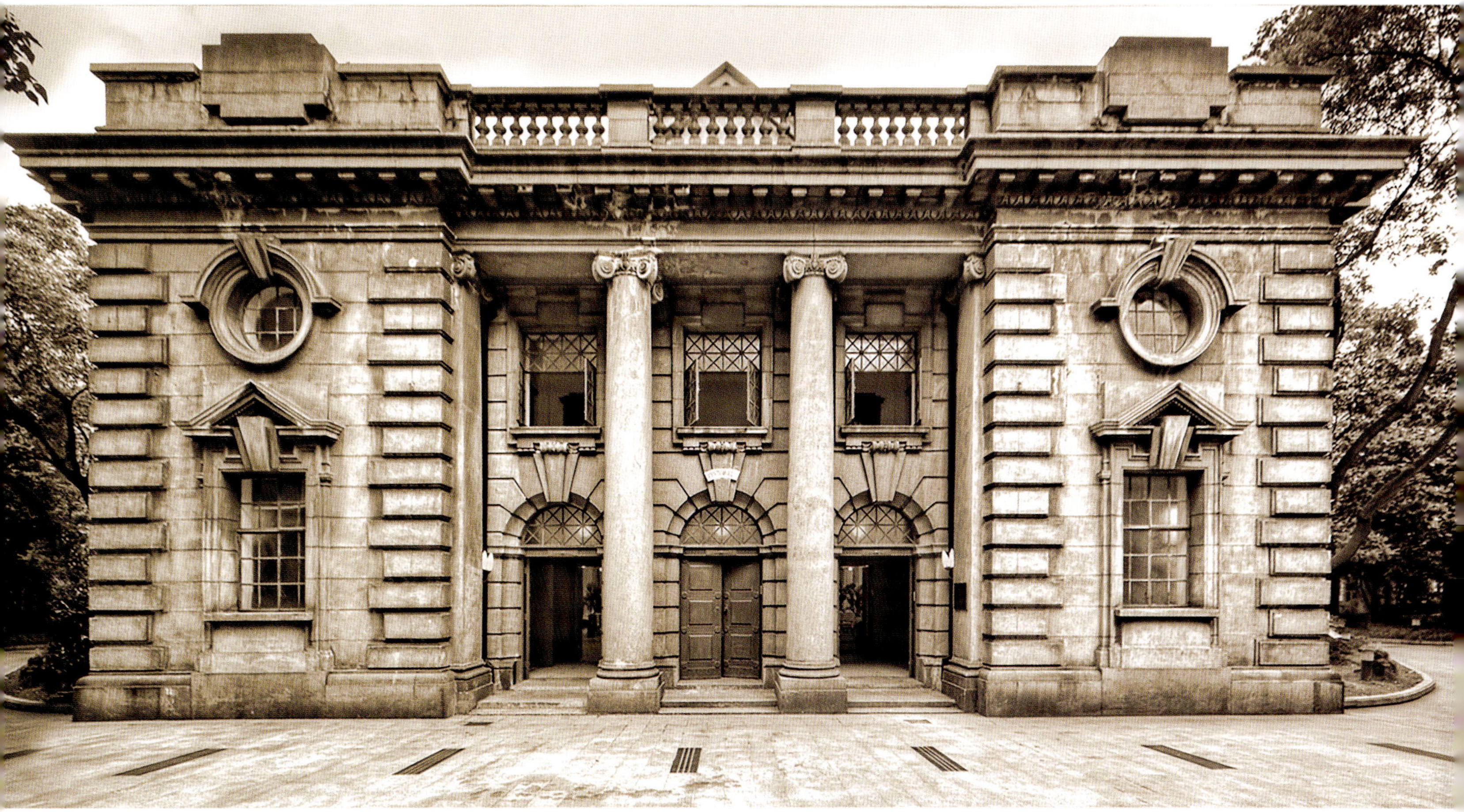

Ohel Rachel Synagogue, Shanghai, 1920, Robert Bradshaw Moorhead and Sidney Joseph Halse, architects, photographed in 2010.

Shanghai

Among the treaty ports, Shanghai was the prize, as its superb location promised huge profits from the transshipment of opium. A thriving walled city since the Ming dynasty, with moats, water gates, gardens, and temples, Shanghai flourished long before the British arrived. After the First Opium War, the British established the International Settlement, where they were joined by the Americans in 1863. Between the British enclave and the Chinese city stood the French Concession. Foreigners benefited from the status of extraterritoriality, which meant that they were subject only to the laws of their own respective countries. Elias David Sassoon was the first of his family to arrive, in 1850, shuttling between Shanghai, Hong Kong, and Guangzhou. Selling opium and piece goods in exchange for tea and silk, he broadened the firm's commercial offerings, opening the first of many offices of David Sassoon & Co. His own firm, E. D. Sassoon & Co., was founded in 1867.[45] In the early years, health conditions were dire and the mortality rate high.[46] Not surprisingly, one of the first things built by the Sassoons for the growing Baghdadi community was the Jewish cemetery (1862).

The Sassoons were also interested in the old community of Chinese Jews in Kaifeng, who were assimilated. In a rare Hebrew letter, dated October 31, 1850, sent to them by Isaac Faraj ben Reuben ben Jacob, the Baghdadi Jewish trader inquired about their well-being and religious practices. The letter is endorsed in Chinese: "If you have a letter [in reply to this] send it to Shanghai town care of Sassoon Company," indicating that he may have been one of the first employees of the Shanghai office.[47]

Since Westerners could not own land, leases kept changing hands as buildings were erected and torn down to make way for bigger ones. At first there were one- or two-story houses in the compradoric style along the Huangpu River. By the late 1870s, houses gave way to three-story office buildings, some with mansard roofs, prominently sited along the Bund, as the riverfront came to be called by the British. Over the years, the foreign enclave began to grow from a hastily improvised port, inhabited largely by men, to a burgeoning city. More cosmopolitan and tolerant

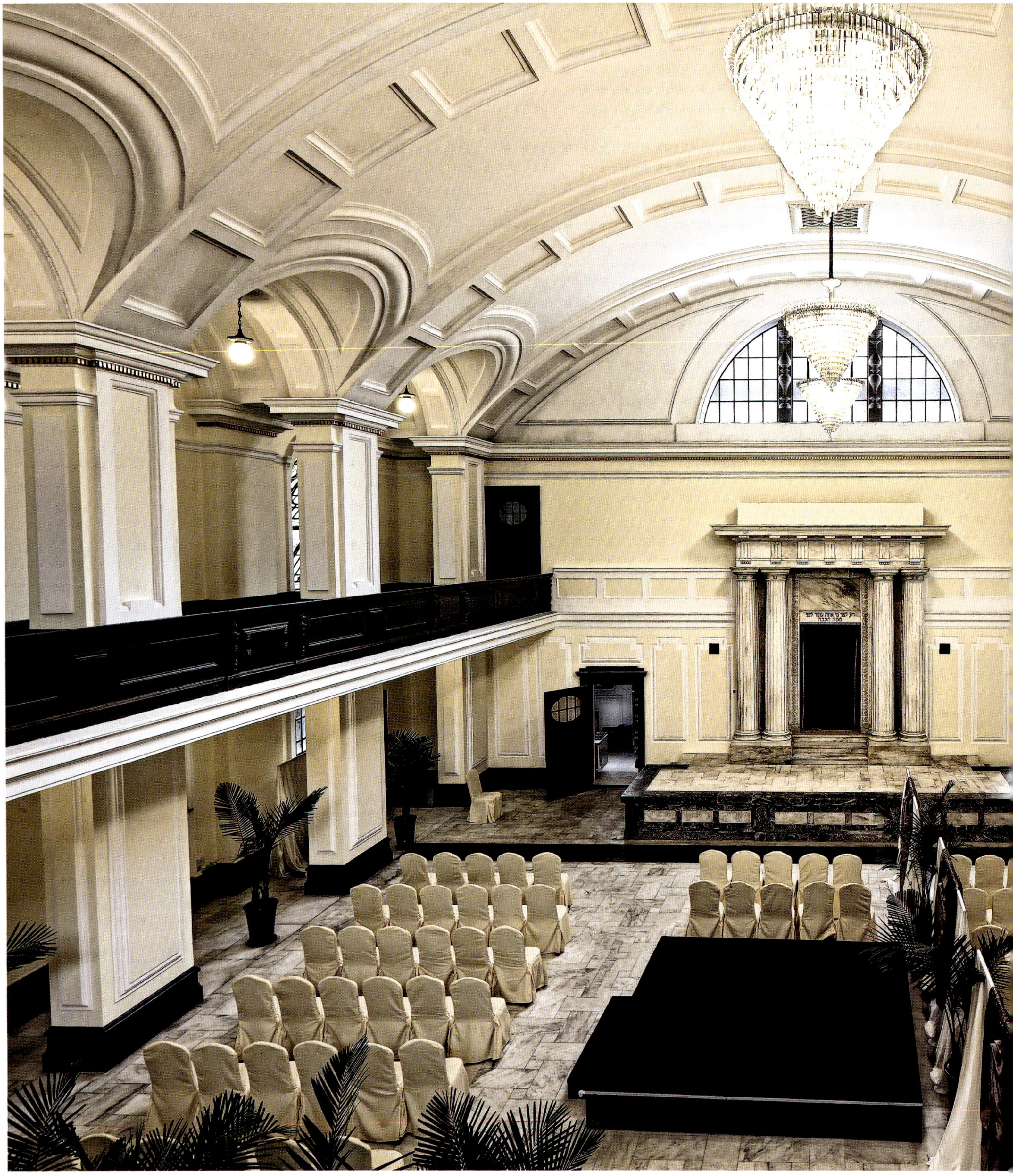

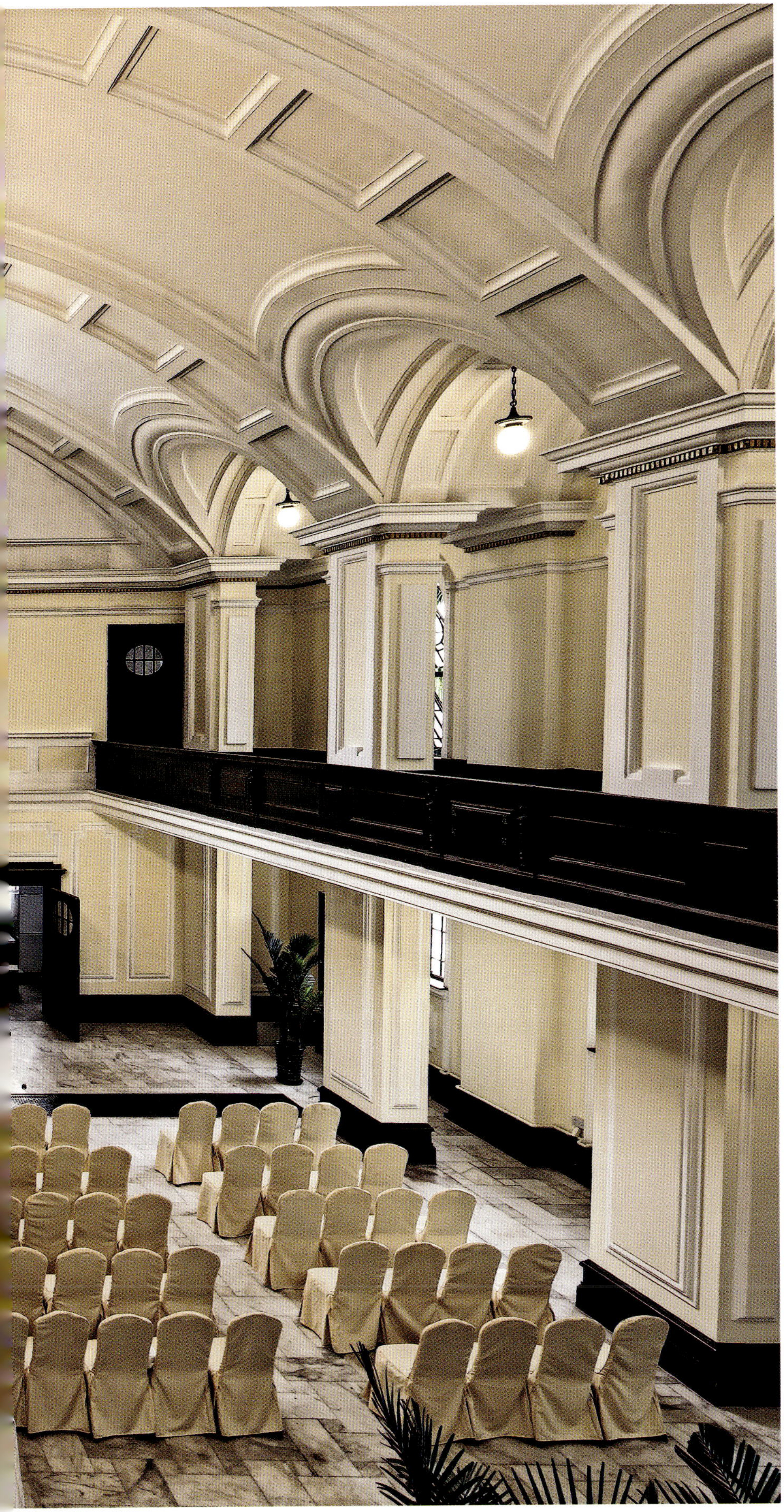

than colonial India or Hong Kong, Shanghai was exciting. Every Chinese ethnic group was represented. Although it was never a colony, colonialism ruled in this intersection of three empires, where the French and the British loved to flaunt their imperial status. In the International Settlement, dominated by the British, the police force was made up of Indians from the Raj; in the French Concession, *tirailleurs* from Vietnam were brought in to defend the enclave.

By the first decade of the twentieth century, about fifty Baghdadi families were working for the two Sassoon firms. They were not a homogenous group but split by class between the affluent, anglicized merchants and the poorer, less acculturated workers who remained attached to the customs of their homeland in Mesopotamia. Ohel Rachel, Shanghai's first permanent synagogue, was donated by Jacob Sassoon in memory of his wife, opening in 1920, four years after his death. Designed by Robert Bradshaw Moorhead and Sidney Joseph Halse, its exterior is articulated with an almost Mannerist sensibility, with rusticated corners and enormous oeils-de-boeuf and keystones. The compound later included a mikvah, a playground, and a school. Furnishings were provided by the congregation. Each seat had the name of the donor in English, a sign of the anglicization of wealthy Baghdadis.[48]

Unlike his uncles who lived temporarily in Shanghai but longed for the comforts of Mumbai, Victor flourished in the city's bracing, international atmosphere. When he arrived, the old port city had become an industrial metropolis. Commerce and stockage of goods along the Bund had given way to banks, insurance companies, and financial institutions. Victor slowly transferred assets from India and cannily diversified the firm's portfolio. Rising property prices made real estate a great engine of profit. Seeing the rise in tourism, he turned to the hospitality industry, creating luxury hotels and rental properties, and investing in transportation, breweries, and laundries. Key to his growing financial empire was his expansion into construction by acquiring Arnhold & Co., a leader in engineering supplies and building materials, particularly lumber. The firm was folded into the new Cathay Land Company, Ltd., which oversaw the new building ventures of E. D. Sassoon & Co.[49]

In Shanghai's heady multiethnic mix, Baghdadis did not have to conform. Different

Ohel Rachel Synagogue, Shanghai, interior, photographed in 2010.

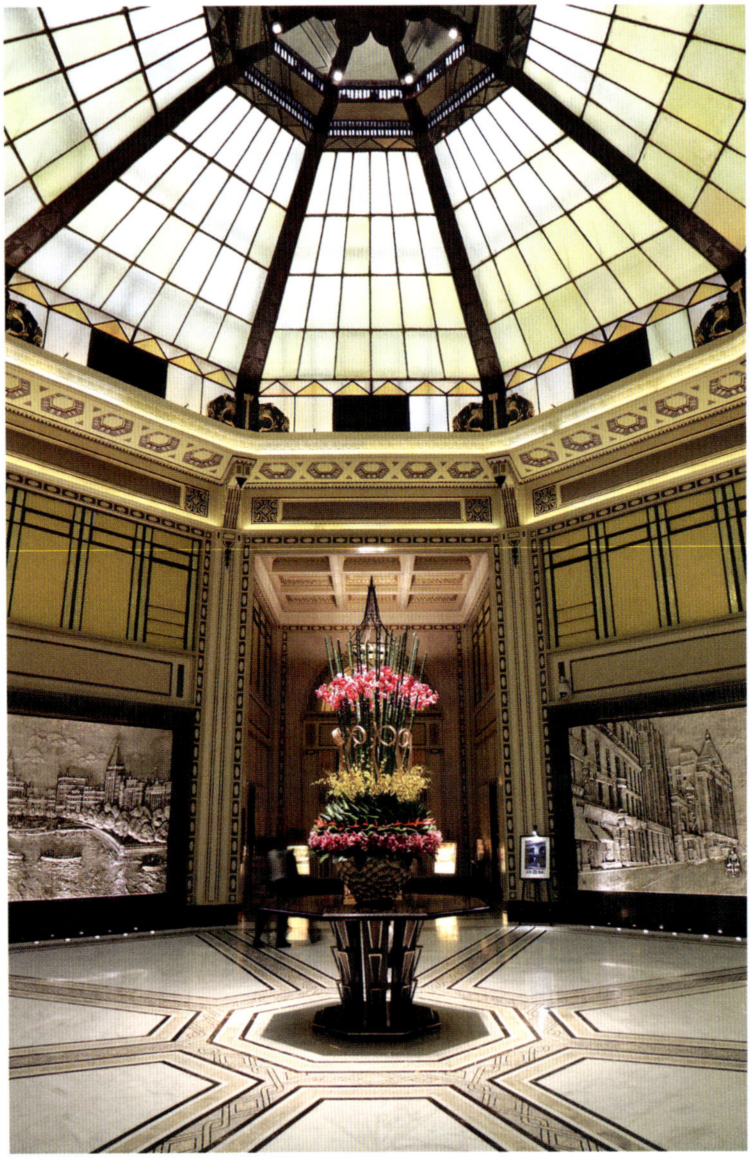

Fairmont Peace Hotel, Shanghai, 1926–29, Palmer and Turner, architects, rotunda.

OPPOSITE
Sassoon House, Shanghai, 1926–29, Palmer and Turner, architects. The top floors house the Cathay Hotel, now the Fairmont Peace Hotel.

nationalities chose architectural styles that spoke to them of their pasts: there were Gothic Revival, Renaissance, and Byzantine churches; eclectic Spanish villas; and a Mozarabic garage. Banks and insurance buildings along the waterfront followed the Beaux-Arts. Many architects and clients, both foreign and Chinese, preferred Art Deco and the International Style, which reflected the edgy tempo of modern life.

With supreme self-confidence, Victor set the tone, using advanced technology to erect stylistically innovative buildings for new social uses. Sassoon House (1926–29), to this day the best known landmark on the Bund, caused a stir when it opened. The broad thoroughfare had become a world-famous boulevard where foreign firms and nations could advertise their power through architecture. Designed by George Leopold Wilson, of the prestigious architectural firm Palmer and Turner, the building included an arcade for luxury shops and banks on the ground floor. Above were the offices of E. D. Sassoon & Co. and the American Women's Club, and from the fourth floor up, the Cathay Hotel (now the Fairmont Peace Hotel), with restaurants, ballrooms, nightclub (the Tower), and roof garden.[50]

The interior had exquisite decorative features, often inspired by Chinese art, a welcome departure from the classicizing details found on buildings along the Bund. Expensive suites were decorated in Indian, Chinese, Japanese, French, Jacobean, and Georgian styles. The high quality of local and foreign craftsmanship was on display: wall paintings, mosaics, stained glass, as well as opalescent lighting by Lalique. At the crossing of the arcades, a great glass rotunda floats effortlessly above marble floors. Expertly restored by architect Tang Yuen in 2007, the building is still extremely

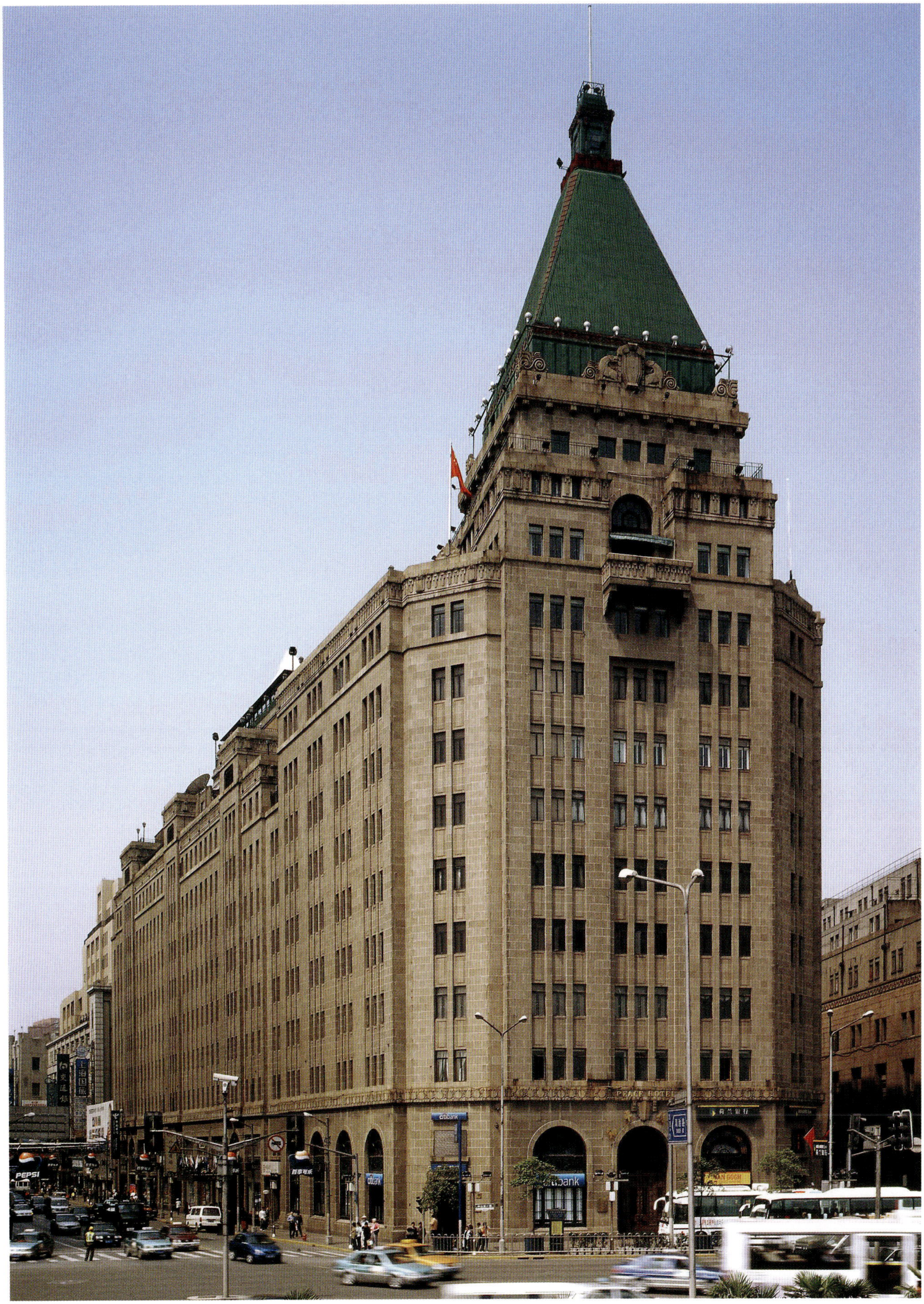
PEPSI

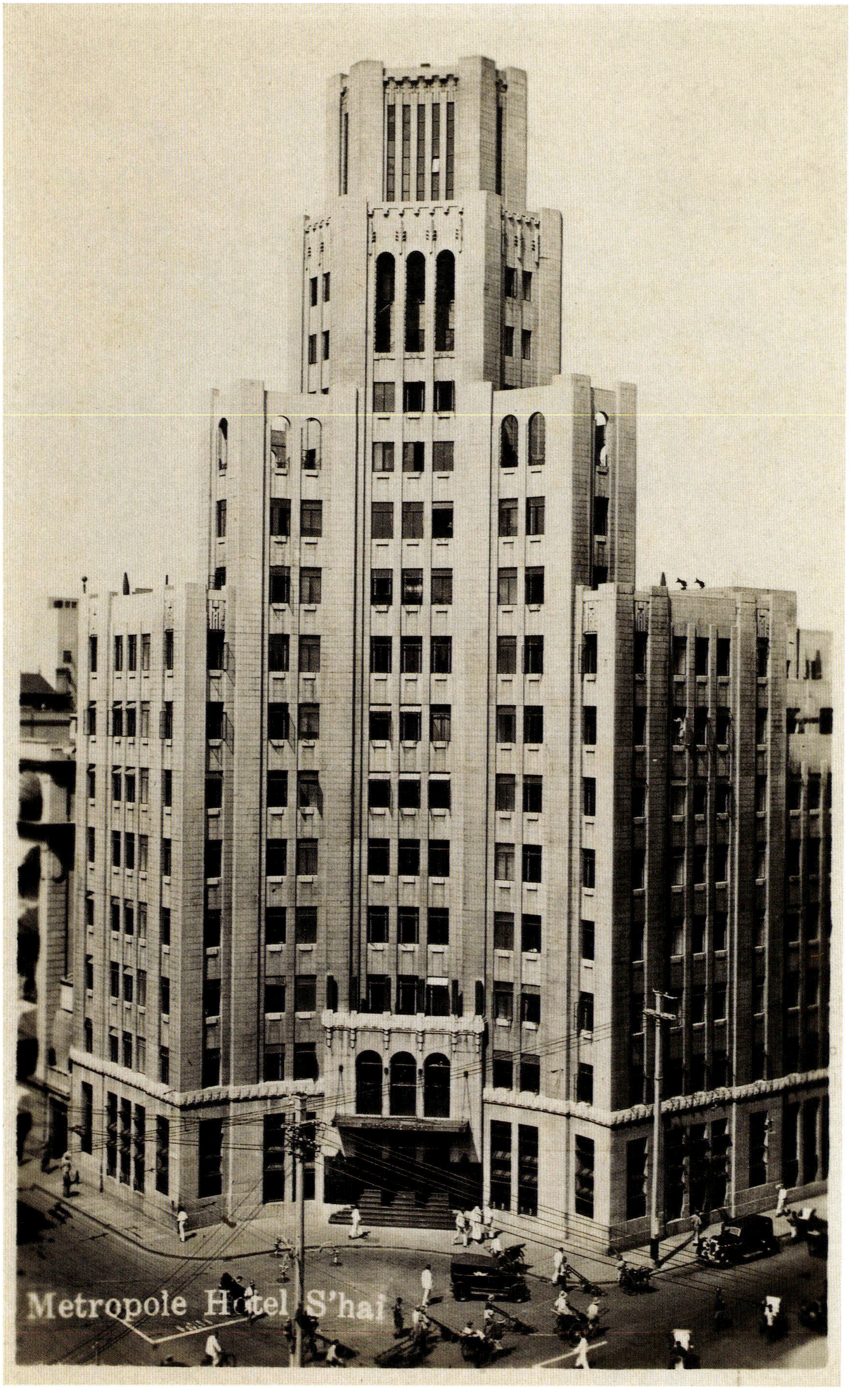

The Metropole Hotel, Shanghai, 1931–33, Palmer and Turner, architects.

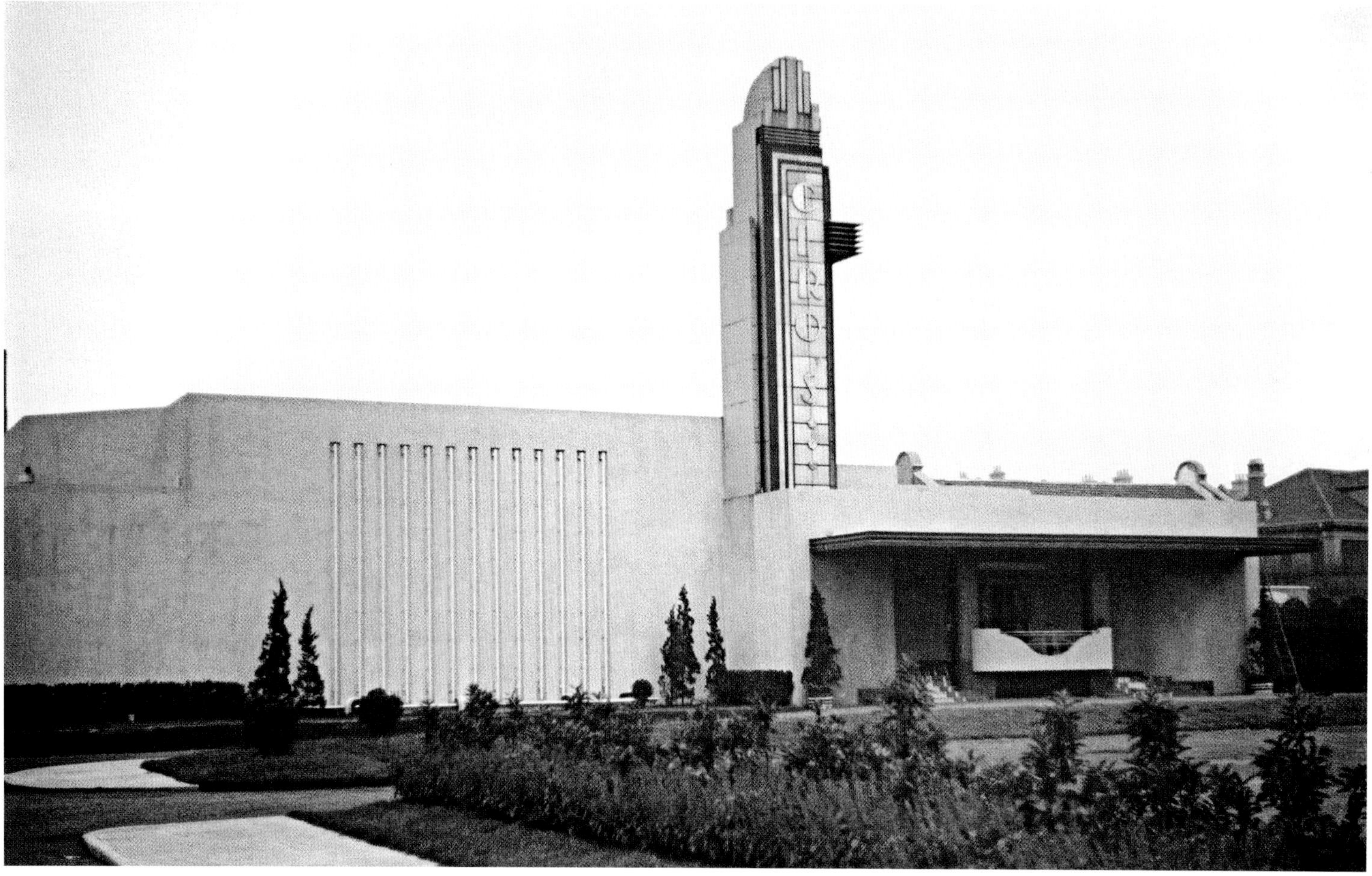

Ciro's nightclub, Shanghai, 1936, Palmer and Turner, architects.

beautiful, although some of the original decorative features have been lost.[51]

With Sassoon House, Sin Jin Kee, Victor's Chinese contractor, created the tallest building on the Bund. Until then, the muddy soil of the city ruled out skyscrapers. Even modest high-rises had to make use of concrete rafts supported by piles—1,600 in the case of Sassoon House—which could sustain a steel skeleton and reinforced concrete. Clad in granite and embellished with Art Deco motifs, the building, with its sleek verticality and division into base, shaft, and capital, resembles the American skyscrapers that Victor had seen in New York.[52]

Victor proceeded to build even taller Art Deco skyscrapers, all by Palmer and Turner, on the spongy, waterlogged soil of Shanghai. The fourteen-story Metropole Hotel and its twin, Hamilton House (1931–33), likewise built by Sin Jin Kee, were designed like bookends. In an imaginative urban gesture, their concave façades frame Fuzhou Road at a busy intersection with Jiangxi Road.[53] Both are setbacks, tapering upward, with roof gardens and terraces, and boasted sprinkler systems and rubbish chutes. The interiors were extremely stylish, with marble and hardwood floors, and Art Deco lighting fixtures. Following the mixed-use formula used on the Bund, Hamilton House had offices, hotel rooms, and rental apartments, and offered meals.

In the French Concession, Victor erected several high-end buildings. Grosvenor House (1929) followed the ziggurat fashion of New York skyscrapers, rising to twenty-one stories. In response to Shanghai's thriving film industry, Victor also commissioned the Austro-Hungarian architect Charles Henry Gonda (Károly Goldstein) to design the Art Deco Cathay Cinema (1932), which could seat more than a thousand people. Victor completed the eighteen-story Cathay Mansions, begun by Arnhold & Co. Designed by Palmer and Turner and built by Wing Kor Sung & Sons, it had problems of subsidence, endemic to the city's marshy soil. An unusual residence hotel, it had shops at ground level, public rooms, and private suites with lifts that carried meals to the guests.[54] Its neo-Tudor exterior was at variance with the advanced technology employed by its engineer, Abraham Levenspiel. Ciro's nightclub (1936), by Palmer and Turner, was a huge attraction when it was unveiled,

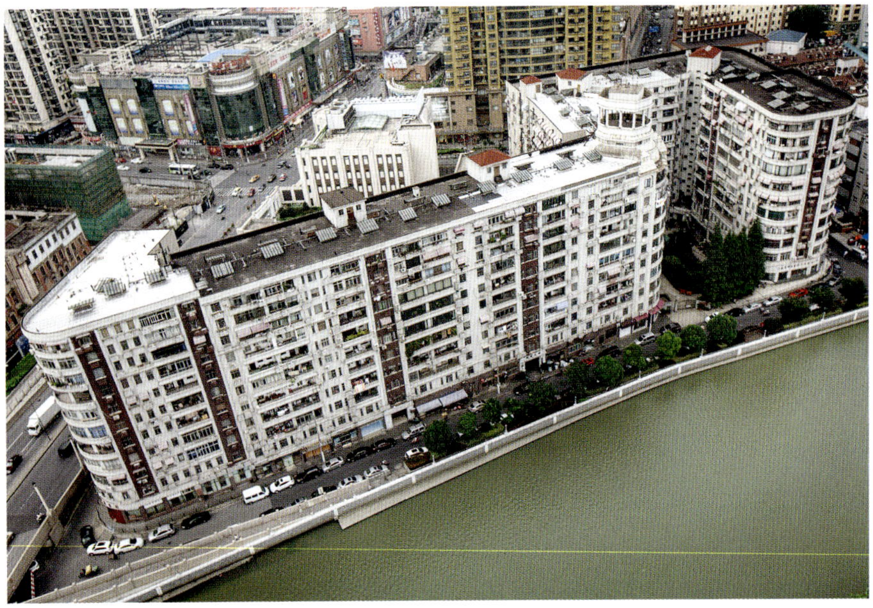

The Embankment Building, Shanghai, 1935, Palmer and Turner, architects.

OPPOSITE
Victor Sassoon's Shanghai residence, Eves, 1933, Palmer and Turner, architects, photographed by Victor Sassoon, Victor Sassoon Diary, November 18, 1933, Dallas, Southern Methodist University, DeGolyer Library.

with its sleek, neon-lit Art Deco tower and abstract ornament. Another commission by Victor, the Embankment Building (1935), rises on the edge of Suzhou Creek with an unprecedented quarter-mile-long façade, offering apartments, offices, and a swimming pool on the ground floor.

Though he lived mostly in the Cathay Hotel, Victor built a picturesque villa on the outskirts of the city in 1933. Known as "Eves," after his initials (Ellice Victor Elias Sassoon), it had a half-timbered "Tudor" façade with windows of leaded glass. The interior, with exposed rafters, had a spacious two-story hall with a large fireplace and inglenook.[55] The garden, designed by Palmer and Turner, had a creek, two lakes, an island, rustic bridges, and artificial knolls executed by Koo Ah Dong & Brothers.

David Sassoon & Co. also embraced modern architecture and in 1938 inaugurated Magnet House, an office building designed by Emmanuel Gran of Davies, Brooke and Gran.[56] The Baghdadis—Sassoons, Kadoories, Ezras, and Silas Hardoon—certainly contributed to the architectural beauty of the International Settlement and the French Concession. Shanghai, however, was a vibrant *Chinese* city. A great incubator for Chinese culture, it was the center of its publishing industry, film, theater, literature, and the arts. The intelligentsia blossomed. By the early twentieth century, ninety-eight percent of the foreign enclaves of exclusivity was inhabited by the Chinese. Thousands had sought refuge in these protected zones during the Small Swords and Taiping rebellions (1850–64). By 1931, according to the census, almost one million Chinese lived in the International Settlement and 422,000 in the French Concession. Both foreign and Chinese developers, including the Sassoons, made money building traditional housing (*lilong*) for the Chinese. Interestingly, the Sassoons also had Japanese-style rental flats for non-Japanese residents. A swollen population of impoverished Chinese workers who toiled in industry lived throughout the foreign and Chinese areas.[57]

Life in this wealthiest of the treaty ports gave a strong impetus to Chinese capitalism. Merchants, bankers, and industrialists made fortunes, adopting upscale lifestyles in the settlements. Nevertheless, they suffered constant discrimination in their own country. Until June 1928, the Chinese were not allowed in parks under foreign jurisdiction unless they were servants accompanying their employers.[58] Nor were they welcome in many restaurants, clubs, and racecourses patronized by foreign elites. Such deep-rooted patterns of inequality helped fan the flames of a nascent nationalism that began to challenge colonial practices and slowly changed equality of access.

Non-Europeans were on both sides of the divide. Wealthy Baghdadis undoubtedly donated to Chinese causes: Victor gifted $70,000 to the National Medical College established by the Chinese, the only foreigner, along with Elly Kadoorie, to contribute to this important initiative. Victor also gave key jobs in his firms to well-known Chinese figures.[59] His hotels and nightclubs were open to the Chinese who were often invited to his parties, but both the Cathay Hotel and Hamilton House had segregated bathrooms and were angrily criticized by the Chinese who frequented them.[60] Yet like other minorities, the Baghdadis also

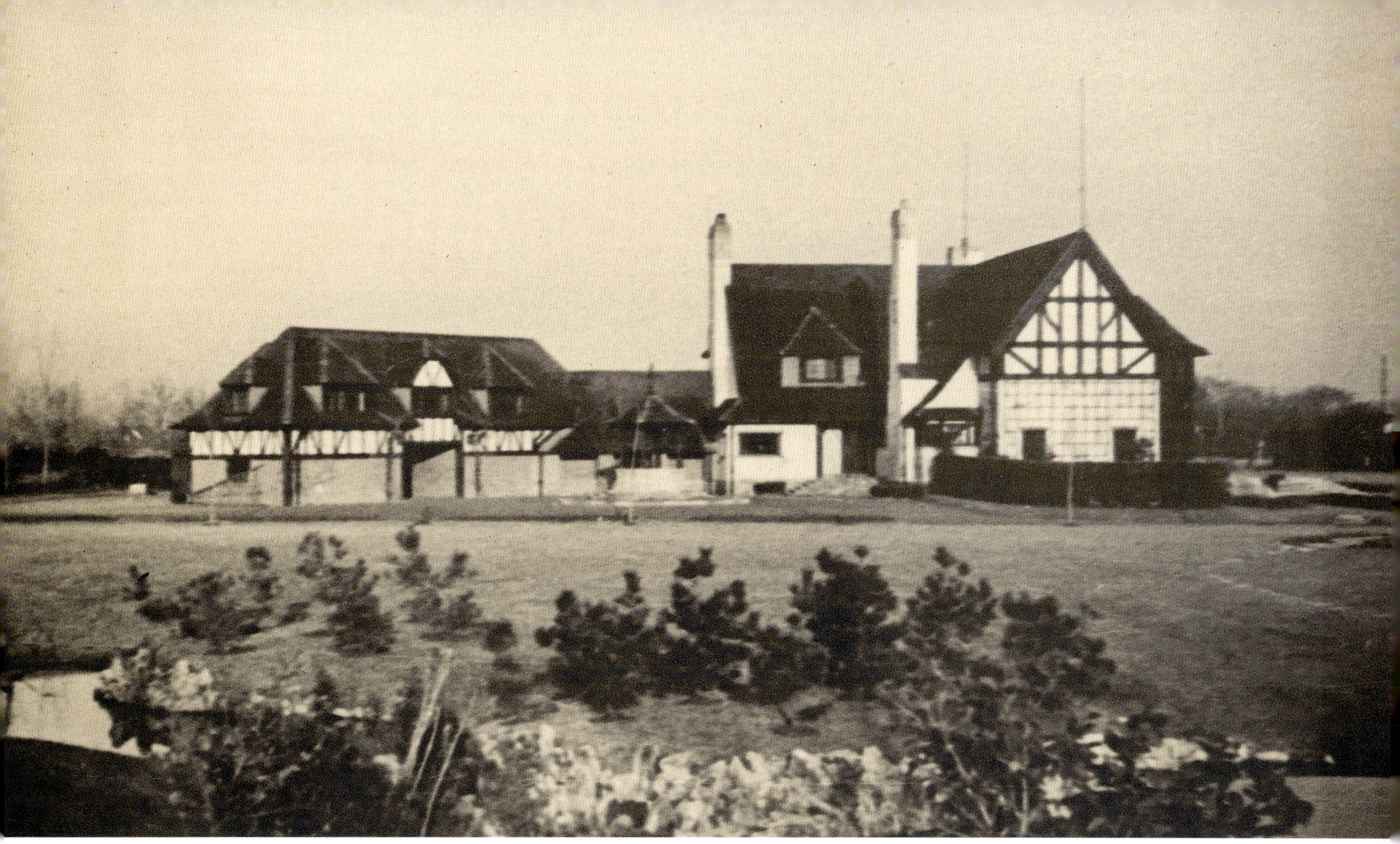

Japanese-style flats for non-Japanese residents, Shanghai, 1937, from an album of the Shanghai properties belonging to the Sassoon family, Norfolk, UK, Houghton Hall Collection.

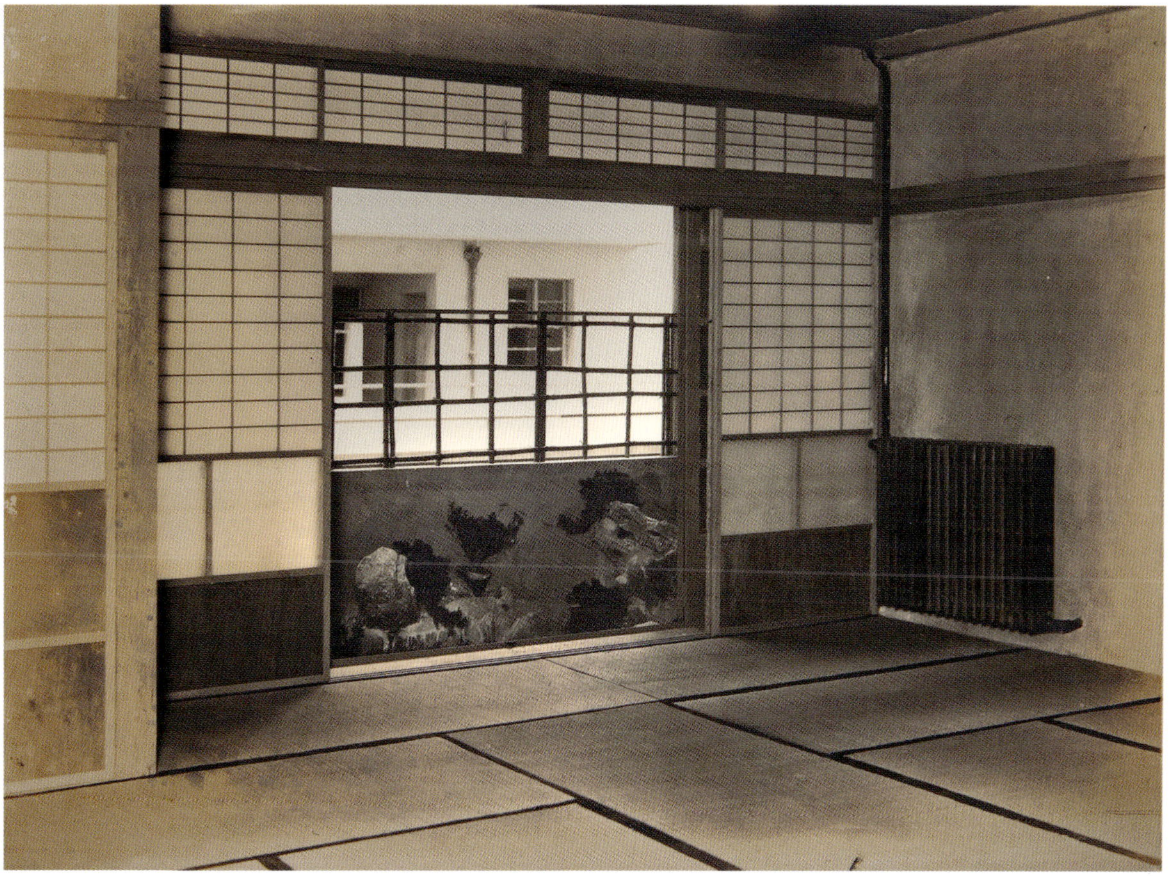

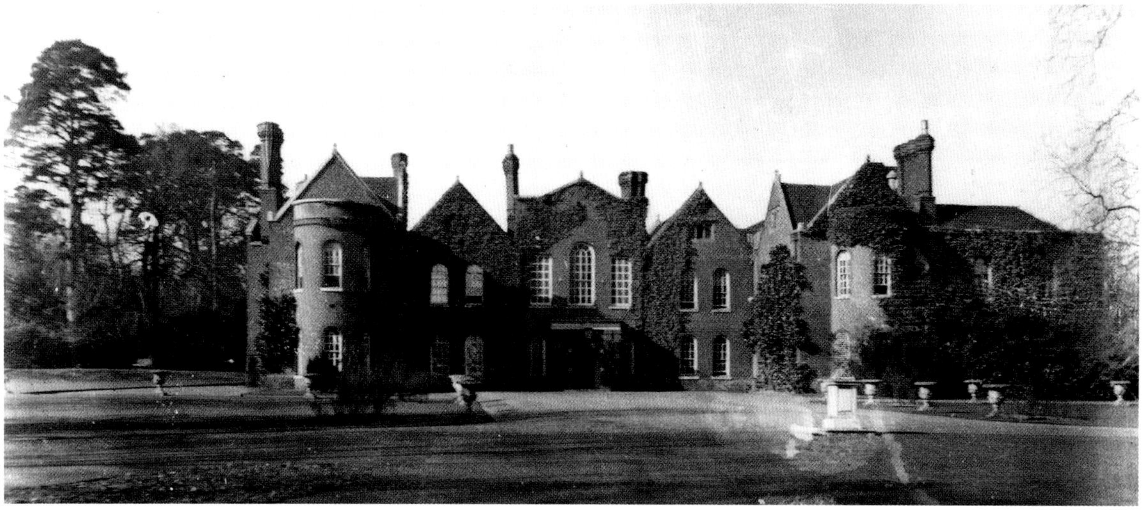

Sassoon David Sassoon's residence, Ashley Park, Surrey, England, built in 1605, rebuilt several times, and demolished in 1920.

suffered discrimination. While the imposing Cercle Sportif Français admitted "minorities," including the Chinese, and women, the exclusive Shanghai Club functioned as a gatekeeper of racialist practices. Even Victor, the most famous host in the foreign community, was sometimes greeted with chants of "Back to Baghdad! Back to Baghdad!" on entering a bar in the 1930s.[61] As *Fortune* magazine put it in 1935, "the crusty diehards of the British colony still look askance at his exuberance and sniff at his ancestry. In England he may hobnob with Princes, but in Shanghai, where the Old Guard is almost provincial, there are circles that he cannot enter, partly because he is a Jew, partly because the British deplore his flight from taxation as not quite sporting."[62] A member of several clubs, he was kept out of many British social events by the same people who came to his own fabulous parties. In 1911, the Jewish community built its own club on a prestigious but small site on Nanjing Road, designed by the well-known architectural firm Lafuente and Wootten. In 1920, when Elly Kadoorie built a club that was to be the grandest of all, it was destroyed by fire: authorities suspected arson.[63]

England

In hindsight, all these cities—Mumbai, Hong Kong, Shanghai—were way stations on that long process of acculturation by which the Sassoons gradually changed their identity from "Judeo-Arabic to Judeo-British."[64] While David Sassoon's grandsons were doing their stints in the East, six of his sons moved to London. In 1858, Sassoon David established a beachhead for the family firm. After opening an office in Leadenhall Street, where the East India Company had its headquarters, he bought a distinguished Tudor estate in Surrey, Ashley Park, possibly built by Cardinal Wolsey. He also acquired a superb townhouse at 17 Cumberland Terrace, John Nash's exquisite neoclassical gem. The introspective and scholarly "S. D." was extremely successful in expanding the commercial network and was soon joined by his younger brother Reuben, who took over the business in 1867 after Sassoon David's sudden death.

Conscious of the Sassoons' standing, Reuben established himself with his family and mother in a classical townhouse in Belgrave Square. The elegant terraces had been designed between 1825 and 1840 by a prominent Sephardic architect, Elias George Basevi (1794–1845), Disraeli's first cousin.[65] Among many modern conveniences, the house had a hydraulic, leather-padded elevator that took the horses up to their stables on the top of the house. Reuben loved horses, and his most beautiful stallion served as the model for the equestrian statue of the Prince of Wales that the family donated to Mumbai. The interior of the house was richly appointed and included Reuben's collection of Chinese and Japanese embroideries.[66] Warm, gregarious, and endowed with an astonishing gift for mathematics, Reuben kept a superb table and cellar, entertaining his titled guests lavishly. Sharing the Sassoons' passion for music, he held several concerts in his home. Ovide Musin, the Belgian violinist and composer, warmly recalled a musical soirée at Reuben's house when he, the composer Camille Saint-Saëns, and the cellist Gustave Libotton played.[67] Reuben was the first Sassoon to open his house to art exhibitions on behalf of charities.

The other brothers acquired stately homes in London's fashionable areas. Sent by his father to study in London, Arthur, David Sassoon's fifth son,

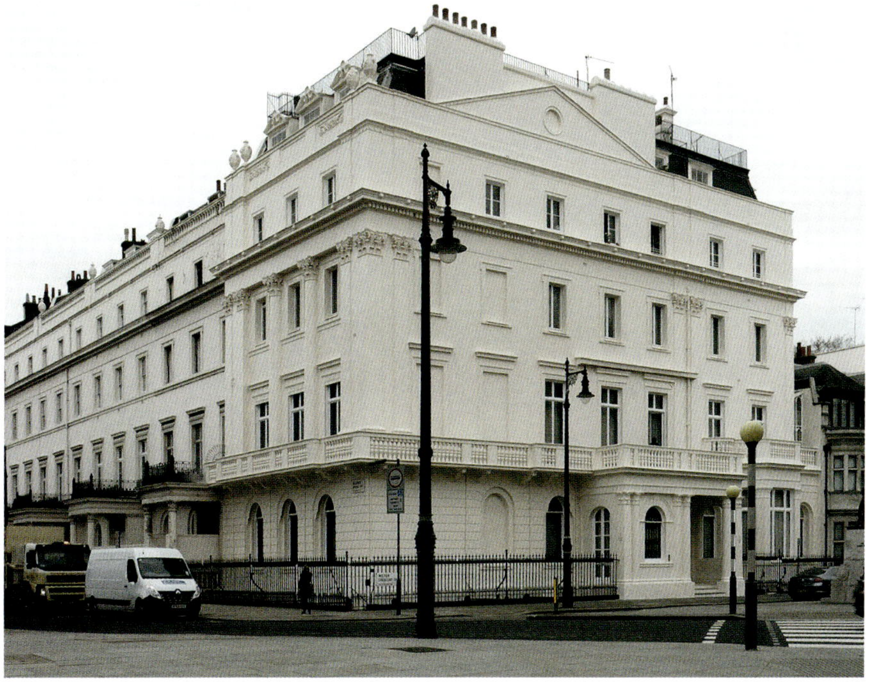

Reuben Sassoon's residence in London, 1 Belgrave Square, 1825–40, Elias George Basevi, architect.

spent a few years in Hong Kong and Shanghai. After his marriage to the glamorous Louise Perugia in 1873, he moved to 2 Albert Gate, a building designed by Thomas Cubitt. It had an imposing staircase and a superb music room; Johann Strauss Jr. led his orchestra there, probably in the ballroom.[68] Albert Abdullah came to test the waters before moving there permanently in 1875, after being knighted in 1872 and receiving the Freedom of the City of London a year later. As head of the family, he acquired a magnificent mansion at 25 Kensington Gore, originally commissioned by the British banker and philanthropist Samuel Montagu, who was deeply involved in Jewish causes. The wooden paneling in the dining room, inlaid with ivory and ebony, came from the Pavilion of the Prince of Wales at the Paris exhibition of 1878, as did the tapestries flanking the fireplace ("Ye Merrie Wives"). In 1880, when Albert Abdullah gave a reception for the prince, the entrance hall and staircase were exquisitely decorated with a grotto, a cascade, water lilies, and a fernery.[69]

This same prodigal hospitality continued at Brighton, where family members bought homes facing the elegant promenade along the shore. There they hosted dinners for royalty, politicians, and eminent personalities from the musical and theatrical worlds. King Edward was particularly close to Reuben, and to Arthur and his lovely wife, Louise, with whom he often stayed. (King Edward was also a frequent guest of the Arthur Sassoons

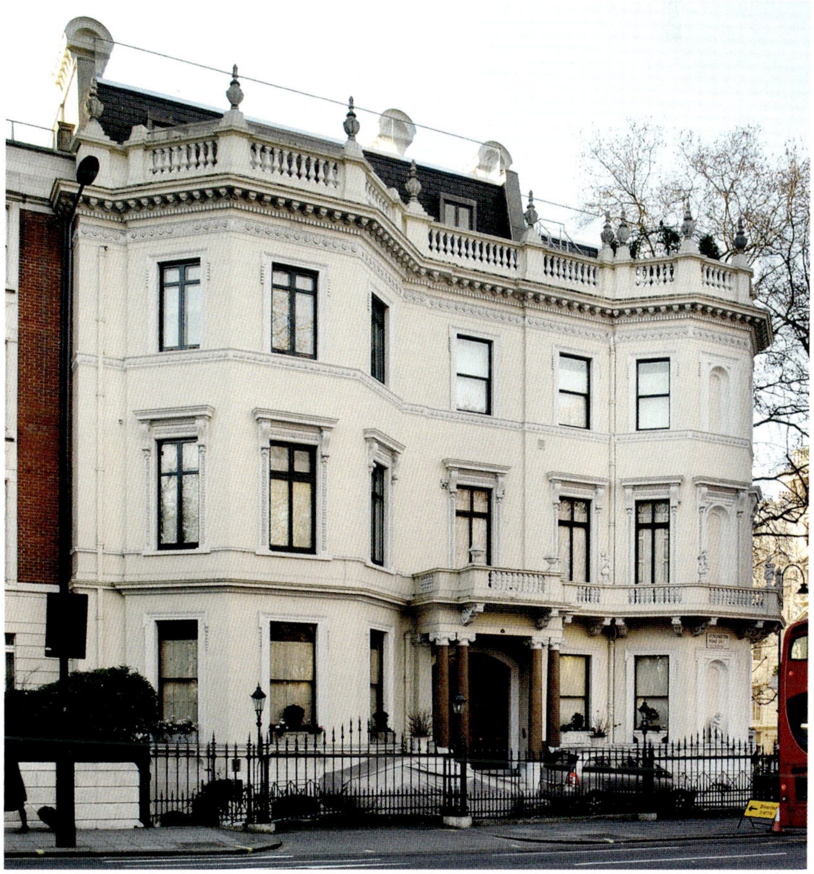

Albert Abdullah's London residence, 25 Kensington Gore, 1873–75, Samuel Whitfield Daukes, architect.

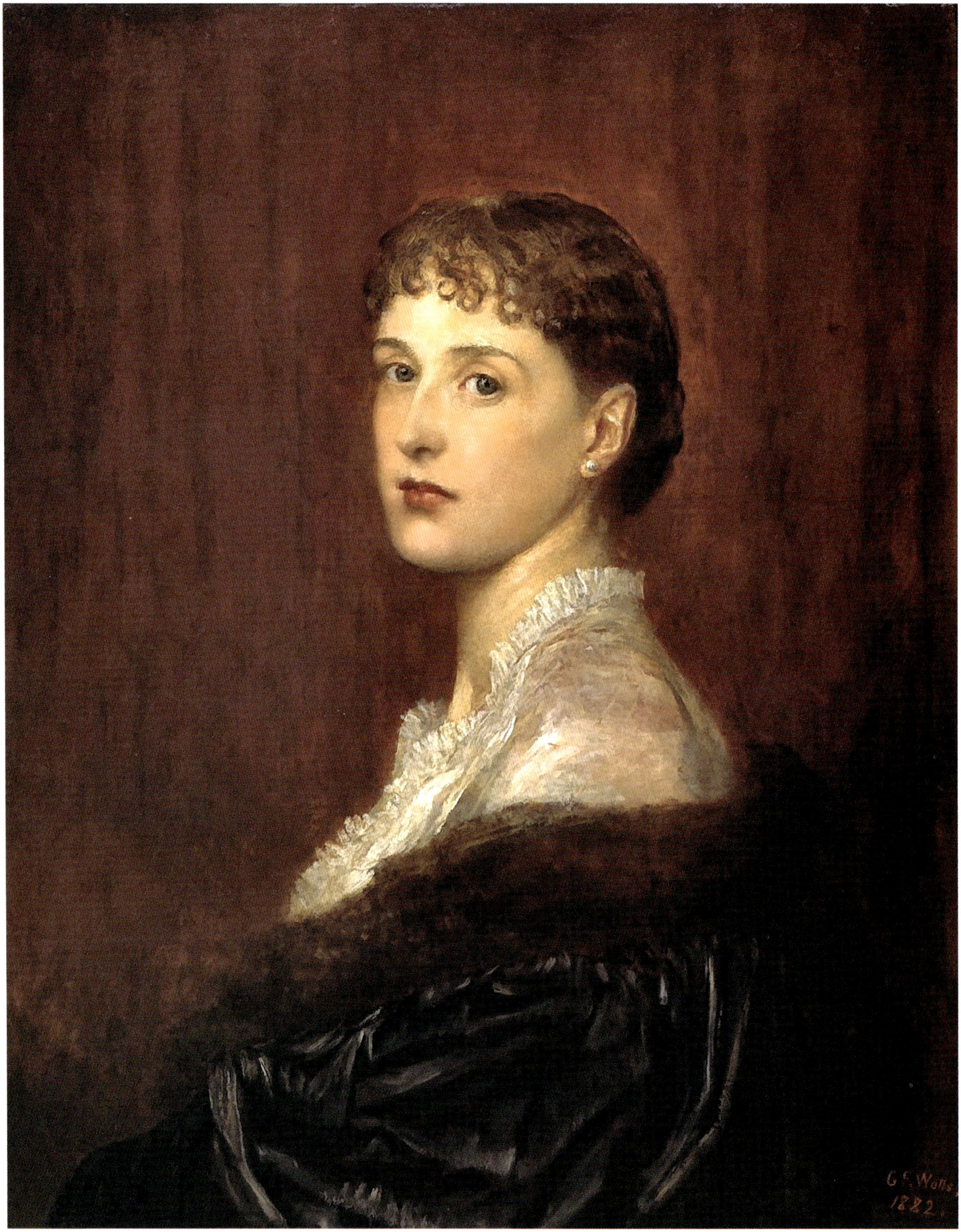
G F Watts
1882

OPPOSITE
George Frederic Watts, *Mrs. Arthur Sassoon,* 1882, oil on canvas, 26 × 21 in. (66 × 53.3 cm), London, Tate, presented by Mr. and Mrs. Arthur Sassoon, 1929. Louise Sassoon's younger sister Marie married Leopold de Rothschild.

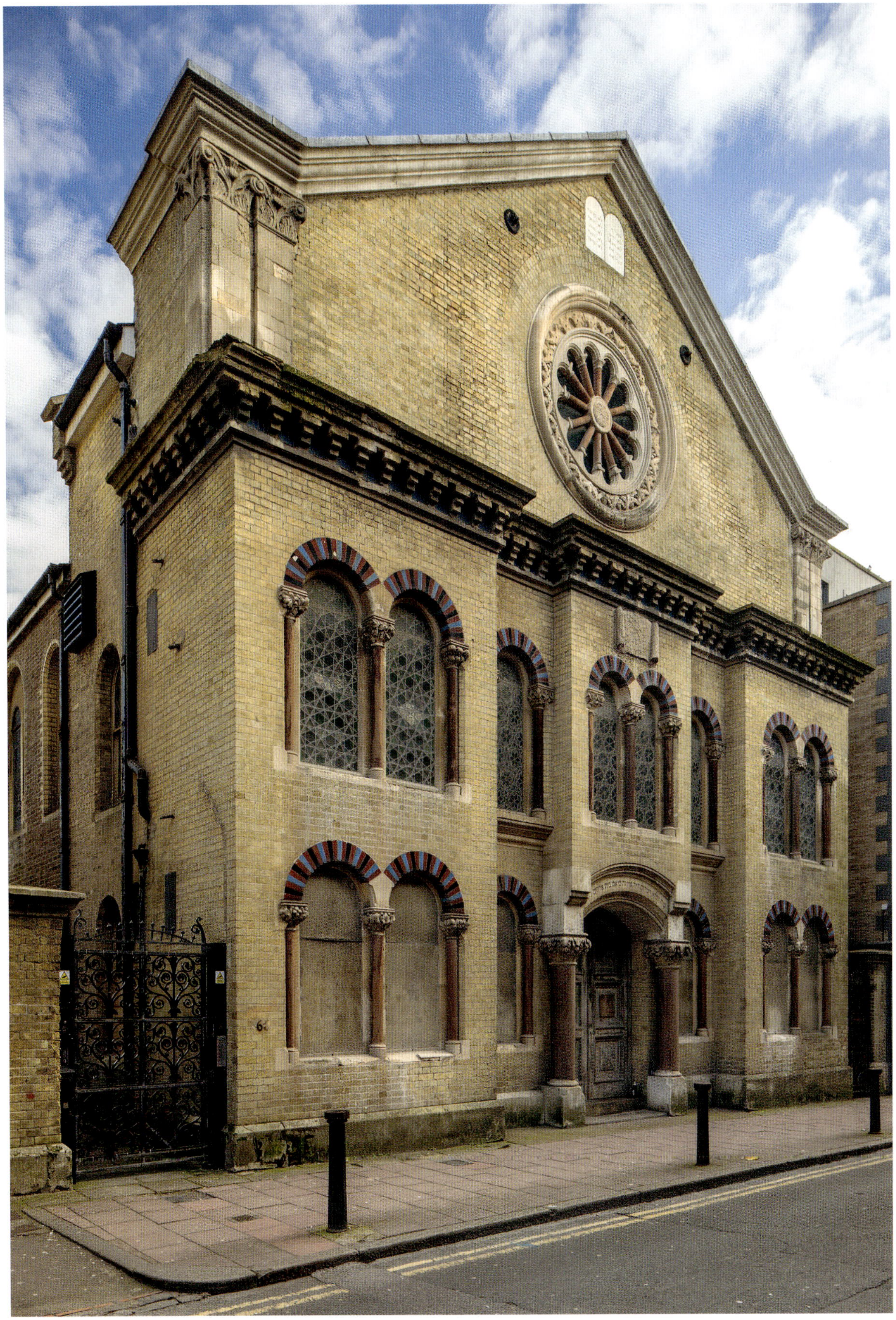

Middle Street Synagogue, Brighton, 1874–75, Thomas Lainson, architect.

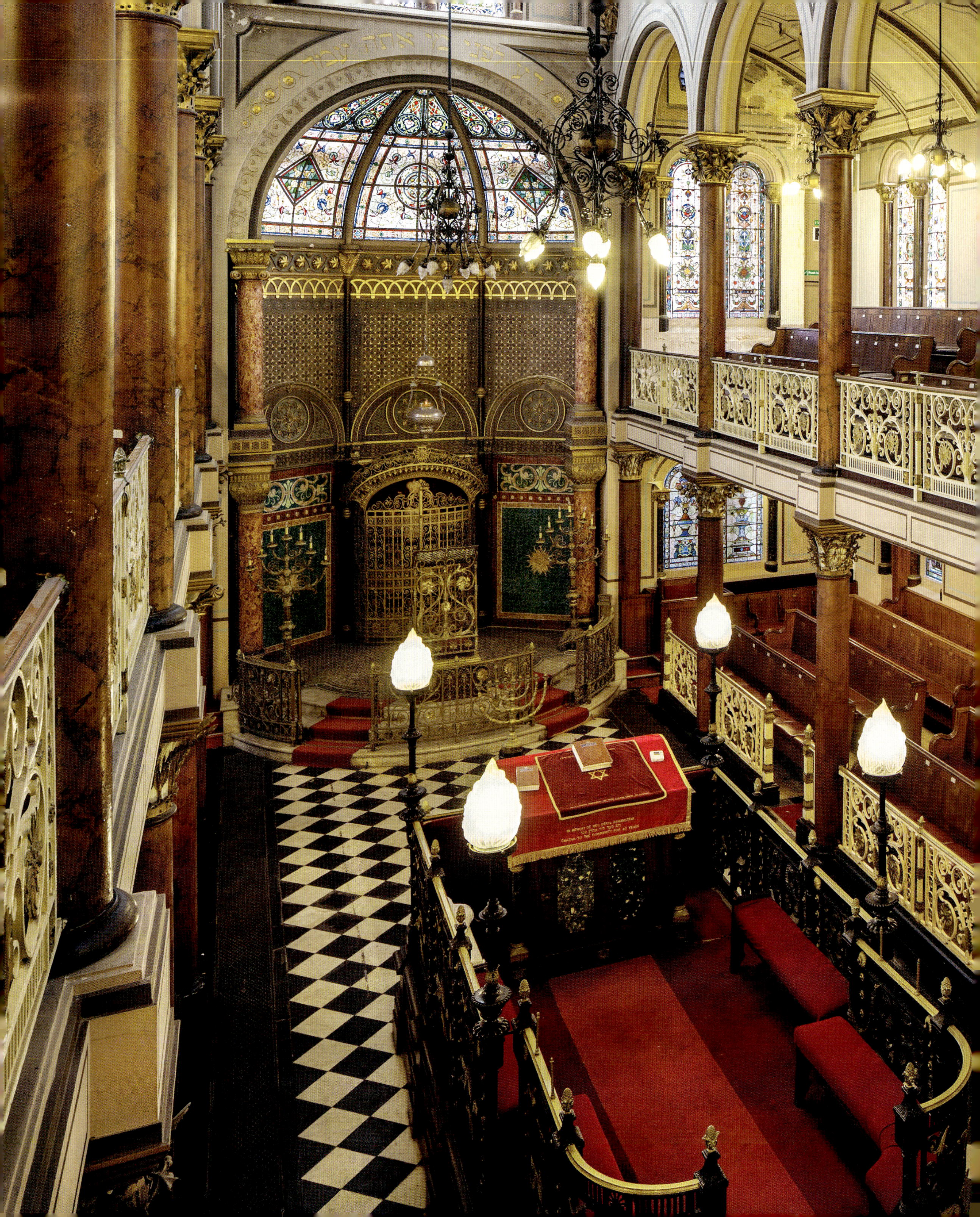

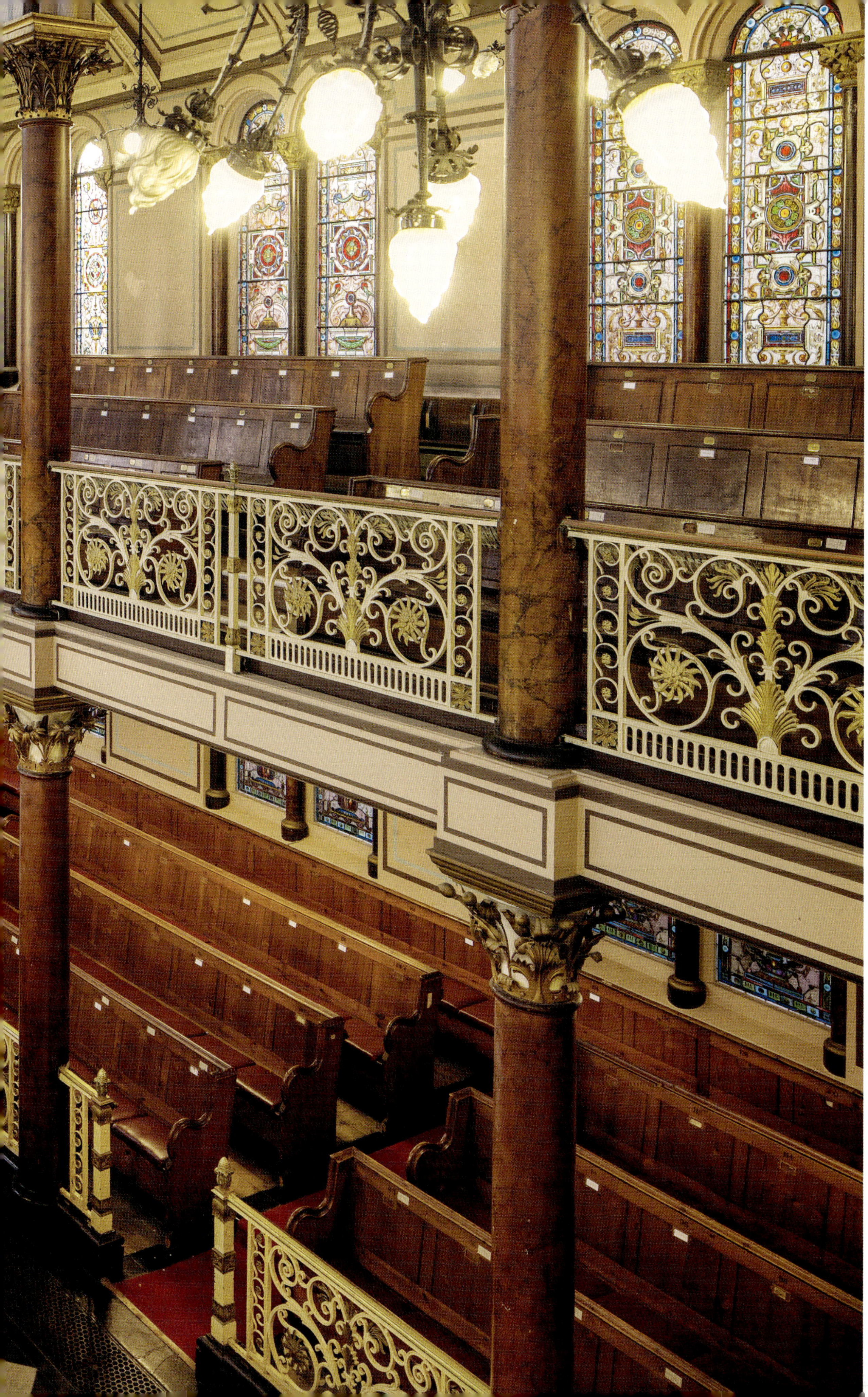

Middle Street Synagogue, interior view from the women's gallery.

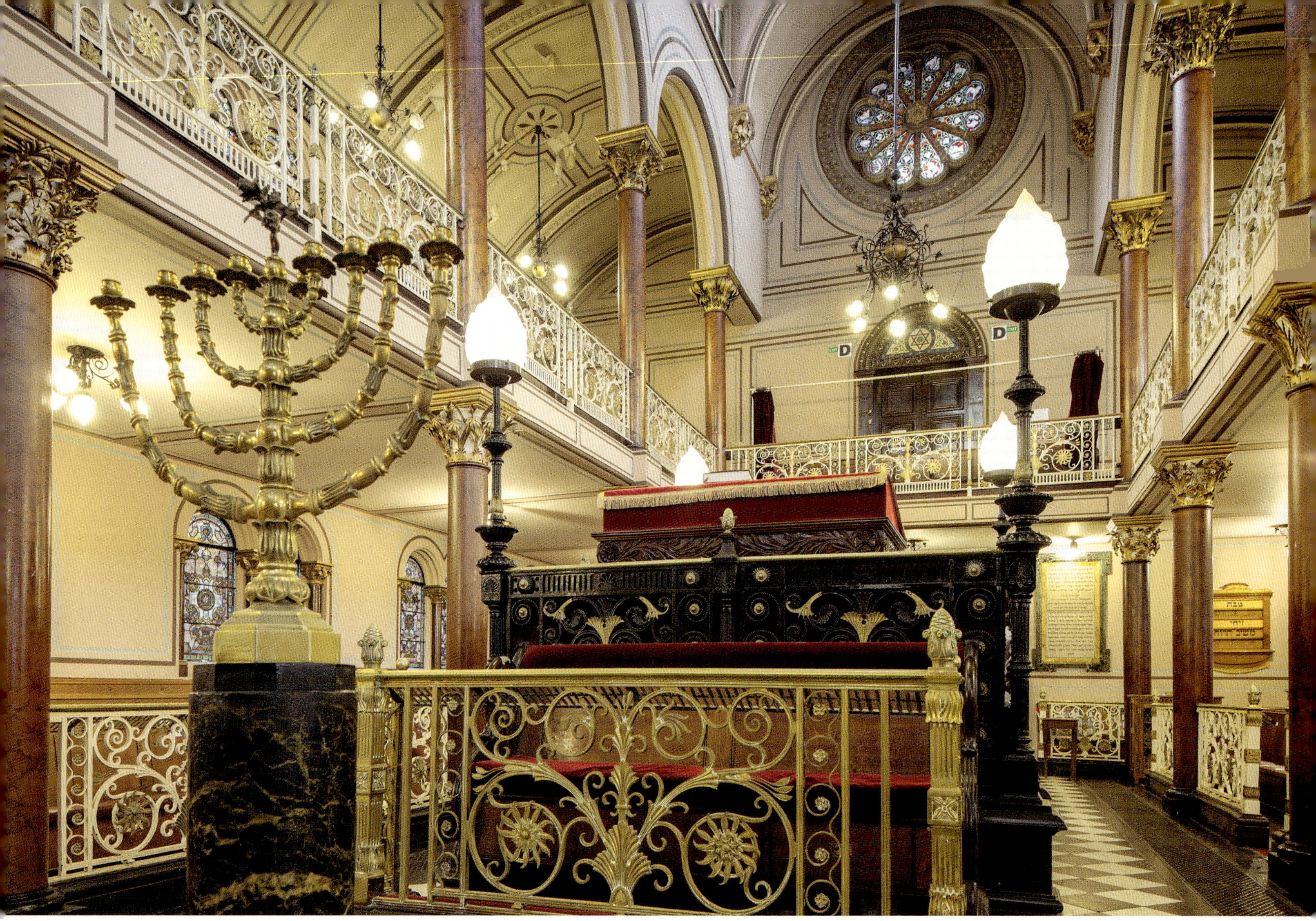

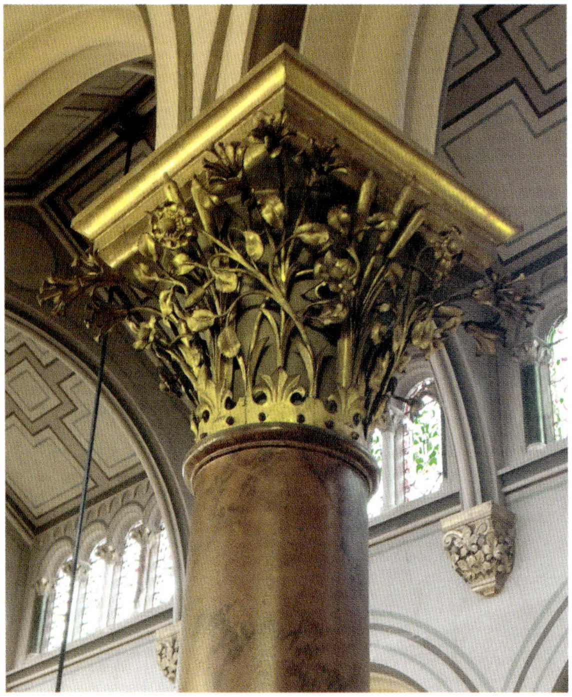

Middle Street Synagogue, detail of the capitals in hammered copper.

Middle Street Synagogue, interior. The bimah with brass decoration was dedicated by Meyer Sassoon to commemorate his marriage to Mozelle Gubbay in 1892. The stained-glass rose window was donated by the brothers Reuben, Arthur, and Aaron Sassoon.

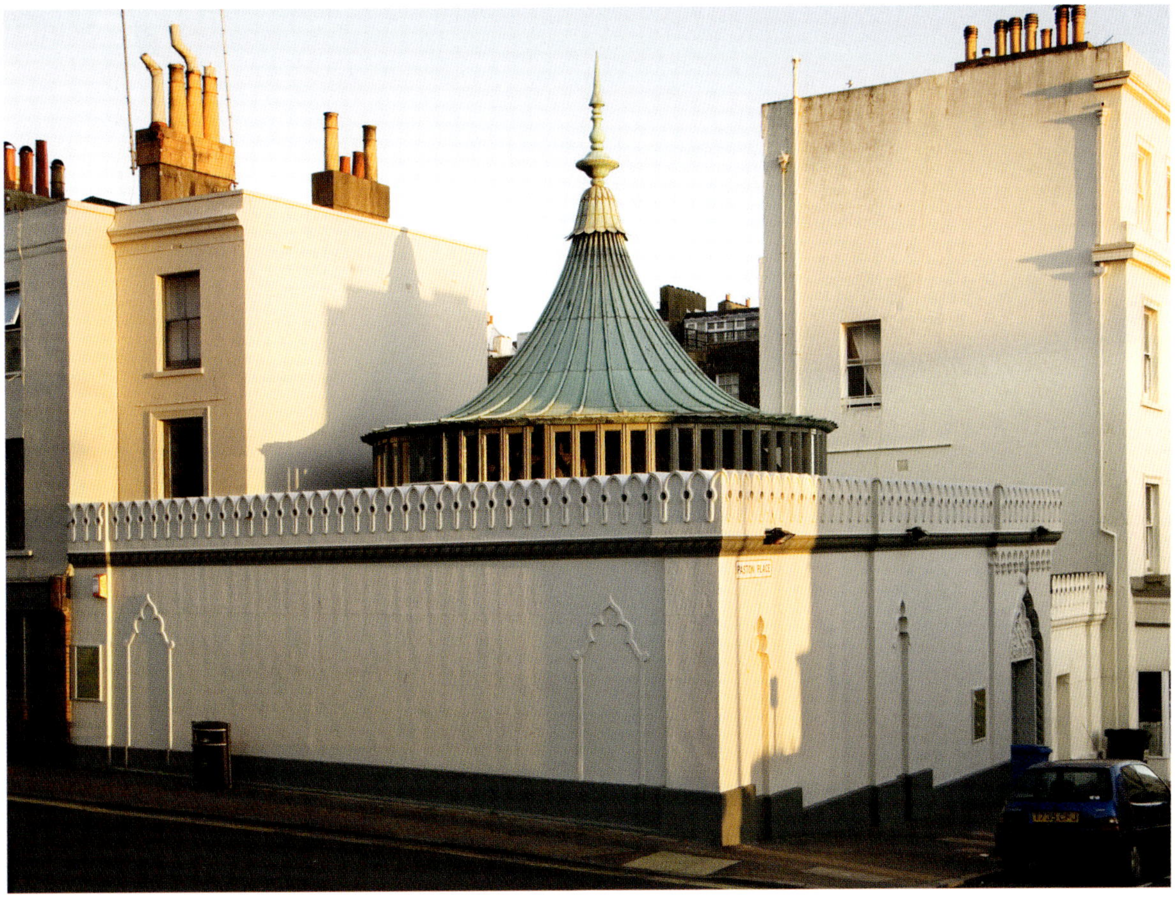

The mausoleum of Albert Abdullah Sassoon, Brighton, built 1892, later converted to the Hanbury Arms pub.

at Tulchan Lodge in Scotland.) Reuben hosted notable personalities, including the premier, Arthur Balfour, who was convalescing from illness.

In Brighton, the Sassoons were major donors—followed by the Rothschilds, the Mocattas, and the Montefiores—to the beautiful Middle Street Synagogue (1874–75), designed by Thomas Lainson. The exterior is eclectic, with its Islamic architectural allusions present in medieval Spanish synagogues. The rose window references the Gothic, and the short columns and composite capitals the Romanesque. The contrast between the expensive but modest façade and the magnificent interior could not have been greater.[70] The nave, surrounded by galleries on three sides, builds up momentum until it reaches the bimah at the center and the Torah ark at the east end, where the beauty of the ornamentation attains new heights. The play between the light that streams through stained or tinted windows, the richly gilded surfaces, and metal capitals envelops visitors in a resplendent blaze.

In 1887, Albert Abdullah gifted the graceful brass lectern on the occasion of his son Edward's marriage to Aline de Rothschild; his brothers Reuben, Arthur, and Aaron donated the rose window, the Decalogue window, and part of the apse window in memory of their mother, Farha. The brass decoration of the bimah came from Meyer Sassoon, who wished to commemorate his marriage to Mozelle Gubbay in 1892. Edward gave two stained-glass windows in honor of his father, who died in 1896.[71] Louise also donated two stained-glass windows in the women's gallery, and Arthur was honored with two more. The family also paid for the electrification of the synagogue, electroliers, new sanctuary gates, and a Torah scroll.

In 1892 Albert Abdullah, who had retired to Brighton, erected a mausoleum for the family, a one-story building by an unknown architect, not far from his home. Crowned by an unusual copper dome tapering to a finial once sheathed in gold leaf, and with emphatically Mughal crenellations, it was inevitably termed "Indo-Saracenic." Albert Abdullah may have been inspired by two Orientalist buildings nearby: John Nash's famous Royal Pavilion (1815–23), built for George, Prince of Wales, and Amon Henry Wilds's Western Pavilion (1827–28).

After his father left for Brighton, Edward, Albert Abdullah's only surviving son, moved to

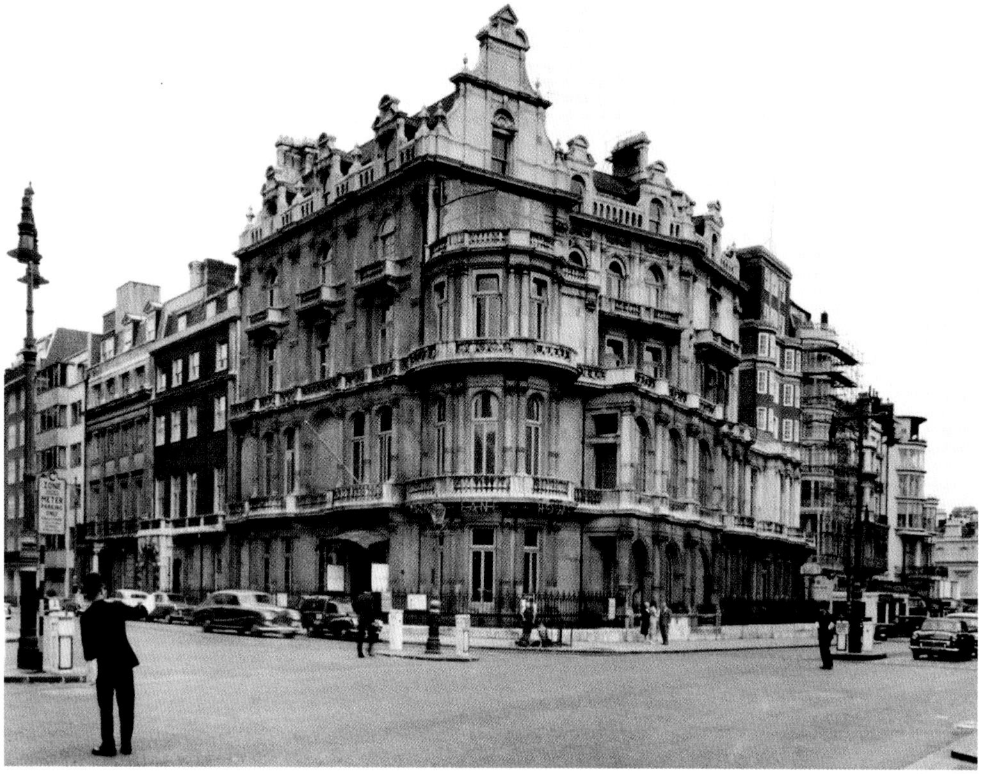

25 Park Lane, built 1895–96, destroyed in the early 1960s, and photographed c. 1960, T. H. Smith and C. E. Sayer, architects, Westminster City Archives.

25 Kensington Gore. As neither he nor his wife liked it, his uncle Reuben found the young couple a home in 25 Park Lane. The rather garish mansion had been built by the South African Randlord Barney Barnato.[72] Aline put her refined taste to work, removing crude allegorical statues from the eclectic façade and remodeling the interior. Priceless eighteenth-century furnishings were brought from the parental mansion of the Rothschilds in Paris. But it was their son, Philip, who would transform the interior into a superb setting for dinners, balls, and art exhibitions.[73] With this fourth generation, the anglicization of the Sassoon family was complete: the long letting-go of Baghdad.

Park Lane would play a seminal role in Philip's political career, and he remodeled it extensively, filling the house with sumptuous furniture; Aubusson, Gobelin, and Persian carpets; tapestries; and Chinese porcelain. All period reproductions bought by his mother were removed. In the dining room and antechamber, Philip installed Rococo paneling originally from the Palais Paar in Vienna and now in the Metropolitan Museum of Art, New York. Philip Tilden, his architect, built a recessed gallery overlooking the marble staircase, with oyster-colored mirrored glass. The large drawing room was given a new monumentality: Aline's white and gilt paneling was replaced and the ceiling raised to accommodate Regency oak boiserie from a French château. Two magnificent Brussels tapestries gave the space added resonance. In his luxuriously appointed rooms, Philip achieved a perfect integration of painting, architecture, and the decorative arts: a Gesamtkunstwerk.[74] Yet with its emphasis on French furnishings, Park Lane remained associated with his mother.

The Catalan artist Josep Maria Sert was commissioned to execute murals for the ballroom. *Caravans of the East* (1921), an overpowering concoction of elephants, camels, palm trees, and exotically attired turbaned crowds, exemplified Sert's baroque imagination.[75] Fifty panels of shimmering gray-blue, pink, and black on a silver background are now in the Museu Nacional d'Art de Catalunya in Barcelona, but the glass ceiling with swirling clouds is gone. The effect was breathtaking. The art critic Henry McBride declared: "The ballroom of Sir Philip Sassoon must be M. Sert's masterpiece. In it he destroys architecture by means of mirrors at the corners of the walls and ceilings and in various places, and the romantic scene of his fancy erects itself against these space enhancing glasses."[76] Sert's work appears as a silvery blur in Charles Sims's painting of Philip's sister, Sybil, in the ballroom.

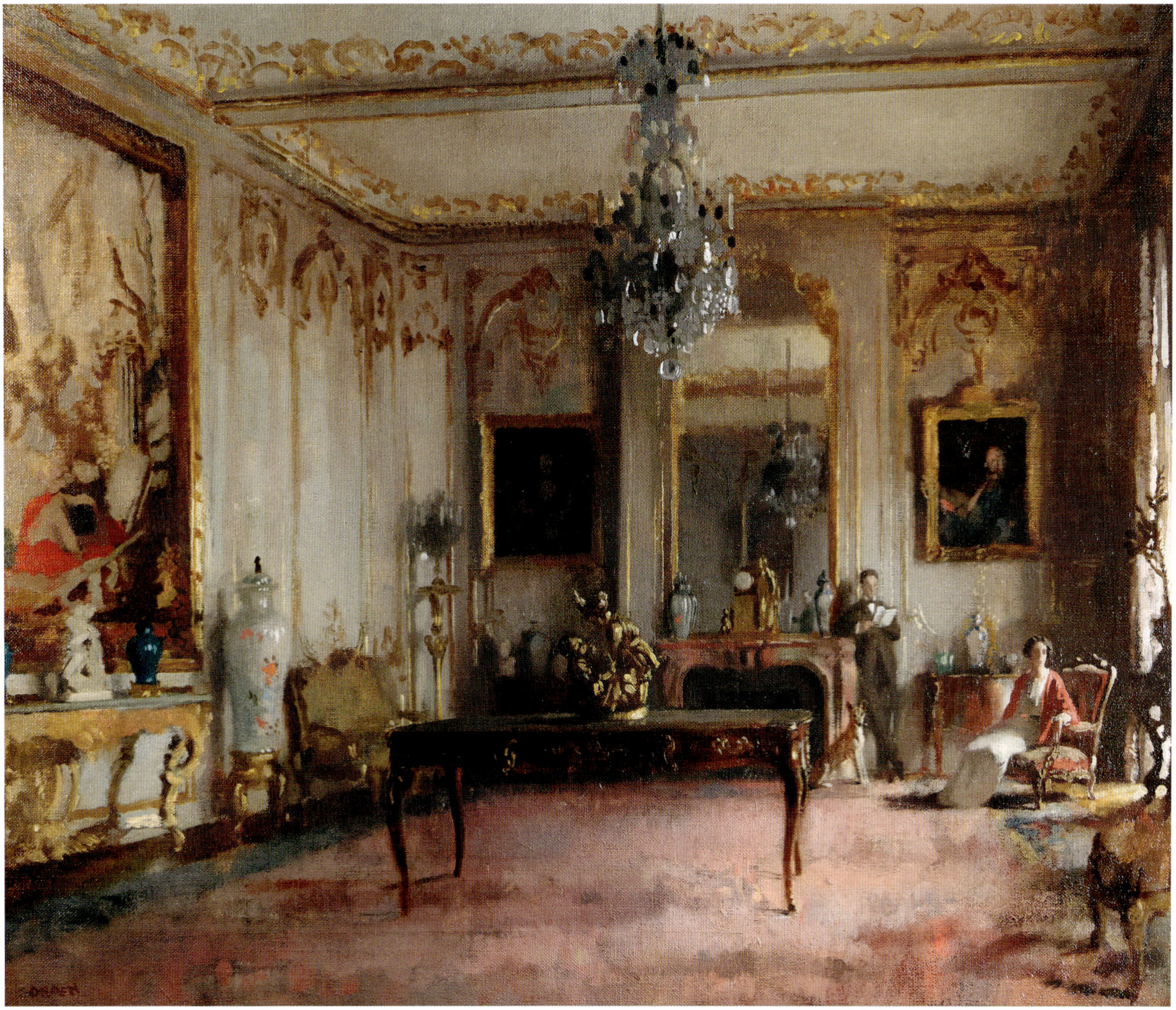

William Orpen, *The Drawing Room at 25 Park Lane*, 1913, oil on canvas, 19 × 23½ in. (48.3 × 59.7 cm), private collection. Philip Sassoon is depicted with his sister, Sybil, at his London residence, decorated by their mother, Aline.

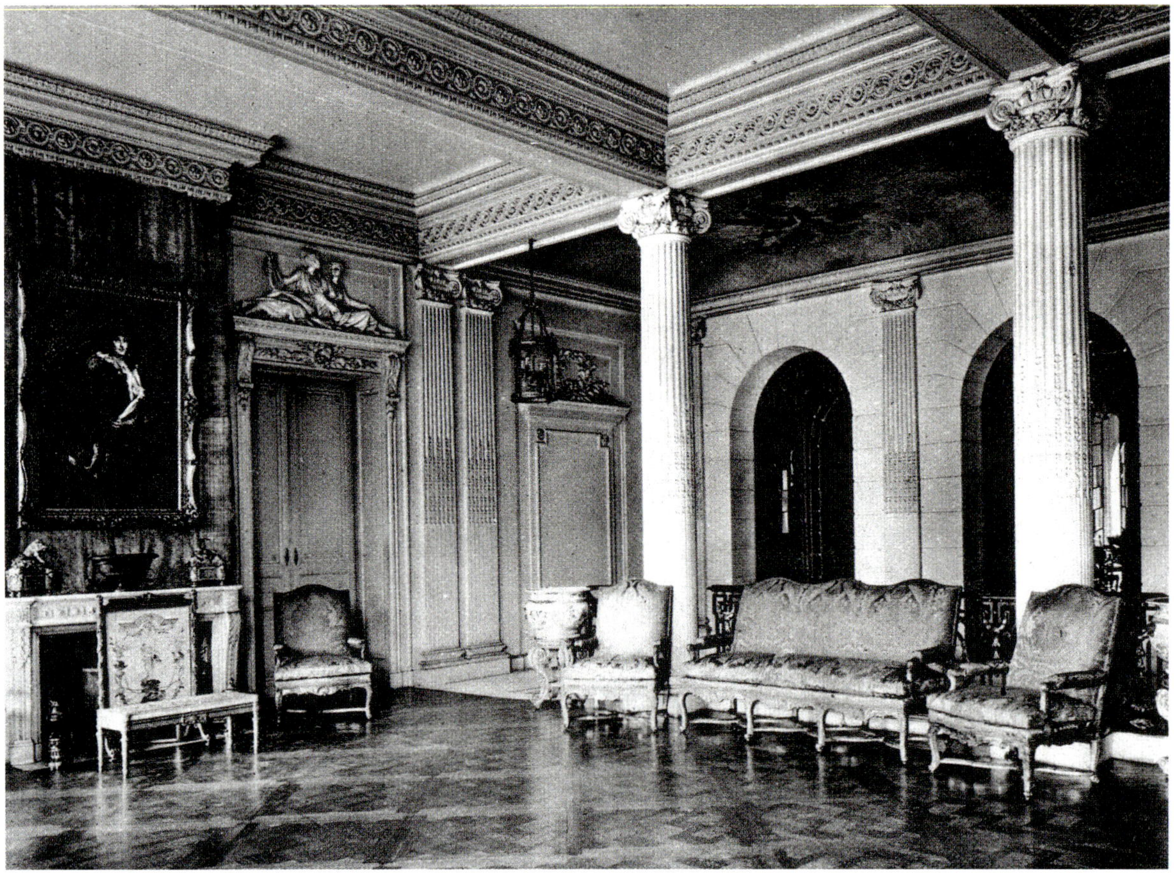

The upper landing at 25 Park Lane, with John Singer Sargent's portrait of Aline Sassoon at left, published in the *Illustrated London News*, September 23, 1922.

OPPOSITE
Ernest Howard Shepard, *The Drawing Room at Park Lane*, 1923, oil on canvas, 29 × 24½ in. (73.7 × 62.2 cm), private collection. The painting shows the room as redecorated by Philip Sassoon.

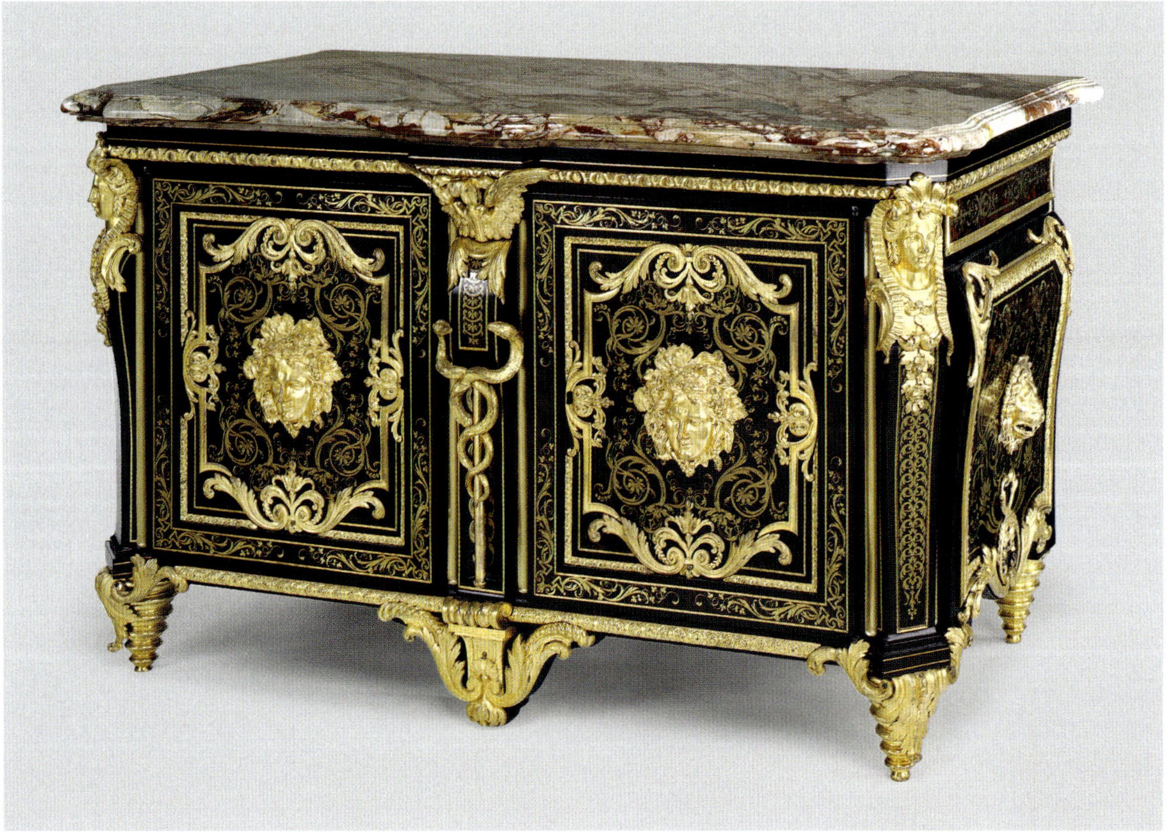

Attributed to André-Charles Boulle, cabinet, 1710–15, oak and fir veneered with ebony, amaranth, kingwood, brass, and tortoiseshell, with gilt-bronze mounts and a marble top, 32½ × 55¼ × 28½ in. (82.6 × 140.3 × 72.4 cm), Los Angeles, J. Paul Getty Museum, formerly in the Philip Sassoon Collection. The cabinet is seen in Ernest Howard Shepard's *The Drawing Room at Park Lane*, and was shown in the exhibition *Three French Reigns*, organized by Philip Sassoon and Hannah Gubbay in 1933.

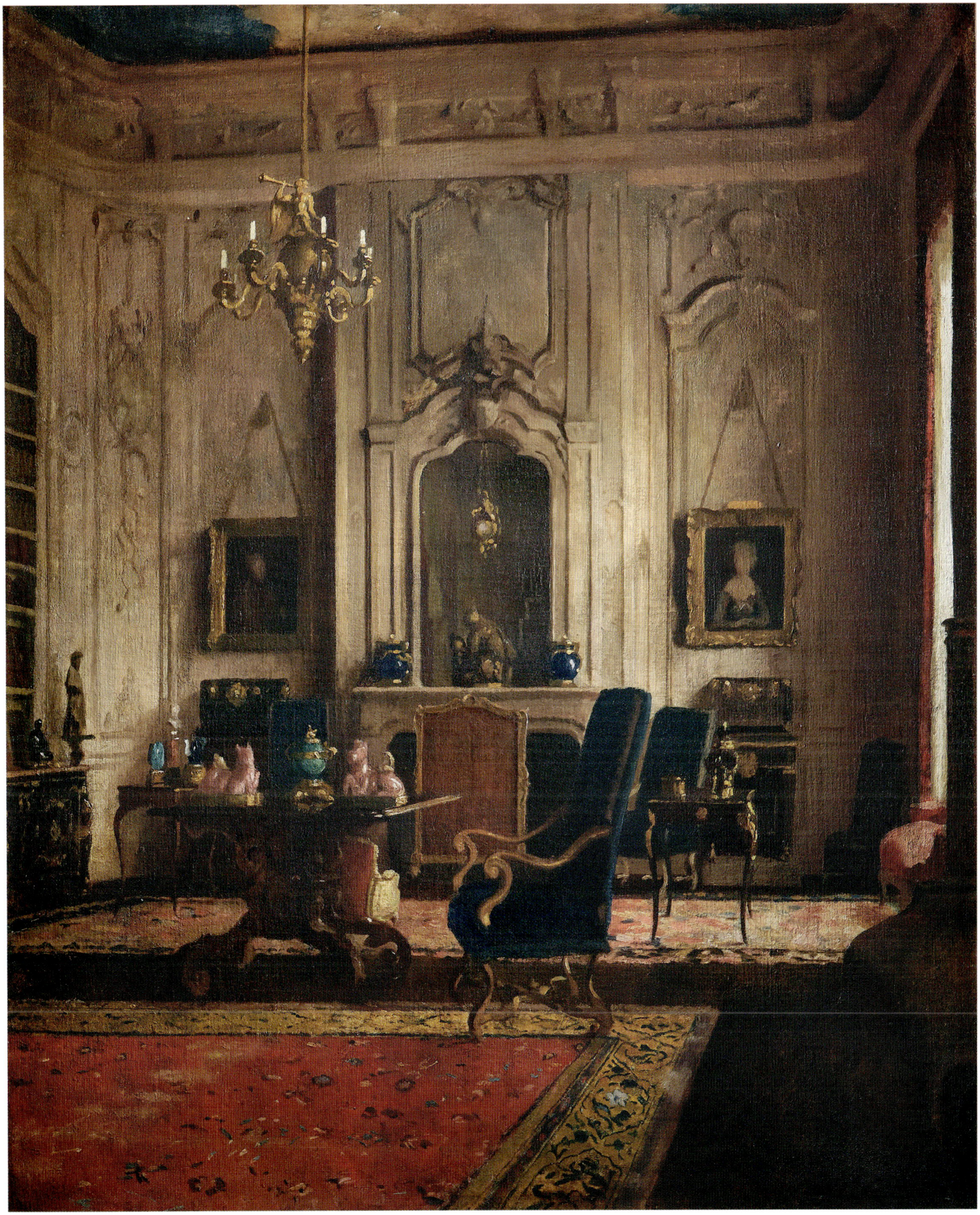

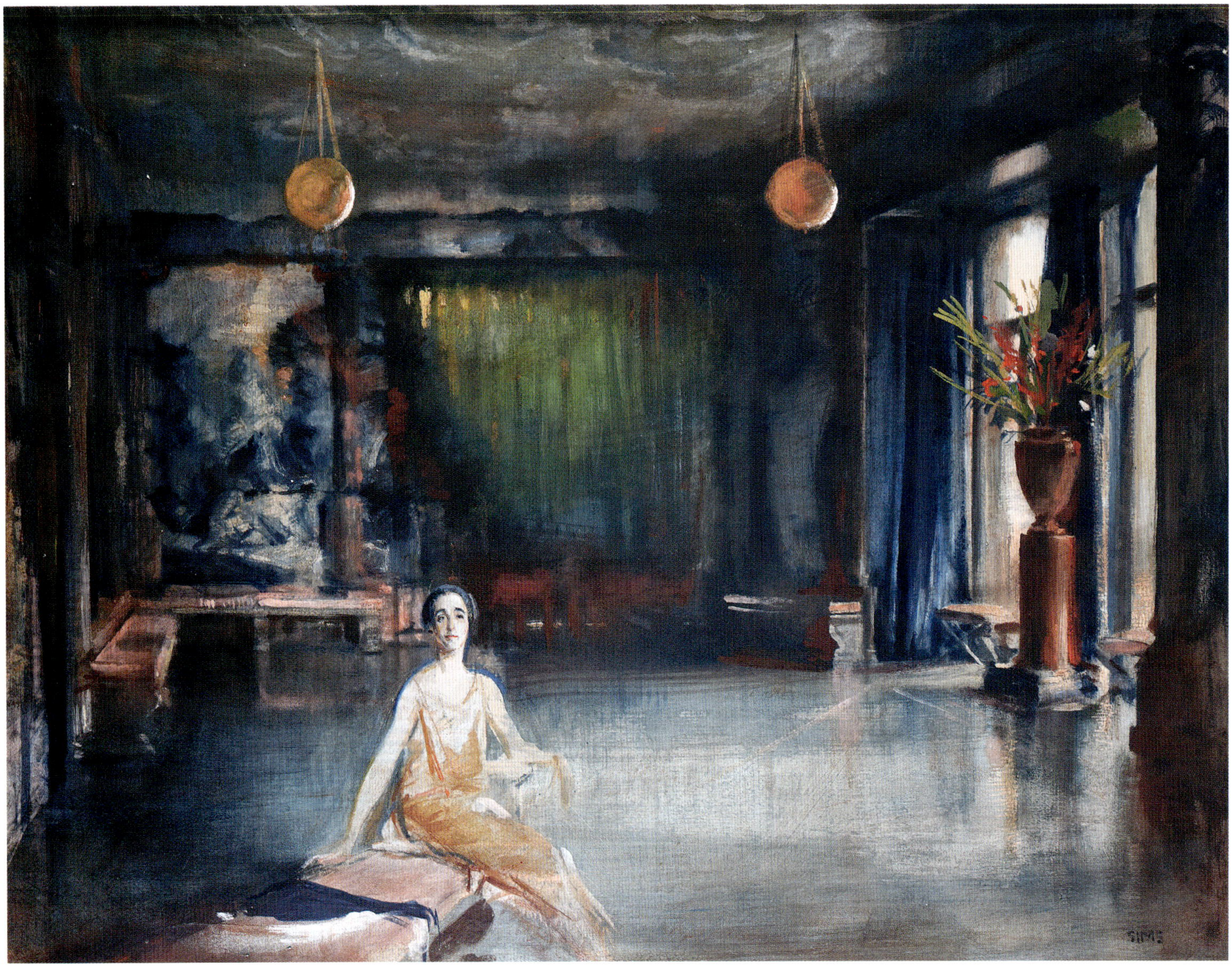

Charles Sims, *The Ballroom at 25 Park Lane with Sybil Sassoon,* c. 1923, oil on canvas, 20 × 26¾ in. (50.8 × 67.9 cm), private collection.

OPPOSITE
Josep Maria Sert, *Caravans of the East,* later renamed *Caravans from the Orient* (one wall of four), 1921, oil and silver leaf on wood, 55 ft. 9¼ in. × 21 ft. 4 in. (170 × 65 m), Barcelona, Museu Nacional d'Art de Catalunya, purchased 1980.

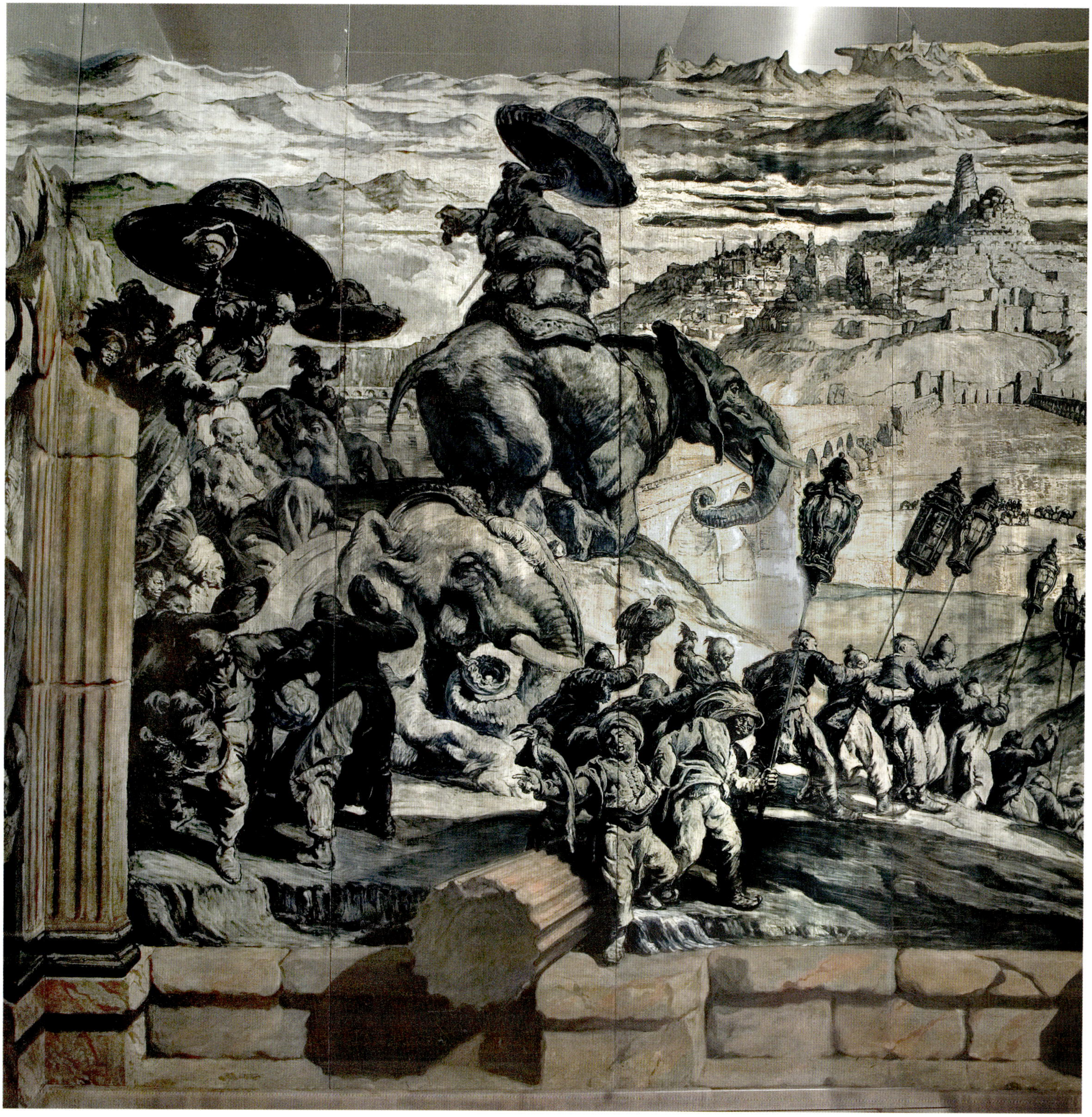

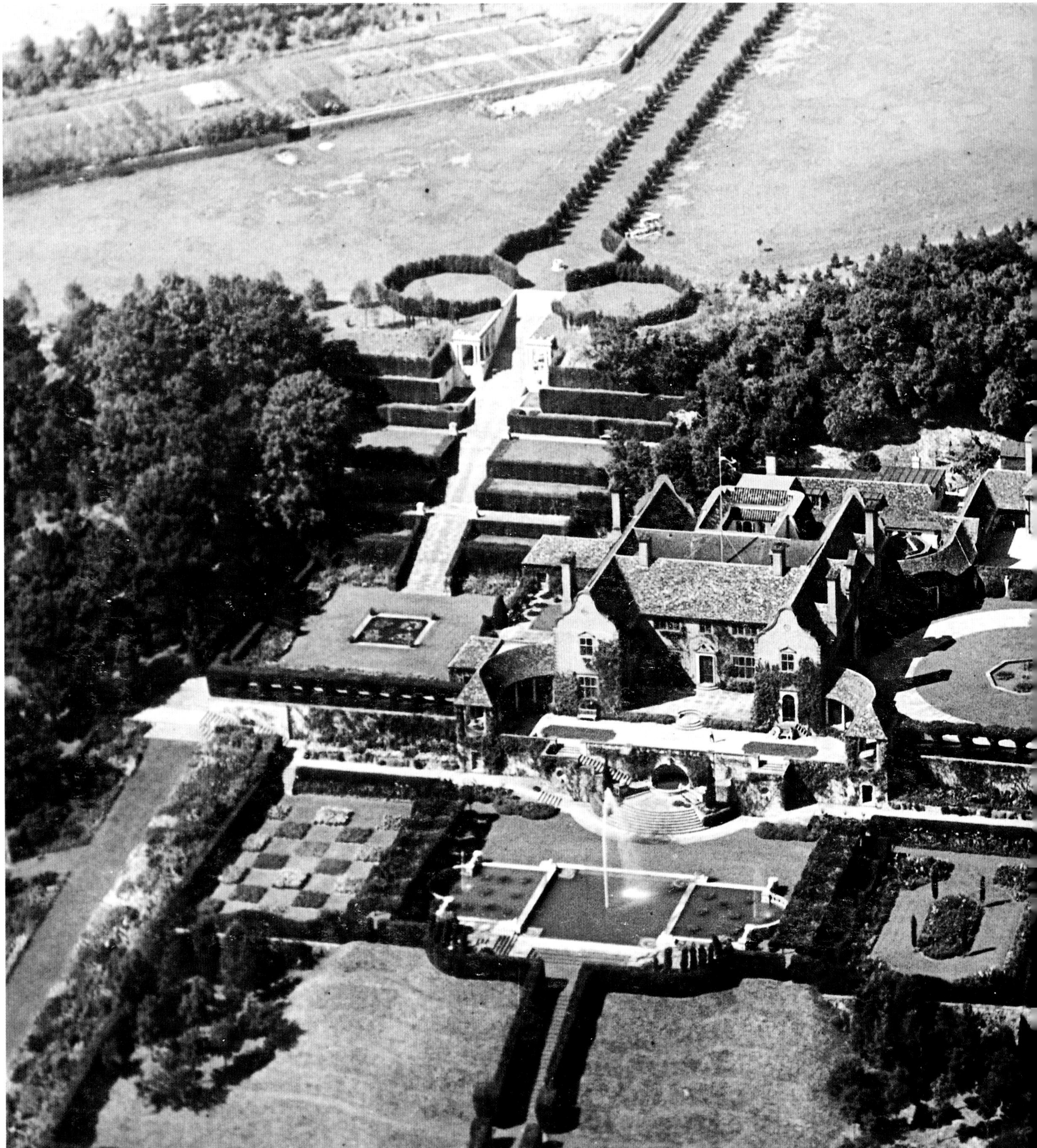

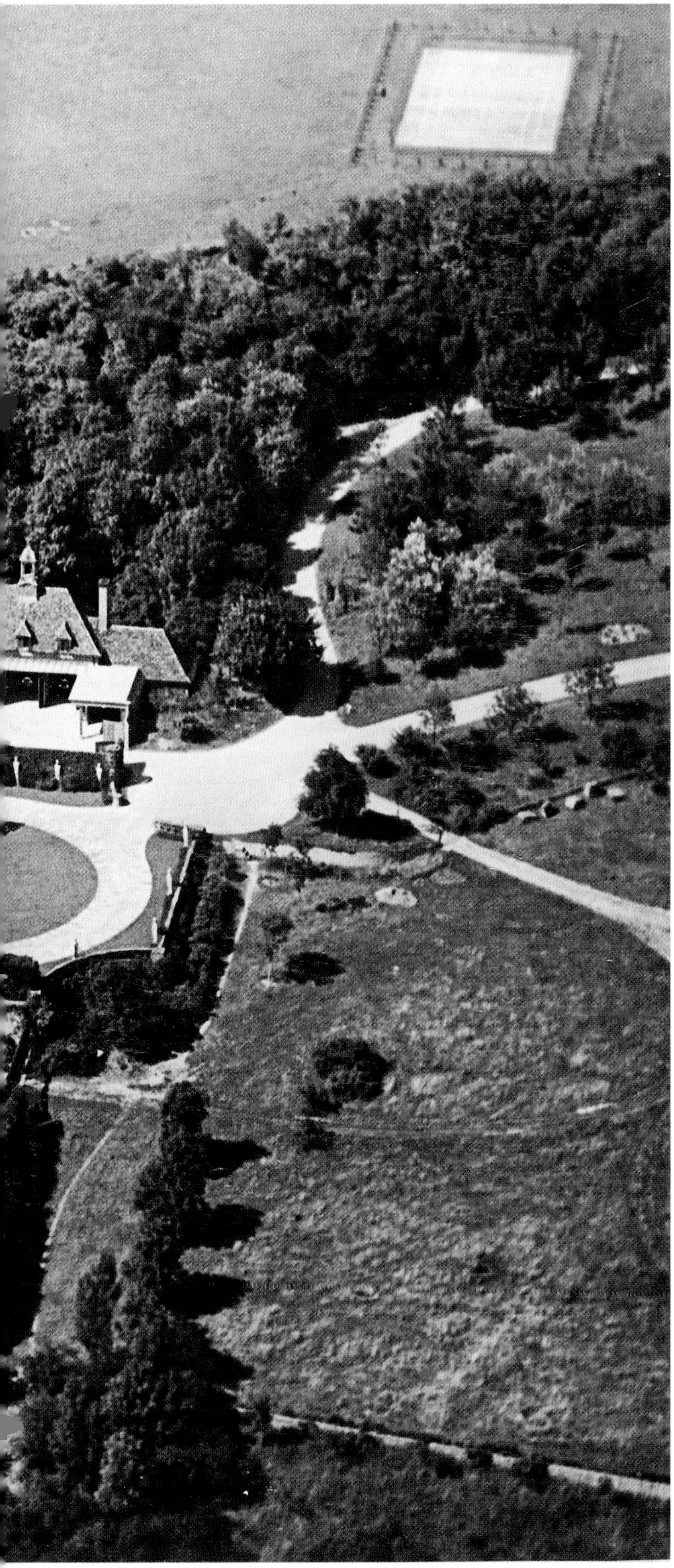

Port Lympne, the country home of Philip Sassoon, seen from the air, 1926, from the Port Lympne visitors' book, vol. I, 1919–28, private collection.

Port Lympne

After becoming a parliamentarian for Hythe in 1912, Philip bought 270 acres in Kent with a breathtaking view of Romney Marsh and, across the Channel, France, his mother's homeland. Once partly covered by sea, the area had been the site of a Roman port, Portus Lemanis, a historical trace that would resonate in the home Philip was about to build, Port Lympne. Herbert Baker, at the time a major figure in British architecture, was asked to design the house, initially called Belcaire, which was completed in 1914. Old bricks gave it a certain patina, but the exterior was modest, with its Cape Dutch gables reminiscent of Baker's work in colonial South Africa. Baker, already working with Lutyens in India, had little time to spare, and the house was finished by Ernest Willmott.[77]

Philip had grander plans. Immediately after the war, he asked Tilden to add several features: a "Moorish" courtyard, a bathing pool, and monumental exterior steps. The contrast between Baker's unimaginative exterior and Philip's whimsical interiors—an exciting amalgam of non sequiturs—is refreshing. Far from London, Philip could give free rein to a fantasy that Park Lane would not have led one to expect. "Here at Lympne," wrote Tilden, "all was to be new and forceful, pulsing with the vitality of new blood. Only in its empirical splendour was there to be reminiscence of the Roman Legions, the four-hundred-year occupation of Britain, the link with Rome itself, and thence back to Greece through the ages."[78]

On the ground floor, the rooms were like so many microcosms, independent of one another. Baker's small library remained untouched, with silvered Wren-period woodwork flecked with gold and books in red Morocco bindings. Tilden created a second library, a small octagon of unpolished sycamore and limewood, covered with a dome lit by windows. Another addition was a delightful courtyard inspired by Muslim architecture in Spain. Two superimposed arcades of slender marble

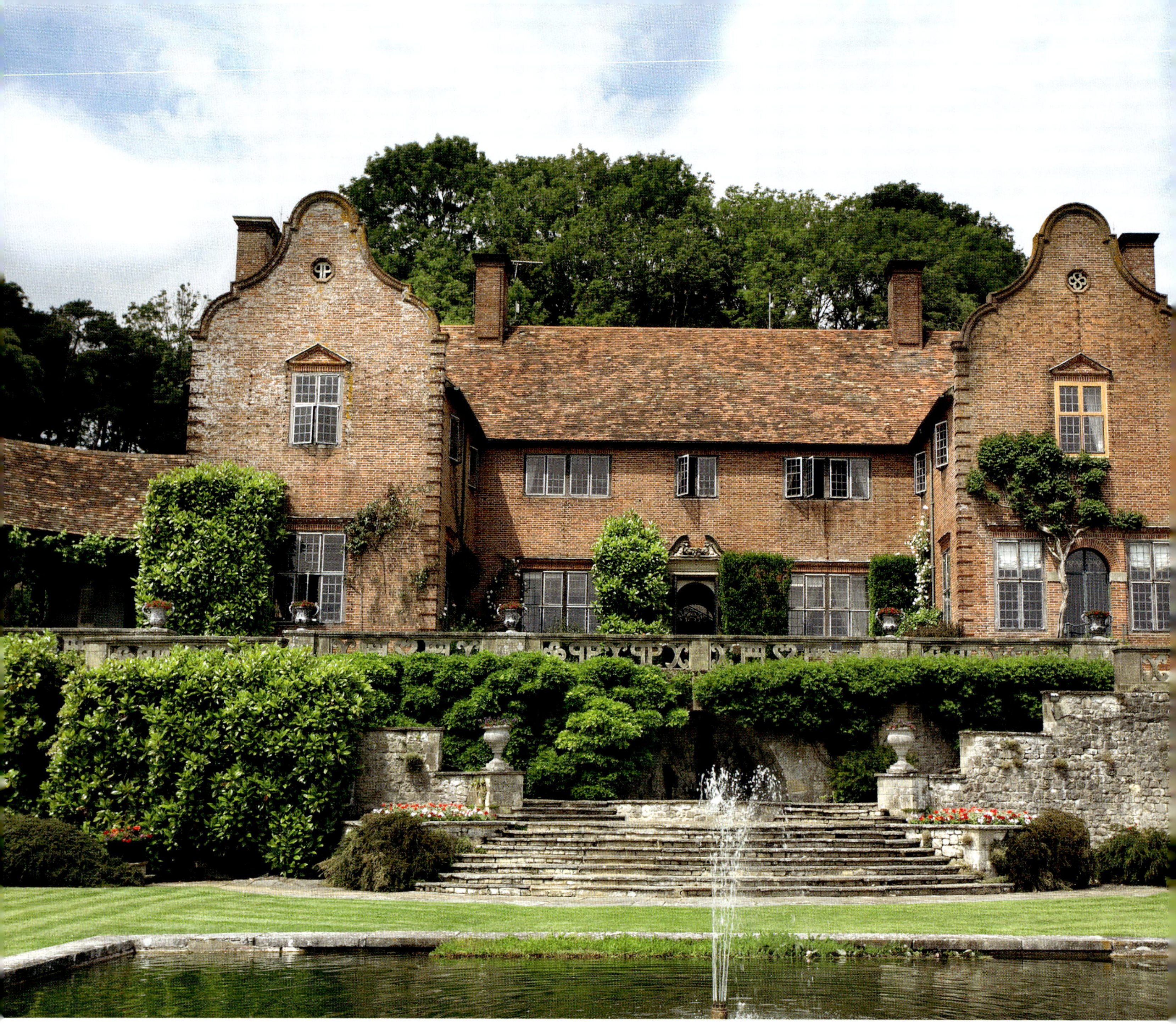

Port Lympne, Kent, 1914, Herbert Baker, architect. Designed by Herbert Baker, Port Lympne was completed by Ernest Willmott; Philip Tilden made significant changes in the early 1920s.

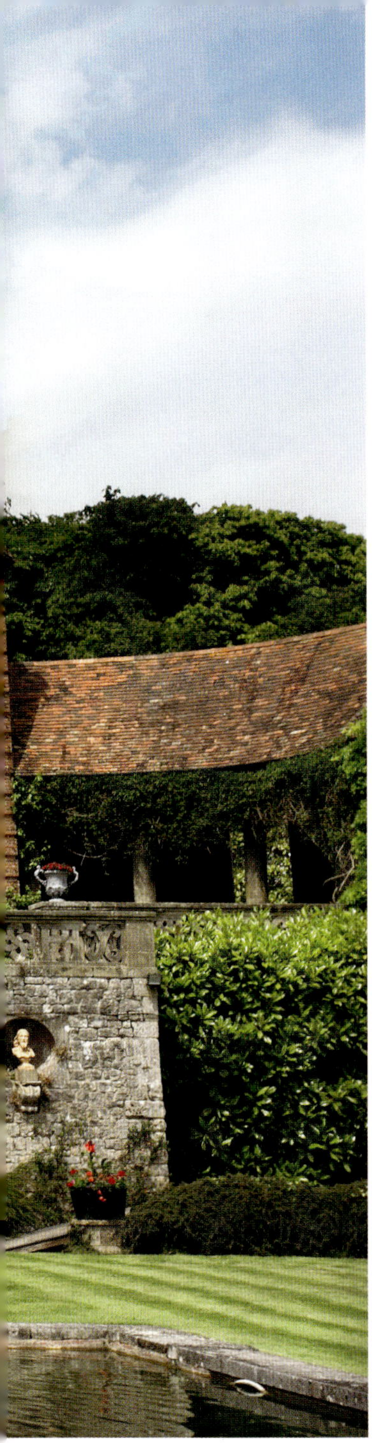

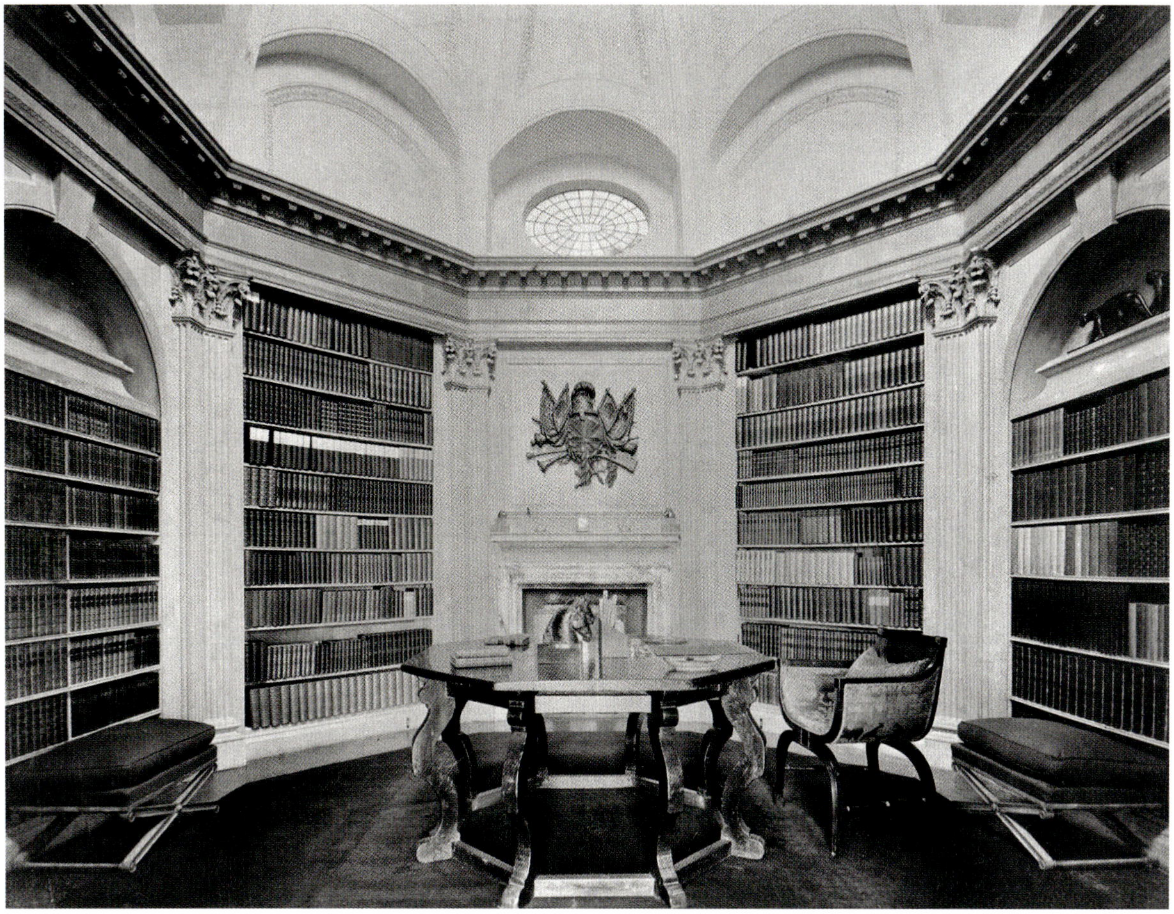

ABOVE
The octagonal library at Port Lympne, designed by Philip Tilden, 1923, published in *Country Life*, May 26, 1923.

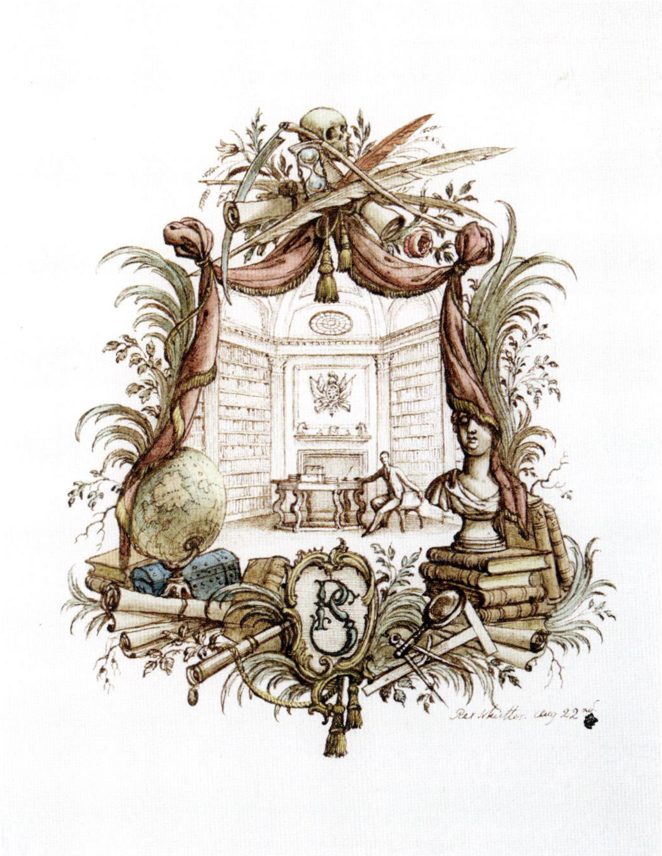

Rex Whistler, vignette of the octagonal library, Port Lympne, 1930, from the Port Lympne visitors' book, vol. II, 1929–38, ink and watercolor on paper, 12 × 9¼ in. (30.5 × 23.5 cm), private collection.

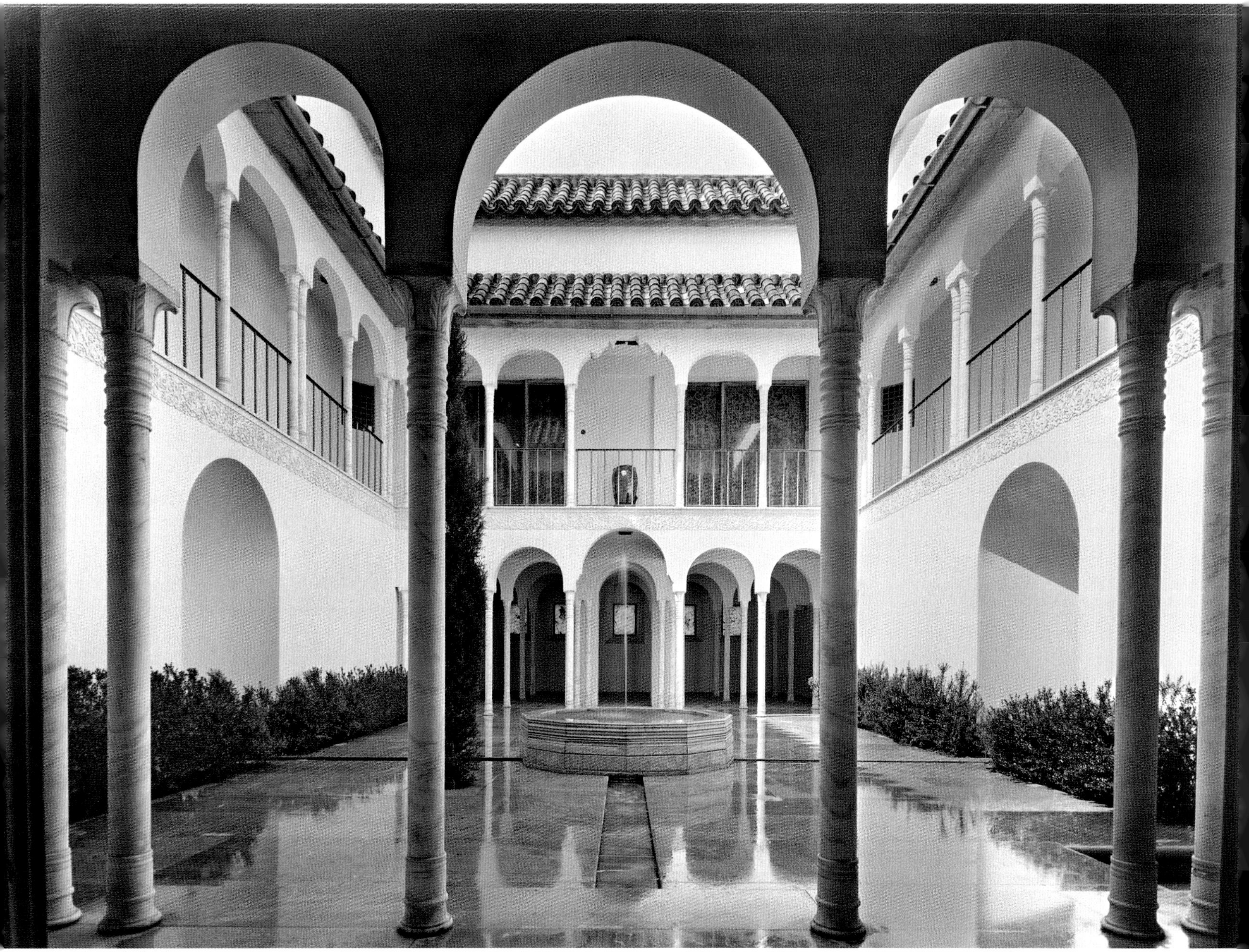

The "Moorish" courtyard, Port Lympne, designed by Philip Tilden, 1923, published in *Country Life,* May 26, 1923.

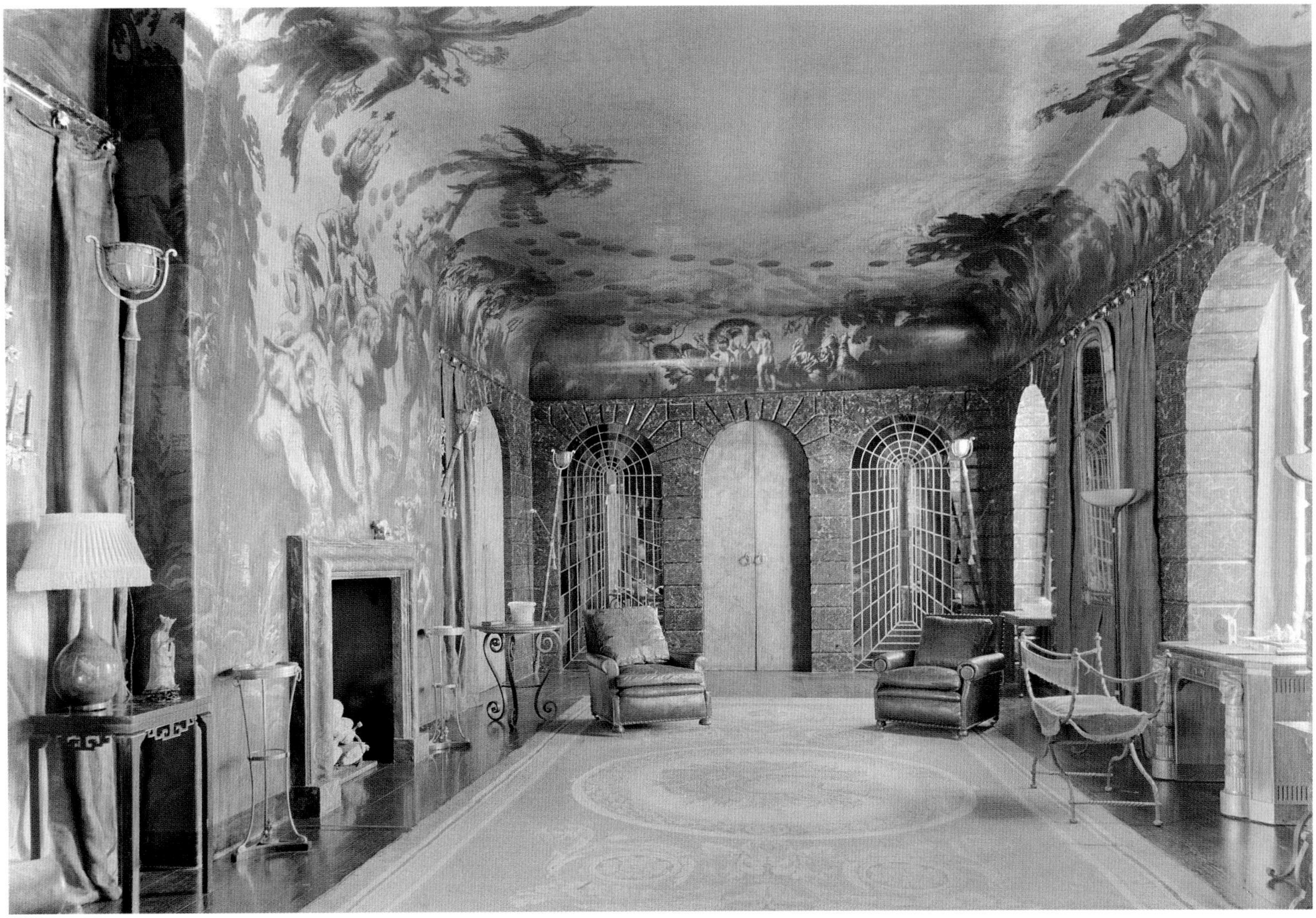

Murals by Josep Maria Sert in the drawing room at Port Lympne, painted in 1914–15, later destroyed by Philip Sassoon, published in *Country Life*, May 26, 1923.

columns marked the main axis on either end. Bright green tiles, onyx-glazed windows, thin channels of water crossing at a central fountain, and myrtle hedges: "Spain in Kent."[79]

For the drawing-room murals, Philip chose Sert, then at the height of his fame. A member of Paris high society, Sert had worked for prominent personalities, including Philip's grandfather Baron Gustave de Rothschild, at his Château de Laversine. Port Lympne displayed the delirious Orientalism that would later encompass the ballroom at Park Lane. France, personified by a naked woman, and the Allies, represented by children, were being attacked by two German eagles, while two enormous elephants representing India came to their rescue, an interesting reference to a family past usually ignored by Philip. Painted in 1914–15, the allegory was timely, if oppressive. Rising seamlessly past the walls into the coved ceiling, the brownish monochromatic paintings on a gold background overpowered the space. Following Sargent's advice, Tilden painted the end walls moss brown veined with gold, interrupted by windows in trompe l'oeil.[80]

In May 1920, British Prime Minister David Lloyd George decided to hold a conference at Port Lympne with French Prime Minister Alexandre Millerand to decide on German war reparations, the first of several.[81] It was a major coup for Philip, who had just become Lloyd George's private secretary. Millerand and his staff were delighted at the comforts of Lympne and the attentions of a Parisian-born host with superb French chefs. Sert's décor, like that of Tiepolo, teetered dangerously between beauty and the grotesque, hovering uneasily over the French and British delegations as

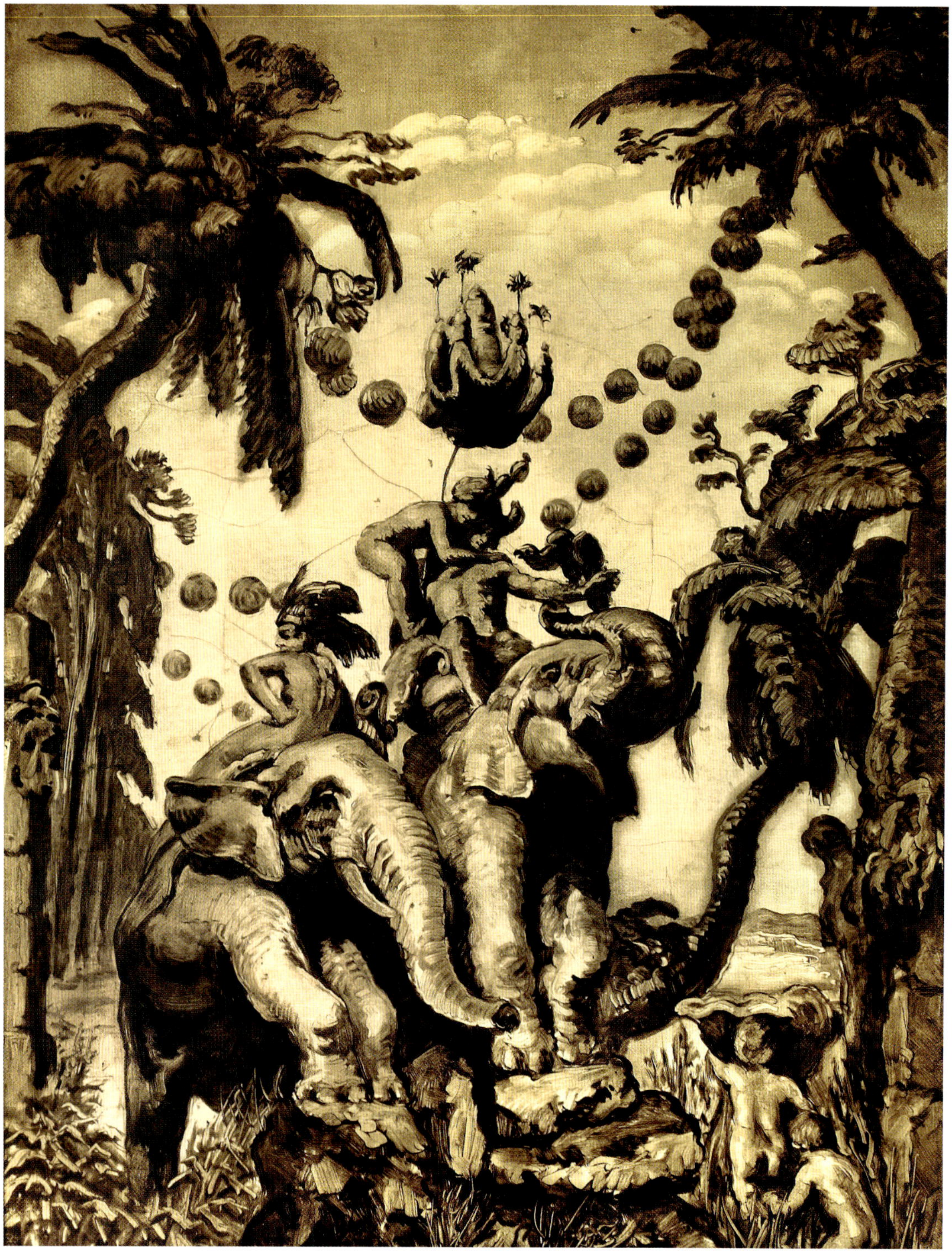

Josep Maria Sert, sketch for *The Indies Coming to the Rescue of the Allies,* 1914–15, oil on gold ground on plywood panel, 27½ × 21⅝ in. (70 × 55 cm), courtesy of Emeric Hahn Gallery.

they negotiated. Philip found the paintings monstruous and had them whitewashed and replaced by Sargent's watercolors. Only a vigorous oil sketch survives.

Philip had not given up on painted walls. Asked to do the dining room, Philpot produced an "Egyptian" frieze below the ceiling. Pressed close to the picture plane like an Assyrian bas relief, it also recalls Minoan and Egyptian art, as well as Greek vase painting. With their parallel gestures and chiastic poses, the stylized, hieratic figures resemble those of the Russian impresario Sergei Diaghilev's ballet *Afternoon of a Faun* (1912), choreographed by Vaslav Nijinsky, whom both Philip and Philpot admired. The Black figures, originally naked, eroticized, and almost always shown at work, appear to be enslaved: "a frieze of negroes," wrote Kenneth Clark. As Philpot left the murals dangling above white walls, Tilden painted them lapis lazuli: "an undulating blue, never quite green;

Josep Maria Sert, *The Indies Coming to the Rescue of the Allies,* mural, published in *Country Life*, May 26, 1923.

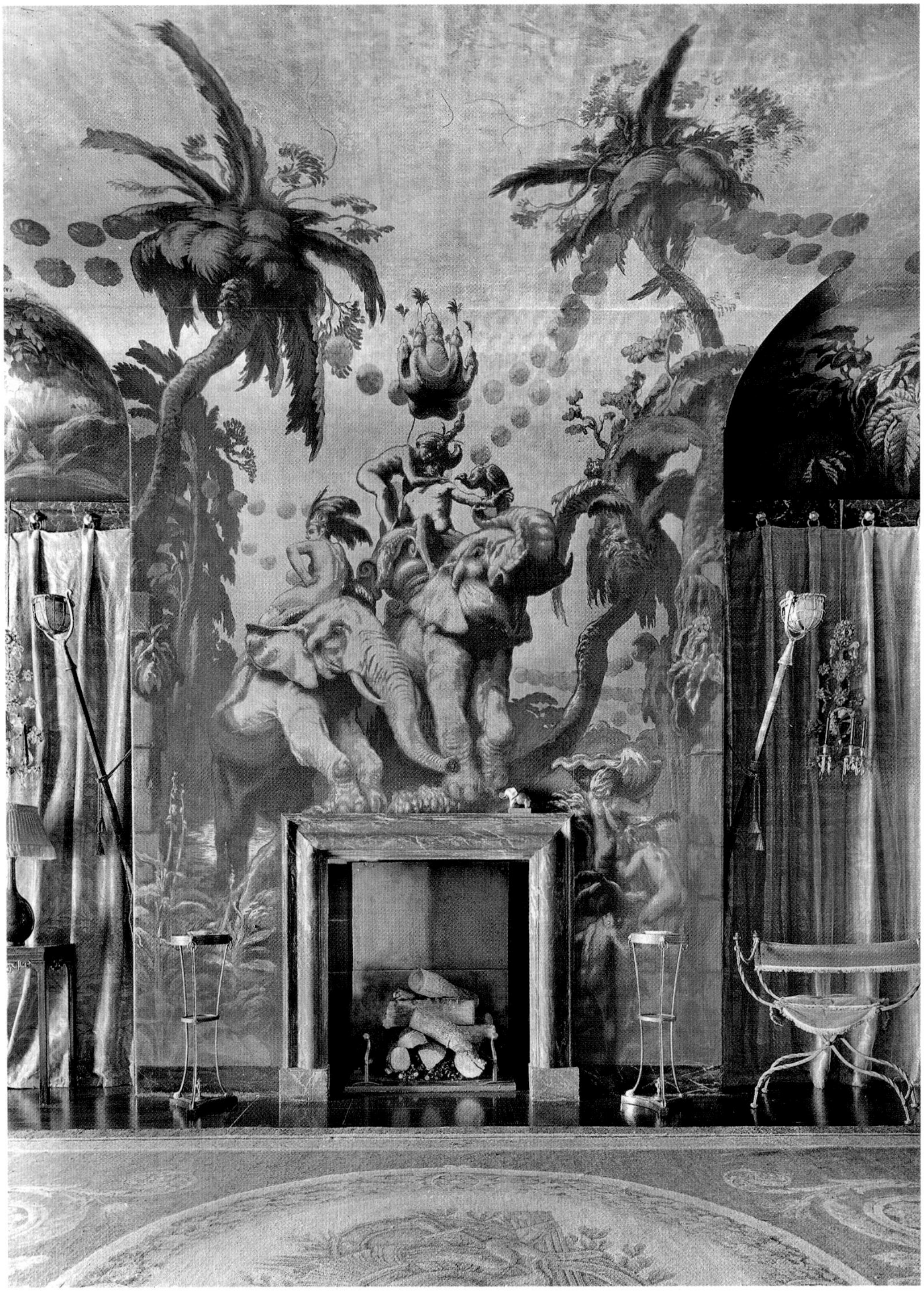

a living wall of moving color." An opalescent pink ceiling, and gilt winged chairs with jade cushions, heightened the room's bold color contrasts, reminiscent of the Ballets Russes and probably chosen by Philip himself.[82] The Regency console was designed by Tilden; the chairs, evocative of Russian neoclassicism, possibly by Baker.

In the celebrated tent room (1930–32), Rex Whistler created a charming Georgian capriccio. Philip's book *The Third Route* (1929), relating his journey by air to India through Egypt, Sudan, and Iraq, had a map illustrated by Whistler. And as a trustee of the Tate, Philip knew Whistler's murals for the institution that now shock for their depiction of enslaved Black children and caricatures of Chinese figures.[83] Unlike the dining room with its daring color contrasts, here everything is serene, bathed in soft golden light. As a mural painter, Whistler was a keen student of architecture. One can recognize St. Martin-in-the-Fields,

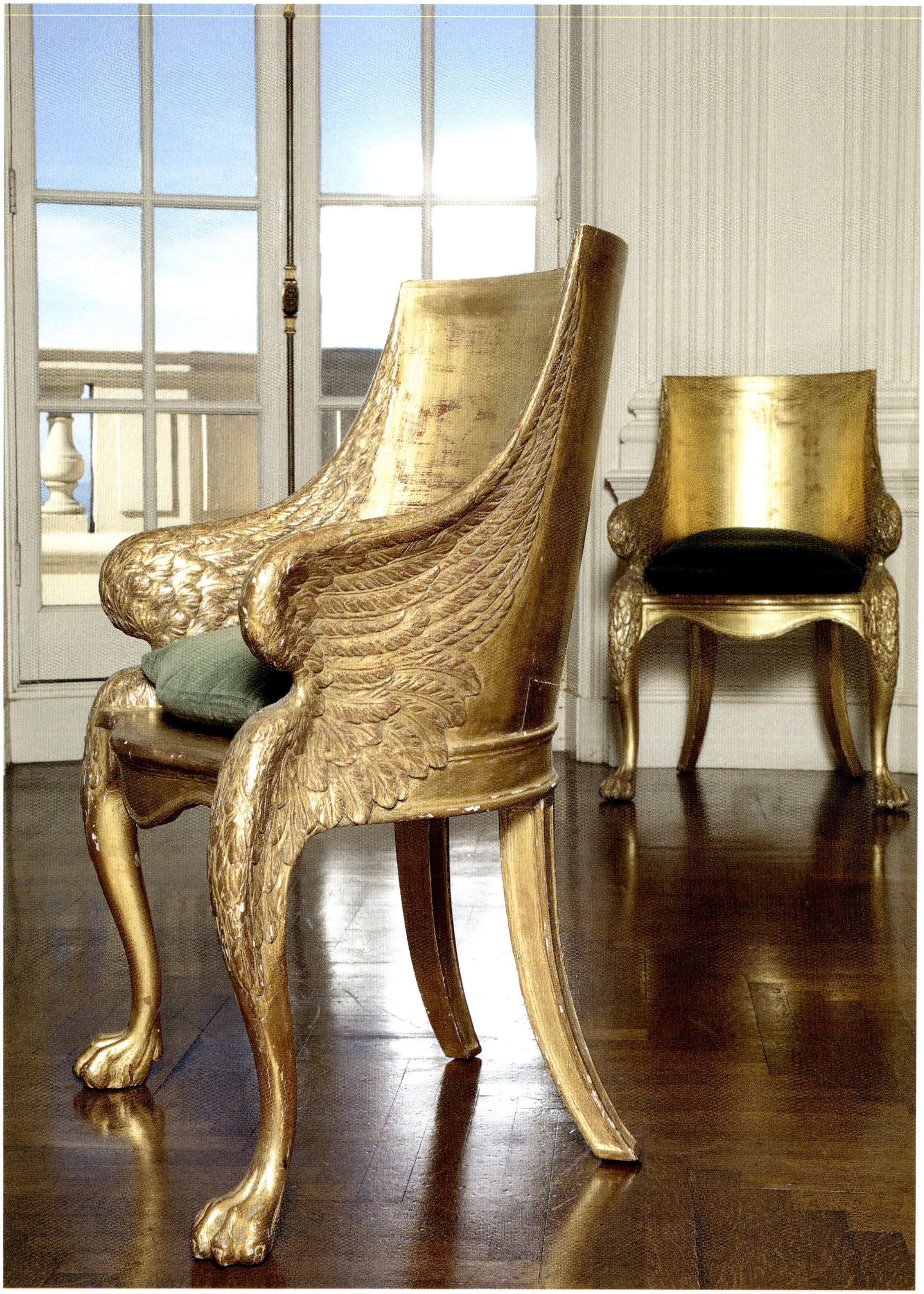

A Russian neoclassical armchair for the dining room at Port Lympne, c. 1910, carved and gilt wood, 36 in. high (91.4 cm), probably after a design by architect Herbert Baker.

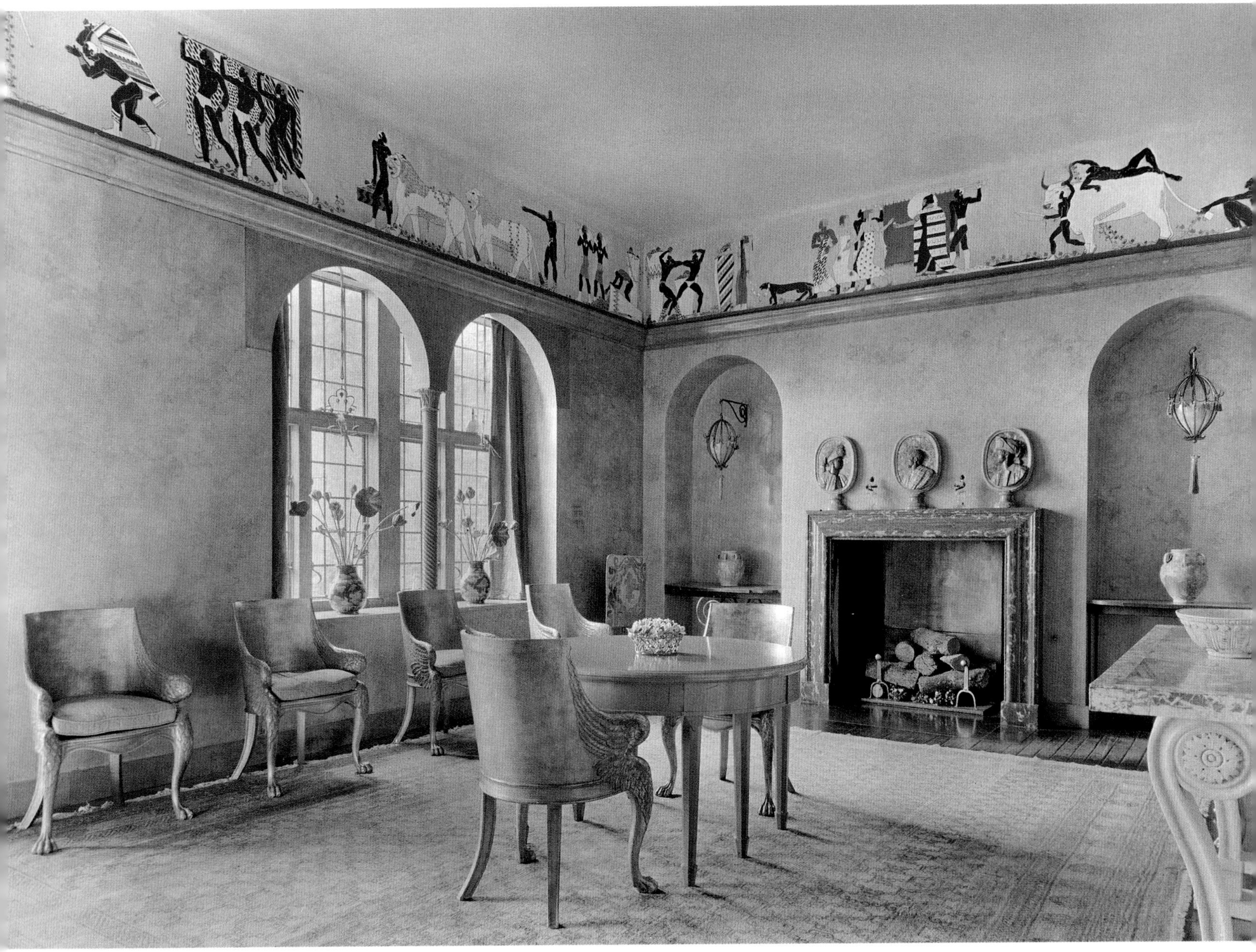

The dining room at Port Lympne with a frieze by Glyn Warren Philpot, c. 1920, published in *Country Life*, May 26, 1923. While Black men were portrayed with sympathy and dignity in Philpot's paintings, this frieze clearly shows racialized bodies.

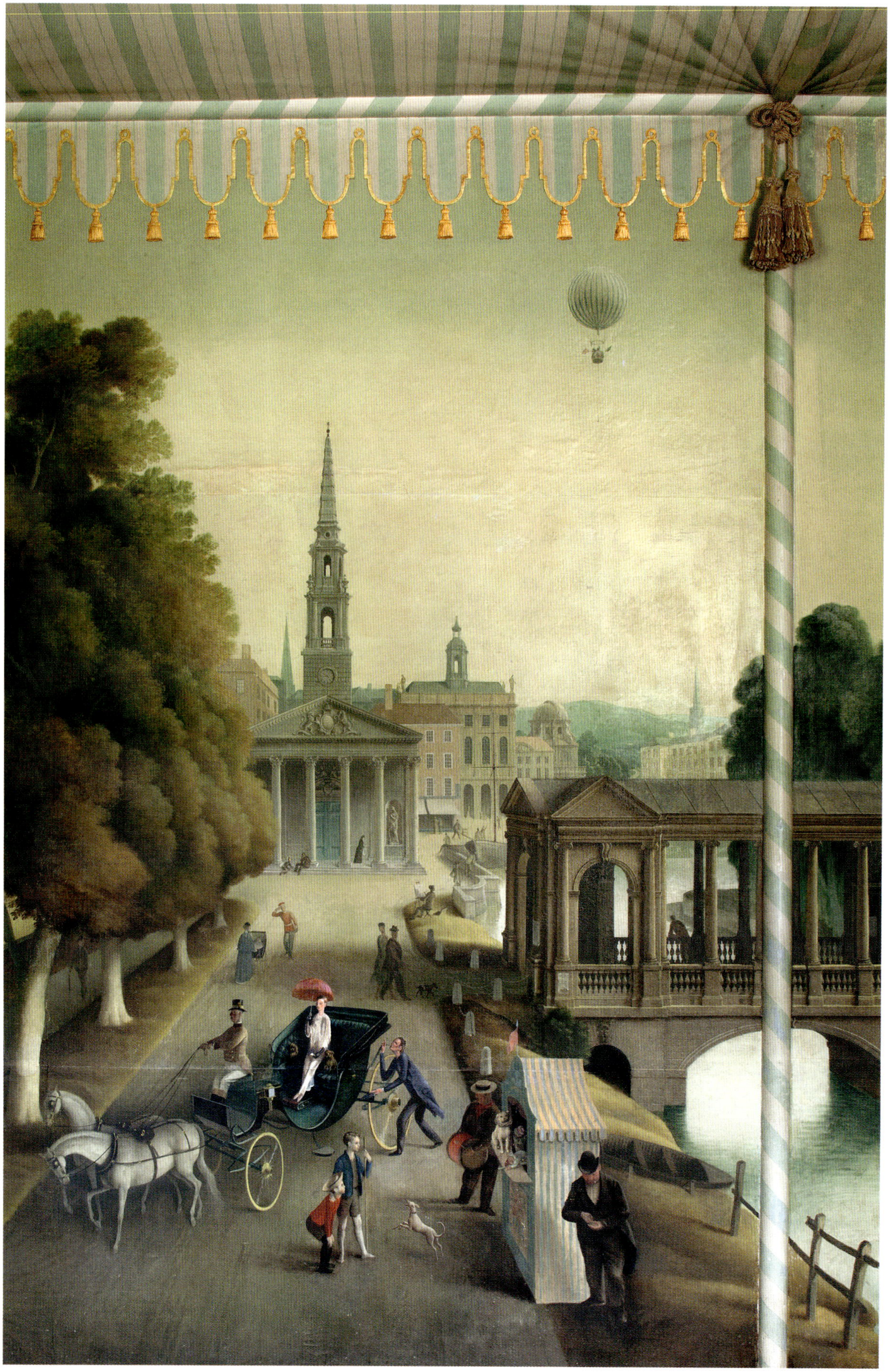

Detail of Rex Whistler's tent room, showing the church of St. Martin-in-the-Fields and the Palladian bridge at Wilton.

OPPOSITE
The tent room at Port Lympne, designed in 1930–32 by Rex Whistler, published in *Country Life*, February 4, 1933.

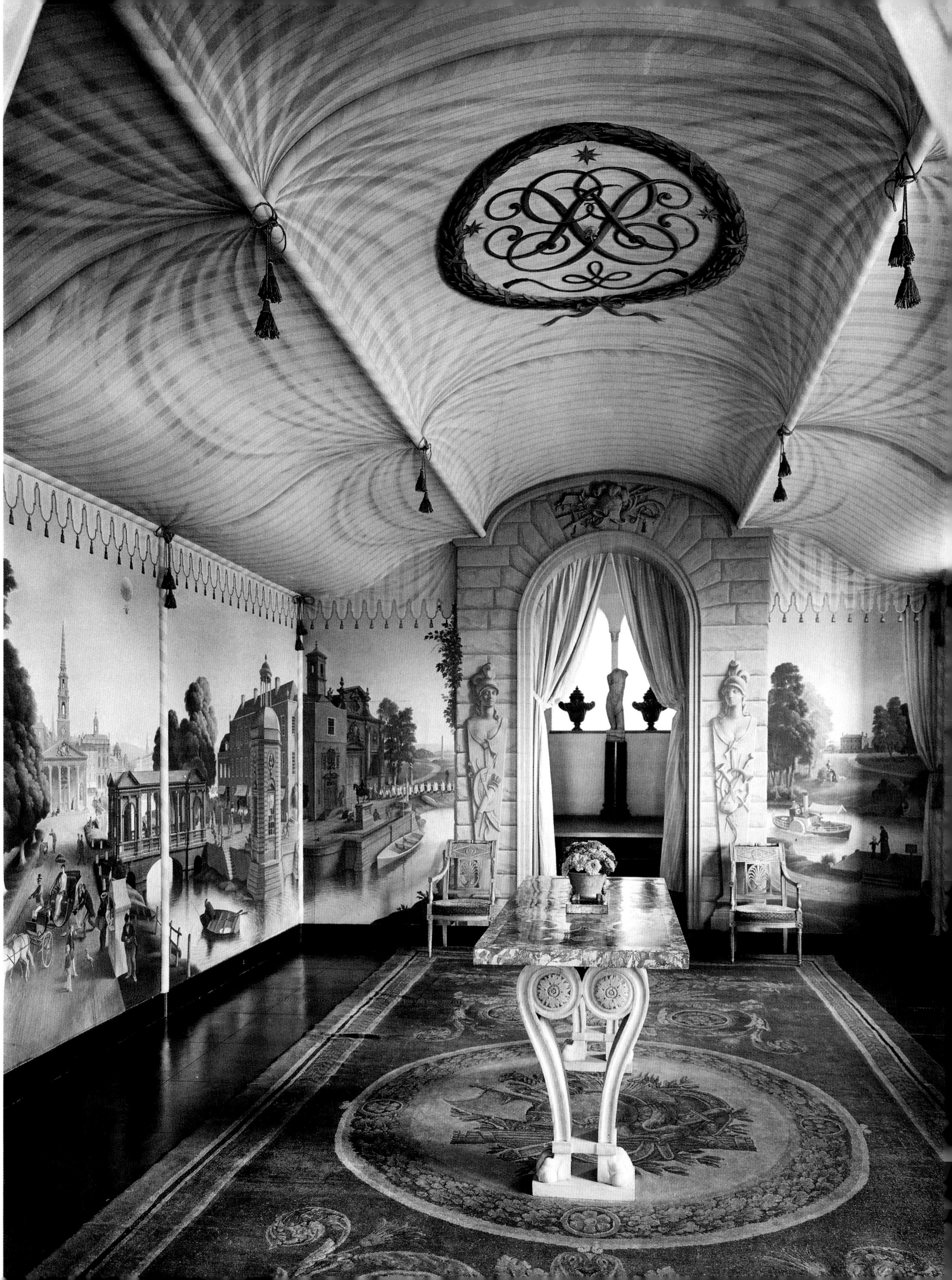

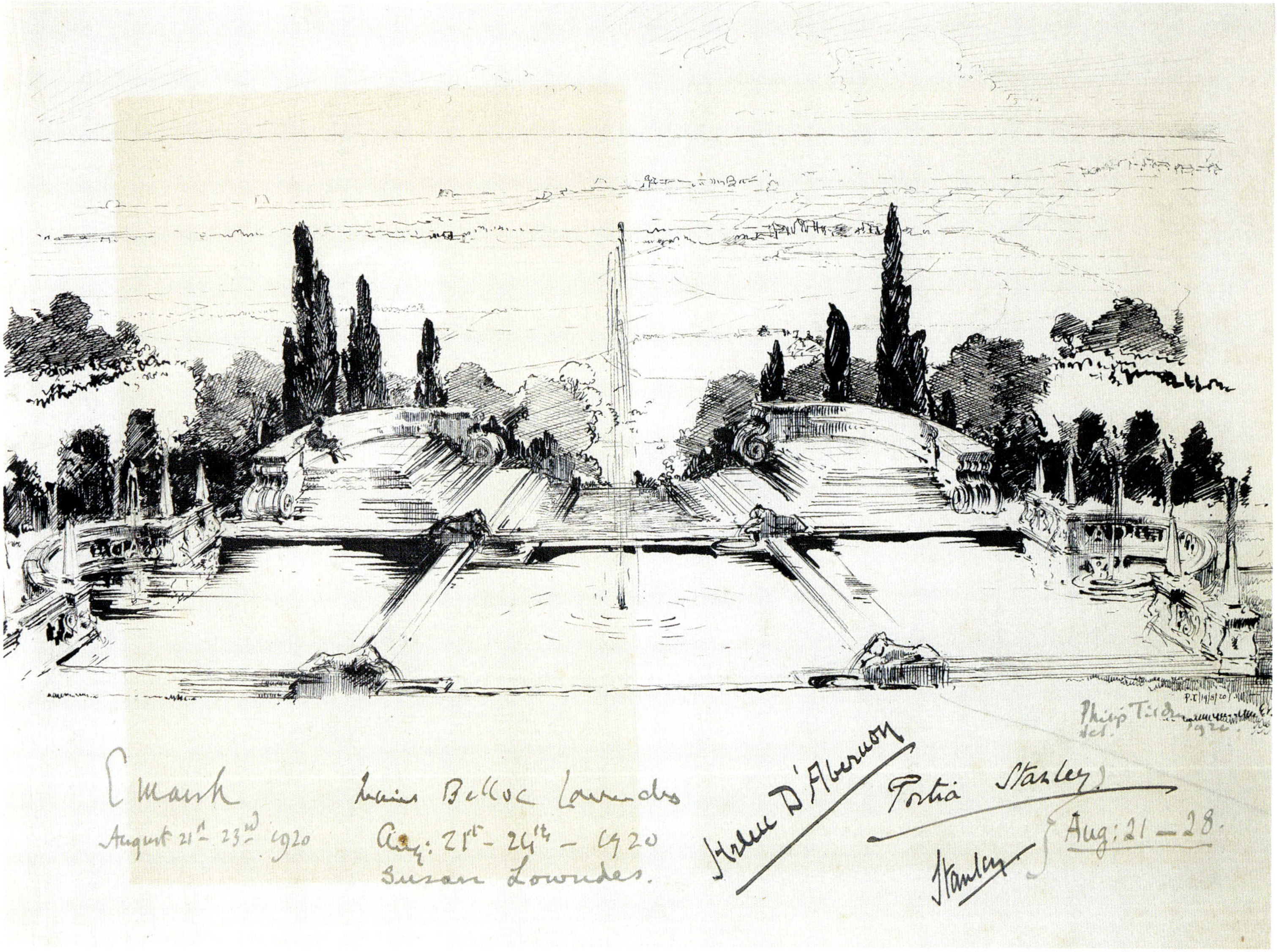

the Palladian bridge at Wilton, Lord Berners's Faringdon House, and even Whistler's poster for Philip's exhibition *The Age of Walnut*.[84] To heighten the trompe l'oeil, real tentpoles and tassels are juxtaposed with the painted cloth tent.

On the western side of the house, Tilden's superb staircase, culminating in two small *tempietti*, alluded to the Roman history of Portus Lemanis. Contemporary critics understood that Tilden's steps succeeded in evoking the genius loci.[85] Regrettably, Baker returned from India and, horrified with the additions to his house, was so scathing in his criticism that Philip destroyed the temples.[86] Tilden was no more successful with his beautiful bathing pool: a square fountain flanked by two slightly raised pools terminating in exedras and quadrant-shaped terraces. Perched precariously above Romney Marsh, it was "the grandest of English water parterres."[87] Here Tilden evoked a different Rome from that of his monumental steps. The quadrants, echoing the curves of the semicircular pools, have something of the preciosity of Hadrian's Villa in Rome. Unfortunately, only the square fountain in the center remains. The rest was too heavy for the site and had to be destroyed due to subsidence.

Sketch of fountains at Port Lympne, 1920, designed by Philip Tilden, from the Port Lympne visitors' book, vol. I, 1919–28, ink on paper, 12 × 9¼ in. (30.5 × 23.5 cm), private collection.

Sketch for Port Lympne's Roman steps, designed by Philip Tilden, from the Port Lympne visitors' book, vol. I, 1919–28, ink on paper, 9¼ × 12 in. (23.5 × 30.5 cm), private collection.

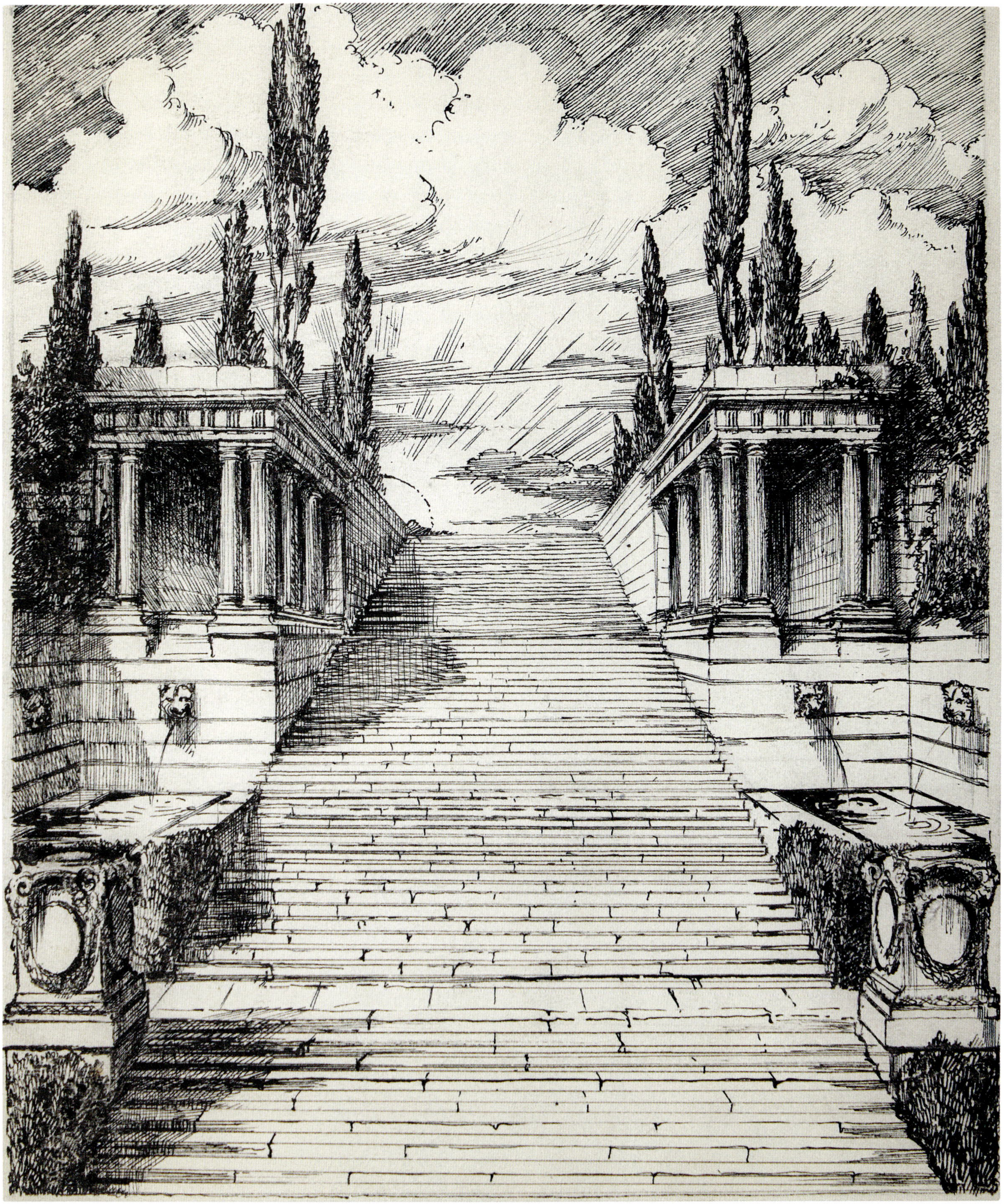

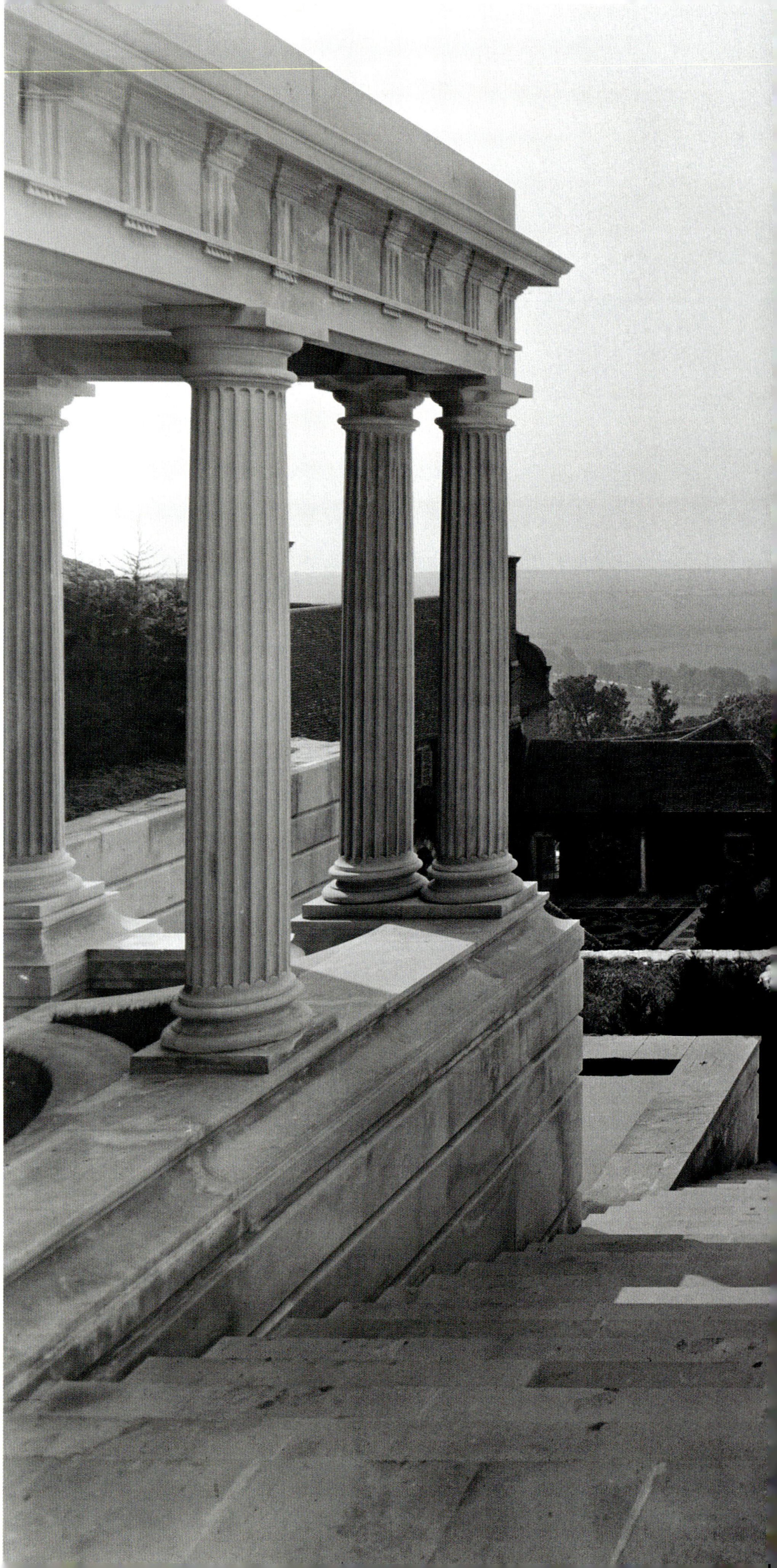

The Roman steps with *tempietti* at Port Lympne, 1921, published in *Country Life,* May 19, 1923.

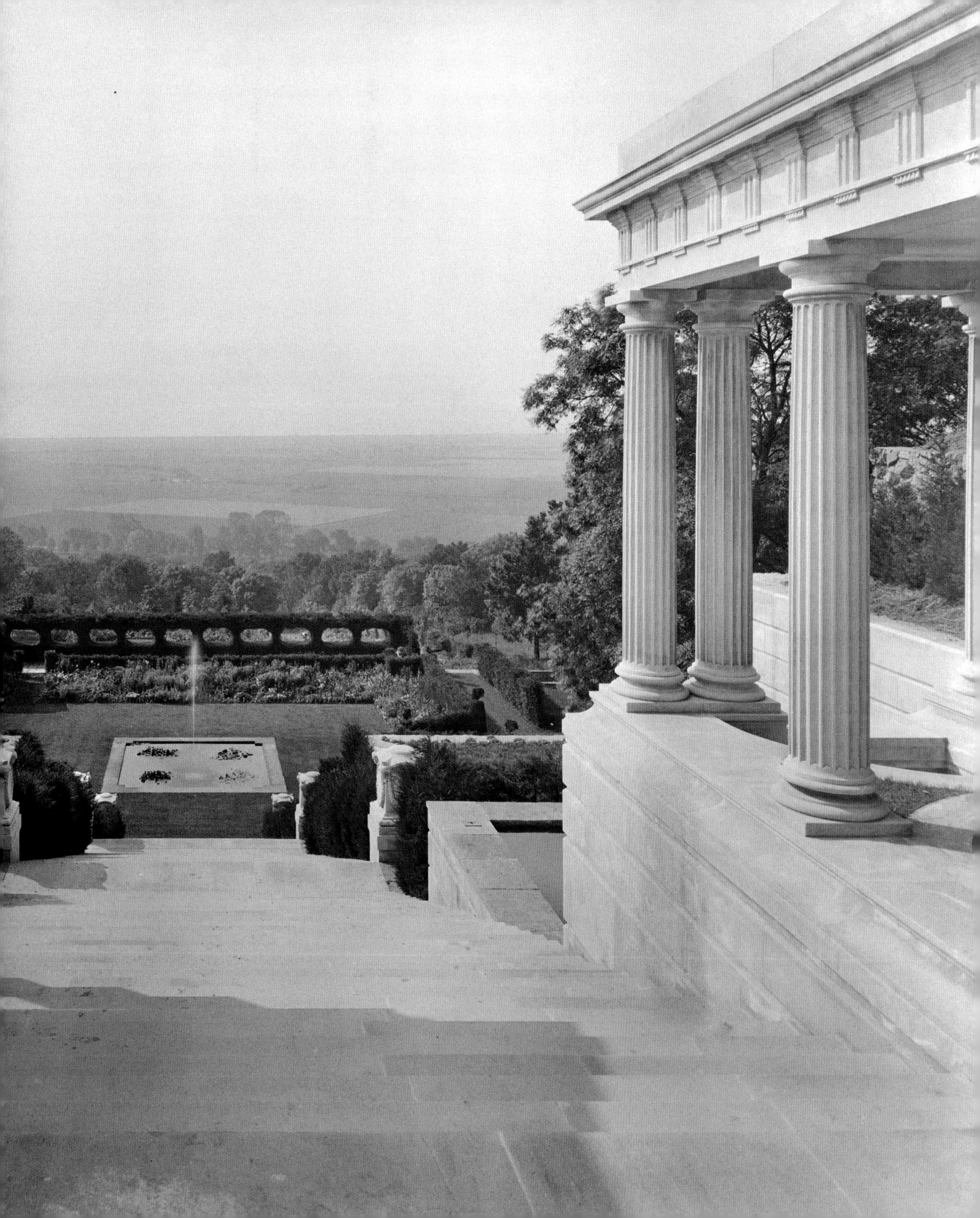

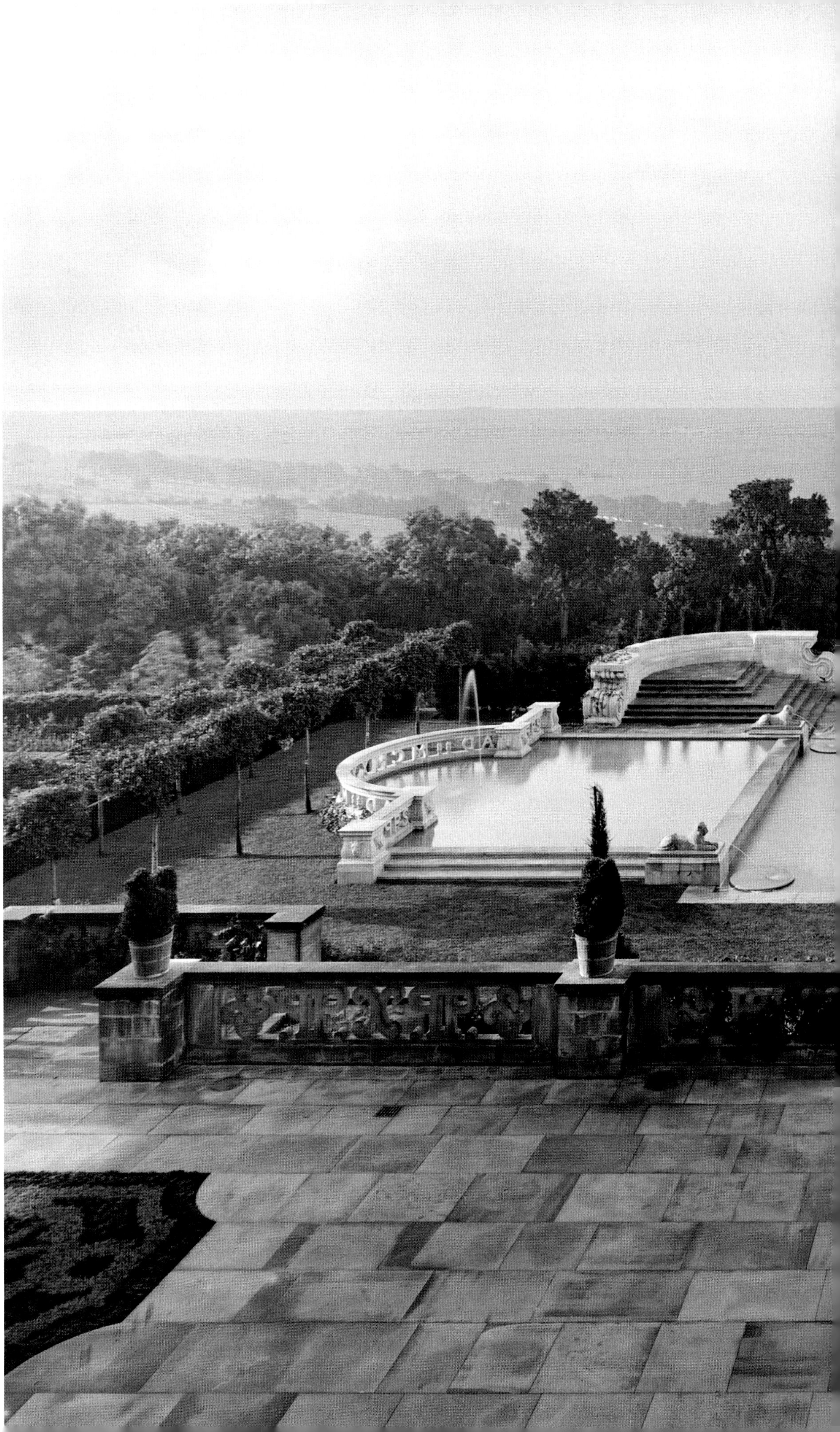

The bathing pool and fountain at Port Lympne, designed by Philip Tilden, c. 1921, published in *Country Life,* May 19, 1923.

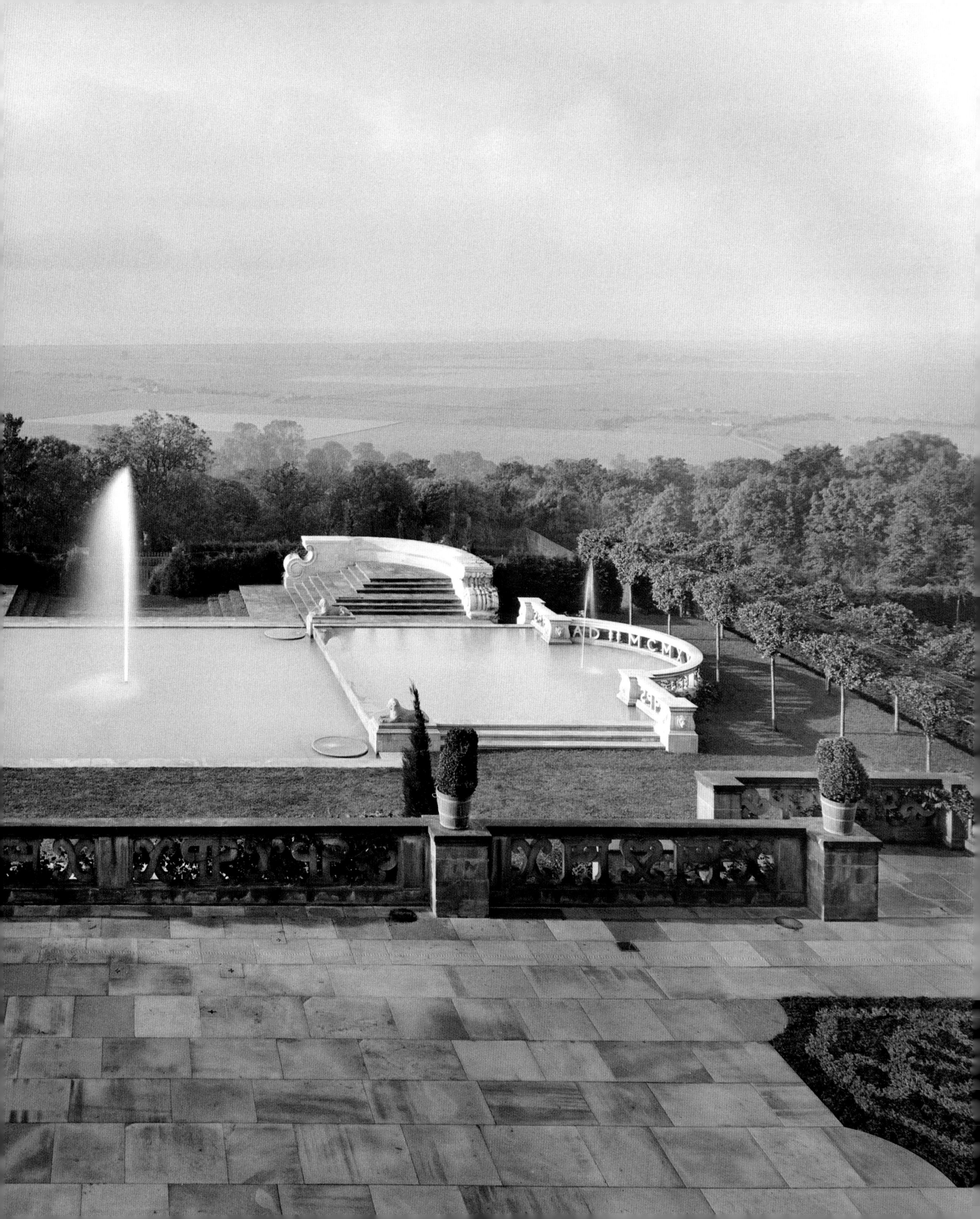
A D I M C M X

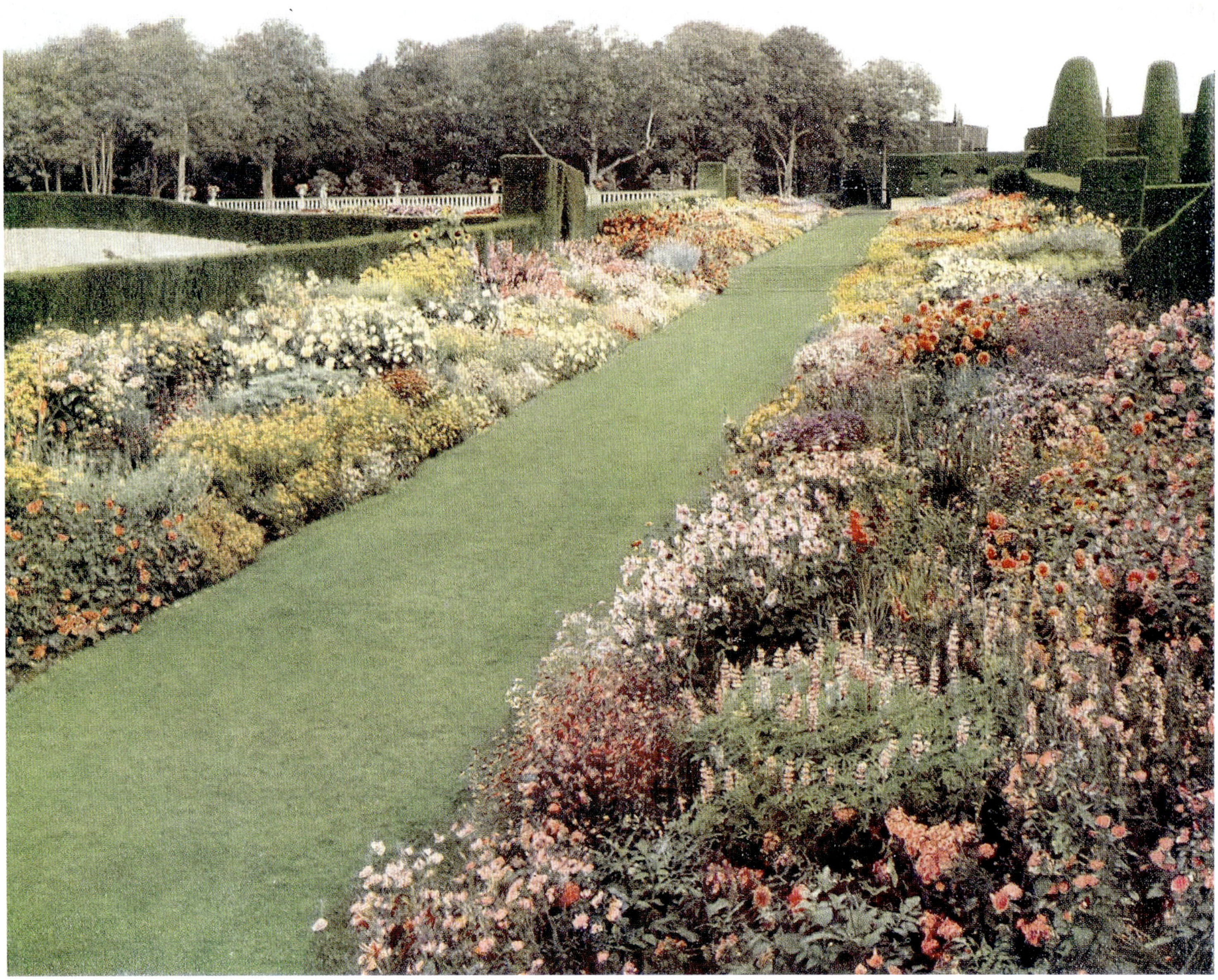

The Gardens

Philip loved the site, which was so resonant with history. Around the circular entrance court, he added caryatids from Stowe. To exploit the sharp incline of the terrain, "a cataract of gardens," all different, showed the house, Roman steps, terraces, and courtyards to best advantage.[88] This was the work of Norah Lindsay, a socialite who designed gardens for wealthy clients. Her herbaceous borders, aflame with color, were a great attraction in late summer, when Philip opened the gardens to the public. Russell Page, one of the twentieth century's great practitioners, described her unusual chessboard garden: "the flower squares were set nine inches below the turf squares so that when in full bloom all was at the same level. It was this

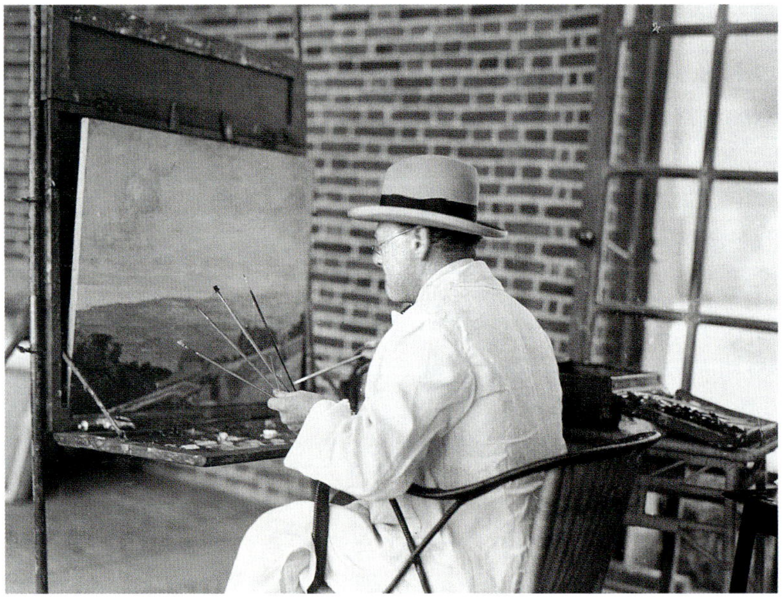

ABOVE RIGHT
Winston Churchill, *The Terrace at Port Lympne, Kent*, c. 1925, oil on canvas, 25 × 29 15/16 in. (63.5 × 76 cm), on loan from the Honorable Mary Spencer-Churchill, Lady Soames, Chartwell, Kent, UK, National Trust.

BELOW RIGHT
Winston Churchill, *The Living Room at Sir Philip Sassoon's House, Port Lympne, with Lady Pamela Smith, later Lady Hartwell (d. 1982)*, 1921, oil on canvas, 20 1/16 × 24 3/16 in. (51 × 61 cm), on loan from the Honorable Mary Spencer-Churchill, Lady Soames, Chartwell, Kent, UK, National Trust.

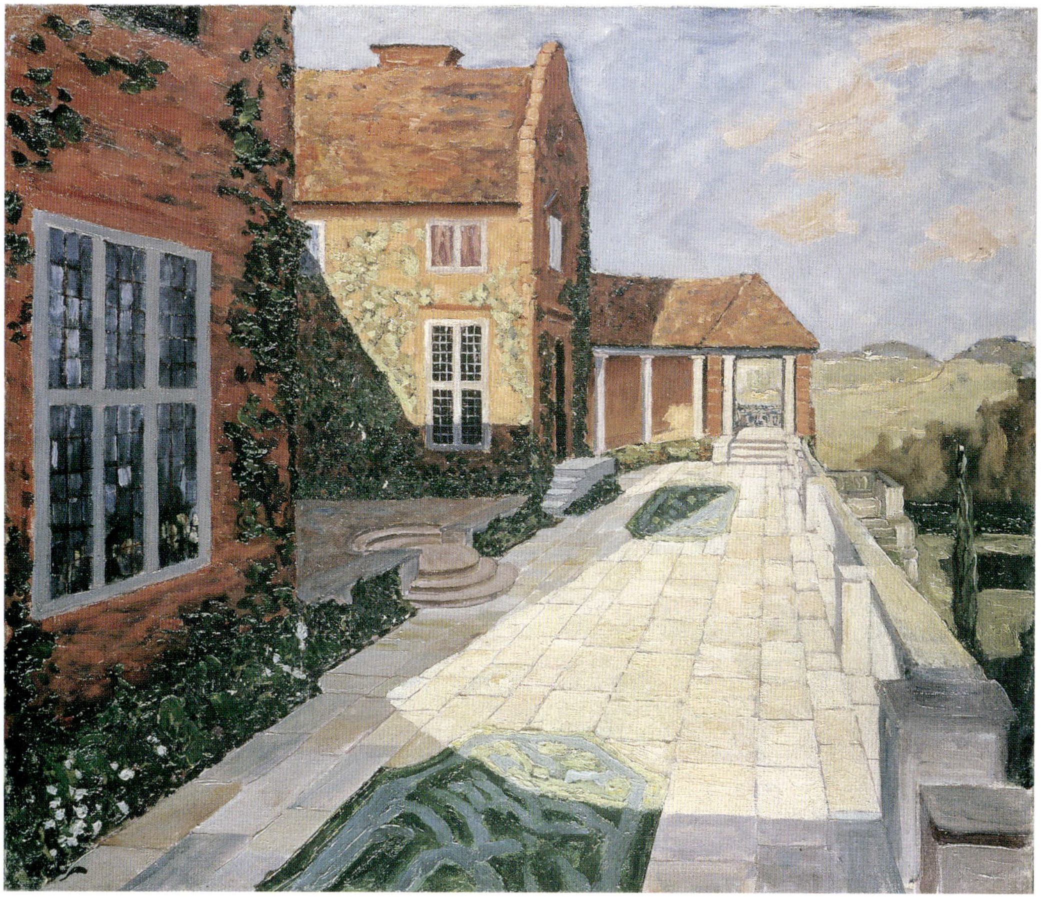

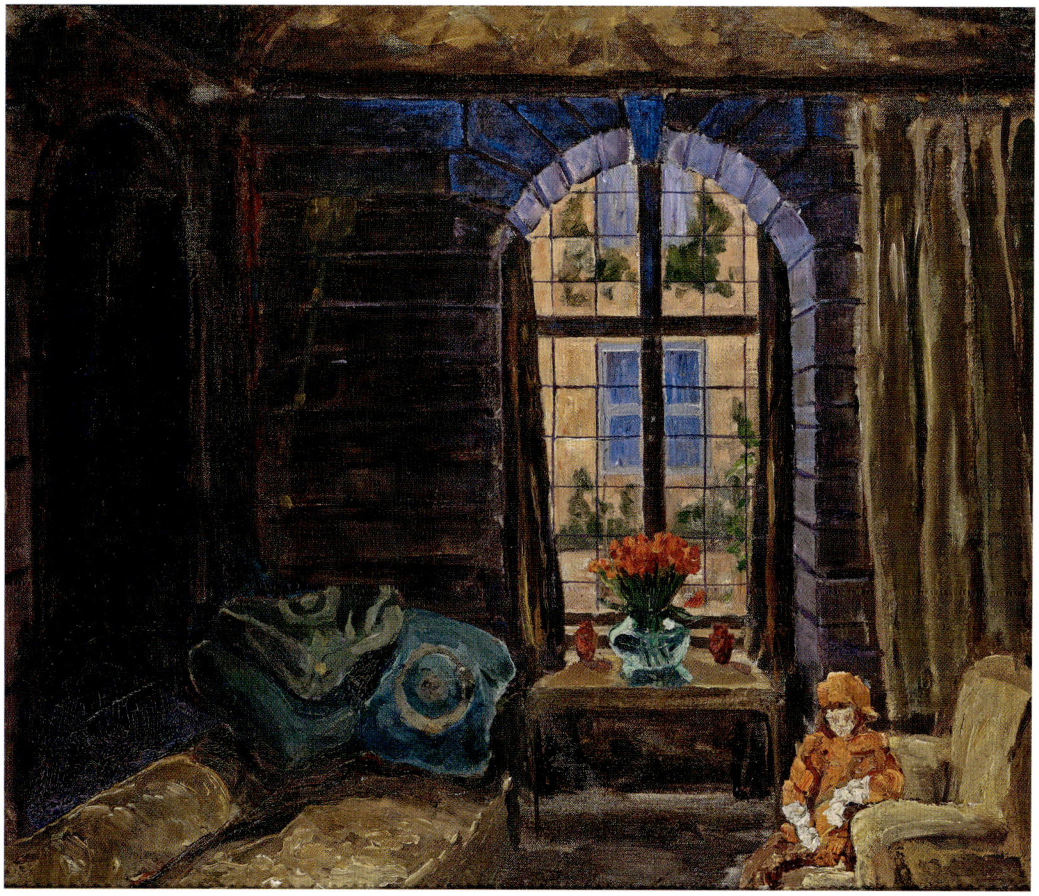

OPPOSITE ABOVE
Flower borders by the garden designer Norah Lindsay, 1929, published in *Country Life,* March 14, 1936.

OPPOSITE BELOW
Winston Churchill painting during a visit to Port Lympne, 1926, when he was Chancellor of the Exchequer, from the Port Lympne visitors' book, vol. I, 1919–28, private collection.

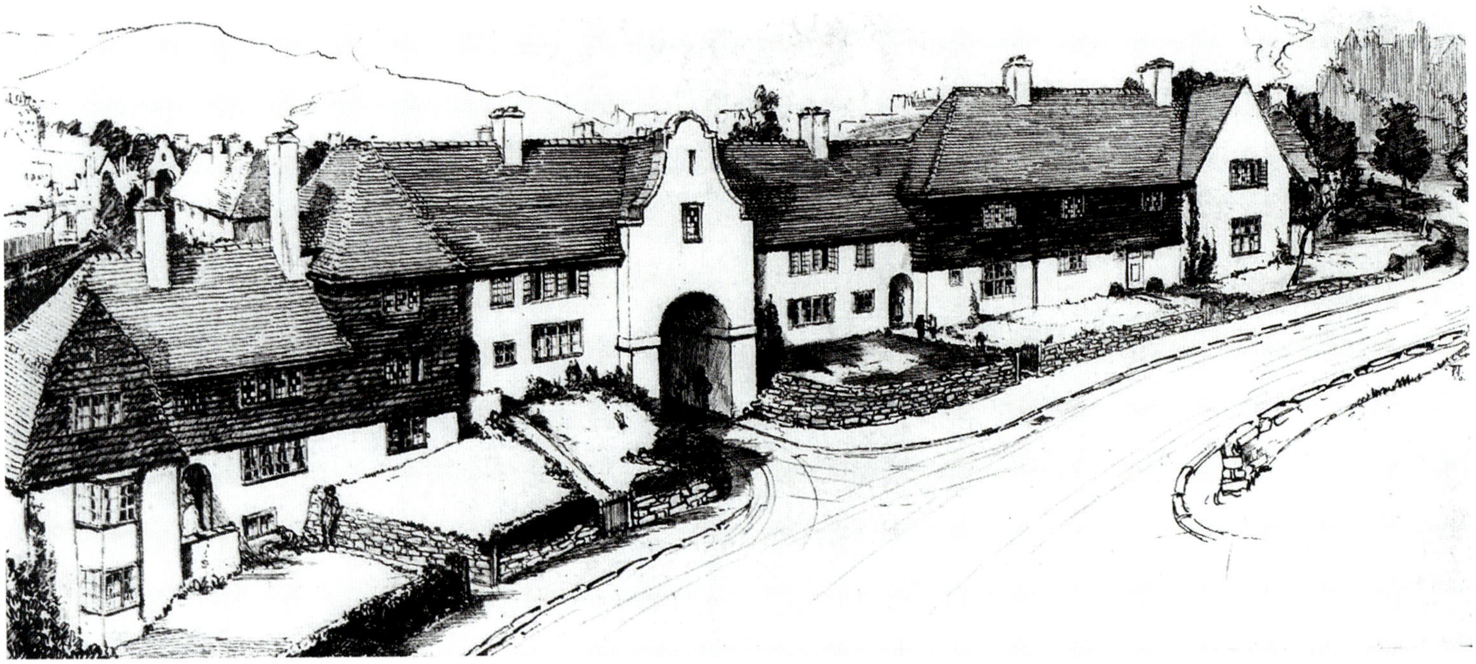

refinement which gave elegance to a basically simple pattern."[89] Both native and exotic species were used throughout the grounds, as well as aromatic plants. For Tilden, Lindsay had that "pristine touch of genius that put scents and colours in their places."[90]

On weekends, Port Lympne was filled with friends, family, and politicians. Winston Churchill, a pampered guest, painted Philip's houses several times. Requisitioned during World War II to serve the airmen, Port Lympne was vandalized and is now a safari park belonging to the Aspinall Foundation.

The Durlocks

While working on Port Lympne, Philip built a small community of affordable rental units—the Durlocks—for local fishermen in his Folkestone constituency in response to the housing crisis. After securing funds to engage the firm of Culpin and Bowers, who had extensive experience in public housing, Philip located a vacant lot overlooking the harbor. As the steep gradient required extensive leveling, the plan made the most out of the site, differentiating the elevations to avoid repetitiveness. The design, which had been examined by a committee of housewives from the neighborhood, blended well with the context. There were thirty-three units in all, grouped in the manner of a small garden city, each with two or three bedrooms and its own plot of land.[91] Philip's sister, Sybil, laid the first stone in 1919.

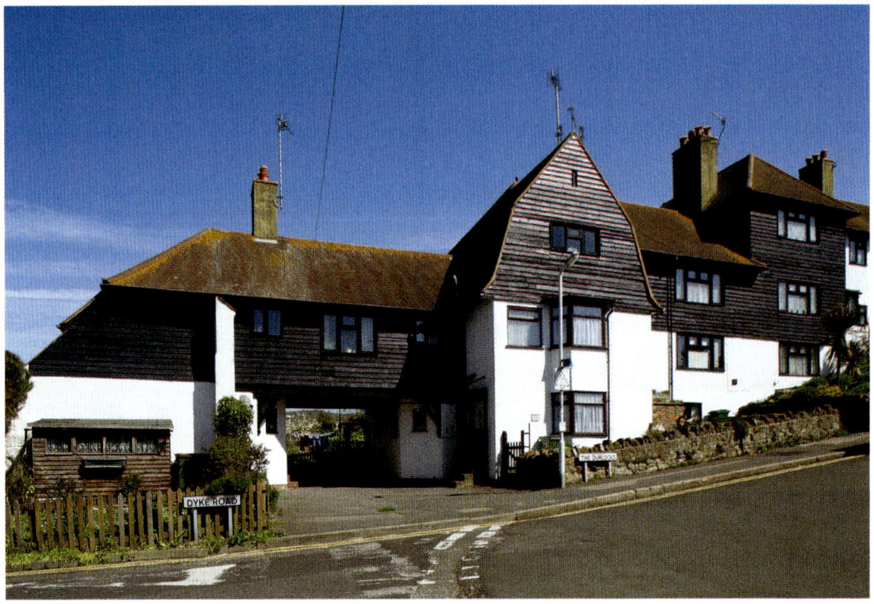

Sketch of the Durlocks, Folkestone, Kent, published in *Country Life*, December 25, 1920.

The Durlocks, Folkestone, Kent, 1921, Ewart G. Culpin and Robert Steuart Bowers, architects.

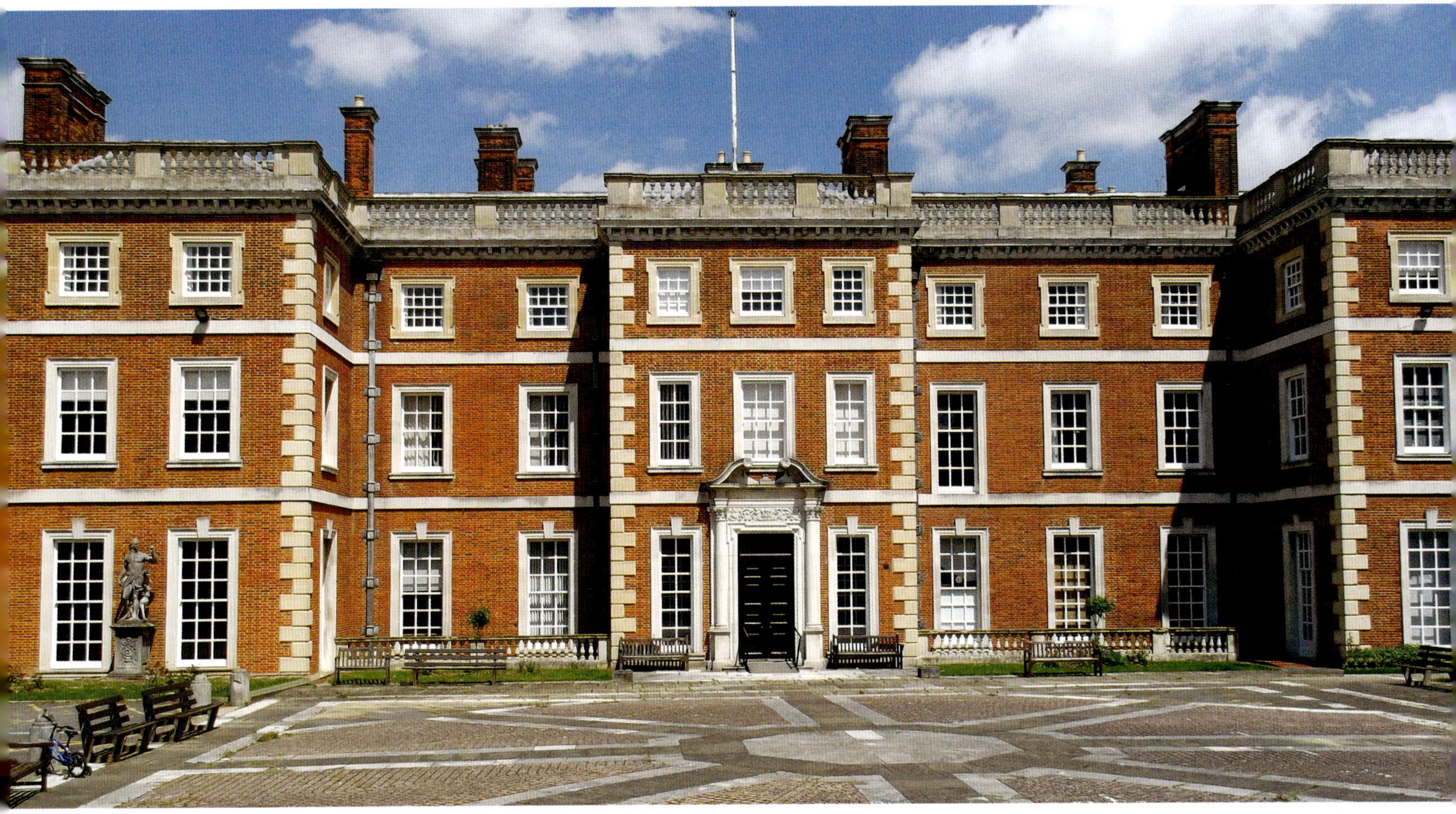

Trent Park

Thirteen miles from London, Philip's parents had bought a lease on Trent Park, an old Georgian house, rebuilt several times. Philip acquired the leasehold in 1923.[92] With his knowledge of eighteenth-century architecture, Philip began to transform the heavy-handed Victorian exterior into a grand Georgian retreat. He refaced the exterior using rose-colored bricks and stones from Devonshire House, originally designed by William Kent, and demolished in 1924. Tearing down the entrance, Philip recycled the balustrade, replaced Victorian windows with classical-looking ones, raised the north façade, and added a terrace with a commanding view of the lake.[93] If Park Lane was associated with France in its luxurious furnishings, Trent Park was rooted in English history.

Trent's remodeling seems to have been done without an architect, Philip having made the decisions in consultation with friends and experts. He added a library to the south side to make the building symmetrical but left the disposition of rooms unchanged. Stately doorframes and pediments impart grandeur to the interiors, and critics admired the enfilade of elegant rooms, luxurious furnishings, Chinese and Delft porcelain, japanned furniture, and conversation pieces. Availing himself of the brisk trade in architectural salvage, he bought statues, obelisks, columns, and lions for the gardens, and architectural details from Stowe, Wrest Park, Chesterfield House, and Milton Abbey.[94] Once again, Whistler provided several decorative elements for the walls, painted in oil on wood: monograms, trophies, mythological figures, and dolphins.[95]

One thousand acres of parkland, then thought to be the work of noted eighteenth-century landscape designer Humphry Repton, gave Philip the chance to create gardens remarkable for their unusual combinations of color and texture, and expert use of the terrain. Wisely leaving the lawns intact, with their broad vistas sloping down to the lake, he scattered smaller gardens and parterres throughout the wooded areas, carefully coordinating vistas and eye-catchers. The unstructured charm of a lush water garden and lily ponds offered a perfect contrast to the formal gardens. East of the house, an eighteenth-century–style orangery by Colonel

Trent Park, North London, built in 1777, rebuilt by Philip Sassoon in the mid-1920s.

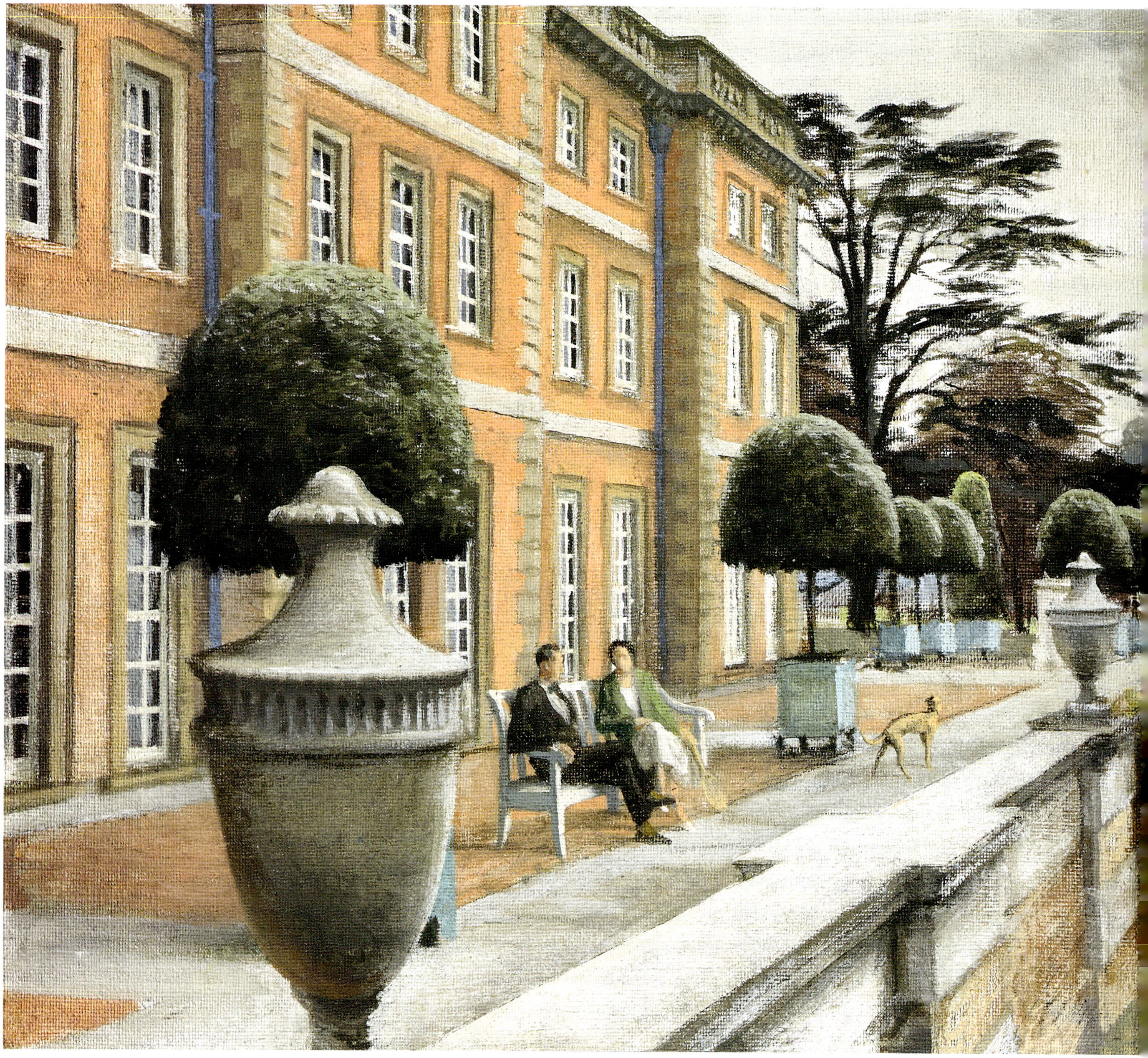

Rex Whistler, *Philip and Hannah on the Terrace at Trent Park with Their Whippet, Blazer,* 1934, oil on canvas, 9¾ × 13¾ in. (24.8 × 34.9 cm), private collection.

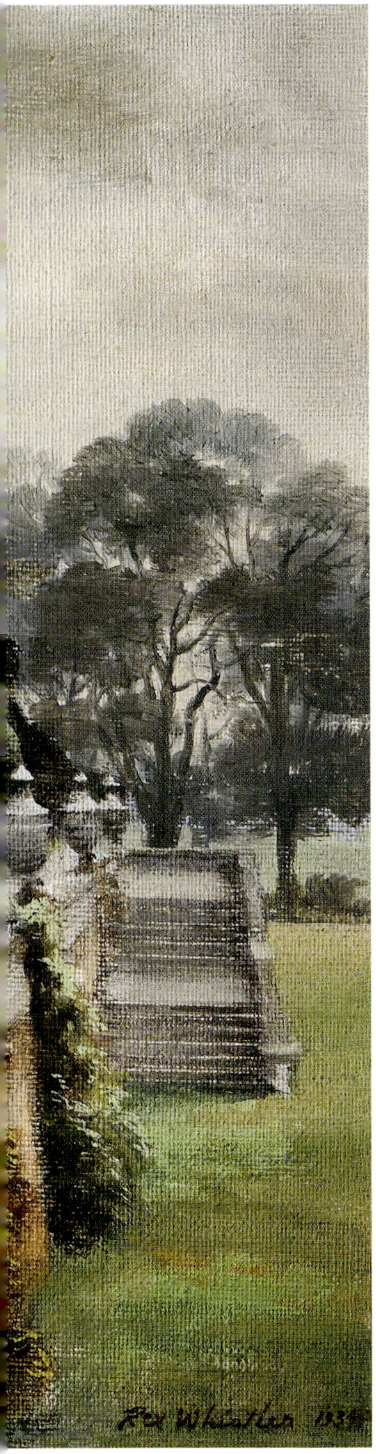

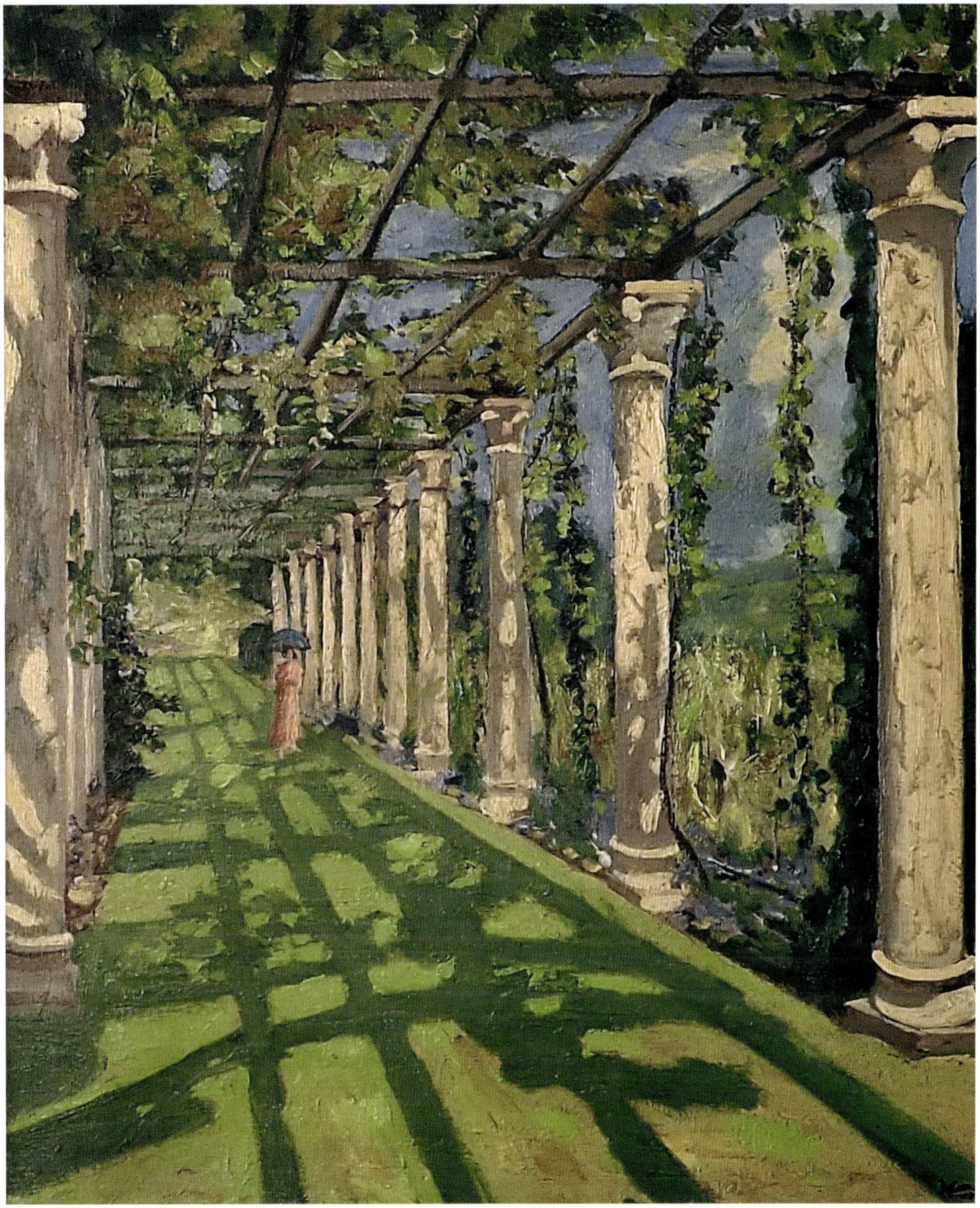

Winston Churchill, *The Terrace at Trent Park (Wisteria Walk)*, 1935, oil on canvas, 24 × 20 in. (61 × 50.8 cm), private collection. Clementine, Churchill's wife, can be seen strolling with a parasol.

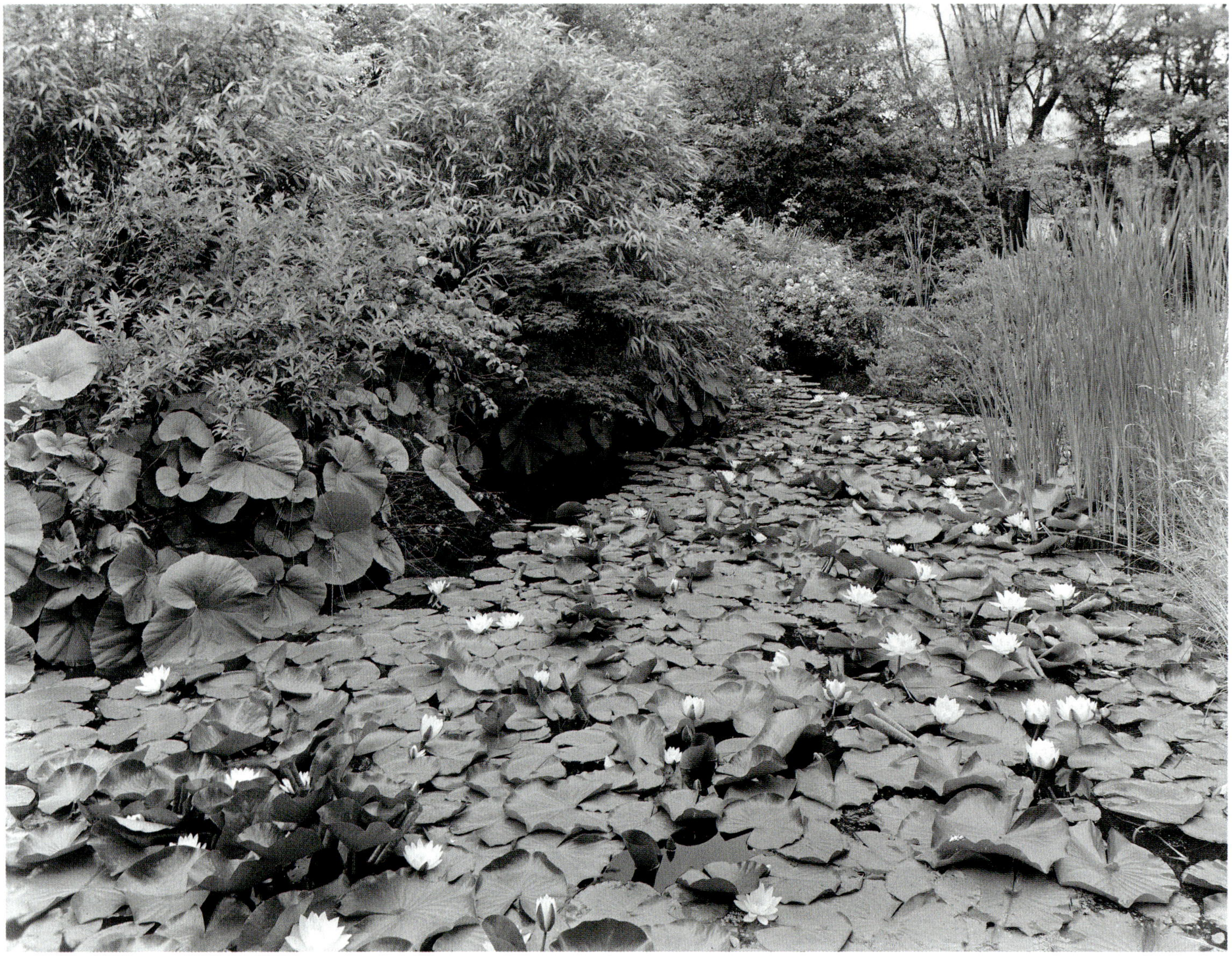

Reginald Cooper overlooks a swimming pool. Not far rose the marble columns of Wisteria Walk, painted by Churchill. When the gardens opened to the public, Norah Lindsay's herbaceous borders attracted thousands "with their barbaric splendour of coloring and luxuriance of bloom."[96]

As one of the great hosts of his day, Philip combined his public and private lives, welcoming friends, family, and statesmen alike. Given its proximity to London, Trent Park was used often by cabinet ministers, members of the royal family, and celebrities. Everything was added for their comfort and enjoyment: a golf course, tennis courts, and an airfield. The historian Christopher Hussey, doyen of manor houses, described it as "a great country house in the pure English tradition." It was a building, he adds, "at once dignified and unpretentious, practical and yet civilised."[97]

But being anglicized did not necessarily guarantee acceptance. In England, the Sassoons had arrived at the center of empire, yet they were caught between privilege and prejudice. In the biting words of the British politician and historian Harold Nicolson, Philip was "a strange, lonely, un-English little figure, flitting about among these vast apartments." Even Philip's friend Lord Boothby

The water garden at the lower end of the lake, Trent Park, published in *Country Life,* January 10, 1931.

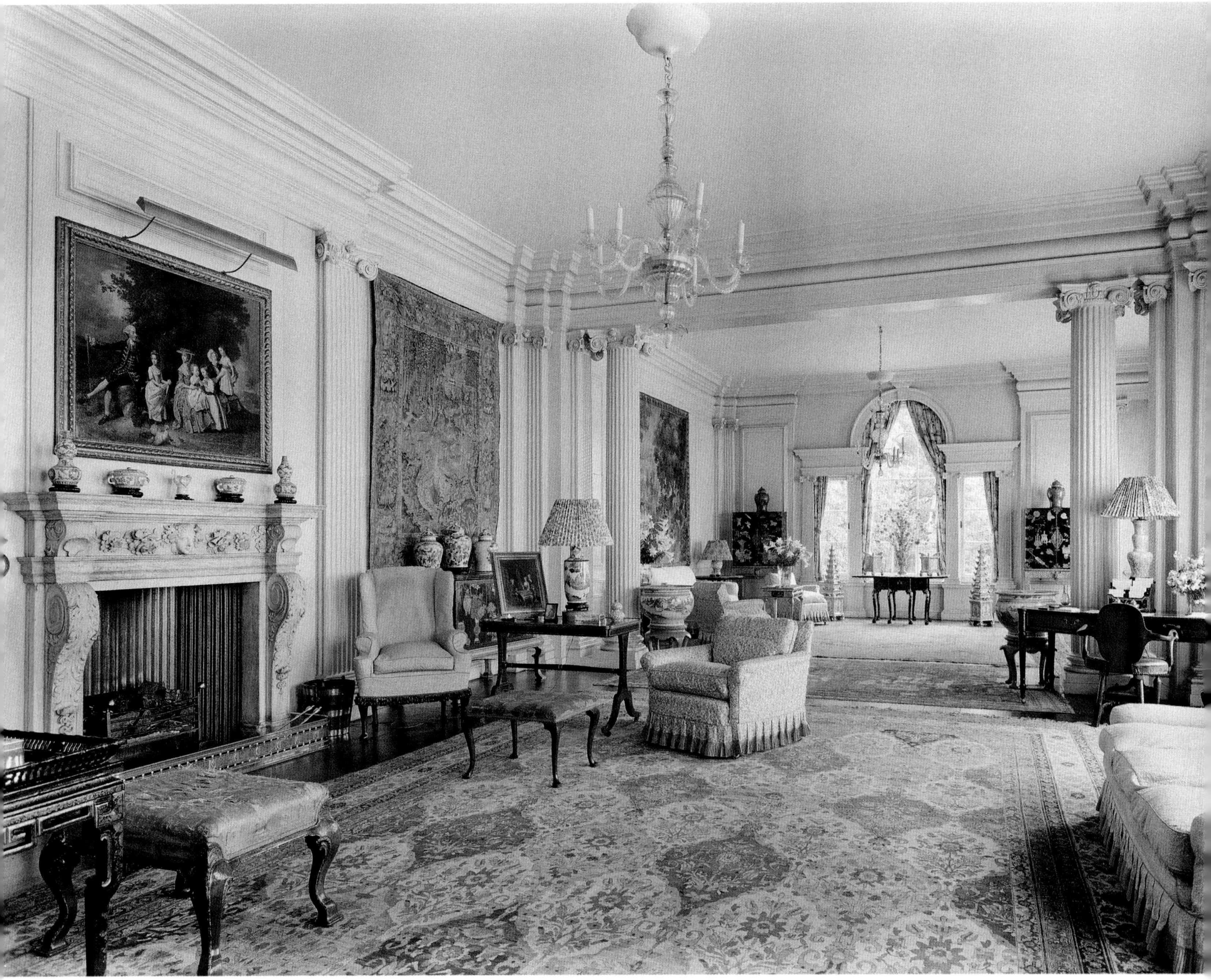

The drawing room at Trent Park, photographed in 1931, published in *Country Life*, January 17, 1931. *The Colmore Family* by Johan Zoffany hangs above the fireplace.

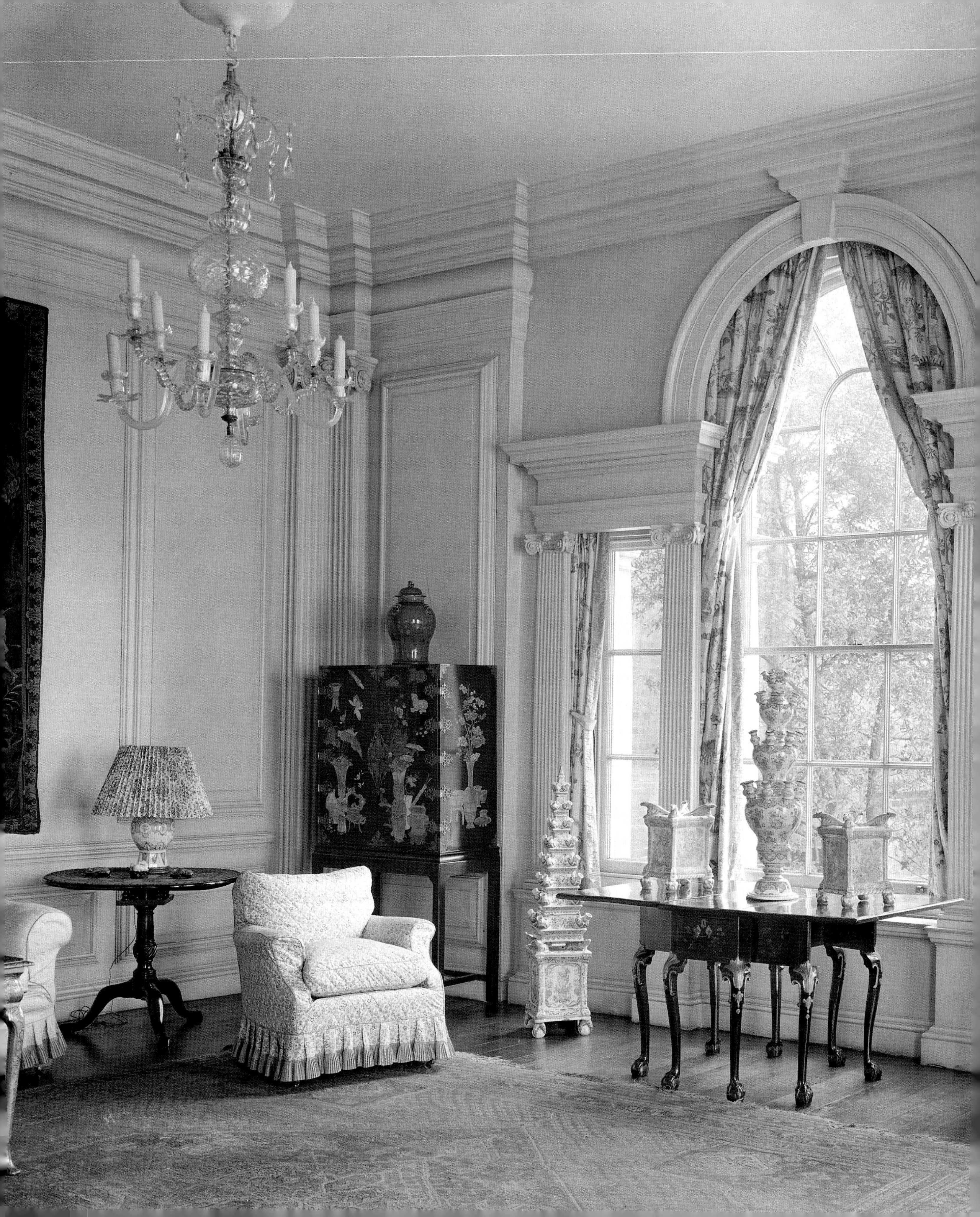

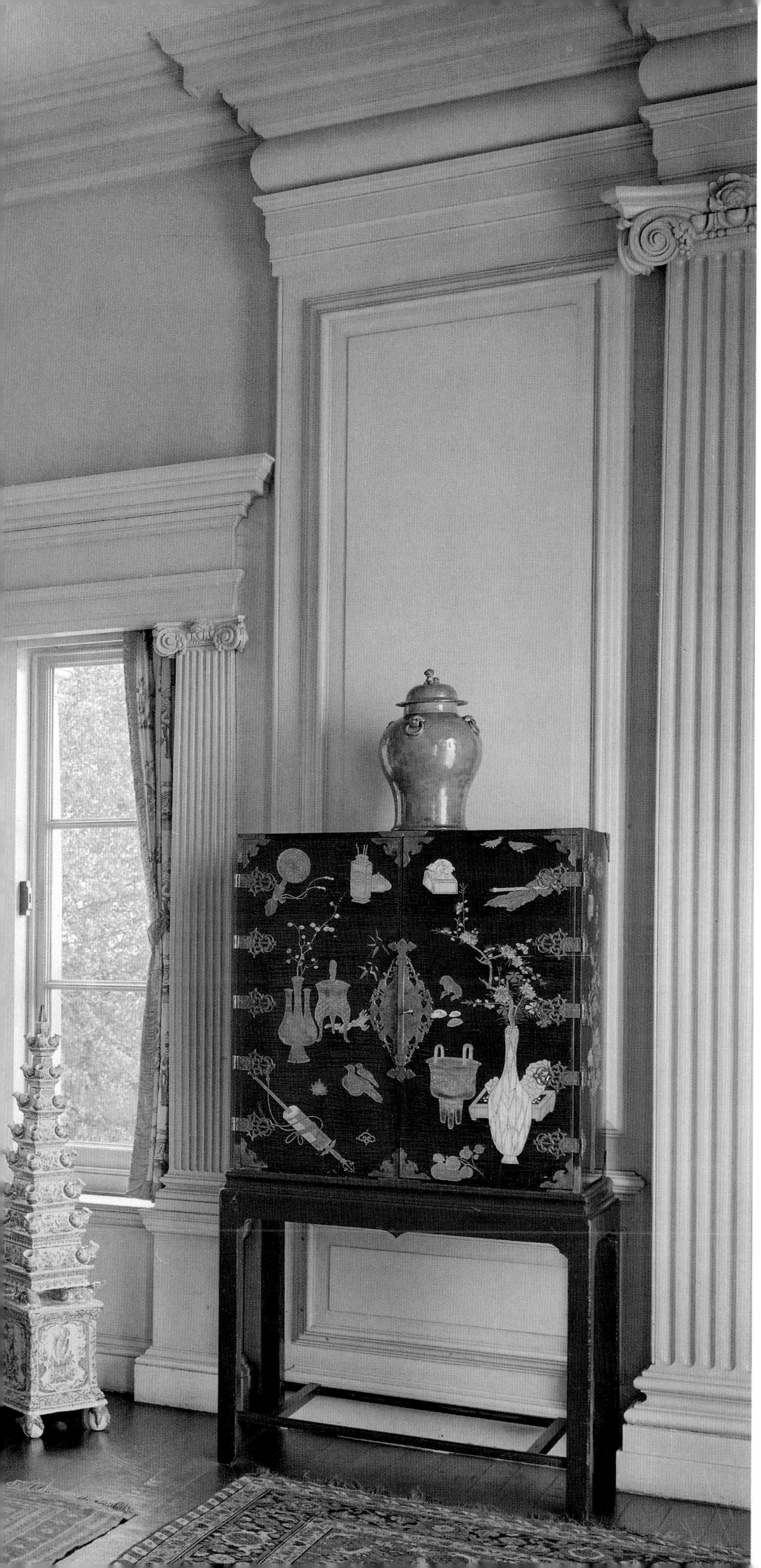

The drawing room at Trent Park with japanned furniture and Delft flower holders, published in *Country Life*, January 17, 1931.

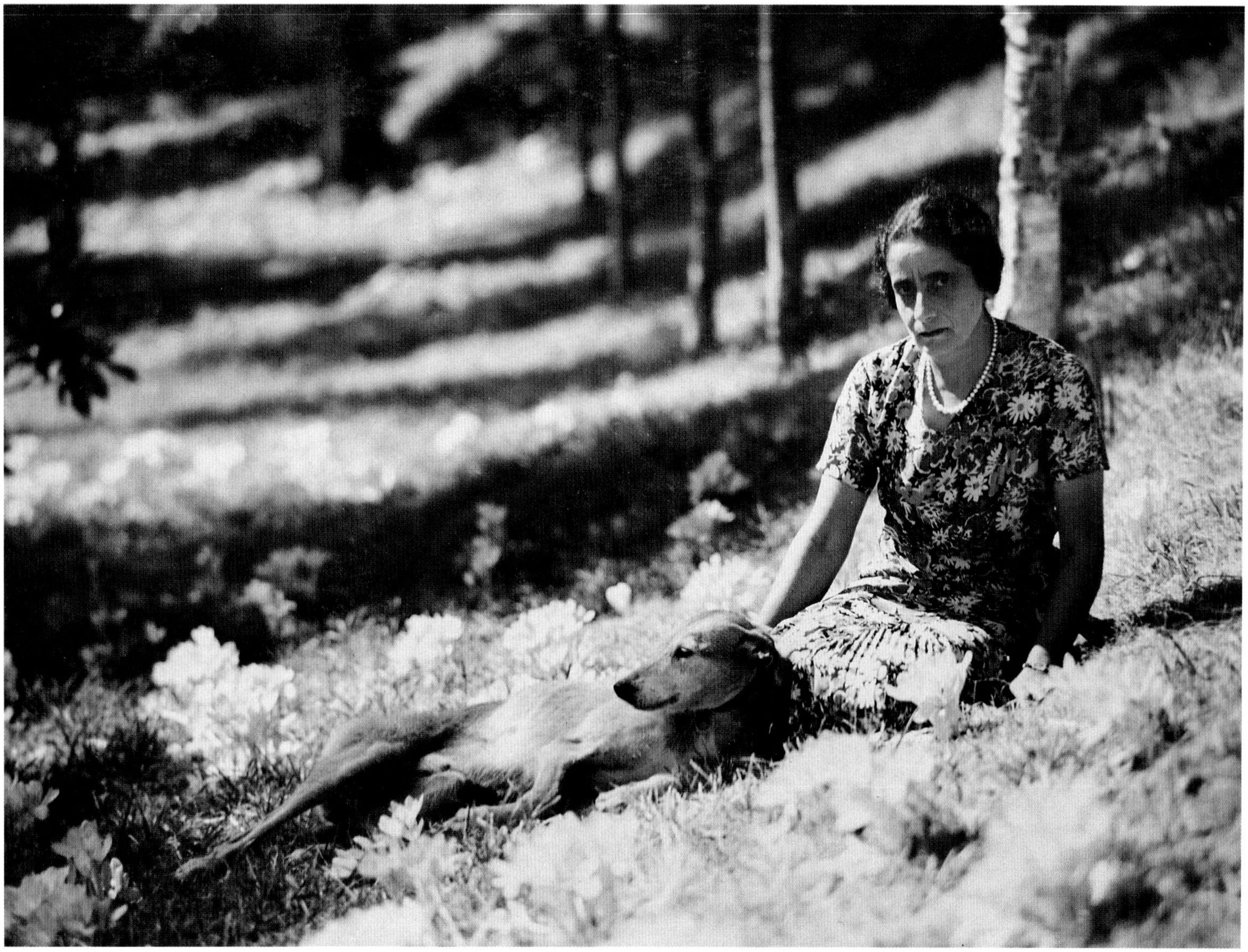

Hannah Gubbay at Port Lympne, 1934, from the Port Lympne visitors' book, vol. II, 1929–38, private collection.

claimed that "he was not part of England, and whatever gods he worshipped were not our gods." Behind their backs, the Sassoons were the target of persistent antisemitism: "an underbred Whitechapel Jew," wrote Virginia Woolf of Philip to her sister Vanessa Bell in 1929.[98] Hannah Gubbay, who inherited Port Lympne, and was possibly seen as a proxy for Philip, also received her share. "Mr. Gubbay a dear little man," wrote the novelist Alice Dudeney, who often stayed at Port Lympne, "but so palpably Oriental—the palms of his hands looking as if they were sprinkled with soot. Mrs. Gubbay handsome: in the short-necked Jewish way but . . . take off her fine clothes and her ropes of pearls, put her behind a banana stall in the East End on a Saturday night—and there you are! Dozens of her anywhere."[99] Rex Whistler, who saw Hannah while working at Port Lympne and Trent Park, told his brother Laurence, "I do wish Hannah wouldn't say, 'I've been working like a black.' She *is* a black!"[100] If true, this recollection, recounted by a third party, years after events, suggests that discrimination cut both ways.

Mozelle

Mozelle Sassoon also entertained guests lavishly at her Château de Port-Breton on the French coast, a magnificent property facing the sea, surrounded by a landscaped park à la française. During high season, she hosted Churchill and members of the royal family. Designed by René Aillerie, architect of the town of Dinard, and completed in 1923, the château is a massive granite structure with projecting bays flanking the entrance. The roof, interrupted by dormers and chimneys, was heavily damaged during World War II, but the interior is

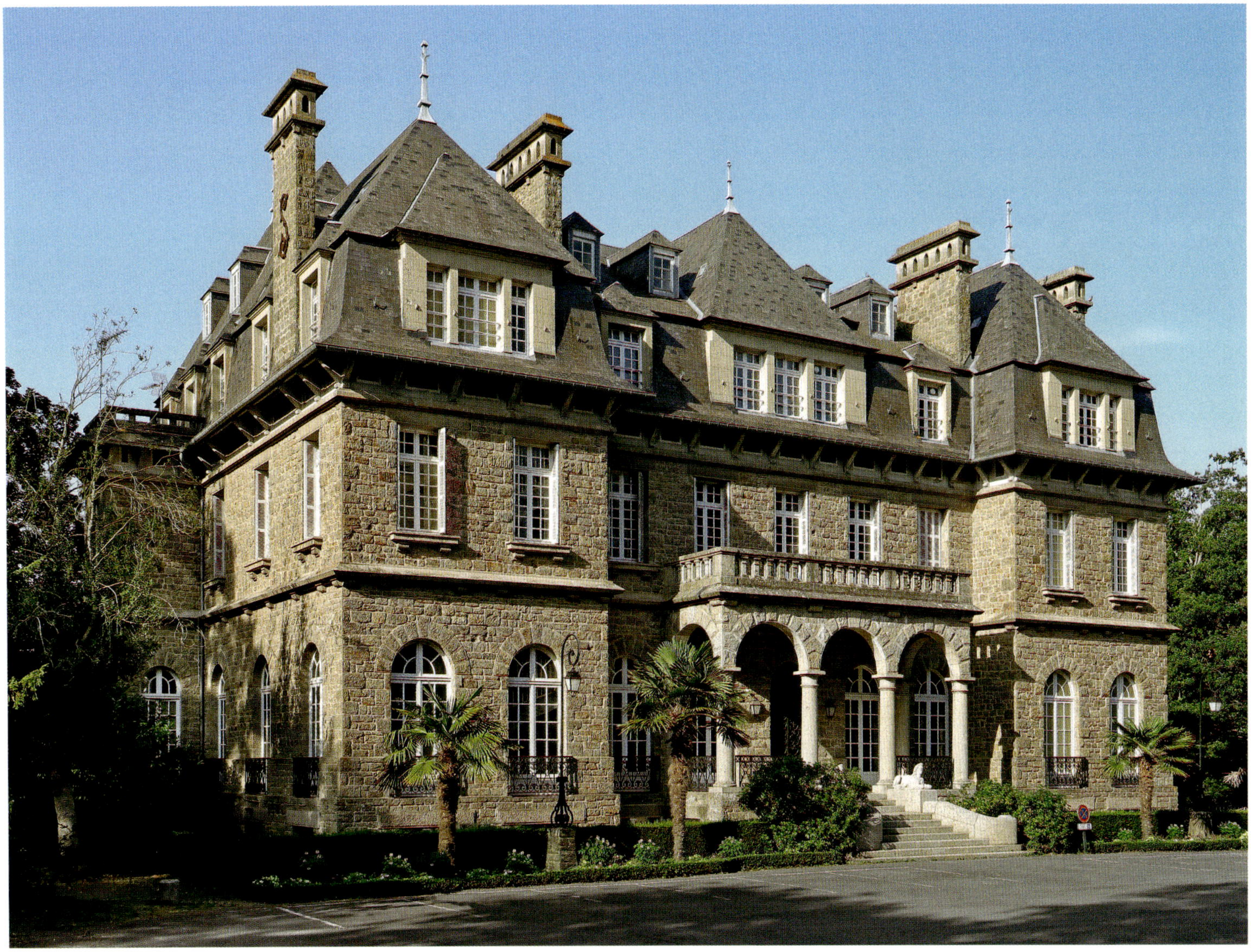

The Château de Port-Breton, Dinard, France, 1923, René Aillerie, architect.

still intact, with its suite of fine reception rooms overlooking the gardens.

While Port-Breton followed local tradition in both elevation and massing, a decade later Mozelle commissioned a crisp, abstract prism that epitomized the tenets of the architectural avant-garde. When her son, Reginald Ellice Sassoon, died in a horse-riding accident in 1933, she decided to honor his memory with a five-story apartment building for workers: the R. E. Sassoon House.[101] In consultation with Elizabeth Denby, an expert on inner-city poverty, Mozelle selected Maxwell Fry as architect. From the start, Denby and Fry wanted the building to deliver a new form of social housing. With her knowledge of working-class life and the needs of women, Denby ensured that all flats had model kitchens with practical, time-saving equipment.[102] The façade, layout, and use of standardized parts clearly reveal the influence of German experiments in working-class housing by Ernst May and especially Walter Gropius, with whom Fry was to collaborate on his next low-income project.[103] The long, cantilevered balconies provide tenants with access to their flats in front, and on the garden side, a modicum of private space outdoors. Glass corner windows, still a novelty at the time, dematerialized the edges of the façade. The Vitrolite mural, by the émigré German Jewish artist Hans Feibusch, represents a horseman, an allusion to Reginald.

A milestone in modern British architecture and social housing between the wars, the sleek International Style building was featured in the 1937 exhibition *Modern Architecture in England* at New York's Museum of Modern Art. That Mozelle should have agreed to such a cutting-edge design is remarkable. As the first modernist working-class apartment building in Britain, Sassoon House

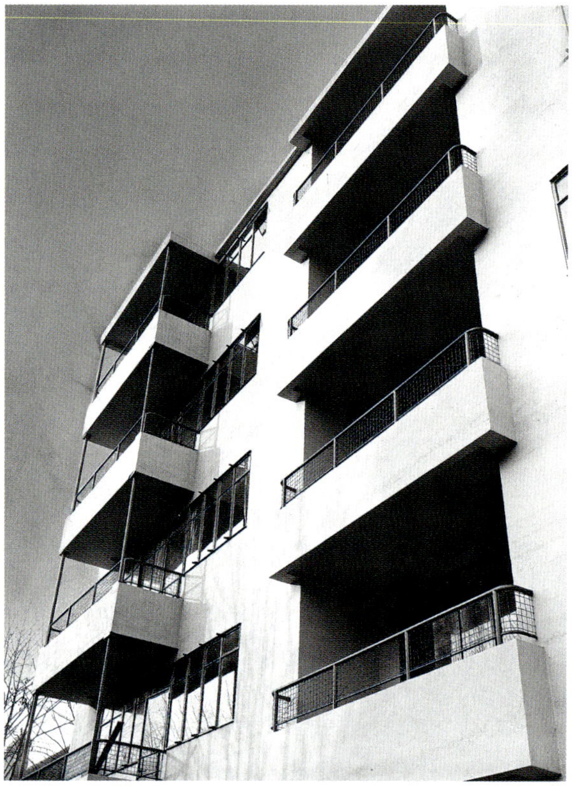

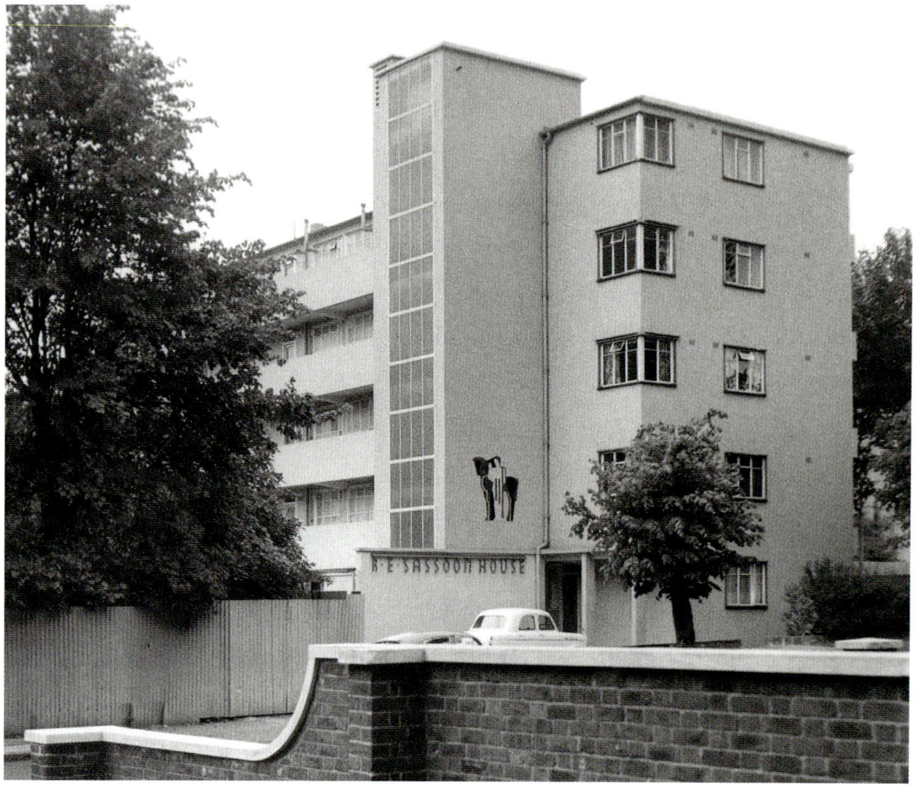

made a significant contribution to British architecture and shows the importance of women as patrons. Appropriately, given Mozelle's place of birth, the building was inaugurated in 1934 by a family friend, Samuel Hoare, Secretary of State for India.[104]

Throughout their journey from Iraq to India, China, and ultimately England, the Sassoons inhabited a world of extraordinary cultural fluidity and proved remarkably adept in navigating its currents. Their linguistic skills; sprawling web of familial, intra-Jewish, and transnational contacts; as well as their seasoned command of trade circuits made them highly attractive to the colonial powers. Although their dependence on the British entailed political and cultural accommodation, the Sassoons charted a cautious path that also revealed sensitivity to regional populations. Even their innumerable social, religious, and cultural benefactions reflected new patterns of Jewish philanthropy that balanced local and global concerns.[105] With the decision to settle in England, family aspirations were channeled through a singularly English context, though with Continental admixtures that drew on family alliances in France. Even those buildings closely tied to their Jewish identity were now folded into social and political aspirations that were distinctly British. This is reflected in their homes, as well as in their commitments and contributions to cultural enlightenment and social welfare.

TOP LEFT
The R. E. Sassoon House, Peckham, South London, 1934, commissioned by Mozelle Sassoon, Maxwell Fry, architect, in collaboration with the social housing expert Elizabeth Denby.

TOP RIGHT
The entrance to Sassoon House with a 1934 equestrian artwork in Vitrolite by Hans Feibusch.

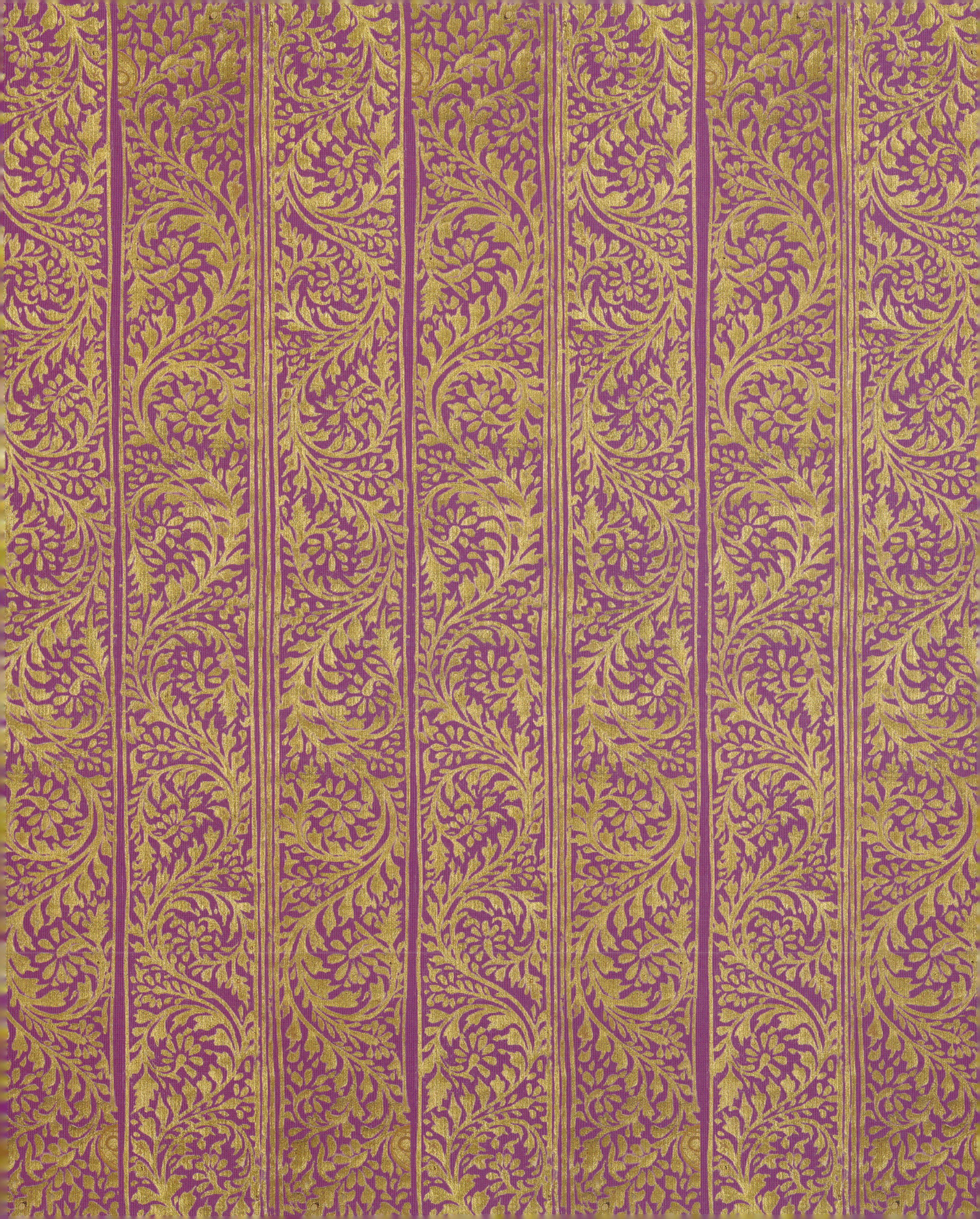

Epilogue

It was the far-reaching British Empire that enabled the Sassoons to prosper, but in the end, it was to Britain itself that they showed their loyalty. Fourteen grandsons and great-grandsons of David Sassoon fought for the British during World War I. The five Sassoon brothers from Ashley Park enlisted. Victor Sassoon served with the Royal Flying Corps, but a flying accident during a reconnaissance exercise in 1916 left him with chronic pain and on crutches for the rest of his life. Several family members were wounded. Hamo Sassoon (1887–1915), Siegfried's brother, died at Gallipoli. Three great-grandsons earned the Military Cross: Siegfried; Mozelle's son, Reginald; and Arthur Sassoon, grandson of Sassoon David. We know less about the Sassoon women during World War I, but many volunteered for jobs that were open to them. Louise Sassoon was head of the Officers' Clothing Branch of the Officers' Families Fund and also volunteered for the Queen's Work for Women Fund. Sybil worked on behalf of the war effort for three and a half years and was one of the prime movers behind the Women's Royal Naval Service (WRNS). Among many initiatives, she ordered miniature Qur'ans encased in metal to be given out to Muslim troops serving with the Allied Forces. Mozelle Sassoon (granddaughter of Sassoon David), whose five brothers enlisted, worked at the Walton Branch of the War Supply Depot.[1]

Siegfried became the voice of a generation traumatized by the scenes of carnage and the unspeakable horror of trench warfare. His defiant letter of protest, "A Soldier's Declaration," published in *The Times* of London on July 31, 1917, and read aloud in Parliament, nearly earned him a court-martial. Thanks to the intervention of his fellow poet-soldier Robert Graves, and the army's reluctance to condemn a decorated war hero, he was sent to recover at Craiglockhart, Scotland, where he would meet and mentor another of the war's great poets, Wilfred Owen. Siegfried's verses, jotted down in mud-spattered booklets under terrible circumstances, struck a nerve. Even a disapproving Churchill could recite several of Siegfried's poems by heart.

And through some mooned Valhalla there
will pass
Battalions and battalions, scarred from hell;
The unreturning army that was youth.[2]

Philip, two years younger than Siegfried, whom he only met in 1925, was a second lieutenant with the Royal East Kent Yeomanry and served as private secretary to Field Marshal Douglas Haig. As a member of Parliament, Philip had connections to the government that were of great help to the commander in chief. He was

Louise Sassoon sewing to benefit the Officers' Families Fund, January 1, 1920, photograph by Wakefields, Chiswick and Brentford, London, Imperial War Museums.

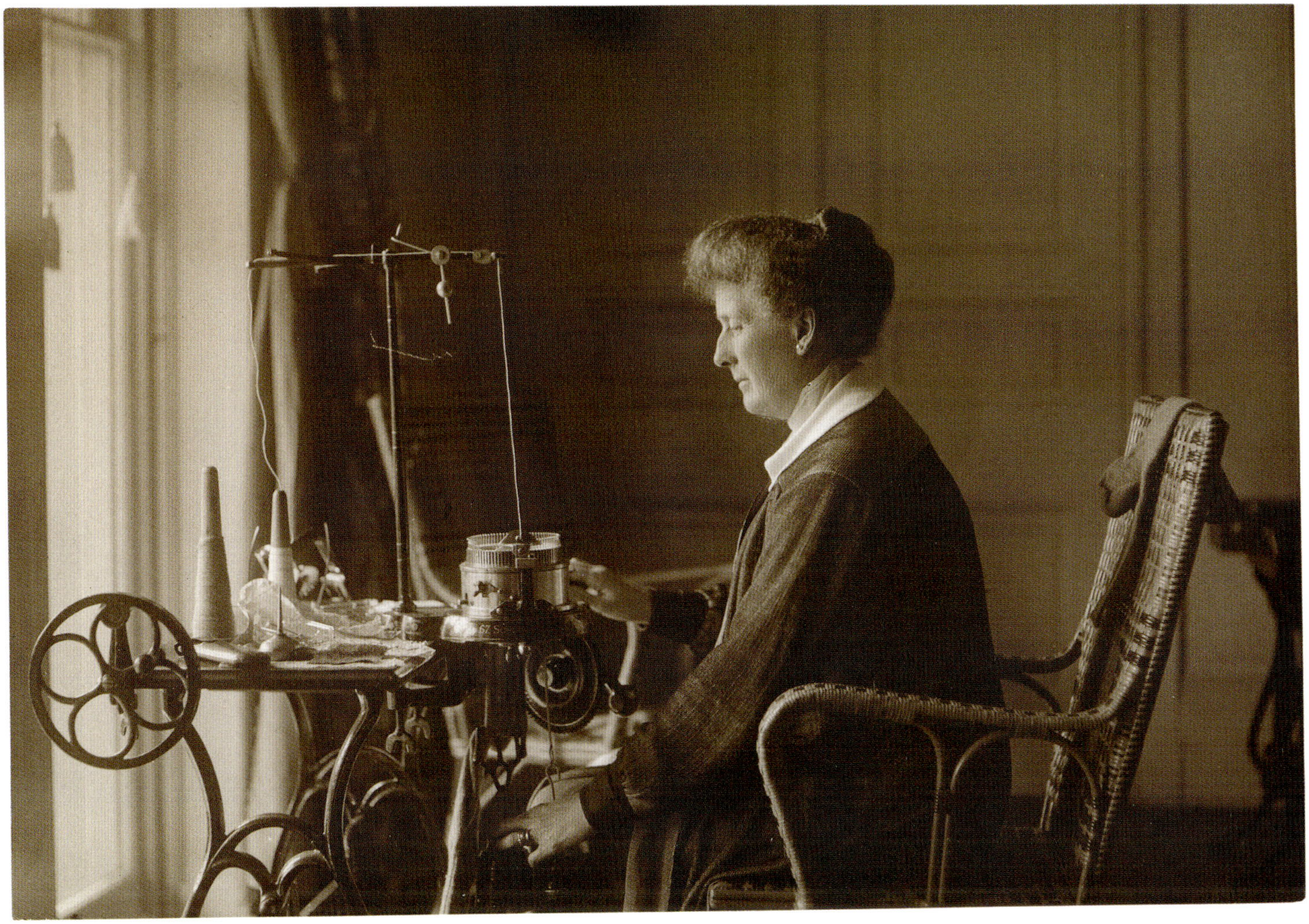

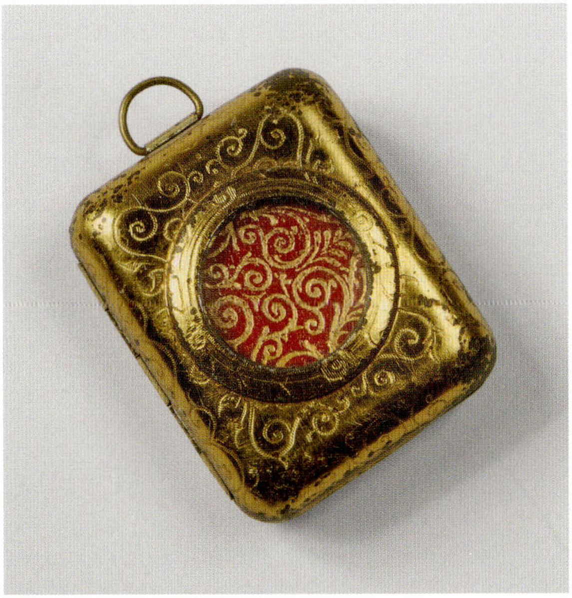

A miniature Qur'an, published in Glasgow, 1900, 2 × 1½ × ½ in. (5.1 × 3.8 × 1.3 cm), Norfolk, UK, Houghton Hall Collection. During World War I, Sybil Sassoon, Countess of Rocksavage, donated these miniature Qur'ans for distribution to Muslim soldiers fighting for the British.

RIGHT
The poet Siegfried Sassoon in military uniform, c. 1916, Cambridge University Library, UK, ms. Add. 7973/S57a.

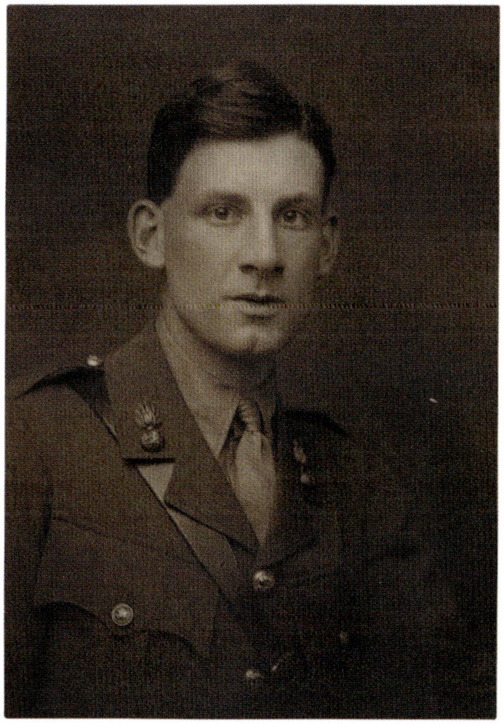

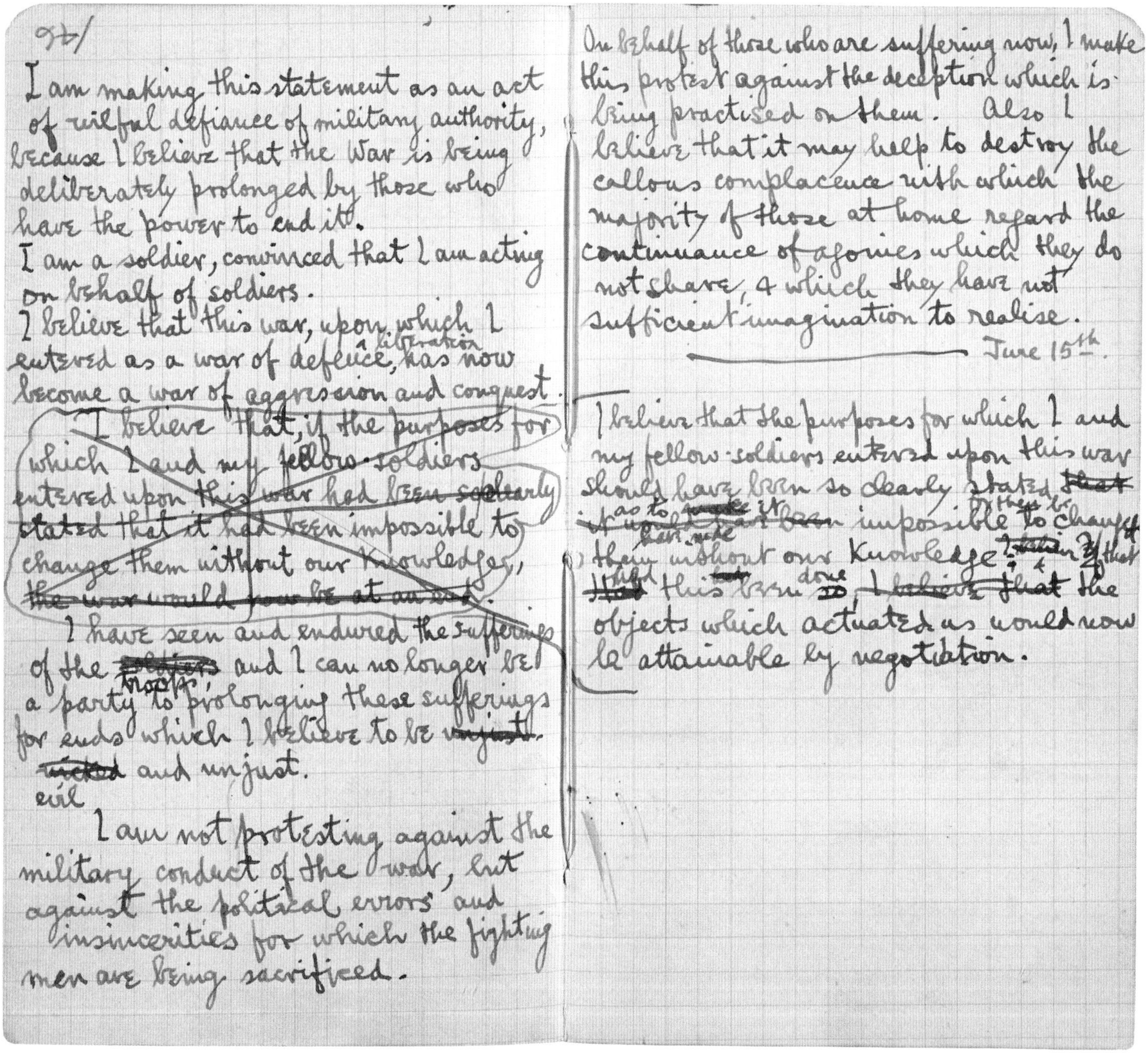

I am making this statement as an act of wilful defiance of military authority, because I believe that the War is being deliberately prolonged by those who have the power to end it.

I am a soldier, convinced that I am acting on behalf of soldiers.

I believe that this war, upon which I entered as a war of defence & liberation, has now become a war of aggression and conquest.

~~I believe that, if the purposes for which I and my fellow-soldiers entered upon this war had been so clearly stated that it had been impossible to change them without our knowledge, the war would now be at an end.~~

I have seen and endured the sufferings of the troops, and I can no longer be a party to prolonging these sufferings for ends which I believe to be evil and unjust.

I am not protesting against the military conduct of the war, but against the political errors and insincerities for which the fighting men are being sacrificed.

On behalf of those who are suffering now, I make this protest against the deception which is being practised on them. Also I believe that it may help to destroy the callous complacence with which the majority of those at home regard the continuance of agonies which they do not share, & which they have not sufficient imagination to realise.

June 15th.

I believe that the purposes for which I and my fellow-soldiers entered upon this war should have been so clearly stated as to have made it impossible to change them without our knowledge; & that if this been done the objects which actuated us would now be attainable by negotiation.

Draft of Siegfried Sassoon's statement against the conduct of the war in his journal, April 11–June 2, 1917, Cambridge University Library, UK, ms. Add. 9852/1/10, fols. 46r–45v.

OPPOSITE
Siegfried Sassoon and Robert Graves, photographed in September 1920 by Lady Ottoline Morrell, vintage snapshot print, 2½ × 1⅞ in. (6.2 × 4.9 cm), London, National Portrait Gallery, purchased with help from the Friends of the National Libraries and the Dame Helen Gardner Bequest.

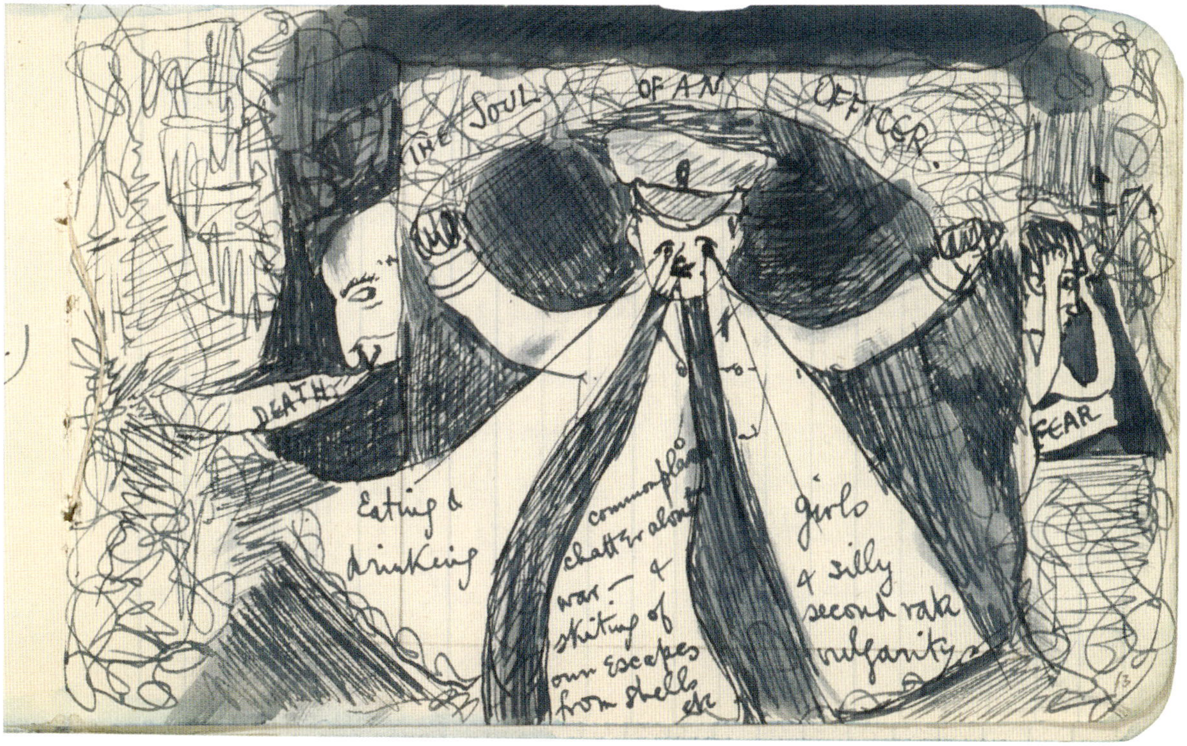

"The Soul of an Officer," in Siegfried Sassoon's journal, June 26–August 12, 1916, Cambridge University Library, UK, ms. Add.9852/1/7, fol. 3r.

BELOW
Page of a letter from Robert Graves to his fellow soldier-poet Siegfried Sassoon, Cambridge University Library, UK, ms. Add.9852/1/6/4. Graves wrote from Mametz Wood during the Battle of the Somme, July 17, 1916. The text expresses dreams of good times at war's end, concluding, "In old Baghdad we'll call a halt / At the Sassoons' ancestral vault."

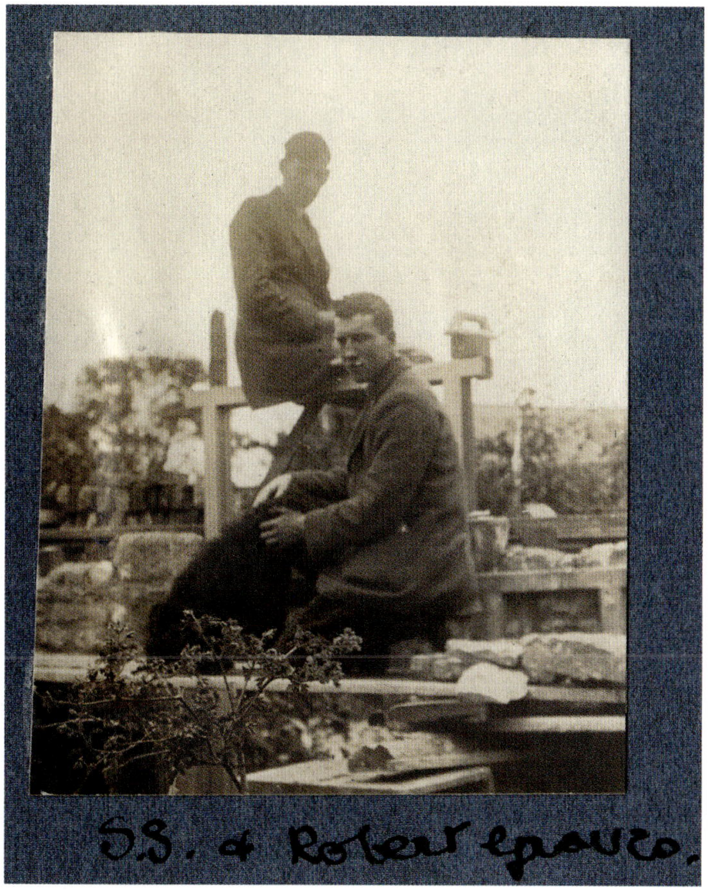

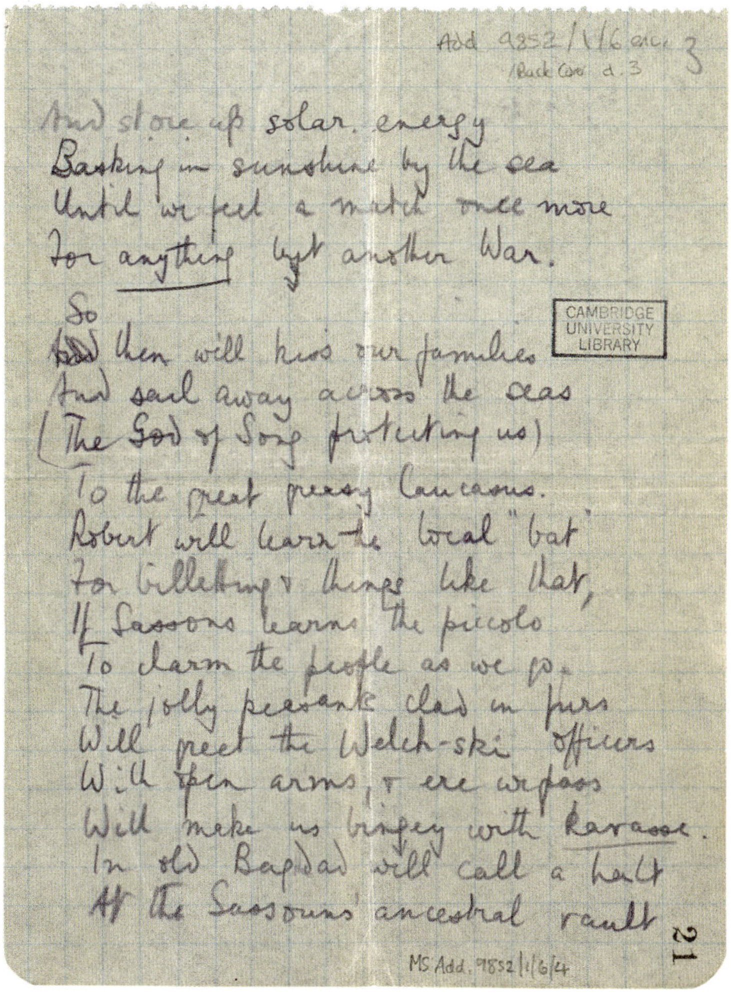
Add 9852/1/6 3
And store up solar energy
Basking in sunshine by the sea
Until we feel a match once more
For anything but another War.

So
We then will kiss our families
And sail away across the seas
(The God of Song protecting us)
To the great greasy Caucasus.
Robert will learn the local "bat"
For billeting & things like that,
If Sassoon learns the piccolo
To charm the people as we go.
The jolly peasants clad in furs
Will greet the Welch-ski officers
With open arms, & ere we pass
Will make us bingey with Kavasse.
In old Bagdad we'll call a halt
At the Sassoons' ancestral vault
21

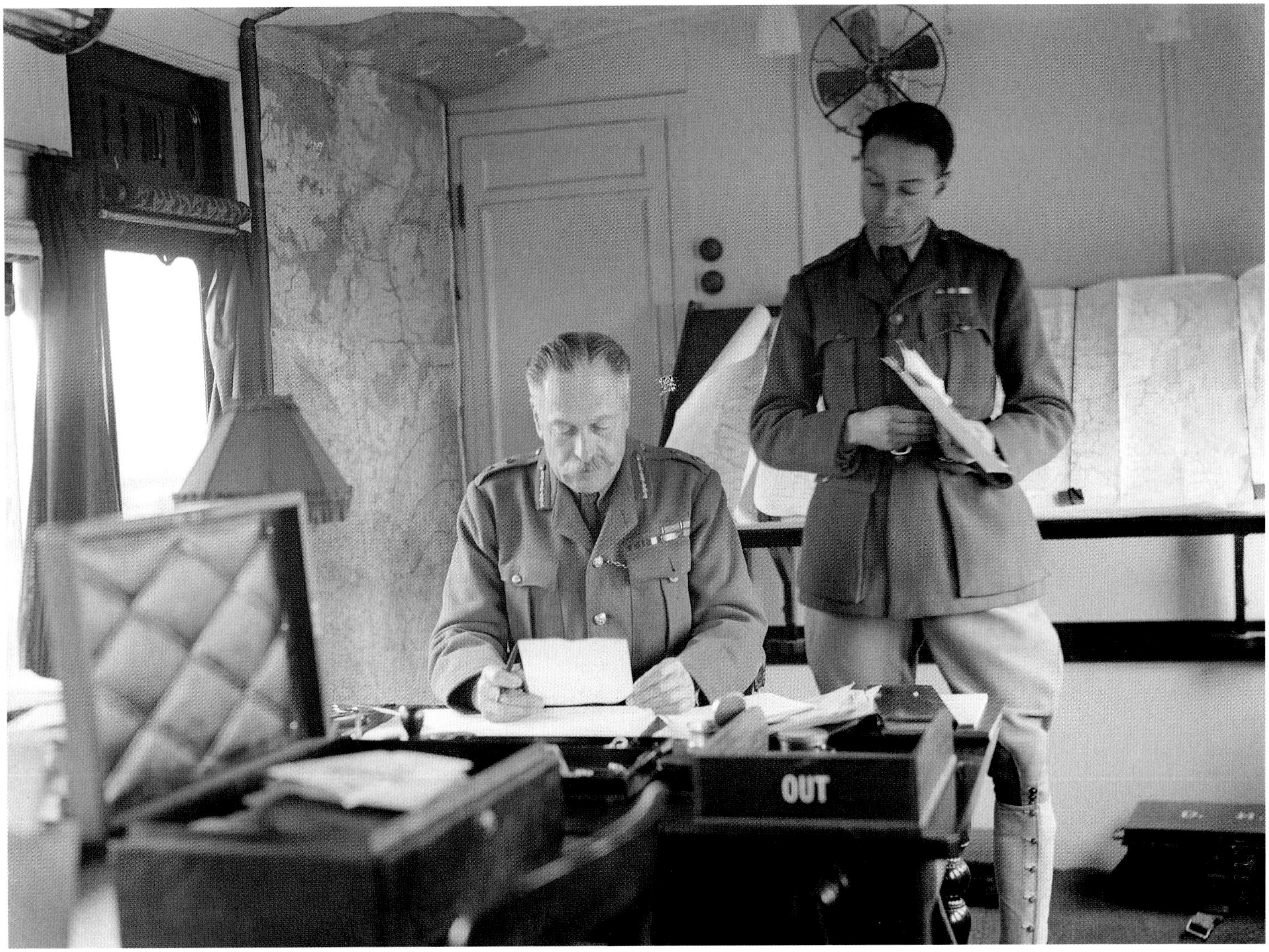

British Field Marshal Douglas Haig and Second Lieutenant Philip Sassoon, his private secretary, photographed during World War I by Ernest Brooks, London, Imperial War Museums.

fluent in French, and his Rothschild relations in France certainly contributed to Haig's table at Pas-de-Calais, where they were headquartered. It was Philip who facilitated the visit of artists John Singer Sargent, William Orpen, Henry Tonks, and William Rothenstein to the front to portray the horrors of war. Orpen would later express his gratitude in the preface to his published war journal for the "opportunity that was given to me to look and see the fighting man, and to learn to revere him and worship him—that is the only serious thing."[3] Sargent's dramatic canvas *Ruined Cathedral at Arras* was later acquired by Philip and copied by Churchill, an amateur painter and his frequent guest, while Rothenstein's devastated landscapes would become emblematic of the magnitude of human loss.

OPPOSITE
Philip de László, *Sir Philip Sassoon*, 1915, oil in canvas, 35 × 28 in. (88.9 × 71.2 cm), Norfolk, UK, Houghton Hall Collection.

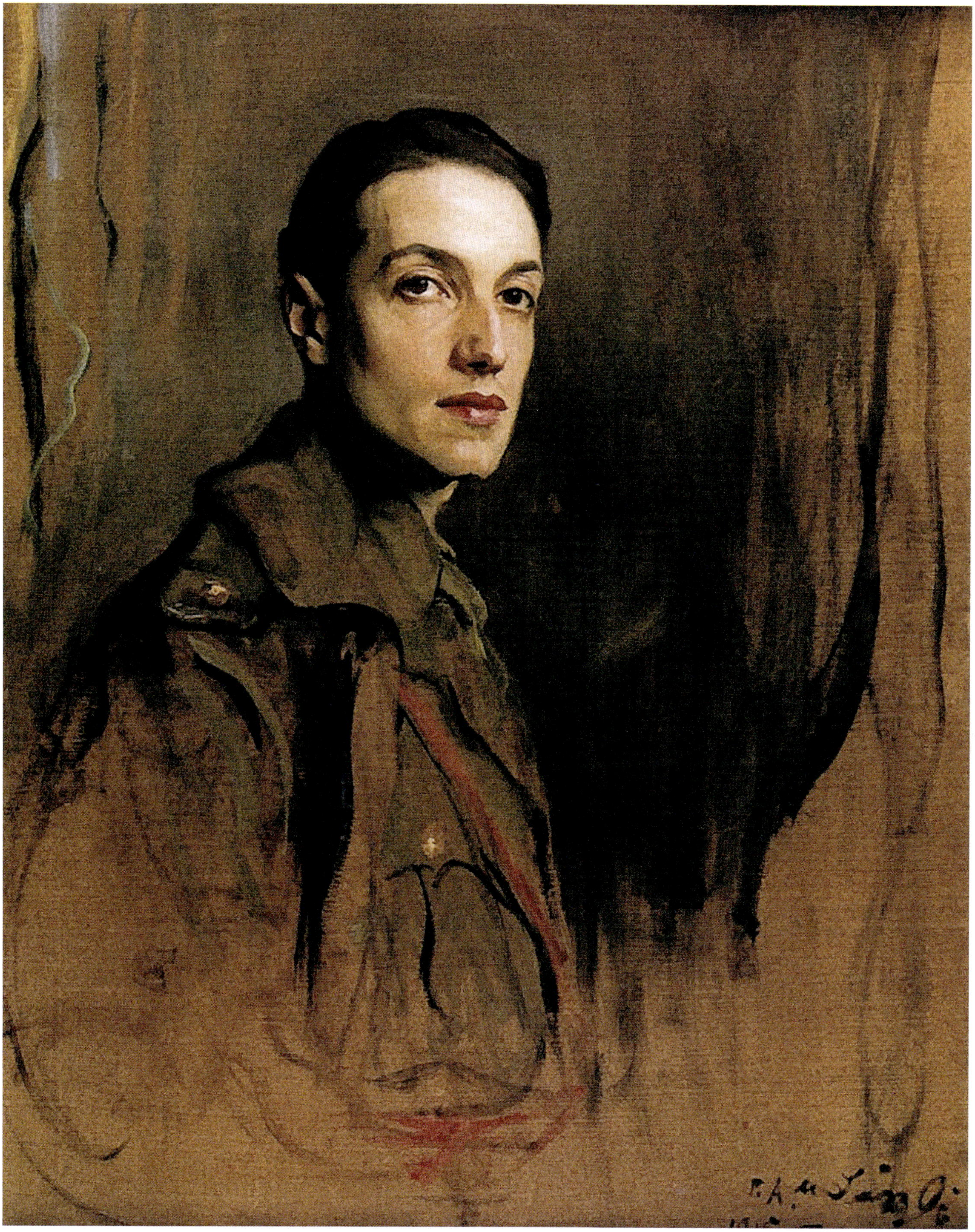

William Orpen, *Man with a Cigarette,* 1917, pencil, chalk, and watercolor on paper, 23 × 17½ in. (58.4 × 44.4 cm), London, Imperial War Museums.

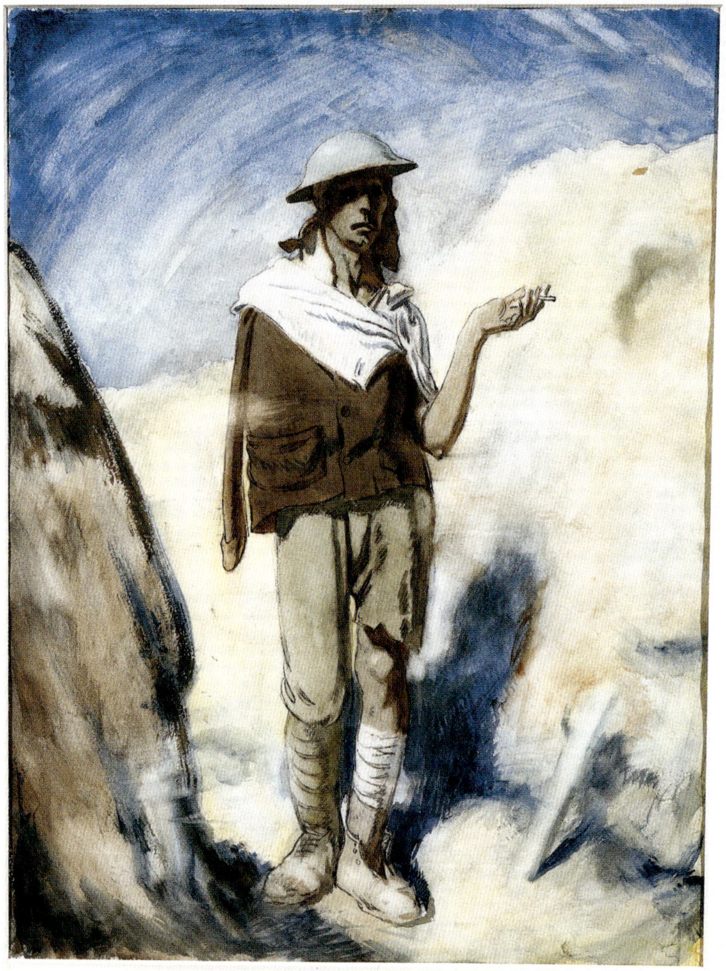

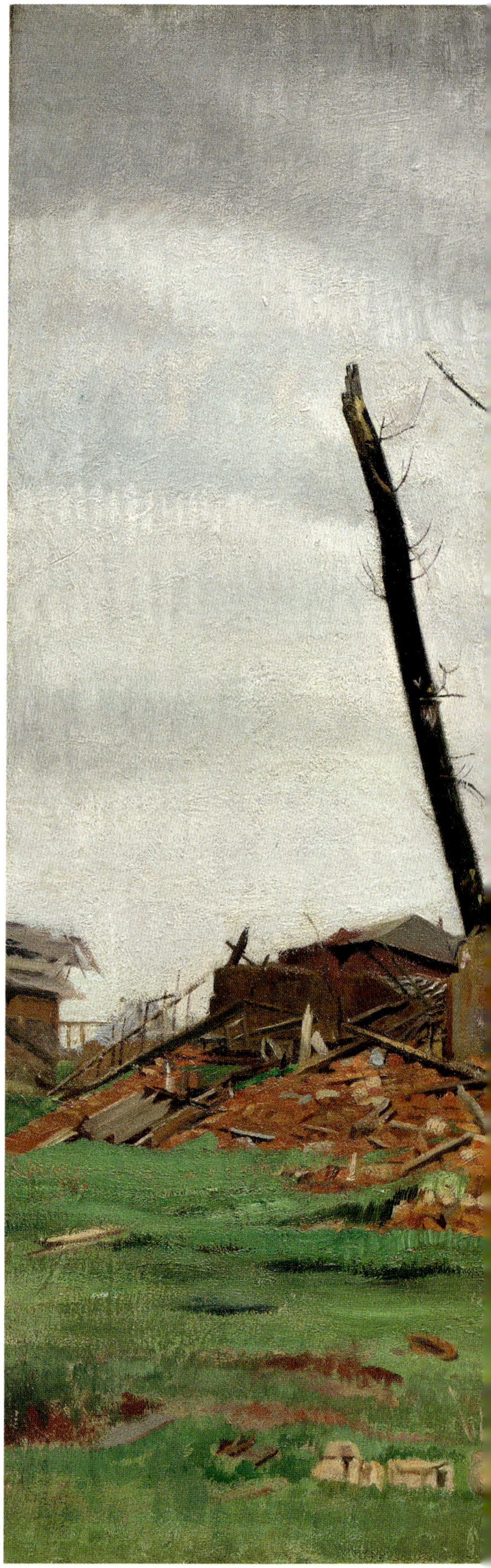

BELOW
Henry Tonks, *An Underground Casualty Clearing Station, Arras, France,* August 1, 1918, oil on canvas, 22⅛ × 28⅛ in. (56.3 × 71.6 cm), London, Imperial War Museums. Near the end of the war, Philip Sassoon enabled Tonks and John Singer Sargent to visit the Western Front as war artists. The painters toured the area from July to October 1918. Tonks, who had been trained as a doctor, depicted the wounded with stark realism.

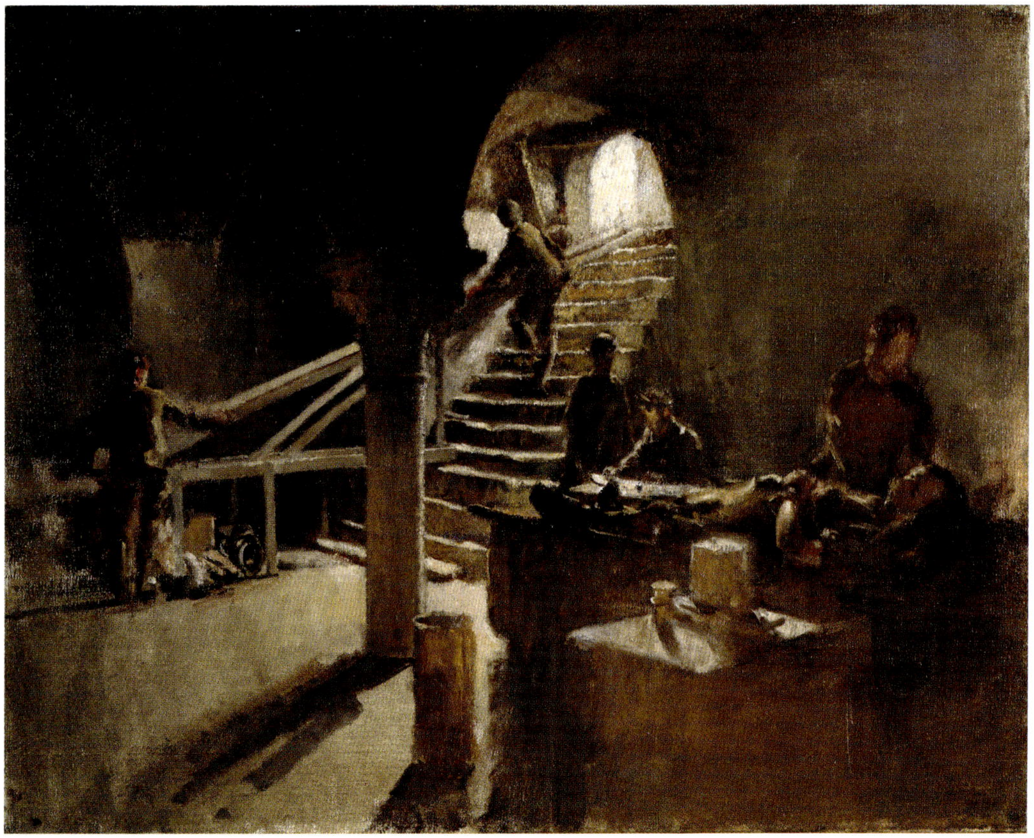

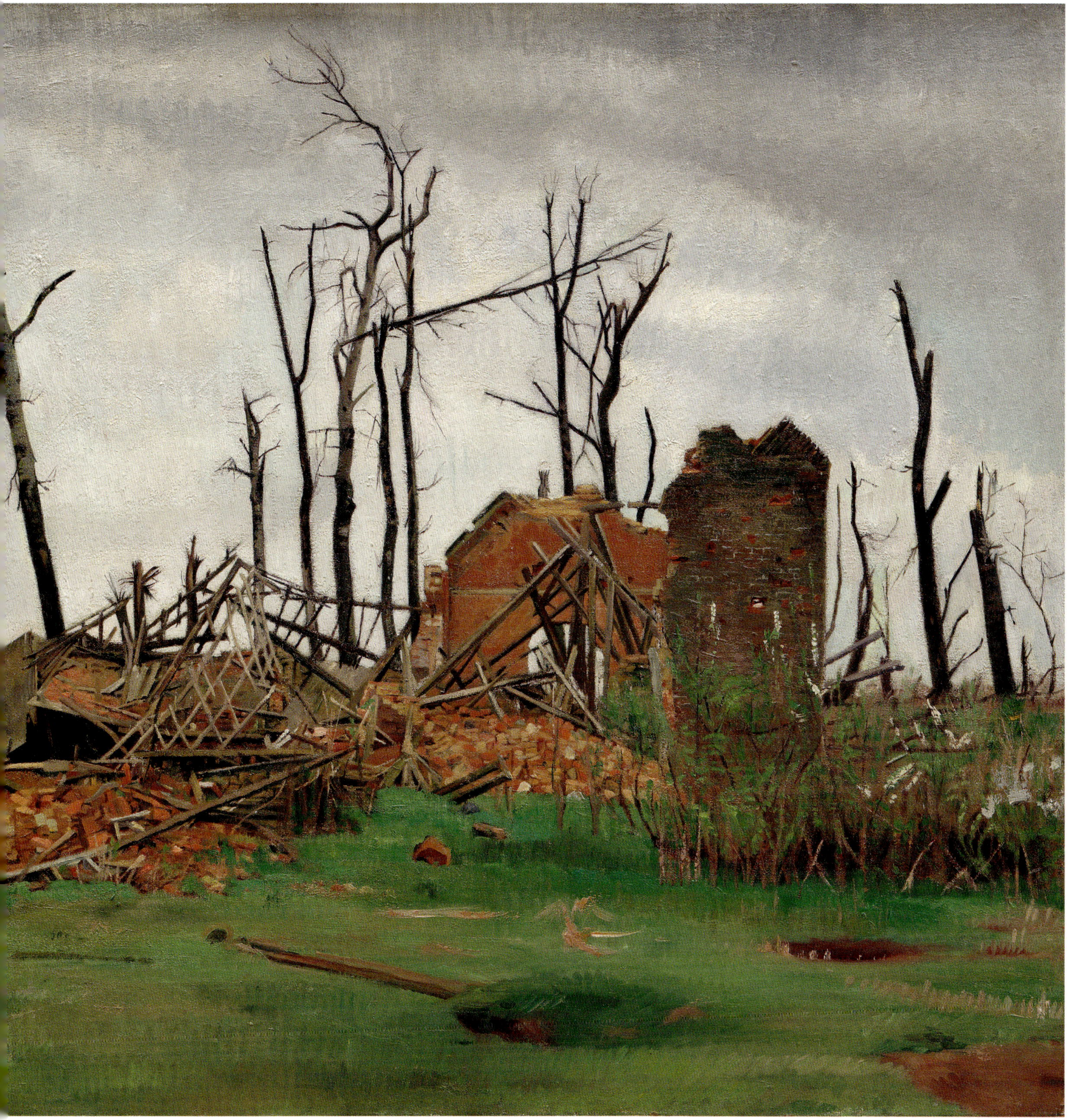

William Rothenstein, *Ruins at the Front,* 1918, oil on canvas, 29⅞ × 40⅛ in. (76 × 102 cm), London, Imperial War Museums.

During World War I, Rothenstein gained access to the front to record the devastation firsthand with the help of Philip Sassoon.

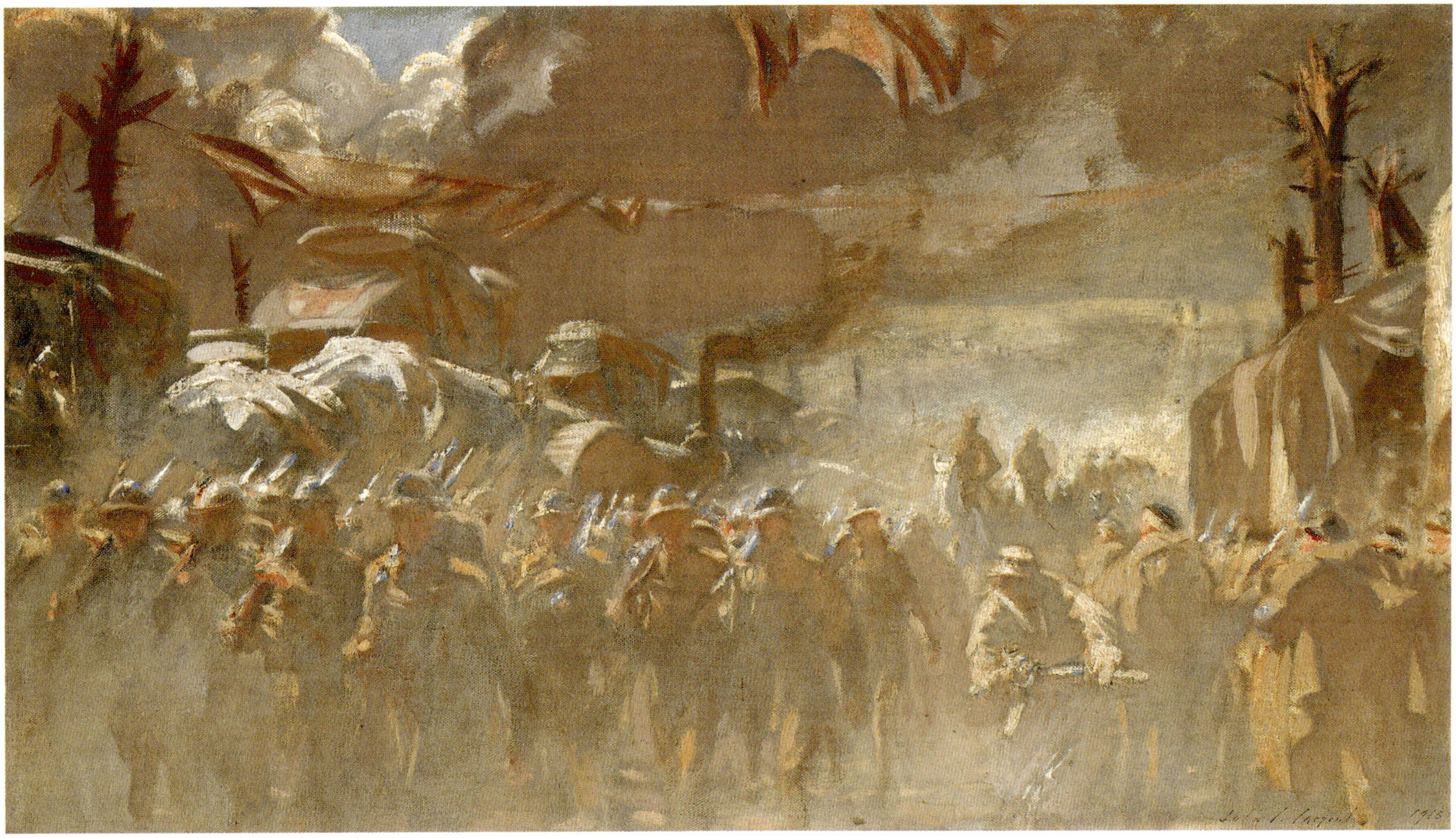

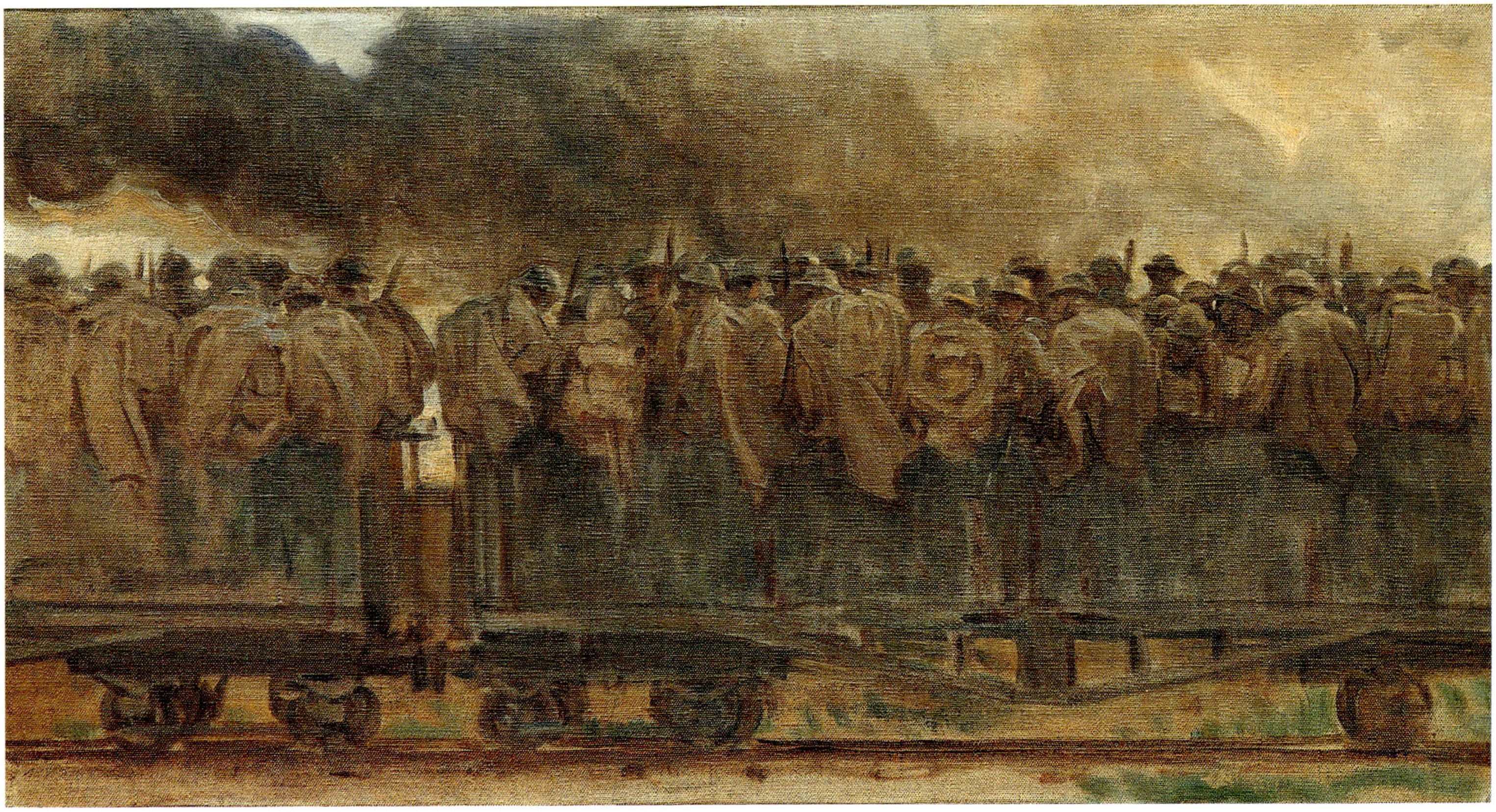

OPPOSITE
John Singer Sargent, *The Road*, 1918, oil on canvas, 15 × 26½ in. (38.1 × 67.3 cm), Boston, Museum of Fine Arts, the Hayden Collection—Charles Henry Hayden Fund.

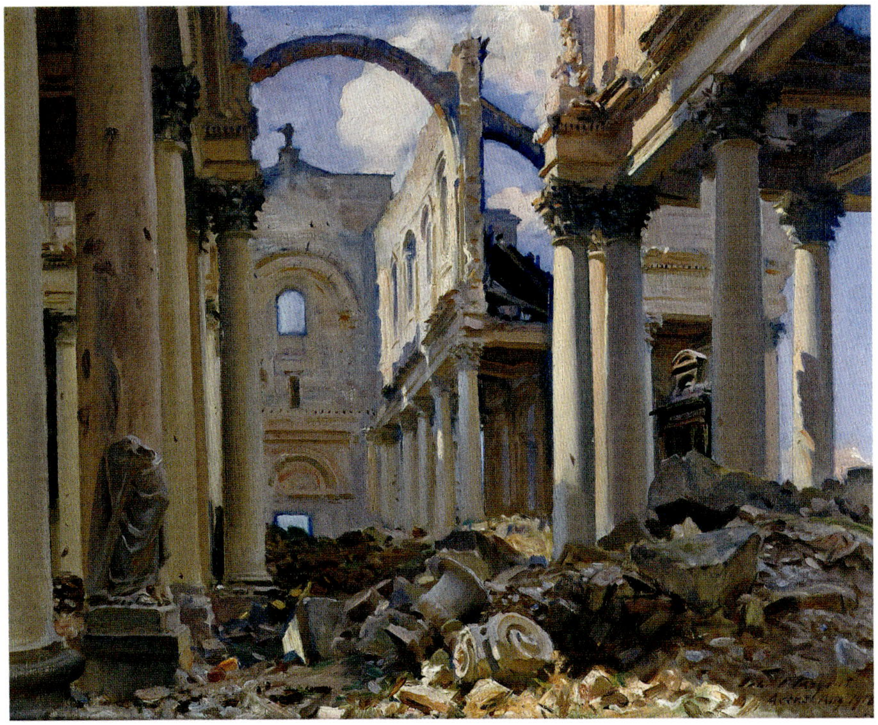

John Singer Sargent, *Ruined Cathedral at Arras,* 1918, oil on canvas, 21½ × 27½ in. (54.6 × 70 cm), Norfolk, UK, Houghton Hall Collection, formerly in the Philip Sassoon Collection.

OPPOSITE
John Singer Sargent, study for *Gassed*, 1918, oil on canvas, 14½ × 27¾ in. (36.8 × 70.5 cm), Norfolk, UK, Houghton Hall Collection, formerly in the Philip Sassoon Collection. *Gassed*, one of the most emblematic artworks of World War I, captures the horror and misery of soldiers blinded by mustard gas. Together with Henry Tonks, Sargent witnessed the aftermath of a gas attack in August 1918.

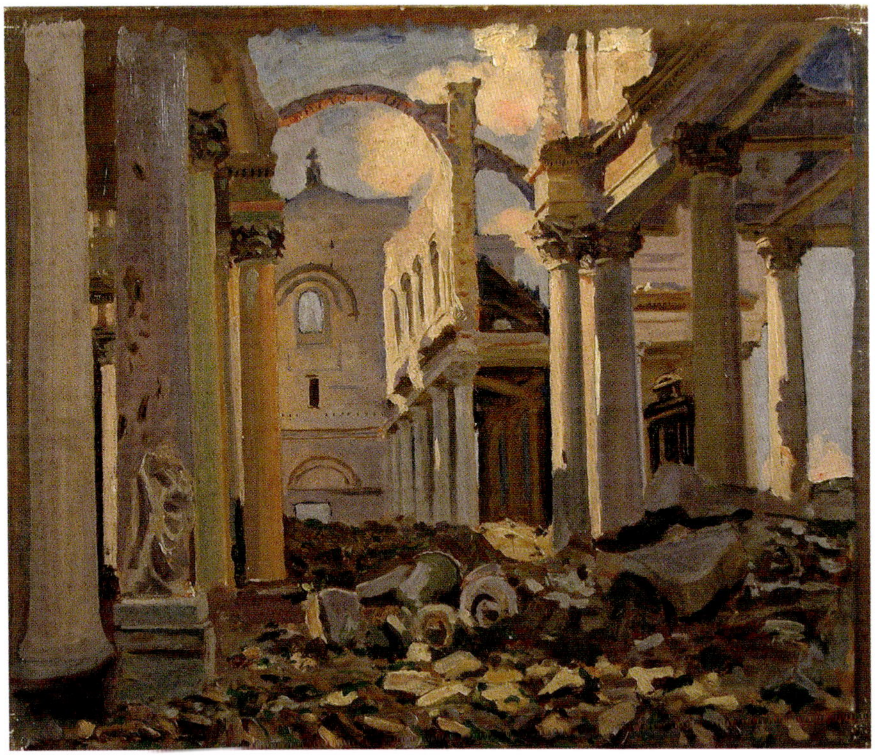

Winston Churchill, *Ruins of the Cathedral of St. Vaast, Arras, 1918* (after John Singer Sargent), 1920s, oil on canvas, 25 × 30 in. (63.5 × 76.2 cm), Chartwell, Kent, UK, National Trust.

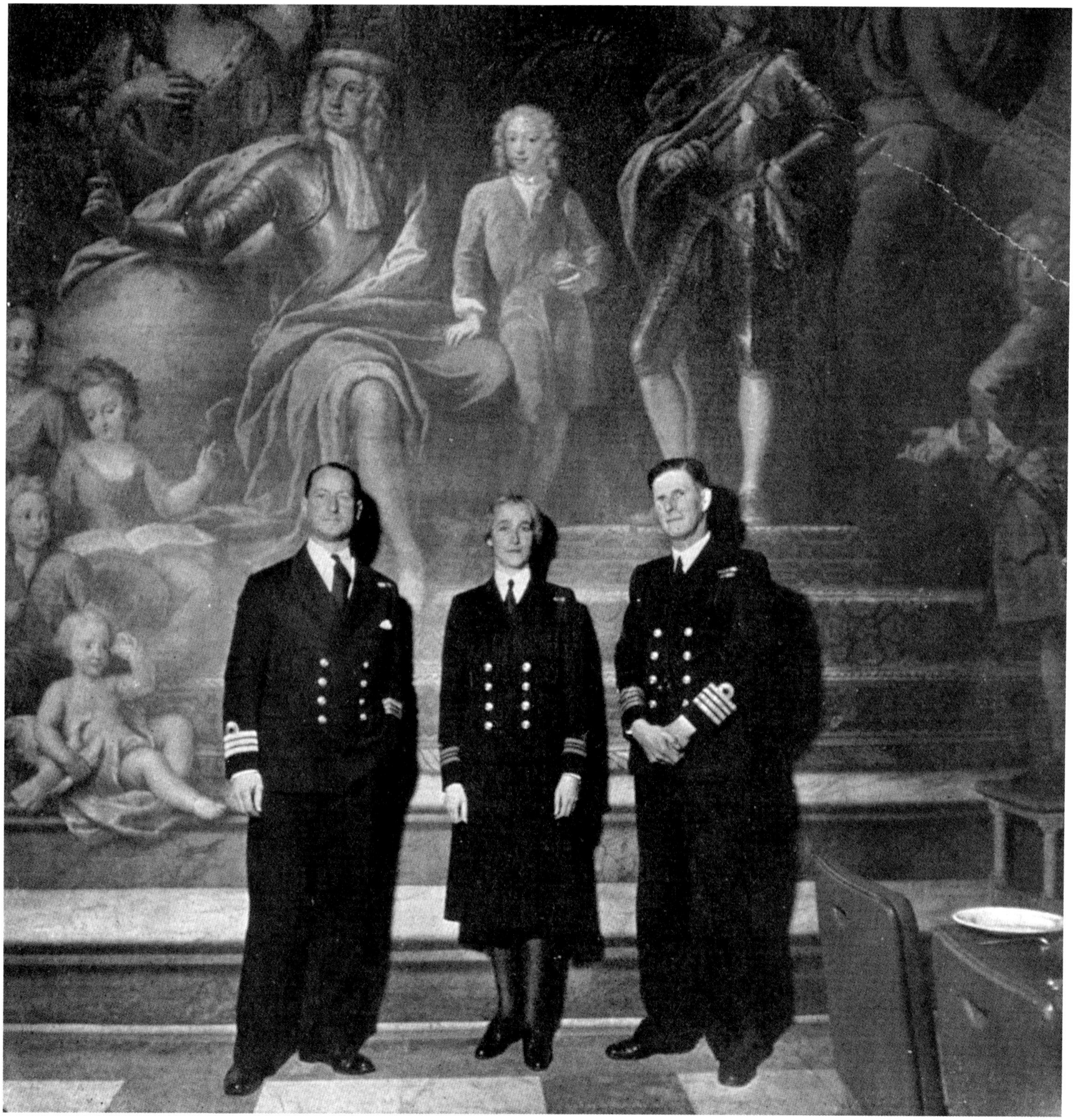

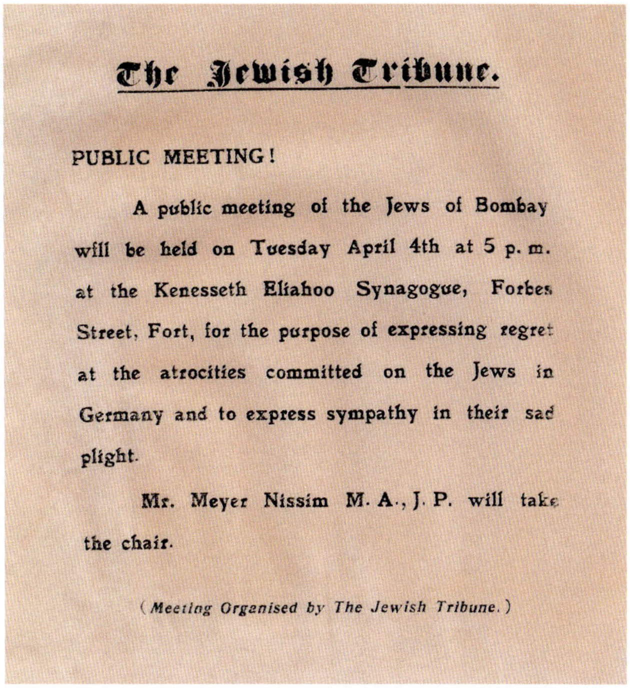

The Jewish Tribune.

PUBLIC MEETING!

A public meeting of the Jews of Bombay will be held on Tuesday April 4th at 5 p. m. at the Kenesseth Eliahoo Synagogue, Forbes Street, Fort, for the purpose of expressing regret at the atrocities committed on the Jews in Germany and to express sympathy in their sad plight.

Mr. Meyer Nissim M. A., J. P. will take the chair.

(*Meeting Organised by The Jewish Tribune.*)

Announcement of a meeting at the Keneseth Eliyahoo Synagogue in Mumbai, convened by Meyer Nissim, great-grandson of Albert Abdullah Sassoon, and organized by *The Jewish Tribune*, to rally support for the Jews of Germany, 1933.

OPPOSITE
Sybil Sassoon, Lady Cholmondeley, Chief Officer, WRNS, with Captain J. C. Davis, RN, OBE, and Captain of the College, and Commander J. R. d'Oyly, RN, in Sir James Thornhill's Painted Hall, photographed by Cecil Beaton, published in *Country Life*, April 26, 1941.

During World War II, the Sassoons contributed to the war effort in various ways. Several of the men enlisted; the women signed up to help, including Sybil Cholmondeley, who served as chief staff officer in the WRNS from 1939 to 1946. Louise became the first Jewish woman to receive the Commander of the Order of the British Empire for her work.[4] In Shanghai, Victor repeatedly gave large sums to help the British War Fund, donating one million dollars in 1939 to be paid in installments every month. He also sold sapphires and jade necklaces to help buy more fighter planes for the British.[5] Like Philip and Victor, Percival believed in a strong air force, and in 1940, he spent a year in the United States studying aircraft production. In 1941, on his way to India, Percival was in Shanghai at the time of the attack on Pearl Harbor on December 7. Captured by the Japanese, he spent nine months under house arrest before being exchanged for Japanese prisoners in Mozambique.

But World War II would also show the family's deep concern for the plight of their fellow Jews. When Adolf Hitler became chancellor of Germany in 1933, the Sassoons in London, Mumbai, Kolkata, and Shanghai sprang into action, donating substantial funds to assist Jewish refugees. When the Council for German Jewry began to raise money for children in 1938, Mozelle and her nephew Victor donated £25,000, a huge sum at the time. A year later, Christie's had a sale to aid Lord Baldwin's Fund for Refugees, which helped finance the Kindertransport. Philip, Sybil, and Hannah all gifted works of art to the sale, but Mozelle was the biggest donor and the chief buyer.[6] Her terracotta bust of a child by the eighteenth-century French sculptor Jean-Antoine Houdon fetched the highest price.

India and above all China were among the few countries that accepted Jewish refugees when almost all others closed their doors to them with stringent quotas. Roughly 2,000 made their way to India, mostly to Mumbai, Kolkata, and Chennai, where they were received and assisted by local Jewish communities. Largely from Austria and Germany, the refugees included physicians, engineers, merchants, industrialists, musicians, artists, and filmmakers, who would make major contributions to India. In Mumbai, several Sassoon buildings were used to organize support for Jewish evacuees, including the Keneseth Eliyahoo Synagogue and the E. D. Sassoon building, the Indian headquarters of Victor's firm, E. D. Sassoon & Co., which helped the Jewish Relief Association. The Chinchpokli cemetery, founded by Elias David Sassoon, has many tombs of Ashkenazi refugees who arrived at this time. Meyer Nissim, a former mayor of Mumbai and great-grandson of Albert Abdullah Sassoon, helped drum up support for the refugees. When the Japanese attacked Pearl Harbor, Victor was in Mumbai and remained there for several months. As president of the Jewish Hospitality Committee, he maintained a strong presence in the city, funding several initiatives such as a Passover seder held in 1944 in one of the Baghdadi schools for 400 Jewish refugees and servicemen.[7]

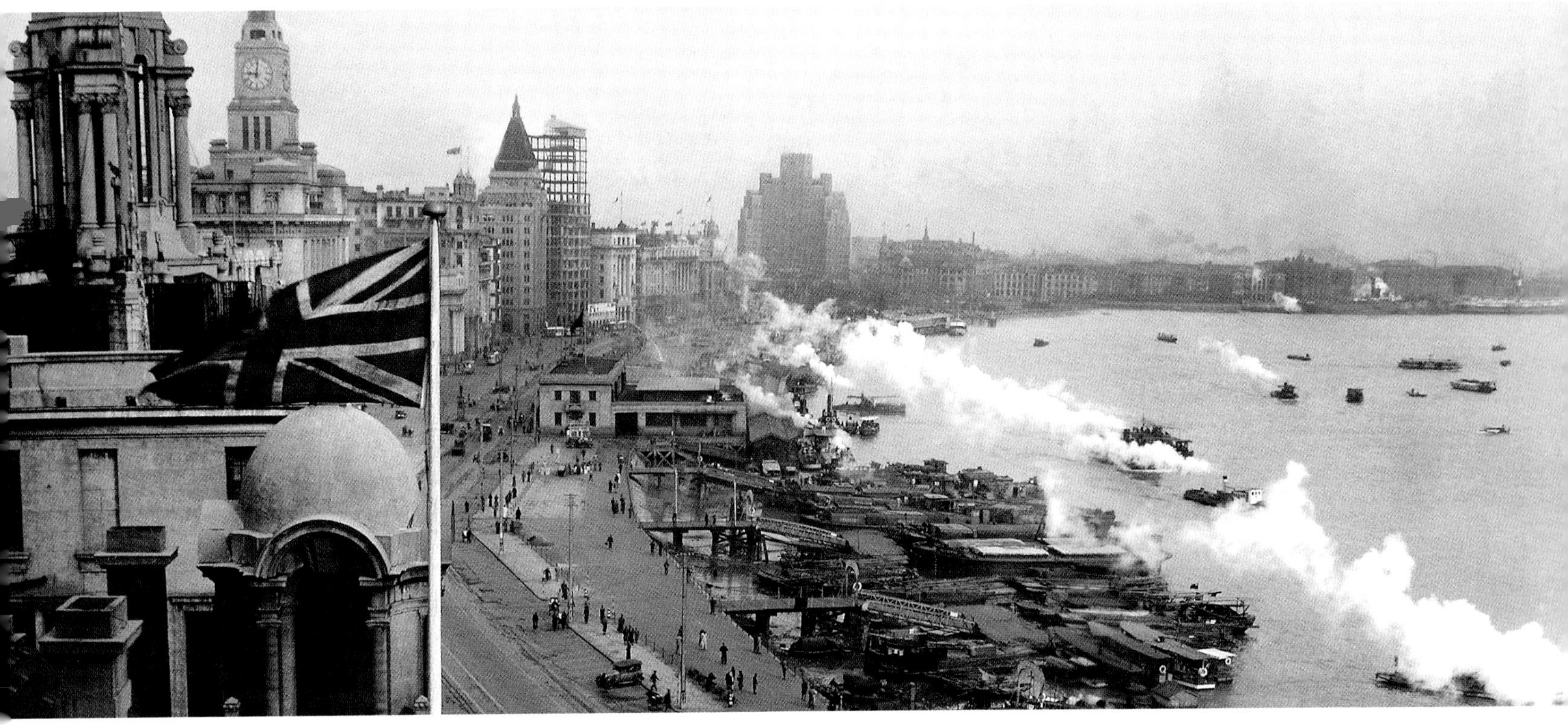

Shanghai offered a far more complicated situation. In a letter to Yvonne FitzRoy, the private secretary to the Marchioness of Reading, dated March 6, 1932, Victor described Shanghai under Japanese attack: "the actual scene of fighting looks like the ruins of Ypres," he wrote, alluding to the devastation inflicted on the Belgian city during World War I.[8] The Japanese would bombard Shanghai extensively in 1937. Almost two decades had elapsed since his flying accident, and though no longer fit for active service, Victor had found a new mission for his old photography hobby, capturing in film and photo the political situation in Shanghai. Although they did not occupy the International Settlement and the French Concession, the Japanese effectively ruled the city. When the Jewish community asked for funds from abroad to help refugees whose homes and businesses had been destroyed, several high-standing members of Jewish organizations overseas held that help was not necessary, given the wealth of the community. David Solomon Sassoon, among others, responded that the Jews of Shanghai were not "suffering any pecuniary difficulties." Yet a year earlier, when Rabbi Solomon David Sassoon, David Solomon's son, approached Victor for help with money for Jewish causes, Victor wrote four checks of £1,000, a substantial sum.[9]

The first significant wave of Jewish refugees from Germany began to arrive in 1938 and received a warm welcome from the local Baghdadi Jewish community. As the numbers of refugees from all parts of Central Europe escalated sharply, they became a cause of concern among those already living in the International Settlement. The opposition they faced "took on the character of a universal conspiracy," wrote David Kranzler, as "the governments of the United States, Britain and France, and their major Jewish organizations, such as the American Jewish Joint Distribution Committee and HICEM-HIAS [Hebrew Immigrant Aid Society], attempted to curtail the flight of Jews from Germany to Shanghai."[10] At the Evian conference in July 1938, delegates from thirty-two countries refused to let in more Jewish refugees, with the exception of the Dominican Republic. In May of that year, Victor had visited President Getúlio Vargas in Brazil to interest him in a scheme of settling Central European Jews in that country, but Vargas was not interested.[11]

In Shanghai, fear of the economic consequences of the influx of refugees came from the International Settlement, the Municipal Council, and the Jewish community, split by different cultural and religious backgrounds. The city was overwhelmed by the growing number of new arrivals. There was also fear that the stream of immigrants would lead to anti-Jewish sentiment. Jewish leaders, including Victor, worked with Jewish organizations in other countries, local

The Bund in Shanghai, c. 1936 or 1937, seen from the roof of the Asiatic Petroleum Building, photograph by Leonard Dombroski. The Bund, a word of Indo-Persian derivation possibly introduced by Baghdadi Jews, designates the waterfront or embankment along the treaty ports, lined with imposing buildings.

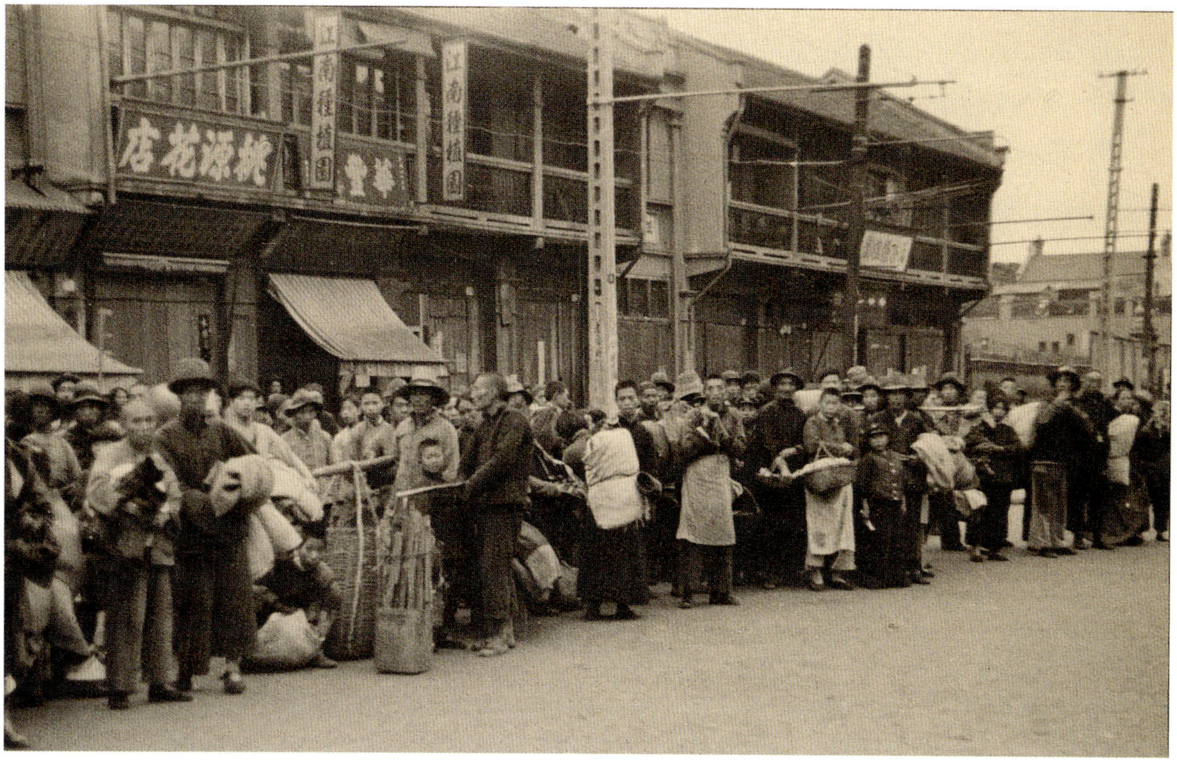

Chinese crowds in Shanghai, photographed by Victor Sassoon in 1937, from his album "China and Second Sino-Japanese War, 1937–1939," Sir Ellice Victor Elias Sassoon Papers and Photographs, Dallas, Southern Methodist University, DeGolyer Library.

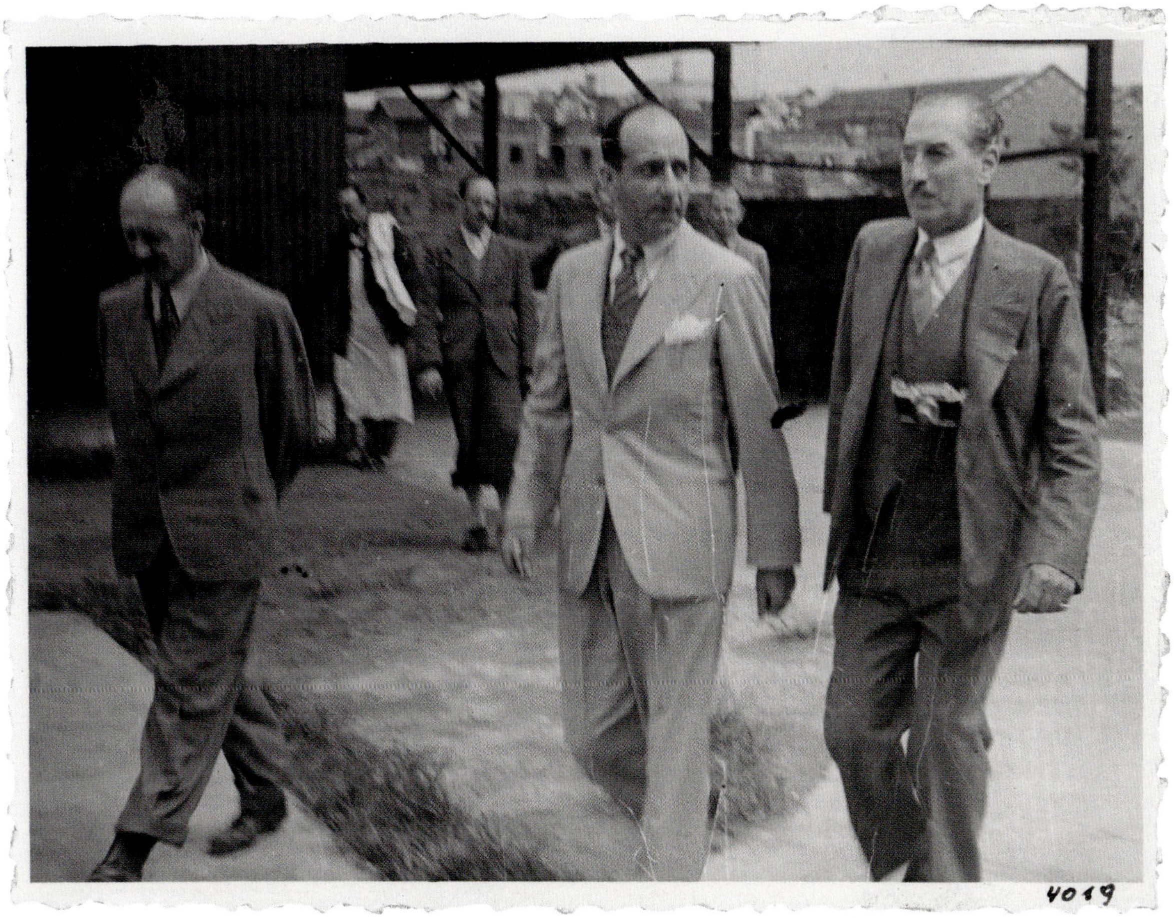

Ellis Hayim, center, and Victor Sassoon, with his camera, right, Shanghai, c. 1940, photographed by D. St. Koenig (?), New York, American Jewish Joint Distribution Committee Archive. Ellis Hayim was a member of a Baghdadi Jewish family that had made its way to China via India for business. Both men contributed funds to assist Jewish refugees from Nazi Europe in Shanghai.

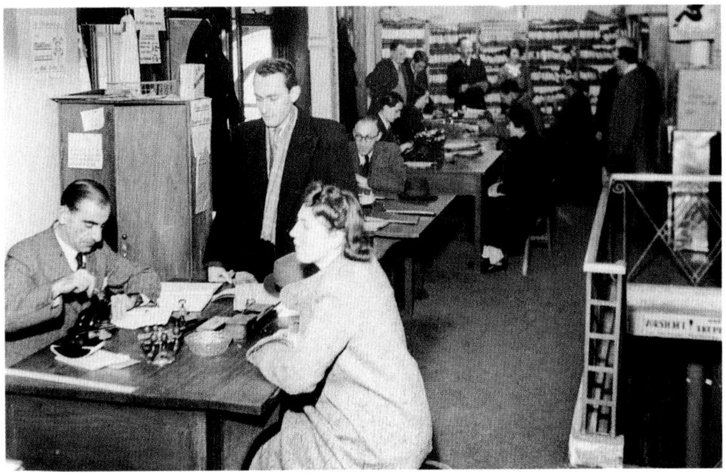

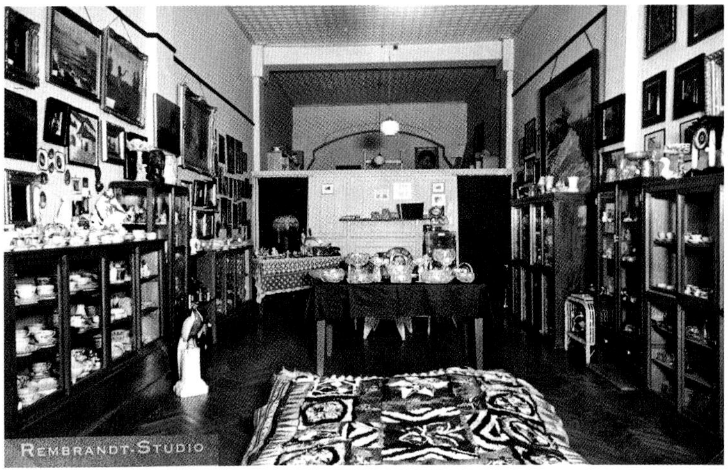

consular authorities, and even the Japanese to curtail further immigration.[12]

In the meantime, thousands had to be housed and fed. Wealthy Baghdadi Jews (Victor Sassoon, the Kadoories, the Hayims, the Ezras, the Abrahams) and several others raised funds to support the Jews who arrived from Europe with the help of many other Shanghai residents such as Michael Speelman and Paul Komor. Victor set aside the first floor of his Embankment Building to register, feed, and temporarily house new arrivals, even though it lacked the requisite sanitary facilities. As this was hardly sufficient for the influx of refugees, he allocated his former Aeroconcrete Company for bachelors and a few couples. At the luxurious Sassoon House, several offices were assigned to the International Committee for European Immigrants. There was also a thrift shop where refugees could sell valuables. As the International Settlement feared that highly educated Jews arriving from Europe might take jobs away from established foreigners, Victor co-founded the International Committee for Granting Relief to European Refugees in August 1938, giving $150,000 to help them open businesses of their own. For the Ward Road Heim, which housed 1,200 refugees, he donated bales of cotton for sheets. He also gave $10,000 a month to feed the refugee children in need. Exactly a year later, in August 1939, the Japanese forbade the entry of more immigrants.[13]

Pearl Harbor would change the situation of the refugees dramatically. All foreigners were rounded up and interned. In 1943, the stateless refugees—Germany had withdrawn nationality from all Jews—were consigned to Hongkou (formerly Hongkew), a poor residential area that had been partly destroyed during the hostilities of 1937. Known as the Shanghai Ghetto, it was home to 100,000 Chinese, many of whom lived in the same buildings as the 18,000 Jewish refugees.[14] Arthur Rothstein, an American Jewish photographer, had been serving in the U.S. Army in China during World War II. In 1946 he became chief photographer for the United Nations Relief and Rehabilitation Administration and recorded the organization's humanitarian efforts in postwar China. Through his stark images of the living conditions in Hongkou, Rothstein sought to raise awareness of the plight of his fellow Jews whose status at war's end had changed from "stateless refugees" to "displaced persons."

Nothing bears better testimony to the loyalty of the Sassoons to British endurance and to Jewish survival than their multiple contributions during these tragic years when both were at their greatest risk. With the end of the Raj in 1947, many of the Sassoons remaining in Mumbai and Kolkata began to depart for England, and in 1948, just before the Communist takeover in China, Victor left Shanghai for good. Through the prism of two world wars and the Holocaust, the journey of the Sassoon family became intertwined with global events unimaginable when David Sassoon left Baghdad in 1830. The long journey of a Baghdadi Jewish family that had been forced to leave the ancestral shores of the River Tigris, sought haven along the waters of the Indian Ocean, and navigated the perilous currents of the Pearl River delta in China, was gradually coming to an end along the Thames.

ABOVE LEFT
Members of the International Committee for European Immigrants in Shanghai at work in their office at Sassoon House, Washington, DC, United States Holocaust Memorial Museum, courtesy of Valerie S. Komor.

ABOVE RIGHT
The interior of the thrift shop set up at Sassoon House to facilitate the sale of personal property owned by Jewish refugees. Both images c. 1938–42, from a photograph album prepared for Paul Komor, Honorary Consul for Hungary in Shanghai, who was secretary of the committee, Washington, DC, United States Holocaust Memorial Museum, courtesy of Valerie S. Komor. The International Committee was founded in August 1938 with the financial help of Victor Sassoon to support Jews seeking haven in Shanghai as war approached in Europe.

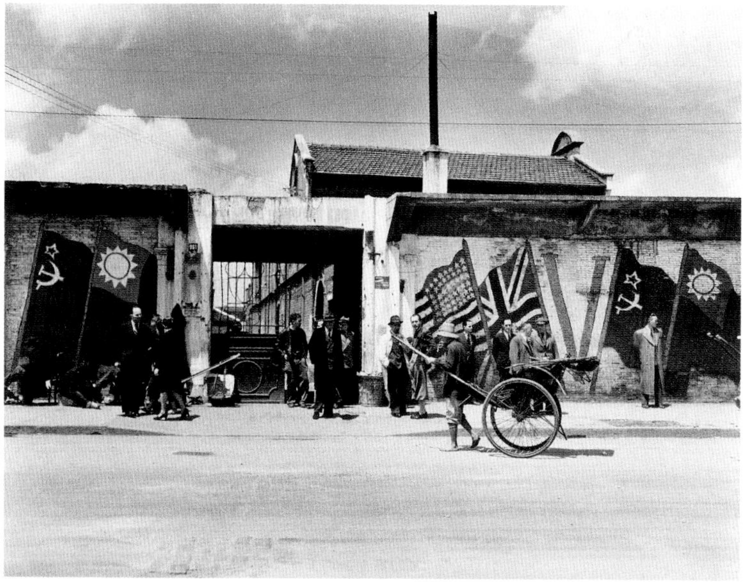

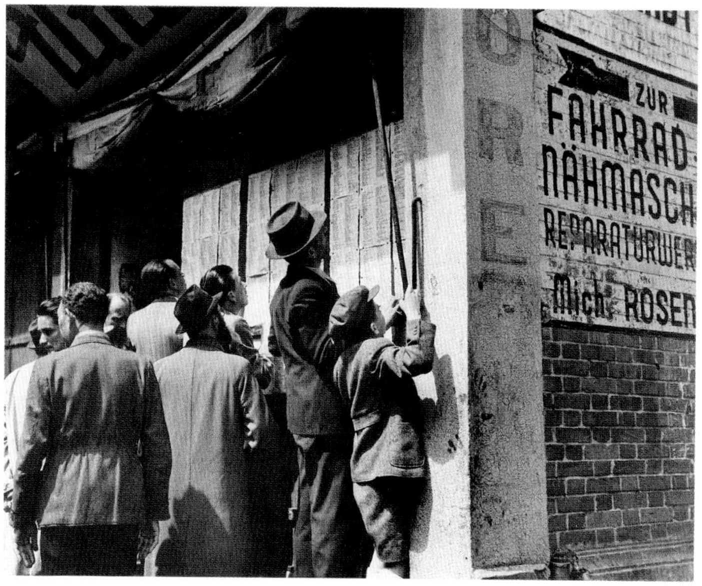

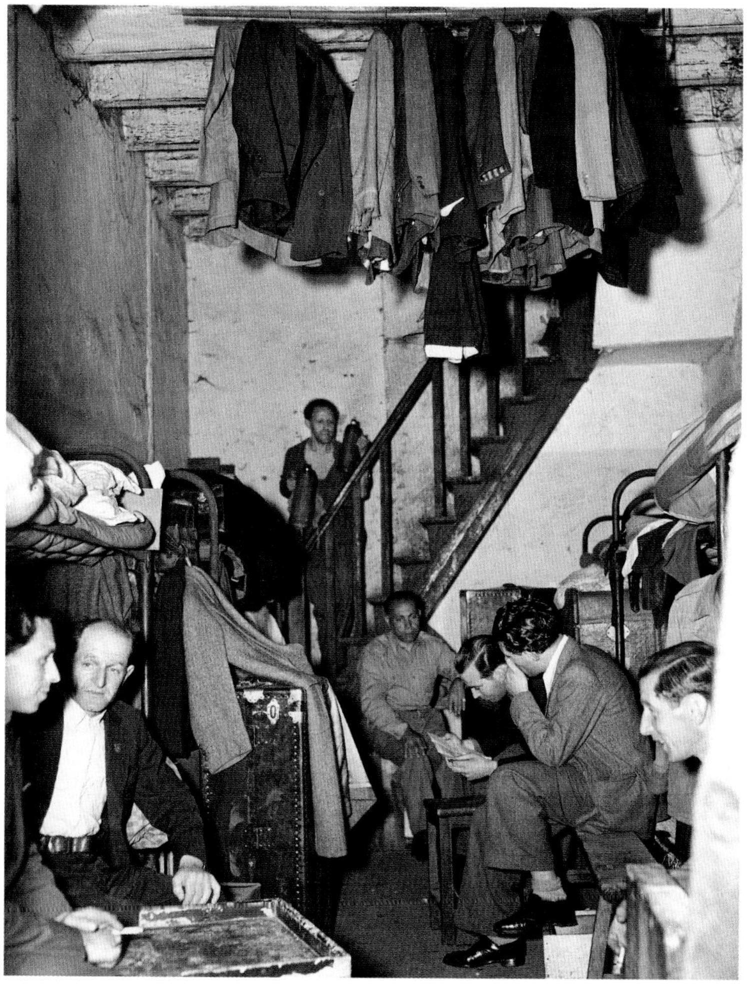

In 1946 Arthur Rothstein photographed the crowded refugee camp at Hongkou (formerly Hongkew), a district of Shanghai, adding notes about each image.

TOP LEFT
The entrance to the camp, with the photographer's comment, "Entrance to Hongkew refugee camp is decorated with flags of China, Russia, England and America. The flags were painted by refugee artists immediately after V–J Day."

TOP RIGHT
Refugees look at a list of survivors, with Rothstein's inscription, "Looking anxiously for the names of those relatives and friends who may have survived Hitler's death houses in Europe are these refugees who escaped to Shanghai in time. They are now awaiting repatriation or a transfer to another country. In the meantime, UNRRA [the United Nations Relief and Rehabilitation Administration] is helping to care for them."

LEFT
"Jammed into eight camps, German and Austrian refugees live out of steamer trunks. Clothing is hung from the ceiling to save space. UNRRA has erected Quonset huts to alleviate the housing shortage." New York, Jewish Museum, gift of the Arthur Rothstein Family.

NOTES

Introduction

A word on Indian and Chinese names and terms: except in quotations we have used standard pinyin romanization of Chinese names. Similarly, Indian place names are modernized and the older spellings offered in parentheses where useful. This is a colonial story told in a postcolonial context and it bears noting that some of the current approaches to transliteration are not without their own colonialist or imperialist undercurrents.

1. James Clifford, "Diasporas," *Cultural Anthropology* 9, no. 3 (1994): 314.

2. David Solomon Sassoon, the famed bibliophile and collector of Hebrew manuscripts, who researched his family extensively, refutes categorically the theory of a Sephardic origin. See David Solomon Sassoon, *Ohel Dawid: Descriptive Catalogue of the Hebrew and Samaritan Manuscripts in the Sassoon Library, London* (London: Oxford University Press, 1932), 585, no. 800 (hereafter *Ohel Dawid*). On David Solomon's visit to Baghdad in 1910, see David Solomon Sassoon, *Masa' Bavel: Be-tseruf 'inyanim le-toldot ha-ḳehilah ha-Yehudit be-Bagdad*, ed. Meir Benayahu (Jerusalem: Azriel, 1954–55), 126 (hereafter *Masa*). For the ketubbah, see *Ohel Dawid*, 377, no. 204, there dated 1765 instead of 1764 (the wedding was held on 1 Tevet 5525=December 25, 1764). See also *Masa*, 203–5; David Solomon Sassoon, *A History of the Jews in Baghdad* (Letchworth: S. D. Sassoon, 1949; reprint ed., Simon Wallenberg Press, 2006) (hereafter *History*), 116–18. The wedding must have been a lavish affair judging by the extraordinary amount of jewelry and other articles itemized as part of the dowry in the *tosefet ketubbah* or codicil, written in Arabic.

3. See the pioneering work of Yaron Ben-Naeh, "The Sassoon Family: Jewish Tujjars between East and West in the Nineteenth Century," lecture delivered at the International Conference on Commercial Networks, University of Haifa, June 5–7, 2006.

4. Maisie Meyer, "Baghdadi Jewish Merchants in Shanghai and the Opium Trade," *Jewish Culture and History* 2, no. 1 (1999): 60–61. For a recent in-depth study of the family's economic, commercial, and financial history, see Joseph Sassoon, *The Global Merchants: The Enterprise and Extravagance of the Sassoon Dynasty* (London: Allen Lane, 2022; hereafter, *Global Merchants*).

5. *Ohel Dawid*, 401, no. 538. The document is reproduced in Rachel Manasseh, *Baghdadian Jews of Bombay: Their Life and Achievements; A Personal and Historical Account* (Great Neck, NY: Midrash Ben Ish Hai, 2013), 57.

6. For the prayer, see *Ohel Dawid*, 447, no. 475. The text was microfilmed; see https://www.nli.org.il/en/manuscripts/NNL_ALEPH000133991/NLI. We are grateful to Prof. Yaron Ben-Naeh at the Hebrew University of Jerusalem for his invaluable help with the research of this unique text. For justification of the opium trade, investigation of the trade, and the moral issues surrounding it, see *Global Merchants*, 44–45, 163–66, 178–80, 189, 228–30. See also Meyer, "Baghdadi."

7. See *Global Merchants*, 39.

8. *Ohel Dawid*, 576–77, no. 12.

9. These points are raised in Linda Colley, "How British Is It?" *New York Review of Books*, September 23, 2021, 36.

Chapter 1: From Commissioners to Collectors

1. The three Torah cases are reproduced in *Masa*, plates 11–12. See also *Masa*, 123–25, 208; David Solomon Sassoon, "The History of the Jews in Basra," *The Jewish Quarterly Review* 17, no. 4 (April 1927): 429 (hereafter "Basra"); and *Ohel Dawid*, 570, no. 5. For an in-depth study on the sacred graves in Iraq, see Avraham Ben-Ya'akov, *Kevarim kedoshim be-Vavel Te'urim shel ḳivre ishim mi-tekufat ha-Tanakh, ha-Talmud veha-ge'onim* (Jerusalem: Hotsa'at Mosad ha-Rav Ḳuḳ, 1973). For the scrolls in memory of Reuben and Amam, see *Ohel Dawid*, 578–79, no. 16. On David Salomon's visit to Baghdad, see *Masa*, 123–25.

2. *Masa*, 129 and n. 117.

3. Reading the date on the pair of finials has proved challenging. The pair was offered for sale at Sotheby's Tel Aviv, *A Collection from the Sassoon Family Estate*, October 25 and 27, 2000, 33, and dated there to 1760. Later, the date was revised to c. 1742. We would like to thank Sharon Weiser-Ferguson, senior curator in the Jack, Joseph, and Morton Mandel Wing for Jewish Art and Life, at the Israel Museum, Jerusalem, for reexamining the finials and providing us with a confirmed 1741/42 date. The single finial was sold at Sotheby's Tel Aviv, *A Collection from the Sassoon Family Estate*, October 25 and 27, 2000, 32. On the curtain, see *History*, 167; Avraham Ben-Ya'akov, *Perakim be-toldot Yehude Bavel: Korot 'anaf ehad mi-mishpahat Sason ha-Bagdadit* (Jerusalem: Olam ha-Sefer ha-Torani, 1989), 1:170 (hereafter *Perakim*).

4. On the pilgrimage standard, see *Ohel Dawid*, 569, and "Basra," 431. On the ceremony, see *Masa*, 228–29, and for the miracle, see "Basra," 430. On the embroidered cover, see *Ohel Dawid*, 546, no. 882; 568–69, Inscriptions, no. 4; and *Masa*, 160.

5. For a view of the synagogue and for its dedicatory inscriptions, see *Masa*, 266 and 154, and *Ohel Dawid*, 568, Inscriptions, no. 4. In *Masa* (p. 156) David Solomon writes: "On Shabbat morning the second of Kislev [5671] (=December 3, 1910) we went to the David Sassoon synagogue where I was given to read the *Maftir* [the section from the Prophets following the Torah reading]. The Torah portion was read from a Torah scroll donated by my great grandfather Sheikh Sassoon." No other mention is made of this Torah scroll and of whether it was kept in a decorated case. For a bequest by David Sassoon of a building to the Alliance Israélite of Baghdad, see *Global Merchants*, 107, 350n80, and *Alliance Israélite Universelle: Écoles de Bagdad*, Anniversary Album (1932). David Solomon Sassoon found the Alliance's curriculum too secular. When he was in Baghdad in 1910, he intended not to visit its schools but, without his knowledge, "they brought me to the school, which was a branch of the Alliance school in Baghdad. I saw a very strange spectacle. In one of the classes the pupils were learning the Hebrew Bible bare headed, from a teacher with a long beard, turban, and long coat." (*Masa*, 152). See also *History*, 171. The copy of *Sefer Zikhron Yerushalayim* was auctioned at Kestenbaum & Company, *Rare & Excellent Hebrew Printed Books: From the Library of Artur A. Marx*, June 17, 2021, 210. While the Sassoons contributed to religious causes in Ottoman Palestine, family members differed on their support of Zionism. See *Global Merchants*, 195–96, 238–39.

6. Rachel's baby, Elias, died on February 4, 1886. Rachel may have been familiar with Yemenite Jewish practices through her Yemenite Jewish housekeeper. See Avraham Ben-Yaakov, *Yehude Bavel ba-tefutsot* (Jerusalem: R. Mas, 1985), 83–84, n. 15 (hereafter *Yehude*). On the pilgrimage to Rabbi Shabazi's grave and synagogues to pray for offspring, see Haya Bar-Itzhak, *Israeli Folk Narratives: Settlement, Immigration, Ethnicity* (Detroit: Wayne State University Press, 2005), 51–53.

7. Mozelle Sassoon's diary is excerpted in "The Sassoons' Return Visit to Baghdad," *The Scribe* 74 (Autumn 2001), http://www.dangoor.com/74007.html. In the Sassoon collection was a copy of an 1883 decision by the Rabbinical Court of Baghdad "concerning the use of the Holy Scrolls belonging to Sheikh Sason b. Saleh b. David and Sheikh Mordecai b. David Hakkohen on special occasions in the Great Synagogue in Baghdad," stating the continuation of these privileges that had been contested by some community members (*Ohel Dawid*, 389, no. 211, item O; *Masa*, 126–27).

8. The set was auctioned at Sotheby's New York, *Sassoon: A Golden Legacy*, December 17, 2020, 38. See also *Perakim* 1: 123, 426–27, 653, 729. On Mozelle (Sassoon) Ezra's donation, see *Ohel Dawid*, 570, no. 5; "Basra," 425.

9. See Bracha Yaniv, "The Story behind a Baghdadi Torah Case," in *Windows on Jewish Worlds: Essays in Honor of William Gross, Collector of Judaica on the Occasion of His Eightieth Birthday*, ed. Shalom Sabar, Emile Schrijver, and Falk Wiesemann (Zutphen: Walburg Pers Algemeen, 2020), 297 (hereafter Yaniv). For the inscription, see *Ohel Dawid*, 579, no. 16. On the Chinese origin of the Torah case, see *Perakim*, 123 and n. 38. On the disparity in dating, see Sotheby's, *Sassoon: A Golden Legacy*, 38 (notes by Sharon Liberman Mintz). Several Torah cases of this type are known, including an earlier one in the Gross Collection (see Yaniv, 287–98); one at the Jewish Museum, New York, c. 1850–85 (2016–18); and one at the North Carolina Museum of Art dedicated in 1907/8 (G.80.3.5). The Mumbai Torah scroll in case was dedicated by Rachel Sassoon in 1905/6; see www.midrash.org/world/india/albums/125/jpg_keneseth-eliyahoo-125-mumbai-1845.htm.

10. On Ezekiel Gubbay, see *Masa*, 179, and *Yehude*, 96, 100–102. On his miniature manuscripts, see *Ohel Dawid*, 227, no. 58; 240–43, no. 57; 836–37, no. 903.

11. See A. G. Grimwade, A. F. Kendrick, R. D. Barnett, Temple Williams, and E. Croft-Murray, *Treasures of a London Temple: A Descriptive Catalogue of the Ritual Plate, Mantles, and Furniture of the Spanish and Portuguese Jews' Synagogue in Bevis Marks* (London: Taylor's Foreign Press, 1951), 64, XXXL. We thank warden Dr. Francis Treuherz and his wife, Rachel Montagu, assistant archivist at

Bevis Marks, for their warm reception during our visit to Lauderdale Road Synagogue. As per verbal communication with Ms. Montagu, the Torah scroll was probably removed from its case, which has yet to be located. See also Joseph Jacobs and Lucien Wolf, *Catalogue of the Anglo-Jewish Historical Exhibition, Royal Albert Hall, 1887* (London: F. Haes, 1887), no. 2043 (hereafter *Anglo-Jewish*). A silver eternal lamp hanging today in front of the Torah Ark at the Lauderdale Road Synagogue was dedicated by Reuben Sassoon's wife, Kate (née Ezekiel), almost two decades later, as stated in the English inscription: "Presented to the Spanish and Portuguese Synagogue by Mrs. Reuben Sassoon on her recovery from a dangerous illness, London 5637 (1876)."

12. The collecting of Hebrew manuscripts, however, had a longer history. Most notable among Jewish bibliophiles was Rabbi David Oppenheimer (1664–1736), whose extensive holdings are in the Bodleian Libraries.

13. *Anglo-Jewish*, vii; and "The Historic Anglo-Jewish Exhibition in London, 1887," in Natalia Berger, *The Jewish Museum: History and Memory, Identity, and Art from Vienna to the Bezalel National Museum* (Leiden: Brill, 2018), 66–91. See also Cecil Bloom, "The Politics of Immigration, 1881–1905," *Jewish Historical Studies* 33 (1992–94): 187–214.

14. *Anglo-Jewish*, 207, xi, ix. On Sassoon David, see Stanley Jackson, *The Sassoons: Portrait of a Dynasty* (1968; London: Heinemann, 1989), 38 (hereafter Jackson), and Cecil Roth, *The Sassoon Dynasty* (London: Robert Hale Limited, 1941), 191–92 (hereafter Roth). Two manuscripts once owned by Sassoon David became part of his nephew David Solomon Sassoon's holdings—an Arabic poetry collection, or diwan, copied in Baghdad in the nineteenth century, and a compilation of Hebrew liturgical poems in a nineteenth-century Kochi hand. See *Ohel Dawid*, 478, no. 247; 246, no. 605. We are grateful to Dr. Nadhra Naeem Khan at Lums University in Lahore for translating the Persian inscriptions in the miniature portrait of Sassoon David Sassoon.

15. For all works lent by Joseph Sassoon, see *Anglo-Jewish*, nos. 1392 (Torah scroll in silver case), 1416a, 1546, 1616 (candlesticks), 1806–8, 1830–31 (wedding rings), 1844, 1854, 1888, 1893, 2100 (Sephardic mahzor), 2109, 2124, 2125, 2130, 2131. The candlesticks (no. 1616), dated to the seventeenth century, were likely made a century later; a parallel can be found in the Jewish Museum, New York (F 1847 a-b). On the Esther scroll in silver gilt case (no. 1807), see also Sotheby's, *Sassoon: A Golden Legacy*, 1. On the forgery of Jewish wedding rings, see Vivian B. Mann, "The First English Collector of Jewish Wedding Rings and Their Dealers," *Images* 11 (2018): 177–85. At the time of the *Anglo-Jewish Historical Exhibition*, Joseph Sassoon had probably already sold a Hebrew manuscript dated 1385—a "Commentary of Rashi on Kidushin"—to the British Museum in 1885 (now British Library Or 2891), with the sale recorded on fol. ii v of the manuscript: "Bought of J. Sasson [*sic*] 11 June 1885." On his auctioned paintings, see Christie, Manson and Woods, *Pictures by Old Masters Forming a Portion of the Bretby Heirlooms*, May 31 and June 3, 1918, 28–29, 193–202.

16. *Anglo-Jewish*, nos. 2031–65, 210. Shalom Sabar, "The Illuminated *Ketubbah*," in Orpa Slapak, *The Jews of India: A Story of Three Communities* (Jerusalem: Israel Museum [1995]), 187 (hereafter *Jews of India*).

17. Several Judaica pieces were kept by the descendants and are today in the collection of the Salomons Museum at Broomhill, Tunbridge Wells, Kent, in the former country home of the Salomons family; see http://www.thecivicsociety.org/Salomons1035.htm#Jud.

18. See *Anglo-Jewish*, 128–30, and illustrations facing pp. 91 and 130. The shields are listed as part of dressed Torahs 2035, 2038, and 2040. Two of the shields sold at Sotheby's, *Sassoon: A Golden Legacy*, 26–27 (descriptions by Sharon Liberman Mintz), and the third was auctioned at Sotheby's Tel Aviv, *A Collection from the Sassoon Family Estate*, October 25 and 27, 2000, 34. See also Richard McBee, "The Mystery of the Sassoon Torah Shields," in *Mosaic*, February 10, 2021. The shields are now in the Israel Museum, Jerusalem (148/35), the Museum of Fine Arts, Boston (2021.58), and a private collection.

19. For examples of Torah shields created in Galicia, see Rafi Grafman, *Crowning Glory: Silver Torah Ornaments of the Jewish Museum, New York* (New York: Jewish Museum, 1996), nos. 136ff; for a finer Torah shield and a pair of Torah finials probably created in Lviv (Lemberg), see nos. 174 and 339. The Torah crown (no. 463) is also published in Maurice Berger, Joan Rosenbaum, Vivian B. Mann, and Norman L. Kleeblatt, *Masterworks of the Jewish Museum* (New York: Jewish Museum, 2004), 116–17.

20. *The Statist: A Journal of Practical Finance and Trade*, November 1894, 573. The sales were publicized in *The Atheneum*. The issue on June 24, 1905, advertised the June 29 sale of "A Casket of Jewels the Property of Reuben D. Sassoon Esq., deceased, and Jewels from Private Sources," and the one on July 8, 1905, announced the July 13 auction "Silver Plate the Property of Reuben D. Sassoon Esq., deceased, and others." The following year, the April 28, 1906, issue mentioned the May 2, 1906, auction "Important Jewels, the Property of the Late Lady Currie, the late Mrs. Reuben Sassoon, Mrs. A. H. Graves and others." Avraham Ben-Ya'akov mentions that Reuben liked to accent his attire with jewels, which may account for a sale devoted in part to his jewelry. See *Yehude*, 289.

21. "Most of the gravestones and the ceremonial art he received from his uncle Reuben," *Perakim* 1: 170–71, and *Yehude*, 289; Harry M. Rabinowicz, *Treasures of Judaica* (South Brunswick, NJ: Thomas Yoseloff, 1971), 143; Whitechapel Art Gallery, *Exhibition of Jewish Art and Antiquities* (London: 1906), nos. 130–79 (hereafter *Whitechapel*).

22. We thank Filine Wagner and Holly Robertson at the Whitechapel Art Gallery Archive for sharing extensive information on the exhibition. The contributing Sassoons are listed on a printed solicitation for further subscriptions, which is in the archive. David Solomon Sassoon is listed as a committee member in *Whitechapel Gallery: Report, 1906*, 10.

23. See *Anglo-Jewish*, no. 2044; *Whitechapel*, no. 150.

24. See David Cholmondeley and Andrew Moore, *Houghton Hall: Portrait of an English Country House* (New York: Skira Rizzoli, 2014), 298–99.

25. See *Whitechapel*, 80, nos. 31, 40; 40, no. 567; and *Anglo-Jewish*, no. 1058. Isaac Sassoon, possibly a descendant of David Sassoon's brother Simon, also lent a number of Judaica works to the exhibition.

26. See *Whitechapel*, 1, and Juliet Steyn, "The Complexities of Assimilation in the 1906 Whitechapel Art Gallery Exhibition 'Jewish Art and Antiquities,'" *Oxford Art Journal* 13, no. 2 (1990): 45.

27. *Whitechapel*, 1–2, and *Whitechapel Gallery: Report, 1906*, 9. See also "The Jewish Exhibition," *The Jewish Chronicle*, November 2, 1906; and "Jewish Art Exhibition opened at Whitechapel," *Daily Chronicle*, November 7, 1906.

28. On David Solomon's loans to the exhibition, see *Whitechapel*, nos. 180–91. It is difficult to ascertain whether the tombstones had been in Reuben's collection. David Solomon was interested in old inscriptions, which he recorded avidly and collected whenever possible, including tombstones—he acquired two in Iraq in 1910 (*Masa*, 152, 167). For David Solomon's early collecting, see *Ohel Dawid*, ix, xiii, 577, no. 1, and *Whitechapel*, no. 185; this scroll was sold at Christie's Amsterdam, *Silver, Judaica, Russian Works of Art and Objects of Vertu*, November 13, 2001, 373. For Reuben's scroll, see *Anglo-Jewish*, no. 2061. For Arthur and Louise's ketubbah, see *Ohel Dawid*, 383, no. 501; for three parallels, see Shalom Sabar, *Ketubbah: Jewish Marriage Contracts of the Hebrew Union College Skirball Museum and Klau Library* (Philadelphia and New York: Jewish Publication Society, 1990), 169–74 and nos. 92, 94–95. For the marriage contracts of Frederick and Mozelle, see *Ohel Dawid*, 382, no. 457; 385, no. 502. For the Esther scroll from Rabbi Joseph Hayyim, see *Ohel Dawid*, 557–58, no. 2, and David Solomon's diary *Divrei David*, 651, excerpted in *Perakim* 2 (hereafter *Divrei*).

29. For a brief overview of his collection, which also comprised printed books, including many incunabula and books on parchment, see *Perakim* 1:167–71; and H. Rabinowicz, "The Sassoon Treasures," *The Jewish Quarterly Review* 57, no. 2 (October 1966): 136–53, later edited and reprinted in Rabinowicz, *Treasures of Judaica*, 121–44.

30. *Ohel Dawid*, ix–xii and 14–15, no. 16; David Solomon Sassoon, "Hebrew Manuscripts from Spain," *Jewish Chronicle Literary Supplement*, May 29, 1925. In 2004 the manuscript was in a London private collection, according to Katrin Kogman-Appel, *Jewish Book Art between Islam and Christianity: The Decoration of Hebrew Bibles in Medieval Spain* (Leiden: Brill, 2004), 149 (hereafter *Jewish Book Art*). For images, see the Index of Jewish Art, https://cja.huji.ac.il/browser.php?mode=set&id=1900.

31. *Jewish Book Art*, 148–50, 154, 156–57, 162–63, 192; *Divrei*, 700.

32. *Ohel Dawid*, 275–76, nos. 225–27.

33. *Ohel Dawid*, 1–2, no. 508. On this Bible and the other two created by Merwas, see *Jewish Book Art*, 88–90.

34. *Ohel Dawid*, xlviii, 21, no. 199. The manuscript is today in the British Library (Or 14054) and has been digitized; http://www.bl.uk/manuscripts/FullDisplay.aspx?ref=Or_14054.

35. See *History*, 167–68, 183; *Masa*, 200; and *Jews of India*, 159.

36. *Ohel Dawid*, xxii, 6–14, no. 368; and *Divrei*, 660. The manuscript has been unavailable to scholars and few of its decorated pages have been published. See Bezalel Narkiss, *Hebrew Illuminated Manuscripts* (Jerusalem: Keter, 1969), 72–73. Katrin Kogman-Appel has studied the manuscript and its scribe and illuminator extensively. See her *Jewish Book Art*, 150–54; 163–64; Kogman-Appel, "The Scholarly Interests of a Scribe and Mapmaker in Fourteenth-Century Majorca: Elisha ben Abraham Bevenisti Cresques's Bookcase," in *The Late Medieval Hebrew Book in the Western Mediterranean: Hebrew Manuscripts and Incunabula in Context*, ed. Javier del Barco (Leiden: Brill, 2015), 148–81; Kogman-Appel, "Calligraphy and Decoration in the Farhi Codex (Sassoon coll. no. 368, Majorca, 1366–83)," in *Sephardic Book Art of the Fifteenth Century*, ed. Luís U. Alfonso and Tiago Moita (London: Harvey Miller, 2019), 13–33; and Kogman-Appel, *Catalan Maps and Jewish Books: The Intellectual Profile of Elisha Ben Abraham Cresques (1325–1387)* (Turnhout: Brepols, 2020).

37. *Ohel Dawid*, xi–xii. See also Kogman-Appel, "Calligraphy and Decoration," 13. On the use of the honorific *mikdashyah* for lavish Sephardic Hebrew Bibles, see *Ohel Dawid*, 528, footnote and p. 1017, stating that the term had been used for centuries by Arabic-speaking Jews to demark biblical codices. See also David Stern, "The Hebrew Bible in Europe in the Middle Ages: A Preliminary Typology," in *JSIJ* [Jewish Studies, an Internet Journal] 11 (Ramat Gan: Bar-Ilan University, 2012): 235–322.

38. *Ohel Dawid*, x–xi.

39. *Ohel Dawid*, 24, nos. 330–31. The *taj* was sold at Sotheby's New York, *Sassoon: A Golden Legacy*, 56, and is now owned by Les Enluminures Ltd., New York. See www.textmanuscripts.com/medieval/yemenite-pentateuch-159662?inventorySearch=0&p=54. For the use of the term *taj* to designate Hebrew Bibles from Yemen, see David Stern, "On the Term *Keter* as a Title for Bibles: A Speculation about Its Origins," in *Meḥevah le-Menaḥem: Studies in Honor of Menahem Hayyim Schmelzer*, ed. Shmuel Glick, Evelyn M. Cohen, and Angelo M. Piattelli (Jerusalem: JTS-Schocken Institute for Jewish Research, 2019), *259–*73.

40. *Ohel Dawid*, 19–21, no. 506. The manuscript was auctioned in 1899 at the sale of De Castro's property following his death a year earlier. See Julie-Marthe Cohen, "David Henriques de Castro Mzn: A Collector in Nineteenth-Century Amsterdam," *Studia Rosenthaliana* 33, no. 1 (1999): 42. The Pentateuch was purchased at the De Castro auction by Spinossa Catella, an affluent buyer or agent, who, according to Cohen, acquired it on behalf of David Solomon Sassoon. Given that in 1899 Sassoon was in the very early stages of his collecting career, this is unlikely. Moreover, the Pentateuch was catalogued as no. 506 in the Sassoon collection, which only reached 500 manuscripts at the end of World War I (see *Ohel Dawid*, xii).

41. *Ohel Dawid*, 20.

42. *Ohel Dawid*, xlvii, 1084–85, no. 1043. Now Braginsky Collection BC 345, https://braginskycollection.com/portfolio/mishneh-torah/. See also Anna Nizza and Sarit Shalev-Eyni, *Maimonides: A Legacy in Script* (Jerusalem: Israel Museum, 2018), 42–45, no. 4. We are grateful to Anna Nizza for kindly providing information about this manuscript and others formerly owned by David Solomon Sassoon.

43. *Ohel Dawid*, x and 92–93, nos. 72–73, now in the National Library of Israel (Heb. 4°5703). See also Nizza and Shalev-Eyni, *Maimonides*, 30–33, no. 1. For a recent analysis of Maimonides's autograph manuscripts, see Edna Engel, "The Evolution of Maimonides' Handwriting" (in Hebrew), *Pe'amim* 150–52 (2018): 349–71 (with older bibliography there).

44. One volume (ms. Pococke 295), including Seder Nezikin and Seder Kodashim, was acquired from the Orientalist and Professor of Arabic and Hebrew at Oxford Edward Pococke (1604–91), who had purchased it while serving as chaplain in Aleppo in the early 1630s. Years after, the second volume with Seder Zeraim (ms. Hunt. 117) was acquired by the Bodleian Library from Robert Huntington (1637–1701), another English clergyman, Orientalist, and manuscript collector who held a chaplaincy in Aleppo in the 1670s.

45. *Divrei*, 668.

46. *Ohel Dawid*, 996–98, no. 1047. See also Ilana Tahan, *Hebrew Manuscripts: The Power of Script and Image* (London: British Library, 2007), 126–27; Nizza and Shalev-Eyni, *Maimonides*, 84–78 (Hebrew pagination); and Gabrielle Sed-Rajna, "Hebrew Manuscripts of Fourteenth Century Catalonia and the Workshop of the Master of St. Mark," *Jewish Art* 18 (1992): 125. See also the following articles by Katrin Kogman-Appel: "Hebrew Manuscript Painting in Late Medieval Spain: Signs of a Culture in Transition," *Art Bulletin* 84, no. 2 (June 2002): 246–72, and "The Decoration of Maimonides' Writings in Manuscripts from Spain" (in Hebrew), *Pe'amim* 97 (2004): 56–57. For the interrelation between the creation of altarpieces and manuscripts in medieval Spain, see Thomas F. Glick and Vivian B. Mann, *Uneasy Communion: Jews, Christians, and the Altarpieces of Medieval Spain* (New York: Museum of Biblical Art, 2010), 106–18.

47. *Ohel Dawid*, 303–4, no. 514. Auctioned at Sotheby's Zurich, *Thirty-Eight Highly Important Hebrew and Samaritan Manuscripts from the Collection Formed by the Late David Solomon Sassoon*, November 5, 1975, 11. See Evelyn M. Cohen, "Three Sephardic *Haggadot* and a Possible Missing Link," in *Jewish Studies in a New Europe: Proceedings of the Fifth Congress of Jewish Studies in Copenhagen 1994*, ed. Ulf Haxen, Hanne Trautner-Kromann, and Karen Lisa Goldschmidt Salamon (Copenhagen: Det Kongelige Bibliotek, 1998), 142–51; Iris Fishof, "A Legacy on Parchment: The Sassoon Spanish Haggadah," *The Israel Museum Journal* 10 (1992): 9–14; and Bezalel Narkiss, *Hebrew Illuminated Manuscripts* (Jerusalem: Encyclopedia Judaica, 1969), 62–63. For the letter sent to David Solomon Sassoon from M. Lipschutz, see Sassoon Haggadah in Ktiv site of Hebrew manuscripts: https://web.nli.org.il/sites/NLI/English/digitallibrary/pages/viewer.aspx?&presentorid=MANUSCRIPTS&docid=PNX_MANUSCRIPTS990001341290205171-1#|FL49806055 (p. 4). The censor's signature appears on p. 332 of the Sassoon Haggadah. See also William Popper, *The Censorship of Hebrew Books* (New York: Knickerbocker Press, 1899), 104, and plate IV, no. 3.

48. *Ohel Dawid*, 234, no. 363. The Haggadah was auctioned at Sotheby's New York, *Important Judaica*, December 22, 2015, 19.

49. The Esther scroll was auctioned at Sotheby's Tel Aviv, *A Collection from the Sassoon Family Estate*, April 9, 1999, 12. Its dimensions correspond with those of Esther scroll no. 190 in *Ohel Dawid*, 558—the entry also mentions that the scroll is decorated with "portraits of the various people and scenes of the Megillah." The Esther scroll is now in the Braginsky Collection (BCS 58). See Evelyn M. Cohen, Sharon Liberman Mintz, Emile Schrijver, and Elka Deitsch, *A Journey through Jewish Worlds: Highlights from the Braginsky Collection of Hebrew Manuscripts and Printed Books* (Amsterdam: Universiteit van Amsterdam, 2009), 274–77, no. 97.

50. *Ohel Dawid*, 473–76, no. 614. The manuscript is in the British Library (ms. Or. 13704) and it is digitized: www.bl.uk/manuscripts/FullDisplay.aspx?ref=Or_13704. See Vera Basch Moreen, *Miniature Paintings in Judaeo-Persian Manuscripts* (Cincinnati: Hebrew Union College Press, 1985), 40, 49–50; idem, "A Supplementary List of Judeao-Persian Manuscripts of the British Library," *The British Library Journal* 21 (1995): 73; and Vera Basch and Orit Carmeli, *The Bible as a Judeo-Persian Epic: An Illustrated Manuscript of Imrani's Fath-Nāma* (Jerusalem: Yad Ben-Zvi Press, 2016). See also Ilana Tahan, *Hebrew Manuscripts: The Power of Script and Image* (London: British Library, 2007), 138–39; and "A Judeo Persian Epic, the Fath-Nāma (Book of Conquest)," British Library Asian and African Studies Blog, September 27, 2017, https://blogs.bl.uk/asian-and-african/2017/09/a-judeo-persian-epic-the-fath-nama-book-of-conquest.html.

51. *Ohel Dawid*, 424–25, no. 56. Now in the collection of the Dorot Jewish Division of the New York Public Library [**P (ms. Heb. 190)]. See Leonard Singer Gold, *A Sign and a Witness: 2,000 Years of Hebrew Books and Illuminated Manuscripts* (New York: New York Public Library, 1988), 67. The manuscript has been digitized. See https://digitalcollections.nypl.org/items/77f3a6e0-a5ee-0133-c454-00505686d14e. Gershom Scholem commented on the manuscript in *Kiryat Sefer* 10 (1933): 169.

52. *Ohel Dawid*, 1041–43, no. 823. The manuscript was later owned by the Carl Alexander Floersheim Trust for Art and Judaica (Bermuda) and is now in the Rare Book and Manuscript Library, University of Pennsylvania, Philadelphia (LJS 57) and is digitized. See http://dla.library.upenn.edu/dla/medren/pageturn.html?q=LJS%2057&id=MEDREN_9948521743503681&. See also Karl A. F. Fischer, Paul Kunitzsch, and Y. Tzvi Langermann, "The Hebrew Astronomical Codex MS. Sassoon 823," *The Jewish Quarterly Review*, n.s. 78, nos. 3–4 (January–April 1988), 253–92. The manuscript was featured in 1992 in the Jewish Museum, New York, exhibition *Convivencia: Jews, Christians, and Muslims in Medieval Spain* and published in the accompanying catalogue (no. 31).

53. *Ohel Dawid*, xii.

54. *Divrei*, 709; Rabinowicz, *Treasures of Judaica*, 144.

55. The Binger Haggadah is now in the Braginsky Collection (BC 285). See https://braginskycollection.com/portfolio/hijman-binger-haggadah/. See also H. Rabinowicz, "The Sassoon Treasures," *The Jewish Quarterly Review* 57, no. 2 (October 1966): 149.

Chapter 2: Art

1. Abigail Green, "The 'West' and the Rest: Jewish Philanthropy and Globalization to c. 1880," in *Purchasing Power: The Economics of Modern Jewish History*, ed. Rebecca Kobrin and Adam Teller (Philadelphia: University of Pennsylvania Press, 2015), 160.

2. "The Royal Academy: Second Notice," *Manchester Guardian*, May 7, 1883, 6 (originally published in *The Observer*). See Eilat Negev and Yehuda Koren, *The First Lady of Fleet Street: The Life of Rachel Beer; Crusading Heiress and Newspaper Pioneer* (New York: Bantam Books, 2011); and Lucy Masterman, ed., *Mary Gladstone (Mrs. Drew): Her Diaries and Letters* (New York: E. P. Dutton, 1930), 287.

3. Negev and Koren, *First Lady*, 203–34; and Eloise Forestier, "Rachel Beer, the Dreyfus Case, and the *Observer*: The 'Sponge Metaphor,'" *Victorian Periodicals Review* 52, no. 3 (Fall 2019): 518–39.

4. Negev and Koren, *First Lady*, 5–6, 178, 249–51, 275; and Christie, Manson & Woods, *The Collection of Modern Pictures & Drawings of the British and Continental Schools, the Property of the Late Mrs. Rachel Beer*, July 22, 1927. For Constable's *Salisbury from the Fields*, see Guillaume Faroult, *De Gainsborough à Turner: L'âge d'or du paysage et du portrait anglais dans les collections du Musée du Louvre* (Milan: Silvana, 2014), 5.

5. See Hugh Belsey, *Thomas Gainsborough: The Portraits, Fancy Pictures, and Copies after Old Masters* (New Haven: Yale University Press, 2019), 2: 711, no. 768; Alex Kidson, *George Romney: A Complete Catalogue of His Paintings* (New Haven: Yale University Press, 2015), 1: 131, no. 247; Kenneth Garlick, *Sir Thomas Lawrence: A Complete Catalogue of the Oil Paintings* (Oxford: Phaidon, 1989), 217, no. 453 (the sitter was born Harriet Beckford and the portrait was probably done shortly before her marriage in 1807 to Henry Seymer, later Henry Ker-Seymer, also cited as Ker-Seymour); David Mannings, *Sir Joshua Reynolds: A Complete Catalogue of His Paintings; The Subject Pictures Catalogued by Martin Postle* (New Haven: Yale University Press, 2000); and F. J. B. Watson, *The Wrightsman Collection: Furniture, Gilt Bronze and Mounted Porcelain, Carpets*, vol. 2 (New York: Metropolitan Museum of Art, 1966), 309.

6. Christie, Manson & Woods, *Catalogue of Ancient and Modern Pictures and Water-Colour Drawings*, November 18, 1955, 111–13. For the portrait of Robert Hamby, see John Hayes, "Unknown Early Gainsborough Portraits," *The Burlington Magazine* 107, no. 743 (February 1965): fig. 5 and pp. 65, 74; and Belsey, *Thomas Gainsborough*, 431, no. 433.

7. Mannings, *Sir Joshua Reynolds*, 1: 169, no. 523. It was recently sold at auction with her portrait of Mme. Delahaye by the French miniaturist and portrait painter Antoine Vestier (1740–1824), and a flower painting by the Austrian artist Anton Weiss (1801–1851).

8. Christie's London, *Julians Park and Six Private Collections*, June 8, 2021, 230–33, 235, 237.

9. For Philip's work in the Air Ministry, see Damian Collins, *Charmed Life: The Phenomenal World of Philip Sassoon* (London: William Collins, 2016), 155–201.

10. Philip produced two catalogues for each show: one, complete but unillustrated, had information on every object on view. Another, of the same format, given out as a souvenir, had excellent black-and-white reproductions of many works, and listing each work's title, artist, and lender.

11. On October 7, 1932, Jacques Seligmann wrote to Philip with a list of collectors who owned French eighteenth-century paintings, offering to help with loans of his own as well. Archives of American Art, Smithsonian Institution, Jacques Seligmann & Co. records, 1904–1978, bulk 1913–1974, box 86, folder 4.

12. Philip Sassoon, "Foreword," *Loan Exhibition of English Conversation Pieces, in Aid of the Royal Northern Hospital at 25 Park Lane, March 4th to 30th (inclusive) 1930* (Clapham Park, England: Battley Bros., 1930), n.p. For the term, see Chin-Jung Chen, "From Genre to Portrait: The Etymology of the 'Conversation Piece,'" *The British Art Journal* 13, no. 2 (Autumn 2012): 82–85. The exhibition led to a series of books and articles on the subject, including Sacheverell Sitwell, *Conversation Pieces: A Survey of English Domestic Portraits and Their Painters, with Notes on the Illustrations by Michael Sevier* (London: B. T. Batsford, 1936), dedicated to Philip; and *English Conversation Pictures of the Eighteenth and Early Nineteenth Centuries, with an Intro. and Notes by Dr. G. C. Williamson, and a Foreword by Sir Philip Sassoon* (London: B. T. Batsford, 1931).

13. David Bindman and Helen Weston, "Court and City: Fantasies of Domination," in *The Image of the Black in Western Art*, vol. 3, *From the "Age of Discovery" to the Age of Abolition*, part 3, *The Eighteenth Century*, ed. David Bindman and Henry Louis Gates Jr. (Cambridge, MA: Harvard University Press, 2011), 164–66; and Mary Webster, *Johan Zoffany, 1733–1810* (New Haven: Yale University Press, 2011), 161–63.

14. See J., "French Furniture at the Exhibition of 'Three French Reigns,' 25, Park Lane," *Country Life*, February 25, 1933, 204–6. Though not offering art-historical criticism, Marthe Bibesco, a friend of Philip's, covered the exhibition with a superbly illustrated account in her "Trois règnes: Louis XIV, Louis XV, Louis XVI," *La Renaissance* 16, no. 6 (June 1933): 121–43.

15. See Peter Stansky, *Sassoon: The Worlds of Philip and Sybil* (New Haven: Yale University Press, 2003), 202; and M. Chamot, "Gainsborough as a Landscape Painter," *Country Life*, February 29, 1936, 215.

16. For Philpot, see J. G. P. Delaney, *Glyn Philpot: His Life and Art* (Aldershot, UK: Ashgate, 1999), 51. Simon Martin, *Glyn Philpot: Flesh and Spirit*, with an intro. by Alan Hollinghurst (Chichester: Pallant House Gallery, 2022), was published as the present volume was in press.

17. Jews "formed a significant presence on many boards of trustees and in learned societies." Silvia Davoli and Tom Stammers, "Jewish Collectors and Collecting: An Introduction," *Journal of the History of Collections* (2019), https://academic.oup.com/jhc/pages/jewish-collectors.

18. Quoted in Collins, *Charmed Life*, 147.

19. See Hannah Gubbay's letter to *The Times*, March 12, 1936; and the letter by Grace Boyce to Kenneth Clark, June 28, 1934, National Gallery Archive.

20. Roth, *Sassoon Dynasty*, 14.

21. Frank Davis, "The Gubbay Bequest at Clandon Park," *The Antique Collector* 43, no. 6 (December 1972–January 1973), 313.

22. See *Early English Needlework and Furniture* (1928), *The Age of Walnut* (1932), *Reynolds* (1937), and *The "Old London"* (1938); "The Exhibition of Needlework at 25, Park Lane," *Country Life*, March 3, 1928; "Rare Historical Exhibits," *The Times*, March 6, 1928, 13; "An Exhibition of Needlework at 25, Park Lane," *Country Life*, March 10, 1928; and "The Age of Walnut Exhibition at No. 25 Park Lane," *Country Life*, February 20, 1932, 199.

23. Claire Dumortier and Patrick Habets, *Porcelaine de Tournai: Le service d'Orléans*, preface by Antoinette Faÿ-Hallé (Brussels: Racine, 2004), 35–38.

24. Gervase Jackson-Stops, *The Gubbay Collection: Clandon Park, Surrey* (London: National Trust, 1973), 4. See also "Little Trent Park," *The Antique Collector* (November–December 1950): 208.

25. Davis, "Gubbay Bequest at Clandon Park," 313; M. J., "Mrs. David Gubbay's Collection of Mirrors," *Country Life*, February 15, 1930, 259–62.

26. G. Bernard Hughes, "Exoticism of English Japanners," *Country Life*, June 9, 1966, 1459, 1462.

27. Stanley Jackson, *The Sassoons* (New York: Dutton, 1968), 190.

28. Sarah B. Sherrill, "The 'Landskip' Identified in an English Fire-Screen Panel, 1750–1755," *Studies in the Decorative Arts* 6, no. 1 (Fall–Winter 1988–99): 95, 98–99. The information in this paragraph is indebted to Sherrill.

29. John Cornforth and Gervase Jackson-Stops, "The Gubbay Collection at Clandon," *Country Life*, April 29, 1971, 1004 (emphasis mine); and John Pope-Hennessy, "Mrs. David Gubbay," *The Times*, March 2, 1968, 10.

30. Davis, "Gubbay Bequest at Clandon Park," 312; and Clifford Musgrave, "Clandon Park, Surrey, and Mrs. Gubbay's collections," *The Connoisseur* 181, no. 729 (November 1972): 155.

31. David Yudelman, "Trust will lose most of £1m," *The Times*, January 8, 1969, 1.

32. Roth, *Sassoon Dynasty*, 186.

33. See her letter to Joseph Duveen, October 6, 1935, now at the Getty, informing him that she wanted to return the painting "The Horsley Children," by George Romney: "I have tried to get used to it but without success." Philip, a friend of Duveen's, was outraged and thought Duveen should make her pay, but Duveen refused, as Mozelle was Philip's and Hannah's cousin; https://rosettaapp.getty.edu/delivery/DeliveryManagerServlet?dps_pid=IE1003027.

34. Philip and Kenneth Clark had considered acquiring *La Belle Strasbourgeoise*, also thought to be by David. As Clark's budget at the National Gallery was too low, he hoped Philip would buy it himself. See Clark's letter to Grace Boyce, Philip's secretary, dated March 25, 1936, National Gallery Archive. A signed version of this painting was recently sold at Christie's on September 15, 2020.

35. Thomas Blake Clark, *Omai, First Polynesian Ambassador to England: The True Story of His Voyage There in 1774 with Captain Cook; of How He Was Feted by Fanny Burney, Approved by Samuel Johnson, Entertained by Mrs Thrale & Lord Sandwich and Painted by Sir Joshua Reynolds* (San Francisco: Colt Press, 1940: the Reynolds portrait appears as the frontispiece. The title published in Mannings's catalogue raisonné, "Young Black in a Turban" (no. 2002, fig. 1010), is problematic: portraits of white men never mention their color. Sara Blad, "Head of a [___] Man: How the British Museum Continues to Center Whiteness When Describing Prints of Black and White Men," *The Courtauldian* (November 2020); www.courtauldian.com/single-post/head-of-a-___-man.

36. "Eighteenth-Century Works of Art: Exhibition at Home of Mrs. Meyer Sassoon," *The Times*, March 12, 1935, 21.

37. Faith Dennis, "French Snuffboxes in the Wentworth Collection," *The Metropolitan Museum of Art Bulletin* 3, no. 10 (June 1945): 244.

38. Rosalind Savill, "François Boucher and the Porcelains of Vincennes and Sèvres," *Apollo* 115, no. 241 (March 1982): 162–70.

39. Roth, *Sassoon Dynasty*, 187; "British Institute in Paris," *The Times*, October 13, 1927, 13, and January 19, 1928, 11; and *Nature* 183 (December 26, 1936), 1106–7. See also Susanna Avery-Quash with Christine Riding, "Two Hundred Years of Women Benefactors at the National Gallery: An Exercise in Mapping Uncharted Territory," *Journal of Art Historiography* 23 (2020): 16–17, 45, http://epapers.bham.ac.uk/3397/; and Humphrey Wine, "Mrs. Mozelle Sassoon (1872–1964)," National Gallery, London, www.nationalgallery.org.uk/research/research-resources/national-gallery-catalogues/former-owners-of-the-eighteenth-century-french-paintings/mrs-mozelle-sassoon.

40. Tom Stammers, "Women Collectors and Cultural Philanthropy, c. 1850–1920," *19: Interdisciplinary Studies in the Long Nineteenth Century* 31 (2020): 1–4; Davoli and Stammers, "Jewish Collectors and Collecting"; and Meaghan Clark and Francesco Ventrella, "Women's Expertise and the Culture of Connoisseurship," *Visual Resources* 33, nos. 1–2 (2017): 2, 5.

41. For the oil portraits, see Richard Ormond and Elaine Kilmurray, *John Singer Sargent: The Later Portraits* (New Haven: Yale University Press, 2003), 3: nos. 531, 566, 603–4 (Sybil); and no. 494 (Flora).

42. Ormond and Kilmurray, *John Singer Sargent*, fig. 145.

43. Cholmondeley and Moore, *Houghton Hall*, 216, 218; and Stansky, *Worlds of Philip and Sybil*, 39, fig. 37, and 182.

44. Cholmondeley and Moore, *Houghton Hall*, 215–16; Stansky, *Worlds of Philip and Sybil*, 39.

45. "The Transition from Palace to Museum: The Palace Museum's Prehistory and Republican Years," *China Heritage Newsletter* 4 (December 2005), n.p.

46. Stacey Pierson, "From Market and Exhibition to University: Sir Percival David and the Institutionalization of Chinese Art History in England," in *Collecting China: The World, China, and a History of Collecting*, ed. Vimalin Rujivacharakul (Newark: University of Delaware Press, 2011), 132.

47. Percival David, *The Shōsō-in* (London: Eastern Press, 1932).

48. H. S. Hansford, "Obituary," *Bulletin of the School of Oriental and African Studies* 28, no. 2 (1965): 473.

49. Percival David, ed. and trans., *Chinese Connoisseurship: The Ko Ku Yao Lun; The Essential Criteria of Antiquities* (New York: Praeger, 1971); see also Jessica Rawson's review of this work in "Chinese Connoisseurship," *Modern Asian Studies* 9, no. 3 (1975): 428–31.

50. Pierson, "From Market and Exhibition to University," 135.

51. Jason Steuber, "The Exhibition of Chinese Art at Burlington House, London, 1935–36," *Burlington Magazine* 148, no. 1241 (August 2006): 528.

52. Naturally, notions of what constitutes Chinese art have changed steadily over time, and given the sharp rise of Chinese collectors, they no longer reflect purely Western ideas. Stacey Pierson, "The China Collectors," *Apollo* 186, no. 658 (November 2017): 81.

53. Pierson, "From Market and Exhibition to University," 132.

54. Rosemary Scott, "Sir Percival David's Yuan Ceramics," *Arts of Asia* 39, no. 3 (2009): 87–88; Stacey Pierson, *Collectors, Collections, and Museums: The Field of Chinese Ceramics in Britain, 1560–1960* (Oxford: P. Lang, 2007), 147.

55. Bruce Christman, "Technical Note on the Raft Cup," *Bulletin of the Cleveland Museum of Art* 81, no. 10 (December 1994): 402–7; J. Keith Wilson, "The Fine Art of Drinking: The Chinese Silversmith Zhu Bishan and His Sculptural Cups," *Bulletin of the Cleveland Museum of Art* 81, no. 10 (December 1994): 381.

56. Stacey Pierson, *Percival David Foundation of Chinese Art: A Guide to the Collection* (London: Percival David Foundation of Chinese Art, School of Oriental and African Studies, University of London, 2002), 17.

57. Translated by Robert E. Harrist, Jr., "Ch'ien Hsüan's *Pear Blossoms*: The Tradition of Flower Painting and Poetry from Sung to Yüan, *Metropolitan Museum Journal* 22 (1987): 64. The interpretation of this work is complex and disputed; it hinges on Qian Xuan's politics after the fall of the Southern Song to the Mongols.

58. Wen C. Fong, "The Modern Chinese Art Debate," *Artibus Asiae* 53, nos. 1–2 (1993): 303.

59. Maxwell K. Hearn, *How to Read Chinese Paintings* (New York: Metropolitan Museum of Art, 2008), 6–7.

60. Ellice Victor Sassoon and Sydney E. Lucas, *The Catalogue of the Sassoon Chinese Ivories*, 3 vols. (London: Country Life, 1950), 1: IX; Jackson, *Sassoons*, 213; Phillip Allen, "Sir Victor Sassoon and His Chinese Ivories," in Rose Kerr, Allen, and Shih Ching-Fei, *Chinese Ivory Carvings: The Sir Victor Sassoon Collection* (London: Scala, 2016), 31.

61. "The Sassoon Ivories," *Times Literary Supplement*, May 25, 1951, 320. Unsigned, but written by Leigh Ashton.

62. For this issue, see Jessie Park, "Made by Migrants: Southeast Asian Ivories for Local and Global Markets, ca. 1590–1640," *Art Bulletin* 102, no. 4 (2020): 66–89.

63. Derek Gillman, "Ming and Ching Ivories: Figure Carving," in *Chinese Ivories from the Shang to the Qing: An Exhibition Organized by the Oriental Ceramic Society Jointly with the British Museum* (London: British Museum Publications, 1984), 41.

64. Sydney E. Lucas, *The Catalogue of Sassoon Chinese Ivories in Three Volumes: Prospectus* (London: Country Life, c. 1950), n.p.; Wen Fong, *The Lohans and a Bridge to Heaven* (Washington, DC: Smithsonian Institution/Freer Gallery of Art, 1958), 17–19.

65. Quoted in Kerr, Allen, and Shih Ching-Fei, *Chinese Ivory Carvings*, 188.

66. Phillip Allen, "Sir Victor Sassoon and His Chinese Ivories," 34–35.

67. For Siegfried Sassoon's reminiscences of his aunt Rachel, see his *The Old Century and Seven More Years* (London: Faber and Faber, 1938), chaps. 5 and 7.

68. Max Egremont, *Siegfried Sassoon: A Biography* (London: Picador, 2005), 449–50.

69. "Christ in the Carpenter's Shop," *The Nation & The Atheneum*, July 9, 1921, 541.

Chapter 3: Architecture: A Scattered Legacy

1. Recent scholarship has called attention to the relationship between colonialism and the Jews. See Ethan B. Katz, Lisa Moses Leff, and Maud S. Mandel, *Colonialism and the Jews* (Bloomington: Indiana University Press, 2017); David Feldman, "Jews and the British Empire c. 1900," *History Workshop Journal* 63, no. 1 (2007): 70–89; and Sarah Abrevaya Stein, "Modern Jewries and the Imperial Imagination," *AJS Perspectives* (Fall 2005): 14–16.

2. Adam Mendelsohn, "Not the Retiring Kind: Jewish Colonials in England in the Mid-Nineteenth Century," in Katz, Leff, and Mandel, *Colonialism and the Jews*, 83.

3. Aníbal Quijano, "Coloniality and Modernity/Rationality," *Cultural Studies* 21, nos. 2–3 (2007): 169.

4. Mumbai had a large population of enslaved peoples of different origins. Those of the Baghdadis came from Arabic-speaking tribes, and according to his grandson, David Sassoon manumitted one Salem, in 1843, "using a formulary familiar to students of the Talmud." David Solomon Sassoon, *A History of the Jews in Baghdad* (n.p.: Simon Wallenberg, 2006), 211. See also *Ohel Dawid*, 972, no. 897.

5. Joan Roland, *Jews in British India: Identity in a Colonial Era* (Hanover, NH: University Press of New England, 1989), 15; and Amar Farooqui, "Urban Development in a Colonial Situation: Early Nineteenth-Century Bombay," in *Economic and Political Weekly* 31, no. 40 (October 5, 1996): 2746–59.

6. Dinshaw Edulji Wacha, *Shells from the Sands of Bombay, Being My Recollections and Reminiscences, 1860–1875* (Bombay: K. T. Anklesaria, 1920), 396 and 397. The role of the Sassoons in Mumbai's architecture can be found largely in literature specializing on the Indian Jews. Kenneth X. Robbins and Pushkar Sohoni, *Jewish Heritage of the*

Deccan: Mumbai, the Northern Konkan, and Pune (Mumbai: Jaico Publishing House, 2017); and Shaul Sapir, *Bombay: Exploring the Jewish Urban Heritage* (Mumbai: Spenta Multimedia, 2013).

7. Joan G. Roland, "Negotiating Identity in a Changing World: From British Colonialism to Indian Independence," in *The Baghdadi Jews in India: Maintaining Communities, Negotiating Identities and Creating Super-Diversity*, ed. Shalva Weil (Abingdon, Oxon: Routledge, 2019), 21.

8. In the absence of written documents, the exact date of their arrival has plagued scholars. Schifra Strizower, *The Bene Israel of Bombay: A Study of a Jewish Community* (New York: Schocken Books, 1971), 10–20.

9. Smita Dalvi, "Architecture as Social History: Jewish Built Heritage in Bombay and the Konkan," *TEKTON* 5, no. 2 (September 2018): 66.

10. Roland, *Jews in British India*, 20.

11. Walter J. Fischel, "Bombay in Jewish History in the Light of New Documents from the Indian Archives," *Proceedings of the American Academy for Jewish Research* 38–39 (1970–71): 138–39.

12. Quoted in Christine E. Dobbin, *Urban Leadership in Western India: Politics and Communities in Bombay City, 1840–1885* (London: Oxford University Press, 1972), 23.

13. Elizabeth E. Imber, "A Late Imperial Elite Jewish Politics: Baghdadi Jews in British India and the Political Horizons of Empire and Nation," *Jewish Social Studies* 23, no. 2 (Winter 2018): 52 and 77. Jael Silliman, *Jewish Portraits, Indian Frames: Women's Narratives from a Diaspora of Hope* (Hanover, NH: University Press of New England, 2003); and Jael Silliman, "Crossing Borders, Maintaining Boundaries: The Life and Times of Farha, a Woman of the Baghdadi Jewish Diaspora (1870–1958)," *The Journal of Indo-Judaic Studies* 1, no. 1 (April 1998): 57–79.

14. Shaul Sapir, "Jewish Schools, Their Entrepreneurs and Their Educational Landscape in Bombay," in Weil, ed., *Baghdadi Jews in India*, 85.

15. Roland, *Jews in British India*, 69–70.

16. Jackson, *Sassoons*, 99–100. "A Woman Banker in India," *The Woman's Journal* (Boston), September 17, 1898, 303.

17. Sten Nilsson, *European Architecture in India, 1750–1850*, trans. Agnes George and Eleonore Zettersten (London: Faber, 1968), 126–27; St. Martin-in-the-Fields was influential because Gibbs had reproduced detailed engravings of plan, section, and elevation in his *Book of Architecture* (1728). Dalvi, "Architecture as Social History," 52.

18. Christopher W. London, *Bombay Gothic* (Mumbai: India Book House, 2002), 58. For the importance of local labor, see Partha Mitter, "The Early British Port Cities of India: Their Planning and Architecture Circa 1640–1757," *JSAH* 45, no. 2 (June 1986): 96.

19. "India," *Illustrated London News*, January 28, 1865, 79; "Statue of David Sassoon," *Illustrated London News*, July 17, 1869, 76; Jackson, *Sassoons*, 43.

20. Robbins and Sohoni, *Jewish Heritage of the Deccan*, 107. For the tombstone of David Sassoon, see *Perakim* 1: 48, fig. 33.

21. *Illustrated London News*, August 2, 1879, 118. For the use of segregated hospitals by European and Indian philanthropists (but not Baghdadi Jews), see Preeti Chopra, *A Joint Enterprise: Indian Elites and the Making of British Bombay* (Minneapolis: University of Minnesota Press, 2011), 128–48.

22. By 1869, the family had built more than fifty buildings in Mumbai alone and thirty-four in Pune. See the two albums of photographs donated by the family to the British Library, Collection Area: Visual Arts, Photo Album 1245/1 and 1245/2.

23. Jackson, *Sassoons*, 47.

24. James Douglas, *Glimpses of Old Bombay and Western India, with Other Papers* (London: S. Low, Marston, 1900), 49.

25. The interior had a full-length portrait of David Sassoon and a bust of Garibaldi. *Handbook of the Bombay Presidency with an Account of Bombay City* (London: John Murray, Albemarle Street, 1881), 185–86.

26. Dalvi, "Architecture as Social History," 63. For the political symbolism of clock towers, see Thomas R. Metcalf, "Architecture and the Representation of Empire: India, 1860–1910," *Representations*, no. 6 (Spring 1984), 55–56.

27. The building attracted attention even in the United States: "David Sassoon Building, Elphinstone High-School, Bombay," in *Scientific American Supplement*, October 1, 1881, 4781. See also *The Builder*, November 20, 1875, 1039–41.

28. The best source is Sapir, *Bombay: Exploring the Jewish Urban Heritage*, 226–30.

29. Farooqui, "Urban Development in a Colonial Situation," 2753.

30. For the family split, see *Global Merchants*, 79–86.

31. Shekhar Krishnan, "Inside Indu Mills: A Textile Museum for Mumbai," *Monthly Archives* (September 2018), https://shekhar.cc/2018/09/; Rajnarayan Chandavarkar, *The Origins of Industrial Capitalism in India: Business Strategies and The Working Classes in Bombay, 1900–1940* (Cambridge, UK: Cambridge University Press, 1994), 386; Roland, *Jews in British India*, 135; "Miscellaneous," *London and China Telegraph*, August 8, 1892, 6.

32. In London, Albert Abdullah changed his will, leaving no provisions for his grandfather's synagogues, schools, reformatory, and hospital. Sapir, *Bombay: Exploring the Jewish Urban Heritage*, 95–97, and "Personal Items," *The London and China Telegraph*, December 12, 1896, 1068.

33. According to the Jacob Sassoon Bombay Jewish Charity Fund (1899), moneys were "for the benefit of all poor Jews and Jewesses resident in Bombay (not being Beni Israel Jews or Black Jews from Cochin who are hereby expressly excepted)." Joan G. Roland, *The Jewish Communities of India: Identity in a Colonial Era* (New Brunswick, NJ: Transaction, 1998), 72. The same held true for the trust deed of his wife, the Lady Rachel Sassoon Dispensary.

34. In 2003, the school had 600 students, 80% of whom were Muslim, 10% Jewish (Bene Israel), and 10% of other religions (mainly Parsis and Hindus). Rachel Manasseh, *Baghdadian Jews of Bombay: Their Life and Achievements; A Personal and Historical Account* (Great Neck, NY: Midrash Ben Ish Hai, 2013), 188.

35. Imber, "A Late Imperial Elite Jewish Politics," 61; Shalva Weil, "Super-diversity among the Baghdadi Jews of India," in *The Baghdadi Jews in India: Maintaining Communities, Negotiating Identities, and Creating Super-Diversity*, ed. Weil (New York: Routledge, 2019), 14.

36. Metcalf, "Architecture and the Representation of Empire," 60; Sapir, *Bombay: Exploring the Jewish Urban Heritage*, 242–44.

37. For Jacob's speech, see "The Jacob Sassoon Hospital in Poona," *Israel's Messenger*, August 24, 1906, 11.

38. On these issues, see Chopra, *Joint Enterprise*, 128–29.

39. Jackson, *Sassoons*, 109–10. Flora, too, was inoculated and organized her women friends, spreading the word among Jewish, Parsi, and other communities.

40. Sapir, *Bombay: Exploring the Jewish Urban Heritage*, 137–38. Sir Sassoon David Hospital is situated on the grounds of the J.J. Hospital in Byculla.

41. Maisie J. Meyer, "Sir Ellice Victor Elias Sassoon, 3rd Bart.," in *Shanghai's Baghdadi Jews* (Hong Kong: Blacksmith Books, 2018), 270, 276.

42. As Western traders did not usually speak local languages, they used middlemen—the compradors—to mediate between themselves and the Chinese.

43. Caroline B. Plüss, "Sephardic Jews in Hong Kong: Constructing Communal Identities," *Sino-Judaica: Occasional Papers of the Sino-Judaic Institute* 4 (2003): 61; Katrina McDougall and Bruce Pettman, *The Ohel Leah Synagogue, Hong Kong: Its History and Conservation* (Hong Kong: Jewish Historical Society of Hong Kong, 2000), 13–25.

44. Carl T. Smith, *A Sense of History: Studies in the Social and Urban History of Hong Kong* (North Point, Hong Kong: Hong Kong Educational Publishing, 1995), 407.

45. Nevertheless, the two firms joined forces when necessary to advocate for their common interests. See the letter written in Shanghai, June 13, 1886, now in the Cambridge University Library, UK (ms. JM B7/37/10764).

46. Chiara Betta, "The Baghdadi Jewish Diaspora in Shanghai: Community, Commerce and Identities," *Sino-Judaica: Occasional Papers of the Sino-Judaic Institute* 4 (2003): 85.

47. David Solomon Sassoon, "Inscriptions in the Synagogue of Kai-Fung-Foo," *The Jewish Quarterly Review* 11, no. 2 (October 1920): 143.

48. Maisie J. Meyer, *From the Rivers of Babylon to the Whangpoo: A Century of Sephardi Jewish Life in Shanghai* (Lanham, MD: University Press of America, 2003), 12; Chiara Betta, "Marginal Westerners in Shanghai: The Baghdadi Jewish Community, 1845–1931," in *New Frontiers: Imperialism's New Communities in East Asia, 1842–1953*, ed. Robert Bickers and Christian Henriot (Manchester: Manchester University Press, 2000), 38; and Maisie J. Meyer, "The Sephardi Jewish Community of Shanghai 1845–1939 and the Question of Identity" (PhD diss., University of London, 1994), 104.

49. Marie-Claire Bergère, "'The Other China': Shanghai from 1919 to 1949," in *Shanghai: Revolution and Development in an Asian Metropolis*, ed. Christopher Howe (Cambridge, UK: Cambridge University Press, 1981), 6; Meyer, "Sir Ellice Victor Elias Sassoon, 3rd Bart.," 271; Stephanie Po-yin Chung, "Floating in Mud to Reach the Skies: Victor Sassoon and the Real Estate Boom in Shanghai, 1920s–1930s," *International Journal of Asian Studies* 16 (2019): 10.

50. Victor decided to install a hotel on the top floors after construction began. Edward Denison and Guang Yu Ren, *Building Shanghai: The Story of China's Gateway* (Chichester: Wiley-Academy, 2006), 141; Chung, "Floating in Mud to Reach the Skies," 11. Years later, the Russian Jewish architect Emmanuel Moiseevich Gran, who then worked for Palmer and Turner, claimed credit for the Cathay Hotel. He was the architect of the Ashkenazi synagogue, destroyed in 1985; https://sites.google.com/view/russianshanghai/architects/a-k/e-m-gran.

51. Denison and Ren, *Building Shanghai*, 141–44; Peter Hibbard, *The Shanghai Bund: China Faces West* (Hong Kong: Odyssey, 2007), 253–55.

52. "Shanghai's New Billion-Dollar Skyline," *Far Eastern Review* (June 1927): 260; Jon W. Huebner, "Architecture on the Shanghai Bund," *Papers on Far Eastern History* 39 (March 1989): 130; Lynn Pan, *Shanghai Style: Art and Design between the Wars* (San Francisco: Long River Press, 2008), 220. The high-rises also signaled the rise of America's imperial power in the Pacific. Leo Ou-fan Lee, *Shanghai Modern: The Flowering of a New Urban Culture in China, 1930–1945* (Cambridge, MA: Harvard University Press, 1999), 9–10.

53. This idea came from seventeenth-century Rome, where the churches of Santa Maria dei Miracoli and its twin, Santa Maria in Montesanto, frame the Via del Corso.

54. Meyer, *From the Rivers of Babylon*, 72; Denison and Ren, *Building Shanghai*, 152–53.

55. "Country House for Sir V. Sassoon," *Israel's Messenger*, January 1, 1934, 4.

56. "Modern Shanghai—Jewish Contributions, IX," *Israel's Messenger*, October 18, 1938, 3.

57. Bergère, "'The Other China,'" 12–13; for Shanghai's modern Chinese culture, see Lee, *Shanghai Modern*, passim; Marie-Claire Bergère, *Histoire de Shanghai* (Paris: Fayard, 2002), 123. The Chinese and foreign populations in the city were 3,096,856, and 59,285, respectively. Huang Ching-Shu, "Building a New Shanghai," in *The China Weekly Review*, May 9, 1931, 363.

58. Robert A. Bickers and Jeffrey N. Wasserstrom, "Shanghai's 'Dogs and Chinese Not Admitted' Sign: Legend, History, and Contemporary Symbol," *China Quarterly* 142 (June 1995): 445.

59. *Israel's Messenger*, July 12, 1938, 20; Robert Bickers, *Britain in China: Community, Culture and Colonialism, 1900–1949* (Manchester: Manchester University Press, 1999), 190.

60. "Hamilton House: One of Finest Buildings in Past Two Seasons: Modern Structure on Foochow and Kiangse Roads Boasts Latest Devices in Apartment Equipment for Convenience of Guests, Office Holders," *China Press*, June 22, 1933, A5.

61. Rena Krasno, "Nobody Said Not to Go: The Life, Loves, and Adventures of Emily Hahn," *Points East* 16 (March 2001): 10.

62. "The Shanghai Boom," *Fortune* (January 1935), 38.

63. "Fire at Jewish Club," *The North-China Herald*, May 8, 1920, 333.

64. Silliman, "Crossing Borders, Maintaining Boundaries," 57.

65. Edward Jamilly, "Anglo-Jewish Architects, and Architecture in the 18th and 19th Centuries," *Transactions (Jewish Historical Society of England)* 18 (1953–55): 133. Jamilly adds that Basevi almost certainly converted.

66. Mary Eliza Haweis, *Beautiful Houses, Being a Description of Certain Well-Known Artistic Houses* (New York: Scribner & Welford, 1882), 75–76, 72.

67. Ovide Musin, *My Memories* (New York: Musin Publishing, 1920), 85. Reuben was also a good friend of the composer Arthur Sullivan.

68. Roth, *Sassoon Dynasty*, 126. Jackson, *Sassoons*, 69.

69. "Sir Albert Sassoon at Home," *The Times of India*, January 22, 1885, 6.

70. Sharman Kadish, "The 'Cathedral Synagogues' of England," *Jewish Historical Studies* 39 (2004): 55.

71. Godfrey Gould and Michael Cook, *Brighton Jewry 250: An Anthology of the Brighton and Hove Jewish Community 1766–2016* (Hove: Jewish Historical Society of England, Sussex Branch, 2016), 37–38.

72. For the important role of Britain's Jews in the world of architecture and real estate, see Edward Jamilly, "Patrons, Clients, Designers and Developers: The Jewish Contribution to Secular Building in England," *Jewish Historical Studies* 38 (2002): 75–103.

73. From his father and grandfather, Philip inherited Park Lane, Trent Park, Shorncliffe Lodge (Sandgate), Alvie Lodge in Kincraig (Scotland), and Sans Souci (Mumbai).

74. James Parker, "The Hôtel de Varengeville Room and the Room from the Palais Paar: A Magnificent Donation," *Metropolitan Museum of Art Bulletin* (November 1969): 143–44; Philip Tilden, *True Remembrances: The Memoirs of an Architect* (London: Country Life, 1954), 39–40; Marc Fecker, "Sir Philip Sassoon at 25 Park Lane: The Collection of an Early Twentieth-Century Connoisseur and Aesthete," *Journal of the History of Collections* 31, no. 1 (2019): 151–70. See also E.H.S., "Sir Philip Sassoon's House in the French Style," *Illustrated London News*, September 23, 1922, 469–71; and James Knox, "Not Our Gods: Philip Sassoon at 25 Park Lane," *Country Life*, November 17, 1994, 50–53. The tapestries, misidentified as representations of the Duke of Marlborough's campaigns, are now known to be fragments of the *Art of War*. Fecker, "Sir Philip Sassoon at 25 Park Lane," 161–62.

75. "Sir Philip Sassoon. Bt., Aesthete, Connoisseur, Patron," in *Works of Art from Collections of the Cholmondeley Family and the Late Sir Philip Sassoon, Bt from Houghton* (London: Christie's, 1994), xx.

76. *The Flow of Art: Essays and Criticisms of Henry McBride* (New York: Atheneum, 1975), 185–86.

77. Herbert Baker, "Recent Domestic Architecture: Sir Philip Sassoon's House at Lympne," *The Architectural Review* 52, no. 311 (October 1, 1922): 90.

78. Tilden, *True Remembrances*, 42. Not everyone liked the interiors. Baker, wrote Kenneth Clark, was "a polite and thoughtful man with a positive genius for errors of design; in his public buildings every proportion, every cornice, every piece of fenestration was (and unfortunately still is) an object lesson in how not to do it. Port Lympne was no exception, and Philip's taste for interior decoration had not improved matters." Clark, *Another Part of the Wood: A Self Portrait* (New York: Harper & Row, 1974), 221.

79. Christopher Hussey, "Port Lympne—II. Kent," *Country Life*, May 26, 1923, 720.

80. Tilden, *True Remembrances*, 43.

81. Oswald Mosley, then an MP and later head of the British Union of Fascists, attacked Lloyd George for holding a conference at Philip's villa, where the "abrasions of controversy could be soothed" by a "liberal application of precious ointment from the voluptuous Orient." Oswald Mosley, *My Life* (London: Nelson, 1968), 143.

82. Delaney, *Glyn Philpot*, 114; Clark, *Another Part of the Wood*, 221; Tilden, *True Remembrances*, 43; Hussey, "Port Lympne—II. Kent." Simon Martin's book, *Glyn Philpot: Flesh and Spirit* (Chichester: Pallant House Gallery, 2022) came out when this book was in press.

83. According to the minutes of the board, Philip had opposed giving the commission to Whistler. Clare A. P. Willsdon, *Mural Painting in Britain 1840–1940: Image and Meaning* (Oxford: Oxford University Press, 2000), 369.

84. Rex Whistler, "Problems of the Stage Designer," in *Footnotes to the Theatre*, ed. R. D. Charques (London: Peter Davies, 1938), 120–23; Hugh Cecil and Mirabel Cecil, *In Search of Rex Whistler: His Life and His Work* (London: Frances Lincoln, 2012), 80–85.

85. Christopher Hussey, "Port Lympne—I. Kent," *Country Life*, May 19, 1923, 684.

86. "I was at the time away in India for many months in the year, and Sassoon, eager and impulsive, with a keen artistic imagination, which lacked a sense of proportion, employed artists to decorate rooms of the house, and overweigh the garden with heavy stone fountains, terraces and temples in the manner which he had admired in Paris or in Spain." Herbert Baker, *Architecture & Personalities* (London: Country Life, 1944), 139.

87. Brent Eliott, "Historical Revivalism in the Twentieth Century: A Brief Introduction," *Garden History* 28, no. 1 (Summer 2000): 24.

88. Russell Page, *The Education of a Gardener* (New York: New York Review Books, 2007), 92.

89. Page, *Education of a Gardener*, 128.

90. Tilden, *True Remembrances*, 34; see also Hussey, "Port Lympne—I. Kent," 683.

91. J. C. B., "A Folkestone Housing Scheme," *The Architectural Review* 50 (December 1, 1921): 146; R. Randal Phillips, "Sir Philip Sassoon's Housing Scheme," *Country Life*, December 25, 1920, 862–63.

92. Stansky, *Worlds of Philip and Sybil*, 163. As Stansky points out, in the eighteenth century, the estate had been owned by the Earl of Cholmondeley.

93. Patrick Campbell, *Trent Park: A History* (London: Middlesex University Press, 1997), 29.

94. These included a Georgian staircase designed by William Kent. Campbell, *Trent Park*, 32.

95. Nikki Frater, "Rex Whistler (1905–1944): Patronage and Artistic Identity" (PhD diss., University of Plymouth, 2015), 189–93.

96. G. C. Taylor, "The Wild Garden at Trent Park," *Country Life*, February 21, 1931, 237.

97. Christopher Hussey, "Trent Park—I, Hertfordshire," *Country Life*, January 10, 1931, 44.

98. Harold Nicolson, *Diaries and Letters: 1930–1939*, ed. Nigel Nicolson and Joanne Trautmann (London: Collins, 1966), 73; Robert Boothby, *I Fight to Live* (London: Victor Gollancz, 1947), 48; *The Letters of Virginia Woolf*, vol. 4, *1929–31*, ed. Nigel Nicolson (London: Hogarth Press, 1978), 47.

99. Quoted in Stansky, *Worlds of Philip and Sybil*, 158–59. No source given.

100. Laurence Whistler, *The Laughter and the Urn: The Life of Rex Whistler* (London: Weidenfeld and Nicolson, 1985), 202. Emphasis in original.

101. Born in Shanghai, Reginald lived in India but returned to Britain for horse racing, the great passion of his life.

102. Elizabeth Darling, "'The star in the profession she invented for herself': A Brief Biography of Elizabeth Denby, Housing Consultant," *Planning Perspectives* 20, no. 3 (2005): 278–80; Elizabeth Denby, "Women and Kitchens," *Design for Today* 1 (1933): 113–15. Denby was no doubt aware of the standardized Frankfurt kitchen, designed by Austrian architect Margarete Schütte-Lihotzky for Ernst May's workers' housing in Frankfurt.

103. Maxwell Fry, "Harmony out of Discord," *RIBA Journal* 86 (1979): 527.

104. "Blocks of Flats of Many Storeys," *The Times*, November 17, 1934, 9. "R. E. Sassoon House: Working-Class Flats in St. Mary's Road, Peckham," *Architects' Journal*, November 29, 1934, 824.

105. Caroline Plüss, "Globalizing Ethnicity and Multi-local Identifications: The Parsee, Indian Muslim, and Sephardic Trade Diasporas in Hong Kong," in *Diaspora Entrepreneurial Networks: Four Centuries of History*, ed. Ina Baghdiantz McCabe, Gelina Harlaftis, and Ioanna Pepelasis Minoglou (New York: Berg, 2005), 248; Abigail Green, "The 'West' and the Rest: Jewish Philanthropy and Globalization to c. 1880," in *Purchasing Power: The Economics of Modern Jewish History*, ed. Rebecca Kobrin and Adam Teller (Philadelphia: University of Pennsylvania Press, 2015), 155.

Epilogue

1. Roth, *Sassoons*, 211; Kathleen Woodward, "The Life Story of the Queen of England," *Ladies' Home Journal* 43, no. 12 (December 1926): 101; Stansky, *Worlds of Philip and Sybil*, 83; and Michael Dane, *The Sassoons of Ashley Park* (Walton-on-Thames: M. Dane, 1999), 87.

2. Siegfried Sassoon, *Collected Poems, 1908–1956* (London: Faber and Faber, 1961), 61.

3. Sir William Orpen, *An Onlooker in France, 1917–1919* (London: Williams and Norgate, 1921), v.

4. "Obituary," *Jewish Chronicle*, August 2, 1943.

5. *Israel's Messenger*, November 10, 1939, 10; and Meyer, *From the Rivers of Babylon*, 209; Maisie Meyer, "The Global Reach of Shanghai's Baghdadi Jews," in *China and Ashkenazic Jewry: Transcultural Encounters*, ed. Kathryn Hellerstein and Lihong Song (Berlin: De Gruyter Oldenbourg, 2022), 157.

6. Atina Grossmann, "Trauma, Privilege, and Adventure in Transit: Jewish Refugees in Iran and India," *Colonialism and the Jews in German History: From the Middle Ages to the Twentieth Century*, ed. Stefan Vogt (London: Bloomsbury Academics, 2022), 253–79; "German Jewry Fund," *The Times*, December 23, 1938, 10; "Lord Baldwin's Fund for Refugees," *The Times*, May 25, 1939, 13; and "Odds and Ends Bring £4,477," *Palestine Post*, June 2, 1939, 12.

7. Meyer, "Sir Ellice Victor Elias Sassoon, 3rd Bart.," 289–90; and Walter Bergwerk, "Seder in Bombay in 1944," *Journal of the Association of Jewish Refugees* (May 2011): 3, https://ajr.org.uk/wp-content/uploads/2018/02/2011_May.pdf.

8. Letters to Yvonne FitzRoy from Sir Victor Sassoon (with enclosures), British Library, India Office Records and Private Papers mss. Eur. E312/4 Folios 62–63.

9. Meyer, *From the Rivers of Babylon*, 197; and Jackson, *Sassoons*, 238.

10. The first families actually arrived in 1933, but larger numbers did not come until 1938. Avraham Altman and Irene Eber, "Flight to Shanghai, 1938–1940: The Larger Setting," *Yad Vashem Studies* 28 (2000): 53; and David Kranzler, *Japanese, Nazis and Jews: The Jewish Refugee Community of Shanghai, 1938–1945* (Hoboken, NJ: KTAV, 1988), 152.

11. The Dominican Republic wanted to rehabilitate its image after the government massacred thousands of Haitians in 1937. For Victor's meeting with the president of Brazil, see the "Unedited stenographic typescript of a luncheon conversation between Sir Victor Sassoon and Henry B. Sell," February 1943, 2, now in the DeGolyer Library, Southern Methodist University (Ag2011.0005). Victor's words about his meeting with Vargas, written five years after the fact, have to be taken with caution. "They are a very lazy nation," he wrote of the Brazilians. "They don't want to work hard. . . . They realize if once virile immigrants began coming in, their day would be over." The same year, 1938, Victor had "purchased 10.000 square miles of land in South America whereon to settle expropriated Jews from Germany and Austria." "Sir Victor Sassoon's Handsome Achievement," *Israel's Messenger*, August 12, 1938, 13.

12. Kranzler, *Japanese, Nazis and Jews*, 158–59; Marcia Reynders Ristaino, *Port of Last Resort: The Diaspora Communities of Shanghai* (Stanford, CA: Stanford University Press, c. 2001), 144–47; Irene Eber, *Jewish Refugees in Shanghai 1933–1947: A Selection of Documents* (Göttingen: Vandenhoeck & Ruprecht, 2018), 76; and Wang Jian, "Tracking the Exact Number of Jewish Refugees in Shanghai," *China and Ashkenazic Jewry: Transcultural Encounters*, 136. Altman and Irene Eber, "Flight to Shanghai," 65–68; Kranzler, *Japanese, Nazis, and Jews*, 268–69.

13. Ristaino, *Port of Last Resort*, 119; Eber, *Jewish Refugees in Shanghai 1933–1947*, 241; and Kranzler, *Japanese, Nazis and Jews*, 271.

14. Kranzler, *Japanese, Nazis and Jews*, 491. The exact number of Jewish refugees is under constant discussion in the scholarly literature. The Committee for Assistance of European Jewish Refugees gave the number as 23,310 in 1940. "Annual Jewish Refugee Committee Report," *Israel's Messenger* (February 21, 1941), 9.

INDEX

Italicized page numbers indicate images.

A

Aillerie, René, 222–23, *223*
Albert, Prince Consort, 142, *142–43*
Alma-Tadema, Laura, 66
Amam (née Gubbay, wife of Sheikh Sassoon), 24
antisemitism, 43, 163, 168, 178–80, 218–22, 238
architecture, 136–224; adapting to European colonial environment, 136, 141, 157, 163; the Durlocks, 214, *214*; in England, 180–220, *180–224*; in France, 222–23, *223*; in Hong Kong, 166–68, *166–69*; in India, 136–65, *138–55*; in Mumbai, 136–44, *138–47*, 246n6, 247n22; Port Lympne, *194–214*, 195–214; in Pune, *148–55*, 149–52, 247n22; in Shanghai, *170–79*, 171–80; Trent Park, 215–18, *215–21*. *See also specific members of Sassoon family and structures by location*
art collecting, 62–134, 245n17; Rachel Sassoon Beer, 62–66, *63*, *66–68*; Percival Sassoon David, 118–26, *118–27*; Hannah Gubbay, 94–96, *96–97*; Frederick Sassoon, 69–70, *69–71*; Leontine Sassoon, 72, *72–73*; Siegfried Sassoon, 132–34, *134*; Sybil Sassoon, 105–8, *108–11*; Victor Sassoon, 129–30, *130–31*. *See also specific members of Sassoon family and types of art*
Art Deco, 174, *177*, 177–78
Ashkenazi, 22, 34, 36, 42, 168, 237

B

Bachelier, Jean-Jacques: *A Marmoset Taking Sweets on a Painted Commode (The Thieving Marmoset)* (attrib.), 70
Baghdad, 16–18, 20, 22, 24–25, 62, 88; Beit "Abu-Reuben" (Sassoon home), 16, *18*, 88
Baghdadi Jews, 136–39, 159, 163, 165, 173–74, 178, 238
Baker, Herbert, 88. *See also* Port Lympne
Bakst, Léon, 84
Balfour, Arthur, 187
Ballets Russes, 84, 133, 201
Barnato, Barney, 188
Basevi, Elias George, 180, *181*
Bassa, Ferrer, 55
Beaton, Cecil, photographs of Sybil Sassoon, *117*, *236*
Beaux-Arts, 174
Beer, Frederick, 62–66
Beer, Julius, 65–66
Beer, Rachel Sassoon, 62–66; art collection of, *63*, 66, *66–68*; as journalist and poet, 65, *65–66*; marriage of, 62–65; portrait of, *64*, 66, *67*; Siegfried and, *64*, 65–66, 132, 133, 246n67
Beerbohm, Henry Maximilian ("Max"), 105, 132, *133*, 134; *Self-Portrait*, *109*
Berkshire (England): Pope's Manor, 98
Berners, Lord, 132, 206
Boehm, Joseph Edgar: Prince of Wales statue, *145*, 157, 180
Boltraffio, Giovanni Antonio: *Portrait of a Youth*, 76
Bomberg, David, 84
Bonheur, Rosa, 66
Boothby, Robert, 218–22
Boucher, François, 101; *The Old Dovecote*, 99–100
Boudin, Eugène: *The Laundresses*, 96
Boulle, André-Charles, *190*
Bowers, Robert Steuart, 214, *214*
Boyce, Grace, 80
Brazil, 238, 249n11
Britain. *See* England
Bronzino, 34
Burne-Jones, Edward, 62

C

Campbell, Colen, *110*
Campbell, John, 144, *144–47*, 157, *158–59*
Casteels, Pieter, III, 72
Cathay Land Company, 173
Chelsea porcelain, 90, 100, *102*
China: Communist takeover, 240; First Opium War (1839–42), 18, 130, 166; Palace Museum (Beijing), 118; Taiping Rebellion (1850–64), 178; Treaty of Nanjing (1842), 166. *See also* Hong Kong; Shanghai
Chinese art and collectibles, 75, *92–93*, 93, 118–30, *118–31*, 180, 215; Bodhisattva Guanyin figure, *128*, 129; bowls, 120, *121*; boxes, *131*; casket, 130, *131*; cups, 120–21, *122*; "David vases," *118*, 119; embroideries, 180; *famille rose* moon flask, 119–20, *120*; handscrolls, 121–26, *124–27*; ivory figures, *128*, 129–30, *130–31*; mortar, *131*; *Night-Shining White* (Han Gan), 125–26, *126–27*; *In the Palace* (after Wenju), 124; *Pear Blossoms* (after Qian Xuan), 124–25, *124–25*; plate, wooden with lacquer decoration, 121, *123*; *Scholars of the Liuli Hall*, 124; table screen, 129, *130*
Cholmondeley, George, Earl of Rocksavage ("Rock"), 105, *105*, 108, *110–11*, *112*
Cholmondeley, Sybil, Marchioness of Rocksavage (née Sassoon), 90, 105–8, 214; autograph book of, 105–8, *108–9*; background of, 75, 105; Houghton Hall and, 108, *110–11*; Jewish refugees, aid for, 237; marriage of, 105; miniature Qur'ans distributed by, 226, *227*; portraits/photographs of, 105–8, *105*, *112–17*, *189*, *192*, *236*; Siegfried and, 132; World War I and, 226, *227*; World War II service of, *236*, 237
Churchill, Winston, 214, 222, 226; photograph of, *212*; paintings by, 214, 230; *The Living Room at Sir Philip Sassoon's House, Port Lympne, with Lady Pamela Smith*, *213*; *The Terrace at Port Lympne, Kent*, *213*; *The Terrace at Trent Park (Wisteria Walk)*, *217*, 218
Clark, Kenneth, 80, 84, 200, 245n34, 248n78
Constable, John, 66; *Salisbury from the Fields*, 66, *68*
Constable, William George, 80
Cooper, Reginald, 218
Corot, Jean-Baptiste-Camille, 66; *Moonlit Landscape*, *63*, 66; *Return of the Hayers to Marcoussis*, *68*; *Souvenir of Roquemaure in the Gard* (with Daubigny), 66, *66*
Council for German Jewry, 237
Courbet, Gustave, 66
Cresques, Elisha ben Abraham Bevenisti, 51
Cubitt, Thomas, 181
Culpin, Ewart G., 214, *214*

D

Dadd, Julian and Richard, 134
Danckerts, Hendrick, 42
Daubigny, Charles-François: *Souvenir of Roquemaure in the Gard* (with Corot), 66, *66*
Daukes, Samuel Whitfield, 181, *181*
David, Percival Sassoon, 75, 118–26, *118–27*; bequests of, 119; publications by, 118–19; World War II and, 237. *See also* Chinese art and collectibles
David Sassoon & Co., 75; Baghdadi Jews employed by, 18, 139, 173; business rivals of, 18–20, *21*; Chinese locations of, 18, 166, *166*, *170*, 171, 178; Hannah overseeing charitable work of, 139; London office, 20; opium trade and, 18–22; textile industry and, 159, *161*
Davies, Martin, 81
Dawud Pasha, 16–18
decorative arts, 75, 90; bowls, 96, *96–97*; boxes, *20*, *74*; candlesticks, *104*; Fabergé bonbonnière, *75*; fire screen, 94, *95*; mantelpiece ornaments, 93, *93*; Meissen theater figure, *102*; mirrors, 93; needlework, 94, *95*; pail with birds, *92*, 93; parrot on domed rockwork base, *92*, 93; scent bottles, 100, *102*; Sèvres cabaret set, 101, *102*; snuffboxes, *74*, 100, *100*; tureen (lidded), liner, and stand, *101*; vases and two covers, 101, *103*. *See also* Chinese art and collectibles; furniture
de Gunzburg family, 22, 34
Delaunay, Jules-Élie: *Personification of Spring*, *108*
Denby, Elizabeth, 223, 249n102
Diaghilev, Sergei: *Afternoon of a Faun*, 200
Ditchburn, David William, 165
Douglas, James: *Glimpses of Old Bombay and Western India with Other Papers*, *137*
Dreyfus affair, 65, *65*
Drouias, François-Hubert, 100
Ducrollay, Jean, 100, *100*
Durlocks, 214, *214*
Duveen, Joseph, 108
Duveen Brothers, 80

E

E. D. Sassoon & Co.: Ballard Estate offices, 165; founding, 157–59, 171; Hong Kong office, 166, *167*; Jacob Elias as head of, 159; Jewish refugees in World War II, aid for, 237; Shanghai office, 173–74; textile industry and, 159, *160*, 165; Victor as head of, 75, 165
Eastern European Jews. *See* Ashkenazi
East India Company, 136, 141, 180
Edward, Prince of Wales (later Edward VIII), 90, *90*, 94
Edward VII (king of Great Britain; Prince of Wales): Albert Abdullah's reception for (1880), 181; Gainsborough exhibition loans by, 81; Mumbai statue of (called Kala Ghoda), *145*, 157, 180; Mumbai visit (1875), *138*, 139, 157, 165; Sassoon family and, *74*, 75, 181
Elphinstone, John, 119, 141
Elphinstone, William Mountstuart, 119, 152–57
England: Aliens Act (1905), 42; architecture in, 180–222, *180–224*; as home of Sassoon family, 22, 224, 240
Ephrussi family, 9
Esterhazy, Ferdinand, 65, *65*
exhibitions: *Anglo-Jewish Historical Exhibition*, Royal Albert Hall (London, 1887), 32–36, 42–44; Belgrave Square home of Reuben hosting, 180; *Exhibition of Jewish Art and Antiquities*, Whitechapel Art Gallery (London, 1906), 42–44; *International Exhibition of Chinese Art*, Royal Academy, Burlington House (London, 1935–36), *118*, 119, 121; *Modern Architecture in England*, Museum of Modern Art (New York, 1937), 223; Paris Universal Exhibition (1878), 181
exhibitions at 25 Park Lane, London, 76–81, 84, 245n10; *The Age of Walnut*, 90, *90*, 206; *Conversation Pieces*, 80, 96; *Early English Needlework and Furniture*, 80, 94; *The Four Georges*, 81; *Gainsborough*, 81; *Old English Plate*, 80, *80*, *97*; *Porcelain through the Ages*, 119; *Reynolds*, 76, 81; *Three French Reigns*, *76*, 81, 98, *190*
Ezra, Alfred, 70
Ezra, Mozelle (née Sassoon), 30, *48*, 132
Ezra, Muriel (née Sassoon), 70
Ezra family, *48*, 136, 178, 240

F

Feibusch, Hans, 223, *224*
Fragonard: *A Young Girl Reading*, *76*
France: Château de Port-Breton, 222–23, *223*
Frere, Henry Bartle, 136–38, 144, 152
Fry, Maxwell, 223–24, *224*
furniture, 93–94; armchairs, Russian neoclassical, 201, *202*; cabinets, 94, *94*, *190*; chinoiserie, 94; dining room, *203*; japanned furniture, 93–94, *94*, 215, *220–21*; Leontine Sassoon's collection, 72

G

Gainsborough, Thomas, 72, 76, 80; *The Artist with His Wife and Daughter*, 81, *82*; exhibition of, 81; *Mrs. David Richards*, 69–70, *69*; *Self-Portrait*, 81, *83*
Gao Pian, 129
Gatty, Hester, 133
George IV (king of Great Britain), *74*, 101
George V (king of Great Britain; Prince of Wales), 80, 81, 163, 165, *165*, 187
George VI (king of Great Britain) and family, *89*
Georgian art and architecture, 90, 133, 174, 201, *205*, 215, *215*, 249n94
Germain, Thomas, *101*
Gertler, Mark, *133*
Gibbs, James, *110*, 141, 247n17
Gladstone, Mary, 62
Gladstone, William Ewart, 144
Gonda, Charles Henry, 177
Gosse, Sylvia, 134
Gostling, David Ebenezer, 142–44, *144–47*, 159, *164*
Gothic architecture, 157, 159, *186*, 187
Gothic Revival. *See* neo-Gothic architecture
Gran, Emmanuel, 178, 248n50
Graves, Robert, 226, *229*
Gropius, Walter, 223
Gubbay, David, 75, 96, 222
Gubbay, Hannah (née Ezra), 75, 90–97, 104; assisting in Philip's exhibitions, 76, 90; bequests of, 97; birds theme and, 92, *93–94*, *95*; critics on her collecting, 96–97; decorative arts collected by, 90–93, *92–93*, 96, *96–97*; furniture pieces of, 93–94, *94*; homes of, 90; Jewish refugees, aid for, 237; paintings acquired by, 94–96; portrait/photograph of, *91*, 96, *216*, *222*; royal associations of, *74*
Gubbay family, 32

H

Hahn, Reynaldo, 75
Haig, Douglas, 226–30, *230*
Halpert, Edith, 9
Halse, Sidney Joseph, *171–73*, 173
Hamby, Robert, 72
Han Gan, 125–26, *126–27*
Hayim, Ellis, *239*, 240
Hayyim, Joseph, 30
Henry Ellis (opium ship), 20
Hobson, Robert Lockhart, 118–19
Hogarth, William, 76, 80
Holbein, Hans: *A Lady with a Squirrel and a Starling (Anne Lovell?)*, 108, *117*
Hong Kong, 18, 166–68, *166–69*, 171; as central hub for Sassoon businesses, 166; David Sassoon & Co. office, 166, *166*; E. D. Sassoon & Co. office, 166, *167*; Ohel Leah Synagogue, 168, *169*; Shelley Street Synagogue, 168, *168*
hospitality industry, 173
Houdon, Jean-Antoine, 237
Humphrey-Owens, Elizabeth Mary, 129

I

Impressionists, 9
India, 136–65; decorative arts from, 96, *96–97*; George V visits to (1905–6; 1911–12), 163, *165*; independence of, 165, 240; Jewish refugees in World War II in, 237; Mahabaleshwar summer homes, 152, 159; plague outbreak (1896), 165, 247n39. *See also* Mumbai; Pune
Indo-Saracenic architecture, 163–65, *165*, 187, *187*
Ingres, Jean-Auguste-Dominique: *Odalisque with Slave*, 76
International Committee for European Immigrants, 240, *240*
International Style, 174, 223, *224*
Israel, 25, 55, 98

J

Japan, 18, 118, 130, 166, 237–38
Jardine, Matheson & Co., 18, *21*
Jeejeebhoy, Jamsetjee, 139, 142, 152
Jewish ceremonial art and Judaica, 24–60; astrological works, 57–59, *59*; Book of Judges decorated page, *54*; bridegroom robe, 32, *33*; Cairo Genizah fragments (Karaite texts), *49*, 49–50; candlesticks, 34, 243n15; constellation map, *59*; De Castro Pentateuch, 52, 244n40; Esther scrolls, 34, *36*, 43–44, *44–45*, 57, *57*, 243n28, 244n49; Fahri Codex, 50–51; *Fath-Nāma* (Book of Conquest), 57, *58*; Hagaddah, 32, 55–57, *56*, 60, *60*; *Ishban Kashtah* page, *60*; Kabbalistic literature, 57, *58*; ketubbah (Baghdad, 1764), 16, *19*, 34–36; ketubbah (London, 1894), *47*; ketubbah (Mumbai, 1853), 34, *37*; ketubbah (Mumbai, 1859), 34, *38*; ketubbah (Pune, 1870), *48*; ketubbah (Trieste, 1873), 44, *46*; Maimonides's works, 53–55, *55*; Masoretic Bibles, table of differences among, 50, *51*; *Perek Shira*, 41; Rashba Bible, *49*; Samaritan calendrical treatises, 59, *60*; Sephardic Hebrew Pentateuch (fifteenth century), 50; Song of Songs word panel, *53*; standard carried in pilgrimage, 25, *26*; Toledo (Spain) Bible, 50, *50*; tomb of Prophet Ezekiel, 24–25, *25–26*; Torah and haftarah scrolls with cases, 24, 27–32, *31*, 34, 242n9 (Ch. 1); Torah ark curtain inscription and plaque, 25, 27, *28–29*; Torah finials, 24–25, *25*, 36, *39*, 42, *43*, 242n3 (Ch. 1); Torah shields, *40–41*, 41–42, 243n18; wedding rings, 34, 243n15; Yemenite Pentateuch, 51–52, *52*
Jewish refugees, 33–34; in World War II, 237–40, 249n14. *See also* Ashkenazi
John, Augustus, 84
Jones, Inigo, 88
Judah family, 57

K

Kadoorie family, 168, 178, 180, 240
Kaifeng Jews, *170*, 171
Kent, William, 94, *110*, 215, 249n94
Kindertransport, 237
Kipling, John Lockwood: David Sassoon medallion portrait, 144, *144*
Kneller, Godfrey, 34
Kolkata (formerly Calcutta), 18, 136, 138, 237, 240

L

Lainson, Thomas, *183–86*, 187
Lambah, Abha Narain, 159, *164*
Largillière, Nicolas de: *La Belle Strasbourgeoise*, 98–99, *99*, 245n34
László, Philip de: *Sir Philip Sassoon*, 84, *231*
Lavery, John, 84
Lawrence, Thomas: *Mrs. Harriet Ker-Seymour*, 70, *71*, 245n5
Leighton, Frederic, 62
Leonardo da Vinci, 104
Libotton, Gustave, 180
Lindsay, Norah, gardens designed by, 212–14, *212*, 218, *218*
Lloyd George, David, 199, 248n81
London (and environs): Ashley Park, 34, 180, *180*; 1 Belgrave Square, 42, 180, *181*; Bevis Marks synagogue, 32, 46; British Museum, 119, 129, 130; Clandon Park, *97*; 17 Cumberland Terrace, 180; 25 Kensington Gore, 181, *181*, 188; 12 Kensington Palace Gardens, *112*; Letchworth, 42, 60; Middle Street Synagogue (Brighton), *183–86*, 187; National Gallery, 104; 25 Park Lane, 76, 108, 188, *188–92*, 199, 215, 248nn73–74; R. E. Sassoon House (Peckham), 223–24, *224*; Sassoon business offices in, 180; Trent Park, 76, 90, 96, 215–18, *215–21*; University of London, 119
Lucas, Sydney Edward, 129
Lutyens, Edwin, 88, 165, *165*, 195

M

Maimonides, 53–55, *55*
Mannerism, *171–73*, 173
Manship, Paul, 105–8, *108*
Martincourt, Étienne, *104*
Mary, Queen Consort, *74–75*, 75, 80, 90, 94, 163
Maurois, André, 81
May, Ernst, 223
Mayer, Jean-Ghislain-Joseph, *92*, 93
Meissen porcelain, 90, *102*
Melville, William: *Portrait of David Sassoon* (attrib.), *17*
Millais, John Everett: *Christ in the House of His Parents (The Carpenter's Shop)*, 65–66, 134
Millerand, Alexandre, 199
Mocatta family, 144, 187
Molecey, George Twigge, 152–57, *156*
Montagu family, 144, 181
Montefiore family, 187
Moorhead, Robert Bradshaw, *171–73*, 173
Morrell, Ottoline, 132, *133*, *229*
Morris, James, 159
Moses ben Jacob ben Mordecai ben Jacob ben Moses, 57
Mumbai (formerly Bombay), 136–44, *138–47*, 247n22; Alexandra Mill, 159; background of, 136–38; Baghdadi Jews in, 18, *18*, 32, 138–39, 165, 246n4; Bene Israel, 34, 36, 138–39, 141, 159, 163; Braganza Hall, 159, *162–63*; clock towers, 142, *143*, 152, 247n26; David Sassoon Benevolent Institution, 142; David Sassoon Industrial and Reformatory Institution, *139*, 141; David Sassoon Library, 142–44, *144–47*; Dr. Bhau Daji Lad Museum, 142, *142–43*, 157; E. D. Sassoon building, 237; Elphinstone Technical High School and Elphinstone College, *144–45*, 152–57, *156*, 247n27; Gateway of India, 163–65, *165*; Jewish cemetery, 157, *157*, 163, 237; Jewish refugees of World War II in, 237; Keneseth Eliyahoo Synagogue, 159, *164*, 237; Magen David Synagogue, 22, *140–41*, 141–42, 149; Malabar Hill residences, 157, *158–59*; Royal Institute of Science, 163; Sans Souci mansion, *138*, 139–41, 152; Sassoon Docks, 152; Sassoons relocating to and businesses in, 18, 22, 136, 138, 159; Sir Jacob Sassoon High School, 163, 247n34; Sir Sassoon David Hospital, 165. *See also* Pune
Musin, Ovide, 180
Muslim-Jewish-Christian exchange in medieval Iberia, 59, *59*

N

Nash, John, 180, 187
Nattier, Jean-Marc, 100
Neoclassicism, 70, *71*, 180, 201, *202*
neo-Gothic architecture, 144, *144*, *148–50*, 149, 151–52, *151–53*, *156*, 165, 174
neo-Renaissance architecture, 159, *164*
New Delhi (India), 88, *89*
Nijinsky, Vaslav, *86*, 200
Nissim, Meyer, 237, *237*
Noble, Matthew: Prince Albert statue, 142, *142–43*
Norfolk, England: Houghton Hall, 75, 108, *110–11*

O

opium trade, 9, 18–20, 136, 165–66, 171
Oppenheimer, David, 243n12
Orientalism, 99, *99*, 165, *165*, 187, 199
Orpen, William, 84, 105, 230; *The Drawing Room at 25 Park Lane*, 188, *189*; *Man with a Cigarette*, 230, *232*; *The Play Scene from Hamlet*, 108; *Self-Portrait*, *108*; *Sybil Sassoon, Countess of Rocksavage*, 108, *116*
Ottoman Empire, 9, 16, 18, 27, 242n5 (Ch. 1)
Owen, Wilfred, 226

P

Palestine, 27, 60, 242n5 (Ch. 1)
Parisot, Pierre, 94, *95*
Parsis, 136, 138, 139, 168

Pater, Jean-Baptiste, 42; *L'Escarpolette*, 99; *Fête Champêtre*, 99, *100*
Pearl Harbor attack (1941), 237, 240
philanthropy, 139, 224, 242n5 (Ch. 1); Alliance Israélite of Baghdad, 27, 242n5 (Ch. 1); art bequests, 62; Collège A. D. Sassoon, 27; cultural, 101–4; Hillah synagogue, 27; Jerusalem synagogue, 27; Jacob Elias Sassoon, 142, 159–65, *164–65*, 247n33; Albert Abdullah Sassoon and, 152, 247n32; David Sassoon and, 141, 149; Reuben Sassoon and, 180, 187; Victor Sassoon and, 178; Whitechapel exhibition, 42; in World Wars, 226–30, 237–40
Philpot, Glyn Warren, 84, 105, 132–33; *Head of Billy*, 84, *87*; *Nijinsky before the Curtain*, 84, *86*; Port Lympne frieze, 84, 200–201, *203*; *Siegfried Sassoon*, *132*, 132–33
Pithou, Pierre-Nicolas, 101, *103*
Port Lympne (Kent), *194–214*, 195–214; Baker as designer, 88, 195, *196–97*, 206, 248n78, 248n86; bathing pool and fountains, 195, 206, *206*, *210–11*; Churchill's paintings of, *212–13*, 214; courtyard, 195–99, *198*; dining room furniture, 201, *202–3*; dining room with frieze, 200–201, *203*; drawing room murals, 84, *193*, *199*, 199–200, *201*; exterior vs. interior design, 195, 248n78; gardens, *212*, 212–14; Hannah Gubbay and, 90, *222*; Lloyd George-Millerand conference held at, 199–200, 248n81; octagonal library, 195, *197*; staircase with *tempietti*, 195, 206, *207–9*; tent room, *10*, 201–6, *204–5*; Tilden as designer, 195, *196–98*, 199–201, 206, 214; Whistler and, *10*, 96, *197*, 201–6, *204–5*, 248n83
Proust, Marcel, 75
Pune, 44, *148–55*, 149–52, 247n22; buildings by David Sassoon in, 149; Ohel David Synagogue, *48*, *148–50*, 149–51; Sassoon General Hospital, 149–51, *151*; Sassoon mausoleum in, 149, *150*; buildings by Jacob Sassoon in: Ashley House (Jacob's residence), 159; Jacob Sassoon Hospital for Europeans, 165; buildings by Victor Sassoon in, 165; residence of Albert Abdullah: Garden Reach mansion, 152, *152–53*, 247n25

Q

Qian Xuan, 124; *Pear Blossoms*, 124–25, *124–25*, 246n57

R

Raphael, Ernest G., 42
Raphael, Flora Cecilia (née Sassoon), 105, *106*
Rashi, 52
Renaissance architecture, 159, 174
Repton, Humphry, 215
Reynolds, Joshua, 76; *Andrew Drummond of Ridgeway* (attrib.), 72, *72*, 245n7; exhibition of, 76, 81; *Portrait of Miss Bullock* (attrib.), 70; *Portrait of Nelly O'Brien* (studio), 70; *Young Man in a Turban* (previously called Omai), 99, *99*, 245n35
Rocksavage, Countess of. *See* Cholmondeley, Sybil
Rocksavage, Earl of. *See* Cholmondeley, George
Rollos the Elder, Philip, *80*
Romanesque architecture, *184–86*, 187
Romney, George, 245n33; *Hester, Countess of Clanricarde*, 70, *70*
Ross, Ethel, 66
Rothenstein, William: *Ruins at the Front*, 230, *232–33*
Rothschild, Gustave de, 75, 199
Rothschild family, 9, 22, 81, 144, 187–88, 230. *See also* Sassoon, Aline
Rothstein, Arthur, 240, *241*
Roussel, Pierre, 72
Rubens, Peter Paul, 66

S

Saint-Saëns, Camille, 180
Saleh ben David ben Jacob (Sassoon's ancestor), 16, *19*
Salomons, Philip, 36, 41, 42, 243n17
Sargent, John Singer, 9, 76, 96, *105*, 105–8, 199–200, 230; *Aline de Rothschild, Lady Sassoon*, *107*, *190*; David Gubbay charcoal drawing, *96*; *Gassed* (study), 230, *234*; *Hand of Philip Sassoon*, 84, *84*; *Head of a Capri Girl*, *77*; *Mrs. Ernest G. Raphael* (Flora Cecilia Sassoon), 105, *106*; *Philip Sassoon*, *76*, 84; *The Road*, 230, *234*; *Roman Architecture*, *78*; *Ruined Cathedral at Arras*, 230, *235*; *Sir Philip Sassoon*, 84, *85*; *Sybil, Countess of Rocksavage* (1913), 105, *114*; *Sybil, Countess of Rocksavage* (1922), 105, *115*; *Sybil Sassoon* (1910), *8*, 105, *113*
Sason ben Saleh ben David (David Sassoon's father, known as Sheikh Sassoon), 24, 27, 242n7 (Ch. 1)
Sassoon, Aaron, 187
Sassoon, Albert Abdullah, 27, 34, 247n32; architectural projects of, 152–57, *156*; death/mausoleum of, 187; Garden Reach residence of, 152, *152–53*, 247n25; Indian nobility and, 139, 152; Kensington Gore residence of, 181, *181*; knighthood and honors, 152, 181; in London, 181; photograph of, *22*; Prince of Wales statue commissioned by, *145*, 157, 180
Sassoon, Alfred Ezra, 132
Sassoon, Aline, Lady Sassoon (née de Rothschild), 42; autograph book of, 105, *108*; marriage of, 187; Park Lane residence of, 188, *189*; portrait of, *107*, *190*
Sassoon, Arthur (1840–1912), 34, 42, 43–44, *74*, 75, 180–81, 187
Sassoon, Arthur (S.D.'s grandson), 226
Sassoon, David: architectural projects of, 27, 136–51, *137–51*; British citizenship and family coat of arms of, 20, *20*; death/mausoleum of, 149, *150*; desk seal of, *20*; letter with signature of, *21*; move from Baghdad to Mumbai, 16–18, 22, 240; as patriarch, 16, 22; portraits/photographs of, *17*, 20, *22*, *137*; in Pune, 149–51; Sans Souci mansion of, *138*, 139–41; trading business of, 18–22; Woolner bust and statue of, 142, *143*, 144, *147*, 247n25. *See also* David Sassoon & Co.; Pune
Sassoon, David Solomon, 16, 20, 24–25, 36, 42–60, 238, 242n2 (Intro), 242n5 (Ch. 1), 243n14, 243n28; *Ohel Dawid* (catalogue of his collection), 43–44, 59–60
Sassoon, Edward Albert, 42, 157, 187–88
Sassoon, Edward Elias, 72, 75, 168
Sassoon, Elias David (E. D.), *22*; in China to establish trade, 18, 166, 171; Mumbai Jewish cemetery and, 157, *157*, 237. *See also* E. D. Sassoon & Co.
Sassoon, Farha (née Hyeem), 187
Sassoon, Flora (née Gubbay), 27–30, *30*, 42, 139, 157, 247n39
Sassoon, Flora/Farha (née Reuben), *35*, 132
Sassoon, Frederick, 42, 44, 69–70, *69–71*, 168
Sassoon, Hamo, 226
Sassoon, Hannah (née Moise), 27, 139
Sassoon, Jacob Elias: as head of E. D. Sassoon & Co., 159; mausoleum of, *157*; philanthropy and architectural projects of, 142, 159–65, *164–65*, 247n33; residences of, 159, *162–63*; Sir Jacob Sassoon High School, 163, 247n34; synagogues commissioned by, 168, *169*, *171–73*, 173
Sassoon, Joseph, 34
Sassoon, Leontine (née Levy), 72, *72–73*
Sassoon, Louise (née de Gunzburg), 34, 105
Sassoon, Louise (née Perugia), 187; marriage of, 44, *46*, 181; portrait/photograph of, *182*, *227*; royal associations of, 181; World War I and, 226, *227*; World War II and, 237
Sassoon, Meyer Elias, 75, 98, 101, 168, 187
Sassoon, Mozelle (1853–1922). *See* Ezra, Mozelle
Sassoon, Mozelle (1855–1952), 132
Sassoon, Mozelle (1884–1921), 27, 44
Sassoon, Mozelle (née Gubbay; 1872–1964), 75, 98–104; Château de Port-Breton and, 222–23, *223*; Jewish refugees aided by, 237; marriage/lifestyle of, 98, 101, *186*, 187; paintings acquired by, *98–100*, 98–101, 245n33; philanthropy of, 101–4, 237; porcelains of, 100–101, *102–3*; R. E. Sassoon House and, 223–24, *224*; royal associations of, *74*, 222
Sassoon, Mozelle (S.D.'s granddaughter), 226
Sassoon, Philip, 75–88; art collection and curatorial work of, 42, 75–84, *76–87*, 99, 245n10; bequests of, 90, 108; career of, 75, 88, 188; Durlocks housing project and, 214, *214*; Park Lane residence of, 76, 81, *117*, 188, *188–92*, 199, 215, 248n73; Port Lympne and, 195–206; portraits/photographs of, *76*, 84, *84–85*, *89*, *105*, *133*, *216*, *230–31*; Siegfried and, 132–33; *The Third Route*, 88, *89*, 201; Trent Park residence of, 76, 90, 96, 215–18, *215–21*, 248n73; World War I service of, 226–30, *230–31*; World War II aid from, 237. *See also* exhibitions at 25 Park Lane; Port Lympne
Sassoon, Rachel. *See* Beer, Rachel Sassoon
Sassoon, Rachel (née Isaac), 27, 173; mausoleum of, *157*
Sassoon, Rachel (wife of Jacob), 32
Sassoon, Reginald Ellice, 223, 226, 249n101
Sassoon, Reuben, 24, 32, 41–42, 44, 76, 105, 180, 187–88; *Anglo-Jewish Historical Exhibition* and, 34–36, 42, 44; Belgrave Square residence of, 180, *181*; children of, 42; horses and, 180; marriage of, 34, *38*; philanthropy of, 180, 187; royal associations of, *74*, 75, 181
Sassoon, Sassoon David (S. D.), 20, *22*, 32, 34, *35*, 62, 75, 180, 243n14
Sassoon, Siegfried: art collection of, 132–34, *134*; Graves and, 226, *229*; marriage of, 133; Philip and, 132–33; poetry by, 9, 226; portraits/photographs of, 65, *65*, *132–33*, *227*, *229*; Rachel and, *64*, 65, 66, 133, 246n67; "A Soldier's Declaration" (protest letter), 226, *228*; "The Soul of an Officer," 226, *229*
Sassoon, Solomon David (1841–1894), 157, *158–59*
Sassoon, Solomon David, Rabbi, 60, 238
Sassoon, Victor, 75, 173–80; architectural projects of, 174–78, *174–79*; Brazil as possible haven for Jewish refugees and, 238, 249n11; Chinese ivories of, *128*, 129–30, *130–31*; Eves residence of, 178, *179*; as head of E. D. Sassoon & Co., 75, 165; Jewish refugees aided by, 237–40; in Mumbai and Pune, 165; philanthropy of, 178, 237; as photographer, 88, *88–89*, 238, *239*; relocation to England, 240; in Shanghai, 75, 165, 173–80; Sir Victor Sassoon Chinese Ivories Trust, 129; World War I service of, 226; World War II and, 237–40
Sassoon family: antisemitism and, 163, 168, 180, 218–22; British loyalty/self-identity of, 22, 180, 188, 224, 226, 240; coat of arms, 20, *20*, 139; diaspora and, 16, 62, 224, 240; family tree, 6–7; Jewish identity of, 240; mausoleums in Pune, Mumbai, and Brighton, 149, *150*, *157*, 187, *187*; Mizrahi origin, 16; origins of, 16, 242n2; philanthropy of, 224; photographs of, *4*, *154*; wealth of, 18, 24, 134, 157–59, 163; women of, 22, 62, 139, 224, 226; World War II aid from, 237; World War II and, 9. *See also* art collecting; Baghdad; England; Hong Kong; London; Mumbai; Pune; Shanghai; *individual family members, residences, and family businesses*
Scott, McClelland and Company, 142, *143*, 144
Seligmann, Jacques, 80, 245n11

Sert, Josep Maria, 84; *Caravans of the East* (later *Caravans from the Orient*), 188, *193*; *The Indies Coming to the Rescue of the Allies*, 199–200, *199–201*
Sèvres porcelain, 42, 90, 100–101, *102–3*
Shanghai, 18, *170–79*, 171–80, 248n57; Baghdadis in, 178–80, 238; Bund, 171, 173–74, 177, 238, *238*; Cathay Cinema, 177; Cathay Hotel (now Fairmont Peace Hotel), 174, *174–75*, 178, 248n50; Cathay Mansions, 177; Chinese inhabitants, restrictions in, 178; Ciro's nightclub, 177, *177*; David Sassoon & Co. offices in, *170*, 171; Embankment Building, 177–78, *178*, 240; Eves villa, 178, *179*; Grosvenor House, 177; Hamilton House, 177–78, 248n53; International Settlement and French Concession, 171, 173, 177–78, 238–40; Japanese attack/takeover of, 238; Japanese-style flats, 178, *179*; Jewish cemetery in, 171; Jewish World War II refugees and Shanghai Ghetto, 238–40; Magnet House, 178; Metropole Hotel, *176*, 177–78; multiethnicism of, 173–74; Ohel Rachel Synagogue, *171–73*, 173; Sassoon House, 174–77, *175*, 240, *240*; Shanghai Club, 180; Victor in, 75, 165, 173–80
Shepard, Ernest Howard, 84; *The Drawing Room at Park Lane*, 188, *191*
Sheth, Jagannath Shanker, 142
Sims, Charles: *The Ballroom at 25 Park Lane with Sybil Sassoon*, 108, 188, *192*
slavery, 81
Steer, Philip Wilson, 84, 134
Strauss, Isaac, 34
Strauss, Johann, Jr., 181

T
Tang Yuen, 174
Tessier, Louis: *A Marmoset Taking Sweets on a Painted Commode (The Thieving Marmoset)* (attrib.), *70*
textile industry, 18, 75, 159, *160–61*, 165
Thaddeus, Henry Jones: *Rachel Sassoon Beer*, 66, *67*
Tilden, Philip, 188, 214. *See also* Port Lympne
Tonks, Henry, *235*; *An Underground Casualty Clearing Station, Arras, France*, 230, *232*
Tournai porcelain, 90, *92*, *93*
Trent Park, 76, 90, 96, 215–18, *215–21*
trompe l'oeil, 199, *199*, *205*, 206
Troy, Jean-François de, 76, *99*
Tudor architecture, 178–80, *179–80*

U
United Nations Relief and Rehabilitation Administration, 240, *241*

V
van Dyck, Anthony, 69
Velázquez, Diego, 76
Vernet, Claude-Joseph, 42, 134; *The Waterfalls at Tivoli*, *134*
Vieillard, André Vincent, 101, *102*
Vincennes porcelain, 90, 101
Vuillard, Édouard, 9

W
Wallraf, Muriel (née Sassoon), 70
Wallraf, Paul, 70
Walpole, Robert, 108, *110–11*
Waterhouse, Ellis, 80, 81
Watts, George Frederic, 62; *Mrs. Arthur Sassoon*, *182*; *Orpheus and Eurydice*, *62*
Wertmüller, Adolf Ulric: *Jean-Jacques Caffieri*, 98, *98*
Whistler, Rex, 84, 132–33, 222; *Hannah Gubbay*, *91*, *96*; *Philip and Hannah on the Terrace at Trent Park with Their Whippet, Blazer*, *216–17*; Trent Park, 215. *See also* Port Lympne
Wilds, Amon Henry, 187
Wilkins, Henry Saint Clair, *148–53*, 149–52
Willmott, Ernest, 195, *196–97*
Wilson, George Leopold, 174–77, *175*
Wilson, Richard: *Lake, Ruin, and Pine Trees* (attrib.), *72*
Wittet, George, 163–65, *165*
Wolmark, Alfred, 43
women: as art connoisseurs/patrons, 62, 96–97, 104, 224; Baghdadi in Mumbai, 139; in World Wars, 226, 237
Woolf, Virginia, 222
Woolner, Thomas: bust and statue of David Sassoon, 142, *143*, 144, *147*, 247n25
Wootton, John, 108
World War I, 226–30, *227–35*
World War II, *236–41*, 237–40

Y
Yang Mao, 121, *123*
Yemenite Jews, 51–52, *52*, 242n6 (Ch. 1), 244n39

Z
Zhou Wenju, 124
Zhu Bishan, 120–21, *122*
Zoffany, Johan, 76, 80; *The Colmore Family*, *219*; *The Family of Sir William Young*, 80–81, *81*; *Richard Henry Alexander Bennett*, *79*; *Samuel Foote as Major Sturgeon and Robert Baddeley as Sir Jacob Jollop in "The Mayor of Garratt,"* 94–96

The copyright holders, photographers, and sources of visual material other than the owners indicated in the captions are listed below. Every reasonable effort has been made to supply complete and correct credits; if there are errors or omissions, please contact the Jewish Museum so that corrections can be addressed in any subsequent edition. Material in copyright is reprinted by permission of copyright holders or under fair use. Images may be listed in more than one location. Page numbers are **BOLD**.

Copyrights
© Buildington, London: **181 bottom.** © Christie's Images Limited: **44–45, 70, 72.** © Churchill Heritage Ltd: **213 top and bottom, 235 bottom.** © Country Life / Future Publishing Ltd: **10, 94 left and right, 197 top, 198, 199, 201, 202, 203, 204, 205, 208–9, 210–11, 212 top, 214 top, 218, 219, 220, 221.** © Fitzwilliam Museum, Cambridge, UK: **122 top.** © Historic England Archive: **187.** © Illustrated London News Ltd / Mary Evans: **190 top.** © Israel Museum, Jerusalem: **25 right, 53, 56 top.** © Museu Nacional d'Art de Catalunya, Barcelona: **193.** © Museum of Fine Arts, Boston: **40–41, 98, 234 top.** © Trustees of the British Museum: **120, 128 left, 130 left and right, 131 top left and top right.** © ÜberRaum Architects, London: **181 top.** © Victoria and Albert Museum, London: **39 left and right, 80, 96, 97, 121, 128 right, 131 bottom left and bottom right.**

Image Providers and Sources
Abha Narain Lambah Associates: **164 top.** Adrian Sassoon, London: **102–3.** Alamy Stock Photo: **140, 143 left, 144 left, 147 top and bottom, 164 bottom, 169 top, 183, 184, 185, 186 top.** American Jewish Joint Distribution Committee: **239 bottom.** Architectural Press Archive / RIBA Collections: **224 left and right.** Artefact / Alamy Stock Photo: **68 top, 78, 107.** Art Resource, NY: **68 bottom, 124–25, 126–27.** Artvee: **69.** Beinecke Rare Book and Manuscript Library, Yale University: **64.** Bibliothèque Nationale de France, Gallica: **76 bottom.** Braginsky Collection, Zurich: **54, 57, 60 right.** Bridgeman Images: **8, 22, 84, 110–11, 113, 114, 116.** British Library: **cover, 4, 58 top, 137, 139, 143 right, 144–45, 150, 151, 154, 155, 156, 158–59, 162–63.** British Museum: **120, 128 left, 130 left and right, 131 top left and top right.** By permission of the Syndics of Cambridge University Library: **21, 49, 65 left, 227 bottom right, 228, 229 top, 229 bottom right.** Cecil Beaton / Condé Nast: **117, 236.** Center for Jewish Art, Jerusalem: **186 bottom.** ChinaImages / Depositphotos: **175.** Chronicle / Alamy Stock Photo: **176.** Cleveland Museum of Art: **122 bottom, 123, 134.** CNMages / Alamy Stock Photo: **174.** CPA Media Pte Ltd / Alamy Stock Photo: **238.** Curtis Brown, London: **213 top and bottom, 235 bottom.** *Daily Mirror*, March 11, 1939, 26: **89 bottom.** Dinodia Photos / Alamy Stock Photo: **138, 142, 156.** Elmbridge Museum, Elmbridge Borough Council: **180.** ephotocorp / Alamy Stock Photo: **148.** Fitzwilliam Museum, Cambridge, UK / Art Resource, NY: **132.** Emeric Hahn Gallery: **200.** GL Archive / Alamy Stock Photo: **83.** IanDagnall Computing / Alamy Stock Photo: **82.** Images of Kent / Alamy Stock Photo: **196–97.** Imperial War Museums: **227 top, 230, 232 top and bottom, 232–33.** incamerastock / Alamy Stock Photo: **77.** Jewish Museum, New York: **18 top, 26 left, 28, 29, 38, 160, 241 top left and right and bottom left.** *Jewish Tribune*, Bombay, April 4, 1933: **237.** J. Paul Getty Museum: **101, 104, 190 bottom.** Jono David / HaChayim HaYehudim Jewish Photo Library: **157.** Kedem Auction House Ltd: **30, 44–45.** *Lady's Realm: An Illustrated Monthly Magazine*, vol. 13, p. 355: **188.** Library of Congress, Prints & Photographs Division: **26 right.** Mei-fei Elrick and University of Bristol Library, Special Collections (www.hpcbristol.net): **177.** Metropolitan Museum of Art: **100 bottom, 102 bottom left and bottom right.** Museum of Fine Arts, Boston: **40, 41, 98, 234 top.** National Gallery of Ireland: **66.** National Library of Australia: **99 right.** National Library of Israel: **55.** National Portrait Gallery, London / Art Resource, NY: **73, 133 top left, top right, and bottom, 229 bottom left.** National Trust Images: **92 left, 93, 235 bottom.** National Trust Photolibrary / Alamy Stock Photo: **92 right, 95.** New York Public Library Digital Collections: **58 bottom.** Niday Picture Library / Alamy Stock Photo: **81.** Norton Simon Museum: **100 top.** NTRVT: **103 bottom.** Painters / Alamy Stock Photo: **106, 115, 182, 231.** Picture Art Collection / Alamy Stock Photo: **63, 91, 99 left.** Private collection: **35, 67.** ProQuest Historical Newspapers: *The Guardian* and *The Observer*: **65 right.** Qilai Shen / New York Times / Redux: **178.** Richard Mahoney: **217 right.** Royal Academy of Arts, London: **118 left.** Royal Collection Trust: **74 top left, top right, center, and bottom, 75, 152–53.** Royal Ontario Museum: **161.** Smith Archive / Alamy Stock Photo: **90.** Sotheby's New York: **31, 33, 36, 37, 43, 52, 47, 56 bottom, 170 top, 202.** Southern Methodist University Libraries, DeGolyer Library: **179 top, 239 top.** Süddeutsche Zeitung Photo / Alamy Stock Photo: **88.** Tate Images: **85.** United Kingdom Department for Digital, Culture, Media & Sport: **86.** United States Holocaust Memorial Museum: **240 left and right.** University of Pennsylvania, Penn Libraries: **19, 46, 47, 48, 59.** University of Toronto Libraries, Thomas Fisher Rare Book Library: **50.** Wikimedia Commons: **118 right, 141, 165, 170 bottom.**

Photographers
Avshalom Avital: **25 right.** Ardon Bar-Hama: **53, 54, 55, 57, 60 right.** Sandra Bornstein: **169 bottom.** Lynn Bradshaw: **215.** David Brown: **71.** Rangan Datta: **141.** Anil Dave: **140.** Jono David: **157.** James O. Davies: **187.** Sylvain Deleu: **102–3.** Anand Diwadkar: **148.** Sarah Duncan: **214 bottom.** Noshir Gobhai: **164 top.** Philip Goldberg: **171, 172–73.** Richard Goodbody Inc.: **26 left.** Barney Hindle: **17, 87, 105, 134, 189, 191, 192, 194–95, 197 bottom, 206, 207, 216–17, 222.** Pete Huggins: **20 top, center, and bottom, 76 top, 79, 89 top, 108 top left, top right, and bottom, 109, 112, 166–68, 179 bottom, 227 bottom left, 234 bottom, 235 top.** Erich Lessing: **68 bottom.** Nadia Mackenzie: **92 left.** Elena Odareeva: **144 left.** Ekaterina Oleshkevich: **186 bottom.** Satish Parashar: **164 bottom.** Anthony Parkinson: **92 right.** David Pearson: **147 bottom.** Hira Punjabi: **143 left.** Primo Dul Ravel: **147 top.** Joe Ravi: **146.** Boaz Rottem: **169 top.** Sascha Schröder: **223.** Alex Shams: **25 left.** Qilai Shen: **178.** Kevin Standage: **149.** Slawek Staszczuk: **183, 184–85, 186 top.** Charles Thomas: **235 bottom.** Sam Waigand: **217 right.**

This book has been published in conjunction with the exhibition *The Sassoons*, organized by the Jewish Museum, New York, March 3–August 13, 2023.

Jewish Museum, New York
Director of Publications: Eve Sinaiko
Editor: Susan Higman Larsen
Proofreaders: Marian Appellof, Bruno George, James Waller

Yale University Press
Editor, Art and Architecture: Amy Canonico
Production Manager: Sarah Henry

Designed by Miko McGinty
Set in Centra and Maiola by Tina Henderson
Printed in Malaysia

Jewish Museum
1109 Fifth Avenue
New York, New York 10128
thejewishmuseum.org

Yale University Press
P.O. Box 209040
New Haven, Connecticut 06520-9040
yalebooks.com/art

Library of Congress Control Number: 2022945853
ISBN 978-0-300-26430-2

A catalogue record for this book is available from the British Library.

The paper in this book meets the requirements of ANSI/NISO Z39.48-1992 (Permanence of Paper).

10 9 8 7 6 5 4 3 2 1

Cover, frontispiece, and page 4: members of the Sassoon family in Pune, India, 1869; see pages 154–55. Page 8: Sybil Sassoon sketched by John Singer Sargent; see page 113. Page 10: the tent room at Port Lympne; see page 205.